# Computer Communications and Networks

For other titles published in this series, go to
www.springer.com/series/4198

The **Computer Communications and Networks** series is a range of textbooks, monographs and handbooks. It sets out to provide students, researchers and non-specialists alike with a sure grounding in current knowledge, together with comprehensible access to the latest developments in computer communications and networking.

Emphasis is placed on clear and explanatory styles that support a tutorial approach, so that even the most complex of topics is presented in a lucid and intelligible manner.

Maciej Drozdowski

# Scheduling for Parallel Processing

 Springer

Maciej Drozdowski
Poznan University of Technology
Inst. Computing Science
ul. Piotrowo 2
60-695 Poznan
Poland
Maciej.Drozdowski@cs.put.poznan.pl

*Series Editor*
Professor A.J. Sammes, BSc, MPhil, PhD, FBCS, CEng
Centre for Forensic Computing
Cranfield University
DCMT, Shrivenham
Swindon SN6 8LA
UK

ISSN 1617-7975
ISBN 978-1-4471-2508-2        e-ISBN 978-1-84882-310-5
DOI 10.1007/978-1-84882-310-5
Springer Dordrecht Heidelberg London New York

British Library Cataloguing in Publication Data
A catalogue record for this book is available from the British Library

*Cover design*: SPi Publisher Services

Printed on acid-free paper

Springer is part of Springer Science+Business Media (www.springer.com)

# Preface

## Overview and Goals

This book is dedicated to scheduling for parallel processing. Presenting a research field as broad as this one poses considerable difficulties. Scheduling for parallel computing is an interdisciplinary subject joining many fields of science and technology. Thus, to understand the scheduling problems and the methods of solving them it is necessary to know the limitations in related areas. Another difficulty is that the subject of scheduling parallel computations is immense. Even simple search in bibliographical databases reveals thousands of publications on this topic. The diversity in understanding scheduling problems is so great that it seems impossible to juxtapose them in one scheduling taxonomy. Therefore, most of the papers on scheduling for parallel processing refer to one scheduling problem resulting from one way of perceiving the reality. Only a few publications attempt to arrange this field of knowledge systematically.

In this book we will follow two guidelines. One guideline is a distinction between scheduling models which comprise a set of scheduling problems solved by dedicated algorithms. Thus, the aim of this book is to present scheduling models for parallel processing, problems defined on the grounds of certain scheduling models, and algorithms solving the scheduling problems. Most of the scheduling problems are combinatorial in nature. Therefore, the second guideline is the methodology of computational complexity theory.

In this book we present four examples of scheduling models. We will go deep into the models, problems, and algorithms so that after acquiring some understanding of them we will attempt to draw conclusions on their mutual relationships. Hence, this book is also intended to give generalizations on scheduling models, their problems, and algorithms.

## Target Audiences

This book may be helpful for researchers in parallel computing, operating systems, management science, and applied mathematics. We hope that this book may be also useful for lecturers and advanced students in the above fields.

A necessary prerequisite to reading this book is understanding basic concepts in computer hardware, programming, operating systems, parallel processing, and discrete mathematics. Knowledge of the notions from combinatorial optimization, computational complexity, and parallel application performance metrics would ease reading the book.

## Organization and Features

The book is organized in the following way. Chapters 1, 2, and 3 set the stage for discussing scheduling models. Four examples of scheduling models are presented in Chaps. 4 to 7. Conclusions on applicability of scheduling models are drawn in Chap. 8. A more detailed description of the following chapters is given below.

In Chap. 1 fundamental scheduling concepts which appear throughout the book are introduced. The relation between scheduling models, problems, algorithms, and schedules is clarified.

In Chap. 2 selected notions related to graph theory are introduced to avoid ambiguity in further chapters. The methodology of computational complexity theory is outlined. It is a framework for scheduling as a combinatorial optimization problem. Finally, basic metrics of parallel application performance are introduced.

Chapter 3 is dedicated to the technological aspects of scheduling for parallel processing. Scheduling determinants posed by hardware, programming environments, and widely understood operating systems are discussed. We examine the perception of and support for scheduling in parallel systems. This chapter shows how highly abstract scheduling policies are determined by the underlying hardware and software.

Chapter 4 is dedicated to scheduling parallel applications on the grounds of the classic deterministic scheduling theory. We present the notions, concepts, and algorithms that are most immediately applicable in parallel processing. A reader not familiar with the scheduling theory may find here many concepts and definitions shared by other models in the book. The classic scheduling theory has developed in many directions which are applicable in parallel processing. Selected extensions of the classic theory are discussed.

Chapter 5 examines the parallel task model. In the parallel task model a task may be executed by several processors simultaneously. The internal structure of the task is unknown to the scheduler. However, the scheduler may know some of the task requirements. Several types of parallel tasks are analyzed: rigid tasks which require a fixed number of processors, moldable tasks which may be executed on several alternative numbers of processors but the actual number of used processors is selected by the scheduler before starting the application, malleable tasks which may change the number of used processors during runtime, multiprocessor tasks which require a *set* of processors, and tasks requesting a certain processor interconnection shape (for instance mesh or hypercube). This chapter may be interesting for designers of operating systems and queuing systems for supercomputing facilities.

Chapter 6 examines scheduling with communication delays. A parallel application is a collection of sequential communicating processes (tasks) here. If two tasks are executed on different processors, and the first one is producing some data for the second one, then a communication delay arises as a result of transferring data from one processor to the other. Scheduling algorithms must take into account costs of communication delays. The algorithms presented in this chapter may be interesting for programmers, developers of parallel applications, and designers of compilers.

In Chap. 7 scheduling divisible loads is discussed. This model applies to scheduling parallel applications which can be divided into parts of arbitrary sizes, which in turn can be processed independently on remote computers. The assumption about arbitrary divisibility means in practice that the grains of parallelism are fine. Independent computing on remote computers means that there are no data dependencies between the grains of parallelism. This model has been applied to schedule parallel applications in various processor interconnection networks, and in systems with limited memory, to minimize the cost of parallel execution, and to analyze performance of parallel computer systems. The content of this chapter may be useful for developers of parallel applications and designers of parallel systems.

Finally, in Chap. 8 we return to the initial division of the research area into domains of scheduling models. We study the relations between models, problems, and algorithms using the knowledge presented in the earlier chapters.

This book presents ideas and concepts rather than proofs of the theorems. Moreover, we will only outline some methods which are too complex to be presented in fine detail. Still, we hope that the given description will be sufficient to grasp the idea of the presented algorithms, allowing the readers to code them if necessary.

Many scheduling algorithms presented in this book are heuristics solving hard combinatorial problems. We do not compare the performance of the proposed heuristic methods, as it may be taken for granted that there are instances for which certain heuristics perform well. On the other hand, discussing generality of such results is beyond the scope of this book.

The algorithms considered in this book are presented in the order they appeared in print. The index at the end of the book may be helpful in finding a particular algorithm.

With the exception of a few symbols like the number of tasks $n$, number of processors $m$, schedule length $C_{max}$, the notation is local for the chapters. The symbols which are frequently used are summarized in Appendix A.

### Acknowledgements

Writing this book would not be possible without help from many people.

I would like to thank my family for supporting me and giving courage to go through the process of writing this book.

I am very grateful to Danuta Marek, Ewa Nawrocka, Joanna Radke, and Jerzy Nawrocki for providing access to publications not so easily accessible in my workplace. I direct my special thanks to Krystyna Ciesielska, and Jan Kniat for their efforts in improving the quality of this book.

I am also very indebted to Jacek Błażewicz, Lixin Gao, Klaus Jansen, Arnaud Legrand, Cynthia Phillips, Christope Picouleau, Thomas Robertazzi, Arnold Rosenberg, Frédéric Vivien, Yakov Zinder, for providing and discussing some of their old and more recent publications.

Writing this book was partially supported by grant NN519 1889 33 of Polish Ministry of Science and Higher Education.

October 2008                                                                  *Maciej Drozdowski*

# Contents

# Chapter 1
# Introduction

In this chapter, we introduce scheduling for parallel processing as a field of knowl-edge. We define and distinguish abstract scheduling concepts and their real imple-mentations. General descriptions are given here because details of many scheduling notions differ in various scheduling paradigms. Examples of scheduling problems are given to demonstrate that scheduling is essential for efficient use of parallel com-puters. Finally, we introduce the concept of a scheduling model which is crucial to the structure of this book.

## 1.1 Field of Scheduling for Parallel Processing

This book is dedicated to scheduling for parallel processing. Scheduling is usually associated with such applications as production and transportation planning, timetabling, vehicle routing, staff rostering, sport events planning, etc. More gener-ally, scheduling can be considered as managing the execution of jobs (manufacturing operations, transportation operations, computer applications, sport events, etc.) which require certain resources (workers, tools, energy, CPUs, memory, bandwidth, etc.) in such a way that certain optimality and/or feasibility criteria are met. Thus, the problems of managing activities are similar in many application areas, including scheduling programs in a computer. Operational research is a more general research area studying efficient management of complex systems, and as such it encompasses scheduling.

Parallel processing (or parallel computing) is a field in computer science related to the application of many computers running in parallel to solve computationally intensive problems. The main goal of parallel processing is to provide users with performance which no single computer may deliver. Though the concept of parallel processing is very old, this area is still experimental in nature. It may be attributed to the fact that many new ideas that may increase the speed of computation are formed and verified in parallel processing. Hence, parallel processing is tightly coupled with the advances in computer hardware and networking.

M. Drozdowski, *Scheduling for Parallel Processing*, Computer Communications and Networks, DOI 10.1007/978-1-84882-310-5_1,
© Springer-Verlag London Limited 2009

The methods of representing and analyzing scheduling problems are rooted in discrete mathematics. Consequently, the tools for solving such problems are a subject of combinatorial optimization.

It can be concluded that scheduling for parallel computing is an interdisciplinary subject which brings together computer science, computer hardware, discrete mathematics, operational research, and other fields. Therefore, limitations in one field determine the possible solutions in other areas. For example, parallel applications are in practice limited by computer hardware and software. The nature of parallel applications influences scheduling models (cf. Fig. 1.2). The scheduling models, and the way of representing them mathematically, determine the computational hardness of obtaining optimum solutions (schedules). The schedules determine performance of parallel processing: response time, speed, fairness, quality of service, etc. The awareness of these relations and constraints will allow us to see the considered problems in a broader perspective.

Now we set off on a journey which encompasses thousands of publications and a myriad of ideas, to gain some broader view of scheduling for parallel processing, and, hopefully, to discover some generalizations.

## 1.2  Basic Scheduling Notions

In this section, we introduce basic theoretic concepts related to scheduling, and we distinguish them from their real implementations.

### 1.2.1  Scheduling Theory Notions

A *task* is the smallest schedulable entity. Depending on the scheduling model and the level of abstraction, in a real computer system, it can be a thread in a process, a process, a set of processes, a communication, a set of communications. Let $n$ denote the number of tasks, and $\mathcal{T}$ the set of tasks. Some tasks may be started only after the completion of some other task(s). Hence, the set of tasks may be partially ordered. This partial order can be represented as a directed acyclic graph which we will call a *task graph* or a *task precedence graph* (see Sect. 2.1 for explanation of graph theory concepts). A set of tasks forming a task graph will be called a *job*.

A *processor* or *processing element* (PE) is the smallest active entity executing the tasks. In other words, a processor represents a device necessary to execute the tasks. It can be, e.g., one of the cores in a CPU, a CPU, a whole computer, a set of computers. Let $\mathcal{P}$ denote the set of processors, and $m$ their number. Processors may be connected with each other in a specific way. This may be taken into account while solving a scheduling problem to minimize communication costs. Mutual connections of the processors may be represented as a graph with nodes corresponding to the processors and edges corresponding to the communication links. This type of graph will be called *host graph*. *Resources* are the means and instruments, beyond the processor, required by the tasks for their execution. Memory, communication bandwidth, critical sections are examples of the resources.

A *schedule* is an assignment of the tasks to processors and resources in time. In other words, a schedule is a function from time intervals on processors and resources to the tasks. Consequently, a processor (or a resource) can be used by only one task at a given time moment. A *Gantt chart* is a graphical representation of a schedule (see Fig. 4.1).

### 1.2.2 Computer Systems Notions

By a *parallel application* we mean all forms of computations which can be executed in parallel. A parallel application may consist of a single process, or a set of communicating processes. A *process* is an operating system entity. A process owns some amount of memory and other computer system resources which are isolated from other processes. Since a process is usually equivalent to a running program, we will use words program and process interchangeably. A *thread* is an active execution entity which exists within a process. Threads of the same process are not isolated from each other, but they share memory image, and resources of the hosting process. Therefore, thread communications and synchronizations may be faster, as they need not involve the operating system. A thread may own some limited amount of memory, e.g., execution stack or its local variables. We assume that a process has at least one thread. Therefore, we will use the term "thread" in text where both thread and process can be referred to. As already mentioned, threads, processes, and parallel applications correspond with the scheduling notions of tasks, or jobs.

Threads communicate with each other. A communication may result if one thread requires some input data computed in some other thread. Communications may also result from synchronizations or accessing shared global variables. Thus, communications introduce precedence in thread execution. The set of precedences between the computations in the threads corresponds with arcs in a task graph. In some cases thread communication pattern is known before starting the application. In other cases this pattern develops at runtime and cannot be reliably predicted.

In this book the term *parallel system* will refer to all classes of parallel computers from multicore CPUs to wide area computational grids comprising distributed and heterogeneous installations owned by mutually unrelated institutions. The scheduling concept of a processor may have various realizations. As mentioned before, it can be a core in the CPU, the CPU, a whole computer, or a distributed computer system. The terms *host* or *node* are also used in many publications to denote a computer system with one or many CPUs. Note, however, that *node* is a graph-theoretic notion and is always used with respect to some graph. Hence it may cause confusion depending on what is represented by the graph. We will use one of the terms: CPU, host, computer, to distinguish the scheduling concept of a processor from its implementation.

CPUs and computers communicate with each other. By *interconnection* we will mean the hardware communication network connecting CPUs or computers. The structure of the real interconnection [3, 6] may be complex and not always known. Therefore, on one hand interconnection corresponds with the scheduling concept of a host graph, on the other hand they are not necessarily one-to-one equivalent.

From the point of view of an operating system [5, 7, 9] this book is dedicated to scheduling policies rather than to the low-level mechanisms used to implement them. The terms parallel and distributed processing (or computing) will be used interchangeably with a tacit assumption that at least two concurrently executing threads exist in a parallel application. Some researchers distinguish parallel and distributed computations on the basis of distance, communication delay, or hardware vs. software implementation of communication mechanisms. We believe that independently of the above issues fundamental scheduling problems remain the same.

## 1.3  Why We Need Scheduling

Parallel systems are not used to their full potential if the applications are not properly scheduled. Below we give examples where simple ad hoc solutions are not good choices.

*Example 1.1.* A commonly used scheduling scheme is First-In-First-Out (FIFO), or First-Come-First-Served (FCFS). It assigns programs to the computers in the order of the request arrival. Consider a parallel system with $m$ computers, and a sequence of $m$ applications requesting all $m$ processors for one unit of time, interleaved with applications requesting just one processor for $a$ units of time (see Fig. 1.1). A schedule (Fig. 1.1a) constructed according to the FIFO rule has a lot of idle time, which means that computing resources are wasted. A more efficient schedule is shown in Fig. 1.1b. It is $\frac{m(a+1)}{m+a}$ times shorter, and this fraction may be made arbitrarily big by changing $m$ and $a$. Hence the FIFO scheme may be arbitrarily bad. On the other hand, in the second schedule applications are not processed in the order in which they were submitted, which is unfair. Thus, a more advanced schedule may be needed as a compromise between fairness and efficient utilization of the computers.

*Example 1.2.* Suppose a parallel application consists in searching for a pattern in a big number of pictures. Pictures are analyzed independently of one another. Processing $V$ pictures takes time $VA$. Transferring this number of pictures from the storage

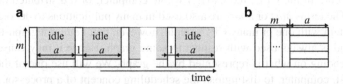

**Fig. 1.1** Example of a schedule on $m$ processors obtained by (**a**) FIFO and (**b**) some other method

on a server to a remote computer takes time $CV$. Time $CV$ cannot be reduced even if we use many computers because the storage server has only one network interface with limited speed. A commonly used scheme for distributing this kind of computations is *equipartitioning*, i.e. dividing the work equally between the working computers. Suppose we have two computers working with equal speed. Thus, the whole work is done in $CV + \frac{AV}{2}$ units of time. Suppose now that the two computers are not identical. For example, the second computer has smaller core memory and substitutes it with out-of-core storage. As a consequence, it is $k$ times slower than the first computer. Then the schedule length is $CV + \frac{AVk}{2}$. It can be arbitrarily big compared to the previous schedule length. We see that equipartitioning is not a good choice here because it does not take into consideration resource heterogeneity. An ad hoc solution is to assign to the second computer $k$ times fewer pictures than to the first one. But this is not a good solution either, because the reduced number of pictures may now fit in the core memory of the second computer. Then, there is no need of using out-of-core storage on the second computer. As a result this computer will compute faster and will finish earlier, while the first computer will be overloaded.

We conclude from the above examples that simple algorithms are not always good solutions. Thus, there is a need for judicious planning and coordination of the applications running on parallel computers.

## 1.4  Problems, Models, Algorithms, and Schedules

In this section, we explain how the structure of this book follows from models, problems, and algorithms for scheduling parallel computations. First, we will explain why such a structure is needed, and how difficult it is to find one. Then, we explain the relations between the scheduling models, problems, algorithms, and schedules.

In presenting a research field as broad as scheduling for parallel processing it is useful to introduce some systematic classification of the analyzed phenomena, because it gives a logical, consistent partition of a body of knowledge. The partitions may be analyzed separately until nothing is left. Such efforts were made in the past [1, 2, 4, 8]. However, human imagination does not follow straight lines of taxonomies. Nor are there any divisions between ideas which could not be crossed. New concepts that are bridging seemingly disparate worlds are fuzzing classifications. Some approaches that do not fit the taxonomy are often left out. Consequently, the classifications tend to be disputable. Scheduling is no exception here. On the other hand, it is indeed necessary to introduce some guidelines in the presentation of a body of knowledge. To solve this dilemma we decided to, primarily, discuss methods typical of certain scheduling models. Thus, scheduling problems and algorithms are presented within some scheduling model. The second guideline is the methodology of the computational complexity theory, which is introduced in Sect. 2.2.

Let us now introduce the concept of scheduling model and its relation to real scheduling problems, algorithms, and schedules (cf. Fig. 1.2). The issue of

**Fig. 1.2** Mutual relationships of the real scheduling problem, scheduling model, theoretical scheduling problems, algorithms, and schedules

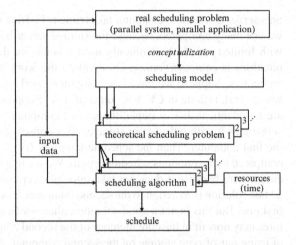

scheduling a real parallel application on an existing computer system can be reduced to a question "what should I do to have my computation finished on this parallel computer in the shortest possible time?". Posing and answering questions like this constitute real scheduling problems.

A schedule is a practical answer to the above question. Schedules are constructed by scheduling algorithms. But not every scheduling algorithm fits any real scheduling problem. The general comprehension of a real scheduling problem (computers, application, their interactions) and the way it should be solved constitutes a scheduling model. In other words, a scheduling model is a conceptualization transforming applications and systems into algorithms. Within a scheduling model special cases may be considered. These special cases are commonly called scheduling problems in the literature. We will preserve this meaning in this book. Note that word *problem* is now used in two meanings: to refer to a *real* scheduling problem and a *theoretical* scheduling problem. The domain of a real scheduling problem comprises real world objects: parallel applications, parallel computers, their users, communication networks, etc. The domain of theoretical scheduling problems encompasses tasks, task graphs, processors, host graphs. It may be also said that theoretical scheduling problems are defined on the grounds of a certain scheduling model unifying all such problems by shared way of understanding the real scheduling problem. Hence, the theoretical scheduling problems can be also called instances of a scheduling model. In the further presentation we will drop the word "theoretical" when it is obvious that we are referring to the theoretical scheduling problems.

Needless to say, any algorithm can operate only within the limits of available information and time. Thus, a scheduling algorithm needs data about the application and the parallel computing system. Moreover, the algorithm requires certain resources. In this book we concentrate on just one crucial resource, the time. Hence, it follows that computational complexity theory is particularly important in assessing the quality of algorithms and difficulty of scheduling problems. Finally, to implement a schedule constructed by the scheduling algorithm, adequate instrumentation and control structures are required in the real computer system and the application.

Let us finish this section with examples of a real scheduling problem, scheduling models, theoretical scheduling problems, and scheduling algorithms. Consider Example 2 from Sect. 1.3. In this example we assumed that the whole volume $V$ of pictures can be divided into two parts of arbitrary sizes. This is one possible way of perceiving this real scheduling problem. Hence, it allows us to define one scheduling model. However, analyzing one picture is not so easily divisible. In some cases, e.g., when the number of pictures is small, it is more convenient to treat the analysis of one picture as one task. Since pictures differ, the tasks they correspond to have different processing times. If the interconnection is very fast then communication times needed to deliver pictures to the processors can be neglected. Thus, the whole scheduling problem boils down to assigning tasks to processors in such a way that the length of a schedule is as short as possible. This is an example of another scheduling model for the same real scheduling problem.

Suppose that for some reason it was decided that the second model is more adequate (we introduce a scheduling model of this kind in Chap. 4). Theoretical scheduling problems defined on the grounds of this model may differ, e.g., in referring to homogeneous or heterogeneous processors. The difference in processing speed of the processors introduces at least two theoretical scheduling problems: one with identical processors and one with processors of different speeds. Now let us remain with the first problem with identical processors. This problem can be solved by a number of algorithms (cf. Sect. 4.3.1.1). Since this problem is computationally hard there are scheduling algorithms which construct optimum schedules in exponential time and algorithms which construct feasible schedules in polynomial time.

# References

1. I. Ahmad, Y.-K. Kwok, M.-Y. Wu, and W. Shu. CASCH: A tool for computer-aided scheduling. *IEEE Concurrency*, 8(4):21–33, 2000.
2. T.L. Casavant and J.G. Kuhl. A taxonomy of scheduling in general-purpose distributed computing systems. *IEEE Transactions on Software Engineering*, 14(2):141–154, 1988.
3. A.L. Decegama. *The Technology of Parallel Processing. Parallel Processing Architectures and VLSI Hardware Volume I*. Prentice-Hall, Englewood Cliffs, 1989.
4. F. Dong and S.G. Akl. Scheduling algorithms for grid computing: State of the art and open problems. Research Report 504, Queen's University School of Computing, Kingston, Ont., Canada, 2006.
5. E.F. Gehringer, D.P. Siewiorek, and Z. Segall. *Parallel Processing: The Cm* Experience*. Digital Press, Bedford, 1987.
6. M.D. Grammatikakis, D.F. Hsu, and M. Kraetzel. *Parallel System Interconnections and Communications*. CRC Press, Boca Raton, 2001.
7. R. Levin, E.S. Cohen, W.M. Corwin, F.J. Pollack, and W.A. Wulf. Policy/mechanism separation in HYDRA. In *ACM Symposium on OS Principles*, pages 132–140, 1975.
8. M. G. Norman and P. Thanisch. Models of machines and computation for mapping in multicomputers. *ACM Computing Surveys*, 25(3):263–302, 1993.
9. A.S. Tanenbaum. *Modern Operating Systems*. Prentice-Hall. Upper Saddle River NJ, 2001.

# Chapter 2
# Basics

In this chapter, we present notions shared across the book. The purpose of this chapter is not only to define terms and notions, which may be known to the reader, but also to disambiguate some of them. Graph theory models are often used in scheduling. Therefore, we will introduce basic definitions of the graph theory. Most of the scheduling problems have combinatorial nature. Hence, elements of the computational complexity theory providing guidelines in analyzing combinatorial optimization problems are outlined. Then, selected methods solving hard combinatorial problems are discussed. Finally, basic metrics of parallel performance are presented.

## 2.1 Selected Definitions Form Graph Theory

Graph representations are ubiquitous in scheduling. In this section, we give definitions of selected graph-theoretic concepts and graph classes often used to embody scheduling problems. For a complete treatment the reader should refer to one of the many publications on the graph theory.

*Graph* is a pair $G = (\mathcal{V}, \mathcal{E})$, where $\mathcal{V}$ is a set of nodes also called vertices, and $\mathcal{E}$ is a set of edges. An edge is a two-element set of nodes from $\mathcal{V}$. For example, $\{i, j\} \in \mathcal{E}$ denotes an edge between nodes $i, j$. Note that as there is no order between the objects in set $\{i, j\}$, and edge $\{i, j\}$ is not directed. A *directed graph* is a pair $G = (\mathcal{V}, \mathcal{A})$, where $\mathcal{V}$ is again a set of nodes, and $\mathcal{A}$ is a set of arcs. An arc is a pair $(i, j) \in \mathcal{A}$. As there is an order of objects in a pair, or in a sequence, arcs have orientation, and $i$ precedes $j$. Therefore, arc $(i, j)$ can be equivalently denoted $i \rightarrow j$. In a directed graph, a node without predecessors is called *entry, source,* or *input* node, and a node without successors is called *exit, sink, terminal,* or *output* node. In scheduling graphs are used to represent interconnections of computer systems or the order of executing tasks within a job. Let us emphasize that *node* is a graph-theoretic notion, and it is always used with respect to some graph. Thus, a node may be a computer in a graph representing computer network or a task in a task graph.

M. Drozdowski, *Scheduling for Parallel Processing*, Computer Communications and Networks, DOI 10.1007/978-1-84882-310-5_2,
© Springer-Verlag London Limited 2009

A *degree* of node $i \in \mathcal{V}$ denoted by $deg(i)$ is the number of edges incident with this node. We will denote by $deg(G) = \max_{i \in \mathcal{V}} deg(i)$ the *degree* of the whole graph $G$. In the case of directed graphs it is necessary to distinguish the number of arcs starting or ending in a certain node. Thus, we will denote $indeg(i)$ the number of arcs inbound to node $i$, and $outdeg(i)$ the number of arcs starting from node $i$.

A path in a directed graph is a sequence of nodes $(a_1, \ldots, a_k)$ such that $a_i \in \mathcal{V}$ for $i = 1, \ldots, k$, $(a_i, a_{i+1}) \in \mathcal{A}$ for $i = 1, \ldots, k - 1$. A cycle in a directed graph is a path $(a_1, \ldots, a_k)$ such that $(a_k, a_1) \in \mathcal{A}$. For undirected graphs definitions are analogous, but edges $\{a_i, a_{i+1}\}$ are used instead of arcs $(a_i, a_{i+1})$.

A graph *weighted on nodes* is a graph in which each node has associated a number. A graph *weighted on arcs* (or edges) is a graph in which each arc (or edge) has a number associated. There are also graphs weighted on arcs and on nodes. Weights of the nodes and arcs have immediate interpretation in the task graph. The weight of a node is a processing time of a task represented by the node. The weight of an arc may represent duration of the communication time, or amount of data, transferred between the tasks. The sum of the weights along some path can be interpreted as a distance. Depending on the application, the weight of the nodes, or of the arcs, or both, can be added up along the path to calculate the distance. The longest path without cycles is called a *critical path*. Note that a precise definition of the critical path depends on the way of calculating the distance in the graph.

Now we will define certain graph classes which are common in scheduling. A *directed acyclic graph (DAG)* is a directed graph without cycles. Observe that the precedence of tasks in a job can be conveniently represented as a DAG.

An acyclic graph is a called a *tree* if it is not directed. A DAG is an out-forest if and only if for every node $i$ there is at most one node $j$ for which arc $(j, i)$ exists in $\mathcal{A}$. Analogously, a DAG is an in-forest if and only if for every node $i$ there is at most one arc $(i, j) \in \mathcal{A}$. The node without predecessors in the out-forest, or a node without the successors in the in-forest, is called a *root*. The in-forests or out-forests with only one root are called in-trees or out-trees, respectively. An example of an out-tree is shown in Fig. 2.3 (see page 21), and of an in-tree in Fig. 4.5a (page 66). Terminal nodes of an out-tree, and entry nodes of an in-tree, are called *leaves*. The *height* of an in- or out-tree is the number of arcs on the longest path in the tree. The height, or *level*, of a node in a tree is defined in various ways in various publications. It can be defined as the distance to/from the root or to/from the leaves. The distance can be counted in arcs (as stated above for the tree height), the total weight of the arcs, the total weight of the nodes, or the sum of both weights. Hence, care must be taken when referring to the node level. In the further discussion we follow the original definitions used in the algorithms.

Special cases of directed trees are single level trees whose nodes are either leaves or a root. A single level out-tree is often called *fork, branch, send*, star graph. A single level in-tree is often called *join, merge, receive* graph. A DAG comprising in- and out-trees is called an opposing forest.

A *series–parallel graph* is defined recursively. A single vertex is a series–parallel graph. *Series* construction connects two series–parallel graphs one after another. *Parallel* construction juxtaposes series–parallel graphs. Thus, series–parallel graphs may be equivalently represented as trees of the decomposition operators. The leaves of the decomposition tree are the vertices of the series–parallel graph, while the other nodes of the tree represent series and parallel operations. The above general idea of recursively composing a series–parallel graph leaves open details which differ in many publications. Fixing the details results in graph classes which are not equivalent. Hence, care must be taken when referring to the series–parallel graphs. Now we will distinguish types of series–parallel graphs. We will use terminology from [15].

In the first, most general definition, the series and the parallel constructions are binary operators. Let $\mathcal{G}_1 = (\mathcal{V}_1, \mathcal{A}_1, \mathcal{I}_1, \mathcal{O}_1)$, $\mathcal{G}_2 = (\mathcal{V}_2, \mathcal{A}_2, \mathcal{I}_2, \mathcal{O}_2)$, be two series–parallel graphs, where $\mathcal{V}_i$ are the sets of nodes, $\mathcal{A}_i$ are the sets of arcs, $\mathcal{I}_i \subseteq \mathcal{V}_i$ are the entry nodes, $\mathcal{O}_i \subseteq \mathcal{V}_i$ are terminal nodes, for $i = 1, 2$.

Series–parallel graphs (or general series–parallel graphs) are defined as follows:

- A single vertex is a series–parallel graph.
- Series composition of two series–parallel graphs $\mathcal{G}_1, \mathcal{G}_2$ is defied as follows:

$$ser(\mathcal{G}_1, \mathcal{G}_2) = (\mathcal{V}_1 \cup \mathcal{V}_2, \mathcal{A}_1 \cup \mathcal{A}_2 \cup (\mathcal{O}_1 \times \mathcal{I}_2), \mathcal{I}_1, \mathcal{O}_2)$$

- Parallel composition of two series–parallel graphs $\mathcal{G}_1, \mathcal{G}_2$ is defied as follows:

$$par(\mathcal{G}_1, \mathcal{G}_2) = (\mathcal{V}_1 \cup \mathcal{V}_2, \mathcal{A}_1 \cup \mathcal{A}_2, \mathcal{I}_1 \cup \mathcal{I}_2, \mathcal{O}_1 \cup \mathcal{O}_2)$$

An example of a series–parallel graph defined in the above way is shown in Fig. 2.1a. Its decomposition tree is shown in Fig. 2.1b. Note that there may be several decomposition trees of one series–parallel graph. Series–parallel graphs are DAGs, and in a series composition it matters which task is preceding which. Therefore, series operator is not commutative and the decomposition trees are oriented in this sense that the left and the right operands of the series construction are distinguished. A special subclass of the series–parallel graphs are *series–parallel-1 graphs* (SP1 graphs) which allow in the series construction that $|\mathcal{I}_2| = 1$ or $|\mathcal{O}_2| = 1$. Note that SP1 graphs generalize trees.

A subclass of SP1 series–parallel graphs are *series–parallel-11* graphs (SP11 graphs) defined as follows:

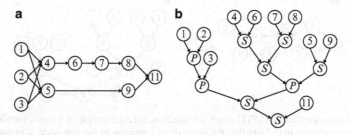

**Fig. 2.1** Series–parallel graph construction. (**a**) An example of a series–parallel graph. (**b**) Its decomposition tree. $P$ denotes parallel and $S$ series constructions

- A single vertex is an SP11 graph.
- Let $\mathcal{G}_i$, for $i = 0, \ldots, k + 1$, be SP11 graphs, and $a = \min\{1, k\}$. Then graph

$$\mathcal{G} = (\cup_{i=0}^{k+1} \mathcal{V}_i, \cup_{i=0}^{k+1} \mathcal{A}_i \cup (\mathcal{O}_0 \times \cup_{i=1}^{k} \mathcal{I}_i) \cup (\cup_{i=a}^{k} \mathcal{O}_i \times \mathcal{I}_{k+1}), \mathcal{I}_0, \mathcal{O}_{k+1}) \quad (2.1)$$

is also SP11 graph.

It follows from the above definition that SP11 graphs have single entry and single terminal nodes. Thus, SP11 graphs do not include all trees. Equation (2.1) is general enough to define both serial and parallel constructions. By convention it may be said that when $k \in \{0, 1\}$ the resulting DAG is a series concatenation of two or three SP11 graphs. By convention it may be also said that for $k > 1$ Eq. (2.1) defines a parallel construction of graphs $\mathcal{G}_1, \ldots, \mathcal{G}_k$ preceded by a fork graph rooted in the terminal node of $\mathcal{G}_0$, and succeeded by a join graph rooted in the entry node of $\mathcal{G}_{k+1}$. Note that this convention has consequences in the arity of the SP11 graph operators. The series constructions are binary or ternary operators, parallel construction is at least quaternary. An example of SP11 graph and its decomposition tree is shown in Fig. 2.2a and b, respectively. SP11 graphs as a subclass of series–parallel graphs may be constructed using the general definition of series–parallel graphs. In such a case decomposition trees of SP11 are binary trees. However, the representation based on Eq. (2.1) with decomposition trees of higher arity is used by some algorithms presented in this book.

There are also other definitions of series–parallel graphs where the exit nodes and entry nodes are unified. For example, in parallel construction entry nodes of $\mathcal{I}_1, \mathcal{I}_2$ are unified to a single node, and exit nodes of $\mathcal{O}_1, \mathcal{O}_2$ are unified to one exit node. Unless stated otherwise, in this book we will mean SP11 graphs when referring to the series–parallel graphs. Where possible, it will be pointed out that the considered methods are applicable to more general types of the series–parallel graphs.

Series–parallel graphs are a special kind of precedence constraints in scheduling because in many cases partial schedules built for the components of the series–parallel graph may be used to compose an optimum schedule for the whole graph. Thus, by traversing the decomposition tree from the leaves, where scheduling is trivial in most cases, to the root an optimum schedule may be constructed.

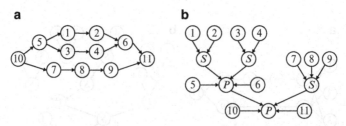

**Fig. 2.2** Series–parallel-11 (SP11) graph construction. (**a**) An example of a series–parallel graph. (**b**) Its decomposition tree. Note that the order of arcs arriving in the tree node is important. By convention $P$ denotes parallel ($k > 1$ in Eq. (2.1)) and $S$ series construction ($k = 0, 1$ in Eq. (2.1))

An *interval order* is a directed graph whose nodes can be mapped to intervals of real numbers such that for all $(i, j) \in \mathcal{A}$ the interval assigned to $i$ completely precedes the interval assigned to $j$.

In a *bipartite graph* the set of nodes can be partitioned into two subsets $\mathcal{V}_1, \mathcal{V}_2$ such that all edges $\{i, j\} \in \mathcal{E}$ satisfy $i \in \mathcal{V}_1, j \in \mathcal{V}_2$. In the case of directed bipartite graphs all arcs $(i, j) \in \mathcal{A}$ satisfy $i \in \mathcal{V}_1, j \in \mathcal{V}_2$.

A *clique*, or a *complete graph*, is a graph in which $\forall i, j \in \mathcal{V}, \{i, j\} \in \mathcal{E}$. In other words, clique is a graph with all possible edges.

A *matching* in a graph is set $M \subseteq \mathcal{E}$ such that no pair of edges in $M$ is incident with the same vertex.

## 2.2  Methodology of Complexity Theory

In this section, we outline the framework of the computational complexity theory for analyzing combinatorial optimization problems. Extensive presentation of this subject can be found, e.g., in [16, 38, 43]. Understanding this methodology is important because it guides research in combinatorial optimization problems. Many scheduling problems have combinatorial nature, and hence computational complexity theory is an essential tool in analyzing them.

Before going into definitions, let us informally present the basic ideas of the computational complexity. Many problems in discrete mathematics, combinatorial optimization, and consequently in computer science, expose exponential growth of the running time of the algorithms solving them, when the size of the problem is growing. Though these algorithms are correct, they are virtually unusable even for medium problem sizes. This phenomenon is sometimes called combinatorial explosion. Of course, one would prefer to use effective algorithms which have more moderate running times. Unfortunately, it seems that the difficulty in solving such problems is associated with the problems themselves, rather than with the deficiency of the solution method or the implementation. Such problems are called *intractable* or *computationally hard*. According to the current state of knowledge no methods are known to solve intractable problems effectively. By *effective methods* we mean the algorithms with running times bounded by a polynomial in the size of the problem. Computational complexity theory provides techniques for identifying computationally hard problems, and then suggests strategies for solving them. Though recognizing intractability of some problem is a pessimistic result, it is a "fact of life" because most of the scheduling problems are computationally hard. Three standard approaches are applied in dealing with hard problems: strive for the solution optimality at considerable cost, or sacrifice the optimality for the sake of effective algorithm, or try simplifying the problem hoping that the resulting solution is still useful. In the second case a *heuristic* or *approximation* algorithm is sought for. In some cases it is even possible to give guarantees of the heuristic solution quality. Obviously, one would prefer as strong quality guarantees as possible.

Unfortunately, providing certain types of quality guarantees may be as hard as solving some problem to optimality. Now we will formulate the main notions of the computational complexity theory which are referred to in this book.

## 2.2.1  Problems, Machines, Complexity Functions

For the purposes of this book combinatorial problems can be divided into decision problems, search problems, and optimization problems. Informally a *decision problem* can be defined as a set of parameters such as numbers, sets, graphs, etc. and a question for which only "yes" or "no" answers are allowed. Alternatively, decision problem $\Pi$ can be defined as a set of instances $D_\Pi$, and set $Y_\Pi \subseteq D_\Pi$ for which the answers are positive. A decision problem may be interpreted in a yet another way: It is a language which comprises all strings encoding instances from $Y_\Pi$ written according to a given encoding rule $e$, using symbols from some given alphabet $\Gamma$. A *search problem* $\Pi$ is defined by a set of its instances $D_\Pi$ and a set of admissible solutions $Z_\Pi(I)$ for each instance $I \in D_\Pi$. A decision problem $\Pi_D$ can be formulated as a search problem when $Z_{\Pi_D}(I) = \{\text{"yes"}\}$ for $I \in Y_{\Pi_D}$, and $Z_{\Pi_D}(I) = \{\text{"no"}\}$ if $I \notin Y_{\Pi_D}$. In *optimization problem* not only the set of instances $D_\Pi$ and the set of admissible solutions $Z_\Pi(I)$ for all $I \in D_\Pi$ are given, but also function $f(I, z)$ whose values are numbers is defined for all $I \in D_\Pi, z \in Z_\Pi(I)$. Function $f$ determines how good a solution $z$ is for input data $I$. Function $f$ is called *optimality criterion*, or *objective function*, and should be either minimized, or maximized, by the selection of solution $z$ for the given instance $I$.

Computational complexity theory classifies problems on the basis of the relation between execution time of the fastest algorithm solving the problem and problem size. Therefore, universal methods of expressing problem size and algorithm execution time are necessary. The length $N(I)$ of a string encoding instance $I$ according to some encoding rule, and using a given set of symbols, is a universal measure of problem size. What particular encoding rule and symbol alphabet are applied is not important for recognizing hard and easy problems. However, it is required that numbers are encoded at base greater than 1, and the string has no redundant symbols. The function $f(N(I))$ of the execution time of some algorithm in the size of the problem is called *computational complexity function* or *complexity* in short. For simplicity of presentation we will assume that basic arithmetic operations, such as addition, multiplication, can be performed in constant time. An algorithm with complexity bounded by a polynomial in problem size is called *polynomial* or *effective* algorithm. The algorithms whose complexity cannot be bounded in this way are called *exponential*. The main components of algorithm complexity can be conveniently expressed by the $O$ notation. Some complexity function $f(n)$ is $O(g(n))$ if $\exists C > 0, n_0, \forall n > n_0, f(n) < Cg(n)$. For example, $15.2n^2 + 103n + 0.1$ is $O(n^2)$. Informally, $O$ notation expresses an asymptotic upper bound of function $f(n)$. There is also $\Omega$ notation used to express asymptotic lower bounds. Function $f(n)$ is $\Omega(g(n))$ if $\exists C > 0, n_0, \forall n > n_0, Cg(n) < f(n)$. If function $f(n)$ is bounded asymptotically both below and above by function $g(n)$, then $\Theta$ notation is used. More formally, $f(n)$ is $\Theta(g(n))$ if $\exists\, C, C' > 0, n_0, \forall n > n_0, Cg(n) < f(n) < C'g(n)$.

The running time of an algorithm can be measured on a variety of computing systems. Let us mention two examples: deterministic turing machine (DTM) and random access machine (RAM). DTM is a simple model of a computer. It has a tape, where symbols may be recorded and read from, and an automaton which guides the machine behavior. RAM resembles contemporary computers. It has a program, random access memory, input, and output streams. DTM and RAM are realistic computer models, because such machines can be feasibly built. All realistic computers are equivalent in this sense that a polynomial algorithm on one realistic model can be simulated in polynomial time on any other realistic machine [16].

There are also machines which cannot be built, according to the current state of knowledge. Nondeterministic turing machine (NDTM) is one example. NDTM differs from DTM only in additional generating module which can guess a string allowing for solving some problem. More explicitly, the string may encode a solution of the problem. An algorithm on NDTM is polynomial if the stage of recording the guessed solution and checking it can be performed in polynomial time. Since NDTM and DTM differ only in the generating module, it can be informally said that DTM is a subset of NDTM. Since NDTM cannot be built (according to the current state of knowledge), its purpose is not solving problems, but defining certain classes of problems. Now we are ready to define complexity classes.

## 2.2.2   Basic Complexity Classes

**Definition 2.1.** **P** is a class of decision problems which can be solved in polynomial time on DTM.

Thus, problems in **P** can be solved in polynomial time on any realistic computer. One would expect to define the class of hard problems analogously, i.e. as these which cannot be solved in polynomial time. Unfortunately, such a definition would incorporate an assumption that hard problems cannot be solved in polynomial time. Still, this remains unknown. Thus, the definition of the class of hard decision problems is more involved. First, we define a class of problems with compact solution strings. Then, we define the subset of the hardest problems in this class.

**Definition 2.2.** **NP** is a class of decision problems which can be solved in polynomial time on NDTM.

Hence, **P** $\subseteq$ **NP** because what is solvable in polynomial time on DTM is also polynomially solvable on NDTM. Whether **P** $=$ **NP** and all hard problems can be solved in polynomial time, or **P** $\neq$ **NP** and hard problems require exponential algorithms remain one of the open problems in mathematics and computer science.

**Definition 2.3.** A polynomial transformation of problem $\Pi_1$ to $\Pi_2$ (denoted $\Pi_1 \propto \Pi_2$) is a function $f : D_{\Pi_1} \to D_{\Pi_2}$, satisfying the following:

(1) $\forall\, I \in D_{\Pi_1}$, $f(I)$ can be computed on DTM in polynomial time in $N(I)$
(2) $I \in Y_{\Pi_1} \iff f(I) \in Y_{\Pi_2}$

Note that polynomial transformation preserves polynomial time solvability of the problems (condition 1) and positive answer (condition 2). Consequently, it is possible to solve problem $\Pi_1$ by polynomially transforming its instances to $\Pi_2$. If the algorithm solving $\Pi_2$ is polynomial, then also $\Pi_1$ can be solved in polynomial time.

**Definition 2.4.** Problem $\Pi_1$ is NP-complete (NPc in short) if $\Pi_1 \in$ NP, and $\forall\, \Pi_2 \in$ NP, $\Pi_2 \propto \Pi_1$.

Observe that we did not define **NPc** problems as having exponential algorithms, but as those that are the hardest in class **NP**, because any problem in **NP** can be solved by a polynomial transformation to some **NPc** problem. It is generally accepted *hypothesis* that **P** $\neq$ **NP**, and **NPc** problems must be solved by exponential algorithms. The class of **NPc** problems comprises, e.g., Satisfiability, Partition, Hamiltonian Circuit [16], and thousands of other problems. By use of the transitivity of polynomial transformation one my prove that some problem $\Pi_3$ is **NPc** by constructing a polynomial transformation $\Pi_2 \propto \Pi_3$ from a known **NPc** problem $\Pi_2$ to problem $\Pi_3$.

For some **NPc** problems algorithms with complexity $O(p(N(I), Max(I)))$ exist, where $p$ is a polynomial in problem size $N(I)$, and $Max(I)$ is the value of some number given in the instance. Such algorithms are called *pseudopolynomial*. These are not polynomial algorithms, because $Max(I)$ is not polynomially bounded by the length of a string encoding value $Max(I)$ (numbers are encoded radix $>1$). Yet, pseudopolynomial algorithms may be practical in solving some hard problems if $Max(I)$ is small. Unfortunately, unless **P** $=$ **NP**, pseudopolynomial algorithms cannot be formulated for a class of *strongly* **NP**-*complete* (sNPc in short) problems. These are defined as follows.

**Definition 2.5.** Let $p$ be a polynomial in $N(I)$. Let $\Pi_p$ be a subproblem of $\Pi$ obtained by restricting $D_\Pi$ to instances satisfying $Max(I) < p(N(I))$. Problem $\Pi$ is **NP**-complete in the strong sense if $\Pi \in$ NP, and $\Pi_p$ is **NP**-complete.

If $\Pi$ has a pseudopolynomial algorithm, then subproblems $\Pi_p$ in the above definition are polynomially solvable. Consequently, pseudopolynomial algorithms can be constructed only for **NPc** problems *not* satisfying $\forall\, I \in D_\Pi$, $Max(I) < p(N(I))$ for any $p$.

The above complexity classes have been defined for decision problems. But one may argue that most of the scheduling problems are optimization problems. The results of the preceding discussion apply also to optimization problems because all decision problems have their decision version. By asking if for instance $I$ solution $z$ exists with $f(I, z) \leq y$ (in minimization), where $y$ is some threshold value, one obtains a decision version $\Pi_D$ of an optimization problem $\Pi$. Furthermore, the decision version $\Pi_D$ cannot be harder than $\Pi$, because a hypothetic algorithm $A$ solving $\Pi$ solves also $\Pi_D$ when supplemented with a comparison $f(I, z) \leq y$. Consequently, optimization problem cannot be tractable when its decision counterpart is intractable. Now we will define the class of hard search problems.

**Definition 2.6.** By a *polynomial Turing reduction* of search problem $\Pi_1$ to a search problem $\Pi_2$ (denoted $\Pi_1 \propto_T \Pi_2$) we mean algorithm $A$ solving problem $\Pi_1$ on DTM by use of some hypothetical procedure $P$ solving problem $\Pi_2$ such that $A$ is polynomial-time provided that $P$ can be executed in polynomial time by DTM.

**Definition 2.7.** Search problem $\Pi_1$ is **NP**-hard (**NPh** in short) when there exists some **NPc** problem $\Pi_2$ (formulated as a search problem) such that $\Pi_2 \propto_T \Pi_1$.

Since optimization problems are also search problems, consequently Definitions 2.6 and 2.7 apply also to optimization problems. Note that Definition 2.6 describes, e.g., the procedure of solving some decision version of a problem by use of an algorithm solving the optimization version. Problem $\Pi_1$ in Definition 2.7 cannot be solved in polynomial time unless $\mathbf{P} = \mathbf{NP}$. Thus, **NPh** problems are at least as hard as the problems in class **NP**. It can be shown that for many combinatorial problems the relation between complexity of the decision and the optimization version is even tighter. That is, the optimization version is not harder than the problems in class **NP**. Analogously to the class of s**NPc** problems, a class of problems **NP**-hard in the strong sense (s**NPh** in short) can be defined as such problems $\Pi$ which have a subproblem $\Pi_p$ which instances satisfy $\forall\, I \in D_{\Pi_p}, Max(I) < p(N(I))$ and $\Pi_p$ is **NPh**. For the end of complexity class considerations, let us mention that a hierarchy of increasingly difficult complexity classes exists beyond class **NP**. There are also other complexity classes built around different concepts than the ones discussed above [16, 38].

## 2.2.3   Approximability of Hard Problems

Determining complexity class of some problem is not the end of the analysis procedure. An optimization problem which is **NPh**, or s**NPh**, still has to be solved. As it was mentioned before, the computational complexity theory suggests three options: (1) find optimum solution which costs time, (2) find feasible solution fast which costs quality, and (3) try simplifying or reformulating the problem. The third option is a research strategy intending to delineate the border between the most general problems which are still computationally tractable and the simplest problems which are already hard.

A solution $z^* \in Z_{\Pi}(I)$ is optimum (for minimization) if $\forall\, z \in Z_{\Pi}(I)$, $f_{\Pi}(I, z^*) \leq f_{\Pi}(I, z)$. Let $A(I)$ denote the value of a solution delivered by some algorithm $A$ for instance $I$. An *optimization* algorithm finds an optimum solution for each instance of the problem, i.e. $\forall\, I \in D_{\Pi}, A(I) = OPT(I)$, where $OPT(I) = f(I, z^*)$.

An optimization algorithm has practical sense only if it has low-order polynomial complexity. Unfortunately, for computationally hard problems, only exponential optimization algorithms are known in the current state of knowledge (unless $\mathbf{P} = \mathbf{NP}$). Optimization algorithms of computationally hard problems are also called *enumerative* because in the worst case they may generate all possible solutions.

We will outline the second option now. An *approximation* algorithm, or *heuristic*, finds an admissible solution $\forall I \in D_\Pi, z \in Z_\Pi(I)$. Approximation algorithms trade quality for time. Thus, these algorithms make sense only if they have low-order running time. A measure of the approximation algorithm quality is the distance of its solutions from the optimum. In most of the cases it is expressed as *absolute performance ratio* (also called worst-case performance ratio, worst-case performance guarantee, or approximation ratio)

$$R_A = \inf\{r \geq 1 : \forall I \in D_\Pi, R_A(I) \leq r\} \tag{2.2}$$

or *asymptotic performance ratio*

$$R_A^\infty = \inf\{r \geq 1 : \exists N \in Z^+, \forall I \in \{I \in D_\Pi : OPT(I) \geq N\}, R_A(I) \leq r\} \tag{2.3}$$

where $R_A(I) = \frac{A(I)}{OPT(I)}$ for minimization and $R_A(I) = \frac{OPT(I)}{A(I)}$ for maximization. An algorithm with performance ratio $k$ is called $k$-approximate. The performance ratio $R_A$ is called to be *tight* if $\exists I \in D_\Pi, R_A(I) = R_A$. Let us note that a very similar notion of a $k$-competitive algorithm is used for online algorithms. A $k$-*competitive* algorithm builds a solution online (i.e. using only the currently available partial information) which is at most $k$ times worse than the optimum solution built by an algorithm with the complete knowledge of the given instance.

For some problems randomized approximation algorithms are known. In such cases the quality of the approximate solution is a random variable. For a randomized algorithm $A$ and instance $I$ the expected ratio $E(R_A(I))$ is calculated, where the expectation is taken over the random bits used in the algorithm. Performance ratio $ER_A$ of randomized algorithm $A$ is defined as a supremum of $E(R_A(I))$.

At this point computational complexity theory guides analysis of combinatorial optimization problem toward admissible approximation algorithm performance ratios. It is desirable to construct approximation algorithms with as good performance ratios as possible. If for a problem no algorithm with bounded performance ratio exists, then the problem is *inapproximable*. If an algorithm with a constant performance ratio exists for problem $\Pi$, then $\Pi$ is said to belong to class *APX*. For some problems even better approximation algorithms can be constructed. A *polynomial time approximation scheme* (PTAS) is an approximation algorithm which has absolute performance ratio $1 + \varepsilon$, and complexity bounded by a polynomial in $N(I)$, for any fixed $\varepsilon > 0$. A *fully polynomial time approximation scheme* (FPTAS) is an approximation algorithm which has absolute performance ratio $1 + \varepsilon$, and complexity bounded by a polynomial in $N(I)$, and $\frac{1}{\varepsilon}$ for any $\varepsilon > 0$. The quest for better and better approximation algorithms ends when some approximation algorithm meets a lower bound on possible performance ratios for a certain problem. Such lower bounds (if known) are also important indication on the nature of the solved problem.

Heuristic algorithms can be evaluated experimentally. Performance of certain algorithms depends very much on the input instances. It is not hard to imagine that some heuristics will perform well for certain types of instances. Unfortunately, there are no generally accepted ways of conducting experiments and generating representative test instances. Often simple probability distributions of the instance parameters do not represent reality sufficiently precisely. There are correlations between instance elements. For example, tasks running longer may require more processors and memory, short tasks may be submitted to the scheduler more often than long tasks. Hence, there is a need for benchmark instances of scheduling problems. The results obtained in experimental studies have limited portability between systems, and instances. Consequently, experimental findings must be taken with care. Due to the above concerns, we do not present results from the empirical tests comparing performance of the heuristics.

We conclude this section by itemizing the steps of combinatorial optimization problem analysis according to the methodology of computational complexity. Let $\Pi$ be an optimization problem and $\Pi_D$ its decision version.

1. Is $\Pi$ solvable in polynomial time? If "yes" then stop: $\Pi$ is easy.
2. Is $\Pi_D$ $\in$**NPc**?
   If the answer is unknown the complexity status of $\Pi$ is open.
   If "yes", then $\Pi$ $\in$**NPh**, and both $\Pi_D, \Pi$ are intractable (unless $\mathbf{P} = \mathbf{NP}$), $\Pi$ can be solved by (1) exponential optimization algorithm, (2) polynomial time heuristic, and (3) by simplifying $\Pi$.
3. Is $\Pi$ solvable in pseudopolynomial time?
   If "no", then $\Pi$ $\in$s**NPh**.
4. Is $\Pi$ approximable?
   If "no", then stop: $\Pi$ is inapproximable.
5. Is $\Pi$ $\in$**APX**?
6. Is there a PTAS (or even better an FPTAS) for $\Pi$?

In the next section we present common algorithmic techniques for solving hard combinatorial problems.

## 2.3 Solving Hard Combinatorial Problems

In this section, we present several standard methods used in solving hard combinatorial optimization problems. Note that general frameworks are presented here, while the actual algorithm performance depends very much on applying problem-specific knowledge in the adaptation of the framework to the considered problem. Due to the space limitations, only rudimentary facts are given to make reading this book easier for a reader without combinatorial optimization background.

## 2.3.1   Branch and Bound Algorithm

A detailed description of the Branch and Bound algorithm (B&B in short) can be found, e.g., in [7, 34, 39]. As its name indicates, B&B is composed of at least two elements: *branching* and *bounding* schemes. The branching scheme is a method of partitioning the set of all possible solutions into subsets which are subsequently fathomed. A subset $S$ of solutions is fathomed by either discarding it when it is certain that $S$ does not contain a better solution than the one currently known or by recursively partitioning $S$ into subsets. The procedure of partitioning the set of solutions is continued until some solution is singled out. The branching is completed when all subsets of solutions are fathomed. It is convenient to represent the branching process as a search in a tree. The root of a tree corresponds to the whole solution space $Z_\Pi(I)$. The descendants of a root represent subsets into which $Z_\Pi(I)$ has been partitioned. Analogously, if some node represents subset $S \subseteq Z_\Pi(I)$ of solutions then its descendant nodes represent subsets into which $S$ has been partitioned. Usually, the leaves of the search tree represent solutions. It is common to combine the search in the tree with constructing the solutions. Thus, a root of the tree has an "empty" solution which represents all solutions that can be built. As the search progresses toward the leaves solutions are gradually built. Then, an internal node of the B&B tree represents a partial solution and a leaf is a complete solution.

The number of the nodes grows exponentially with the depth of the search tree, hence there is a need for some method of discarding at least some of them. Here comes the second part of the B&B algorithm that is a bounding scheme eliminating the nodes representing subsets of solutions certainly not comprising a better solution than the one currently known. Suppose that $\Pi$ is a minimization problem. A subset (equivalently a node) $S$ is eliminated on the basis of comparing a lower bound $lb(S)$ on objective function of all the solutions in the subset $S$, with the value of the objective function of some solution which is already known. Such a solution can be found by some heuristic before starting B&B, or it can be one of the complete solutions constructed by the algorithm itself. There are also other means that can be applied to prune the search tree [7, 34, 39]. Properly implemented B&B algorithm finds the optimum solution very quickly for most of the instances, yet it spends exponential time in producing a proof that this solution is indeed optimal. Parallel versions of B&B are also known [9].

Let us finish this section with an example. Assume that we solve a problem of scheduling $n$ independent tasks with different processing times, ready at time 0, without deadlines, for minimum schedule length criterion. Processing times of the tasks are $p_j$, for $j = 1, \ldots, n$. The number of parallel identical processors is $m$. Let us refer to this problem as to $P||C_{\max}$ (the notation of scheduling problems is introduced in Sect. 4.2). The above problem can be solved by assigning tasks from a list to processors, as soon as some processor becomes available. Thus, it can be reduced to the construction of the optimum permutation of the tasks on the list. A search tree can be constructed as follows (cf. Fig. 2.3). The root represents all permutations. It has $n$ successors each representing permutations starting with one of the tasks. Nodes at level $l$ (for $l = 0, \ldots, n$) of the tree are partial permutations

**Fig. 2.3** Example of B&B
tree construction

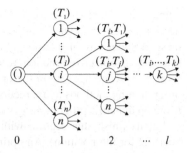

with $l$ leading tasks already selected. The nodes at level $l < n$ have $n - l$ descendants, each representing a permutation constructed by concatenation of the parent permutation with one more task absent in the parent permutation. A leaf of the tree is a complete permutation. The whole tree has $n!$ leaves in the worst case. A lower bound of a node $S$ at level $l$ can be calculated as a sum of the lengths of two parts in the schedule: $lb_1(S)$ for the already determined partial permutation $S$ and $lb_2(S)$ for the tail of the permutation remaining to be constructed. For the tasks in the partial permutation $S$ scheduled on the processors, the earliest time when some processor becomes available is $lb_1(S)$. The remaining tasks need at least $lb_2(S) = \max\{\sum_{j \notin S} \frac{p_j}{m}, \max_{j \notin S}\{p_j\}\}$. Thus, $lb_1(S) + lb_2(S)$ is a lower bound for node $S$.

## 2.3.2   Dynamic Programming

The origins of dynamic programming can be traced back to Bellman's principle of optimality [4], applied in the decision processes. The principle states that for an optimal decision trajectory A $\rightarrow$ B $\rightarrow$ C from a beginning state A to a final state C, every final part B $\rightarrow$ C is also an optimal trajectory from the starting state $B$ to a final state C. Though this statement may seem vague, it declares that the decision process is essentially memoryless, because from the point of view of getting from B to C optimally it does not matter how state B was reached. In other words, starting at any current state, the optimal policy for the subsequent stages is independent of the policies adopted in the previous stages. Bellman's principle can be used to construct the optimum trajectory from every possible state A to B. This makes sense especially when the decision problem has discrete nature, which is often the case of the combinatorial optimization problems. One may start with an initial state $s_0$ representing no decision taken, and find the optimum path to any feasible state accessible from the initial state. This can be repeated for each next pair of decision states $s_i, s_{i+1}$. An optimum path from $s_0$ to $s_{i+1}$ consists of the optimum paths from $s_i$ to $s_{i+1}$, from $s_{i-1}$ to $s_{i+1}$, from $s_{i-2}$ to $s_{i+1}$, etc. By analyzing all possible states of the decision problem, and the optimum ways of progressing from a state to a state, we implicitly analyze all possible paths from an initial state of no decision taken to a final state where an optimum solution is built. The number of such paths is exponential for hard computational problems. Thus, dynamic programming methods for these problems are also exponential algorithms. Very often characteristic of some state $s_i$ (e.g. objective function, resource consumption) can be calculated on the basis of the preceding state in the optimum path. Therefore, it is typical of dynamic programming methods to use recursive equations for calculating such characteristic. More on dynamic programming may be found in e.g. [8].

Let us finish this section with an example. Consider problem $P||C_{max}$ (see Sect. 4.2 for the notation). An optimum schedule is an active schedule, i.e. there is no advantage in delaying tasks, and each task is started as early as possible. Hence, schedule length is determined solely by the sets of tasks assigned to processors. A state of the decision process may be determined by the load $x_i$ of the processor $i$, and the subset $\emptyset \cup \{T_1, \ldots, T_j\}$ of already scheduled tasks, for $j = 0, \ldots, n$. Thus, a state in the decision problem may be represented as a vector $(x_1, \ldots, x_m, j)$. State $(x_1, \ldots, x_m, j)$, for $j > 0$, is accessible from states $(x_1, \ldots, x_i - p_j, \ldots, x_m, j-1)$, for $i = 1, \ldots, m$, which corresponds with assigning task $T_j$ to processor $P_i$. For each of such states it is possible to calculate a characteristic feature which asserts if the state represents a feasible active schedule:

$$f(x_1, \ldots, x_m, j) = \begin{cases} 1 & \text{a schedule exists for tasks } \emptyset \cup \{T_1, \ldots, T_j\} \text{ such} \\ & \text{that processor } P_i \text{ completes computations at } x_i \\ 0 & \text{otherwise} \end{cases}$$

This function can be calculated recursively:

$$f(0, \ldots, 0) = 1; \; f(x_1, \ldots, x_m, 0) = 0, \text{ for } x_i > 0, \; i = 1, \ldots, m$$
$$f(x_1, \ldots, x_m, j) = 0 \text{ if } x_i < 0, \text{ for } i = 1, \ldots, m, \; j = 1, \ldots, n$$
$$f(x_1, \ldots, x_m, j) = f(x_1, \ldots, x_i - p_j, \ldots, x_m, j - 1) \text{ for } x_i = 0, \ldots, C,$$

$i = 1, \ldots, m, j = 1, \ldots, n$, where $C$ is some upper bound on possible schedule lengths. The optimum schedule is determined by a state $(x_1^*, \ldots, x_m^*, n)$ such that $f(x_1^*, \ldots, x_m^*, n) = 1$ and $\forall \{(x_1, \ldots, x_m, n) : f(x_1, \ldots, x_m, n) = 1\}$, $\max_{i=1}^{m} \{x_i^*\} \leq \max_{i=1}^{m} \{x_i\}$. Since function $f(x_1, \ldots, x_m, j)$ has to be calculated for $x_i = 0, \ldots, C$, and $j = 1, \ldots, n$, the complexity of this method is $O(nC^m)$. This is a pseudopolynomial algorithm for a fixed $m$, i.e. for problem $Pm||C_{max}$. The origins of the above method can be found in [40].

### 2.3.3 Linear Programming

Many combinatorial optimization problems can be conveniently expressed as linear programs (LPs). In linear programming it is assumed that the decision variables $x_i$ are numbers. A linear program decrees that a linear function of decision variables be minimized, or maximized, subject to linear constraints. Suppose that the number of variables is $n$, and the number of constraints is $m$. Thus, a linear program may be expressed as follows:

$$\text{minimize} \quad \sum_{i=1}^{n} a_i x_i \tag{2.4}$$

$$\text{subject to} \quad \sum_{i=1}^{n} b_{ij} x_i = c_j \quad \text{for } j = 1, \dots, m \tag{2.5}$$

where $a_i, b_{ij}, c_j$ are given constants. A linear program (2.4)–(2.5) can accommodate weak inequalities ($\leq, \geq$) in the constraints (2.5), e.g. by use of additional relaxing variables. Two fundamentally different versions of linear programming problem can be distinguished: rational LP and integer LP (ILP). In the rational LP, the variables are rational numbers. Let us observe that constraints (2.5) define a convex $n$-dimensional body. Since the objective function (2.4) is linear, the optimum solution of an LP resides in one of the corners of the area defined by (2.5). Which particular corner is optimum obviously depends on $a_i, b_{ij}, c_j$, and it cannot be guessed just from the formal statement of an LP. A practical consequence is that if some problem needs linear programming to be solved, then closed-form solutions (i.e. fixed formulas for $x_i$s) are hard to be expected. The rational LP can be solved in polynomial time [29]. On contrary, the integer LP is computationally hard [16]. In practice rational LP formulations are solved either by simplex method (which is effective on average, but exponential in the worst case) or by interior point methods. Integer LP can be solved by a dedicated branch and cut method, or by one of the standard combinatorial optimization methods such as B&B, or metaheuristics. More information on linear programming may be found in, e.g., [31, 37, 39].

Let us finish this section with an example. We will formulate problem $P||C_{max}$ as an ILP. Let $x_{ij} = 1$ if task $j$ is assigned to processor $i$, and $x_{ij} = 0$ otherwise. Our problem can be formulated as follows:

$$\text{minimize} \quad C_{max} \tag{2.6}$$

$$\text{subject to} \quad \sum_{j=1}^{n} x_{ij} p_j \leq C_{max} \quad \text{for } i = 1, \dots, m \tag{2.7}$$

$$\sum_{i=1}^{m} x_{ij} = 1 \quad \text{for } j = 1, \dots, n \tag{2.8}$$

$$x_{ij} \in \{0, 1\} \tag{2.9}$$

Inequalities (2.7) guarantee that no processor computes after the end of the schedule. By Eq. (2.8) each task is assigned to exactly one processor.

### 2.3.4 Metaheuristics

Metaheuristics are a group of general-purpose methods providing "*meta*" structure for constructing approximation algorithms. This structure has to be adopted to the actual problem. Metaheuristics use various strategies to guide the search for near-optimum solutions. Very often the search consists in a sequence of moves or local perturbations of the search state. For this reason metaheuristics are also called *local search methods*. The problem-specific knowledge must be applied to implement the moves. Many metaheuristics use randomization in their search. Thus, these methods are probabilistic algorithms in most of the cases. Metaheuristics do not examine the whole space of possible solutions as, e.g., B&B algorithm does. In general there is no information when the search is sufficiently broad to stop it. Two types of stopping criteria are frequently used. First, when a satisfactory solution is reached. For example, a feasible graph coloring using a certain number of colors is achieved [26]. Second, when a limit on the amount of computations is reached: a time limit, an upper bound on the number of algorithm iterations, or a limit on the number of iterations without improving the best solution. Metaheuristics usually have specific parameters determining their behavior. Such parameters must be tuned in each implementation. In the following we describe three popular metaheuristics: simulated annealing, tabu search, and genetic algorithm. More information about metaheuristics, local search methods can be found, e.g., in [1, 44].

### 2.3.4.1  Simulated Annealing

The search strategy of *simulated annealing* [6, 30, 33] is an analogy of solid thermodynamic state evolution simulation. In such a simulation [35] particles of a solid make random perturbations which change total energy of the solid. The perturbations decreasing the energy are accepted, while the ones increasing solid energy by $\Delta E$ are accepted with probability proportional to $e^{-\frac{\Delta E}{k_B T}}$, where $k_B$ is Boltzmann constant and $T$ is temperature.

In the case of optimization problems random local moves, or perturbations, are accepted if the quality of the solution is improved. Moves lowering the solution quality by $\Delta y$ are accepted with probability $e^{-\frac{\Delta y}{t}}$, where $t$ is an equivalent of temperature. Thus, deteriorating moves are more accepted when $t$ is high. As the "solid" cools down, temperature is lowered, and accepting a worse solution is less likely. The procedure for increasing and reducing parameter $t$ is specific for the implementation, and is called a *cooling schedule*. Cooling schedules frequently comprise the following steps. Initially temperature $t$ should be big enough to allow visiting all feasible solutions. Hence, $t$ is being increased until certain number of moves, or fraction of moves, is accepted. Then, the temperature starts decreasing. At every temperature level thermodynamic equilibrium should be achieved. This is guaranteed if a certain number of moves are accepted. On the other hand, for low temperatures, the number of try moves may be very big to attain a determined number of accepted moves. Therefore, also an upper limit on the total number of moves at each temperature stage may be imposed.

### 2.3.4.2  Genetic Algorithm

*Genetic algorithm* or *genetic search* is imitating evolution of a genome [22, 36]. Solutions are usually encoded as strings by analogy to encoding of chromosomes. A pool of solutions exists, analogously to a population of individuals. Usually the initial population is randomly generated. Genetic operators transform populations in a direction improving quality of the solutions.

Selection, crossover, and mutation are typical genetic operators which are iteratively applied to the population. *Selection* elects better solutions for the next population. *Crossover* operation generates offspring solutions by randomly combining pieces of the parent strings. In the simplest form of the crossover operation two chromosomes $(a_1, a_2, \ldots, a_n)$, $(b_1, b_2, \ldots, b_n)$ are selected and combined into $(b_1, \ldots, b_{k-1}, a_k, \ldots, a_n)$ and $(a_1, \ldots, a_{k-1}, b_k, \ldots, b_n)$, where $k$ is a randomly chosen crossover point. Though the offspring is constructed in a random manner, the fragments of a string encoding an optimum solution are indirectly discovered and combined due to the selection preferring better solutions. *Mutation* changes randomly some solutions to diversify the search and to escape local optima.

### 2.3.4.3    Tabu Search

*Tabu search* [19–21], for minimization, uses a strategy of progressing in the direction of the biggest decrease, or the smallest increase, of the objective function.

More precisely, tabu search starts from some initial solution $x_0$ and analyzes its neighborhood $S(x_0)$. The best neighbor $x_1 \in S(x_0)$ is selected as the next point to be visited. Analogously, for solution $x_i$ the best solution in neighborhood $S(x_i)$ is selected as the next solution $x_{i+1}$. This strategy may result in cyclic visiting the same pair of solutions if the search process gets trapped in a local optimum. Therefore, a queue of forbidden moves is used which is called a *tabu list*. Banning certain moves may be too prohibitive, especially when the topology of the search space is complex. Therefore, a concept of *aspiration function* has been introduced: Aspiration function calculates how good a new solution should be to accept it even though it is on a tabu list. The length of the tabu list, construction of the neighborhood, and the aspiration function are implementation-specific parameters of this method. Tabu search as described above is not a probabilistic method. However, the search preformed from one initial solution $x_0$ may be not thoroughly enough. Various methods are applied to diversify the tabu search. The simplest way to do it is by restarting the search from random initial solutions.

For the end of this section let us mention that metaheuristics turned out to be very effective in constructing near-optimum solutions of hard combinatorial problems. Hence, it is not a surprise that metaheuristics are quite common in scheduling. This should not be confused, however, with making them work effectively. It still requires a lot of problem-specific knowledge, tuning, and hard work. Addressing such details is beyond the scope and size of this publication. Therefore, we will not present metaheuristics solving particular scheduling problems in this book.

## 2.4    Parallel Performance Metrics

In this chapter, we present basic performance measures related to parallel processing. We simplify the notation by considering only one parallel application.

Let $p(i)$ be the processing time of a parallel application if run on $i$ processors. This function will be called *processing time function* (also called *execution time function* or *execution signature* [5, 11]). By conceiving such a definition of $p(i)$ we tacitly assume that the parallel application can be executed on any number of processors $i$ from one to the maximum available. This is not always true due to the internal structure of the application. Obviously, processing time depends on the computer system: its architecture and speeds of the components. Since the goal of high performance computing is computing as fast as possible, $p(i)$ is the basic parallel performance measure. A usually accepted form of function $p(i)$ is

$$p(i) = a + \frac{b}{i} + c(i) \qquad (2.10)$$

where $a, b$ are constants, and nondecreasing function $c(i)$ represents the cost of using many processors [18, 42, 45].

*Work* of a parallel application executed on $i$ processors is $W(i) = ip(i)$.

A commonly used parallel performance measure is *speedup*, classically [2, 28] defined as

$$\varsigma(i) = \frac{p_{BS}}{p(i)} \qquad (2.11)$$

where $p_{BS}$ is the execution time of the best known sequential algorithm for the considered problem. Since it is often disputed whether comparing two different algorithms makes sense, speedup is more practically defined as [17, 27]

$$\varsigma(i) = \frac{p(1)}{p(i)} \qquad (2.12)$$

Note that speedup is a dimensionless measure. Speedup measures how much application accelerates while using more processors (though it has no acceleration units like m/s$^2$). It quantifies how well the application utilizes processors on the given computer system. Hence, speedup may be considered as an indicator of the application *scalability*, i.e. the ability to compute effectively on growing sizes of the parallel computers. Alternatively, if (2.12) is rewritten to $p(i) = \frac{p(1)}{\varsigma(i)}$, and $p(1)$ is interpreted as the amount of computations, then speedup can be interpreted as an equivalent of processing speed function on $i$ processors. It is confusing to use speedup in this way because $\varsigma(i)$ has no standard units of speed (e.g. km/h, m$^3$/s, FLOPS, tps, etc.). Thus, considerable care must be taken while referring to speedup.

Various models of speedup were proposed, including famous Amdahl's [3], Gustafson's [25], and Downey's models [12]. Following the form of the execution time function (2.10) speedup is usually a sublinear function. It is often assumed that parallel applications have nondecreasing speedup: $\varsigma(i) \leq \varsigma(i + 1)$ which is equivalent to nonincreasing processing time function: $p(i) \geq p(i + 1)$. Furthermore, it is often assumed that parallel applications have *monotony* or *monotonous penalty* property, which means that processing time function $p(i)$ is nonincreasing, and performed work $W(i)$ is nondecreasing in $i$. Nondecreasing work implies sublinear speedup because:

$$W(i) = ip(i) \le (i+1)p(i+1) = W(i+1) \Rightarrow \frac{i}{i+1} \le \frac{p(i+1)}{p(i)} = \frac{\varsigma(i)}{\varsigma(i+1)}$$

$$(2.13)$$

Hence, $\varsigma(i+1) \le \frac{i+1}{i}\varsigma(i)$. More generally, $\varsigma(ki) \le k\varsigma(i)$. Thus, monotony property is equivalent to sublinear and nondecreasing speedup.

Though it seems counterintuitive superlinear speedup has been reported in the literature. The possibility of superlinear speedup depends on the amount of work performed by a parallel application. Note that a superlinear speedup implies $W(i) = ip(i) < p(1)$. It is often assumed that the work of a parallel application is nondecreasing, but it need not be true in general (even without achieving superlinear speedup) [13, 45]. For example, if the application requires a lot of memory which does not fit into core of a single computer, then $p(1)$ in Eq. (2.12) will be unfairly big because the out-of-core memory will have to be used. On the other hand, $i$ computers together may have sufficient amount of memory to accommodate the application in their core memories.

*Efficiency* $E(i) = \frac{\varsigma(i)}{i}$ is a measure derived from speedup. It can be understood as the fraction of all processors granted to the application which really computes. A different interpretation of efficiency is average work performed by the application per time unit per processor [14], because $p(1)$ may be understood as the amount of work in the application, and $p(i)$ is the execution time. It has been observed that efficiency $E$ of parallel computation, problem size, and the number of used processors $i$ are mutually related (cf. also Sect. 7.12.3). Therefore, *isoefficiency function* $ief(i, E)$ was defined in [23, 24] as the function of the problem size required to maintain efficiency $E$ while using $i$ processors. The efficiency defined in this paragraph should not be confused with $E(\tau)$ – a measure of the fraction of all $m$ processors performing usable work at time $\tau$. This second definition of (momentary) efficiency is used in many online algorithms (e.g. in Chap. 5).

*Parallelism profile* [10, 18, 32, 41, 42] is the number of processors used by a parallel application over time, on an ideal parallel machine with unbounded number of processors. The same function, but measured on a computer with bounded processor

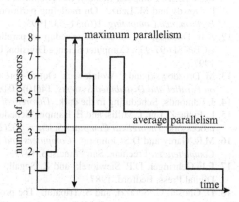

**Fig. 2.4** Example of parallelism profile

number, is called *execution profile*. Maximum parallelism, i.e. maximum usable number, of processors, and average parallelism (average number of used processors) can be computed using the data in parallelism profile (cf. Fig. 2.4).

Maximum and average parallelism are examples of processor numbers which may be assigned to execute a parallel application on a system with limited resources. *Processor working set* (PWS) [18] is another gauge of parallel application performance which defines processor number that may be assigned to execute the application. PWS is the minimum number of processors $i$ at which the ratio $\frac{\varsigma(i)}{1/E(i)}$ is minimum. The rationale behind this particular ratio is that it expresses relation between the gain from parallelism, which is speedup $\varsigma(i)$, and the cost of parallelism, which is inefficiency $\frac{1}{E(i)}$.

# References

1. E. Aarts and J.K. Lenstra. *Local Search in Combinatorial Optimization*. Wiley, New York, NY, 1997.
2. S.G. Akl. *The Design and Analysis of Parallel Algorithms*. Prentice-Hall, Englewood Cliffs, NJ, 1989.
3. G.M. Amdahl. Validity of the single processor approach to achieving large scale computing capabilities. In *AFIPS Conference Proceedings (Atlantic City Apr. 18–20, 1967)*, volume 30, pages 483–485. AFIPS, 1967.
4. R. Bellman. *Dynamic Programming*. Princeton University Press, Princeton, NJ, 1957.
5. M. Calzarossa and G. Serazzi. Workload characterization: A survey. *Proceedings of the IEEE*, 81(8):1136–1150, 1993.
6. V. Cerny. Thermodynamical approach to the traveling salesman problem: An efficient simulation algorithm. *J. Optimization Theory and Applications*, 45:41–51, 1985.
7. E.G. Coffman Jr., editor. *Computer and Job-Shop Scheduling Theory*. Wiley, New York, 1976.
8. T.H. Cormen, C.E. Leiserson, and R.L. Rivest. *Introduction to Algorithms*. MIT Press, Cambridge MA and MCGraw-Hill, New York, 1990.
9. T.G. Crainic, B. Le Cun, and C. Roucairol. Parallel branch-and-bound algorithms. In E.-G. Talbi, editor, *Parallel Combinatorial Optimization*, pages 1–28. Wiley, Hoboken NJ, 2006.
10. D.E. Culler and Arvind. Resource requirements of dataflow programs. In *Proceedings of the 15th Annual International Symposium on Computer Architecture (ISCA'88)*, pages 141–150, 1988. IEEE, Computer Society, Los Alamitos, CA, USA.
11. L. Dowdy and M. Leuze. On modeling partitioned multiprocessor systems. *Journal of High Performance Computing*, 1(6):31–53, 1993.
12. A.B. Downey. A model for speedup of parallel programs. Technical Report Report No. UCB/CSD-97-933, Computer Science Division, University of California, Berkeley, CA 94720, 1997.
13. M. Drozdowski and P. Wolniewicz. Out-of-core divisible load processing. *IEEE Transactions on Parallel and Distributed Systems*, 14(10):1048–1056, 2003.
14. J. Edmonds. Scheduling in the dark. *Theoretical Computer Science*, 235(1):109–141, 2000.
15. L. Finta, Z. Liu, I. Millis, and E. Bampis. Scheduling UET-UCT series–parallel graphs on two processors. *Theoretical Computer Science*, 162(2):323–340, 1996.
16. M.R. Garey and D.S. Johnson. *Computers and Intractability: A Guide to the Theory of NP-Completeness*. Freeman, San Francisco, 1979.
17. E.F. Gehringer, D.P. Siewiorek, and Z. Segall. *Parallel Processing: The $Cm^*$ Experience*. Digital Press, Bedford, 1987.
18. D. Ghosal, G. Serazzi, and S. Tripathi. The processor working set and its use in scheduling multiprocessor systems. *IEEE Transactions on Software Engineering*, 17(5):443–453, 1991.

19. F. Glover. Tabu-search part i. *ORSA Journal on Computing*, 1(3):190–206, 1989.
20. F. Glover and M. Laguna. *Tabu Search*. Kluwer Academic, Boston, 1997.
21. F. Glover and M. Laguna. Tabu search. In D.-Z. Du and P.M. Pardalos, editors, *Handbook of Combinatorial Optimization*, volume 3, pages 621–757. Kluwer Academic, Dordrecht, The Netherlands, 1998.
22. D.E. Goldberg. *Genetic Algorithms in Search, Optimization and Machine Learning*. Addison-Wesley, Reading, MA, 1989.
23. A.Y. Grama and V. Kumar. Scalability analysis of partitioning strategies for finite element graphs: A summary of results. In *Proceedings of Supercomputing '92*, pages 83–92. IEEE Computer Society, Los Alamitos, CA, USA, 1992.
24. A. Gupta and V. Kumar. Performance properties of large scale parallel systems. *Journal of Parallel and Distributed Computing*, 19(3):234–244, 1993.
25. J.L. Gustafson. Reevaluating Amdahl's law. *Communications of the ACM*, 31(5):532–533, 1988.
26. A. Hertz and D. de Werra. The tabu search metaheuristic: How we used it. *Annals of Mathematics and Artificial Intelligence*, 1:111–121, 1990.
27. K. Hwang. *Advanced Computer Architecture: Parallelism, Scalability, Programmability*. McGraw-Hill, New York, 1993.
28. J. Jájá. *An Introduction to Parallel Algorithms*. Addison-Wesley, Reading, MA, 1992.
29. L.G. Khachiyan. A polynomial algorithm in linear programming (in Russian). *Doklady Akademii Nauk SSSR*, 244:1093–1096, 1979.
30. S. Kirkpatrick, C.D. Gelatt Jr., and M.P. Vecchi. Optimization by simulated annealing. *Science*, 220(4598):671–680, 1983.
31. B. Korte and J. Vygen. *Combinatorial Optimization: Theory and Algorithms*. Springer, Berlin, Heidelberg, 2002.
32. M. Kumar. Measuring parallelism in computation-intensive scientific/engineering applications. *IEEE Transactions on Computers*, 9(37):1088–1098, 1988.
33. P.J.M. Laarhoven and E.H.L. Aarts, editors. *Simulated Annealing: Theory and Applications*. D. Reidel, Dordrecht, The Netherlands, 1987.
34. J.K. Lenstra. *Sequencing by Enumerative Methods*. Number 69 in Mathematical Centre Tracts. Matematisch Centrum, Amsterdam, 1977.
35. M. Metropolis, A. Rosenbluth, M. Rosenbluth, A. Teller, and E. Teller. Equation of state calculations by fast computing machines. *Journal of Chemical Physics*, 21:1087–1092, 1953.
36. Z. Michalewicz. *Genetic Algorithms + Data Structures = Evolution Programs*. Springer, Berlin, Heidelberg, 1996.
37. J.E. Mitchell, P.M. Pardalos, and M.G.C. Resende. Interior point methods for combinatorial optimization. In D.-Z. Du and P.M. Pardalos, editors, *Handbook of Combinatorial Optimization*, volume 1, pages 189–297. Kluwer Academic, Dordrecht, The Netherlands, 1998.
38. C.H. Papadimitriou. *Computational Complexity*. Addison Wesley, Reading, MA, 1994.
39. C.H. Papadimitriou and K. Steiglitz. *Combinatorial Optimization: Algorithms and Complexity*. Prentice-Hall, Englewood Cliffs, NJ, 1982.
40. M. Rothkopf. Scheduling independent tasks on parallel processors. *Management Science*, 12(5):437–447, 1966.
41. V. Sarkar. *Partitioning and Scheduling Parallel Programs for Multiprocessors*. MIT Press, Cambridge MA, 1989.
42. K.C. Sevcik. Application scheduling and processor allocation in multiprogrammed parallel processing systems. *Performance Evaluation*, 19:107–140, 1994.
43. Wikipedia. Computational complexity theory. http://en.wikipedia.org/wiki/ Computational_complexity_theory, 2008 [online accessed 29 September 2008].
44. Wikipedia. Metaheuristic. http://en.wikipedia.org/wiki/Metaheuristic, 2008 [online accessed 29 September 2008].
45. J.L. Wolf, J. Turek, M.-S. Chen, and P.S. Yu. A hierarchical approach to parallel multiquery scheduling. *IEEE Transactions on Parallel and Distributed Systems*, 6(6):578–590, 1995.

# Chapter 3
# Vision of Scheduling in Parallel Systems

In this chapter, we examine vision of scheduling parallel applications which exist at various levels of computer systems. In other words this chapter is dedicated to the technical foundations of scheduling in parallel computing. We will study three elements of a parallel system: hardware, programming environment, i.e. programmer abstraction of the parallel system, and runtime environments. The purpose of this study is to find clues on scheduling problems that need to be solved, the approaches that may be viable, and limitations imposed on scheduling models. The following issues may be interesting: Is there any particular support for scheduling parallel applications? How much scheduling flexibility is left to a user of the application? Can the application be suspended, assigned to a selected processor, or migrated to a different processor? Are there any guarantees of executing parts of the application in parallel in real time? What data can be practically collected for the scheduling algorithms?

## 3.1 Hardware

In this section, we discuss elements of a parallel system hardware which may influence the scheduling decisions. We will concentrate on CPUs, memory, and the interconnection. One important issue is if the parallel system hardware can be easily partitioned between coexisting parallel applications. A good partitioning design should support locality of hardware usage such that coexisting tasks do not interfere with one another.

### 3.1.1 CPU

Contemporary CPU contains parallelism in various forms. The simplest form of parallelism is using wide words. This form of parallelism is so ordinary that some do not even consider it parallelism. A realization of the SIMD class of parallel

M. Drozdowski, *Scheduling for Parallel Processing*, Computer Communications
and Networks, DOI 10.1007/978-1-84882-310-5_3,
© Springer-Verlag London Limited 2009

computers from Flynn's classification [25] are MMX, 3DNow!, SSE, AltiVec instruction sets which allow to perform the same operation on a packed group of numbers. CPUs use parallelism also in the instruction execution. Pipelined execution of the instruction stages (fetch, decode, execute, etc.) is another example of parallelism. To overcome performance disadvantages of pipeline processing (filling, stalls, emptying, synchronizations) speculative instruction execution, branch prediction techniques were invented which are yet other examples of instruction level parallelism (ILP). Though ILP is an excellent scheduling research area, we do not present scheduling at the instruction level in this book.

General-purpose CPUs support multiple threads of execution by multithreading and multicore designs. Before introduction of such CPUs, threads were managed by the operating system or a user application. This does not seem to have changed so far despite supporting operating system functionality in the hardware of a CPU. It seems to be a natural choice in a design of a general-purpose CPU, not necessarily dedicated to high performance computations, to give as much flexibility as possible to the higher level scheduling policies. Efficient hardware mechanisms, such as fast context switch, are the design goals. Within the limits of CPU hardware resources (replicated registers, functional units) partitioning a CPU between the threads is possible. Thus, contemporary commercially available CPUs do not prefer any particular policy of parallel application scheduling.

High performance computing systems are sometimes extended by Field Programmable Gate Array (FPGA) systems. FPGA reconfigurable systems [12] accelerate execution of small parts of code lending itself to hardware implementation. Contemporary FPGA coprocessors work as slaves to the standard CPUs. Thus, such facilities may be considered an additional resource required by a task.

### 3.1.2   Memory

Memory system is another element of a parallel computer which may influence scheduling decisions. Current computer systems use hierarchic memory designs. At the top of memory hierarchy are CPU registers which have the shortest access time, but are available in the smallest number. At the bottom of the hierarchy there are slow but spacious external storage devices such as hard disks, tapes, or networked file systems. Generally, the higher in the memory hierarchy we get, the shorter access times are experienced, and the smaller amount of memory is available. Transferring datasets from one memory level to another may be a time-consuming operation limiting profitability of thread or process migration. For example, a thread executed on a certain CPU may accumulate data and instructions in the cache of the processor on which it is executed. The time needed to transfer this dataset to the core memory may be longer than the sheer time of migrating the thread control structures from one processor to some other processor. Therefore, by using cache a thread executed on some processor builds a kind of affinity to this processor. This kind of phenomenon is called *cache affinity* or *processor affinity* because cache hardware is usually attached to CPUs. Hence, it may be advantageous to execute a thread always on the same CPU. In this case CPUs, though parallel and identical, may be understood as dedicated devices. Similar situation takes place when a big dataset, e.g. a file with measurements or a database, is held by a particular computer. Due to the communication delays it may be counterproductive to transfer the dataset to a different computer for processing. A more effective option is to process the dataset on the computer where the dataset resides. Processor affinity may arise in the case of vector CPUs. The main application of the vector hardware is solving linear algebra problems [3, 8], which are the building blocks of many numerical analysis tools. Vector CPUs process whole blocks of numbers (i.e. pieces of matrices) in a pipelined fashion [39]. The pipelined functional units of a vector CPU, such as adders, multipliers, memory access units, can be chained together to compute more complex operations. Setting up and filling with data a compound network of pipelined functional units are time consuming. Hence, also in the case of vector processors, it may be profitable to keep a processor dedicated to a particular application to reduce the setup costs.

We conclude that due to the use of hierarchical memory (but not only) processor affinity phenomena may arise which, in turn, may decree that some CPUs or computers be treated as dedicated for execution of particular tasks.

Limitations on memory partitioning can result from both hardware and runtime environment (e.g. operating system, communication libraries). Hardware determines where and how memory modules are attached in the computer system. On top of the hardware architecture operating system may impose its own view of the memory. There are two most common opposite choices.

(1) Independent memory modules are connected to the processors via an interconnection not preferring any processor (e.g. a bus, a multistage interconnection). Consequently, memory access time is uniform for all processors. This type of design is called a *multiprocessor*, or Symmetric MultiProcessor (SMP), or it is said that it supports Shared Memory Processing (also abbreviated to SMP), or Uniform Memory Access (UMA) time. It is possible to maintain single computer-wide image of the memory. This idea is used by such operating systems as IRIX, Solaris, Windows, Linux, and other. Operating systems and memory management hardware are flexible enough to support sharing memory by multiple programs. Thus, there are no hard technological restrictions on arbitrarily partitioning memory of a parallel computer. Of course, there may be efficiency limitations. It is not reasonable to partition memory between too many tasks which may result in big number of page faults, and consequently slower computations.

(2) Memory modules are bound to the CPUs. Consequently, memory access time depends on the location of the memory block. Local accesses are faster than the remote ones. What is more, nonlocal access time is correlated with the distance between the processor and remote memory. This type of design is often called a *multicomputer*, or a Massively Parallel Processing (MPP) system, or it is said that memory is distributed, or that it has nonuniform memory access (NUMA) time. On $m$ computers there are $m$ separated memory images managed by $m$ independent operating systems. Considering efficiency of communication it is reasonable to partition memory together with the CPUs.

Still, some operating systems provide distributed shared memory [75]. This means that a different view of memory exists in the hardware architecture than in the runtime environment. In such systems it is possible to use memory units available on processors not directly executing the parallel application (e.g., operating system service servers, monitors). In the current case, partitioning of memory is ambiguous and depends on the operating system, runtime libraries, or the application.

We close memory partitioning discussion with a conclusion that memory is arbitrarily partitionable and imposes no restrictions on scheduling decisions in SMP systems, or it is partitioned as processors in MPP systems.

### 3.1.3  Interconnection

Parallel system interconnections determine communication efficiency. Information passed from one CPU, or computer, to another one should be delivered as quickly as possible. Yet, the topology of the interconnection hardly ever is a complete graph (clique) nor is the communication link bandwidth infinite. Thus, messages of some parallel application compete for communication medium both with other messages from the same application and with the messages from other applications. A message may have to cross some particularly busy part of the network, though the message neither originates from nor is destined to this part of network. Such a message experiences substantial delay which could be avoided if a different routing were selected. Thus, message routing should untangle communication paths as much as possible. It has been confirmed in many studies [13, 46, 48, 71] that execution time of parallel applications is shorter if the threads are located close to each other. This dependence was particularly severe in the systems with processor to processor communication links only (such as Transputers in the 1980s). Only the neighboring processors could communicate effectively using hardware. Any longer data path needed handling by software in the intermediate processors. This decreased performance of the computations. Progress in networking lessened importance of application thread location. For example, in a dedicated wormhole routing network, dependence of the communication time on the distance between the sender and the receiver is not very strong [55]. Still, a correlation between the number of messages contending for communication medium [10, 48], or the average message distance [13], and the communication time exists. Thus, executing different applications in compact and mutually separated parts of the network seems a reasonable decision to eliminate network congestion by messages of different applications. Such assignment of application to the network nodes is called *contiguous* processor allocation. However, there is a trade-off: the time spent waiting for a specific compact part of the network may exceed the gains from contiguous allocation. Therefore, *noncontiguous* allocations may be advantageous in certain situations. To eliminate competition from messages of the same application several mutually nonexclusive options are available. For example, selecting communication paths which are colliding as little as possible, assigning links with the highest

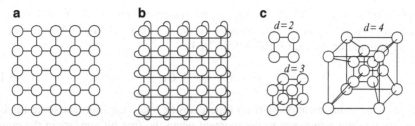

**Fig. 3.1** Examples of (**a**) two-dimensional mesh, (**b**) two-dimensional toroidal mesh, and (**c**) two-, three-, four-dimensional hypercubes

bandwidth to connect threads communicating most actively, designing dedicated group communication algorithms. It can be summarized that communication interconnection can influence scheduling decisions in at least two ways:

(1) How the interconnection is partitioned between the applications?
(2) How the task graph is mapped into the interconnection?

The way of solving the first issue depends on the type of a parallel system. If the topology of the interconnection is unknown, or it is uncontrollably shared by many users, then not much can be done to separate parallel applications from each other on the grounds of the interconnection structure. This is the case of geographically distributed systems owned by different institutions, such as the grid systems. The situation is different when the interconnection topology is known, and pieces of the network can be isolated for certain applications. Meshes and hypercubes are the interconnection topologies most commonly referred to in scheduling literature (see Fig. 3.1). In *d-dimensional mesh* connected computer of size $a_1 \times \cdots \times a_d$, a CPU has coordinates $(x_1, \ldots, x_d)$, where $0 \leq x_i \leq a_i - 1$, and has neighbors with coordinates $(x_1, \ldots, x_i \pm 1, x_d)$, where $x_i \pm 1$ is restricted to $\{0, \ldots, a_i - 1\}$ for $i = 1, \ldots, d$. If the neighbor address components $x_i \pm 1$ are calculated modulo $a_i$, then a *d-dimensional torus* is defined. A *d-dimensional hypercube* can be considered a $d$-dimensional toroidal mesh with two processors along each dimension (i.e. $\forall i, a_i = 2$). A whole zoo of parallel computer system interconnection topologies have been proposed [22, 32] to minimize communication costs, to maximize reliability, or to aid execution of some algorithms. It seems that the ease of partitioning and managing subnetworks received less attention. Yet, the scheduling decision must take into account possible ways of partitioning the given interconnection architecture into simple contiguous processor allocations. For example, it would be preferable if a parallel application executed in a hypercube-connected system were allocated a subcube of CPUs, in a two-dimensional mesh-connected system it received a rectangular submesh. Partitioning and scheduling in interconnection topologies is discussed in Sects. 5.6 and 5.7.

The second issue of mapping tasks to the interconnection again depends on the type of the parallel system and available information. It is possible to construct a mapping from task graph arcs to the routes if the interconnection is well known. Conversely, if the interconnection is unknown or beyond the control of the application, it is convenient to abstract the interconnection by using a model of communication delay. Typically, communication delay $\tau$ in a dedicated link is a sum of several components [1,9,15,16,21,55,57,64]:

$$\tau = S + D\nu + C\alpha \tag{3.1}$$

where $S$ is communication start-up time elapsing since the moment some thread requests sending a message to the moment when the first bit appears in the communication medium, $D$ is a delay introduced by each node on the message route, $\nu$ is the number of the intermediate nodes on the route, $C$ is inverse of bandwidth, and $\alpha$ is message length. Examples of start-up times for various systems are given in Table 3.1. Values of the parameters in Eq. (3.1) perceived by an application on a certain parallel system are different in different parallel programming environments. In some communication delay models also $C$ depends on distance $\nu$.

Construction of communication strategies may be driven by the relations between the components in Eq. (3.1). For example, if $S$ dominates in $\tau$, then it is disadvantageous to send data in many pieces. One long message combining the data of all the pieces would be delivered faster. Big $D\nu$ discourages sending long-distance messages and vice versa; small $D\nu$ means that the distance to the receiver

**Table 3.1** Examples of communication start-up values

| (Year) | System | $S$ | Reference |
|--------|--------|-----|-----------|
| (1991) | Cray-C90 | 108 ns | [37] |
| (1992) | iPSC/860 | 205 μs[a] | [36] |
| (1992) | Touchstone Delta | 132 μs[b] | [37] |
| (<1993) | Inmos T800, Occam, hardware link | 6 μs | [36] |
| (1995) | Inmos T805, software routing | 1.4 ms | p.c. |
| (1993) | Meiko CS-2, Parmacs | 87.2 μ | [37] |
| (1998) | Meiko CS-2, MPI | 71 μ | [26] |
| (1995) | various Sun workstations: SLC, IPX, SparcClassic, PVM | 636±86 ms | [23] |
| (<1997) | Intel Paragon | 231 μs[c] | [10] |
| (1997) | IBM SP2, PVM, | 205±144 μs | [23] |
| (1999) | homogeneous PCs: Pentium-200MMX, WinNT, PVM | 248±35 ms | [23] |
| (2001) | SGI Origin 3800, MPI | 18±1 μs | p.c. |
| (2005) | SFTP: California–The Netherlands | 8.5 s | [79] |

[a] Messages longer than 100B.
[b] Longer than 512B.
[c] Longer than 8640B.
p.c. – private communication.

node is meaningless. Consequently, for small $D$, in scattering computations it may be advantageous to send the work far from the node of origin, and then to redistribute the work (see e.g. Sect. 7.2.3).

Let us note that formula (3.1) is an optimistic estimation because most of the communication networks work according to the best-effort rule, and there are no deterministic guarantees on the upper limit of the communication time.

Another representation of communication delay introduced in log $P$ model of parallel machine [21] imposes limits on the bandwidth of the communication subsystems of the sender and the receiver. After initiating one communication, the next communication cannot be started in the following $g$ time units. log $P$ model is presented in more detail in Sects. 6.2.2 and 6.9.

As mentioned at the beginning of this section, messages traversing the same communication link suffer from additional delays resulting from sharing the communication medium. A common sense is that bandwidth $\frac{1}{C}$ decreases to $\frac{1}{Cn}$ when $n$ data paths share the link. This may be true if messages share the whole bandwidth fairly, and no quality of service mechanisms exist. However, it has been experimentally demonstrated [15] that in wide area networks bandwidth not necessarily decreases with growing number of connections between two hosts. Hence, it may be advantageous to design scheduling algorithms which open many parallel connections between the hosts. Embedding application threads and communications into the topology with the goal of minimizing communication costs for a single parallel application is discussed in Chap. 6 and Sect. 7.2.

We finish this section with an observation that out of the three considered elements of computer hardware, processor interconnection has the most evident impact on scheduling decisions.

## 3.2 Programming Environments

The creators of languages and programming environments for parallel processing implanted some vision of the parallel system, and possibly delegated to the programmer or the user some scheduling performance optimizations. Thus, some scheduling decisions may be left open to a programmer or to the user of a parallel application. In this section, we discuss various parallel programming environments and their view of scheduling. Some overview of parallel programming environments may be found, e.g., in [5, 27].

Inter-process communication (IPC) is one of the fundamental requirements for coordinating parts of a parallel application. Consider, e.g., a UNIX shared memory programming library. It is possible to create a shared memory block (by shmget()), attach/detach to the memory space of some other process (shmat/ shmdt), or remove it (shmctl). Using these functions, and other synchronization libraries (e.g. semaphores), it is possible to coordinate processes and implement a parallel application task graph. Yet, there is no explicit vision of process scheduling.

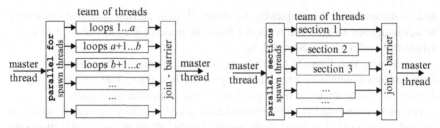

**Fig. 3.2**   The idea of thread parallel execution in OpenMP

Some more control over the thread execution is given in programming libraries such as POSIX threads (`pthreads`) [33]. It is possible to create a thread by `pthread_create()`. Similar functionality existed before `pthreads` [5]. Analogously, starting a process from other process is possible by use of `fork()` UNIX system call. Thus, it is possible to create a thread or process from within the application. However, thread or process execution placement and timing depends on the operating system or the thread library implementation. Furthermore, in `pthreads` it is possible to set some scheduling attributes: policy and thread priority (`pthread_setschedparam()`). Possible policies are: the default system scheduling policy `SCHED_OTHER` and special policies `SCHED_FIFO`, `SCHED_RR`. `SCHED_FIFO` executes a thread until it yields the processor by itself, it is interrupted by a higher priority thread, or it blocks on an I/O request. `SCHED_RR` extends the `SCHED_FIFO` by executing threads of certain priority for a time quantum in a round-robin fashion. Unfortunately, these policies may have different implementations and characteristic in various systems.

OpenMP is a thread programming environment which originated in 1997 with the intention of exploiting parallelism in loop execution or in independent code sections of numerical analysis applications executed on SMP systems. OpenMP specification [58] covers compiler directives, libraries, and environment variables. Regions of code which can be executed in parallel are explicitly declared. The master thread of execution is spawned at the beginning of the parallel block, and the parallel threads are joined at an implicit barrier at the end of the parallel block (cf. Fig. 3.2). For example, a group of different blocks of code to be executed in parallel can be declared as follows:

```
#pragma omp parallel sections [clause1 clause2 ...]
{
#pragma omp section
structured-block1
#pragma omp section
structured-block2
...
}
```

Parallel execution of one loop is declared as follows:

```
#pragma omp parallel for [clause1 clause2 ...]
for-loop
```

The above *clauses* declare, among other, the number of running threads, managing thread local and shared variables. Thus, a programmer of an OpenMP application is responsible for controlling the number of threads, which are equivalent to independent tasks. However, the number of real CPUs executing the threads may depend on the implementation of the OpenMP and the operating system. Surprisingly, clause `schedule` (*kind, chunk*) declares how the loops (iterations) are divided into chunks and distributed among the threads. Loop scheduling is discussed in Sect. 7.10.2.

Linda [14] is a parallel processing coordination language based on the abstract concept of tuple space which is an equivalent of the associative distributed shared memory. Tuples have a name and 0 or more values. Linda defines six operations for inserting tuples, reading or removing them from the tuple space. One of them (`eval()`) is used to start a process which calculates some value and inserts it into the name space. Hence, it is possible to start execution of a task, but the actual placement and timing of the execution depends on the environment hosting a Linda program. There are also other environments derived from Linda [50, 67].

A different view of parallelism management is conveyed in high performance Fortran (HPF) [38]. HPF, developed in 1992–1997, was created with similar objectives as OpenMP. Namely, supporting data parallelism in processing big arrays of numbers. A particular attention has been paid to the distribution of the data as it affects performance. The address space is distributed shared memory. A programmer has been granted a set of directives which advise the compiler on scattering the arrays to the processors. It is possible to declare co-allocation of the arrays (`ALIGN` directive), rect-linear arrangement of processors (`PROCESSORS` directive), distribution of the arrays onto processors (`DISTRIBUTE` directive), or independence of some loop iterations (`INDEPENDENT` directive). The method of mapping the processor arrays to real CPUs is left to the implementation. For example, the following code:

```
REAL A(100,100), B(100,100), C(100,100)
!HPF$ PROCESSORS P(4), Q(2,2)
!HPF$ DISTRIBUTE A(BLOCK,*) ONTO P
!HPF$ DISTRIBUTE C(*,CYCLIC) ONTO P
!HPF$ DISTRIBUTE B(BLOCK,BLOCK) ONTO Q
!HPF$ ALIGN B(*,:) WITH A(:,*)
```

declares three arrays A, B, C of floating point numbers, and two arrangements of the processors: chain P of 4 processors and a two-dimensional mesh Q of $2 \times 2$ processors. Rows of array A and columns of C are distributed on processors P. Quarters of B are mapped on mesh Q as shown in Fig. 3.3. It is recommend to store rows of A on the same processor as the corresponding columns of B (cf. Fig. 3.3). We conclude that in HPF PROCESSORS directive implicitly defines tasks as abstract processors and a host graph by the rect-linear processor arrangement. The number of tasks is a constant defined during the compilation. The communications are also implied by the references to arrays which are assigned to different processors. The mapping of the processors to CPUs is lax because it is delegated to the HPF implementation. The optimizations in the schedule are done by minimizing the number of nonlocal

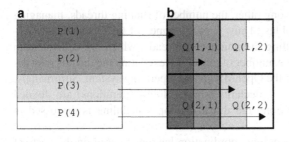

**Fig. 3.3** Example distribution and alignment of arrays in HPF

array references. These optimizations are explicitly declared in the code in the form of data distribution and co-allocation. Potentially, a compiler may achieve further optimizations by exploiting the rect-linear structure of the declared processors and mapping them into a real interconnection.

Parallel virtual machine (PVM) [61, 74] is a milestone of distributed processing environments. It originated in 1989 as a heterogeneous distributed computing project with the goal of harnessing multiple Unix workstations into a single computing facility. PVM is a runtime environment and a library. Each computer making up a virtual machine runs a `pvmd` daemon which is a contact point for the applications running on the computer. `pvmd` provides message routing and process control. The library part is an application interface allowing for message passing, spawning and coordinating processes, setting up the virtual machine. PVM implements the concept of sequential communicating processes. The parallel application consists of a set of distributed processes which exchange data by explicit programmer declared communications. The range of functions provided by PVM allows for constructing arbitrary control structures. Similarly, process management and parallel machine configuration functions let set up the PVM arbitrarily from the available computers, and alter it during the execution. Let us now outline some PVM functions dedicated to process and computer management.

Function `pvm_addhost(char **hosts,...)` adds computers to PVM. Analogously, function `pvm_delhosts(char **hosts,...)` removes computers from PVM. Parameter `hosts` is a list of computers. Thus, either the programmer must know the set of the computers, or some other mechanism must exist in the computer system which substitutes this knowledge.

`pvm_spawn(char*task,char*argv[],intflag,char*where,...)` initiates a new process where binary code is given in parameter `task`, with arguments in `argv`, on machines specified by `where` and `flag`. For example, `flag=0` means that PVM should select the target computer. If `flag=1`, then `where` specifies Internet address of the host. For `flag=2`, `where` specifies computer platform. `flag=16` means that the program will be started on a computer selected from an MPP system. Important facts of `pvm_spawn()` are that the executable files must be accessible on the target computers, and the programmer must be aware of the mechanism of computer selection.

pvm_notify() requests information from PVM on processes which exited PVM, computers joining, and leaving PVM.

pvm_config() provides information on the computers constituting the PVM, and pvm_tasks() on the running tasks.

pvm_reg_rm() allows for intercepting resource management calls from other processes to implement some original scheduling policy.

PVM extensions which adapt this environment to a particular parallel computer system or to some batch processing system exist. Let us conclude the outline of PVM with an observation that this system allows for managing the parallel computer, and for assigning a given task to a particular computer. However, a considerable knowledge is required on the structure of the application (e.g. task graph) and on the configuration of the computers making up the virtual machine.

Message Passing Interface (MPI) [52,53] is a newer parallel programming library specification which is built on the experience of PVM, but with slightly different objectives (see [34]). One of the differences is a method of invoking a new process. Function int MPI_Comm_spawn(char *command, char *argv[], int maxprocs,MPI_Info info, ...) starts maxprocs copies of executable code command with arguments argv. Parameter info indicates where and how the processes are to be executed. It is a set of key-value string pairs passed to the runtime environment. MPI standard reserves some keys in info for requesting the computers. These are: host for hostname and arch for an architecture (platform). However, the meaning of the values is implementation specific. Thus, instead of dictating where and what processes are executed, this decision is deferred to the runtime environment. Such a solution has an advantage of system independence, because the programmer need not know the configuration of the parallel system. On the other hand, this design choice gives weaker guarantees of process allocation and parallel execution in real time. In MPI 1.1 a concept of process topologies has been introduced. The process topologies may better reflect the processes' communication pattern and may aid the runtime environment in mapping the host graph to the real interconnection such that communication cost is minimized. Functions MPI_Cart_create() and MPI_Graph_create() can be used to create Cartesian communication topology and arbitrary graph, respectively. Thus, MPI designers recognized the need for communication cost minimization by scheduling done at the level of the runtime environment.

Modern programming environments provide support for distributed processing. Java RMI, Microsoft.NET Remoting, are built on the concept of Remote Procedure Call (RPC) [33,75]. It allows for passing arguments and executing code on a remote computer. Hence, these environments give the programmer a flexibility equivalent with message passing environments. Furthermore, executable code can be deployed from within the application, which is not as easy in, e.g., PVM or MPI.

We finish this section with some observations. Parallel programming environments give the programmer various degrees of freedom in the construction of task graphs. In message passing environments (PVM, MPI), the task graph has a free and explicit form. In OpenMP, it is bounded by the form of the parallel blocks of code. In HPF it is implied by the data references. Hence, control structures can be expressed in the parallel programming environments. It is not surprising because these environments were constructed with the goal of ensuring correct implementation of control structures, and consequently the task graphs. The number of tasks used by an application may be fixed before the runtime (HPF) or changed during the application execution (the rest of environments). As for the processor allocation it is possible to select particular computers or some architecture (PVM, MPI). On the other hand, the decisions on task and CPU binding may be taken by the runtime environment (in all environments). Then it is deferred to subsystems of parallel computers where specific information on system configuration is accessible. Some indications on embedding of the task graph into the interconnection can be expressed in HPF and MPI. None of the parallel programming environments assumes parallel execution in real time. OpenMP, `pthreads`, and standard UNIX libraries were initially created for SMP systems. Linda and HPF were designed around two different concepts of distributed shared memory. PVM, MPI originated as multicomputer environments. Note that these environments were created for different memory models, and simultaneously give different degrees of freedom in process placement. Hence, different concepts of memory management in parallel processing implicitly influence scheduling.

## 3.3   Runtime Environments

By a runtime environment we mean the parallel system infrastructure managed by the owner(s) of the system. Runtime environment scheduling decisions are in general beyond the control of the application, or the user. The parallel application may only indicate some scheduling preferences to the operating system which has exclusive control of the resources. As it has been observed in the previous section many scheduling decisions are deferred to the runtime environments. In this section, we discuss the support for particular application scheduling. We examine what information may be available to undertake a scheduling decision and the assumptions that may be reasonably justified in designing the scheduling algorithms. The scheduling algorithms are discussed in the following chapters. Example structure of a parallel system runtime environment is shown in Fig. 3.4. The hardware of

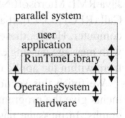

**Fig. 3.4** Structure of application–operating system interaction

the parallel system may have various nature: these can be SMP, MPP systems or computer clusters. Operating systems bind CPUs, memory, and other resources to threads and processes. Depending on the construction of the computer system and its operating system, the application may call the resource management system services. Parallel computing systems are expensive facilities shared by many users and applications. Therefore, a stack of resource managers may exist to ensure complex resource use restrictions and policies (Fig. 3.6). We discuss the resource managers stack in Sect. 3.3.2.

### 3.3.1  Operating System Peculiarities

Current operating systems use multitasking. Therefore, preemption and task migration are generally possible, in particular in homogeneous systems, such as SMP and some MPP systems. Operating systems of such computers usually have a global queue of executable processes ordered by their priority. The global queue is managed by multilevel feedback algorithm [7, 18, 51, 68], or similar, which decreases priority and increases time quantum during the process lifetime. The processes/threads are distributed to local CPU queues. To improve resource utilization, operating system attempts to balance the number of processes/threads assigned to the CPUs. The operating system is not aware of the internal structure of the applications and little guarantees can be obtained for simultaneous execution of the threads/processes of the application. To improve parallel performance several mechanisms have been introduced which affect scheduling.

An attempt to transfer a thread/process from one CPU to another may be disadvantageous for the application performance. A restriction on task migration may be a result of the cache affinity discussed in Sect. 3.1. Therefore, some operating systems allow for binding processes or threads to CPUs. For example, in Linux an application may be bound to a CPU by use of the function `sched_setaffinity(pid_t pid,...,unsigned long *mask)` which sets affinity of process `pid` to processors specified in the bit vector `mask`. In Microsoft Windows (post NT 4.0) similar functionality is offered by functions `SetProcessAffinityMask()` and `SetThreadAffinityMask()`. A processor set can be defined in Tru64 Unix and then selected processes can be assigned to run on this set of processors only [19]. Similar functionality exists in HPUX 11. In IRIX 6.2 [69] the operating system kernel calculates process affinity as a fraction of fixed length time interval used by the process on the CPU. If this fraction is sufficiently big then the process is executed on the same CPU. We conclude that by the use of the affinity functions the programmer and the user may have some control over the assignment of the tasks to the CPUs.

Another scheduling peculiarity related to parallel applications is *gang scheduling* or *coscheduling*. When a parallel application is executed in a time-sharing system, the threads of the application may communicate. However, the speed of communication may depend on the speed of context switching. For example (cf. Fig. 3.5),

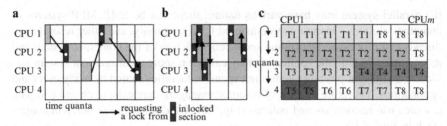

**Fig. 3.5** Communicating threads (**a**) without, (**b**) with coscheduling. (**c**) Ousterhout matrix

threads may be accessing a critical section guarded by a lock. When the critical section is used by some thread which is descheduled because its time quantum expired, then other threads attempting to access the critical section must wait until the context switch. A solution is to execute the threads/processes of the same parallel application in parallel in real time. This scheduling scheme is called gang scheduling or coscheduling. Some of the algorithms implementing gang scheduling use Ousterhout matrix [28, 59] (see Fig. 3.5b). In the matrix columns represent CPUs and rows correspond to time quanta. The threads are placed as entries in the matrix. A low-level mechanism of operating system switches on the processors the threads aligned in the rows. A high level scheduling algorithm decides about number of rows in the matrix and placement of the threads in the matrix. We present such algorithms in Sect. 5.3.3. The number of rows is also the number of applications sharing the CPU, and is often called a degree of *coallocation* or *multiprogramming*. The number of rows should not be too big because high level of CPU sharing decreases performance of the memory system. Ideally, the parallel application should have its threads in one row. It has been observed that the performance of the parallel applications running under gang scheduling generally improves [24, 28, 80].

Gang scheduling is possible in several SMP and MPP systems. It has been applied in 1970s in the experimental Medusa operating system of Cm* [28]. In SGI IRIX operating system thread coscheduling was possible when requested by a parallel application by use of schedctl(SCHEDMODE,SGS_GANG) function. IRIX 5.1 insured parallel execution of the threads by increasing the priority of the threads in the local CPU queues when the first thread of the application entered execution on some CPU [6]. It was observed that even in the heavy load conditions 72% of the coscheduled application runtime was truly parallel. Yet, this implementation of gang scheduling by boosting the priority of the threads at the local CPU queues resulted in an unfair preference given to parallel applications with many threads. This has been changed in the latter versions of IRIX. Gang scheduling is also possible in HPUX 11 for the applications using MPI or pthreads library. It is invoked by setting on MP_GANG environment variable.

We conclude that it is possible to execute a parallel application on many CPUs in real time, as long as the coscheduling is supported by the operating system. Coscheduling may be equally well applied in MPP systems or clusters of workstations to improve performance of actively communicating applications. Over the years terms of gang scheduling or coscheduling became understood more generally as guaranteed parallel execution in real time. For more details on the internals of parallel system schedulers see, e.g., [6, 45].

## 3.3.2 Resource Managers

A stack of managers may control parallel systems resources (cf. Fig. 3.6). At the bottom of the stack local operating system resource managers (e.g. HP PRM [35], IBM WLM [40], SGI Miser [70], Sun SRM [72]) enforce limits on CPU, memory, I/O usage. Distributed resource managers (DRM) (such as Condor [20], IBM LL [41], LSF [60], PBS [2], Sun SGE [73], TORQUE [76]) manage submissions of the applications to computer clusters by sequencing the applications and assigning computers. These applications are usually batch applications executed without human interaction. The picture of resource stack hierarchy is blurred, however, by the fact that some DRM systems can share work and submit jobs to each another. There are attempts to hide the complexity of diverse platforms and to integrate the resources in a unified computing Grid. We will analyze what information on the submitted applications is accepted by these systems, what scheduling attributes are allowed and enforced.

### 3.3.2.1 Local Resource Managers

The standard time-sharing system schedulers (e.g. UNIXes, or Windows) order the applications according to their priorities [18, 51, 68]. The applications with higher priority receive CPU time quanta more often than the lower priority applications. The applications with the same priority receive CPU time quanta with equal frequency. There are also mechanisms to avoid starvation of the low priority applications. Consequently, the fraction of CPU computing power is defined implicitly in relation to higher, equal, and lower priority running applications. Therefore, the real fraction of CPU received by a program, i.e. the number of CPU time quanta used over a period of time, is often hard to predict.

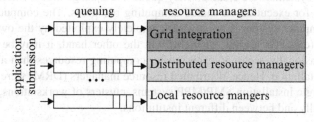

**Fig. 3.6** Resource managers stack

More advanced local resource managers partition the resource space (space sharing) and/or in time (time sharing). This is also called [49], respectively, slot-based and/or threshold-based control of the resources. Thus, e.g. CPUs may be divided into subsets, across boundaries of which a parallel application cannot span. Such partitions may be defined in relation to the underlying interconnection topology. In the case of time multiplexing, the local resource manager may enforce assignment to an application of a fraction of the resource accumulated over time. For example, Sun Resource Manager (SRM) [72] uses a hierarchy of user groups and users to which the shares of the total CPU resource are assigned. All the CPU shares are owned by the tree root. These shares may be arbitrarily distributed between the root direct descendants which are representing groups of users. The share allowances assigned to a certain node (group of users) may be divided between its successors (users or groups of users). In *fair share scheduling (FSS)* the distribution of CPU power between the actually running user applications will be proportional to the assigned CPU shares. For example, if the currently working users A, B, C are assigned shares $x$, $y$, $z$ of the total CPU resource, then their applications will receive fractions $\frac{x}{x+y+z}$, $\frac{y}{x+y+z}$, $\frac{z}{x+y+z}$ of the total CPU power, respectively. Each node of the resource ownership hierarchy may have a restriction on the usage of memory and the number of simultaneously executable processes. It is possible to define processor sets and permanently assign some users or applications to thus defined processor partitions. Similar functionality exists in HP Process Resource Manager (PRM) [35], IBM Work Load Manager (WLM) [40] which additionally allows for specifying disk I/O bandwidth restrictions. SGI Miser [70] defines queues with restricted memory sizes, processor numbers, and time segments within the time intervals reserved by the system queue. Thus, it is possible to reserve a fraction of CPU time for a particular queue. In conclusion, it may be stated that the advanced local resource managers guarantee a fixed fraction of CPU power (consequently also speed of computation), amount of memory, and in some cases also the I/O bandwidth. A comparison of capabilities for various local resource managers can be found in [49].

### 3.3.2.2   Distributed Resource Managers

High performance computing systems are shared by many users. One user of such a system is able to consume the computing power completely. To share the computers fairly, batch systems were created. They queue and manage the submissions of the applications for execution on shared computing resources. The computing power at some computer system is not always completely exploited by the owner of the installation (e.g. PCs are idle at night). On the other hand, it may be necessary to have occasionally access to even greater computing resources than available at the local installation. Hence, distributed resource managers (DRM) were created to integrate single installation SMP/MPP systems, clusters of workstations, dispersed geographically and between different institutions.

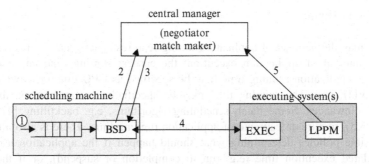

**Fig. 3.7** Starting an application by a distributed resource manager

Typically, an application is managed by a distributed batch system in the following way [40,41,62,65,78] (see Fig. 3.7).

1. An application is submitted to a scheduling machine with a description of the required resources.
2. Batch scheduling daemon (BSD) contacts a central manager presenting the resource requirements of the submitted application.
3. On the basis of the available information on the computers, their availability, performance and use policies, a set of resources is selected for application execution, and this information is passed back to the BSD managing the submission.
4. BSD claims the resources on the target computer(s) from execution manager (EXEC), and if successful, it transfers the application binaries, and starts the execution.
5. Information on the performance of the local machine and admissible use policies are periodically advertised to the central batch manager by local policy and performance managers (LPPM).

This rough description does not present the whole complexity and functionality of current distributed batch systems. It is also necessary to control user access to the resources, guarantee security of the computations, transfer files necessary for the application execution (called stage-in) and collect results (stage-out), redirect I/O streams, record accounting information, monitor machine performance and availability, etc.

Distributed batch systems enforce certain kinds of limits on the resource usage as well as some scheduling features important for defining scheduling algorithms. Some requirements for scheduling characteristics of distributed batch systems were presented in [66], and then used to compare several distributed batch systems [43, 49,56,63]. A survey of batch systems existing at the beginning of 1990s may be found in [44]. We present some of the scheduling attributes from [44,66], as well as add some new ones.

Application Timing

A user may define a set of application timing features. These may be restrictions on the interval of application execution: the earliest starting time and a deadline. The application running time may be specified as CPU time or as wall (i.e. real world) time. The running time may be specified to economize on the resource allowances. Some batch scheduling algorithms, e.g. backfilling [47] (cf. Sect. 5.3.3), require an estimate of application running time. There is also a range of possible policies determining what should happen if the application uses up its declared execution time (e.g. run to completion or suspend), or if the declared execution interval does not fit anywhere (e.g. retry scheduling, ignore, reject submission). Some batch systems allow to specify even more sophisticated information. For example, Moab Workload Manager [17] allows for specifying application execution time on various numbers of processors. This is done by a list of pairs (CPU number, execution time). For example, submission msub -1 trl=2@500:4@250:8@125:16@62 job.cmd requests job.cmd to be run on two CPUs for 500 s, or on four CPUs for 250 s, etc.

Application Resource Requirements

Most of the systems allow to indicate the number of required CPUs, particular computer to run an application, architecture (CPU type), operating system, amount of necessary memory (distinction between core, virtual, shared memory may exist), disk space (in /tmp or local directories). This information may be provided for a whole application and for each process of the application. It is also possible to detail other local resources such as necessary libraries (e.g. .dll) or software with limited number of licenses available at one site only. A more advanced feature is process *coallocation*. In the current context, coallocation means executing two or more processes of the same application on the same computer. More generally, coallocation is sharing of a resource by several processes or applications (e.g. by time multiplexing). Coallocation should not be mixed with coscheduling (gang scheduling). If the target machine is known to be a computer with multiple CPUs, then some DRMs allow for declaring the extent of coallocation by specifying the number of processes on the computer which is often called task/application *geometry*. In Load Leveler [41] process coallocation may be declared in more specific way. For example, statement task_geometry={(0,1,7) (3,6) (5,4) (2)} means that out of 8 processes to be put on 4 CPUs, the processes with identifiers 0, 1, 7 are to be coallocated, similarly processes 3 and 6 are to be coallocated, etc.

Schedule Attributes

The possibility of constructing schedules depends on the ability of enforcing schedule characteristics by batch scheduling systems. *Advanced resource allocation* consists in the reservation of a set of resources (e.g. CPUs, memory, network bandwidth) for a certain interval in the future. Note that such a feature is very useful, because it allows for implementing practically arbitrary schedule on the available computers. Deterministic scheduling theory (see Chap. 4) defines *preemption* as ability to suspend execution of a task, and restart it without additional costs, possibly on a different processor. Implementing this simple idea is quite involved especially in a distributed system, and is usually divided into several steps. First an application must be suspended. A suspended application may still occupy the resources (memory, disk, software licenses) expecting to be resumed soon. Application state must be recorded before it can be migrated to a different set of computers. This process is called *checkpointing*. Checkpointing can be implemented in the operating system, or by the programmer using special runtime libraries. After checkpointing the sate of the application execution can be moved to a different set of resources, which is called *migration*. Transferring a running application is a nontrivial task especially when the originating and the target machines are different platforms, a set of processes were created on the machine, the application had open I/O channels, or it is a parallel application (when messages are in the communication channels, the state of the application may be unobservable). Thus, though preemption, checkpointing, and migration are supported by most of the current distributed batch systems, restrictions may exist on the scope of their applicability. Another feature of distributed batch systems is the support for *coscheduling*. Most of contemporary distributed batch systems support coscheduling because execution of parallel applications written, e.g., in PVM, MPI, OpenMP, is possible. Precedence constraints between processes of an application, often called task dependencies, may be specified in most of DRMs.

### DRM Algorithms

To implement some schedule on a DRM it may be necessary to know the method of matching the applications with the computers and the algorithm building a schedule. Typically, applications are considered according to some priority concept. Priority may be given by the system administrator on the institutional importance basis, on the basis of submission waiting time, resources required or already consumed. DRM first filters out the systems a submitting user is not authorized to use. Then, a set of required resources is compared, item by item, with the set of resources provided by the potential target machines. In Condor [62] application and machine matching is supported by *classified advertisements* which allow specifying not only the application requirements, but also the target machine usage policy. Furthermore, it is possible to express quantitatively how good a machine is for an application, and vice versa. If there are matches, DRM may attempt balancing the distribution of the computations. Considering available memory, number of CPUs, their speed, and utilization, number of running processes computer score may be calculated [17, 44]. The machines with the best score are proposed as the targets for the application execution. DRM attempts to schedule the application on the target machine availability intervals. Scheduling algorithms used by DRM are [42]: FIFO (FCFS), backfilling (see Sect. 5.3.3), Fair Share Scheduling (see the previous section). If scheduling procedure is not successful, the DRM may restart the resource selection procedure several times. DRMs often distinguish computers (called *nodes*) and their CPUs. Since different DRMs use different models of the parallel systems, some concepts do not map one-to-one between them.

It can be concluded that current distributed batch systems support construction of quite detailed schedules including timing and resource indications.

### 3.3.2.3   Grid Integration

As already mentioned some DRMs can submit application to one another. Such work sharing is possible if several issues are adequately addressed. The scheduling concepts and terminology differ in the DRMs. This requires considerable effort in preparing system interfaces. Hence, there are efforts to standardize the way of sharing the computing resources. The standardization is led by such bodies as Global Grid Forum [29], Globus Alliance [30], and Unicore Forum [77]. The problems of Grid resource management, current state of the art, are broadly discussed in book [54]. Here we will only outline resource specification capabilities related to scheduling.

In the Globus Resource Allocation Manager Resource Specification Language (GRAM RSL) [31] it is possible to express number of requested CPUs, and wall times, minimum and maximum memory sizes required. In GGF Distributed Resource Management Application API (DRMAA) [11] application submission attributes are (among other): earliest start time, absolute termination time, wall clock time limit (includes suspension time, the application is terminated after exceeding it), soft wall clock time limit (estimate of the execution time for the scheduler), job run duration hard limit (how long the application may be in running state until it should be terminated), job run duration soft limit (estimation of the application running state duration for the scheduler). GGF Job Submission Description Language (JSDL) [4] allows for detailed specification of application resource requirements. A submission may define more than one resource requirement. Out of the multiple submission elements, the following seem to be important for the scheduling purposes:

CandidateHosts – a list of computers eligible for running the application
HostName – the name of a particular computer to execute the application
IndividualCPUTime – the number of CPU seconds required in one resource
IndividualCPUCount – the number of CPUs required in a resource
TotalCPUTime – the number of CPU seconds required by the whole application
TotalCPUCount – the number of CPUs used by the whole application

It is also possible to specify CPU architecture, operating system, various file system features, memory requirements. These specifications mentioned above may be subject of further development in the future.

We conclude that also in the Grid resource managers extensive information on the application timing and resource requirements can be specified.

# References

1. A. Alexandrov, M.F. Ionescu, K.E. Schauser, and C. Scheiman. LogGP: Incorporating long messages into the LogP model for parallel computation. *Journal of Parallel and Distributed Computing*, 44(1):71–79, 1997.
2. Altair Engineering Inc. PBS Professional 7.1. http://www.altair.com/software/pbspro.htm, 2006 [online accessed 5 August 2006].
3. E. Anderson, Z. Bai, C. Bischof, S. Blackford, J. Demmel, J. Dongarra, J. Du Croz, A. Greenbaum, S. Hammarling, A. McKenney, and D. Sorensen. *LAPACK Users' Guide*. SIAM, Philadelphia, PA, third edition, 1999.
4. A. Anjomshoaa, F. Brisard, M. Drescher, D. Fellows, A. Ly, S. McGough, D. Pulsipher, and A. Savva. Job Submission Description Language (JSDL) specification version 1.0. http://www.gridforum.org/documents/GFD.56.pdf, 2005 [online accessed 5 August 2006].
5. R.G. Babb II, editor. *Programming Parallel Processors*. Addison-Wesley Reading MA, 1988.
6. J. Barton and N. Bitar. A scalable multi-discipline, multiprocessor scheduling framework for irix. In D. Feitelson and L. Rudolph, editors, *Proceedings of the 1st Workshop on Job Scheduling Strategies for Parallel Processing. LNCS*, volume 949, pages 45–69, Springer Berlin, 1995.
7. L. Becchetti, S. Leonardi, A. Marchetti-Spaccamela, G. Schäfer, and T. Vredeveld. Average case and smoothed competitive analysis of the multi-level feedback algorithm. In *Proceedings of the 44th Annual IEEE Symposium on Foundations of Computer Science (FOCS'03)*, pages 462–471, 2003.
8. BLAS Technical Forum. Basic linear algebra subprograms technical forum standard. *International Journal of High Performance Applications and Supercomputing*, 16(1), 2002. http://www.netlib.org/blas/blast-forum/blas-report.pdf [online accessed 5 August 2006].
9. J. Błażewicz and M. Drozdowski. Distributed processing of divisible jobs with communication startup costs. *Discrete Applied Mathematics*, 76(1–3):21–41, 1997.
10. S.H. Bokhari and D.M. Nicol. Balancing contention and synchronization on the Intel Paragon. *IEEE Concurrency*, 5(2):74–83, 1997.
11. R. Brobst, W. Chan, F. Ferstl, J. Gardiner, J.P. Robarts, A. Haas, B. Nitzberg, H. Rajic, and J. Tollefsrud. Distributed Resource Management Application API specification 1.0. http://www.ggf.org/documents/GFD.22.pdf, 2004 [online accessed 5 August 2006].
12. D. Buell, T. El-Ghazawi, K. Gaj, and V. Kindratenk. High-performance reconfigurable computing. *IEEE Computer*, 40(3):23–27, 2007.
13. D.P. Bunde, V.J. Leung, and J.Mache. Communication patterns and allocation strategies. In *Proceedings of the 18th International Parallel and Distributed Processing Symposium (IPDPS'04)*, page p.248b, 2004.
14. N. Carreriro and D. Gelertner. Linda in context. *Communications of the ACM*, 32(4):444–458, 1989.
15. H. Casanova. Network modeling issues for GRID application scheduling. *International Journal of Foundations of Computer Science*, 16(2):145–162, 2005.
16. Y.-C. Cheng and T.G. Robertazzi. Distributed computation with communication delay. *IEEE Transactions on Aerospace and Electronic Systems*, 24(6):700–712, 1988.

17. Cluster Resources Inc. Moab workload manager administrator's guide ver. 4.5. http://
    www.clusterresources.com/products/mwm/docs/, 2006 [online accessed 5 Au-
    gust 2006].
18. E. G. Coffman and L. Kleinrock. Feedback queueing models for time-shared systems. *Journal
    of the ACM*, 15(4):549–576, 1968.
19. Compaq Computer Corporation. Processor sets, Tru64 UNIX version 5.1 reference
    pages. http://h30097.www3.hp.com/docs/base_doc/DOCUMENTATION/V51_
    HTML/MAN/MAN4/0202____.HTM, 2000 [online accessed 1 July 2006].
20. Condor Team. Condor high throughput computing. http://www.cs.wisc.edu/
    condor/, 2006 [online accessed 5 August 2006].
21. D.E. Culler, R.M. Karp, D. Patterson, A. Sahay, E.E. Santos, K.E. Schauser, R. Subramonian,
    and T. Eicken. LogP: A practical model of parallel computation. *Communications of the ACM*,
    39(11):78–85, 1996.
22. A.L. Decegama. *The Technology of Parallel Processing. Parallel Processing Architectures and
    VLSI Hardware*, Volume I. Prentice-Hall, Englewood Cliffs, 1989.
23. M. Drozdowski and P. Wolniewicz. Experiments with scheduling divisible tasks in clusters of
    workstations. In A. Bode, T. Ludwig, W. Karl, and R. Wismuller, editors, *Proceedings of the
    6th Euro-Par Conference. LNCS*, volume 1900, pages 311–319. Springer Berlin, 2000.
24. D. G. Feitelson and L. Rudolph. Gang scheduling performance benefits for fine-grain synchro-
    nization. *Journal of Parallel and Distributed Computing*, 16(4):306–318, 1992.
25. M.J. Flynn. Very high-speed computing systems. *Proceedings of the IEEE*, 54(12):1901–1909,
    1966.
26. G. Folino, G. Spezzano, and D. Talia. Performance evaluation and modeling of mpi com-
    munications on the Meiko CS-2. In P. Sloot, M. Bubak, and B. Hertzberger, editors,
    *High-Performance Computing and Networking. LNCS*, volume 1401, pages 932–936. Springer
    Berlin, 1998.
27. I. Foster. Languages for parallel processing. In J. Błażewicz, K. Ecker, B. Plateau,
    and D. Trystram, editors, *Handbook on Parallel and Distributed Processing*, pages 92–165.
    Springer, 2000.
28. E.F. Gehringer, D.P. Siewiorek, and Z. Segall. *Parallel Processing: The Cm\* Experience*.
    Digital Press, Bedford, 1987.
29. Global Grid Forum. http://www.ggf.org/, 2001 [online accessed 5 August 2006].
30. Globus Alliance. Globus Toolkit. http://globus.org/toolkit/, 2006 [online ac-
    cessed 5 August 2006].
31. Globus Alliance. GRAM RSL schema documentation. http://www.globus.org/
    toolkit/docs/3.0/gram/rsl-schema.html, 2006    [online accessed 5 August
    2006].
32. M.D. Grammatikakis, D.F. Hsu, and M. Kraetzel. *Parallel System Interconnections and Com-
    munications*. CRC Press, Boca Raton, 2001.
33. J.S. Gray. *Interprocess Communications in UNIX*. Prentice-Hall, Upper Saddle River, NJ,
    1997.
34. W. Gropp and E.L. Lusk. Goals guiding design: PVM and MPI. In *IEEE International Con-
    ference on Cluster Computing (CLUSTER'02)*, pages 257–265, 2002.
35. Hewlett-Packard Development Company, L.P. Process resource manager. http://h20338.
    www2.hp.com/hpux11i/cache/317534-0-0-0-121.html, 2006 [online accessed
    6 August 2006].
36. R.W. Hockney. Performance parameters and benchmarking of supercomputers. In J.J. Dongarra
    and W. Gentzsch, editors, *Computer Benchmarks*, pages 41–63. Elsevier, 1993.
37. R.W. Hockney. The communication challenge for MPP: Intel Paragon and Meiko CS-2. *Par-
    allel Computing*, 20:389–398, 1994.
38. High performance Fortran specification. http://www.netlib.org/hpf/hpf-
    v20-final.ps.gz, 1997 [online accessed 16 May 2006].
39. K. Hwang. *Advanced Computer Architecture: Parallelism, Scalability, Programmability*.
    McGraw-Hill, New York, 1993.

40. IBM Corp. AIX 5L workload manager (WLM). http://www.redbooks.ibm.com/ redbooks/pdfs/sg245977.pdf, 2001 [online accessed 5 August 2006].
41. IBM Corp. IBM LoadLeveler for AIX 5L: Using and administering. http://publibfp. boulder.ibm.com/epubs/pdf/a2278810.pdf, 2001 [online accessed 5 August 2006].
42. D. Jackson, Q. Snell, and M. Clement. Core algorithms of the Maui scheduler. In D. Feitelson and L. Rudolph, editors, *Proceedings of the 7th Workshop on Job Scheduling Strategies for Parallel Processing. LNCS*, volume 2221, pages 87–102, Berlin, 2001. Springer.
43. D.B. Jackson. Grid scheduling with Maui/Silver. In J. Nabrzyski, J.M. Schopf, and J. Węglarz, editors, *Grid Resource Management*, pages 161–170. Kluwer Academic, Dordrecht, The Netherlands, 2004.
44. J.A. Kaplan and M.L. Nelson. A comparison of queueing, cluster, and distributed computing systems. Technical Memorandum 109025, NASA Langley Research Center, 1994. http://citeseer.ist.psu.edu/kaplan94comparison.html.
45. R.N. Lagerstrom and S.K. Gipp. PScheD political scheduling on the CRAY T3E. In D.G. Feitelson and L. Rudolph, editors, *Proceedings of the 3rd Workshop on Job Scheduling Strategies for Parallel Processing. LNCS*, volume 1291, pages 117–138. Springer Berlin, 1997.
46. V.J. Leung, E.M. Arkin, M.A. Bender, D. Bunde, J. Johnston, A. Lal, J.S.B. Mitchell, C. Phillips, and S. Seiden. Processor allocation on Cplant: Achieving general processor locality using one-dimensional allocation strategies. In *Proceedings of the IEEE International Conference on Cluster Computing (CLUSTER'02)*, pages 296–304, 2002.
47. D.A. Lifka. The ANL/IBM SP scheduling system. In D. Feitelson and L. Rudolph, editors, *Proceedings of the 1st Workshop on Job Scheduling Strategies for Parallel Processing. LNCS*, volume 949, pages 295–303, Springer Berlin, 1995.
48. V. Lo, K.J. Windisch, W. Liu, and B. Nitzberg. Noncontiguous processor allocation algorithms for mesh-connected multicomputers. *IEEE Transactions on Parallel and Distributed Systems*, 8(7):712–726, 1997.
49. I. Lumb and C. Smith. Scheduling attributes and Platform LSF. In J. Nabrzyski, J.M. Schopf, and J. Węglarz, editors, *Grid Resource Management*, pages 171–182. Kluwer Academic, Dordrecht, The Netherlands, 2004.
50. N. Matloff. UCTuplets: A Linda programming library and more. http://heather.cs. ucdavis.edu/~matloff/uct.html, 2000 [online accessed 12 May 2006].
51. J.A. Michel and E.G. Coffman Jr. Synthesis of a feedback queueing discipline for computer operation. *Journal of the ACM*, 21(2):329–339, 1974.
52. The Message Passing Interface (MPI) standard. http://www-unix.mcs.anl.gov/ mpi/, 2006 [online accessed 20 June 2006].
53. MPI-2: Extensions to the message-passing interface. http://www.mpi-forum.org/ docs/mpi-20.ps, 1997 [online accessed 20 June 2006].
54. J. Nabrzyski, J.M. Schopf, and J. Węglarz. *Grid Resource Management: State of the Art and Future Trends*. Kluwer Academic, Dordrecht, The Netherlands, 2004.
55. L.M. Ni and P.K. McKinley. A survey of wormhole routing techniques in direct networks. *Computer*, 26(2):62–76, 1993.
56. B. Nitzberg, M. Schopf, and J. Patton Jones. PBS Pro: Grid computing and scheduling attributes. In J. Nabrzyski, J.M. Schopf, and J. Węglarz, editors, *Grid Resource Management*, pages 41–52. Kluwer Academic, Dordrecht, The Netherlands, 2004.
57. M.G. Norman and P. Thanisch. Models of machines and computation for mapping in multicomputers. *ACM Computing Surveys*, 25(3):263–302, 1993.
58. OpenMP application program interface. http://www.openmp.org/drupal/mp-documents/spec25.pdf, 2005.
59. J.K. Ousterhout. Scheduling techniques for concurrent systems. In *Proceedings of the 3rd International Conference on Distributed Computer Systems*, pages 22–31, 1982.
60. Platform Computing Inc. Platform LSF family of products. http://www.platform. com/Products/Platform.LSF.Family/, 2000 [online accessed 5 August 2006].
61. PVM: Parallel Virtual Machine. http://www.csm.ornl.gov/pvm/, 2006 [online accessed 14 June 2006].

62. R. Raman, M. Livny, and M. Solomon. Matchmaking: Distributed resource management for high throughput computing. In *Proceedings of the 7th IEEE International Symposium on High Performance Distributed Computing (HPDC'98)*, pages 140–146. IEEE Computer Society, Los Alamitos, CA, USA, 1998.

63. A. Roy and M. Livny. Condor and preemptive resume scheduling. In J. Nabrzyski, J.M. Schopf, and J. Węglarz, editors, *Grid Resource Management*, pages 135–144. Kluwer Academic, Dordrecht, The Netherlands, 2004.

64. Y. Saad and M.H. Schultz. Data communication in parallel architectures. *Parallel Computing*, 15(11):131–150, 1989.

65. J.M. Schopf. Ten actions when grid scheduling. In J. Nabrzyski, J.M. Schopf, and J. Węglarz, editors, *Grid Resource Management*, pages 15–23. Kluwer Academic, Dordrecht, The Netherlands, 2004.

66. U. Schwiegelshohn and R. Yahyapour. Attributes for communication between grid scheduling instances. In J. Nabrzyski, J.M. Schopf, and J. Węglarz, editors, *Grid Resource Management*, pages 41–52. Kluwer Academic, Dordrecht, The Netherlands, 2004.

67. B.R. Seyfarth, J.L. Bickham, and M.R. Fernandez. Glenda: An environment for easy parallel programming. In *Proceedings of the Scalable High-Performance Computing Conference*, pages 637–641. IEEE Computer Society, Los Alamitos, CA, USA, 1994.

68. A. Silberschatz, J.L. Peterson, and P.B. Galvin. *Operating Systems Concepts*. Addison-Wesley, 1991.

69. Silicon Graphics Inc. REACT real-time programmer's guide. http://techpubs. sgi.com/library/tpl/cgi-bin/getdoc.cgi/0620/bks/SGI_Developer/ books/REACT_PG/sgi_html/ch06.html, 1996 [online accessed 1 July 2006].

70. Silicon Graphics Inc. Irix 6.5 man pages: Miser(5). http://techpubs.sgi.com/ library/tpl/cgi-bin/getdoc.cgi?cmd=getdoc&coll=0650&db=man& fname=5\%20miser, 2006 [online accessed 6 August 2006].

71. V. Subramani, R. Kettimuthu, S. Srinivasan, J. Johnston, and P. Sadayappan. Selective buddy allocation for scheduling parallel jobs on clusters. In *Proceedings of the IEEE International Conference on Cluster Computing (CLUSTER'02)*, pages 107–116. IEEE Computer Society, Los Alamitos, CA, USA, 2002.

72. Sun Microsystems Inc. Solaris Resource Manager. http://www.sun.com/software/ resourcemgr/, 2001 [online accessed 6 August 2006].

73. Sun Microsystems Inc. Sun N1 Grid Engine. http://www.sun.com/software/ gridware/, 2006 [online accessed 6 August 2006].

74. V.S. Sunderam, G.A. Geist, J. Dongarra, and R. Manchek. The PVM concurrent computing system: Evolution, experiences, and trends. *Parallel Computing*, 20:531–545, 1994.

75. A.S. Tanenbaum. *Distributed Operating Systems*. Prentice-Hall, Englewood Cliffs, NJ, 1995.

76. Torque resource manager 2.0. http://www.clusterresources.com/pages/ products/torque-resource-manager.php, 2006 [online accessed 6 August 2006].

77. Unicore Forum. UNICORE Plus final report. http://unicore.org/documents/ UNICOREPlus-Final-Report.pdf/, 2003 [online accessed 3 August 2006].

78. M.Q. Xu. Effective metacomputing using LSF multicluster. In *Proceedings of the 1st International Symposium on Cluster Computing and the Grid (CCGRID '01)*, pages 100–105. IEEE Computer Society, Los Alamitos, CA, USA, 2001.

79. Y. Yang, K. van der Raadt, and H. Casanova. Multiround algorithms for scheduling divisible loads. *IEEE Transactions on Parallel and Distributed Systems*, 16(11):1092–1102, 2005.

80. J. Zahorjan, E.D. Lazowska, and D.L. Eager. The effect of scheduling discipline on spin overhead in shared memory parallel systems. *IEEE Transactions on Parallel and Distributed Systems*, 2(2):180–199, 1991.

# Chapter 4
# Classic Scheduling Theory

In this chapter, we outline the terminology of the classic deterministic scheduling theory. Examples of algorithms for basic problems of scheduling on parallel systems will be presented. Finally, we discuss advantages and disadvantages of this scheduling model. Classic deterministic scheduling theory collected a great body of knowledge which is comprehensively presented in many books, e.g. see [11, 13, 19, 42, 57]. It is neither intended nor possible to cover all this information here. The goal of this chapter is to present basic concepts of the classic deterministic scheduling theory which are shared in the later scheduling models.

## 4.1 Definitions

In this section, we define scheduling notions which originated in the deterministic scheduling theory, but are used also in other models of scheduling parallel applications. A key assumption of the deterministic theory is just *determinism* of input data. Any information necessary to describe the instance of a scheduling problem is, at least in principle, available without any form of uncertainty. This does not mean that data are known a priori and static. Necessary scheduling information may become available, e.g., with the progress of time. It is convenient to define problems of deterministic scheduling theory in terms of the processing environment, tasks, and optimality criterion. Without loss of generality it is assumed that all number parameters are integers. Let us start with the description of the processing environment.

Let $\mathcal{P} = \{P_1, \ldots, P_m\}$ denote the set of processors. Classic theory distinguishes two types of processing environments: *parallel* and *dedicated*. In general parallel processors are able to execute any task. Parallel processors have three subtypes: *identical*, *uniform*, and *unrelated* processors. Identical processors are the same for the tasks. Uniform processors have different speeds $b_i$, which means that all tasks are executed faster or slower according to the processor speed. In the case of unrelated processors, execution time of the task may depend arbitrarily on the processor. The dedicated systems are divided into three types: *open shop*, *flow shop*, and

M. Drozdowski, *Scheduling for Parallel Processing*, Computer Communications and Networks, DOI 10.1007/978-1-84882-310-5_4,
© Springer-Verlag London Limited 2009

*job shop* or *general shop*. These three systems assume agglomeration of tasks in jobs and special order of executing tasks within the job (cf. Sect. 1.2 for task and job definitions). In dedicated systems no two tasks of the same job can be executed simultaneously. In the open and flow shops job $j$ consists of tasks $T_{ij}$, for $i = 1, \ldots, m$, which have to be executed on processors $P_1, \ldots, P_m$, respectively. In the open shop the tasks of a job can be executed in arbitrary order. In the flow shop tasks of a job traverse processors consecutively from the first to the last. In the job-shop routing of the tasks through the processors can be arbitrarily defined for each job. The above idea of dedicated processors originated in the factory production scheduling. Therefore, it is different than dedicated processors in the computer context (e.g. I/O processors, GPUs, or arithmetic coprocessors of the 1980s). Still, some computer equivalents of flow shop, or job shop, can be found. For example, flow shop resembles pipeline execution of instructions in a CPU or computations on blocks of numbers in a vector processor. A parallel application consisting of a sequence of queries which have to go through a set of distributed databases may be an example of the job shop. Unless stated otherwise, in the further text, we will discuss parallel processors.

Set $\mathcal{T}$ of tasks comprises tasks $\{T_1, T_2, \ldots, T_n\}$. Each task $T_j$ $(j = 1, \ldots, n)$ is defined by the following parameters:

*Processing time*. If the task is executed on one of identical processors, then its processing time is denoted $p_j$. On uniform processor $P_i$ processing time is $\frac{p_j}{b_i}$, where $p_j$ is execution time on a processor with standard speed, and $b_i$ is the actual speed of processor $P_i$. On unrelated processor $P_i$ execution time of task $T_j$ is denoted $p_{ij}$. For identical processors we will denote by $p_{\max} = \max_j\{p_j\}$ and $p_{\min} = \min_j\{p_j\}$.

*Ready time* $r_j$ is the time at which $T_j$ arrives to the system.

*Duedate* or *deadline* $d_j$, the time by which $T_j$ should (for a duedate) or must (in case of a deadline) be completed.

*Weight* $w_j$ which represents value of $T_j$.

*Vector of resource requirements* $\overline{R}_j = [R_{1j}, \ldots, R_{sj}]$. Let us assume that there are $s$ different types of resources. $R_{ij}$ is the number of resource $i$ units required by $T_j$.

For jobs comprising tasks the above notation may be adapted by adding new subscripts. For example, task $T_{ij}$, which is the $i$th task within job $j$, may be defined by processing time $p_{ij}$, ready time $r_{ij}$, resource requirement $\overline{R}_{ij}$, etc.

Set $\mathcal{T}$, as a whole, is characterized by the following attributes:

*Precedence constraints* (cf. Sect. 1.2). If some task $T_i$ must be completed before some other task $T_j$ can be started, which is denoted $T_i \rightarrow T_j$, then it is said that there are precedence constraints in set $\mathcal{T}$. Precedences are represented as a directed acyclic graph (DAG) called a *task graph* or a *task precedence graph*. Typically tasks are nodes of the graph, and arcs are precedences. Thus, task graph is a pair $(\mathcal{T}, \mathcal{A})$, where $\mathcal{A}$ is the set of precedence constraints. It is also possible to represent tasks as arcs and states of processing as nodes. The first type of graph is a *task-on-node* representation, the second is called *task-on-arc* representation. Note that flow and job shops imply a chain of precedence constraints between the tasks in a job. We will be saying that a task is *ready*, or *available*, when all its predecessors are completed, and it has already arrived to the system.

If the execution of the tasks can be suspended, and resumed, possibly on a different machine without incurring any costs or delays, then it is said that tasks are *preemptive*. When this is not possible, then the tasks are said to be *nonpreemptive*. With the respect to task suspension and migration, there are no other options in the classic scheduling theory.

*Schedule* is an assignment in time of tasks to processors. A more formal definition of a schedule can be given as follows. Let $[\tau_a, \tau_b)$ be a time interval from $\tau_a$ to $\tau_b$, where $\tau_a < \tau_b$. Let $\mathcal{I}$ be a set of time intervals. Schedule $\mathcal{S}$ can be defined as a relation $\mathcal{S} \subset \mathcal{P} \times \mathcal{I} \times \mathcal{T}$. In other words, schedule is a set of tuples $(i, [\tau_a, \tau_b), j)$ representing execution of task $T_j$ on processor $P_i$ in interval $[\tau_a, \tau_b)$. Let us use symbol $*$ in a certain field of a tuple to denote a subset of $\mathcal{S}$ including all tuples with admissible values of the considered field in $\mathcal{S}$. For example, $\mathcal{S}(i, *, *) = \{([\tau_a, \tau_b), j) : (i, [\tau_a, \tau_b), j) \in \mathcal{S}\}$. Similarly, the set of intervals in schedule $\mathcal{S}$ when $T_j$ is executed on $P_i$ will be denoted as $\mathcal{S}(i, *, j)$. A *feasible* schedule must satisfy the following conditions:

1. No processor executes two different tasks at the same moment. More formally, for any processor $P_i$ and two different pairs $([\tau_a, \tau_b), j), ([\tau_c, \tau_d), k) \in \mathcal{S}(i, *, *)$, either $\tau_b \leq \tau_c$, or $\tau_d \leq \tau_a$.
2. No task is executed by two processors at the same time. Formally, for two different pairs $(h, [\tau_a, \tau_b)), (i, [\tau_c, \tau_d)) \in \mathcal{S}(*, *, j)$, either $\tau_b \leq \tau_c$, or $\tau_d \leq \tau_a$.
3. Nonpreemptive tasks are not preempted, i.e. $\forall T_j \in \mathcal{T}, |\mathcal{S}(*, *, j)| = 1$. Preemptive tasks are preempted limited number of times: $\forall T_j \in \mathcal{T}, |\mathcal{S}(*, *, j)| < \infty$.
4. Precedence constraints are observed, which can be expressed as $T_i \to T_j \Rightarrow \forall (g, [\tau_a, \tau_b)) \in \mathcal{S}(*, *, i), \forall (h, [\tau_c, \tau_d)) \in \mathcal{S}(*, *, j), \tau_b \leq \tau_c$.
5. Task $T_j$ is executed only after $r_j$ ($\forall (i, [\tau_a, \tau_b)) \in \mathcal{S}(*, *, j), \tau_a \geq r_j$). A deadline is a hard limit on the execution interval of $T_j$ ($\forall (i, [\tau_a, \tau_b)) \in \mathcal{S}(*, *, j), \tau_b \leq d_j$). Hence, $T_j$ must be completed before its deadline $d_j$. Exceeding a duedate deteriorates quality of the schedule only.
6. Tasks must be fully executed. On identical processors, this means that total length of the intervals where $T_j$ is executed must add up to $p_j$: $\forall T_j \in \mathcal{T}, \sum_{i=1}^{m} \sum_{[\tau_a, \tau_b) \in \mathcal{S}(i, *, j)} (\tau_b - \tau_a) = p_j$. On uniform processors it can be expressed $\forall T_j \in \mathcal{T}, \sum_{i=1}^{m} \sum_{[\tau_a, \tau_b) \in \mathcal{S}(i, *, j)} b_i (\tau_b - \tau_a) = p_j$. On unrelated processors $\forall T_j \in \mathcal{T}, \sum_{i=1}^{m} \sum_{[\tau_a, \tau_b) \in \mathcal{S}(i, *, j)} \frac{\tau_b - \tau_a}{p_{ij}} = 1$.

Schedules are often represented graphically in the *Gantt charts* which depict tasks executed by the processors along the time lines. Example Gantt chart is shown in Fig. 4.1. The name of the chart follows from H.L. Gantt (1861–1919). A schedule for preemptive tasks is called *preemptive schedule*, and a schedule without preemption is called *nonpreemptive*.

Having determined schedule $\mathcal{S}$, optimality criteria may be defined. Let $c_j$ denote completion time of task $T_j$, i.e. $c_j = \sup_{(i, [\tau_a, \tau_b)) \in \mathcal{S}(*, *, j)} \{\tau_b\}$. Let $t_j =$

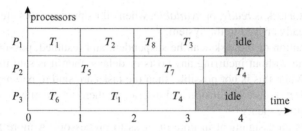

**Fig. 4.1** Example of a Gantt chart

$\max\{0, c_j - d_j\}$ denote tardiness of task $T_j$, and $f_j = (c_j - r_j)$ flow time (sometimes called *response time, stretch, turn-around time*) of $T_j$. Typical optimality criteria are:

- Schedule length (or makespan) $C_{\max} = \max_{T_j \in \mathcal{T}}\{c_j\}$.
- Maximum lateness $L_{\max} = \max_{T_j \in \mathcal{T}}\{c_j - d_j\}$.
- Mean tardiness $\overline{T} = \frac{1}{n}\sum_{j=1}^{n} t_j$.
- Mean weighted tardiness $\overline{T_w} = \frac{\sum_{j=1}^{n} w_j t_j}{\sum_{j=1}^{n} w_j}$. Minimization of $\overline{T_w}$ is equivalent to the minimization of $\sum_{j=1}^{n} w_j t_j$.
- Number of late tasks $U = \sum_{j=1}^{n} u_j$, where $u_j = 1$ if $c_j > d_j$ and $u_j = 0$ otherwise.
- Weighted number of late tasks $U_w = \sum_{j=1}^{n} w_j u_j$.
- Mean flow time $\overline{F} = \frac{1}{n}\sum_{j=1}^{n} f_j$. Since $r_j$ are given in the instance, value of $\sum_{j=1}^{n} r_j$ is constant. Therefore, minimization of $\overline{F}$ is equivalent to the minimization of $\sum_{j=1}^{n} c_j$. Yet, the values of $\sum_{j=1}^{n} c_j$ and $\sum_{j=1}^{n} f_j$ are different and these two criteria are not equivalent from the approximability point of view. Note that $f_j - p_j$ is $T_j$ waiting time. Since $p_j$ are given, the minimization of $\sum_{j=1}^{n} c_j$ is also equivalent to minimizing the average time spent waiting by tasks in the computing environment. Mean flow time is often referred to as *mean turn-around time*.
- Mean weighted flow time $\overline{F_w} = \frac{\sum_{j=1}^{n} w_j f_j}{\sum_{j=1}^{n} w_j}$. Analogously, minimization of $\overline{F_w}$ is equivalent to the minimization of $\sum_{j=1}^{n} w_j c_j$, but they are not equivalent in approximation.

All the above optimality criteria are *regular* which means that they are nondecreasing in $c_j$s. Cost for earliness, i.e. completing a task ahead of its duedate, is an example of nonregular criterion. We discuss new optimality criteria in Sect. 4.4.1. $C_{\max}, L_{\max}$ are often called *minmax criteria* because it is intended to minimize a maximum of some parameter in the schedule. Analogously, $\overline{T}, \overline{T_w}, U, U_w, \overline{F}, \overline{F_w}$ are called *minsum criteria*.

## 4.2   $\alpha|\beta|\gamma$ Notation and Complexity Inference

One of important contributions of the classic deterministic scheduling theory is the notation of scheduling problems proposed in [36], and later extended in various directions to accommodate new models and aspects of scheduling. The notation consists of strings of symbols organized in three fields $\alpha|\beta|\gamma$, describing machine environment, the task system, and the optimality criterion, respectively. We will use symbol ∘ to denote an empty symbol, or a place holder, which will mean that standard assumptions on the problem definition apply.

The first field $\alpha$ has form:

1 – only one processor is considered, or $\alpha_1\alpha_2$ – a set of processors is considered. The first symbol $\alpha_1$ denotes processor type:

$\alpha_1 = P$ – Parallel identical processors

$\alpha_1 = Q$ – Parallel uniform processors

$\alpha_1 = R$ – Parallel unrelated processors

$\alpha_1 = F$ – Flow shop

$\alpha_1 = O$ – Open shop

$\alpha_1 = J$ – Job shop

The second symbol denotes the number of processors:

$\alpha_2 = ∘$ – means that the number of processors is a variable, and is given in the instance of the problem.

$\alpha_2 = m$ – denotes that the number of processors is fixed; $\alpha_2$ may take two forms: it may be a particular number (e.g. 2, 3, . . . ), or it can be just letter "$m$" which means that the number of processors is arbitrary but fixed, i.e. is not given in the instance of the problem.

The second field $\beta = \beta_1, \beta_2, \beta_3, \ldots$ comprises symbols defining the task system. $\beta_1 \in \{∘, pmtn\}$ – Denotes whether tasks are nonpreemptive (for ∘) or preemptive (for $pmtn$).

$\beta_2 \in \{∘, chain, in\text{-}tree, out\text{-}tree, sp, sp1, sp11, prec\}$ – Indicates the type of precedence constraints: ∘ – no precedence constraints, $chain$ – task graph is a chain, $in\text{-}tree, out\text{-}tree$ – task graph is an in- or an out-tree, respectively, $sp, sp1, sp11$ – various types of series–parallel graphs as defined in Sect. 2.1, $prec$ – task graph is arbitrary. Names (or abbreviations) of other types of graphs are often used to represent other types of precedence constraints.

$\beta_3 \in \{∘, p_j = 1, a \le p_j \le b\}$ – Stands for the task processing times: ∘ – task processing times are arbitrary, and given in problem instances, $p_j = 1$ – unit execution time (UET), $a \le p_j \le b$ – Processing times are upper- and lower-bounded by $a$ and $b$, respectively.

$\beta_4 \in \{∘, r_j\}$ – Here symbol ∘ means that all tasks are ready at time 0, and $r_j$ means that tasks have different ready times.

$\beta_5 \in \{∘, d_j\}$ – Symbol ∘ signifies that no task has any deadline, while $d_j$ implies that tasks have different deadlines.

The third field denotes optimality criterion:

$\gamma = C_{\max}$ – Schedule length

$\gamma = L_{\max}$ – Maximum lateness

$\gamma = \sum t_j$ – Mean tardiness
$\gamma = \sum w_j t_j$ – Mean weighted tardiness
$\gamma = \sum u_j$ – The number of late tasks
$\gamma = \sum w_j u_j$ – The weighted number of late tasks
$\gamma = \sum c_j$ – Sum of completion times
$\gamma = \sum w_j c_j$ – Weighted sum of completion times
$\gamma = \sum f_j$ – Mean flow time criterion
$\gamma = \sum w_j f_j$ – Mean weighted flow time criterion
$\gamma = - -$ Denotes that there is no optimality criterion, but a decision problem is considered in which one asks if a feasible solution exists

Note that criteria $L_{\max}, \sum t_j, \sum w_j t_j, \sum u_j, \sum w_j u_j$ imply that duedates are defined for the tasks. In the cases of these criteria symbol $\beta_5 = d_j$ usually is not written in the $\beta$ field.

The $\alpha|\beta|\gamma$ notation not only introduced some method for the enumeration of all possible deterministic scheduling problems, but also allowed for inferring on the complexity classes of the scheduling problems. This is possible on the basis of the relations of generalization and simplification between scheduling problems shown in Fig. 4.2. For these relations polynomial time transformations may be constructed from the problem at the beginning of the arrow to the problem at the end of the arrow. Thus, if a problem at the beginning of the arrow is **NP**-hard, then also the problem at the end of the arrow is **NP**-hard. For example, **NP**-hardness of some scheduling problem on one processor implies **NP**-hardness of the same problem on parallel identical processors (Fig. 4.2a). In general, it can be also concluded that if the problem at the end of the arrow is polynomially solvable, then also its predecessor should be polynomially solvable. Yet, these conclusions should be taken with some care because lengths of the strings encoding the input data of some problem, and its subproblem, may be significantly different. Consequently, polynomially solvable problems may have hard subproblems [12, 67, 71].

The existence of the above complexity relations between the scheduling problems sparked an interest in determining the simplest problems that are already **NP**-hard and the most general problems that are still polynomially solvable. The study of the line separating these two situations become one of the driving forces behind the research in deterministic scheduling theory. Recent results of this research can be found in the repository [14].

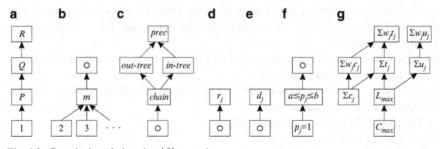

**Fig. 4.2** Complexity relations in $\alpha|\beta|\gamma$ notation

## 4.3   Scheduling Parallel Processors

In this section, we present examples of parallel processor scheduling problems and their classic solutions. Some of the classic algorithms presented below can be generalized in other scheduling models dealing with more general definitions of the task system.

### 4.3.1   $C_{max}$ Criterion

#### 4.3.1.1   Nonpreemptive Schedules

The problem of nonpreemptive scheduling on two processors ($P2||C_{max}$) is **NPh**, and for problem $P||C_{max}$ is s**NPh** [32,44]. According to the current state of knowledge it is hard to expect polynomial time optimization algorithms for **NPh** problems (cf. Sect. 2.2). Thus, it is reasonable to search for simpler problems which are still polynomially solvable, or to look for approximation algorithms. This point of view dictated by the computational complexity theory was, and is, one of the driving forces behind the research in the deterministic scheduling theory. Therefore, in the following, we discuss some special cases solvable in polynomial, pseudopolynomial time, as well as some approximation algorithms.

Problem $Pm||C_{max}$ may be solved in pseudopolynomial time $O(nC^m)$ by a dynamic programming algorithm [62] for any fixed $m$, where $C$ is an upper bound on the schedule length. This algorithm is presented in Sect. 2.3.2.

Problems of scheduling unit execution time (UET) tasks have complexity status depending on the number of processors and the type of precedence constraints. For the simplest UET problem $P|p_j = 1|C_{max}$ it is easy to calculate schedule length $C_{max} = \lceil \frac{n}{m} \rceil$ and the number of tasks on the processors. Thus, it is possible to determine the schedule in polynomial time, but executing the schedule requires exponential time $O(n)$, because the instance of this problem can be recorded using $O(\log n + \log m)$ symbols. Problem $P|p_j = 1, prec|C_{max}$ is s**NPh** [72]. $Pm|p_j = 1, prec|C_{max}$ is one of the open problems in which complexity status is unknown. Simpler problems $P|p_j = 1, tree|C_{max}$, and $P2|p_j = 1, prec|C_{max}$ are solvable in polynomial time. Below we present algorithms for these two cases.

Hu Algorithm [41]

Hu's algorithm solves problem $P|p_j = 1, in\text{-}tree|C_{max}$ using the concept of a task *level*. A task level is the length of the path from the task to the root of the in-tree. The task(s) with the highest level are selected to be executed on available processor(s) first. Hence, it is *highest level first* (HLF) or *level scheduling* algorithm. The case of an out-tree ($P|p_j = 1, out\text{-}tree|C_{max}$) can be solved by inverting the direction

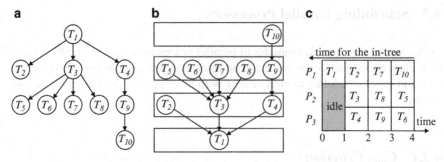

**Fig. 4.3** Hu's algorithm. (**a**) Input out-tree, (**b**) levels in the inverted tree, and (**c**) schedule

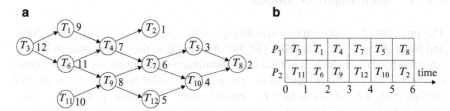

**Fig. 4.4** Coffman–Graham algorithm. (**a**) Precedence constraints and labels, and (**b**) schedule

of the arcs, applying the algorithm for an in-tree, and reading the resulting schedule backward. The complexity of Hu's algorithm is $O(n)$. An instance of this problem and the corresponding schedule can be seen in Fig. 4.3.

Coffman and Graham Algorithm [22]

For two processors UET scheduling problem can be solved in $O(n^2)$ time even for arbitrary precedence constraints (problem $P2|p_j=1, prec|C_{\max}$). This algorithm assigns labels to the tasks from the terminals of the precedence graph to the starting nodes. While labeling the nodes, a list of a node successors' labels is constructed. The labels on these lists are ordered decreasingly. The task with the lexicographically earliest list of the successor node labels is assigned the next label. Tasks are executed as soon as they are ready, but the tasks with bigger labels are given preference. The complexity of this algorithm is $O(n^2)$. An exemplary instance and its solution can be found in Fig. 4.4.

Simple Approximation Algorithms

The analysis of approximation algorithms for scheduling on parallel processors begun in 1960s with the discovery of the *scheduling anomalies* [34] which consist in a counter-intuitive behavior of list scheduling. *List scheduling* algorithms are greedy methods which assign ready tasks from a given list to free processors. Schedules built by list algorithms are active, which means that some ready task is started as soon as some processor is available. These algorithms differ in the way of ordering tasks on the list. It has been observed that for a given list such algorithm may perform worse than expected if, e.g., the precedence constraints are relaxed (some arcs are removed) or processing times of the tasks decrease. On the other hand, for the given precedence constraints, and task processing times, there is an optimum list by use of which the list algorithm would arrive at the optimum solution. It has been shown in [34] that there is a bound $2 - \frac{1}{m}$ on the ratio of the lengths of the two schedules. Hence, an absolute performance ratio for any list algorithm $LS$ solving $P|prec|C_{max}$ is $R_{LS} = 2 - \frac{1}{m}$. It has been also shown in [47] that there is no polynomial approximation algorithm for $P|prec|C_{max}$ with performance ratio better than $\frac{4}{3}$ unless $\mathbf{P} = \mathbf{NP}$. Particular list scheduling algorithms for $P|prec|C_{max}$ build on the ideas of the algorithms by Hu and Coffman–Graham. Algorithm HLFET (Highest Levels First with Estimated Times) [1] gives priority to the tasks with the highest level. Essentially, it is a critical path (CP) algorithm. CP/MISF (Critical Path/Most Immediate Successors First) [45] is a CP heuristic which gives preference to a task with greater number of successors in case of a tie on levels. SCFET (Smallest Co-levels First with Estimated Times) [1] executes tasks in the order of nondecreasing colevels. A colevel of a task is the length of the longest path from any predecessor to the considered task. The longest processing time (LPT) algorithm executes tasks in the order of nonincreasing processing times. For problem $P||C_{max}$ the worst-case performance ratio of LPT is $R_{LPT} = \frac{4}{3} - \frac{1}{3m}$ [35].

Multifit Heuristic

Observe that decision versions of problem $P||C_{max}$ and bin packing problem have similar formulations. Assume that elements to be packed in the bins have sizes $p_j$, and there are $m$ bins of size $y$. Then the decision version of bin packing can be stated as follows: Is there a packing of elements with sizes $p_j$, for $j = 1, \ldots, n$, in at most $m$ bins of sizes $y$. While the decision version of $P||C_{max}$ is: Does there exist a schedule for tasks with processing times $p_j$, for $j = 1, \ldots, n$, on $m$ processors which is not longer than $y$? This close relationship has been exploited in multifit algorithm [26]. Multifit uses first fit decreasing (FFD) algorithm in a binary search over possible schedule lengths. Given $m$ bins (i.e. processors) and bin size $y$ (i.e. schedule length), FFD algorithm packs the tasks in the order of decreasing sizes (which coincides with the LPT order) to the bins with the smallest numbers. If there is no space in any existing bin for the considered task, then a new bin is opened for the current task. FFD fails in assigning tasks to the processors with schedule length $y$, if more than $m$ bins (processors) are used. Multifit uses FFD as an oracle in the binary search for the shortest feasible schedule. The range of checked schedule lengths can be restricted to $[L, 2L]$, where $L = \max\{\frac{1}{m} \sum_{j=1}^{n} p_j, \max_j\{p_j\}\}$. It has been shown that $R_{Multifit} = \frac{13}{11}$ [30,75].

## A PTAS for $P||C_{max}$ [37]

The packing problem can be considered a dual form of $P||C_{max}$. This idea has been generalized in [37] to formulate a PTAS for $P||C_{max}$ using an $\varepsilon$-*dual approximation algorithm*. Here an $\varepsilon$-dual approximation algorithm provides a solution of bin packing problem with at most $m$ bins of size at most $y(1 + \varepsilon)$, if a solution for $m$ bins of size $y$ exists. Thus, if such a dual approximation algorithm is applied in a binary search over the interval of possible (discrete) schedule lengths, then the search stops with a solution of length at most $(1 + \varepsilon)C_{max}^*$, where $C_{max}^*$ is the optimum schedule length. For simplicity of the presentation of the $\varepsilon$-dual approximation algorithm let us assume that bin size $y$ is a unit, and task processing times are expressed using this unit. We will be referring to task processing times rather than element sizes which are more common in bin packing. It can be proved that the algorithm may be defined only for tasks longer than $\varepsilon$. The tasks shorter than $\varepsilon$ can be added to the bins used in the solution for the longer tasks if the occupied space is at most 1, and if it is not possible, then a new bin is opened for the short tasks. It can be shown that this procedure stops with bins of length at most $(1 + \varepsilon)$, and uses the number of bins equal to the maximum of: the number of bins used in the solution for the long tasks, or the optimum number of bins [37]. Let us divide processing times of the tasks into $k = \lceil \frac{1}{\varepsilon^2} \rceil$ equal span intervals $(\varepsilon = l_1, l_2], (l_2, l_3], \ldots, (l_k, l_{k+1}]$, and round the processing times of the tasks to the lower end of the covering interval, i.e. $p_j \in (l_i, l_{i+1}]$ is rounded to $p'_j = l_i$. Let $x_i$ be the number of tasks with length in $(l_i, l_{i+1}]$ present in bin $B$. For a feasibly packed bin $\sum_{T_j \in B} p'_j = \sum_{i=1}^{s} x_i l_i \leq 1$. If the same set of tasks with the original processing times $p_j$ were packed in the bin then the used space would be at most $\sum_{T_j \in B} p_j \leq \sum_{T_j \in B} (p'_j + \varepsilon^2) = \sum_{i=1}^{s} x_i (l_i + \varepsilon^2) \leq 1 + \varepsilon^2 \frac{1}{\varepsilon} = 1 + \varepsilon$, where the last inequality follows from the fact that there are at most $\frac{1}{\varepsilon}$ tasks with processing time greater than $\varepsilon$ in a bin of length 1. Note that for fixed $\varepsilon$ the number $k$ of different rounded task processing times $p'_j$ is also fixed. For a fixed number of task lengths bin packing problem can be solved in polynomial time using dynamic programming. Let $B(a_1, \ldots, a_k)$ be the minimum number of bins needed for packing $a_i$ tasks with processing time $l_i$, for $i = 1, \cdots, k$. $B(a_1, \ldots, a_k)$ can be calculated recursively using formula: $B(a_1, \ldots, a_k) = 1 + \min_{(x_1, \ldots x_k)} B(a_1 - x_1, \ldots, a_k - x_k)$. Since $a_i \leq n$ there are $n^k$ values of $B(a_1, \ldots, a_k)$ which must be tabulated. Each entry is calculated in at most $\lceil \frac{1}{\varepsilon} \rceil^k$ possible values of $(x_1, \ldots, x_k)$. Function $B(a_1, \ldots, a_k)$ can be calculated in time $O((\frac{n}{\varepsilon})^{\lceil \frac{1}{\varepsilon^2} \rceil})$. Thus, there is an $\varepsilon$-dual approximation algorithm for bin packing, and a PTAS with complexity $O((\frac{n}{\varepsilon})^{\lceil \frac{1}{\varepsilon^2} \rceil} (\log n + \log p_{max}))$ for problem $P||C_{max}$. Still, it remains disputable if an algorithm with the complexity of this order is practical.

### 4.3.1.2  Preemptive Schedules

There are close ties between UET nonpreemptive scheduling and the preemptive scheduling. Analogously to the complexity of problem $P|p_j = 1, prec|C_{max}$ also problem $P|pmtn,prec|C_{max}$ is sNPh [72]. Similarly to $Pm|p_j = 1, prec|C_{max}$, the complexity status of problem $Pm|pmtn, prec|C_{max}$ is open. Below we present selected algorithms for preemptive scheduling on parallel processors.

## McNaughton Algorithm [50]

For the simplest preemptive scheduling problem $P|pmtn|C_{max}$ a wrap-around algorithm has been proposed by McNaughton [50]. First, schedule length is calculated $C_{max} = \max\{\max_{j=1}^{n}\{p_j\}, \frac{1}{m}\sum_{j=1}^{n} p_j\}$. Note that it is a lower bound on the schedule length because it cannot be shorter than the longest task or the schedule in which all processors work without idle time. Then, tasks are assigned consecutively, one after another, to the processors starting from $P_1$. If the interval of processing some task on some processor $P_i$ were to exceed $C_{max}$, then the task is divided into two parts: one finishing by $C_{max}$ on $P_i$ and the other which is executed on $P_{i+1}$ starting at time 0. This procedure is repeated for all tasks. The complexity of McNaughton's algorithm is $O(n)$.

## Muntz and Coffman Algorithm [53,54]

Analogously to the nonpreemptive UET case, problems $P2|pmtn, prec|C_{max}$ and $P|pmtn, tree|C_{max}$ are solvable by HLF algorithm of Muntz and Coffman [53,54]. The algorithm for these two problems is based on two concepts: task *level* and *processing capability*. As in the UET case, task level $h(j)$ is the length of the longest path from the task to its furthest successor, where the length of the path is the sum of the processing times of the tasks on the path. Processing capability $\beta_j \in [0, 1]$ is a fraction of processing power assigned to task $T_j$ for some time interval. Processing capability assignment is guided by the following rules:

- If the number $n'$ of the highest level task(s) with unassigned capabilities does not exceed the number of available processors $m'$, then all these tasks receive capability $\beta_j = 1$.
- If $n' > m'$, then all these tasks receive capabilities $\beta_j = \frac{m'}{n'}$.
- If there are still free processors then repeat the procedure by assigning capabilities to the second-highest task(s).

The capability assignments remain valid until one of the events: some task finishes, or the level of some initially higher task drops to the level of some initially lower task. Then, if there are still tasks to be processed, the capabilities are recalculated. The consequence of this way of assigning capabilities is that once the levels of two tasks become equal, they decrease at equal pace. If the tasks are ordered according to their heights, $h(1) \geq h(2) \geq \ldots \geq h(n)$, then this algorithm minimizes in a maximum possible way the $\sum_{i=1}^{j} h(i)$ for $j = 1, \ldots, m$, and the total amount of remaining work $\sum_{i=1}^{n} h(i)$ [24]. The intervals where processing capabilities $\beta_j$ are

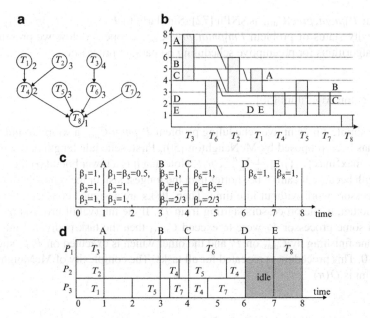

**Fig. 4.5** Applying Muntz–Coffman algorithm. (**a**) Precedence constraints and processing times, (**b**) levels and switching points, (**c**) skeleton schedule with processing capabilities, and (**d**) schedule

constant define a skeleton schedule which can be converted to a normal schedule by McNaughton algorithm. The complexity of Muntz–Coffman algorithm is $O(n^2)$. An example of applying this algorithm is shown in Fig. 4.5.

### Gonzales and Sahni Algorithm [33]

The problem of preemptive scheduling on processors with different speeds may be solved by an algorithm of Gonzales and Sahni [33]. Assume that tasks are ordered according to nonincreasing processing times, i.e. $p_1 \geq p_2 \geq \cdots \geq p_n$, and processors are ordered according to the nonincreasing speeds: $b_1 \geq b_2 \geq \cdots \geq b_m$. Let $PC_i = C_{\max}b_i$ be a *processing capacity* of processor $P_i$. This algorithm is based on the observation that the longest task must fit on the fastest processor, the two longest tasks must fit on two fastest processors, etc., and all tasks must fit on all processors. This observation can be converted to inequalities:

$$\sum_{j=1}^{k} p_j \leq \sum_{i=1}^{k} PC_i \quad \text{for } k = 1, \ldots, m-1 \tag{4.1}$$

$$\sum_{j=1}^{n} p_j \leq \sum_{i=1}^{m} PC_i \tag{4.2}$$

**a**

| task | $T_1$ | $T_2$ | $T_3$ | $T_4$ |
|------|-------|-------|-------|-------|
| $p_j$ | 8 | 5 | 3 | 2 |

| processor | $P_1$ | $P_2$ | $P_3$ |
|-----------|-------|-------|-------|
| $b_i$ | 3 | 2 | 1 |

**b**

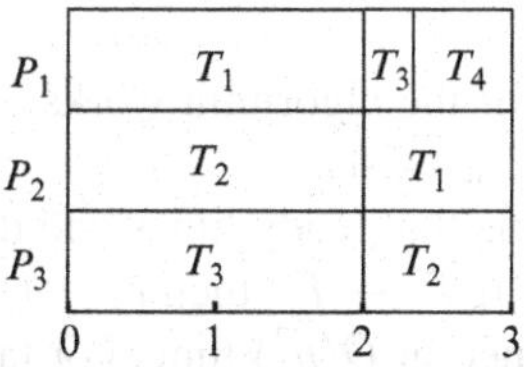

| | | | |
|---|---|---|---|
| $P_1$ | $T_1$ | | $T_3$ $T_4$ |
| $P_2$ | $T_2$ | | $T_1$ |
| $P_3$ | $T_3$ | | $T_2$ |

0          1          2          3

**Fig. 4.6** Gonzales–Sahni algorithm. (**a**) Instance data, and (**b**) a schedule

The above requirements can be used to calculate schedule length

$$C_{\max} = \max\left\{ \max_{k=1}^{m-1}\left\{ \sum_{j=1}^{k} p_j / \sum_{i=1}^{k} b_i \right\}, \sum_{j=1}^{n} p_j / \sum_{i=1}^{m} b_i \right\} \tag{4.3}$$

The algorithm schedule tasks from the longest to the shortest one. Assume that task $T_j$ is about to be scheduled. A pair of processors is found which satisfies $PC_i \geq p_j \geq PC_{i+1}$ (where $i < m$). Then, time moment $x$ is calculated such that processing capacity of $P_i$ in interval $[0, x]$ and processing capacity of $P_{i+1}$ in interval $[x, C_{\max}]$ are equal $p_j$. $T_j$ is scheduled in interval $[0, x]$ on $P_i$ and in $[x, C_{\max}]$ on $P_{i+1}$. A new composite processor with processing capacity $PC_i' = PC_i + PC_{i+1} - p_j$ is constructed from intervals $[0, x]$ on $P_{i+1}$ and $[x, C_{\max}]$ on $P_i$. As a consequence of this way of scheduling $T_j$ value $p_j$ has been subtracted on both sides of one of the inequalities (4.1), and one processor and one task have been eliminated from (4.1). If a pair of processors does not exist (because $PC_m \geq p_j$) then task $T_j$ is executed on $P_m$, and processing capacity of $P_m$ is reduced by $p_j$. Also this action does not violate (4.2). Thus, inequalities (4.1)–(4.2) are invariant of the algorithm. Example application of Gonzales–Sahni algorithm is shown in Fig. 4.6.

### 4.3.2  $L_{\max}$ Criterion

#### 4.3.2.1  Nonpreemptive Schedules

Nonpreemptive scheduling for $L_{\max}$ criterion is sNPh because problem $P||C_{\max}$ is sNPh. Hence, polynomially solvable nonpreemptive scheduling problems should be simpler and may, e.g., involve UET tasks. Problem $P|p_j=1, r_j|L_{\max}$ is solvable in $O(n \log n)$ time by an earliest duedate (EDD) rule, which assigns to the processors ready tasks with the lowest duedate. Problem $P|p_j=1, in\text{-}tree|L_{\max}$ can be solved in $O(n \log n)$ time by calculating modified duedates $d_j' = \min\{\min_{\{k|T_j \to T_k\}}\{d_k' - 1\}, d_j\}\}$ and scheduling ready tasks according to nondecreasing $d_j'$s [13]. The same problem for out-trees ($P|p_j = 1, out\text{-}tree|L_{\max}$) is already sNPh [15].

Garey and Johnson Algorithm for $P2|p_j = 1, r_j, prec|L_{max}$ [31]

The main part of the algorithm works as an oracle checking if a feasible schedule for the given $L_{max}$ exists.

Let us assume that ready times and duedates are consistent with the precedence constraints, i.e. if $T_i \to T_j$, then $r_j \geq r_i + 1$ and $d_i \leq d_j - 1$. Such a modification may be performed in $O(n^2)$ time. For task $T_i$ and integers $s, d$ satisfying $r_i \leq s \leq d_i \leq d$, let $N(i, s, d)$ denote the number of tasks $T_j \neq T_i$ such that $d_j \leq d$, and either successors of $T_i$ or satisfying $s \leq r_j$, The algorithm works on the premise that in a feasible schedule task $T_i$ should be finished before $d - \lceil N(i, s, d)/2 \rceil$, whenever $N(i, s, d) \geq 2(d - s)$. This can be understood as a requirement that $T_i$ should be completed early enough to leave space before duedate $d$ for $T_i$'s successors, and the tasks available only in the interval $[s, d]$. Thus, when the above conditions are fulfilled the duedate is modified to $d_i' = \min\{d_i, d - \lceil N(i, s, d)/2 \rceil\}$.

The subtlety of the algorithm rests in the way of selecting values of $i, s, d$ such that no opportunity for modification of the duedates is missed. A simple approach may consist in brute enumeration of all $i, s, d$. Note that $r_i - r_j < n$ for any $T_i \neq T_j$, otherwise the solution decomposes into two schedules. Analogously, $d_i - d_j \leq n$ for any $T_i \neq T_j$. Therefore, it suffices to check at most $2r$ values of $s, d$. Yet, the algorithm of Garey and Johnson [31] visits only these values which need to be checked. The operation of the algorithm can be viewed as three loops embedded in one another. The outermost loop visits values $d = d_j$ in decreasing order. For a given $d$, the second loop visits $i$, for $d_i \leq d$ in increasing order. For fixed $d, i$ the innermost loop walks over $s$ satisfying $r_i \leq s \leq \max\{d_i, \max_{j=1}^n\{r_j\}\}$. The complexity of the duedate modification algorithm is $O(n^3)$. If the modified duedates are consistent with the ready times, i.e. $r_j \leq d_j' - 1$ for each task $T_j$, then a feasible schedule exists, and it is possible to search for smaller values of $L_{max}$. If the duedates and ready times are inconsistent, then $L_{max}$ should be increased. The optimum $L_{max}$ may be found in $O(\log n)$ calls to the oracle. Hence, the complexity of the whole algorithm is $O(n^3 \log n)$. The optimum schedule can be constructed for the smallest $L_{max}$ for which the oracle gives a positive answer by executing the tasks in the order of nondecreasing modified duedates, while observing precedence constraints.

Example of applying the algorithm is shown in Fig. 4.7. In Fig. 4.7a task graph is shown. For each task the original $r_j, d_j$ are shown (upper line), and modified according to the precedence constraints (lower line). In Fig. 4.7b the intervals of task availability for $L_{max} = 0$ are shown. The algorithm analyzes $d$ decreasing from 6. For fixed $d$, index $i$ is considered increasing from 1. For a given $d, i$, index $s$ is growing from $r_i$ until exceeding $d_i$ or $r_n$. Figure 4.7c presents the duedates $d_j$ for $L_{max}$ with which the algorithm starts and the new duedates $d_j'$ set by the algorithm. As it can be seen for tasks $T_1, \ldots, T_7$ the new duedates are inconsistent with their ready times, and a schedule with $L_{max} = 0$ is infeasible. A feasible schedule for $L_{max} = 1$ is shown is Fig. 4.7d.

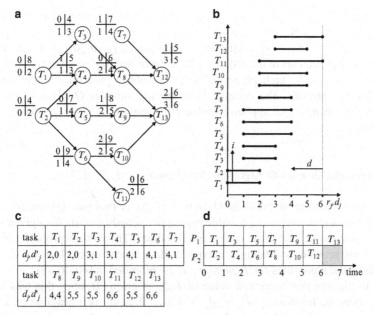

**Fig. 4.7** Garey–Johnson algorithm. (**a**) Instance data, (**b**) intervals of task availability for $L_{max} = 0$, (**c**) original and modified duedates for $L_{max} = 0$, and (**d**) a schedule for $L_{max} = 1$

### 4.3.2.2   Preemptive Schedules

**Horn Algorithm for** $P|pmtn|L_{max}$ [40]

Let $0 = e_0 \leq e_1 \leq e_2 \leq \cdots \leq e_k$ be a sequence of duedates without repetition. The amount of processing task $T_j$ must receive in interval $[0, e_i]$ to be completed in time is at least $\tau(i, j) = \min\{\max\{0, p_j - (d_j - e_i)\}, p_j\}$. Note that if $d_j > e_i$, then $d_j - e_i$ is the amount of processing $T_j$ may receive after $e_i$, and still be completed in time. Otherwise $d_j \leq e_i$, and $p_j$ units of work must have been dedicated to $T_j$ by time $e_i$. Let $N_i = \sum_{j=1}^{n} \tau(i, j)$ be the total amount of work which must be performed on all tasks by time $e_i$ not to miss the original duedates. The optimum value of $L_{max}$ can be calculated as $L_{max} = \max\{\max_{i=1}^{k}\{\frac{N_i}{m} - e_i\}, \max_{j=1}^{n}\{p_j - d_j\}\}$.

Now the problem is to build a feasible schedule for the calculated $L_{max}$. Let $e_i'$ be a modified value of a duedate after adding the above maximum lateness, i.e. $e_0' = 0$, $e_i' = e_i + L_{max}$, for $i = 1, \ldots, k$. The optimum schedule can be built consecutively for the intervals $[0, e_1'], \ldots, [e_{k-1}', e_k']$ using McNaughton algorithm. Still, we have to know lengths of task pieces for each interval. We start with a partial schedule for the first interval. Let $\tau'(i, j) = \min\{\tau(i, j), e_1' - e_0'\}$ and let $i'$ be the maximum index satisfying $\sum_{j=1}^{n} \tau'(i', j) \leq m(e_1' - e_0')$. Length $p_{1j}$ of the piece of task $T_j$ executed in interval $[e_1', e_0']$ should satisfy $\tau'(i', j) \leq p_{1j} \leq \tau'(i'+1, j)$ and $\sum_{j=1}^{n} p_{1j} = m(e_1' - e_0')$. Note that this proposition still leaves freedom of choosing

$p_{1j}$, when $\sum_{j=1}^{n} \tau'(i', j) < m(e'_1 - e'_0)$. The schedule in interval $[0, e'_1]$ can be feasibly built by McNaughton algorithm because $p_{1j} \le \tau'(i' + 1, j) \le e'_1 - e'_0$ and $\sum_{j=1}^{n} p_{1j} = m(e'_1 - e'_0)$. After scheduling pieces $p_{1j}$ in $[0, e'_1]$ the remaining processing requirements of the tasks should be decreased to $p_j = \max\{0, p_j - p_{1j}\}$, also $\tau(i, j)$ should be updated accordingly. The above procedure is repeated for the following intervals. The complexity of the algorithm is $O(n^2)$. Observe that this algorithm can be also applied to solve $P|r_j, pmtn|C_{\max}$ if the schedule is read backward.

### Federgruen and Groenevelt Algorithm for $Q|pmtn, r_j, d_j|-$ [27]

The decision version of problem $Q|pmtn, r_j|L_{\max}$ is problem $Q|pmtn, r_j, d_j|-$ which consists in verifying if a feasible preemptive schedule exists for a given set of uniform processors, task ready times, and deadlines. The method proposed in [27] reduces this problem to finding a maximum flow in a network. In some sense it generalizes the algorithms for $P|pmtn, r_j, d_j|-$ proposed in [40, 46, 73].

Let us assume that some test value of $L_{\max}$ is given. To obey this trial value task $T_j$ must be finished by $d'_j = d_j + L_{\max}$. Thus, $d'_j$ is a deadline of $T_j$ for the current test value of lateness. Let $e_0 < e_1 < \cdots < e_k$ be a sequence of time events in the task system, i.e. ready times and deadlines in increasing order and without repetition. Let $l$ be the number of different processor speeds: $b_1 > b_2 > \cdots > b_l$, and $m_i$ the number of processors with speed $b_i$. It is possible to define processing capacities $PC_{ih} = b_i(e_{h+1} - e_h)$ for processor type $i$, and interval $h$, as in the Gonzales–Sahni algorithm for $Q|pmtn|C_{\max}$ (see in Sect. 4.3.1.2). Processing capacities of the original processors may be viewed as a set of $l$ blocks of processing capacity intervals (see Fig. 4.8). For example, in block $i < l$ there are $m_1 + \cdots + m_i$ processing capacity intervals $[PC_{ih}, PC_{i+1,h}]$ of length $(b_i - b_{i+1})(e_{h+1} - e_h)$ (cf. Fig. 4.8). There are $m$ capacity intervals $[PC_l, 0]$. Thus, processing capacities are decomposed and grouped according to the speeds of processors.

The network (cf. Fig. 4.9) has vertices: source $s$, sink $t$, $n$ vertices $T_j$ corresponding to the tasks, and $lk$ vertices $w_{ih}$ corresponding to $l$ blocks of processing capacities $[PC_{ih}, PC_{i+1,h}]$ in $k$ intervals $[e_h, e_{h+1}]$ of time. Arcs $(s, T_j)$ have

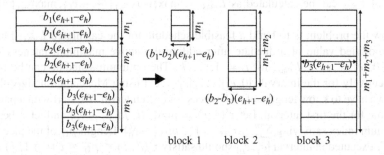

**Fig. 4.8** Decomposition of processor capacities

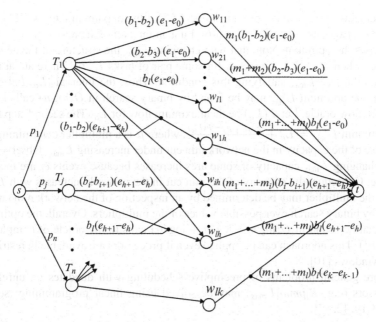

**Fig. 4.9**  Network construction for Federgruen–Groenevelt algorithm

capacity $p_j$. Arcs $(T_j, w_{ih})$ of capacity $(b_i - b_{i+1})(e_{h+1} - e_h)$ exist only if $r_j \leq e_h, r_{h+1} \leq d_j$ for $i = 1, \ldots, l - 1$, $h = 0, \ldots, k - 1$. Arcs $(w_{ih}, t)$ have capacity $(b_i - b_{i+1})(e_{h+1} - e_h)(m_1 + \cdots + m_i)$ for $i = 1, \ldots, l$, $h = 0, \ldots, k - 1$, where $b_{l+1} = 0$. A feasible schedule exists for the given trial value $L_{max}$ if the maximum network flow saturates all arcs $(s, T_j)$. Let us verify that the maximum network flow is equivalent to a feasible schedule. Flows on the arcs represent amounts of work performed on the tasks. Thus, if arc $(s, T_j)$ is saturated then $T_j$ receives the required processing. Flow $\Phi_{(T_j, w_{ih})}$ on arc $(T_j, w_{ih})$ is the amount of work which must be preformed on task $T_j$ in interval $[e_h, e_{h+1}]$ by the processors in processing capacity interval $[PC_{ih}, PC_{i+1,h}]$. Observe that no task receives more work than $PC_{1h} = (e_{h+1} - e_h)b_1$ which is the biggest processing capacity of any processor in interval $[e_h, e_{h+1}]$, because the sum of capacities of all arcs $(T_j, w_{ih})$ for $i = 1, \ldots, l$ is exactly $(e_{h+1} - e_h)b_1$. Any group of $z$ of tasks, where $m_1 + \cdots + m_i \leq z < m_1 + \cdots + m_{i+1}$, cannot receive more processing than $m_1 PC_{1h} + \cdots + (z - m_i)PC_{i+1,h}$ from the $z$ fastest processors. This is guaranteed by the capacities of arcs $(T_j, w_{gh})$ and $(w_{gh}, t)$, for $g = 1, \ldots, m_i$. All tasks together may receive at most $\sum_{i=1}^{m} PC_{ih}$ units of work in interval $[e_h, e_{h+1}]$ which is imposed by the limited capacities of arcs $(w_{ih}, t)$, for $i = 1, \ldots, l$. The above conditions are equivalent to inequalities (4.1) and (4.2) for interval $[e_h, e_{h+1}]$. Hence, a feasible schedule for each interval $[e_h, e_{h+1}]$ can be built by Gonzales–Sahni algorithm solving problem $Q|pmtn|C_{max}$ because inequalities (4.1) (4.2) are satisfied. The network has $2 + n + kl$ nodes, which is $O(nm)$. The complexity of the oracle verifying feasibility of some instance of $Q|pmtn, r_j, d_j|-$ is $O(n^3 m^3)$.

It remains to determine optimum value $L^*_{\max}$ of the maximum lateness. This can be done in two steps as proposed in [46]. First an interval of lateness is found which comprises the optimum. Note that with changing $L_{\max}$ the structure of the network changes when $d_j + L_{\max}$ passes $r_i$ for some pair of tasks $T_i, T_j$. There are at most $O(n^2)$ values of $L_{\max}$ satisfying this condition. Thus, the interval $[L_a, L_b]$ comprising the optimum $L^*_{\max}$ may be found by binary search in $O(\log n)$ calls to the network flow oracle. Let $\Phi(L_a)$ be the maximum flow for $L_a$. The second step finds the optimum $L^*_{\max} = L_a + \frac{\sum_{j=1}^{n} p_j - \Phi(L_a)}{\mu}$, where $\mu$ is a multiplier determining the increase of the capacity in the network min cut under increasing $L_{\max}$. Observe that with changing $L_{\max}$ capacity of some arcs increases because events $e_i$ are moving in time. Consequently, capacity of the min cut in the network increases with $L_{\max}$. Thus, the multiplier may be determined by an inspection of the network min cut for $L_a$ or by binary search over possible values of the multipliers. Overall, the optimum $L^*_{\max}$ can be found in $O(\log n + \log m + \log b_1)$ calls to the oracle of complexity $O(n^3 m^3)$. This approach can be applied even if processors are available in restricted time windows [10].

More general problems of preemptive scheduling with duedates on unrelated processors (e.g. $R|pmtn|L_{\max}$) may be solved using linear programming (see in [11, 13, 19, 42, 57]).

## 4.3.3  $\sum c_j$, $\sum w_j c_j$ Criteria

### 4.3.3.1  Nonpreemptive Schedules

Polynomial Algorithms

Problem $P||\sum c_j$ can be solved by the shortest processing time (SPT) list algorithm which assigns tasks to the processors in the order of nondecreasing processing time.

For uniform processors note that task $T_j$ executed in the $k$th position from the end of task sequence on $P_i$ contributes $\frac{k p_j}{b_i}$ to the objective function $\sum c_j$. Thus, the algorithm for $Q||\sum c_j$ boils down to matching $n$ smallest values $\frac{k}{b_i}$ ordered increasingly (representing positions in the schedules on the processors), with tasks ordered by the LPT rule. The complexity of this algorithm is $O(n \log n)$ for $n \geq m$.

Hu's algorithm (Sect. 4.3.1.1) can be applied to solve $P|p_j = 1, out\text{-}tree|\sum c_j$. Problem $R||\sum c_j$ can be solved by a reduction to finding minimum cost matching in a weighted bipartite graph [16].

Sahni Algorithm for $P2||\sum w_j c_j$ [65]

Let us assume that tasks are ordered according to the weighted shortest processing time (WSPT) rule, i.e. $\frac{w_1}{p_1} \geq \frac{w_2}{p_2} \geq \cdots \geq \frac{w_n}{p_n}$. It can be shown by interchange argument that on each processor separately the optimum schedule obeys the WSPT order. Thus, solving $P2||\sum w_j c_j$ can be reduced to partitioning $\mathcal{T}$ into the subsets executed by $P_1$ and by $P_2$. This problem can be solved by a dynamic program calculating values of tuples $(j, w, c, x)$, representing partitioning of set $\{T_1, \ldots, T_j\}$ such that the sum of weighted completion times is $w$, the processor finishing later has completion time $c$, bit $x$ denotes a change of the processor with the longer processing time. For a given $j$, tuples $(j, w, c, x)$ may be stored in an array with $\sum_{l=1}^{n} p_j$ entries, indexed by values $c$. The algorithm starts with a single tuple $(1, w_1 p_1, p_1, 0)$ for $\{T_1\}$. Let $p = \sum_{l=1}^{j-1} p_l$. For each tuple $(j-1, w, c, x)$ two new tuples are generated: one representing a schedule with $T_j$ on the processor finishing later and one tuple representing a schedule with $T_j$ on the processor finishing earlier. The former tuple is $(j, w + w_j(p_j + c), c + p_j, 0)$. If $p - c + p_j > c$ then the processor finishing later changes and the latter tuple is $(j, w + w_j(p - c + p_j), p - c + p_j, 1)$, otherwise it is $(j, w + w_j(p - c + p_j), p, 0)$. If two tuples $(j, w', c, b')$ and $(j, w'', c, b'')$ have the same third component $c$, then the tuple with greater second component $(w'$ or $w'')$ is discarded. The optimum value of the weighted sum of completion times can be found as a minimum value $w$ among tuples $(n, w, c, b)$. This algorithm can be implemented to run in $O(n \sum_{l=1}^{n} p_j)$ time. It may be generalized to any fixed number of processors (see e.g. [74]).

## Approximation Algorithms

Problems $P2|r_j|\sum c_j$ and $P2||\sum w_j c_j$ are already **NPh** [16] (cf. also [14]). Hence there is a need for good approximation algorithms.

The pseudopolynomial dynamic program for $P2||\sum w_j c_j$ presented in the preceding paragraph may be converted to an FPTAS [65]. Tuples which are close to each other with respect to the optimality criterion are represented by only one tuple. Let $\sum_1$ be the sum of weighted completion times for tasks executed according to WSPT order on a single processor. $\sum_1$ is an upper bound on the optimum value of the criterion in problem $P2||\sum w_j c_j$. Suppose that we divide interval $[0, \sum_1]$ into $\lceil \frac{2n}{\varepsilon} \rceil$ intervals of length $\left\lceil \frac{\varepsilon \sum_1}{2n} \right\rceil$. Now tuples $(j, w, c, x)$ are stored in the order of increasing $w$ rather than $c$ in an array with $\lceil \frac{2n}{\varepsilon} \rceil$ entries. Each entry represents tuples with value $w$ in one of the above intervals. If two tuples were to be stored in the same entry, then the one with bigger $c$ is discarded. The complexity of the algorithm is now $O(\frac{n^2}{\varepsilon})$ because in each stage of the algorithm we have at most $\lceil \frac{2n}{\varepsilon} \rceil$ entries for tuples $(j, w, c, x)$. The error introduced by each tuple substitution is at most the length of the interval $\left\lceil \frac{\varepsilon \sum_1}{2n} \right\rceil$. Since the last set of tuples $(n, w, c, x)$ is result of at most $n$ substitutions, the total error in calculation of the optimality criterion is at most $\frac{1}{2} \varepsilon \sum_1$. It can be shown that the optimum is at least $\sum w_j c_j^* \geq \frac{1}{2} \sum_1$. Thus, the distance from the optimum is at most $\varepsilon \sum w_j c_j^*$.

Existence of FPTASes for many scheduling problems can be derived from the existence of dynamic programming algorithms solving these problems [74]. For

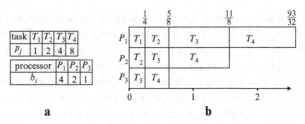

**Fig. 4.10** Example of problem $P|pmtn|\sum c_j$. (**a**) Problem instance, and (**b**) the schedule

example, FPTASes for $Pm||\sum w_j c_j, Qm||\sum w_j c_j$ can be constructed in this way [74]. For problem $P||\sum w_j c_j$ a PTAS has been proposed in [69]. The authors first proposed a PTAS for $P||\sum w_j c_j$ when the ratios of task weight to task processing time are in an interval of constant width, i.e. $\frac{w_j}{p_j} \in [\rho D, D]$, where $0 < \rho \le 1, D > 0$. In the general version of the problem the ratios can be arbitrary. Therefore, the tasks are partitioned into subsets according to the incidence of the ratios with the intervals of exponentially increasing lengths. For each of the subsets a nearly optimal schedule is constructed by the above PTAS for tasks with restricted ratios. Finally, the schedules are concatenated in the order of nonincreasing ratios. On the other hand, problems $P||\sum c_j, R|r_j|\sum c_j, R||\sum w_j c_j$ are hard to approximate and have no PTAS unless **P = NP** [39]. For more results on approximate algorithms for minsum criteria see, e.g., [2, 17, 18, 74].

### 4.3.3.2   Preemptive Schedules

SPT algorithm solves problem $P|pmtn|\sum c_j$. Thus, preemption gives no advantage over $P||\sum c_j$. In the case of uniform processors, i.e. for $Q|pmtn|\sum c_j$, the optimum schedule is built by assigning the task with the shortest remaining time to the fastest processor. This results in a schedule with a stair-case pattern of task assignment. The complexity of the algorithm is $O(nm + n \log n)$. An example of applying this algorithm is shown in Fig. 4.10.

$P2|pmtn, r_j|\sum c_j$ is **NP**h [25]. Unlike $R||\sum c_j$, problem $R|pmtn|\sum c_j$ is s**NP**h [68]. $R|pmtn|\sum c_j$ is one of few problems in which preemptive version is harder than the nonpreemptive equivalent.

## 4.4   Beyond the Classics

Here we present several already classic extensions in the deterministic scheduling theory. These extensions can be also applied to analyze scheduling problems arising in other scheduling models.

### 4.4.1 New Criteria

The classic optimality criteria are not always satisfactory for the decision makers. Therefore, new optimality criteria were defined. Below we give examples.

Scheduling criteria defined in Sect. 4.1 are regular in this sense that reducing completion time of some task does not increase the value of the criterion. However, it is not always profitable to finish a task too early because it may require, e.g., storing products of the task or paying the interest for a credit used to execute the task. Let $e_j = \max\{0, d_j - c_j\}$ be *earliness* of task $T_j$, and $t_j$ be $T_j$ tardiness. The following nonregular criteria were defined on the basis of earliness:

- *Mean earliness* $\overline{E} = \frac{1}{n} \sum_{j=1}^{n} e_j$
- *Mean weighted earliness* $\overline{E_w} = \frac{\sum_{j=1}^{n} w_j e_j}{\sum_{j=1}^{n} w_j}$
- *Earliness-tardiness* [4] $ET = \sum_{j=1}^{n} (w'_j e_j + w''_j l_j)$, where $w'_j, w''_j$ are $T_j$ weights

The last criterion has several versions depending on $w'_j, w''_j$. Sums of $(w'_j e_j + w''_j l_j)^2$ were also studied (see [4] for a survey).

A new scheduling criterion attributed, e.g., to the loss of quality of control in computer monitoring systems is *late work*: $y_j = \min\{\max\{0, c_j - d_j\}, p_j\}$ [9,58]. With the late work the following criteria were defined:

- *Total late work* $Y = \sum_{j=1}^{n} y_j$
- *Total weighted late work* $Y_w = \sum_{j=1}^{n} w_j y_j$

On the grounds of resource managers a set of criteria has been defined which measure how long the applications remain in the system, possibly waiting for service. A classic measure for $T_j$ is flow time $f_j = c_j - r_j$, and the criterion which serves the above purpose is mean (weighted) flow time (cf. Sect. 4.1). Yet, it seems intuitively predictable that long tasks will suffer longer delays until completion than the short tasks. Longer delays are more acceptable for long tasks than for the short ones. Therefore, a special version of weighted flow time was defined which is called *stretch* or *slowdown* $s_j = \frac{f_j}{p_j}$, i.e. $T_j$ flow time normalized to the processing time. A user of an application with stretch $s$ perceives the system as a dedicated machine with speed $\frac{1}{s}$. The new criteria used in this context are [6–8, 28, 29, 52, 55, 59]:

- *Maximum stretch* or *maximum slowdown* $S_{\max} = \max_{j \in T} \{\frac{f_j}{p_j}\}$
- *Mean stretch* or *mean slowdown* $\overline{S} = \frac{1}{n} \sum_{j=1}^{n} \frac{f_j}{p_j}$

There are also bounded slowdown [29,52] which rounds $p_j$ up to some constant to limit the influence of very short tasks on the mean slowdown. Maximum weighted slowdown and mean weighted slowdown criteria were also studied. We will denote mean slowdown by $\sum s_j$ and maximum slowdown $\max s_j$ in the three-field notation. Weighted versions will be denoted $\sum w_j s_j$ and $\max w_j s_j$, respectively.

Maximum (weighted) slowdown and maximum (weighted) flow time can be reduced to scheduling with deadlines. Let $f_{max}$ be the value of maximum flow time of any task in the schedule. By definition $\forall\, T_j, c_j \le r_j + f_{max}$. Similarly, in the case of maximum slowdown: $\forall\, T_j, c_j \le r_j + S_{max} p_j$. This applies also to weighted maximum flow time ($\forall\, T_j, c_j \le r_j + \frac{f_{max}}{w_j}$) and weighted maximum slowdown ($\forall\, T_j, c_j \le r_j + \frac{S_{max} p_j}{w_j}$). If we impose deadlines calculated in the above way we will construct schedules with maximum flow time, or slowdown, not greater than the given values $f_{max}$, or $S_{max}$. Consequently, both maximum (weighted) flow time and maximum (weighted) slowdown essentially boil down to scheduling with ready times and deadlines.

When a parallel application is executed in an unpredictable distributed environment, some of its parts may be delayed which results in a stall of the whole application. More formally, $T_i \to T_j$ and the completion of $T_i$ unexpectedly protracts, or the information about completion of $T_i$ needed by $T_j$ lingers in the network. Consequently, the whole execution of the job comprising $T_i, T_j$ stalls. This phenomenon has been called a *gridlock* [60]. To lessen the severity of such a situation it is advantageous to hide it between other useful computations. For this purpose it is advantageous to have a big pool of tasks ready for execution in each stage of processing the job. Let $E(\tau)$ be the set of ready tasks (i.e. eligible for execution) at time $\tau$. A schedule should be constructed in such a way that for each $\tau$, $E(\tau)$ is as big as possible [49, 60, 61]. This approach may be classified as a new latency-hiding technique.

*Fairness* is a frequently mentioned criterion. However, there is no unanimity in its definition. Fairness is defined in the context of sharing resources by different parties. The resources are fairly shared if they are *equally available* to the parties, or are available in proportion to the support (e.g. payments) given by the parties to the resource owner. This general description still needs a definition of "availability" and "equality". Furthermore, fair scheduling algorithms should not punish any party for any admissible way of using the resources. Fairness definition depends very much on the solved problem and available controls. Let us give examples of what is considered fair and unfair in scheduling.

In networking [20, 56] bandwidth allocation is fair if, for each flow, the received bandwidth is proportional to its share of reservation. Moreover, a flow should not be punished if it takes advantage of consuming unused bandwidth in the channel.

In Sect. 3.3.2 fair share scheduling (FSS) has been mentioned which assigns CPU time to the running applications in proportion to the processors shares defined by the system administrator. The "equity" in scheduling may mean that no application is preferred in any way. In this sense FIFO queuing algorithm is fair. Yet, FIFO is not efficient in utilizing the resources when parallel applications request different numbers of processors (see Sect. 1.3). A scheduling algorithm is unfair if it gives preference to the applications which use resources in a certain way. For example, short running applications may be preferred over long running applications due to time sharing. Small applications requiring few processors may be preferred over big applications requiring a lot of processors because probability of finding a certain number of processors in a parallel computing system decreases with the number of processors. This bias may be overturned by explicitly preferring some type of tasks in the scheduling algorithm. Yet, what is "fair" for one type of tasks is very likely "unfair" for the other task types.

Quantitative measures of unfairness were discussed in [64]. One type of the proposed measures quantifies unfairness in sequencing execution of the tasks. The average delaying of a task by the tasks coming later is used for this purpose. The other measure expresses the difference between the amount of processor resource received and the expected equal share of processing power. Another way of verifying fairness of resource assignment is checking some performance criterion against some parameter of the tasks. A fair schedule should expose no correlation between the criterion value and the task parameters. For example, slowdown should not depend on the number of requested processors or the requested memory size. Such correlation may be verified by statistical tools, or graphically in appropriate charts.

Fairness is expressed in yet another way by applying the concept of equitable dominance [63]. Here the parties sharing resources have their own optimality criteria. Schedules can be represented as points in the space of multiple criteria values. Fair solutions are Pareto optimal (see Sect. 4.4.2) in the criteria space. (More precisely, equitable dominance relation is used in [63], yet it can be reduced to Pareto optimality.)

*Utilization* is a criterion corresponding with the productivity of the computing resources. In the context of resource managers utilization over some interval $\tau$ is a sum of interval lengths in (time $\times$ processors) space when processors work, divided by the available processing power $m\tau$. It is not hard to guess that the more expensive the computing facility is, the closer to 1 the utilization should be. Hence, utilization is a criterion important to the owner of a computing system.

## 4.4.2 Multicriteria Scheduling

Scheduling community is aware that the quality of a schedule is too complex matter to express it with a single number, i.e. a single criterion value. Many criteria have to be taken into account in practice. For example, not only schedule length ($C_{max}$) is meaningful but also the speed of processing perceived by the users is important. The perceived speed of processing can be expressed as mean or maximum slowdown ($\overline{S}$, $S_{max}$, respectively). The amount of resources required by the scheduled tasks, e.g., bandwidth, core memory, storage, etc., is an additional criterion. This situation resulted in formulation of multicriteria scheduling problems. A review of multicriteria scheduling can be found, e.g., in [38]. Here we only outline some key ideas related to multicriteria scheduling.

For the simplicity of presentation, let us assume that there are only two optimality criteria $X_1, X_2$ which have to be minimized. The two criteria can be dealt with in various ways. If one of them, say $X_1$, is more important than the other then it is

**Fig. 4.11** Bicriteria
scheduling and Pareto optimal
solutions

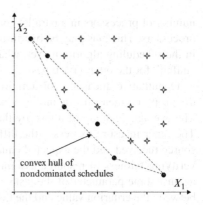

convex hull of
nondominated schedules

possible to find the minimum $X_1^*$ first, and then the minimum of $X_2$ subject to
$X_1 = X_1^*$. This approach is called *hierarchical* or *lexicographical optimization* [38].

A different view of simultaneous minimization of multiple criteria refers to the
concept of nondominated, or Pareto optimal, solutions. Let $X_1(\mathcal{S})$, $X_2(\mathcal{S})$ be values
of the two criteria for schedule $\mathcal{S}$. Schedule $\mathcal{S}$ is *Pareto optimal* or *nondominated* if
there is no feasible schedule $\mathcal{S}'$ such that $X_1(\mathcal{S}') \leq X_2(\mathcal{S})$, or $X_2(\mathcal{S}') \leq X_1(\mathcal{S})$, and
at least one of the inequalities is strict. Intuitively, one criterion cannot be improved
without deteriorating the other criterion. In Fig. 4.11, exemplary set of $(X_1, X_2)$ values is shown. The values for nondominated schedules are marked as bullets. When
the number of feasible schedules is finite, then also the set of Pareto optimal solutions is finite. However, if preemption is allowed, or it is possible to insert idle
times in the schedule, then the number of feasible schedules may be infinite. In such
a case it is convenient to use the *trade-off curve* which contains all Pareto optimal
solutions. The two criteria can be combined using some function $f(X_1, X_2)$. If $f$ is
nondecreasing in both arguments, i.e. $f(X_1, X_2) \leq f(X_1 + a, X_2 + b)$ for $a, b \geq 0$,
then there exists a Pareto optimal solution which minimizes $f$ [38]. If furthermore
$f$ is linear then $f$ is minimized by an *extreme schedule* which is on the lower part
of the convex hull of the set of Pareto optimal solutions [38]. For a decision maker it
may be advantageous to select the most appropriate schedule from the set of Pareto
optimal schedules when function $f$ is not known explicitly. On the other hand, the
set of extreme solutions may be smaller, and hence easier to analyze. Note that
earliness–tardiness $ET$ criterion as defined in the preceding section is an example
of bicriterial scheduling problem with objectives aggregated to a linear function.

Constructing approximate solutions for multicriteria problems may be formulated as searching for solutions which concurrently guarantee fixed bounds on
the worst-case distance from the optimum for each criterion analyzed independently. For instance, it may be required to construct a schedule which concur-
rently guarantees $\frac{X_1}{X_1^*} \leq \alpha$ and $\frac{X_2}{X_2^*} \leq \beta$. A schedule with such characteristic is called
$(\alpha, \beta)$-schedule. It has been shown in [70] that two schedules, $\mathcal{S}_1$ constructed by
an algorithm with approximation ratio $\alpha$ for criterion $C_{\max}$, and $\mathcal{S}_2$ built by an

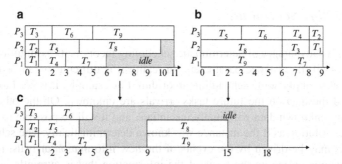

**Fig. 4.12** Construction of $(2\alpha, 2\beta)$ schedule for $(C_{\max}, \sum w_j c_j)$ criteria. (**a**) Schedule $\mathcal{S}_2$ for $\sum w_j c_j$, (**b**) schedule $\mathcal{S}_1$ for $C_{\max}$, and (**c**) schedule $\mathcal{N}$

approximation algorithms with performance ratio $\beta$ for criterion $\sum w_j c_j$, can be converted to a $(2\alpha, 2\beta)$-schedule for a pair of $(C_{\max}, \sum w_j c_j)$ criteria. This can be achieved (cf. Fig. 4.12) by removing from $\mathcal{S}_2$ tasks finishing after $C_{\max}(\mathcal{S}_1)$ resulting in schedule $\mathcal{S}_2'$. Tasks present in $\mathcal{S}_2'$ are removed from $\mathcal{S}_1$ thus forming schedule $\mathcal{S}_1'$. Finally, $\mathcal{S}_2'$ and $\mathcal{S}_1'$ are concatenated into schedule $\mathcal{N}$. To verify that it is a $(2\alpha, 2\beta)$-schedule, note that in schedule $\mathcal{N}$ completion time of task $T_j$ satisfies $c_j(\mathcal{N}) \leq 2C_{\max}(\mathcal{S}_1) = 2\alpha C_{\max}^*$. For criterion $\sum w_j c_j$ note that completion time of $T_j$ remains unchanged if $c_j(\mathcal{S}_2) \leq C_{\max}(\mathcal{S}_1)$, and if $c_j(\mathcal{S}_2) > C_{\max}(\mathcal{S}_1)$, then $c_j(\mathcal{N}) \leq 2C_{\max}(\mathcal{S}_1) \leq 2c_j(\mathcal{S}_2)$. Hence, also the value of the $\sum w_j c_j$ criterion is at most doubled compared to schedule $\mathcal{S}_2$.

In the preceding presentation we assumed that multiple criteria are to be minimized for all the tasks. Yet, it is also possible to define different criteria for different tasks [3, 5]. This is particularly justified if two or more clients share processing environment, and each of them has his/her own set of preferences. In [5] two sets of tasks with two objective functions to be scheduled on a single machine were analyzed. The two objective functions selected from $\{C_{\max}, L_{\max}, \sum w_j c_j\}$ were aggregated to a linear function. In [3] complexity of the following problems was analyzed: finding the optimum schedule for one client criterion on the condition that the other condition is bounded, finding a Pareto optimal schedule, and finding all Pareto optimal schedules. Processing environments examined in [3] were: single processor, two processor flow shop, and two processor open shop. The criteria were selected from: $\sum w_j c_j$, $\sum u_j$, and $f_{\max} = \max_j\{f(c_j)\}$, where $f(c_j)$ is any nondecreasing function of $T_j$ completion time.

Extensions of $\alpha|\beta|\gamma$ notation have been proposed to accommodate bicriterial scheduling. Unfortunately, it seems that there is no generally accepted form of the extension [3, 5, 38]. Problems involving lexicographical optimization are denoted $\alpha|\beta|Lex(X_1, X_2)$, where $X_1, X_2$ are the criteria [38]. If the objectives are aggregated into a given function $f$ then $\alpha|\beta|f(X_1, X_2)$ has been used. Notation $\alpha|\beta|X_1 : X_2$ has been used in [3] for the problem of minimizing $X_1$ for constrained $X_2$. When all the nondominated solutions are to be found $\alpha|\beta|\epsilon(X_1, X_2)$ and $\alpha|\beta|X_1 \circ X_2$ were used in [38] and [3], respectively.

### 4.4.3   Online Scheduling

One of the disadvantages of deterministic scheduling theory is its assumption on the certainty of all the instance parameters. In reality it is difficult to gather arbitrary information to apply some scheduling algorithm. For example, it is hard to predict future, and the data on the future tasks arrivals are unknown. On the other hand, the initially unknown data will finally instantiate, and it will be possible to analyze ex post the solution as if the instance was known deterministically. The scheduling algorithms may be driven by the events of the new information arrivals, and may make decisions online on the basis of the information that is currently available. In this context two questions arise: (1) Can we build an optimum solution online, i.e. with a partial instance data only? (2) If the answer is negative, can we build a *competitive* (cf. Sect. 2.2) algorithm for the studied problem?

Let us give examples of different answers to the first question. Consider problems $1|r_j, pmtn|L_{max}, 1|r_j, pmtn|\sum c_j$. The first problem is solved by EDD rule (cf. Sect. 4.3.2). The second problem is solved by the Shortest Remaining Processing Time (SRPT) rule which assigns to the processor a task with the smallest remaining amount of work. Thus, these problems can be solved to optimality by online algorithms if task data become available at the task arrival. On contrary consider an instance of problem $P2|pmtn, r_j|L_{max}$ in Fig. 4.13 from [23]. Tasks $T_1, T_2, T_3$ are known at time 0, and the remaining tasks may arrive in different scenarios. Suppose tasks $T_1, T_2$ are scheduled at time 0, then if tasks $T_4, T_5$ arrive at time $\tau = 1$ no schedule exists that all tasks meet their duedates (Fig. 4.13a). However, if we started with $T_2, T_3$, then an optimum schedule could have been constructed as in Fig. 4.13b. Suppose we start with $T_2, T_3$, then at $\tau = 2$ tasks $T_6, T_7$ arrive, and at least one of $T_1, T_6, T_7$ cannot be finished in time (Fig. 4.13c). Have we started with $T_1, T_2$, then an optimum schedule could have been constructed as in Fig. 4.13d. Consequently, whatever decision we make at $\tau = 0$, an adversary scenario exists which leads to nonoptimal schedule. Thus, no optimization online algorithm may exist for problem $P2|pmtn, r_j|L_{max}$ without knowing the future.

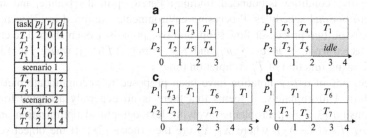

**Fig. 4.13** Nonexistence of online optimization algorithm for $P2|pmtn, r_j|L_{max}$. Scenario 1: (**a**) nonoptimal schedule, (**b**) optimal schedule. Scenario 2: (**c**) nonoptimal schedule, (**d**) optimal schedule

If an optimum solution cannot be constructed online, then a question arises how much we lose in relation to the optimum. Therefore, competitiveness guarantees are examined for the online algorithms similarly to the analysis of the worst-case approximation ratio of the off-line algorithms. Many classic scheduling algorithms can be applied online. The $2 - \frac{1}{m}$ approximation ratio for problem $P||C_{\max}$ (Sect. 4.3.1.1) applies also in the online case if we know the tasks but not their processing times. For the online version of problem $P|pmtn, r_j | \sum f_j$, where we learn about task data as they arrive, no online algorithm may exist with competitiveness $\Omega(\max\{\frac{p_{\max}}{p_{\min}}, \frac{n}{m}\})$. These lower bounds are asymptotically met by the SRPT rule [48]. Thus, SRPT is an *optimal online algorithm* in this sense, that its (worst-case) competitiveness meets the lower bound. Competitiveness guarantees of SRPT have been obtained also for the stretch criterion defined in the previous section. For the online versions of problems $1|pmtn, r_j | \sum s_j$ and $Pm|pmtn, r_j | \sum s_j$, SRPT rule is 2-competitive and at most 14-competitive, respectively [55]. If a constant competitiveness can be achieved for a problem, a new question arises what is the minimum amount of information needed to obtain these performance guarantees. This has led to a distinction of nonclairvoyant, semiclairvoyant, and clairvoyant online algorithms [6, 7, 51, 59]. A nonclairvoyant algorithm assumes no knowledge of task processing times even after $T_j$ arrival. A semiclairvoyant algorithm learns some range of $p_j$, and a clairvoyant algorithm knows $p_j$ at $T_j$ arrival.

On the other hand, if satisfactory competitiveness does not follow from the nature of the problem itself, then can we buy it somehow? For this purpose various *resource augmentation* techniques were proposed [43, 59]. These techniques allow using some more resources, e.g., more processors, faster processors, to guarantee better competitiveness of an algorithm. Other paradigms of online scheduling, analysis techniques, and main results for online scheduling can be found in surveys [59, 66].

To denote various online scheduling problems we will be using an extension of $\alpha|\beta|\gamma$ notation which is quite nonstandard (cf. [59]).

- $oll$ – Stands for *online-list*. In this case tasks are scheduled online one by one, which means that the algorithm works online by irrevocably scheduling tasks from some queue or list. The characteristic of the current task becomes known only after scheduling the previous tasks from the list.
- $olt$ – Abbreviation for *online-time*. Tasks arrive to the system over time. The ready times of the tasks are unknown. The scheduler is unaware of the existence of a task and its attributes until it arrives. Some of the task parameters may become known only after their arrivals.

To facilitate expressing different forms of online scheduling, not covered by the above two ($oll, olt$) paradigms, we will also add $\neg$ symbol before the task parameter which is unknown to the scheduler. For example:

- $\neg p_j$ – Means that processing time of a task becomes known only after completion of the task (equivalent of nonclairvoyance in [59]).
- $\neg prec$ – Denotes that precedence constraints become known only after a predecessor task releases its immediate successors.

We will not use $\neg r_j$ together with $olt$, as the lack of knowledge on ready times follows from the formulation of the $olt$ case.

## 4.5   Remarks on the Classic Scheduling Theory

We hope that at his point the reader has some understanding of the foundations and the methodology of the classic deterministic scheduling theory. Now it is possible to point out its advantages and deficiencies.

Classic deterministic scheduling theory established widely accepted terminology and methodology. It is very useful in classifying scheduling problems. Therefore, it is a starting point and a reference for extensions accommodating features of new problems arising in practice. A huge body of knowledge has been accumulated over the years which is covered in many books (e.g. [11, 13, 19, 21, 42, 57] to mention a few). This is a heritage which cannot be underestimated. Coupling of $\alpha|\beta|\gamma$ notation, complexity theory, and complexity inference gave the research a guidance and structure. The idea that all scheduling problems can be enumerated and fathomed one by one was radical and innovative in its time. Overall, classic deterministic scheduling theory is a very successful scheduling model.

There is no rose without a thorn, however. The sheer assumption of determinism, or complete knowledge about the state of computer system and parallel application, is difficult to fulfill in practice. It may be argued to what extent and under what conditions this assumption is realizable. Yet, it is not hard to imagine situations that this assumption is not fulfilled. Therefore, various approaches, e.g. online scheduling, have been proposed to represent lack of data or its uncertainty.

Filling gaps in the complexity classification of scheduling problems arising in $\alpha|\beta|\gamma$ notation was, and is, a driving force of many scientific investigations. Consequently, great part of the deterministic scheduling theory is laid along the border between hard and easy cases, while surveys on scheduling often recite what problem is still easy and which one is already hard (this book is no exception). Some researchers believe that as a by-product of $\alpha|\beta|\gamma$ notation some scheduling problems were created which have little practical meaning. Recent breakthroughs in approximation algorithms initiated similar investigations along the lines of approximability and inapproximability of scheduling problems.

Deterministic scheduling theory arose in the context of factory production optimization, and later was adapted on the grounds of computer applications. Consequently, some classic scheduling notions do not match perfectly the meaning commonly used in computer science (e.g. dedicated processors). Furthermore, some characteristic features of computing systems, such as communication delays, cannot be expressed conveniently in the classic theory.

As probably in any theory, simplifications have been made. For example, tasks can be either preemptive or nonpreemptive, while in reality a more diverse spectrum exists: some tasks may be preempted, some not, preemption may be possible at some cost which then may depend on the distance of migration. Some models of dedicated systems are too simple to tackle scheduling realities, therefore more complex settings were studied such as reentrant and parallel flow shops, systems with multiple servers. Furthermore, performance of a real parallel system has too complex nature to be represented by a single number. Hence, multicriteria scheduling problems were analyzed.

The deficiencies of the classic deterministic scheduling theory have been addressed in many extensions. Some of them are present in the following chapters.

# References

1. T.L. Adam, K.M. Chandy, and J.R. Dickson. A comparison of list schedules for parallel processing systems. *Communications of the ACM*, 17(12):685–690, 1974.
2. F. Afrati and I. Milis. Designing PTASs for MIN-SUM scheduling problems. *Discrete Applied Mathematics*, 154(4):622–639, 2006.
3. A. Agnetis, P.B. Mirchandani, D. Pacciarelli, and A. Pacifici. Scheduling problems with two competing agents. *Operations Research*, 52(2):229–242, 2004.
4. K.R. Baker and G.D. Scudder. Sequencing with earliness and tardiness penalties: A review. *Operations Research*, 38(1):22–36, 1990.
5. K.R. Baker and J.C. Smith. A multiple-criterion model for machine scheduling. *Journal of Scheduling*, 6:7–16, 2003.
6. L. Becchetti, S. Leonardi, A. Marchetti-Spaccamela, and K. Pruhs. Semi-clairvoyant scheduling. *Theoretical Computer Science*, 324:325–335, 2004.
7. M. Bender, S. Muthukrishnan, and R. Rajaraman. Improved algorithms for stretch scheduling. In *13th Annual ACM-SIAM Symposium on Discrete Algorithms*, pages 762–771, 2002.
8. V. Berten, J. Goossens, and E. Jeannot. On the distribution of sequential jobs in random brokering for heterogeneous computational grids. *IEEE Transactions on Parallel and Distributed Systems*, 17(2):113–124, 2006.
9. J. Błażewicz. Scheduling preemptible tasks on parallel processors with information loss. *Technique et Science Informatiques*, 3:415–420, 1984.
10. J. Błażewicz, M. Drozdowski, P. Formanowicz, W. Kubiak, and G. Schmidt. Scheduling preemptable tasks on parallel processors with limited availability. *Parallel Computing*, 26:1195–1211, 2000.
11. J. Błażewicz, K. Ecker, E. Pesch, G. Schmidt, and J. Węglarz. *Scheduling Computer and Manufacturing Processes*. Springer, Heidelberg, New York, 1996.
12. J. Błażewicz and M. Kovalyov. The complexity of two group scheduling problems. *Journal of Scheduling*, 5:477–485, 2002.
13. P. Brucker. *Scheduling Algorithms*. Springer, Berlin, 1995.
14. P. Brucker and S. Knust. Complexity results for scheduling problems. http://www.mathematik.uni-osnabrueck.de/research/OR/class/, 2006 [online accessed 9 November 2006].
15. P.J. Brucker, M.R. Garey, and D.S. Johnson. Scheduling equal-length tasks under treelike precedence constraints to minimize maximum lateness. *Mathematics of Operations Research*, 2(3):275–284, 1977.
16. J. Bruno, Jr. E.G. Coffman, and R. Sethi. Scheduling independent tasks to reduce mean finishing time. *Communications of the ACM*, 17(7):382–387, 1974.
17. C. Chekuri and S. Khanna. Approximation algorithms for minimizing average weighted completion time. In J.Y. Leung, editor, *Handbook of Scheduling: Algorithms, Models, and Performance Analysis*, pages 11.1–11.30. CRC Press, Boca Raton, 2004.
18. C. Chekuri, R. Motwani, B. Natarajan, and C. Stein. Approximation techniques for average completion time scheduling. *SIAM Journal on Computing*, 31(1):146–166, 2001.

19. P. Chrétienne, E.G. Coffman Jr., J.K. Lenstra, and Z. Liu, editors. *Scheduling Theory and Its Applications*. Wiley, Chichester-England, 1995.
20. J. A. Cobb, M.G. Gouda, and A. El Nahas. Time-shift scheduling: Fair scheduling of flows in high speed networks. In *Proceedings of the 1996 International Conference on Network Protocols (ICNP '96)*, pages 6–13, 1996.
21. E.G. Coffman Jr., editor. *Computer and Job-Shop Scheduling Theory*. Wiley, New York, 1976.
22. E.G. Coffman Jr. and R.J. Graham. Optimal scheduling for two-processor systems. *Acta Informatica*, 1(3):200–213, 1972.
23. M.L. Dertouzos and A. Ka-Lau Mok. Multiprocessor on-line scheduling of hard-real-time tasks. *IEEE Transactions on Software Engineering*, 15(12):1497–1506, 1989.
24. M. Drozdowski. New applications of the Munz and Coffman algorithm. *Journal of Scheduling*, 4(4):209–223, 2001.
25. J. Du, J.Y.-T. Leung, and G.H. Young. Minimizing mean flow time with release time constraint. *Theoretical Computer Science*, 75(3):347–355, 1990.
26. Jr. E.G. Coffman, M.R. Garey, and D.S. Johnson. An application of bin-packing to multiprocessor scheduling. *SIAM Journal on Computing*, 7(1):1–17, 1978.
27. A. Federgruen and H. Groenevelt. Preemptive scheduling of uniform processors by ordinary network flows. *Management Science*, 32(3):341–349, 1986.
28. D.G. Feitelson and L. Rudolph. Evaluation of design choices for gang scheduling using distributed hierarchical control. *Journal of Parallel and Distributed Computing*, 35(1):18–34, 1996.
29. D.G. Feitelson and L. Rudolph. Metrics and benchmarking for parallel job scheduling. In D.G. Feitelson and L. Rudolph, editors, *Job Scheduling Strategies for Parallel Processing. LNCS*, volume 1459, pages 1–24. Springer, Berlin, 1998.
30. D.K. Friesen. Tighter bounds for the multifit processor scheduling algorithm. *SIAM Journal on Computing*, 13(1):170–181, 1984.
31. M.R. Garey and D.S. Johnson. Two-processor scheduling with start-times and deadlines. *SIAM Journal on Computing*, 6:416–426, 1977.
32. M.R. Garey and D.S. Johnson. *Computers and Intractability: A Guide to the Theory of NP-completeness*. Freeman, San Francisco, 1979.
33. T. Gonzalez and S. Sahni. Preemptive scheduling of uniform processor systems. *Journal of the ACM*, 25(1):92–101, 1978.
34. R.L. Graham. Bounds for certain multiprocessing timing anomalies. *Bell System Technical Journal*, 45(2):1563–1581, 1966.
35. R.L. Graham. Bounds on multiprocessing timing anomalies. *SIAM Journal on Applied Mathematics*, 17(2):416–429, 1969.
36. R.L. Graham, E.L. Lawler, J.K. Lenstra, and A.H.G. Rinnoy Kan. Optimization and approximation in deterministic sequencing and scheduling: A survey. *Annals of Discrete Mathematics*, 5:287–326, 1979.
37. D.S. Hochbaum and D.B. Shmoys. Using dual approximation algorithms for scheduling problems: Theoretical and practical results. *Journal of the ACM*, 34(1):144–162, 1987.
38. H. Hoogeveen. Multicriteria scheduling. *European Journal of Operational Research*, 167:592–623, 2005.
39. H. Hoogeveen, P. Schuurman, and G.J. Woeginger. Non-approximability results for scheduling problems with minsum criteria. *INFORMS Journal on Computing*, 13(2):157–168, 2001.
40. W.A. Horn. Some simple scheduling algorithms. *Naval Research Logistics*, 21:177–185, 1974.
41. T.C. Hu. Parallel sequencing and assembly line problems. *Operations Research*, 9(6):841–848, 1961.
42. J.Y. Leung. *Handbook of Scheduling: Algorithms, Models, and Performance Analysis*. CRC Press, Boca Raton, 2004.
43. B. Kalyanasundaram and K. Pruhs. Speed is as powerful as clairvoyance. In *Proceedings of 36th Annual Symposium on Foundations of Computer Science (FOCS'95)*, pages 214–221, 1995.
44. R.M. Karp. Reducibility among combinatorial problems. In R.E. Miller and J.W. Thatcher, editors, *Complexity of Computer Computations*, pages 85–104. Plenum Press, New York, 1972.

45. H. Kasahara and S. Narita. Practical multiprocessor scheduling algorithms for efficient parallel processing. *IEEE Transactions on Computers*, 33(11):1023–1029, 1984.
46. J. Labetoulle, E.L. Lawler, J.K. Lenstra, and A.H.G. Rinnoy Kan. Preemptive scheduling of uniform machines subject to release dates. In W. R. Pulleyblank, editor, *Progress in Combinatorial Optimization*, pages 245–261. Academic Press, New York, 1984.
47. J.K. Lenstra and A.H.G. Rinnoy Kan. Complexity of scheduling under precedence constraints. *Operations Research*, 26(1):22–35, 1978.
48. S. Leonardi. A simpler proof of preemptive total flow time approximation on parallel machines. In E. Bampis, K. Jansen, and C. Kenyon, editors, *Efficient Approximation and Online Algorithms. LNCS*, volume 3484, pages 203–212. Springer, Berlin, 2006.
49. G. Malewicz, A.L. Rosenberg, and M. Yurkewych. Toward a theory for scheduling dags in internet-based computing. *IEEE Transactions on Computers*, 55(6):757–768, 2006.
50. R. McNaughton. Scheduling with deadlines and loss functions. *Management Science*, 6(1):1–12, 1959.
51. R. Motwani, S. Phillips, and E. Torng. Non-clairvoyant scheduling. *Theoretical Computer Science*, 130(1):17–47, 1994.
52. A.W. Mu'alem and D.G. Feitelson. Utilization, predictability, workloads, and user runtime estimates in scheduling the IBM SP2 with backfilling. *IEEE Transactions on Parallel and Distributed Systems*, 12(6):529–543, 2001.
53. R.R. Muntz and E.G. Coffman Jr. Optimal preemptive scheduling on two-processor systems. *IEEE Transactions on Computers*, 18(11):1014–1020, 1969.
54. R.R. Muntz and E.G. Coffman Jr. Preemptive scheduling of real-time tasks on multiprocessor systems. *Journal of the ACM*, 17(2):324–338, 1970.
55. S. Muthukrishnan, R. Rajaramany, A. Shaheen, and J.E. Gehrke. Online scheduling to minimize average stretch. In *Proceedings of 40th Annual Symposium on Foundations of Computer Science (FOCS'99)*, pages 433–443. IEEE, 1999.
56. N. Ni and L.N. Bhuyan. Fair scheduling in internet routers. *IEEE Transactions on Computers*, 51(6):686–701, 2002.
57. M. Pinedo. *Scheduling: Theory, Algorithms, and Systems*. Prentice-Hall, Englewood Cliffs, 1995.
58. C.N. Potts and L.N. Wassenhove. Single machine scheduling to minimize total late work. *Operations Research*, 40:586–595, 1992.
59. K. Pruhs, J. Sgall, and E. Torng. Online scheduling. In J.Y. Leung, editor, *Handbook of Scheduling: Algorithms, Models, and Performance Analysis*, pages 15.1–15.42. CRC Press, Boca Raton, 2004.
60. A. Rosenberg. On scheduling mesh-structured computations for internet-based computing. *IEEE Transactions on Computers*, 53(9):1176–1186, 2004.
61. A. Rosenberg and M. Yurkewych. Guidelines for scheduling some common computation-dags for internet-based computing. *IEEE Transactions on Computers*, 54(4):428–438, 2005.
62. M. Rothkopf. Scheduling independent tasks on parallel processors. *Management Science*, 12(5):437–447, 1966.
63. K. Rządca. *Resource Management Models and Algorithms for Multi-Organizational Grids*. Ph.D. thesis, Institut National Polytechnique de Grenoble and Polish-Japanese Institute of Information Technology, 2007.
64. G. Sabin and P. Sadayappan. Unfairness metrics for space-sharing parallel job schedulers. In D. Feitelson, E. Frachtenberg, L. Rudolph, and U. Schwiegelshohn, editors, *Proceedings of 11th Workshop on Job Scheduling Strategies for Parallel Processing. LNCS*, volume 3834, pages 238–256, Springer, Berlin, 2005.
65. S. Sahni. Algorithms for scheduling independent tasks. *Journal of the ACM*, 23(1):116–127, 1976.
66. J. Sgall. On-line scheduling. In A. Fiat and G. Woeginger, editors, *Online Algorithms: The State of the Art. LNCS*, volume 1442, pages 196–231. Springer, Berlin, 1998.
67. Y. Shafransky. Notions of a problem and subproblem in operations research under the complexity analysis. In *Proceedings of 10th International Workshop on Project Management and Scheduling (PMS'06)*, pages 319–324, Poznań, Poland, 2006.

68. R. Sitters. Two NP-hardness results for preemptive minsum scheduling of unrelated parallel machines. In K. Aardal and B. Gerards, editors, *Proceedings of IPCO 2001. LNCS*, volume 2081, pages 396–405, Springer, Berlin, 2001.
69. M. Skutella and G. Woeginger. A PTAS for minimizing the weighted sum of job completion times on parallel machines. In *Proceedings of the 31st Annual ACM Symposium on Theory of Computing (STOC'99)*, pages 400–407, 1999.
70. C. Stein and J. Wein. On the existence of schedules that are near-optimal for both makespan and total weighted completion time. *Operations Research Letters*, 21:115–122, 1997.
71. V.G. Timkovsky. Reducibility among scheduling classes. In J.Y.Leung, editor, *Handbook of Scheduling: Algorithms, Models, and Performance Analysis*, pages 8.1–8.42. CRC Press, Boca Raton, 2004.
72. J.D. Ullman. NP-complete scheduling problems. *J. Computer System Science*, 10:384–393, 1975.
73. V.G. Vizing. Minimization of the maximum delay in servicing systems with interruption. *U.S.S.R. Computatioanl Mathematics and Mathematical Physics*, 22(3):227–233, 1982.
74. G. Woeginger. When does a dynamic programming formulation guarantee the existence of a fully polynomial time approximation scheme (FPTAS)? *INFORMS Journal on Computing*, 12(1):57–74, 2000. see also Electronic Colloquium on Computational Complexity, 2001, Report TR01-084, ISSN 1433-8092.
75. M. Yue. On the exact upper bound for the multifit processor scheduling algorithm. *Annals of Operations Research*, 24(1):233–259, 1990.

# Chapter 5
# Parallel Tasks

In this chapter, we study the scheduling model of parallel tasks. It is assumed that a parallel task may use more than one processor at the same time. This relaxation departs from one of the classic scheduling assumptions (Sect. 4.1). Before proceeding with the further presentation let us comment on the naming conventions. Different names have been used for the parallel tasks and their special cases. These were concurrent, multiprocessor, multiversion, malleable, moldable, rigid, and parallel tasks [29, 86, 100, 175]. One name often denotes different things. We adopt, and slightly extend, the naming convention of [100]. Reviews of parallel task scheduling can be found, e.g., in [32, 39, 81, 82, 100, 227]. Some results on the complexity of parallel task scheduling problems are collected in [42]. Proceedings of JSSPP workshop [92] are a rich source of knowledge on parallel task scheduling.

This chapter is organized as follows. In the next section, we present practical reasons for introducing parallel task model. In Sect. 5.2 we formally define variants of the model, which are studied in the following sections. In the last section, we discuss odds against, and in favor of the parallel task model.

## 5.1 Parallel Tasks in Practice

In this section, we discuss practical motivation for various forms of parallel tasks.

### 5.1.1 Parallel Applications

Many methods of solving scientific and engineering problems expose potential parallelism. This parallelism is expressed in a certain programming environment, and finally a parallel application is executed on some computing platform. The structure of data dependencies and communications in the parallel application may be complex to optimize by the general-purpose scheduler of the operating system.

M. Drozdowski, *Scheduling for Parallel Processing*, Computer Communications and Networks, DOI 10.1007/978-1-84882-310-5_5,
© Springer-Verlag London Limited 2009

Therefore, it is a reasonable design decision to delegate optimization of the internal structure schedule to the application itself. Thus, the programmer, the compiler, and the runtime environment are responsible for scheduling the application internals. The operating system provides room for parallelism, namely, the processors.

If the application is executed on an SMP system with UNIX, Windows, or a similar operating system with single image of the memory (Sect. 3.1), then thread (or process) creation, suspension, resuming, and termination are possible and relatively easy. A parallel application can create threads or processes at will, yet it is the operating system scheduler that decides if and which threads are executed in parallel in real time. Thus, the number of used CPUs can be changed at the runtime. In the (time × processors) space the parallel application is shaped or bent by the operating system as a ductile metal. Applications in which number of used CPUs can be changed at the runtime are called *malleable tasks* [100]. The application may signal to the operating system that it wants to be executed in parallel in real time by requesting gang scheduling (a.k.a. coscheduling, see Sect. 3.3.1). Then, if gang scheduling were perfectly implemented the application would be a rigid rectangle in the (time×processors) space.

Situation is different when a parallel application is executed on an MPP system managed by some distributed resource manager. Here the costs of migration are much higher, and hence threads hardly ever migrate. Consequently, also the number of used CPUs cannot be easily changed, and has to be set before the application start. Thus, while the application is running, it is a rectangle in the (time×processors) space. Many parallel applications can be adapted to using various numbers of processors, which is confirmed by surveys of supercomputer users [63]. Exploiting this potential depends on the programmer and the programming environment. We described in Sect. 3.3.2.2 how the admissible processor numbers can be expressed in certain distributed resource managers. Let us call *application size* the number of used CPUs. In MPP systems, even if it is possible to run the final program code on various numbers of CPUs, the application size must be chosen before starting it, and cannot be changed during runtime. Depending on who chooses application size two types of tasks were distinguished [100]. *Rigid tasks* – here the number of required processors is specified external to the scheduler, e.g. by the user, and must be made available throughout the whole application runtime. *Moldable tasks* – within constraints set by the application, the size is decided by the scheduler, and is not changed until termination of the application. A third type of *evolving tasks* has been distinguished in [100]. These are the applications which go through phases and change the number of used CPUs themselves, as it may be seen on parallelism profiles (Fig. 2.4). In this book we do not consider evolving tasks as a new type of parallel task because they may be viewed as chains of rigid tasks.

Parallel applications submitted to MPP systems have specific features [63, 96, 178]. Relatively many applications are sequential (approx. 15–40%, see Fig. 5.1). Bigger sizes are less probable than small ones. About 60–84% of applications have sizes which are powers of 2 (Fig. 5.1). This phenomenon has been attributed to several nonexclusive reasons. For example, packing application sizes into the range of available CPUs is computationally easy if sizes are power of 2 [65], interconnection

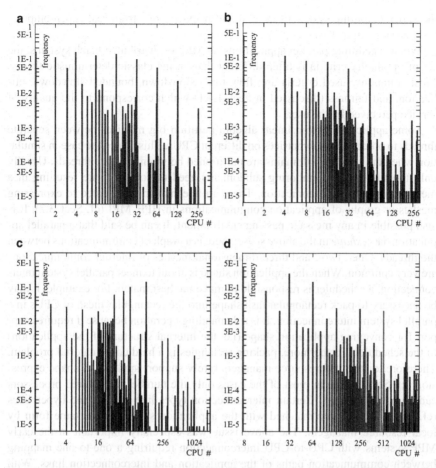

**Fig. 5.1** Frequency of submissions vs. number of used CPUs. (**a**) San Diego Supercomputer Center (SDSC), Intel Paragon, 1994–1995; (**b**) Cornell Theory Center, IBM SP2, 1996–1997; (**c**) LANL, Origin 2000, 1999–2000; (**d**) SDSC, IBM p655/p690, 2004–2005. Data source [95]

may be conveniently partitioned using power of 2 sizes in some designs (e.g. in hypercubes), the inertia of batch system submission interfaces, or users' sense of "round numbers" [63]. Various models of parallel application running times were suggested [96, 178]. However, application running times are not uniform, and big values of running times are often truncated by system administrators imposing limits on the application execution times. A correlation between runtime and application size has been observed: applications using more CPUs run longer. Memory usage and application sizes are also related because applications using more CPUs also use more memory [94]. This may be a result of the fact that in MPP systems memory is tightly coupled with CPUs, and partitioned together with CPUs (see Sect. 3.1.2). Consequently applications requiring more memory also have to use more CPUs. A comprehensive summary of the attributes of parallel applications submitted to the supercomputing systems can be found in [96]. Logs from real supercomputer installations can be found at [95].

When scheduling parallel applications on MPP or distributed batch systems, the set of optimality criteria is often different than in the classic deterministic theory. Most commonly used criteria are: flow time, slowdown, bounded slowdown, utilization, and fairness (discussed in Sect. 4.4.1) which correspond to the quality of service perceived by the user.

Some applications from linear algebra partition big matrices between separate threads to process the submatrices on different CPUs. This is also the case in simulation when the simulated domains are partitioned between separate threads. Usually only threads in the neighboring subdomains need to communicate resulting in a mesh structure of communication. There are mechanisms dedicated to expressing meshes or graphs of application communications in HPF, MPI (cf. Sect. 3.2). It is also possible in any message passing environment. It can be said that a parallel application has a *shape* in the above sense: there is a graph of communications between the threads. One-, two-, and three-dimensional meshes of internal communications are very common. When the application shape is about to meet parallel system interconnection, a scheduler is responsible to make the best match. For example, it may be necessary to pack rectangular task shape into the rectangular mesh of CPUs in a parallel system interconnection. It is a demanding operation because it requires support for conveying application shape (i.e. the internal structure of the application) to the scheduler. Furthermore, packing rectangles is a hard combinatorial problem. Therefore, distributed resource managers rarely support application shape expression (cf. Sect. 3.3.2). In most of the cases only the number of required processors can be communicated. Certain interconnection types like meshes and hypercubes (cf. Sect. 3.1.3) can be matched with the application shapes of the same form by local resource managers. The above issue was especially important in the early MPP systems with CPU-to-CPU interconnection requiring a one-to-one mapping between communication paths of the application and interconnection links. With the progress in parallel computer hardware this matter becomes less critical, but for some parallel applications there is a strong correlation between execution time and the spread of communicating threads (we discussed it in Sect. 3.1.3). Hence, contiguous processor assignments are still advantageous.

In distributed processing according to master–worker or master–slave paradigm, it is possible to adapt the application to the changing number of available processors. This is particularly pertinent to algorithms with data parallelism, i.e. involving similar computations on great number of data units. Examples are research projects conducted by distributed.net, SETI@Home, or applications on BOINC platform. The fact that computers are joining, and leaving the computing work force, is especially important for distributed resource managers, such as Condor (Sect. 3.3.2), harnessing power of idle workstations. Applications of this type may be considered malleable tasks by the distributed resource manager.

In some situations not the number of required processors is important, but the *set* of processors. This may be the case of processor affinity (Sect. 3.1.2), affinity to a particular computer resulting from the dataset transfer times. Similar situation takes place when the application needs a specific set of resources: network connections, dedicated processors (GPUs, FPGAs), libraries, licenses. This constitutes a qualitatively different type of parallel tasks requiring a *set* of processors, or resources, in parallel. We will call such applications *multiprocessor tasks*.

## 5.1.2 Bandwidth and Storage Allocation

Another area of application for parallel task model is bandwidth and storage management.

At the low level of abstraction data flows in computer networks are streams of packets. However, in many cases, it is more convenient to reason about the data flows in terms of requested and allocated bandwidth [15, 74, 141, 183]. Bandwidth is calculated as the amount of data sent over certain period of time. For example, multimedia streaming applications require quality of service in the form of guaranteed bandwidth. There are communication media (e.g. ATM networks) which provide the flows with guaranteed bandwidth. Thus, in the (time × bandwidth) space flows occupy positions analogous to tasks in (time × processors) space. If the requested bandwidth allocation is maintained throughout the whole flow lifetime, then the flow may be considered a rigid task. However, a variability of bit rate exists in many types of multimedia flows. Transferred data are usually buffered at the receiver. Momentary bandwidth fluctuations can be smoothed by using data accumulated in the receiver buffer [104]. The unused bandwidth may be consumed by other flows [64]. Consequently, router scheduling algorithms may shape the area occupied by a certain flow in (time × bandwidth) as for a malleable task. Spectrum allocation is a related problem arising in managing radio communication. Dynamic storage allocation [144, 235] is also similar to bandwidth allocation. It consists in assigning memory blocks of certain sizes to the requesting applications. In the (time × memory addresses) space allocations are equivalent to rigid tasks. Thus, there are analogies between bandwidth, spectrum, and storage allocation, and parallel application scheduling.

Some limited set of results on bandwidth/storage allocation are transferrable to scheduling of parallel tasks on identical processors. Despite the similarities, there are cases when the above analogies are deceptive. For example, a single file broadcast may service several requests for the file. It is rather rare situation that a single run of a program satisfies different requests which usually provide different inputs to the program. Storage or bandwidth units are uniform for the requests, but even identical CPUs may be different for the threads if cache affinity is built. Many network protocols have built in ability to abort and retry a communication. The same approach in the case of parallel applications would be an unacceptable waste of computing power. The optimality criteria used in bandwidth allocation are often different than in scheduling parallel applications. Since bandwidth, spectrum, and storage management are beyond the scope of this book, we will not analyze scheduling problems corresponding with them.

### 5.1.3   Reliable Computing

Testing and reliable computing were the areas where the need for scheduling parallel tasks has been postulated first [29, 77, 148].

For example, in the production phase of computer disks two computers were used simultaneously: one to stimulate the device and one to collect and analyze the output signals [77]. This resulted in a requirement for timely scheduling the tests. Similarly, pairs of processors may test each other [148]. Many electronic devices have built-in self-tests (BIST) which are run at the boot up time to verify the device healthy status [68]. BIST tasks consist in first verifying one functional unit by some other functional unit. If the results are correct groups of positively verified units are used to test more complex structures in the device. Note that the tests may be different for different units, the units cannot substitute each other under the tests, and all units have to be subject to some tests. It may be said that tasks (the tests) are preallocated to the processors. Thus, a *set* of processors is simultaneously required. Consequently, tests provide an example of scheduling multiprocessor tasks.

Many computing systems require increased reliability. This can be achieved in hardware and software [108, 145, 213]. Software failures may be masked by running redundant replicas of the same code or by executing different code variants solving the same problem [138]. The results may be elected by voting. The number of executed replicas may be fixed [111] or selected by the scheduler to maximize some reliability measure [138]. The replicas or variants should run synchronized to maintain system determinism. Various degrees of synchronization are possible [108, 145]. Thus, scheduling replicated and multiversion codes pose various forms of parallel tasks. If the synchronization is tight, and the number of replicas, or variants, is fixed then the tasks may be considered rigid. If the number of replicas/variants is set by the scheduler then the tasks are moldable. If the synchronization is loose, then the reliable applications may be considered malleable tasks.

## 5.2   Assumptions and Definitions

In this section, we define parallel task scheduling problem more formally. In general, notions and the notations of the classic scheduling theory are inherited here. The crucial extensions specify how the parallel processors are used, and what is the dependence of the processing time on the number of allocated processors.

### 5.2.1   Types of Parallel Tasks

In defining various types of parallel tasks a key distinction is whether tasks require just some *number* of processors, some number of processors in a particular *shape*, or a *set* of processors in parallel. When tasks require just a *number* of processors we distinguish the following parallel task types [100].

**Rigid Tasks** Here the number of required processors is given and fixed. Let $size_j$ denote the number of processors required by task $T_j$. We will call tasks requiring $i$ processors, $i$-tasks. Since task size cannot be changed, processing time of rigid task $T_j$ may be denoted $p_j$ without ambiguity. We will denote by $T^i$ the set of $i$-tasks, and the number of such tasks as $n_i$.

**Moldable Tasks** In the case of moldable tasks the number of required processors, within some constraints set by the task, is chosen by the scheduler before starting the task, and is not changed until the task termination. Let $p_j(i)$ denote execution time of $T_j$ on $i$ processors. The set of allowed task sizes may be limited. Let us denote by $X_j$ the set of sizes admissible for task $T_j$, by $X_j(i)$ the $i$th admissible size (we assume that $X_j(i) < X_j(i+1)$), by $\delta_j = \max\{i \in X_j : p_j(i) < \infty\}$ the maximum number of usable processors for $T_j$. We will denote by $i_j$ the number of processors selected for executing task $T_j$, and by $\bar{i}$ the vector of processor allotments of all the tasks.

**Malleable Tasks** We assume that the number of processors used by a malleable task is chosen by the scheduler, and can be changed at runtime. The task may accept new processors when available, and release processors to the system at its request. Note that this requires some infrastructure for incorporating a new processor, or safely removing an application from a processor. This can be done in various ways. Transparently for the application, as migration of threads in a time sharing operating system or as migration of a whole computing environment in some virtualized computer. This can be also attained by checkpointing (Sect. 3.3.2) requiring substantial cooperation of the application. A support for task preemption and migration is essential. In technological sense, malleability generalizes preemption. Therefore, we believe that from the scheduling point of view malleable tasks are qualitatively different than other types of parallel tasks. The range of usable task sizes may be restricted to $\delta_j$ due to technical constraints, or due to a deterioration in the performance of computation.

As mentioned before, we do not distinguish evolving tasks defined in [100] as a separate type because such tasks can be represented as chains of rigid tasks. Our naming convention is different than in some publications which call (our) moldable tasks as malleable.

As discussed in Sect. 5.1.1 some tasks may have *shape* adjusted to the underlying interconnection topology. Parallel tasks with shape require contiguous set of processors in the specific type of interconnection. The following types of task shapes are most common.

**Mesh** Task $T_j$ with mesh shape may require one-, two-, or three-dimensional mesh of processors of sizes $x_j$, $(x_j, y_j)$, $(x_j, y_j, z_j)$, respectively. We will be writing 1D-, 2D-, 3D-mesh, respectively, when referring to a mesh of the corresponding dimension. Let $m, (m_1, m_2), (m_1, m_2, m_3)$ denote sizes along respective dimensions of 1D-, 2D-, 3D-mesh processor network. The whole processor network will be called *machine mesh* or *system mesh*. In the 2D-meshes we will be saying that the first dimension (i.e. of $x_j$ and $m_1$) is horizontal direction, and the second one is vertical direction. In some publications scheduling of the tasks with 1D-mesh shape is introduced implicitly by requiring to allocate to the tasks contiguously numbered processors. The problem of scheduling 1D-mesh tasks is equivalent to a two-dimensional *strip packing problem*. In the two-dimensional strip packing problem rectangles are put on a strip of material of a given width such that the height of the rectangle stack is minimum. In our case tasks are rectangles with dimensions $(size_j, p_j)$, the material strip has width $m$, and schedule length $C_{max}$ is the height of the rectangle stack. A survey on strip packing problem can be found in [177].

**Cube** Task $T_j$ with cube (or hypercube) shape requires a compact hypercube of dimension $cube_j$, i.e. $2^{cube_j}$ processors.

Before proceeding to the further definitions let us comment on a fine distinction between rigid tasks requiring some number of processors and tasks with shape. It is apparent that scheduling rigid tasks is something different than scheduling tasks with 2D-mesh shape because geometric properties of 2D-mesh tasks must be taken into account. Yet, it is less obvious that rigid tasks are different than 1D-mesh tasks requiring contiguous processors. Let us first point to possible sources of the confusion. Firstly, in many papers on scheduling rigid tasks, it is implicitly assumed that processors are allocated contiguously. Consequently, many algorithms declared for tasks requiring $size_j$ processors are also correct algorithms for scheduling in 1D-meshes. The second reason of confusion is the use of buddy processor allocation systems, e.g., in algorithms DHC [97], DQT [122], and some algorithms in Sect. 5.6.1. The idea of buddy allocation systems comes from memory management algorithms [144, 195], and is quite commonly applied to manage processor sets. In such systems ranges of processor indices are recursively divided between scheduling controllers. An advantage of buddy systems is that index ranges correspond to subnetworks of particular topology, and the problem of finding appropriate subnetwork for a task with shape boils down to finding a number of processors. Thus, in buddy systems tasks with shape and tasks that require just some number of processors are managed identically. Note, however, that in buddy systems rigid tasks are managed as if they had shape. Buddy systems may be generalized to manage processor systems without any underlying interconnection topology. This may further blur the distinction between the two types of parallel tasks. Consequently, rigid tasks and 1D-mesh tasks may be easily mixed. However, these types are not equivalent as was demonstrated in [87,226]. Namely, noncontiguos schedules may be shorter than contiguous schedules for tasks with the same sizes and processing times. An example of such a situation is shown in Fig. 5.2. The schedule in Fig. 5.2b is a feasible and optimum schedule for rigid tasks, but is not a feasible schedule for 1D-mesh tasks.

A schedule for 1D-mesh tasks of certain size is also a correct schedule for rigid tasks of the same size. Yet, a correct schedule for rigid tasks is not necessarily correct for 1D-mesh (cf. Fig. 5.2). Thus, for rigid tasks, a better schedule may exist than for tasks with shape requiring the same processor numbers. This has consequence for approximability of the scheduling problems, i.e. for the existence of approximation algorithms with certain values of the worst-case performance ratios. Approximability upper bounds obtained for 1D-meshes are applicable for rigid

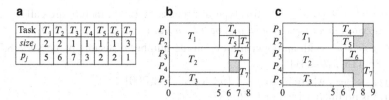

**Fig. 5.2** Example of noncontiguous and contiguous processor allocation. (**a**) Task data. (**b**) A noncontiguous schedule. (**c**) A contiguous schedule

tasks. All approximability lower bounds obtained for rigid tasks are valid approximability lower bounds for tasks with shape. While presenting results on scheduling rigid and 1D-mesh tasks we will preserve the classification in the original publications. Yet, we will point to rigid and moldable task scheduling methods, which can be applied in 1D-mesh case.

To avoid creating excessive number of parallel task categories we do not distinguish moldable tasks with shape. These will be included in the section on moldable tasks or tasks with shape according to the classification in the original source. Again, such cases will be clearly indicated.

Tasks requiring a set of processors simultaneously will be called *multiprocessor tasks*. It is often said that tasks requiring a set of processors are *preallocated* to the processors. Two types of multiprocessor tasks can be distinguished:

**Single Mode Multiprocessor Tasks** It is assumed that the set of processors required by a task is given and fixed. We will denote by $fix_j$ the set of processors required by task $T_j$. Let $\mathcal{T}^A$ denote the set of tasks requiring processors in set $A$, i.e. $\mathcal{T}^A = \{T_j : fix_j = A\}$. We will say that tasks in set $\mathcal{T}^A$ are of type $A$. When there is no ambiguity we will call the single mode tasks just multiprocessor tasks.

**Multimode Multiprocessor Tasks** Alternative sets of processors may be used to execute a multimode task. Let $set_j$ denote the family of processor sets which may process $T_j$. We will denote by $p_{ij}$ the processing time of $T_j$ executed on processors in set $fix_i \in set_j$. Each alternative $(fix_i, p_{ij})$ defines a mode for executing $T_j$. Observe that multimode tasks are more general than moldable tasks, because requiring $i$ processors can be represented as all modes including subsets of $m$ processors with cardinality $i$.

### 5.2.2 Processing Time Functions

Let us now examine the execution time of moldable and malleable tasks as a function of the assigned number of processors. For simplicity of presentation we assume that tasks are not preempted, and the number of used processors is the same through whole runtime. Some clues on the form of processing time function are given in Sect. 2.4. The following types of processing time functions were analyzed in the scheduling literature:

- $p_j(i) = \frac{p_j(1)}{i}$ – tasks with this type of processing time function are called *work preserving*, *ideally parallelizable*, or *fully parallelizable* [89, 102, 229].
- $p_j(i) = \frac{p_j(1)}{i}$, with an upper limit $\delta_j$ on the number of usable processors [8, 73, 80, 85, 115, 229–231].
- $p_j(i) = \frac{p_j(1)}{i^{\alpha_j}}$, where $0 < \alpha_j < 1$ [33, 37, 89, 198, 200].
- $p_j(i)$ is nonincreasing in $i$ [226, 237].
- $p_j(i)$ is nonincreasing in $i$, and work $W_j(i) = i p_j(i)$ is nondecreasing in $i$, these assumptions are often called *monotonous penalty property* [87, 115, 164], this property is equivalent to nondecreasing sublinear speedup (see Sect. 2.4).
- $p_j(i)$ is an arbitrary continuous function of $i$ [234].
- $p_j(i)$ is an arbitrary discrete function of $i$ [86].

If we interpret $p_j(1)$ as the amount of work to be done, then the denominators of the first three expressions for $p_j(i)$ are equivalent to the function of processing speed in the number of assigned processors, or equivalently, speedup $\varsigma_j(i)$ (cf. Sect. 2.4). Speedup $\varsigma_j(i)$ (or processing speed function) is often used instead of the processing time function [33, 37, 89, 200].

Allowing for continuous speedup or processing time functions may result in fractional assignment of processors to the tasks. Depending on the assumed model of processors, such a solution may require special rounding procedure (see e.g. [33]).

When a malleable, or multimode, task is preempted and later restarted on a different set of processors, then it is problematic how to determine progress in the computation. A good solution would be to recourse to the application internal structure, e.g., the number of executed instructions. However, it was our intention to abstract away the internals of the application. Therefore, a different method is needed. In each schedule we can distinguish intervals of time where the assignment of the tasks to the processors does not change. Assume that malleable task $T_j$ is executed for time $\tau$ on $i$ processors. The amount of work done on $T_j$ in this interval is $\frac{\tau}{p_j(i)} p_j(1) = \tau \varsigma_j(i)$ (cf. speedup definition in Eq. (2.12)). The amount of work performed over task $T_j$ in different intervals must sum up to $p_j(1)$. In the case of multimode tasks, the fraction of work on $T_j$ executed for time $\tau$ on processors in set $fix_i$ is $\frac{\tau}{p_{ij}}$. All such fractions of work on $T_j$ must sum to 1.

### 5.2.3  Extension of $\alpha|\beta|\gamma$ Notation

In this section, we introduce new elements in $\alpha|\beta|\gamma$ notation to represent parallel tasks. We also discuss complexity relationships between parallel task scheduling problems.

In Fig. 5.3a we have summarized the generalization/specialization relationships between various types of parallel tasks introduced in Sect. 5.2.1. An extension of $\alpha|\beta|\gamma$ notation for parallel tasks has been proposed [81, 227]. We adapt this notation, and expand it slightly. The following symbols are used in the $\beta$ field to denote task types:

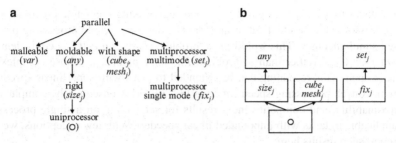

**Fig. 5.3** (a) Types of parallel tasks and their notation. (b) Complexity inference

- *var* – Used for malleable tasks
- *any* – For moldable tasks
- $size_j$ – For rigid tasks
- $cube_j$ – For tasks requiring processors in shape of hypercube
- $1D$-, $2D$-, $3D$-$mesh_j$ – For tasks with shape of one-, two-, three-dimensional mesh, respectively
- $set_j$ – Multimode multiprocessor tasks
- $fix_j$ – Single mode multiprocessor tasks

We will use special symbols to denote the type of processing time function for moldable and malleable tasks. When this function has a simple form, then it will be placed directly in $\beta$ field. For example, in the case of linear speedup notation $p_j(i) = \frac{p_j(1)}{i}$ will be used. More general types of processing time functions are frequently defined with respect to speedup. Therefore, we will use symbols referring to speedup to denote types of processing time functions:

- *Nd* – Nondecreasing speedup, i.e. nonincreasing processing time functions
- *Sub* – Sublinear speedup, i.e. for all tasks $T_j$ work $W_j(i)$ is nondecreasing with $i$
- *NdSub* – Nondecreasing sublinear speedup

If none of these symbols is presented, then it will mean that $p_j(i)$ is an arbitrary discrete function of $i$. Symbol $\delta_j$ in $\beta$ field will denote that upper bounds on the numbers of processors usable by the tasks are defined.

Let us now discuss complexity implications following from the generalization and specialization relationships between certain classes of parallel tasks shown in Fig. 5.3a. Possible polynomial time transformations between scheduling problems are depicted in Fig. 5.3b. Empty symbol ∘ denotes standard (classic) assumptions on the type of tasks. For example, if some moldable task scheduling problem (denoted *any*) is solvable in polynomial time, then the same problem for rigid tasks (denoted $size_j$) is solvable in polynomial time. A hard problem for classic tasks (∘) remains hard for rigid tasks and the tasks with shape.

Note that with linear speedup work of a task is invariant (because $\varsigma_j(i) = \frac{p_j(1)}{p_j(i)} = i$ and $W_j(i) = i p_j(i) = p_j(1)$). In the absence of other constraints, each task may use all processors without additional cost. Then, scheduling malleable and moldable tasks reduces to scheduling on one processor representing the whole processor set. The processors may be identical or uniform because their whole processing power is used simultaneously. This would make problem $Pm|var, prec|C_{max}$ equivalent to $1|pmtn, prec|C_{max}$, rather than to problem $Pm|pmtn, prec|C_{max}$ whose complexity status is open. This reasoning can be extended to tasks with superlinear speedup, i.e. with convex processing speed function [32, 33, 37]. Consequently, complexity, approximability, and competitiveness results for scheduling on a single processor are applicable to tasks with unbounded linear speedup. With few exceptions, we do not report such results here.

Let us further consider a peculiar case of malleable tasks (denoted *var*). Technically, the ability to safely suspend and resume computation is a prerequisite for releasing and adding processors in the computations. In other words, preemption is required for malleability. Classic scheduling with preemption is equivalent to malleable tasks with additional restriction on the number of usable processors ($\forall T_j \in \mathcal{T}, \delta_j = 1$). But the above observations do not imply that classic preemptive scheduling problems are special (simpler) cases of malleable task scheduling problems. For instance, problem $P|pmtn, prec|C_{max}$ is sNPh, but complexity of $P|var, prec|C_{max}$ depends on the type of processing time function. For unbounded linear speedup it is polynomially solvable as the problem of scheduling on one processor. On the other hand, by appropriate selection of processing time function problem $P|var, prec|C_{max}$ can be also made equivalent to $P|size_j, pmtn|C_{max}$ which is NPh. Hence, inferring the complexity of malleable scheduling problems from the complexity of preemptive scheduling problems makes little sense without specifying processing time functions. Consequently, it is hard to say whether preemption is generalized by malleability or not.

For the end of this section let us observe that slowdown criterion, as defined in Sect. 4.4.1, is ambiguous for moldable and malleable tasks. Processing time $p_j(i)$ in the denominator of $s_j$ would bias the slowdown because $p_j(i)$ is usually nonincreasing function of processor number $i$ (cf. Sect. 5.2.2). Moreover, both the denominator and numerator would depend on the schedule which assigns processor numbers to the tasks. This would complicate construction of scheduling algorithms. In the further presentation we adapt the approach from [99, 163] where the flow time is normalized to the processing time on a dedicated system, i.e. $s_j = \frac{f_j}{p_j(m)}$.

## 5.3   Rigid Tasks

In this section, we examine problems of scheduling rigid parallel tasks. Complexity and approximability results will be presented for minmax and minsum criteria. In the last subsection we present heuristics solving problems which do not fit easily in the $\alpha|\beta|\gamma$ notation because they originated with more diversified set of goals than minimizing a single optimality criterion. Though these algorithms have no performance guarantees, they have been evaluated empirically for diversified parallel workloads.

## 5.3.1 $C_{max}, L_{max}$ Criteria

In this section, we analyze rigid task scheduling problems for schedule length and maximum lateness criteria. We study nonpreemptive and preemptive scheduling problems, then heuristics with the worst-case performance guarantees will be presented.

### 5.3.1.1 Nonpreemptive Schedules

We summarize in Table 5.1 the results on **NP**-hardness of nonpreemptive rigid tasks scheduling for $C_{max}, L_{max}$ criteria. References to polynomially, pseudopolynomially solvable cases are presented in Table 5.2. Let us remind that notation $Pm| \ldots$ means that the number of processors is constant. In these tables we use the following notation:

- $C_{max}^*$ – The optimum schedule length
- $\Delta = \max_j \{size_j\}$
- $poly()$ – A polynomial in some variables
- $k$ – The number of precedences in the task graph

**Table 5.1** Hard nonpreemptive rigid task scheduling problems, $C_{max}, L_{max}$ criteria

| Problem | Result | Reference |
|---|---|---|
| $P2\|size_j\|C_{max}$ | **NPh** | from $P2\|\|C_{max} \in$**NPh** |
| $P\|size_j\|C_{max}$ | s**NPh** | from $P\|\|C_{max} \in$**NPh** |
| $P5\|size_j\|C_{max}$ | s**NPh** | [86] |
| $P2\|size_j, chain\|C_{max}$ | s**NPh** | [86] |
| $P2\|size_j\|L_{max}$ | s**NPh** | [161] |
| $P\|size_j, p_j = 1\|C_{max}$ | s**NPh** | [29, 175] |
| $P3\|size_j \in \{1,2\}, p_j = 1, chain\|C_{max}$ | s**NPh** | [35, 175] |
| $P2\|size_j, p_j = 1, chain, r_j\|C_{max}$ | s**NPh** | [43] |

**Table 5.2** Polynomial and pseudopolynomial cases of nonpreemptive rigid task scheduling problems, $C_{max}, L_{max}$ criteria

| Problem | Result | Reference |
|---|---|---|
| $P2\|size_j\|C_{max}$ | $O(nT^2)$ | [86] |
| $P3\|size_j\|C_{max}$ | $O(nT^5)$ | [86] |
| $P4\|size_j \neq 1\|C_{max}$ | $O(nT^4)$ | [79] |
| $P\|size_j \in \{1, \Delta\}, p_j = 1\|C_{max}$ | $O(n)$ | [29] |
| $Pm\|size_j, p_j = 1\|C_{max}$ | $O(n)$ | [29] |
| $Pm\|size_j, p_j = p, r_j\|C_{max}$ | $O(n^{3m})$ | [13] |
| $P2\|size_j, p_j = 1, prec\|C_{max}$ | $O(n^2 + \min\{nk, n^{2.376}\})$ | [5, 175] |
| $P\|size_j \in \{1, \Delta\}, p_j = 1, m.chain\|C_{max}$ | $O(N^2)$ | [36] |
| $P\|size_j \in \{1, m\}, p_j = 1, r_j\|L_{max}$ | $O(poly(n))$ | [14] |

- *m.chain* – Chains of rigid tasks with monotonously decreasing or increasing sizes
- $N$ – The number of chains in the task graph comprising only chains
- $T$ – Is an upper bound on the schedule length

Selected algorithmic techniques for nonpreemptive scheduling of rigid tasks are presented in the following paragraphs.

$Pm|size_j, p_j = 1|C_{\max}$ [29]

This problem can be solved by reduction to integer linear programming. Any schedule for $Pm|size_j, p_j = 1|C_{\max}$ can be treated as a concatenation of unit-length intervals where the set of executed tasks is not changed. Each of the sets of tasks uses no more than $m$ processors. We will be calling such sets of tasks *processor feasible sets*. Processor feasible set $i$ may be represented as vector $\overline{b_i} = (b_1, \dots, b_m)$ of numbers $b_j$ of $j$-tasks executed simultaneously, where $\sum_{i=1}^{m} b_i = m$. The number of different processor feasible sets is equal to the number $p(m)$ of partitions of $m$. Let $x_i$ be the number of processor feasible set $i$ repetitions in a schedule. Thus, problem $Pm|size_j, p_j = 1|C_{\max}$ boils down to decomposing vector $\overline{n} = (n_1, \dots, n_m)$ of certain size task numbers into a minimum number of processor feasible sets. This can be expressed as an integer linear program (ILP).

$$\text{minimize} \sum_{j=1}^{p(m)} x_j \quad \text{subject to} \tag{5.1}$$

$$\sum_{i=1}^{p(m)} x_i \overline{b_i} = \overline{n} \tag{5.2}$$

$$x_i \geq 0 \tag{5.3}$$

There are $m$ constraints and $p(m)$ variables in the above ILP. An exact formula for $p(m)$ is not known. It has been shown that $p(m)$ tends to $\Theta(\frac{e^{\pi\sqrt{2m/3}}}{m})$ as $m \to \infty$. Yet, for fixed $m$ the number of variables is also fixed and the above formulation can be solved in $O((\log n)^c) < O(n)$, where $c$ is a big constant. Implementation of thus constructed schedule requires $O(n)$ time. Whether this can be done in polynomial time depends on encoding of the instance. If for each task $T_j$ its $size_j$ is encoded, then this can be done in polynomial time. If for each size $i \in \{1, \dots, m\}$ the number of tasks is encoded on $O(\log n)$ bits, then sheer implementing of a schedule requires pseudopolynomial (i.e. exponential) time.

$Pm|size_j, p_j = p, r_j|C_{\max}$ [13]

A dynamic programming algorithm with complexity $O(n^{3m})$ was proposed for this problem. Let us assume that $0 = r_1 \leq r_2 \cdots \leq r_n$. It can be shown by interchange argument that tasks of a certain size are ordered according to the nondecreasing values of ready times. In an active schedule tasks are started and completed at times $\tau = r_j + lp$, for $l \in \{0, \ldots, n\}$ [13]. Hence, there are $O(n^2)$ such points in time. In each of such points the number of available processor changes. Let $(\tau_1, \ldots, \tau_m)$ denote processor availability pattern after scheduling some tasks, i.e. one processor is available starting at $\tau_1$, two processors are available at $\tau_2$, etc. Since there are $O(n^2)$ processor availability changes, there can be at most $O(n^{2m})$ processor availability patterns in any schedule. The dynamic programming algorithm computes optimum schedule length by calculating recursive function $C_{\max}(\tau_1, \ldots, \tau_m, j_1, \ldots, j_m)$, where $(\tau_1, \ldots, \tau_m)$ are variables representing processor availability patterns, $(j_1, \ldots, j_m)$ are task variables denoting which tasks of a certain size still remain to be processed. More precisely, only tasks with size equal $s$ ($1 \leq s \leq m$) and index greater or equal $j_s$ remain to be scheduled. There are at most $O(n^m)$ different task variables. If a ready task $T_x$ of size $s$ is appended to a partial schedule with processor availability pattern $(\tau_1, \ldots, \tau_m)$, then processor availability pattern changes to $(\tau_{s+1}, \ldots, \tau_m, \tau_s + p, \ldots, \tau_s + p)$ because schedule is active (the trailing value $\tau_s + p$ repeats $s$ times). Hence schedule length for the partial schedule extended by one task of size $s$ is $C_{\max}(\tau_{s+1}, \ldots, \tau_m, \tau_s + p, \ldots, \tau_s + p, j_1, \ldots, j_{s-1}, x + 1, j_{s+1}, j_m)$. Consequently, $C_{\max}(\tau_1, \ldots, \tau_m, j_1, \ldots, j_m)$ equals

$$C_{\max}(\tau_{s+1}, \ldots, \tau_m, \tau_s + p, \ldots, \tau_s + p, j_1, \ldots, j_{s-1}, x + 1, j_{s+1}, j_m) \qquad (5.4)$$

If no task of size $s$ is ready at $\tau_1$ then $C_{\max}(\tau_1, \ldots, \tau_m, j_1, \ldots, j_m)$ equals

$$C_{\max}(\max\{\tau_1, r_x\}, \ldots, \max\{\tau_m, r_x\}, j_1, \ldots, j_m)$$

where $x$ is the smallest index of a task with size $s$, and $x \geq i_s$. The values of function $C_{\max}()$ are calculated for processor availability pattern and task variables ordered according to the decreasing lexicographic order. In a sense $C_{\max}()$ is calculated from the end of the schedule. For each combination of processor $\tau_1, \ldots, \tau_m$, and task variables $j_1, \ldots, j_m$, all possible sizes $s$ of tasks to be appended to a schedule are evaluated. The value of minimum schedule length is recorded in $C_{\max}(\tau_1, \ldots, \tau_m, j_1, \ldots, j_m)$. Function $C_{\max}(\tau_1, \ldots, \tau_m, j_1, \ldots, j_m)$ is initialized with $\tau_m$, for $j_s = n_s + 1$, and all possible values of $(\tau_1, \ldots, \tau_m,)$. Computation of $C_{\max}()$ finishes with reaching $C_{\max}(0, \ldots, 0)$.

## $P2|size_j, p_j = 1, prec|C_{\max}$ [175]

This problem can be solved by adding all transitive arcs to the task precedence graph $\mathcal{G}$. Complexity of constructing transitive closure is $O(\min\{nk, n^{2.376}\})$, where $k$ is the number of $\mathcal{G}$ arcs, and $nk$ follows from searching the graph, e.g., depth-first from each node. Thus, all tasks from $\mathcal{T}^2$ are bypassed, and can be removed from $\mathcal{G}$. Let $\mathcal{G}'$ be the modified task precedence graph constructed in the above way. Tasks in $\mathcal{G}'$ can

**Table 5.3** Complexity of preemptive rigid task scheduling, $C_{\max}, L_{\max}$ criteria

| Problem | Result | Reference |
|---|---|---|
| $P\|size_j, pmtn, p_j = 1\|C_{\max}$ | **NP**h | [79] |
| $Pm\|size_j, pmtn\|C_{\max}$ | $O(poly(n^m))$ | [29] |
| $Pm\|size_j, pmtn\|C_{\max}$ | $O(n + poly(m))$ | [129] |
| $P\|size_j, pmtn\|C_{\max}$ | $\mathbf{P} \neq \mathbf{NP} \Rightarrow \notin$ s**NP**h | [129] |
| $P\|size_j \in \{1, \Delta\}, pmtn\|C_{\max}$ | $O(poly(n^m))$ | [29] |
| $Q\|size_j \in \{1, \Delta\}, pmtn\|C_{\max}$ | $O(n \log n + nm)$ | [30] |
| $P\|size_j \in \{1, \Delta\}, pmtn\|L_{\max}$ | $O(poly(n^m))$ | [31] |
| $P2\|size_j, pmtn, r_j\|C_{\max}$ | $O(n^2)$ | [82] |
| $P\|size_j \in \{1, \Delta\}, m.chain, pmtn\|C_{\max}$ | $O(n^2)$ | [36] |

be scheduled by Coffman–Graham algorithm (see Sect. 4.3.1.1). Then the parallel tasks may be reinserted in the schedule for $\mathcal{G}'$ observing precedence constraints. The complexity of this algorithm is $O(n^2 + \min\{nk, n^{2.376}\})$.

### 5.3.1.2  Preemptive Schedules

The results on complexity of preemptive rigid task scheduling for $C_{\max}, L_{\max}$ criteria can be found in Table 5.3. In the following we will show that problem $P\|size_j, pmtn, p_j = 1\|C_{\max}$ is **NP**h. The proof is quite simple, and it may give a rough idea of the **NP**-hardness proof structure. Since $P\|size_j, pmtn, p_j = 1\|C_{\max}$ is **NP**h, polynomially solvable cases may exist only for simpler problems. Polynomially solvable cases are outlined in the further text.

**Theorem 5.1.** $P\|size_j, pmtn, p_j = 1\|C_{\max}$ is **NP**h [79].

*Proof.* The hardness of $P\|size_j, pmtn\|C_{\max}$ can be shown by giving a polynomial time Turing reduction (cf. Sect. 2.2) of **NP**c partition problem [110] to our scheduling problem. Partition is formulated as follows: Given a set of positive integers $A = \{a_1, \ldots, a_q\}$, such that $\sum_{j=1}^{q} a_j = 2B$, determine if there is a set $A' \subset A$ such that $\sum_{i \in A'} a_i = \sum_{i \in A - A'} a_i = B$. The reduction from partition instance to $P\|size_j, pmtn\|C_{\max}$: $m = B, n = q, p_j = 1, size_j = a_j$, for $j = 1, \ldots, n$. Determine if there is a schedule of length at most $C_{\max} = 2$. Note that $m C_{\max} = \sum_{j=1}^{n} p_j size_j$, and a feasible schedule of length $C_{\max} = 2$ has no idle time. Therefore, at each time moment $\tau$ the sizes of tasks running in parallel must be equal to $B = \sum_{j \in T(\tau)} size_j$, where $T(\tau)$ is the set of tasks executed at time $\tau$ (see Fig. 5.4). Hence, a positive answer to the scheduling problem implies a positive answer to the partition problem.                                                                                  □

**Fig. 5.4** Illustration to the
proof of Theorem 5.1

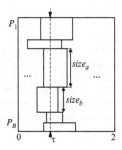

$Pm|size_j, pmtn|C_{max}$ [29]

This problem can be solved by modification of the processor feasible set approach
presented above for problem $Pm|size_j, p_j = 1|C_{max}$. Let $M$ be the number of dif-
ferent processor feasible sets, i.e. sets of tasks which can be processed in parallel
on $m$ processors. Let $Q_j$ be the set of processor feasible sets including task $T_j$, and
$x_i$ the length of an interval in which processor feasible set $i$ is being executed. Our
problem can be expressed as a linear program

$$\text{minimize} \sum_{j=1}^{M} x_j \qquad \text{subject to} \qquad\qquad (5.5)$$

$$\sum_{i \in Q_j} x_i = p_j \quad \text{for } j = 1,\ldots,n \qquad\qquad (5.6)$$

$$x_i \geq 0 \quad \text{for } i = 1,\ldots,M \qquad\qquad (5.7)$$

There are $O(n^m)$ variables and $O(n)$ constraints. Hence, the above approach can be
applied in polynomial time only for fixed number of processors $m$.

$Pm|size_j, pmtn|C_{max}$ [129]

The problem considered in the preceding paragraph can be solved in a more advanced way and with lower complexity. Let us assume that tasks are ordered according to the nonincreasing sizes: $size_1 \geq size_2 \geq \cdots size_n$, and tasks in $T^l$ are ordered
according to the nonincreasing processing time: $p_{a_l} \geq p_{a_l+1} \geq \cdots p_{a_l+n_l-1}$, where
$a_l = 1 + \sum_{i=l+1}^{m} n_i$ is the index of the first task in $T^l$. For simplicity of presentation
we also assume that $n_l > \lfloor \frac{m}{l} \rfloor$ (otherwise some dummy tasks of zero length can be
added). A schedule for our problem is a sequence of processor feasible sets. For each
task size $l$ it is possible to view the sequence as a staircase pattern of $l$-processor
wide stripes (see Fig. 5.5) which we will call $l$-stripes. Let $PC_i^l$ be the length of the
$i$th longest $l$-stripe. Analogously to problem $Q|pmtn|C_{max}$ (see Sect. 4.3.1.2 and inequalities (4.1) and (4.2)) necessary and sufficient conditions for the existence of a
feasible schedule for $l$-tasks are

**Fig. 5.5** (**a**) Original schedule. (**b**) Staircase pattern for 2-tasks. (**c**) Staircase pattern for 1-tasks. The original assignment of tasks to intervals has been preserved to aid understanding construction of the staircase pattern. The staircase pattern is not a schedule

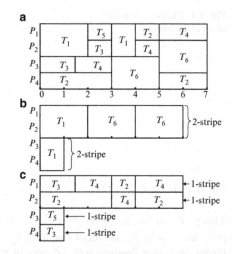

$$\sum_{i=a_l}^{a_l+k-1} p_i \le \sum_{i=1}^{k} PC_i^l \quad \text{for } k = 1, \ldots, \left\lfloor \frac{m}{l} \right\rfloor - 1 \tag{5.8}$$

$$\sum_{i=a_l}^{a_l+n_k-1} p_i \le \sum_{i=1}^{\lfloor \frac{m}{l} \rfloor} PC_i^l \tag{5.9}$$

Again, let $M$ be the number of processor feasible sets, $x_i$ a variable denoting the duration of executing processor feasible set $i$, and $\overline{b_i} = (b_{i1}, \ldots, b_{im})$ a vector representing processor feasible set $i$, where $b_{il}$ is the number of $l$-stripes or $l$-tasks executed in parallel in $i$. Conditions (5.8)–(5.9) can be converted to a linear program:

$$\text{minimize} \sum_{j=1}^{M} x_j \quad \text{subject to} \tag{5.10}$$

$$\sum_{i=a_l}^{a_l+k-1} p_i \le \sum_{i=1}^{M} \min\{b_{il}, k\} x_i \quad \text{for } k = 1, \ldots, \left\lfloor \frac{m}{l} \right\rfloor - 1, l = 1, \ldots, m \tag{5.11}$$

$$\sum_{i=a_l}^{a_l+n_k-1} p_i \le \sum_{i=1}^{\lfloor \frac{m}{l} \rfloor} b_{il} x_i \quad \text{for } l = 1, \ldots, m \tag{5.12}$$

$$x_i \ge 0 \quad \text{for } i = 1, \ldots, M \tag{5.13}$$

The above LP determines duration of executing certain processor feasible sets. In the final schedule processor feasible sets can be concatenated in an arbitrary order. Tasks of size $l$ should be scheduled in the staircase pattern of their $l$-stripes analogously to constructing a schedule for $Q|pmtn|C_{\max}$. Linear programs (5.10)–(5.13) have

$\sum_{i=1}^{m} \lfloor \frac{m}{i} \rfloor \leq m \sum_{i=1}^{m} \frac{1}{i} \leq m(1 + \ln m)$ constraints and $p(m)$ variables, where $p(m)$ is the number of partitions of $m$. Since $p(m)$ grows exponentially with $m$ it seems that (5.10)–(5.13) cannot be solved polynomially in $m$. However, it has been shown in [129] that the separation problem for the dual LP can be solved in $O(m^2 \log m)$ time. This implies that (5.10)–(5.13) can be solved in polynomial time $poly(m)$, though not in $O(\log m)$ which would be required for a polynomial algorithm. The whole problem can be solved in $O(n + poly(m))$ time. However, if $m$ were bounded by a polynomial in $n$ then our problem can be solved in polynomial time. Consequently, it is unlikely that $P|size_j, pmtn|C_{\max}$ is s**NP**h [129]. Similar procedure has been proposed in [86] as a part of an algorithm solving $P|any, pmtn|C_{\max}$.

Both above approaches to $Pm|size_j, pmtn|C_{\max}$ can be generalized to deal with ready times, duedates, processor availability constraints, and malleable tasks [27, 129, 132].

### 5.3.1.3   Heuristics with a Guarantee

The results on approximability of nonpreemptive and preemptive rigid task scheduling for $C_{\max}$, $L_{\max}$ criteria are collected in Table 5.4. Let us explain the notation used in this table. The meaning of $oll$, $olt$, $\neg p_j, \ldots$ has been explained in Sect. 4.4.3 dedicated to online scheduling. The other symbols are:

- $L_{\max}^{MDD}$ – Maximum lateness of a schedule built by the Modified Duedate algorithm.
- $L_{\max}^{*}$ – Optimum value of the maximum lateness.
- $d_{\max} = \max_{j=1}^{n} \{d_j\}$.
- $G = \frac{p_{\max}}{p_{\min}}$.
- $R_X$ – The worst-case performance guarantee of heuristic $X$. The names of the heuristics are explained in the following text. The name is not present in the inapproximability results. For example, $R > l$ means that according to the current state of knowledge no algorithm with worst-case performance guarantee bounded by $l$ can exist, unless e.g. **P** = **NP**, or **ZPP** = **NP**.
- PTAS – Denotes existence of a polynomial time approximation scheme.

The following heuristics are mentioned in Table 5.4 (in the order of appearance):

**LS** – Any list scheduling heuristic.
**Largest Processing Time** (LPT) list scheduling heuristic.

**NonIncreasing Size Longest Processing Time** (NISLPT) [174] This algorithm schedules the tasks according to the nonincreasing sizes, and the tasks with equal size are ordered according to the nonincreasing processing times.

**$H_m$** – Proposed in [167] to solve problem $P|size_j|C_{\max}$ In this algorithm task set is partitioned into subsets $\mathcal{T}_k = \{T_j : \frac{m}{k+1} < size_j \leq \frac{m}{k}\}$, for $k = 1 \ldots, m-1$. Tasks in $\mathcal{T}_k$ are scheduled using any list scheduling algorithm on blocks of $\frac{m}{k}$ processors treated as if they were units.

**Table 5.4**   Approximability of rigid task scheduling, $C_{max}$, $L_{max}$ criteria

| Problem | Result | Reference |
|---|---|---|
| $P\|size_j \leq \Delta, p_j = 1, prec\|C_{max}$ | $R_{LS} = \frac{2m-\Delta}{m-\Delta+1}$ | [175] |
| $P\|size_j\|C_{max}$ | $R_{LPT} = 2 + \frac{p_{max}}{C^*_{max}}$ | [226] |
| $P\|size_j\|C_{max}$ | $R_{NISLPT} = \frac{4\Delta}{3} - \frac{\Delta(\Delta+1)}{6m}$ | [174] |
| $P\|size_j, \neg p_j\|C_{max}$ | $R_{LS} \leq 2 - \frac{1}{m}$ | [103] |
| $P\|size_j, \neg p_j, prec\|C_{max}$ | $R \geq m$ | [102] |
| $P\|size_j \leq \Delta, \neg p_j, prec\|C_{max}$ | $R \geq \frac{2m-\Delta}{m-\Delta}$ | [102] |
| $P\|olt, size_j \leq \Delta, \neg p_j, prec\|C_{max}$ | $R_{LS} = \frac{2m-\Delta}{m-\Delta}$ | [102] |
| $P\|size_j\|C_{max}$ | $\frac{5}{3} \leq R_{H_m} < \frac{31}{18} + \frac{(m-1)p_{max}}{C^*_{max}}$ | [167] |
| $P\|size_j, prec\|C_{max}$ | $R_{LS} \leq \frac{2m-\Delta}{m-\Delta+1}$ | [168] |
| $P2\|size_j, p_j = 1, prec\|L_{max}$ | $L^{MDD}_{max} = \frac{3}{2}L^*_{max} + \frac{d_{max}-1}{2}$ | [43] |
| $P2\|size_j, p_j = 1, prec\|C_{max}$ | $R_{CP} = \frac{3}{2} - \frac{1}{2C^*_{max}}$ | [43] |
| $P\|size_j, p_j = 1, \neg prec\|C_{max}$ | $R_{Level(FF)} = 2.7$ | [26] |
| $P\|size_j, p_j = 1, \neg prec\|C_{max}$ | $R > 2.69103$ | [26] |
| $P\|size_j \leq \frac{m}{2}, p_j = 1, \neg prec\|C_{max}$ | $R_{Level(FF)} = 2.5$ | [26] |
| $P\|size_j, \neg p_j, \neg prec\|C_{max}$ | $R > \max\{\frac{G+1}{2}, 2.69103\}$ | [26] |
| $P\|size_j, \neg p_j, \neg prec\|C_{max}$ | $R_{RRR} = \frac{G}{2} + 4$ | [26] |
| $P\|size_j, \neg p_j, \neg prec\|C_{max}$ | $R_{RRRA} = \frac{G}{2} + 5.5$ | [26] |
| $P\|olt, size_j, \neg p_j\|C_{max}$ | $R_{LS} = 2 - \frac{1}{m}$ | [192] |
| $Pm\|size_j\|C_{max}$ | PTAS, $O(n)$ | [4] |
| $P\|size_j\|C_{max}$ | $R > \frac{3}{2} + \frac{poly(n)}{C^*_{max}}$ | [139] |
| $P\|size_j, pmtn\|C_{max}$ | $R > \frac{3}{2}$ | [139] |
| $P\|size_j, pmtn, r_j\|C_{max}$ | $R_{NIS} = 2 - \frac{1}{m}$ | [139] |
| $P\|size_j, r_j\|C_{max}$ | $R_{LS} < 2$ | [139] |
| $P\|size_j, pmtn, r_j\|C_{max}$ | $R_{LS} < 2$ | [139] |
| $P\|oll, size_j\|C_{max}$ | $R > 2.25$ | [139] |
| $P\|oll, size_j\|C_{max}$ | $R_J < 12$ | [139] |

**Modified Duedate (MDD) [43]** This algorithm is applied to solve problem $P2\|size_j, p_j = 1, prec\|L_{max}$. Duedates $d_j$ of the tasks are modified according to the precedence constraints $\forall(j,k) \in \mathcal{A}, d'_j = \min\{d_j, d_k - 1\}$ and scheduled as soon as possible according to the order of nondecreasing modified duedates $d'_j$ obeying precedence constraints.

**Critical Path (CP) [43]** list scheduling algorithm. Tasks are ordered according to the nonincreasing length of the path from the task to its furthest successor in the precedence task graph.

**Level (FF) [26]** applied to solve problem $P\|size_j, p_j = 1, \neg prec\|C_{max}$, i.e. on-line scheduling UET tasks with unknown precedences. This algorithm packs available tasks with known sizes into $m$ available processor using First Fit (FF) heuristic. Since FF (as any heuristic for bin packing) is not dividing the packed elements into pieces, level(FF) can be also used for 1D-meshes.

---

1: **while** $L_1 \neq \emptyset$ schedule a big task exclusively;
2: **while** not all tasks are finished **do**
3: { **while** $L_2 \neq \emptyset$ **do** schedule small tasks greedily;
4:   **if** $L_1 \neq \emptyset$ **then**
5:     **if** a big task can be scheduled **then** schedule it
6:     **else**
7:       **if** $\alpha(\tau) \geq \frac{1}{2}$ **then** wait for a scheduled task to finish
8:       **else** // start a delay phase
              { collect small tasks that become available during the next 2 units of time;
                schedule those tasks greedily, and then wait for all scheduled tasks to finish;
9:               **while** $L_1 \neq \emptyset$ **do** schedule a big task exclusively;}
10:  **else** wait for the next available task; }

---

**Fig. 5.6** Algorithm RRR (on the basis of [26], copyright (2001), with permission from Elsevier)

**Restricted Runtime Ratio (RRR) [26]** a heuristic used for online scheduling problem $P|size_j, \neg p_j, \neg prec|C_{\max}$ with restricted runtime ratio $G = \frac{p_{\max}}{p_{\min}}$ which is bounded and known. Without loss of generality assume that $p_{\min} = 1$. The set of available tasks is divided into sets of big tasks $L_1 = \{T_j : size_j > \frac{m}{2}\}$ and small tasks $L_2 = \{T_j : size_j \leq \frac{m}{2}\}$. Let $\alpha(\tau)$ denote efficiency of a schedule at time $\tau$, which is fraction of all $m$ processors that is working at time $\tau$. RRR algorithm tries to sustain efficiency greater than or equal to $\frac{1}{2}$. This is done by not starting new small tasks when ready big tasks request more processors than currently available, and efficiency drops below $\frac{1}{2}$. The algorithm is summarized in Fig. 5.6.

**RRR_Adaptive (RRRA) [26]** RRRA is an extension of RRR algorithm to the case when ratio $G$ is bounded, but remains unknown. Hence, $p_{\min}$ is unknown. The algorithm records the shortest processing time $p_{\min}^i$ of any task up to a particular delay phase $i > 0$ (step 8 in RRR), and then collects small tasks that become available in the next $2p_{\min}^i$ time units. In the first delay phase ($i = 0$) the algorithm waits until the completion of all started tasks because $p_{\min}^i$ is not set.

**NonIncreasing Size (NIS) [139]** NIS has been used in [139] for problem $P|size_j, pmtn, r_j|C_{\max}$ in the following way. At ready and completion times the unfinished tasks are scheduled according to the nonincreasing sizes. The idea of scheduling tasks according to the order of nonincreasing sizes appeared in many publications [51, 103, 247], and is often named Largest Job First (**LJF**), Largest Dimension First (**LDF**).

**Johannes heuristic (J) [139]** This is an algorithm for online scheduling tasks one by one. Time is partitioned into intervals $I_i = [2^i, 2^{i+1}], i = 0, \dots$ . Task $T_j$ is put in the first interval $I_i$ at least twice as long as $p_j$ in which $T_j$ feasibly fits. Tasks with $size_j > \frac{m}{2}$ are scheduled as late as possible in $I_i$, while task $size_j \leq \frac{m}{2}$ as early as possible in $I_i$.

## 5.3.2   Minsum Criteria

In this section, we analyze rigid task scheduling problems for minsum criteria. Complexity and approximability of the above problems will be examined.

### 5.3.2.1   Complexity

The results on complexity, polynomially solvable cases, are summarized in Table 5.5. Below, we present an algorithm for problem $Pm|size_j, p_j = p, r_j| \sum c_j$.

$Pm|size_j, p_j = p, r_j| \sum c_j$ [13]

The algorithm of [13] presented in Sect. 5.3.1 can be applied to solve the current problem. The dynamic programming follows the same rules. However, the recursive function should be initialized with 0 (not $t_m$). Equation (5.4) should have the form

$$F(\tau_{s+1}, \ldots, \tau_m, \tau_s + p, \ldots, \tau_s + p, j_1, \ldots, j_{s-1}, x + 1, j_{s+1}, j_m) + t_s + p \quad (5.14)$$

Similar dynamic programming algorithm with complexity $O(n^{3m+1})$ has been proposed for $Pm|size_j, p_j = 1| \sum w_j c_j$ in [84]. Also problems $Pm|size_j, p_j = 1| \sum w_j u_j$ and $Pm|size_j, p_j = 1| \sum t_i$, that is scheduling for the weighted number of late tasks, and for the mean tardiness criteria, are polynomially solvable for fixed $m$ [43] by a reduction to scheduling on fixed number of dedicated processors (problems $Pm|fix_j, p_1 = 1, r_j|\gamma$, where $\gamma \in \{\sum w_j c_j, \sum t_j, \sum w_j u_j\} C_{max}$). Also these problems can be solved in polynomial time for fixed $m$ by dynamic programming algorithms [41] (cf. Sect. 5.8).

**Table 5.5**   Complexity of rigid task scheduling, minimum sum criteria

| Problem | Result | Reference |
|---|---|---|
| $P2|size_j| \sum c_j, n_2 \geq 1$ | **NPh** | [161] |
| $P2|size_j| \sum w_j c_j$ | **sNPh** | [161] |
| $P|size_j, p_j = 1| \sum c_j$ | **sNPh** | [84] |
| $P2|prec, size_j, p_j = 1| \sum c_j$ | **sNPh** | [43] |
| $P2|size_j, p_j = 1, out\text{-}tree| \sum c_j$ | **sNPh** | [249] |
| $P2|size_j, p_j = 1, in\text{-}tree| \sum c_j$ | **sNPh** | [248] |
| $P|size_j, pmtn| \sum c_j$ | **NPh** | [84] |
| $P2|size_j| \sum w_j c_j$ | $O(n(\sum_{j=1}^{n} p_j)^{3n_2+1})$ | [161] |
| $Pm|size_j, p_j = 1| \sum w_j c_j$ | $O(n^{3m+1})$ | [84] |
| $Pm|size_j, p_j = p, r_j| \sum c_j$ | $O(n^{3m})$ | [13] |
| $Pm|size_j, p_j = 1| \sum w_j u_j$ | $O(poly(n^{2^m}))$ | [43] |
| $Pm|size_j, p_j = 1| \sum t_j$ | $O(poly(n^{2^m}))$ | [43] |
| $P2|size_j, p_j = 1, r_j| \sum c_j$ | $O(n)$ | [43] |
| $P2|size_j, p_j = p, r_j| \sum u_j$ | $O(n \log n)$ | [43] |
| $P2|size_j, p_j = p, r_j| \sum t_j$ | $O(n^3)$ | [43] |

#### 5.3.2.2 Nonpreemptive Schedules, Heuristics with a Guarantee

The results on approximability of scheduling rigid tasks for minsum criteria are collected in Table 5.6. The following notations are used in Table 5.6:

- $\sum \hat{u}_j$ – Criterion of maximizing the number of tasks completed before their duedates, studied in [107]. Maximizing $\sum \hat{u}_j$ is equivalent to minimizing $\sum u_j$. However, if all tasks meet their duedates, then $\sum u_j = 0$, and it is hard to calculate relative distance of the approximate solution from the optimum. On the other hand, in all nontrivial cases $\sum \hat{u}_j > 0$.
- $\sum p_j \hat{u}_j$ – Criterion of maximizing the amount of work performed on tasks that meet their deadlines [159]. Analogously to the previous criterion maximizing $\sum p_j \hat{u}_j$ is equivalent to minimizing $\sum p_j u_j$, yet the former simplifies providing approximability results.

Let us introduce the heuristics referred to in Table 5.6.

**Scheduling to Minimize Average Response Time (SMART) [205, 224]** It is a group of heuristics dedicated to scheduling rigid tasks for $\sum c_j$, $\sum w_j c_j$ criteria. A concept of shelf algorithms from two-dimensional packing is used. In two-dimensional strip packing problem rectangles are to be put on a strip of the given width and minimum height. One type of the algorithms for this problem are shelf algorithms. These algorithms pack rectangles at certain height as if on the shelf. If a rectangle cannot be added to the existing shelves, then a new shelf is added for the current rectangle on top of the old ones. Assigning the rectangles to the shelves is performed in the same way as assigning elements to bins in bin packing. Rigid tasks may be viewed as rectangles in processor $\times$ space. Processor number $m$ is the given width of the stripe, $size_j$ is the width, and $p_j$ is the height of task-rectangle. Let us denote by

$S(j)$ – The number of the shelf on which $T_j$ is put

$\mathcal{H}_k = \max_{S(j)=k} \{p_j\}$ – The height of shelf $k$

**Table 5.6** Approximability of rigid task scheduling problems, minimum sum criteria

| Problem | Result | Reference |
|---|---|---|
| $P\|size_j \leq \lceil \frac{m}{2} \rceil\| \sum c_j$ | $R_{LS} \leq 2$ | [223] |
| $P\|size_j\| \sum c_j$ | $4.273 < R_{SMART_{NFIW}} < 32$ | [224] |
| $P\|size_j\| \sum c_j$ | $R_{SMART_{NFIW}} < 9$ | [205] |
| $P\|size_j\| \sum c_j$ | $4.5 < R_{SMART_{FFIA}} \leq 8$ | [205] |
| $P\|size_j\| \sum w_j c_j$ | $6.75 < R_{\gamma - SMART_{NFIW}} < 8.53$ | [205] |
| $P2\|size_j\| \sum w_j c_j$ | $R_{WSPT-H1} \leq 2$ | [161] |
| $P2\|size_j\| \sum c_j$ | $R_{WSPT-H1} \leq \frac{3}{2}$ | [161] |
| $P\|size_j\| \sum p_j \hat{u}_j$ | $R_{H_N} = 5 + \varepsilon$ | [159] |
| $P\|size_j, p_j = 1\| \sum \hat{u}_j$ | $R_{FFIs} = 2$ | [107] |
| $P\|size_j, p_j = 1\| \sum \hat{u}_j$ | $R_{LFIs} = 2 - \frac{1}{m}$ | [107] |
| $P\|size_j, p_j = 1\| \sum \hat{u}_j$ | $R_{HA} = \begin{cases} \frac{3}{2} - \frac{1}{2m} & \text{for odd } m \\ \frac{3}{2} - \frac{1}{2m-2} & \text{for even } m \end{cases}$ | [107] |

$\mathcal{M}_k = |\mathcal{S}^{-1}(k)|$ – The number of tasks on shelf $k$

$\mathcal{U}_k = \sum_{\mathcal{S}(j)=k}\{w_j\}$ – Total weight of tasks on shelf $k$

The general structure of $\gamma - SMART_X$ heuristics is the following:

1. Partition tasks in $\mathcal{T}$ into subsets $\mathcal{T}_k$ according to their processing times such that $\mathcal{T}_k = \{T_j : \gamma^{k-1} < p_j \le \gamma^k\}$. There are at most $1 + \log_\gamma p_{\max}$ such subsets (we assume that $p_{\min} = 1$).
2. Assign tasks in $\mathcal{T}_k$ to shelves according to heuristic $X$ (variants of SMART use different $X$).
3. Order shelves according to nondecreasing values of $\frac{\mathcal{H}_k}{\mathcal{M}_k}$ for $\sum c_j$ criterion and $\frac{\mathcal{H}_k}{\mathcal{U}_k}$ for $\sum w_j c_j$ criterion.
4. If there are contiguous shelves which use less than $m$ processors, then join them. If there are tasks on higher (which means later) shelves that can be feasibly shifted to the lower shelf then shift them.

The $X$ heuristics are modifications of one-dimensional bin packing heuristics assigning tasks of width $size_j$ to bins (shelves) of size $m$. In particular *NFIW* (for *Next Fit Increasing Width*) and *FFIA* (for *First Fit Increasing Area*) were applied, where width is $size_j$ and area is $p_j size_j$. To partition the task set into subsets $\mathcal{T}_k$ $\gamma = 2$ or $\gamma = 1.65$ were used. In [205, 224] heuristics $SMART_{NFIW}$, $SMART_{FFIA}$ with $\gamma = 2$ were proposed for criterion $\sum c_j$ and $1.65 - SMART_{NFIW}$ for criterion $\sum w_j c_j$. *SMART* heuristics have time complexity $O(n \log n)$. Note that SMART algorithms can be also applied in scheduling 1D-mesh tasks.

**WSPT-H1 [161]** A list heuristic for $m = 2$ using modified Weighted Shortest Processing Time order. Tasks are ordered according to the nondecreasing value of $\frac{p_j}{w_j} \frac{size_j}{m}$ and assigned to the first free interval preserving the above sequence.

**$H_N$ [159]** This algorithm maximizes the amount of work of tasks completed before their duedates. Tasks which do not meet duedates are rejected and not executed. The algorithm partitions the set of tasks into $\mathcal{T}_W = \{T_j : size_j > \frac{m}{2}\}$ and $\mathcal{T}_N = \{T_j : size_j \le \frac{m}{2}\}$. Tasks in $\mathcal{T}_W$ must be executed sequentially. Hence, to construct a schedule for them is a matter of selecting tasks that will be executed. An FPTAS from [204] is used for this purpose. Tasks in $\mathcal{T}_N$ are further partitioned into $\mathcal{T}_{NS} = \{T_j : T_j \in \mathcal{T}_N, p_j > \frac{d_j}{2}\}$ and $\mathcal{T}_{NL} = \{T_j : T_j \in \mathcal{T}_N, p_j \le \frac{d_j}{2}\}$. Only $k$ tasks from $\mathcal{T}_{NS}$ are scheduled according to nondecreasing duedates, starting at time $\tau = 0$, where $k$ is the last task satisfying $\sum_{j=1}^{k} size_j \le m$. The remaining tasks from $\mathcal{T}_{NS}$ are rejected. Tasks from $\mathcal{T}_{NL}$ are appended to the schedule of the $k$ tasks from $\mathcal{T}_{NS}$ using EDD heuristic. Out of the two schedules for $\mathcal{T}_N$ and $\mathcal{T}_W$, the one with greater amount of executed work is presented as the final schedule.

**First Fit Increasing Size (FFIs) [107]** It is a list algorithm that orders tasks according to nondecreasing sizes [107]. This order of tasks is also called Smaller Job First (SJF) or NonDecreasing size (NDs).

**Latest Fit Increasing Sizes (LFIs) [107]** This algorithm orders tasks according to nondecreasing sizes, and schedules them as late as possible to meet the duedates (if possible) [107].

**HA [107]** This is hybrid algorithm combining LFIs and EDD [107].

### *5.3.3   Other Heuristics for Rigid Task Scheduling*

Algorithms presented in this section have been compared mainly empirically against various optimality criteria for various workloads. Therefore, they do not fit ideally in the previous parts of this section. Though most of them do not have the worst-case performance guarantees, it should not mislead the reader. These heuristics are simple to implement, and hence, attractive for practical reasons.

**FIFO First In First Out (a.k.a. FCFS – First Come First Served)** The tasks are assigned to the processors by list scheduling in the order of their arrival to the computer system. We present FIFO for completeness of exposition because it cannot be applied alone in any real scheduling system for parallel tasks due to its inefficiency. For example, an alternating sequence of $m$- and 1-processor tasks results in resource utilization of $O(\frac{1}{m})$. On the other hand, FIFO ordering is fair in the sense that the order of servicing tasks is the order of task arrival, and no submission is preferred in any way.

**Backfilling [173]**   to some extent uses the FIFO rule, but it is allowed to start tasks before their FIFO order if they are able to fill the idle processors left by the tasks ahead in the queue. To implement backfilling it is required to provide not only $size_j$, but also some estimation of $p_j$ for each submitted task. The scheduler has information about estimated completion times of the tasks currently running. There are two flavors of backfilling [101, 190, 216]: conservative backfilling and EASY backfilling. **Conservative backfilling** allows the newly arrived task $T_j$ to be started earlier only if it does not violate reservations of the tasks ahead of $T_j$. Thus, tasks which arrived before $T_j$ have fixed processor reservation. In **EASY backfilling** (a.k.a aggressive backfilling) only the task $T_h$ at the head of the queue has fixed reservation. When some task finishes, task $T_h$ can be started. If the number of free processors is insufficient the scheduler calculates the earliest time $\tau$ when $T_h$ can be started. Between the current moment and $\tau + p_j$ some processors may remain idle. These free intervals may be exploited by the tasks which are later in the queue. Observe that short and narrow tasks have better chances of being executed over long and wide tasks. Hence, it may be said that backfilling favors utilization against fairness. Backfilling has been modified in many ways. For example, to reduce mean flow time tasks in the waiting queue may be ordered according to SPT rule, or smallest work first rule, where $p_j size_j$ is task $T_j$ work. Backfilling and its versions were subject of numerous performance studies (see e.g [142, 190, 218, 220]) and implementations [127, 216].

#### 5.3.3.1   Heuristics for Time Sharing Systems

We will present here several heuristics dedicated to parallel systems with time sharing. From some point of view parallel task scheduling methods can be divided into two classes: *space sharing* and *time sharing*. In space sharing applications are given exclusive control of some subset of processors for their whole execution time. Nonpreemptive scheduling algorithms presented before fit space sharing description. A disadvantage of space sharing is that when a thread suspends in I/O, or the application has less parallelism in some moment, then the assigned processor time is wasted. This situation can be avoided in time sharing systems which switch to different applications ready to run. Thus, in time sharing applications are coallocated on the computing nodes, and are multiplexed in time. While solving one problem a different set of challenges is brought by the time sharing systems. For example, which applications should be coallocated, what the sequence of executing them should be, how to schedule gangs of threads, i.e. groups of related threads that frequently communicate, how long the time quantum should be.

Ousterhout matrix (cf. Sect. 3.3.1) is used to represent the assignment of the applications to the nodes (i.e. tasks to processors). The problem is to select processors and the time slot(s) for the task. In the simplest formulation, this can be reduced to bin packing. The processor requirement $size_j$ is the item size, and processor number $m$ is the bin size. This problem has been addressed, e.g., in [93]. The discussed algorithms were bin packing FF, BF, BF-Left-Right, Buddy, and migration algorithms. BF-Left-Right is a modification of BF in which rows in Ousterhout matrix are filled alternatively from left to right, and from right to left, to balance the load of the processors. Migration approach reassigns the tasks in the Ousterhout matrix using FF, whenever a new task arrives, or some old task completes. This last approach may require migration of the running application. The algorithms proposed in [111] allowed for assigning the task in multiple time slots and noncontiguous processor allocations. In the following we present other algorithms for scheduling rigid tasks in time sharing systems.

**Distributed Hierarchical Control (DHC) [97, 98]**  The DHC system has been designed with the following goals: support preemption for interactive rather than batch application execution, support gang scheduling, load balancing, spatial locality of execution for improved caching, lack of centralized control to eliminate bottlenecks, but provide some global coordination when needed.

DHC uses a binary X-tree structure (Fig. 5.7a). It is a binary tree of controllers with lateral connections on the same level. The lateral connections are used for load balancing. The controllers at the first level (counting from the leaves upward) directly manage threads executed on the processors. The requests for execution of an application originate in the processors. A request percolates upward to the level managing sufficient number of processors. Controllers at level $i$ manage $2^i$ processors, and thus, serve the requests of tasks $T_j$ satisfying $2^{i-1} + 1 \leq size_j \leq 2^i$ (with the exception of level 1 managing sizes 1 and 2). At level $i$ satisfying the request, controllers communicate with each other to elect the least loaded one. The number of threads managed in the controller and its subtree is a measure of the load. When the least loaded controller is selected the threads of the application are assigned to the subordinate processors, and are not migrated until the task completion.

The coordination needed for gang scheduling is achieved by simultaneously executing the threads managed on the same level of the tree. Controllers can be in idle, active, or disabled states. In each time moment a front of active controllers

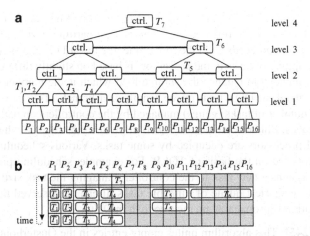

**Fig. 5.7** (**a**) Distributed hierarchical control system with an example of task assignment. "Ctrl." denotes a controller. (**b**) Example of a schedule with selective disabling for tasks with sizes $size_1 = size_2 = 1, size_3 = size_4 = 2, size_5 = 3, size_6 = 5, size_7 = 12$

exists in the DHC tree. The active controllers execute the gangs of applications they manage. The controllers above the front have already executed their threads for the time quantum and are idle. The controllers below the front are disabled, and communicate the demands of their superiors down the tree to the processors. A selective disabling is a mechanism which allows the subordinate controller A to execute its gangs if the superior controller B is not using the processors managed by A. The active front iteratively sweeps down the DHC tree: After level $i$, controllers at level $i - 1$ become active, and after level 1, the procedure is restarted from the root. The time quanta of particular levels may be different, and may themselves be divided between multiple gangs managed by a certain controller. An example schedule shown in Fig. 5.7b was constructed using selective disabling, for the tasks managed by the controllers indicated in Fig. 5.7a.

DHC scheme has some ability to resist failures of the controllers. When an internal controller at level $i$ fails, the controllers at level $i - 1$ can still serve the requests in a smaller size tree. It was assumed in the design of DHC that one thread is executed on one processor. However, DHC can handle also requests to run more threads than the number of processors. In such a case processors have to execute more than one thread of the same application. DHC can be also generalized to manage processor partitions whose sizes are not powers of 2. Design options for DHC regarding topologies of the lateral links between the controllers, distribution of the threads between subtrees when $size_j$ is not a power of 2, lengths of time quanta were examined by simulation in [97, 98].

**Distributed Queue Tree (DQT) [122]** is a partition management scheme similar to the above DHC. DQT uses a simple balanced tree closely related to the underlying topology of the parallel system (DHC uses X-tree structure). In the simplest case, it is a binary tree halving the processor resource with each level, as in the buddy systems [144, 195]. In 2D-meshes it can be a quad-tree and an oct-tree in 3D-meshes. Task sizes are rounded up to the nearest partition size (unlike DHC). The load allocation proceeds from the root of the tree toward the leaves (opposite to DHC). The mapping of tasks to the processors is based on slightly different criteria. In DHC it is intended to balance the subtree load which is the number of threads. On the other hand, in DQT total queue length of a branch (TQLB) is balanced. TQLB is the number of tasks (gangs) managed by the controllers on paths from the root to the leaves. Balanced values of TQLB allow for schedules in which all time quanta on all processors are occupied by some tasks. Various scheduling policies have been proposed on the basis of TQLB. For example, scheduling policy called best fit (BF) assigns a new task to the controller managing the task size which has the system-wide shortest queue of runnable tasks. It can be observed that in DQT more information is propagated up the tree than in DHC.

**Repacking [245]** This algorithm unites empty entries in the Ousterhout matrix by shifting the tasks vertically, i.e. only between time slices, without changing the assigned processor. Assume some initial assignment of the tasks to the matrix entries is given. Each task is executed only in one time slice, which means in one row. When some tasks finish, a block of empty entries remains in one row of the matrix. Such blocks of empty positions in different rows can be glued together to form a longer block of free entries. The method of compacting empty blocks uses so called cuts in time slices. A cut is a position between two columns in the matrix where a task begins or ends, including row ends. A cut is legal in two rows if it does not divide existing tasks into two parts. Thus each task has its assigned processors either to the left or to the right of a legal cut. If there are two rows with empty entries to the left of some legal cut in the first row and to the right of the cut in the second row, then the parts of the rows before (or after) the cut may be swapped. As a result a new bigger block of empty entries is constructed. If all processors (columns) have at least one empty entry, then a completely empty row may be constructed using repacking. Eventually, this empty row may be removed to decrease the degree of coallocation. Example of repacking is shown in Fig. 5.8. Legal cuts are marked in top left figure. The cuts used in swaps are marked with letters A, B, C, D. Repacking may be a basis of processor allocation algorithm. It is possible to use an $m$-entry array, called workload vector, recording the number of empty entries in each column of the matrix. If all entries of workload vector are nonzero then it is known that one row (time slice) can be eliminated by repacking. If we want to find processors for some new task $T_j$, then we have to find a sequence of $size_j$ nonzeros in the workload vector. A disadvantage of workload vector is that verifying this can be done in $O(m)$ time. Therefore, a buddy system has been proposed [245] which records in each tree node the number of empty entries in the managed range of columns if none is zero, and zero otherwise. Consequently, whether a row can be eliminated can be verified in constant time, a set of processors for a new task may be found in $O(\log m)$ time, tree updates are possible in $O(\log m)$. Yet, this buddy extension suffers from weak recognition of neighboring free blocks in different branches of the tree (cf. Sect. 5.6.1 on buddy systems for hypercubes).

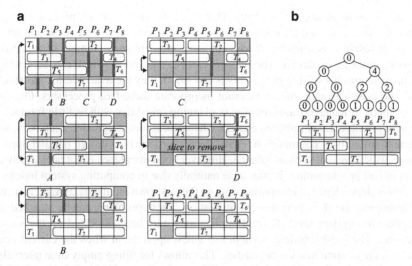

**Fig. 5.8** Repacking algorithm. (**a**) Example of repacking. (**b**) Buddy system with repacking

**Paired Gang Scheduling [236]**  The idea of this algorithm is to match pairs of applications which have different resource requirements. An application which performs a lot of computations should be sharing a processor with application which often uses I/O. The I/O-bound application will not significantly reduce performance of the CPU-bound application. The distinction is done on the basis of statistics on the processor utilization by the application. Usually more than just two applications are run in the parallel system. Therefore, rows of Ousterhout matrix, which may contain several applications, are matched. The rows (time slices) are ordered according to decreasing $\max(x)$, where $\max(x)$ is maximum CPU utilization of a task in the matrix row $x$. The rows are matched starting from both ends of the sorted sequence: the first row (highest CPU utilization) with the last row (smallest CPU utilization), the second row with the penultimate, etc. The match of two rows $x, y$ is realized if $\max(x) + \max(y) + \mu < 100\%$, where $\mu$ is some constant margin. Matching makes sense only if the rows are roughly homogeneous. Otherwise, an odd application with high CPU utilization may deteriorate the effects of the matching. To guarantee homogeneity of the rows, an application with CPU utilization greater than $\min(x) + M$ is removed from row $x$, where $\min(x)$ is the minimum CPU utilization of the applications in $x$, and margin $M = 20\%$ was chosen. The removed application is moved to a different row $y$ with sufficient number of free processors, and where the application utilization fits in range $[\min(y), \min(y) + M]$. If no such slot is found the application will be moved to a new slot. Matching gang-scheduled applications with I/O applications on the basis of CPU utilization was also proposed in [69]. A similar idea of matching applications on the basis of SMP cluster bus utilization (i.e. requested bandwidth to the core memory) has been studied in [147].

**Flexible CoScheduling (FCS) [109]** This algorithm tries to attack processor fragmentation and load imbalance at the low level of operating system scheduling.
Processor resource is fragmented when at some moment some number of free processors cannot be exploited. The reasons can be, e.g., no new task can be started
because the number of free processors is too small, they are available for too short
time, the tasks currently running cannot incorporate these free processors. One of
the methods to manage fragmentation is planning schedules with as little fragmentation as possible. Load imbalance arises when processors assigned to a job perform
different amounts of computation. A standard approach is to design parallel applications which prevent such imbalance. However, load imbalance is not necessarily a
result of bad programming. It may arise naturally due to computing system indeter-
minism or dependence of computing time on the unknown input data. Fragmentation
and imbalance result in poor system utilization. These problems can be attacked at
the operating system level. Several applications may be coallocated on the same
processor. The local scheduler switches to a new application when the current one
blocks in the communication or finishes. This allows for filling empty time intervals
which would otherwise appear because of fragmentation or load imbalance. On the
other hand, parallel applications that communicate often need coscheduling for high
performance.

Algorithm FCS classifies application processes (i.e. tasks in a job) into three
types: CS – which require coscheduling and should not be preempted, F (called
frustrated) – which have enough communication to be classified as CS, but due to
imbalance cannot fully use its alloted CPU time, and DC (called don't care) – which
rarely communicate, can be scheduled independently of other processes of the same
application. DC applications may have arbitrary form in (time × processors) space
like malleable tasks. Therefore FCS can be considered as a scheduler for a mix
of rigid and malleable tasks. The classification of the tasks is based on the average time per communication ($\tau_{comm}$), average CPU time between communications
($\tau_{CPU}$), and time granularity of iterations between synchronizations ($\tau_{comm} + \tau_{CPU}$).
A "phase" diagram of process classification is shown in Fig. 5.9. Threshold values
were selected experimentally. Values of $\tau_{comm}$, $\tau_{CPU}$ are measured in the augmented
MPI library. Process classification is performed after completion of the allotted time
slice using the collected statistics. It can be modified with granularity of several time

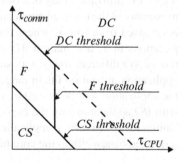

**Fig. 5.9** "Phase" diagram
of FCS process classes (on
the basis of [109], ©[2005]
IEEE)

slices to allow for application start-up and stabilization of communication and computation patterns. Each process starts in CS class. The classification is reset to CS after a long period (order of tens of minutes). In the computing system two types of schedulers cooperate: a single system-wide machine manager (MM) and local node managers (NM). The classification of the processes is done by NMs. MM packs jobs into Ousterhout matrix, and at each time slice sends a message to NMs to switch to the next process. If the new process is in class CS, then it is executed uninterrupted for entire time slice, thus taking advantage of parallel execution in real time. If the next process is in class DC, or F then they are scheduled in a standard way by the local operating system, but F processes are given the highest priority. Synchronous communications use spin-blocking which means that a process waiting for pending communication does not block immediately. To avoid unnecessary context switch it waits for time $\tau_{spin}$ before yielding the processor. $\tau_{spin}$ is a parameter of the algorithm, and was chosen approximately twice the average communication time between a pair of nodes in the system. FCS has advantage of simplicity. Its input data can be easily collected without modifications in the application code. No prior benchmarking of the application is needed. FCS is also an interesting algorithm for at least two reasons. It attempts solving scheduling problem at low level of operating system rather than by high level of abstraction scheduling algorithm. Another interesting feature is that information on application performance is passed from the application, via runtime environment, to the operating system.

## 5.4   Moldable Tasks

In this section, we will study scheduling of moldable parallel tasks. The presentation will follow the lines of computational complexity theory. Namely, the complexity and approximability status of the above problems will be analyzed. In the last subsection, we present a group of heuristics which have no worst-case performance guarantees but are simple to implement and as such have practical value.

### 5.4.1   $C_{max}$ Criterion

#### 5.4.1.1   Nonpreemptive Schedules, Pseudopolynomial Cases

Problem $P5|size_j|C_{max}$ is sNPh. Hence, pseudopolynomial algorithm can be constructed only for $m = 2, 3, 4$ (unless $\mathbf{P} = \mathbf{NP}$). For $P2|any|C_{max}$ and $P3|any|C_{max}$ pseudopolynomial algorithms have been proposed in [86]. In the actual schedule sizes of moldable tasks are already selected, and the tasks can be considered as rigid. Schedules for rigid tasks on two and three processors can be converted to *canonical schedules* depicted in Fig. 5.10. The makespan depends on the lengths of particular blocks of tasks. Hence, this problem can be solved using dynamic programming

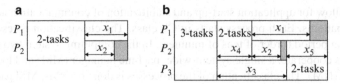

**Fig. 5.10** Canonical schedules (a) $P2|any|C_{\max}$. (b) $P3|any|C_{\max}$

iterating over tasks and task block lengths. In particular, for $P2|any|C_{\max}$ function $F(j, x_1, x_2)$ can be calculated which is the smallest execution time of 2-tasks among the first $j$ tasks such that 1-tasks are executed for $x_1, x_2$ units of time on $P_1, P_2$, respectively. $F(j, x_1, x_2)$ is calculated for $j = 1, \ldots, n$ and $x_1, x_2 = 0, \ldots T$, where $T = \sum_{j=1}^{n} p_j(1)$ is an upper bound on schedule length. $F(j, x_1, x_2)$ can be calculated using recursive equations $F(0, 0, 0) = 0$, $F(0, x_1, x_2) = \infty$ for $x_1 + x_2 \leq T$

$$F(j, x_1, x_2) = \min \left\{ \begin{array}{l} F(j - 1, x_1, x_2) + p_j(2), \\ F(j - 1, x_1 - p_j(1), x_2), \\ F(j - 1, x_1, x_2 - p_j(1)) \end{array} \right\}$$

for $j = 1, \ldots, n, 0 \leq x_1 + x_2 \leq T$. Values of $F(j, x_1, x_2)$ can be calculated in $O(nM^2)$. The optimum schedule has length $\max\{x_1^*, x_2^*\} + F(n, x_1^*, x_2^*)$, where $x_1^*, x_2^*$ satisfy equation $\max\{x_1^*, x_2^*\} + F(n, x_1^*, x_2^*)\} = \min_{x_1, x_2}\{\max\{x_1, x_2\} + F(n, x_1, x_2)\}$. In the case of $P3|any|C_{\max}$ schedule length is controlled by length of six blocks of tasks. Hence $P3|any|C_{\max}$ can be solved in time $O(nT^5)$ by calculation of $F(j, x_1, x_2, x_3, x_4, x_5)$ which is the length of the shortest block of 3-tasks such that the other blocks have lengths $x_1, x_2, x_3, x_4, x_5$ (cf. Fig. 5.10). The recursive equation for $j = 1 \ldots, n, 0 \leq x_1 + x_2 + x_3 \leq \sum_{j=1}^{n} p_j(1), 0 \leq x_4 + x_5 \leq \sum_{j=1}^{n} p_j(2)$ is the following:

$$F(j, x_1, x_2, x_3, x_4, x_5) = \min \left\{ \begin{array}{l} F(j - 1, x_1, x_2, x_3, x_4, x_5) + p_j(3), \\ F(j - 1, x_1 - p_j(1), x_2, x_3, x_4, x_5), \\ F(j - 1, x_1, x_2 - p_j(1), x_3, x_4, x_5), \\ F(j - 1, x_1, x_2, x_3 - p_j(1), x_4, x_5), \\ F(j - 1, x_1, x_2, x_3, x_4 - p_j(2), x_5), \\ F(j - 1, x_1, x_2, x_3, x_4, x_5 - p_j(2)) \end{array} \right\}$$

Other parts of the algorithm are analogous to the 2-processor case. To our best knowledge pseudopolynomial time solvability of $P4|any|C_{\max}$ remains open.

### 5.4.1.2  Nonpreemptive Schedules, Heuristics with a Guarantee

A survey of approximation algorithms for moldable tasks can be found in [87]. The following notations are used in Table 5.7:

* $r = \max_j \max_{\{i, i+1\} \in X_j} \{\frac{X_j(i+1)}{X_j(i)}\}$ – The biggest relative increase of task sizes for two consecutive admissible sizes.

**Table 5.7**   Approximability of moldable task scheduling, $C_{max}$ criterion

| Problem | Result | Reference |
|---------|--------|-----------|
| $P\,\vert any, NdSub\vert C_{max}$ | $R_{Part\_Schedule} = \frac{2}{1-\frac{1}{m}}$ | [16] |
| $P\,\vert any, p_j(i) = \frac{p_j(1)}{i}, \delta_j, prec\vert C_{max}$ | $R_{LS} = \Delta + 1 - \frac{\Delta}{m}$ | [230] |
| $P\,\vert any, p_j(i) = \frac{p_j(1)}{i}, \delta_j, prec\vert C_{max}$ | $R_{ECT} < 2 + \ln \Delta$ | [230] |
| $P\,\vert any, p_j(i) = \frac{p_j(1)}{i}, \delta_j, prec\vert C_{max}$ | $2.5 < R_{ECT} < 3 - \frac{2}{m}$ | [231] |
| $P\,\vert any, NdSub\vert C_{max}, n \le m$ | $R_{PP} = \min\{m, \frac{rm}{m-m'}\}$ | [150] |
| $P\,\vert any, Nd\vert C_{max}$ | $R_{GF-LS} = 2$ | [226] |
| $P\,\vert any, NdSub, pmtn\vert C_{max}$ | $R_{PP} = r$ | [151] |
| $P\,\vert any, NdSub\vert C_{max}$ | $R_{GPA} = 2$ | [115] |
| $P\,\vert any, \neg p_j, p_j(i) = \frac{p_j(1)}{i}, \delta_j, prec\vert C_{max}$ | $R \ge 2 + \frac{\sqrt{4\frac{\Delta^2}{m^2}+1}-1}{2\frac{\Delta}{m}}$ | [102] |
| $P\,\vert any, \neg p_j, p_j(i) = \frac{p_j(1)}{i}, \delta_j, \neg prec\vert C_{max}$ | $R_{PRAM(\alpha)} =$ | |
| | $= 2 + \frac{\sqrt{4\frac{\Delta^2}{m^2}+1}-1}{2\frac{\Delta}{m}}$ | [102] |
| $Pm\,\vert any\vert C_{max}$ | PTAS | [130] |
| $P\,\vert any\vert C_{max}$ | AFPTAS | [128] |
| $P\,\vert any, NdSub\vert C_{max}$ | $R_{2-shelf} = \frac{3}{2} + \varepsilon$ | [87, 189] |
| $P\,\vert any, NdSub, sp\vert C_{max}$ | $R_B = \frac{3+\sqrt{5}}{2} + \varepsilon$ | [164] |
| $P\,\vert any, NdSub, prec\vert C_{max}$ | $R_B = 3 + \sqrt{5}$ | [164] |
| $P\,\vert any, NdSub, prec\vert C_{max}$ | $R_{JZ} = \frac{100}{43} + \frac{100(\sqrt{4349}-7)}{2451}$ | [136] |

- $m'$ – Is the number of controllers in the parallel system, $n \le m' \le m$.
- $\neg p_j$, $p_j(i) = \frac{p_j(1)}{i}$ means that the actual processing time is unknown to the scheduler, but it is known that speedup is linear, i.e. the processing time functions of all tasks are of the form $p_j(i) = \frac{p_j(1)}{i}$.
- AFPTAS stands for asymptotic fully polynomial approximation scheme. It means that a schedule is constructed with $C_{max} \le (1 + \varepsilon)C_{max}^* + O(\frac{1}{\varepsilon^2})$ in time polynomial in $n$, and $\frac{1}{\varepsilon}$ [128].

Below we present selected heuristics referred to in Table 5.7 (in the order of appearance):

**Part_Schedule [16]**   Let us remind that $\bar{i}$ is a vector of processor allotments of the tasks. The algorithm can be summarized in the following steps:

1. Assign to each task one processor, and build a schedule using LPT rule.
2. While $\sum_{i_j>1} i_j < m$ do.
3. {Determine the longest task $T_j$ at the current processor allotments $\bar{i}$. If $p_j(i_j) = C_{max}(\bar{i})$, then increase by one the number of processors used by $T_{j'}$. Construct a new schedule for the new allotments $\bar{i}'$ using LPT rule. If the new schedule length $C_{max}(\bar{i}') > C_{max}(\bar{i})$, then the previous allotment $\bar{i}$ and schedule are restored, and the algorithm stops.}
Algorithm Part_Schedule can be implemented to run in $O(n \log n + nm \log m)$ time.

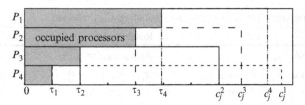

**Fig. 5.11**   Selecting the start time and number of processors in ECT heuristic

**Earliest Completion Time (ECT) [230, 231]**   This is used to schedule moldable
tasks with linear speedup, with limits on parallelism $\delta_j$ and precedences. Tasks are
put on some list, as in list scheduling algorithms. Consider some ready task $T_j$ about
to be scheduled. Some processors are already occupied in some intervals by the
tasks which were scheduled earlier. The busy intervals may be represented as staircase pattern of processor unavailability (see Fig. 5.11). $T_j$ may be started at some
time $\tau_1$ on $m_1$ processors, and completed at $c_j^1 = \tau_1 + \frac{p_j(1)}{\min\{m_1, \delta_j\}}$. At $\tau_2 > \tau_1$ the
number of available processors increases to $m_2 > m_1$, and though $T_j$ would be
starting later, it may be finished earlier at $c_j^2 = \tau_2 + \frac{p_j(1)}{\min\{m_2, \delta_j\}}$. The procedure of
checking alternative starting times may be repeated for the following points when
the availability of processors changes. The task is started at the moment when further waiting for additional free processors does not reduce completion time of the
task. Note that ECT is not really a list scheduling algorithm because tasks may be
delayed and not started as soon as possible. ECT has been independently proposed
in [91], albeit for a different setting.

**Processor Partitioning (PP) [150]**   PP is very similar to algorithm Part_Schedule.
It is used to solve moldable task scheduling problem on a system of $m$ processors
managed by $m' < m$ controllers. It is assumed that $n \leq m'$, and all tasks can be run
in parallel. The algorithm starts with a schedule in which all tasks run in parallel
using one processor. Then, the number of processors used by the task $T_{j'}$ finishing last is increased to the next admissible size. This procedure is repeated until
exhausting the available processors, or reaching $\delta_{j'}$. Processor Partitioning heuristic
has been adapted to the preemptive case and arbitrary number of tasks [151]. Again,
it starts with one processor per task, and constructing a McNaughton's schedule (cf.
Sect. 4.3.1.2). If the length of the schedule is determined by one long task $T_{j'}$, then
the task is assigned the next admissible number of processors $X_{j'}(i + 1)$. Tasks assigned more than one processor are scheduled nonpreemptively, starting at time 0.
The number of processors available for the tasks executed on one processor is decreased by $X_{j'}(i + 1)$, which may result in longer McNaughton's schedule. The
procedure is repeated until exhausting available processors, reaching $\delta_{j'}$, or when
McNaughton's schedule for the tasks on one processor determines the length of the
schedule for all tasks.

**GF-LS [226]**   This algorithm is a tandem of two methods: GF which generates
a family of processor allotments and a list scheduling heuristic. GF generalizes

Part_Schedule to tasks with nondecreasing speedup. The approximability guarantee of GF-LS is obtained on the basis of several results:

(1) A list algorithm solving problem $P|size_j|C_{max}$ builds a schedule of length $C_{max} \leq 2\max\{\frac{\sum_{j=1}^{n} size_j p_j}{m}, p_{max}\}$.

(2) Method GF constructs a set of at most $n(m-1)+1$ allotments. Let $i_j^k$ be the processor number assigned to $T_j$ in iteration $k$. GF assigns $i_j^k$ in the following way: (a) $i_j^1 = \arg\min_i\{p_j(i)i\}$, where $\arg\min_x\{f(x)\}$ is the smallest $x$ which minimizes $f(x)$ and (b) for $k > 1$, let $l = \arg\max_j\{p_j(i_j^{k-1})\}$, where $\arg\max_x\{f(x)\}$ is the minimum $x$ which maximizes $f(x)$, then

$$i_j^k = \begin{cases} i_j^{k-1} & \text{for } j \neq l \\ \arg\min_{i > i_j^{k-1}}\{p_l(i)\} & \text{for } j = l \end{cases}$$

(3) Let $\bar{i}^*$ be the processor allotment in the optimum schedule for $P|any|C_{max}$. At least one of the allotments $\bar{i}^k$ constructed by GF satisfies conditions: (a) Let $l = \arg\max_j p_j(i_j^*)$, then $\forall T_j, p_j(i_j^k) \leq p_l(i_l^*)$ and (b) $\forall T_j, p_j(i_j^k)i_j^k \leq p_j(i_j^*)i_j^*$.

(4) Consequently, at least one of the allotments constructed by GF has sum of areas $\sum_{j=1}^{n} i_j^k p_j(i_j^k) \leq \sum_{j=1}^{n} p_j(i_j^*)i_j^*$, and $\max_j\{p_j(i_j^k)\} \leq \max_j\{p_j(i_j^*)\}$, and the approximability bound 2 of list scheduling holds. More generally, any heuristic H for $P|size_j|C_{max}$ with approximability guarantee in the form $a_1 \sum_{j=1}^{n} i_j p_j(i_j) + a_2 \max_j\{p_j(i_j)\}$, if GF-constructed processor allotment is used, will have the same bound for problem $P|any|C_{max}$. In other words, a tandem of GF-H would have performance guarantee $a_1 + a_2$. This result has been used in [226] to give 2.5-approximate algorithm for the same problem with contiguous processor assignments (which is equivalent to moldable task with 1D-mesh shape).

**Generalized Partition and Assignment (GPA) [115]** It is a heuristic for scheduling moldable tasks with nondecreasing sublinear speedup. GPA assigns the tasks upper bounds $\delta_j$ on the usable processor numbers. Observe that $\delta_j$ is not part of the input data here. The actual processor allotment may be smaller than $\delta_j$. GPA starts with $\forall T_j, \delta_j = 1$, and increases $\delta_j'$ of the task with maximum $p_{j'}(\delta_{j'})$ as long as $p_{j'}(\delta_{j'}) > \frac{\sum_{j=1}^{n} \delta_j p_j(\delta_j)}{m} = \bar{w}$. The procedure is finished if for some task $p_{j'}(\delta_{j'}) < \bar{w}$. GPA divides $m$ processors into partitions called *channels* of sizes $S_i$. Possible sizes are checked in the decreasing order $(m, \ldots, 1)$. For size $S_i$, if $\frac{\sum_{\{T_j : \delta_j \geq S_i\}} p_j(\delta_j)\delta_j}{S_i + \sum_{S_k \geq S_i} S_k} \geq \bar{w}$, then a channel of size $S_i$ is created. Thus, new size $S_i$ channel is added if the previously created channels can be occupied at least until $\bar{w}$. More than one partition of the same size can be created. Task $T_j$ is assigned to a channel $i$ of the greatest size $S_i \leq \delta_j$. If there is more than one channel of the same size, then these channels are loaded with tasks one by one until completion time exceeds $\bar{w}$.

**PRAM($\alpha$) [102]** This method is used to schedule online moldable tasks with linear speedup, limits of parallelism $\delta_j$, and precedence constraints. Here online refers to the fact that processing times are known only when tasks finish. Precedence constraints become known when the predecessor releases its successor tasks. Ready tasks from a given list are started when efficiency falls below $\alpha$, where $\frac{1}{2} < \alpha \leq 1$. The number of processors allotted to $T_j$ is minimum of $\delta_j$ and the number of available processors. The order of the tasks on the list may be arbitrary obeying the precedence constraint. Authors suggest ordering tasks as in the BF heuristic, i.e. starting a task with maximum $\delta_j$ not greater than the number of available processors. The competitiveness guarantee of PRAM($\alpha$) presented in Table 5.7 has been obtained for $\alpha = \frac{1}{2} - \frac{\Delta}{m} + \sqrt{\frac{\Delta^2}{m^2} + \frac{1}{4}}$.

**2-Shelf [87, 189]** This heuristic intends to build a 2-shelf schedule for tasks with nondecreasing sublinear speedup with contiguous processor allocations (i.e. it is also applicable for 1D-meshes). It is a $\frac{3}{2} + \varepsilon$-approximate algorithm with complexity $O(nm \log \frac{n}{\varepsilon})$. A concept of dual approximation algorithm is used. For a given makespan $d$ a $\lambda$-dual approximation algorithm either constructs a feasible schedule of length at most $\lambda d$, or correctly answers that schedule of length $d$ does not exist. By calling such a heuristic $O(\log \frac{1}{\varepsilon})$ times in binary search, a $\lambda(1 + \frac{1}{\varepsilon})$-approximate solution can be delivered. In [87, 189] $\frac{3}{2}$-dual approximation algorithm is proposed. It starts as 2-shelf algorithm. The first shelf has duration $d$, the second shelf has length at most $\frac{d}{2}$. Since the initial schedule for the second shelf may be infeasible, the schedule is modified to make it feasible. Let $\gamma(j, d)$ denote minimum number of processors such that $p_j(\gamma(j, d)) \leq d$. Assume that a schedule of length $d$ exists, then the total amount of work is upper bounded by $md$. The $\frac{3}{2}$-dual approximation algorithm works as follows:

1. Let $\mathcal{T}_S = \{T_j : p_j(1) < \frac{d}{2}\}$; $W = md - \sum_{T_j \in \mathcal{T}_S} p_j(1)$; $\mathcal{T}' = \mathcal{T} - \mathcal{T}_S$.
2. Partition tasks in $\mathcal{T}'$ into sets $\mathcal{T}_1$ of tasks using $\gamma(j, d)$ processors, and $\mathcal{T}_2$ of tasks using $\gamma(j, \frac{d}{2})$ processors. By definition and speedup sublinearity, tasks in the first set have processing times $\frac{d}{2} < p_j(\gamma(j, d)) \leq d$. Set $\mathcal{T}_1$ is supposed to be executed on the first shelf, $\mathcal{T}_2$ on the second. The partition is done by selecting tasks for $\mathcal{T}_1$ using dynamic programming algorithm (similar to knapsack problem), where the task-items have sizes $\gamma(j, d)$ which together cannot exceed knapsack size $m$, simultaneously the area of the tasks is to be minimized. Task $T_j \in \mathcal{T}'$ contributes area $\gamma(j, d) p_j(\gamma(j, d))$ if it is included in $\mathcal{T}_1$, and area $\gamma(j, \frac{d}{2}) p_j(\gamma(j, \frac{d}{2}))$ if it is included in $\mathcal{T}_2$. Let $W^*$ be the minimum area of the tasks obtained by the dynamic programming. If $W^* > W$ then a feasible schedule of length $d$ does not exist and the algorithm stops.
3. If $\sum_{T_j \in \mathcal{T}_2} \gamma(j, \frac{d}{2}) > m$, then apply one of three types of the transformations defined in [87, 189] until $\sum_{T_j \in \mathcal{T}_2} \gamma(j, \frac{d}{2}) \leq m$. This may result in the creation of third "shelf" which starts at time 0 (as the first shelf) and has duration $\frac{3}{2}d$.
4. Shift the tasks executed on the second shelf such that they finish at $\frac{3}{2}d$, and insert tasks from $\mathcal{T}_S$, executed on one processor, in the idle intervals starting from the least loaded processor.

**B [164]** Algorithm B has been proposed for scheduling moldable tasks with sublinear, nondecreasing speedup and precedence constraints. It has been established that performance ratio of list schedule satisfies

$$R_{LS} \leq \min_{1 \leq \Delta \leq \frac{m+1}{2}} \max \left\{ \frac{m}{\Delta}, \frac{2m - \Delta}{m - \Delta + 1} \right\}, \tag{5.15}$$

where $\Delta$ is an upper bound on the processor allotment (note a similar result for rigid tasks by [175] in Table 5.4). It has been also established that this inequality attains values at most $\frac{3 + \sqrt{5}}{2}$ if $\Delta$ is properly selected. Let $\Delta(m)$ be the value for which (5.15) is minimum. Unlike in the case of rigid tasks we have an option of selecting processor allotments, and hence we can influence the longest path in the task graph as well as the total amount of work which were used in deriving (5.15). Therefore, processor allotment $\bar{i}$ is selected which minimizes cost $c(\bar{i}) = \max\{L(\bar{i}), \frac{\sum_{j=1}^{n} i_j p_j(i_j)}{m}\}$, where $L(\bar{i})$ is the longest path in the precedences. Selecting allotment which minimizes the above cost is in itself hard bicriterial discrete time-cost trade-off problem. However, a 2-approximation algorithm is known in the literature for this problem. Hence, there exists a $3 + \sqrt{5}$-approximate algorithm for general precedences which first computes the allotments using the 2-approximation algorithm, reduces them to at most $\Delta(m)$, and schedules the tasks using list algorithm. This result has been improved for two classes of general series–parallel and bounded width task graphs, for which the cost $c(\bar{i})$ can be well approximated. We outline only the simpler case of series–parallel precedences. Let us remind (see in Sect. 2.1) that a (general) *series–parallel graph* (sp) can be represented as a result of applying a sequence of two operators: *Series* connects two series–parallel graphs one after another. *Parallel* merges two series–parallel graphs executed in parallel. A single vertex is a series–parallel graph. Series–parallel graphs may be equivalently represented as binary decomposition trees recording the binary series and parallel operations applied to the subgraphs. The leaves of the tree are the tasks themselves, and the internal nodes represent series and parallel operations. Note that binary decomposition tree of a series–parallel graph may not be unique. Minimum cost $c(\bar{i})$ is calculated by a dynamic programming algorithm tabulating function $F(v, l)$ of the minimum work $\frac{\sum_{j=1}^{n} p_j(i_j)}{m}$ for each node $v$ of binary decomposition tree and each given longest path length $l$. The minimum cost of the whole schedule can be computed from the leaves to the root of the binary decomposition tree in $O(nmX^2)$ time, where $X \leq \sum_{j=1}^{n} p_j(1)$ is an upper bound on cost. This is a pseudopolynomial algorithm which can be converted into FPTAS using standard scaling techniques known, e.g., from knapsack problem. The complexity of the whole algorithm is dominated by computation of the processor allotment, and is $O(n^3 m \frac{1}{\varepsilon})$.

**Jansen and Zhang Heuristic (JZ) [136]** This algorithm is similar in the idea to algorithm B presented above [164]. Also here processor allotments $i_j$ and an upper bound $\Delta(m)$ are calculated first. As in algorithm B the initial allotments are reduced to $\min\{i_j, \Delta(m)\}$, and tasks are scheduled as rigid using list scheduling algorithm.

However here, the allotments are calculated using linear program which minimizes longest path in the precedence graph and the total amount of work. In the linear program each task $T_j$ is represented by $m$ virtual tasks $T_{ji}$ requiring $i$ processors and $p_j(i)$ time. A variable $x_{ji} \leq p_j(i)$ is introduced in the linear program which in some sense is the duration of executing virtual task $T_{ji}$. Yet, only one virtual task can be finally executed. Therefore, fractional solutions $x_{ji}^*$ of the linear program are rounded. If $x_{ji}^* < \rho p_j(i)$, then $x_{ji}$ is rounded to 0. Otherwise, $x_{ji} = p_j(i)$, and $i$ becomes the allotment of $T_j$. $\rho$, $\Delta(m)$ are parameters of the algorithm determined by nonlinear optimization formulation. The performance guarantee in Table 5.7 has been obtained for $\rho = 0.43$ and $\Delta(m) = \frac{93m - \sqrt{4349m^2 - 4300m}}{100}$.

### 5.4.1.3   Nonpreemptive Schedules, Heuristics Without a Guarantee

In this section, we outline some heuristics for scheduling moldable tasks without performance guarantees.

**Multi-Shelf [225]**  It is assumed that tasks are assigned to processors using shelf algorithm. Thus, the problem boils down to the assignment of the tasks to the appropriate shelf. This in turn has been reduced to a knapsack problem with $k$ knapsacks. For $k = 2$ a dynamic programming procedure with complexity $O(m^2 n \log n)$ was proposed. In general case this procedure has exponential complexity in the number of knapsacks (shelves).

**Choudhary, Narahari, Nicol, and Simha Heuristic (CNNS) [59]**  This heuristic is dedicated to scheduling pipelined computations with *series–parallel* (sp) precedences which is a special case of problem $P|any, sp|C_{max}$. Series–parallel graphs have been introduced in Sect. 2.1, and have been reminded in the previous section together with algorithm B. A series–parallel graph may be equivalently represented as binary decomposition tree. The leaves of the tree are the tasks themselves, and the internal nodes represent series and parallel operations. A schedule may be constructed by parsing the tree bottom-up, and merging a pair of tasks into a compound task capturing the characteristic of the pair. For this purpose it is necessary to calculate the length of the shortest schedule of the compound task for each possible number of processors. Parallel construction is realized by PP heuristic [150] (see page 120). In the case of nonpipelined computations, the series construction is simpler because two tasks in series construction may use the same processors one after the other. Then, the processing time of a series compound tasks is the sum of processing times of the merged tasks. Due to the pipelining of computations the series construction needs a specific treatment. A task appended at the end of the pipeline must share processors with the preceding tasks because the preceding tasks will be processing new datasets in parallel with the task on the latter stage, processing the older datasets. Therefore, also for serial construction processing time function is calculated by dynamic programming. The idea of folding up the binary decomposition tree of a series–parallel graph can be applied also in other settings, using different methods for determining characteristics of the compound tasks.

**TSPLIT/ LLIST-B/ HIER [237]** These are heuristics for scheduling in-forests of moldable tasks with nondecreasing speedup ($P|any, Nd, in\text{-}forest|C_{max}$) proposed in [237]. **TSPLIT** (the name is an abbreviation for Tree Split) is a dynamic programming algorithm based on similar ideas as the algorithms for the folding up series–parallel graphs into an equivalent moldable task representing whole jobs. It calculates for a tree the best way of executing it on certain number of processors. In the case of series construction the best execution time on $p$ processors for a task and its predecessors (we have in-forests) is to execute them one after another using at most $p$ processors. In the case of a task with two predecessors $T_l, T_k$ the parallel construction selects the best of the possibilities: the $T_l, T_k$ executed sequentially each using at most $p$ processors, or $T_l, T_k$ executed in parallel $T_l$ on $a$ processors, and $T_k$ on $p - a$ processors, for $a = 1, \ldots, p - 1$. **LLIST-B** – the name comes from Longest List – Bottleneck. LLIST-B uses a subroutine LLIST-NM which schedules rigid tasks. LLIST-NM assigns to the earliest possible starting time one of the ready tasks. LLIST-B selects for each moldable task processor allotment with minimum work $\arg\min_{1 \le i_j \le m}\{i_j p_j(i_j)\}$, and applies LLIST-NM. Then task $T_j'$ is selected which has the greatest amount of idle time in the interval of its execution. The allotment of $T_j'$ is increased to the next admissible value, and the procedure is repeated. LLIST-B iterates until no task has idle time in parallel with its execution. **HIER** (for Hierarchical) is a combination of TSPLIT and LLIST-B which first calculates possible schedules for each tree in the forest using TSPLIT, and then uses LLIST-B to schedule the tasks in the trees. TSPLIT and LLIST-B can be also used separately.

### 5.4.1.4 Nonpreemptive Schedules, Continuous Processing Speed Functions

A different approach to scheduling stems from the control theory using techniques of continuous optimization. It is assumed that progress in processing some task $T_j$ at time $\tau$ is represented by state variable $x_j(\tau)$. $x_j(\tau) = x_j(0) = 0$ for all $\tau$ when the task is not started yet. $x_j(\tau) = x_j(c_j) = p_j$ for all $\tau$ when the task is finished. The progress from the initial to the final state is controlled by processing speed function: $\frac{\partial x(\tau)}{\partial t} = \varsigma_j(i)$, where $\varsigma(i)$ is a continuous differentiable function of processing power $i$. Processing power is a continuous equivalent of the alloted processor number, and may be fractional. Note that a simplifying assumption is made that $\varsigma(i)$ is not a function of time. A number of analytical results have been obtained for this model [32, 140, 198, 233, 234]. For example, independent tasks with convex functions $\varsigma_j(i)$ should be executed one after another using all processors to obtain the shortest schedule. In the case of concave functions, independent tasks, and $C_{max}$ criterion, tasks should be started together, executed in parallel and finished simultaneously. The amount of allotted processors should be $\varsigma^{-1}(\frac{p_j(1)}{M^*})$, where $M^*$ is a root of equation $\sum_{j=1}^{n} \varsigma^{-1}(\frac{p_j(1)}{M}) = 1$.

Scheduling with precedence constraints has been studied in [197–200]. It has been observed that processing power, i.e. processors, can be treated as liquid medium analogous to electric current. Arcs in a task graph operate like wires, and tasks are nonlinear resistors. This led to formulation of scheduling moldable tasks

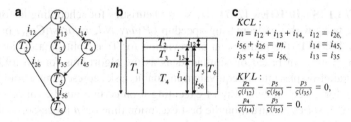

**Fig. 5.12**  (a) Task graph. (b) Form of the schedule. (c) KCL–KCV formulation

problem as finding currents (processing power assignments) and voltages (interval lengths) in electric circuit. In particular, Kirchhoff's Current and Voltage Laws (KCL, KVL, respectively) were used to formulate the problem. KCL equivalent states that the amount processing power pouring into a task is equal to the amount of processing power flowing away from the task. KVL equivalent states that the duration of the tasks around a circuit in the task graph is zero. See Fig. 5.12 for an example. Solving KCL–KVL formulation for arbitrary graphs and nonlinear processing times is nontrivial. Some techniques have been discussed in [197–200]. The problem is easier to solve when all tasks have processing speed function $\forall\, T_j, \varsigma_j(i) = \frac{p_j}{i^\alpha}$, and precedences are a series–parallel graph, i.e. for problem $P\,|any, p_j(i) = \frac{p_j}{i^\alpha}, sp\,|C_{\max}$. Analogously to the method presented in the preceding paragraph for problem $P\,|any, sp\,|C_{\max}$ the binary decomposition tree of a series–parallel graph may be folded up by substituting series and parallel operators with equivalent compound tasks. A task resulting from series construction on $T_j, T_k$ has execution time $p_{j\to k}(i) = \frac{p_i+p_j}{i^\alpha}$. A task resulting from parallel construction on $T_j, T_k$ has execution time $p_{j\|k}(i) = (p_j^{\frac{1}{\alpha}} + p_k^{\frac{1}{\alpha}})^\alpha$, and $T_j, T_k$ are executed in parallel.

### 5.4.1.5   Preemptive Schedules

Let us remind that problem $P\,|size_j, pmtn\,|C_{\max}$ is **NPh**, and is not s**NPh**, while problem $Pm\,|size_j, pmtn\,|C_{\max}$ is solvable in polynomial time for any fixed $m$. Below we present a pseudopolynomial algorithm for problem $Pm\,|any, pmtn\,|C_{\max}$.

$Pm\,|any, pmtn\,|C_{\max}$ [86]

Observe that when the sizes of moldable tasks are finally selected, then a schedule for $Pm\,|any, pmtn\,|C_{\max}$ is also a schedule for some instance of rigid task scheduling problem $Pm\,|size_j, pmtn\,|C_{\max}$. According to formulation (5.10)–(5.13) optimum schedule length for $Pm\,|size_j, pmtn\,|C_{\max}$ is decided by the longest 1-task, sum of processing times of two longest 1-tasks, ..., sum of processing times of all 1-tasks, the longest 2-task, sum of processing times of two longest 2-tasks, ..., sum of processing times of $m$-tasks. Thus, $H = \sum_{i=1}^{m} \lfloor \frac{m}{i} \rfloor \leq m(1 + \ln m)$ numbers control schedule length for $Pm|size_j, pmtn|C_{max}$. To construct a schedule for $P|any, pmtn|C_{max}$, one has to check at most $O(T^H)$ schedules for $Pm|size_j, pmtn|C_{max}$, where $T$ is an upper bound on schedule length. In order to solve only the instances of (5.10)–(5.13) that need to be verified, a pseudopolynomial dynamic program has been proposed which calculates function $F(i, x_1, \ldots, x_{H-1})$ which is the smallest execution time of the first $i$ tasks in $m$-processor mode such that the processing time of the longest task executed in 1-processor mode is $x_1, \ldots,$ the sum of execution times of tasks in $m - 1$-processor modes is $x_{H-1}$. And though construction of $F(i, x_1, \ldots, x_{H-1})$ is quite involved, the whole problem $Pm|any, pmtn|C_{max}$ can be solved in pseudopolynomial for fixed $m$.

## 5.4.2 Minsum Criteria

### 5.4.2.1 Heuristics with a Guarantee

Results on approximability of moldable task scheduling for minsum criteria are collected in Table 5.8. Below we present the heuristics introduced in this table.

**Turek, Ludwig, Wolf, Fleischer, Tiwari, Glasgow, Schwiegelshohn, and Yu Heuristic (TLWFTGSY) [223]** This heuristic has been defined for moldable tasks with nondecreasing sublinear speedup over the range of all $m$ processors. It is built on the basis of several original results:

(1) Assume that processor allotment $\bar{i}$ is given. Consequently, we have problem $P|size_j|\sum c_j$. Let $F^*(\bar{i})$ denote the optimum mean flow time for $\bar{i}$. Note that $F^*(\bar{i}) \geq \max\{A(\bar{i}), H(\bar{i})\}$, where $A(\bar{i}) = \frac{1}{m} \sum_{j=1}^{n} i_j p_j(i_j)(n - j + 1)$, $H(\bar{i}) = \sum_{j=1}^{n} p_j(i_j)$. This lower bound has been improved to $F^*(\bar{i}) \geq A(\bar{i}) + \frac{1}{2}(H(\bar{i}) - W(\bar{i}))$, where $W(\bar{i}) = \frac{1}{m} \sum_{j=1}^{n} i_j p_j(i_j)$.

(2) If for each task $T_j$, $i_j \leq \lceil \frac{m}{2} \rceil$ then list scheduling algorithm builds a schedule with mean flow time at most $F_{LS}(\bar{i}) \leq 2A(\bar{i}) + H(\bar{i}) - 2W(\bar{i}) \leq 2F^*(\bar{i})$.

(3) Reducing any feasible processor allotments to $i'_j = \min\{i_j, \lceil \frac{m}{2} \rceil\}$ and then applying list scheduling algorithm result in a schedule with $F_{LS}(\bar{i}') \leq 2A(\bar{i}) + H(\bar{i}) - W(\bar{i})$.

(4) Let $\bar{i}^*$ be the processor allotment in the optimum schedule for $P|any|\sum c_j$. The allotment which is optimum in the sense of minimum $A(\bar{i}) + \frac{1}{2}(H(\bar{i}) - W(\bar{i}))$

**Table 5.8** Approximability of nonpreemptive moldable task scheduling, minsum criteria

| Problem | Result | Reference |
|---|---|---|
| $P|any, NdSub|\sum c_j$ | $R_{TLWFTGSY} \leq 2$ | [223] |
| $P|any, p_j = \frac{p_j(1)}{i}, \delta_j|\sum p_j(1)\hat{u}_j$ | $R_H = 4.5$ | [159] |

(and hence $A(\bar{i}) + \frac{1}{2}(H(\bar{i}) - W(\bar{i})) \le A(\bar{i}^*) + \frac{1}{2}(H(\bar{i}^*) - W(\bar{i}^*)))$ can be found as minimum weight matching in a bipartite graph. The graph has $n$ vertices representing task and $n$ nodes representing positions of the tasks in the ordering according to the increasing area $i_j p_j(j_i)$. If task $T_j$ is assigned to position $s$ in this order, then $T_j$ contribution to $A(\bar{i}) + \frac{1}{2}(H(\bar{i}) - W(\bar{i}))$ is minimum for $i_j = \arg\min_{1 \le i \le m}\{p_j(i)[1 + \frac{i}{m}(2(n - s) + 1)]\}$. The bipartite graph can be constructed in $O(n^2 + mn)$ time, the minimum weight matching in $O(n^3)$. Hence, the total complexity is $O(n^3 + nm)$. This is also the complexity of the whole heuristic.

Overall, the heuristic consists of the following steps:

1. Find allotment $\bar{i}$ which minimizes $A(\bar{i}) + \frac{1}{2}(H(\bar{i}) - W(\bar{i}))$.
2. Reduce allotments to $i'_j = \min\{i_j, \lceil \frac{m}{2} \rceil\}$.
3. Find the schedule for the resulting $P|size_j| \sum c_j$ using list scheduling.

**H [159]** This heuristic is designed to maximize the amount of work performed on tasks that meet their deadlines. Tasks have linear speedup up to a limit $\delta_j$. Set $T$ is partitioned into $T_L = \{T_j : p_j(\delta_j) \le \frac{d_j}{2}, p_j(1) \le \frac{d_j m}{4}\}$ and $T_S = T - T_L$. Assume that tasks in $T_S$ are ordered according to nonincreasing $d_j$, and $T_k \in T_S$ is the last task such that $\sum_{j=1}^{k} \delta_j \le m$. Tasks $T_j \in T_S$, where $j > k$ are rejected. Start $T_k$ on $\delta_k$ processors at time $\tau = 0$. Tasks $T_1, \ldots, T_{k-1}$ in $T_S$ are started at time $p_k(\delta_k)$ on the processors from pool $P_1, \ldots, P_{\delta_k}$ provided that their duedates can be met. If not, the task is rejected. Tasks from $T_L$ are appended at the end of the schedule by EDD method.

### 5.4.2.2  Heuristics Without a Guarantee

**Maximum Workload Derivative First with Fragment Elimination Heuristic (MWF-FE) [162]** MWF-FE is an algorithm for $P|any, NdSub| \sum u_j$. Let $i_j^{min}$ denote minimum processor allotment necessary to obey the duedate of $T_j$. $dW_j = (i_j^{min} + 1)p_j(i_j^{min} + 1) - (i_j^{min})p_j(i_j^{min})$ is called $T_j$ derivative of work at point $i_j^{min}$. Tasks are scheduled according to the following rules:

(1) The task with the largest $dW_j$ is scheduled first. Ties are broken in favor of the task with smallest duedate.

(2) Processor allotment is smallest possible to meet the duedate.

(3) When some processors remain unassigned because a task $T_l$ scheduled later used more processors than some task $T_j$ scheduled earlier, then the earlier task $T_j$ is assigned all the idle processors, and $T_l$ is rescheduled.

MWF-FE algorithm was evaluated by simulation [162].

## 5.4.3  Other Heuristics for Moldable Task Scheduling

Similarly to the rigid task scheduling problem, a group of heuristics is known which are simple to implement, require little knowledge about the tasks. Therefore, they constitute attractive options in production of computer systems. These heuristics were compared for various optimality criteria and under different workloads in [7, 56, 112, 191, 194, 203]. Hence, they do not fit the above two sections where single optimality criterion was the distinguishing factor. Below we list examples of such heuristics.

**Fixed Processors Per Job (FPPJ) [203, 207]** This divides the $m$ processor pool into a number of equal size static partitions. Let $k$ be the size of the partitions. An arriving task waits until one of the partitions is released, and is allotted $k$ processors.

**Adaptive Partitioning (AP) [56, 112, 203]** The main idea behind AP methods is that partition sizes are adjusted to the system load and available number of processors. Tasks are executed nonpreemptively. When a task arrives to the system and no processor is available, then it is assigned to FIFO queue and waits. Let $n' > 0$ be the number of waiting tasks, $m' > 0$ the number of processors available at the task arrival, or on the completion of some task, $m$ the number of all processors in the system. $n' = 1$ can be assumed when some processors are available at task arrival. In [203] a set of AP algorithms has been proposed that attempt to assign to the tasks some target processor allotment $targetsize_i$. If $m'$ is smaller than the target allotment, then AP waits until this number of processors is free. Processor allotment for at most $m'$ tasks from the head of the queue is: $\min\{targetsize_i, \delta_j\}$. Several versions of AP were defined in [203] depending on the method of calculating $targetsize_i$. For example, in AP$_1$: $targetsize_1 = \max\{1, \lfloor \frac{m}{n'} + 0.5 \rfloor\}$, in AP$_2$: $targetsize_2 = \max\{1, \lfloor \frac{m}{n'+1} + 0.5 \rfloor\}$. There are versions of AP which assign to a task $\min\{1, m', x\}$, where $x$ can be average parallelism, maximum parallelism, or processor working set of $T_j$ (cf. Sect. 2.4). There are also AP policies that calculate target allotment using only the released processors $m'$ not the whole processor pool $m$ [56, 112].

**Adaptive Equipartition (AEP) [7]** This works as AP, but the allotment target size includes all the tasks in the system. The tasks at the head of the FIFO waiting queue are allotted $\min\{\max\{1, \lfloor \frac{m}{n} \rfloor\}, m', \delta_j\}$, where $n$ is the number of all tasks in the system, both running, and waiting.

**AEP(1), AP(1)** – Modification of AEP, AP proposed in [7], for minimizing mean flow time. The modification consists in sorting the tasks in the waiting queue according to SPT rule on $p_j(1)$.

**AEP(2)** – Modification of AEP(1) assuming that waiting tasks are ordered according to SPT, the tasks to be started are assigned $i_j = 1$ processors, the remaining processors (if any) are assigned one by one using *differential rule* which states that a free processor should be assigned to a task which maximizes $p_j(i_j) - p(i_j + 1)$ [7].

**Fair Share (FS) [218]** Waiting tasks are ordered according to SPT. A limit is imposed on usable processor numbers $\delta_j = \frac{mp_j(1)}{\sum_{j=1}^{n'} p_j(1)}$. ECT heuristic with limit $\delta_j$ is used for the task at the queue head. Observe that there is another scheduling policy FSS introduced in Sect. 3.3.2.

**Multiclass Fixed Partitioning (MFP) and Multiclass Adaptive Partitioning (MAP) [191]** The tasks are divided into three classes of small, medium, and large tasks according to the amount of work $i_j p_j(i_j)$ on a certain number of processors. For each task the set of admissible processor allotments $X_j$ is known. MFP($n_s \times m_s, n_m \times m_m, n_l \times m_l$) partitions statically the available processors into $n_k$ partitions with $m_k$ processors (where $k \in \{s, m, l\}$). FIFO queues are maintained for waiting tasks of each class. Smaller tasks may use partitions of bigger classes, but not vice versa. A small task arriving to the system is allotted processors from all partitions, medium tasks from medium and large partitions, large task from large partitions only. When a large task finishes its processors may be assigned to the next large task, or if the large queue is empty, the first task from medium queue is assigned, if also medium waiting queue is empty, then small tasks are assigned. Similarly, when medium queue is empty, small tasks may exploit medium partitions $n_k, m_k$ where $k \in \{s, m, l\}$ are tunable parameters of the algorithm. MAP($[min_s, max_s], [min_m, max_m], [min_l, max_l]$) differs from MFP by adaptively partitioning a pool of $max_k$ processors for each task class $k$. A task from class $k \in \{s, m, l\}$ is assigned processor number from range $[min_k, max_k]$. The actual number of processors is a multiclass version of adaptive policy AP$_4$ defined in [203]. Let $\pi_k$ denote the number of different partitions assigned in the pool $[min_k, max_k]$. If the number of processors that would be requested by $n'_k$ waiting tasks exceeds $max_k$, i.e. when $targetsize_4 n'_k > max_k$, then target partition size is decreased to $targetsize_4 = \max\{min_k, \lfloor \frac{max_k}{n'_k} + 0.5 \rfloor\}$. Otherwise, if the number of free processors in pool $[min_k, max_k]$ is at least $2 targetsize_4$, then one partition is removed from pool $k$, i.e. $\pi_k = \pi_k - 1$, and target partition size is increased to $targetsize_4 = \lfloor \frac{m_k}{\pi_k} \rfloor$. Values of $min_k, max_k$ for $k \in \{s, m, l\}$ are tunable parameters of the algorithm.

*Policies with a maximum*  impose additional maximum on processor allotment. For example, SPT-Max allocates to a task $\max\{MX, \delta_j\}$ processors where $MX$ is the system-wide upper bound.

*Policies with insurance*  intend to leave free processors to accommodate future burst arrivals of the tasks. The number of processors left free decreases with growing length of the queue of waiting tasks. For example, in [203] processors are distributed from a pool of $\lceil m'(1 - k^{n'}) \rceil$ processors, where $0 < k < 1$ is a parameter of the algorithm.

## 5.5  Malleable Tasks

In this section, we examine scheduling malleable tasks, i.e. the tasks which can change the number of used processors during the execution. The presentation will follow not only the distinction by optimality criteria, but also by the speedup function which is an important differentiating feature of malleable task scheduling problems. Let us remind that preemptability follows implicitly from malleability.

## 5.5.1 $C_{max}$, $L_{max}$, max $w_j s_j$ *Criteria*

### 5.5.1.1 Complexity

The results on complexity of selected malleable task scheduling problems are collected in Table 5.9. In the table the following special symbols were used:

- $\varsigma(i)$ – Speedup in processor number $i$ (processing speed function in $i$)
- $\sum s_j$ – Criterion of the sum of the slowdowns (cf. Sect. 4.4.1)
- max $w_j s_j$ – Criterion of the maximum weighted slowdown

Selected polynomially solvable cases are presented below.

$$P \,|\, var, p_j(i) = \tfrac{p_j(1)}{i}, \delta_j \,|\, C_{max} \;\; [85]$$

This problem can be solved by extending McNaughton's rule (see Sect. 4.3.1.2). The length of the schedule is $C_{max}^* = \max\{\max_j\{\tfrac{p_j(1)}{\delta_j}\}, \sum_{j=1}^{n} \tfrac{p_j(1)}{m}\}$. No task uses more than $\delta_j$ processors because $C_{max}^* \delta_j \leq p_j(1)$. The complexity of the algorithm is $O(n)$. Exemplary instance and schedule are shown in Fig. 5.13. Observe that the closest rigid task scheduling problem $P \,|\, size_j, pmtn \,|\, C_{max}$ is **NP**h. Thus, from complexity point of view rigid or moldable tasks are qualitatively different than malleable tasks.

**Table 5.9** Complexity of scheduling malleable tasks, minmax criteria

| Problem | Result | Reference |
|---|---|---|
| $P \,|\, var, p_j(i) = \tfrac{p_j(1)}{i}, \delta_j, chain \,|\, C_{max}$ | s**NP**h | [85] |
| $R \,|\, var, r_j \,|\, \sum s_j$ | s**NP**h | [163] |
| $P \,|\, var, p_j(i) = \tfrac{p_j(1)}{i}, \delta_j \,|\, C_{max}$ | $O(n)$ | [85] |
| $P \,|\, olt, var, p_j(i) = \tfrac{p_j(1)}{i}, \delta_j \,|\, C_{max}$ | $O(n^2)$ | [80, 83] |
| $P \,|\, var \,|\, C_{max}, n \leq m, \varsigma(i) concave$ | $O(n \max\{m, n \log^2 m\})$ | [33, 37] |
| $P \,|\, var, p_j(i) = \tfrac{p_j(1)}{i}, \delta_j, r_j \,|\, L_{max}$ | $O(n^3(\log n + \log m))$ | [229] |
| $Pm \,|\, var, p_j(i) = \tfrac{p_j(1)}{i}, \delta_j, chain \,|\, C_{max}$ | $poly(n)$ | [85] |
| $R \,|\, var \,|\, L_{max}$ | $poly(n, m)$ | [239] |
| $R \,|\, var, r_j, d_j \,|\, \max w_j s_j$ | $poly(n, m)$ | [163] |

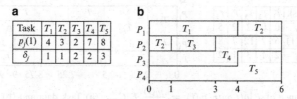

**Fig. 5.13** Instance of $P \,|\, var, p_j(i) = \tfrac{p_j(1)}{i}, \delta_j \,|\, C_{max}$. (**a**) Task data and (**b**) a schedule form $m = 4$

$P|olt, var, p_j(i) = \frac{p_j(1)}{i}, \delta_j|C_{\max}$ [80, 83]

We have a problem of tasks arriving over time. Before $T_j$ arrival the system is un-aware of $T_j$ existence and its data. When $T_j$ arrives at $r_j$ its full data are revealed to the scheduler. The length of the schedule is determined by the tasks, or pieces of tasks that remain to be completed after the last ready time. From the algorithm for $P|var, p_j(i) = \frac{p_j(1)}{i}, \delta_j|C_{\max}$ presented above we know that in this case schedule length is controlled by $\max_j\{\frac{p_j(1)}{\delta_j}\}$ and by $\sum_{j=1}^{n} \frac{p_j(1)}{m}$. Thus, the two values should be made as small as possible before the last task arrival. It has been proved in [83] that classic Muntz–Coffman level scheduling algorithm (cf. Sect. 4.3.1.2) minimizes in maximum possible degree not only $\max_j\{\frac{p_j(1)}{\delta_j}\}$, $\sum_{j=1}^{n} \frac{p_j(1)}{m}$, but also $\sum_{j=1}^{k} \frac{p_j(1)}{\delta_j}$ where $\frac{p_1(1)}{\delta_1} \geq \frac{p_2(1)}{\delta_2} \geq \cdots \geq \frac{p_j(k)}{\delta_k}$. Here $\frac{p_j(1)}{\delta_j}$ is level of task $T_j$. The $n'$ highest level tasks receive $\delta_j$ processors each if the number of free processors $m'$ is sufficient. Otherwise, the free processors are shared in proportion to the maximum width of the task, i.e., task $T_j$ receives allotment $m'\delta_j / \sum_{l=1}^{n'} \delta_l$. The complexity of the algorithm is $O(n^2)$. An example of the problem instance and its solution are shown in Fig. 5.14.

### $P|var|C_{\max}$, Concave Speedup, $n \leq m$ [33, 37]

When $n \leq m$ and speedup $\varsigma_j(i)$ is concave, then it follows from the results of continuous optimal control theory [32, 198–200, 233] that tasks should be started simultaneously, executed in equal pace, and finished together. This requires that task allotments $i_j$ be such that speeds $\varsigma_j(i_j) = \frac{p_j(1)}{C_{\max}}$ are equal. Adding that the allotments cannot exceed processor number $m$ we obtain the equation

$$\sum_{j=1}^{n} \varsigma_j^{-1}(\frac{p_j(1)}{C_{\max}}) = m \tag{5.16}$$

(cf. the section on scheduling moldable tasks with continuous speed functions). Function $\varsigma_j(i)$ is defined only for integer allotments, because processors are discrete. If $T_j$ is executed with two allotments: $i_j$ for time $x$ and $i_j + 1$ for time $y$

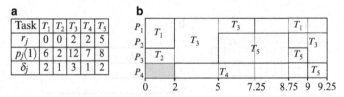

**Fig. 5.14** Instance of $P|olt, var, p_j(i) = \frac{p_j(1)}{i}, \delta_j|C_{\max}$. (**a**) Task data and (**b**) a schedule for $m = 4$. Proportions are not preserved

such that $x + y = z$, then the performed work is $(z - y)\varsigma_j(i_j) + y\varsigma_j(i_j + 1) = z[\varsigma_j(i_j) + \frac{y}{z}(\varsigma_j(i_j + 1) - \varsigma_j(i_j))]$. This means that discrete speedup function can be made continuous and linear between the discrete processor allotments. A scheduling equivalent of fractional processor assignments are two intervals where a task is executed on $i_j$ and $i_j + 1$ processors. This observation results in reducing speedup to a piecewise linear function. For piecewise linear functions $\varsigma_j(i)$ Eq. (5.16) can be solved for $C_{\max}$ and processor allotments $i_j = \varsigma_j^{-1}(\frac{p_j(1)}{C_{\max}})$ in $O(n \max\{m, n \log^2 m\})$ time [37]. Now, a problem is to build a schedule for the potentially fractional allotments. The solution has been proposed in [33]. If $i_j$ is integer for some task then it is a correct allotment, $T_j$ is scheduled in interval $[0, C_{\max}]$ using the allotment. If $i_j$ is fractional, then $T_j$ is processed in two parts: $T_j'$ with allotment $\lfloor i_j \rfloor$ and duration $\frac{(\lceil i_j \rceil - i_j)p_j(1)}{\varsigma_j(i_j)}$ and $T_j''$ with allotment $\lceil i_j \rceil$ and duration $\frac{(i_j - \lfloor i_j \rfloor)p_j(1)}{\varsigma_j(i_j)}$. Note that the work performed in the two parts is $p_j(1)$, and their total duration is $C_{\max}$. $T_j''$ is scheduled first starting at the time when the processor with the smallest number becomes available. This is called southwest corner rule. $T_j'$ immediately follows after $T_j''$ also using the smallest processor number. If $T_j''$ starts at time greater than 0, then some part of $T_j''$ or $T_j'$ will span beyond $C_{\max}$. This part should be wrapped around as in the McNaughton rule and assigned again using southwest corner rule.

$$P|var, p_j(i) = \frac{p_j(1)}{i}, \delta_j, r_j|L_{\max} \quad [229]$$

The problem of minimizing maximum lateness may be reduced to a sequence of decision problems verifying whether a schedule with a given value of lateness $L$ exists. An oracle is based on finding a maximum flow in a network (see Fig. 5.15). Suppose the value of lateness to check is $L$. According or the definition of criterion $L_{\max}$ no task is allowed to be executed after deadline $d_j' = d_j + L$ in a feasible schedule with lateness $L$. Let us sort all the events in the task systems, i.e. ready times $r_j$ and deadlines $d_j'$ according to the increasing value of time. We obtain $l \leq 2n$ time instants $e_0 < e_1 < \cdots < e_l$. The network comprises source $S$ connected with $n$ nodes representing tasks. Arcs $(S, T_j)$ have capacity $p_j$, for $j = 1, \ldots, n$. There is a set of $l$ nodes representing time intervals $[e_{i-1}, e_i]$ for $i = 1, \ldots, l$. A task which arrives at time $e_a$ and has deadline $e_b$ has node $T_j$ connected with interval

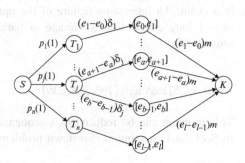

**Fig. 5.15** Network for $P|var, p_j(i) = \frac{p_j(1)}{i}, \delta_j, r_j|L_{\max}$

nodes $[e_a, e_{a+1}], \ldots, [e_{b-1}, e_b]$ by arcs of capacity $\delta_j(e_{a+1} - e_a), \ldots, \delta_j(e_b - e_{b-1})$, respectively. Interval nodes $[e_i, e_{i+1}]$ are connected with the sink $K$ by arcs with capacity $m(e_{i+1} - e_i)$. The maximum flow can be found in $O(n^3)$ time. A feasible schedule exists if the flow value is $\phi = \sum_{j=1}^n p_j(1)$. The values of the flows $\phi_{ij}$ on arcs $(T_j, [e_i, e_{i+1}])$ indicate how much work must be performed on task $T_j$ in interval $[e_i, e_{i+1}]$. A schedule for each interval $[e_{i-1}, e_i]$ can be built using algorithm from problem $P|var, p_j(i) = \frac{p_j(1)}{i}, \delta_j|C_{\max}$. The optimum value of lateness can be found by search over values of $L$. The original algorithm in [229] has complexity $O(n^4 m)$, but this can be improved to $O(n^3(\log n + \log m))$ by use of techniques presented in [160], and, in particular, binary search over multipliers of minimum cut capacities. Minimum cut multipliers are coefficients of linear relation between capacity of min cut and the increase of lateness $L$. Multipliers are integers in range $[1, \sum_{j=1}^n \delta_j]$ and $\sum_{j=1}^n \delta_j \leq nm$. It should not be difficult to apply this algorithm for maximum weighted flow time or maximum weighted slowdown criteria. In the latter case it can be achieved by setting $d'_j = S_{\max} \frac{p_j}{w_j} + r_j$, where $S_{\max}$ is the value of maximum weighted slowdown to be verified.

### $Pm|var, p_j(i) = \frac{p_j(1)}{i}, \delta_j, chain|C_{\max}$ [85]

The problem of scheduling chains of three malleable tasks: sequential ($\delta_{j1} = 1$), parallel ($\delta_{j2} = m$), and sequential ($\delta_{j3} = 1$) has been studied in [85]. This problem is sNPh if the number of processors is arbitrary. However, for a fixed number of processors, it can be solved in polynomial time. Let height of chain $j$ be its work $p_{j1}(1) + p_{j2}(1) + p_{j3}(1)$. Suppose an optimum schedule for at most $m - 1$ chains strictly higher than the $m$th highest chain is known. Then the optimum schedule for all $n > m$ tasks can be constructed in polynomial time by an extension of the Muntz–Coffman level scheduling algorithm. The schedule for the long chains can be reduced to linear programming calculating how much work should be done on each task between the consecutive completions of the tasks in the shortest schedule. Such a linear program can be formulated if we know the sequence of task completions. Since there can be at most $\frac{(2m-2)!}{2^{m-1}}$ such sequences, the optimum sequence can be found in constant time if $m$ is constant. This result can be extended to chains comprising at most a fixed number of tasks. Thus, $Pm|var, p_j(i) = \frac{p_j(1)}{i}, \delta_j, chain|L_{\max}$ can be solved in polynomial time for a fixed number of tasks in a chain. An interesting feature of the optimum schedules is that only at most $m - 1$ long chains take advantage of parallelism, the other tasks are executed sequentially.

### $R|var, r_j, d_j| \max w_j s_j$ [163, 228, 239]

This problem can be reduced to a sequence of linear programs. As pointed out in Sect. 4.4.1, maximum slowdown problems can be reduced to scheduling with deadlines. For a given trial value $S$ of weighted slowdown the completion time of a task should not exceed $c_j = r_j + \frac{Sp_j}{w_j}$. Thus, we may set a modified deadline for each task $d'_j = \min\{d_j, r_j + \frac{Sp_j}{w_j}\}$. Let us assume that we know the range $[S_l, S_u]$ of max $w_j s_j$, and it is such that the sequence of ready times and modified deadlines is fixed. Let $e_0 < e_1 < \cdots < e_l$ be the time moments the events occur. The events related to the ready times and the original deadlines $d_j$ are independent of the tested value of weighted slowdown $S$. Some other events, related to the upper bounds on completion times $r_j + \frac{Sp_j}{w_j}$, depend on $S$. Let $p_{ij}$ denote processing time of $T_j$ on processor $P_i$ solely. Variable $x_{ijk}$ will denote the fraction of task $j$ to be executed on $P_i$ between time moments $e_{k-1}$ and $e_k$. The problem can be reduced to a linear program:

$$\text{minimize } S \quad \text{subject to} \tag{5.17}$$

$$x_{ijk} = 0 \quad \text{for } e_k < r_j, i = 1, \ldots, m, j = 1, \ldots, n \tag{5.18}$$

$$x_{ijk} = 0 \quad \text{for } e_{k-1} \geq d'_j, i = 1, \ldots, m, j = 1, \ldots, n \tag{5.19}$$

$$\sum_{j=1}^{n} x_{ijk} p_{ij} \leq e_k - e_{k-1} \quad \text{for } i = 1, \ldots, m, k = 1, \ldots, l \tag{5.20}$$

$$\sum_{k=1}^{l} \sum_{i=1}^{n} x_{ijk} = 1 \quad \text{for } j = 1, \ldots, n \tag{5.21}$$

$$S_l \leq S \leq S_u \tag{5.22}$$

$$x_{ijk} \geq 0 \tag{5.23}$$

In the above linear program equations (5.18), (5.19) guarantee that tasks are executed between their ready time and modified deadline. A part of the schedule for each processor in each interval between the events fits between them by (5.20). All tasks are fully executed by (5.21), and the sequence of events remains unchanged by (5.22). The schedule can be constructed by executing on processor $P_i$, in interval $k$, a piece of task $T_j$ of length $x_{ijk} p_{ij}$. The sequence of events changes with $S$ at most $O(n^2)$ times, when ready time of some task is equal to the deadline of some other task. The smallest interval of max $w_j s_j$ for which a feasible schedule exists can be found by binary search. Consequently, $R|var, r_j, d_j|$ max $w_j s_j$ is solvable in polynomial time. The linear program verifying feasibility of a schedule for the given deadlines was proposed in [228]. The method of obtaining optimum max $w_j s_j$ was proposed in [163]. A simpler form of the linear program for $R|var|L_{\max}$ was presented in [239].

### 5.5.1.2 Heuristics with a Guarantee

In Table 5.10 phrase *FPTAS(m)* denotes existence of a fully polynomial time approximation scheme, which runs in time polynomial in the length of the input

**Table 5.10**  Approximability of malleable tasks scheduling, $C_{max}$ criterion

| Problem | Result | Reference |
|---|---|---|
| $P\|var, \neg p_j(i)\|C_{max}$ | $R_{SCHEME} = (1 - \frac{1}{m})\mu_m + $ <br> $+ \max\{\frac{1}{m}, \frac{(2-\mu_2)\mu_m}{\mu_2 m}\}$ | [60] |
| $P\|var\|C_{max}$ | $FPTAS(m)$ | [135] |

**Table 5.11**  Approximability of malleable task scheduling, minsum criteria

| Problem | Result | Reference |
|---|---|---|
| $P\|var, \neg p_j(1), p_j(i) = \frac{p_j(1)}{i}\|\sum c_j$ | $R_{RR} = 2 - \frac{2}{n+1}$ | [188] |
| $P\|var, \neg p_j(1), p_j(i) = \frac{p_j(1)}{i}, \delta_j\|\sum c_j$ | $R_{EQ} \leq 2 - \frac{2}{n+1}$ | [73] |
| $P\|var, \neg p_j(1), p_j(i) = \frac{p_j(1)}{i}, \delta_j, chain\|\sum c_j$ | $R_{EQ} \leq 4 - \frac{4}{n+1}$ | [73] |
| $P\|olt, var, \neg p_j(1), p_j(i) = \frac{p_j(1)}{i^{1-\alpha}}, chain\|\sum f_j$ | $1.48^{\frac{1}{\alpha}} \leq R_{EQ} \leq 2^{\frac{1}{\alpha}}$ | [89] |
| $P\|olt, var, \neg p_j(1), p_j(i) = \frac{p_j(1)}{i}, chain\|\sum f_j$ | $R_{EQ} \sim \Omega(\frac{n}{\log n})$ | [89] |
| $P\|var, \neg p_j(1), NdSub, chain\|\sum c_j$ | $e \leq R_{EQ} < 2 + \sqrt{3}$ | [90] |
| $P\|var, \neg p_j(1), NdSub \cup Sup, chain\|\sum f_j$ | $R_{HEQ} \leq 4 + 2\sqrt{3}$ | [90] |
| $P\|var, \neg p_j(1), Nd, chain\|\sum f_j$ | $R_{HEQ'} \sim O(\log n_c)$ | [90] |

instance, and the number of processors $m$ (not $\log m$). This applies to malleable task scheduling problem for which the set of usable processor numbers and processing time functions can be arbitrary. The other heuristics in Table 5.10 is presented below.

**SCHEME [60]**  The name stands for SCHEduling Multiprocessors Efficiently. It is an online algorithm in the sense of not knowing task processing times. The algorithm starts task sequentially using list scheduling heuristic. When less than $m$ tasks remain to be completed, and hence less than $m$ processors are busy, the remaining tasks are executed in any order using all available processors. In the performance ratio in Table 5.10: $\mu_m = \max_j \frac{1}{E_j(m)}$, where $E_j(m)$ is efficiency of $T_j$ executed on $m$ processors as defined in Sect. 2.4.

### 5.5.2  Minsum Criteria

The following notations have been used in Table 5.11:

- $n_c$ denotes the number of chains.
- $NdSub \cup Sup$ means that tasks have nondecreasing and sublinear speedup, or superlinear speedup.

Below we present heuristic scheduling malleable tasks for minimum flow time criterion.

**Round Robin** (RR) is a classic algorithm for one processor which assigns cyclically time quantum $t$ to each task. The results on RR performance on one processor

[188] are applicable for malleable tasks with linear speedup, when the tasks are assigned all $m$ processors. We report them in Table 5.11 because RR is often mentioned in the context of parallel task scheduling. In parallel systems RR usually assigns to a task a number of processors, for some time quantum $t$. Algorithms for parallel systems, presented under the RR name, differ in the assigned processor number, way of managing threads within a parallel application (i.e. tasks within a job) [89, 166, 182].

**Equipartition** (EQ) [89, 90, 182, 222] (also presented under different names in [7, 56, 73, 166, 217]) partitions the processors equally between all the tasks present in the system.

In practical implementations no task is given fewer than one processor. If there are $n_\tau > m$ tasks in the system at time $\tau$, then only first $m$ tasks get a processor, and the remaining tasks wait in FIFO queue. It is not profitable to give a task more processors than its maximum usable number $\delta_j$. For a task with unknown $\delta_j$ we assume it is $m$. Suppose $n_\tau \leq m$. Task $T_j$ is granted processor allotment $i_j = \min\{\max\{1, \lfloor \frac{m - \sum_{l=1}^{j-1} i_l}{n_\tau - j + 1} \rfloor\}, \delta_j\}$, for $j = 1, \ldots, n_\tau$. When new tasks arrive the allotments may be reduced. When some task finishes, they may increase. There are versions of EQ with lower limit on processor allotment $i_{\min} > 1$ [217] and versions which start RR (processor sharing by time multiplexing) if allotments are smaller than 1 [73].

In [89, 90] EQ has been analyzed as an online scheduling algorithm for chains of tasks with unknown processing demand, and exact processing time functions. Only type of speedup function is known. The scheduler is unaware of switching from task to task in a chain. Whole chains, i.e. jobs, are the schedulable entities. Hence, processor allotments are changed $2n_c$ times, where $n_c$ is the number of chains. It was assumed that processor allotments can be real numbers in range $[0, m]$. Only selected results from [89, 90] are presented here and in Table 5.11. In [90] jobs are ready at time 0, and in [89] jobs arrive over time. An important feature of EQ has been observed and exploited. Let OPT denote the optimum scheduler which has complete knowledge about the tasks, and computes schedules in no time. EQ is unaware of the internals of the tasks. If EQ assigns $\frac{m}{n_\tau} > 1$ processors to a task which is sequential, then $\frac{m}{n_\tau} - 1$ processors are wasted. Thus, in the number of finished tasks EQ may lag behind OPT. If EQ lags behind OPT, then compared to OPT the number of unfinished tasks is growing. As a result, processor allotments are decreasing, and fewer processors are wasted. It has been said that EQ self-adjusts the number of processors wasted on tasks that cannot utilize them. EQ has been also examined in using resource augmentation techniques. $EQ^s$ is a version of EQ using $s$-times faster processors, and $EQ_s$ is given $sm$ processors. Given $s = 2 + \varepsilon < 4$ times faster processors $EQ^s$ has competitive ratio at most $2 + \frac{4}{\varepsilon}$, and given $s = 4 + 2\varepsilon$ times faster processors its competitiveness is at most $\frac{16}{s}$ for tasks with linear or nondecreasing sublinear speedup. Alternatively, when $EQ_s$ is given $(2 + \varepsilon)m$ processors then its competitive ratio is at most $2 + \frac{4}{\varepsilon}$, for the same task types.

For the end of EQ presentation let us observe that under heavy load processor allotments reduce to one processor (or even less if time sharing is allowed for allotments smaller than one). This effectively eliminates gains from parallelism.

**Hybrid Equipartition (HEQ, HEQ′) [89,90]**  It is a combination of EQ and RR(or rather gang scheduling). HEQ slices time into intervals of length $t$. For $\frac{t}{2}$ time units $\frac{m}{n_\tau}$ processors are assigned to each of $n_\tau$ jobs unfinished at time $\tau$ which is the beginning of time slice. For the remaining $\frac{t}{2}$ time units each job is assigned $m$ processors for time $\frac{t}{2n_\tau}$. Note that RR on all $m$ processors is in fact the gang scheduling policy known in parallel systems (cf. Sect. 3.3.1). It has been shown that $R_{HEQ} \leq 4 + 2\sqrt{3}$ for chains of tasks with nondecreasing sublinear or superlinear speedup. HEQ′ assigns to the jobs all processor numbers in the range $\frac{m}{n_\tau}$ and $m$ which are powers of 2. Allocating $i = 2^k$ processors to a job, $\frac{m}{i}$ jobs may be executed simultaneously, and $\frac{in_\tau}{m}$ repetitions are needed to execute all $n_\tau$ jobs. Hence, HEQ′ executes each job for $\frac{tm}{in_\tau \log n_\tau}$ time units on $i$ processors. It has been shown in [90] that $R_{HEQ′}$ is $O(\log n)$ for tasks with nondecreasing speedup. A problem with HEQ and HEQ′ is that the above competitiveness results were obtained under the assumption $t \to 0$, i.e. HEQ, HEQ′ need to preempt nearly continuously.

### 5.5.3  Other Heuristics for Malleable Task Scheduling

**Folding [194]**  When a new task $T_j$ arrives to the system, and there are some free processors $m′$, then $T_j$ receives all $m′$ processors. When $m′ = 0$, then task $T_b$ with the biggest processor allotment $i_b > 1$ is preempted and reconfigured to use $\lceil \frac{i_b}{2} \rceil$ processors. The remaining $\lfloor \frac{i_b}{2} \rfloor$ processors are granted to $T_j$. This operation is called folding. If no such $T_b$ task exists, then $T_j$ waits. When some processors are free, and waiting queue is empty, then the free processors are assigned to the task with the smallest processor allotment. The last operation is called unfolding.

**Dynamic Partitioning (DP) [191]**  This heuristic divides tasks into classes of small, medium, and large tasks as in MFP, MAP methods. Large tasks and medium tasks are assumed to be able to reconfigure themselves and shrink the used processor partition. Small tasks are not reconfigured. The tasks that may be requested to shrink the partition are held on the so-called *interruptible list*. After a reconfiguration of task $T_j$ it is removed from this list to avoid reconfiguration thrashing. When a new task $T_j$ of class $k \in \{s, m, l\}$ arrives an attempt is made to allocate for it $t_{appl} = \min\{req_j, \max\{min_k, \frac{m}{n}\}\}$ processors, where $req_j$ is the ideal number of processors requested by $T_j$, $min_k$ is the minimum allotment for tasks in class $k$, $m$ is the number of all processors, and $n$ is the number of all tasks $n$ (both waiting and running). If $t_{appl}$ processors are not available, then tasks on interruptible list are requested to decrease their processor allotment to $\frac{m}{n}$, provided that $\frac{m}{n} \geq min_l, \frac{m}{n} \geq min_m$, and that $t_{appl}$ processors can be collected at all. The processors released when some task is finished are assigned to the waiting tasks on the basis of FF rule. When some processors remain free for time longer than $M$, where $M$ is algorithm parameter, then tasks on interruptible list using less than $\frac{m}{n}$ processors are notified to increase their allotments.

**iScheduler** [232] is a framework constituted by several policies. *Admission policy* determines which applications will be running, which other should wait in FIFO queue. For example, exceeding a limit on the number of simultaneously running jobs may result in queuing the newly arrived jobs. *Harvesting policies* control the source of the processors for the new job. The processors are requested one by one from the running applications. For example, the processors can be requested from each application evenly, from the jobs running for the longest (or the shortest) time, or from the application with the biggest processor allotment. *Distribution policies* manage the processors released by the finished job. There are two main options: either assign the free processors to the running jobs first or to the waiting jobs first. The remaining processors (if any) may be assigned to the other set of jobs. *Control policies* rule the behavior of the iScheduler. For instance, it may be decided to protect new (or old) jobs from being harvested from the processors. To implement iScheduler it was proposed to establish a connection via API between the scheduler and the application. The scheduler should be able to instruct an application to incorporate a new processor, give back a processor, migrate from a processor to a processor, to accept information on the application requirements and costs of changing its scheduled configuration. Though providing such information is generally possible, it may require prior application benchmarking and deep understanding of the application performance determinants.

## 5.6 Tasks with Hypercube Shape

In this section, we examine scheduling parallel tasks with hypercube shape. Before proceeding with the presentation of scheduling on hypercubes, let us first remind the basic features of the interconnection. A hypercube with $m$ processors has $\log m$ dimensions. Nodes of a hypercube are numbered such that the binary representations of the neighboring nodes differ in exactly one bit. Each bit of this representation corresponds to one dimension of the hypercube. For example, to construct a path from one $P_i$ to node $P_j$ it is sufficient to route the path from node to node along the dimensions for which the bits in $i$ xor $j$ are nonzeros. Here xor is a bit-wise exclusive or on binary representations of processor addresses $i$ and $j$. Consequently, the diameter of hypercube is $\log m$. We will refer to hypercube of dimension $k$ as to $k$-cube. Words hypercube, cube will be used interchangeably.

A primary operation in scheduling task $T_j$ on a hypercube computer is selecting a cube with $2^{cube_j}$ processors. A simple solution is to use one of the subcubes with processor indices in ranges $[i2^{cube_j}, \ldots, (i + 1)2^{cube_j} - 1]$, for $i = 0, \ldots, \frac{m}{2^{cube_j}} - 1$. This will guarantee assignment to a subcube of dimension $cube_j$. The leading $(\log m) - cube_j$ bits are the same in the processor numbers. Subcubes of the above kind are called *normal* or *basic*. However, this is not the only possible way of allocating subcubes. More advanced algorithms searching for a free subcube are examined in Sect. 5.6.1. The algorithms presented in Sect. 5.6.2 and the following assume the use of basic subcubes. As we already noted the restriction to using only basic subcubes may blur the distinction between rigid tasks and task with hypercube shape.

### 5.6.1  Subcube Allocation

Here we present heuristics for online selecting a subcube of required dimension. A task requiring a subcube must be allocated the required network of processors before considering the next task, or be rejected (possibly deferred to a waiting queue). We start with this special case of the scheduling problem because the algorithms employed here in the greatest extent expose geometric features of the hypercube. Suppose a $k$-cube is required. The binary representation of processor index has $\log m$ bits. A $k$-cube has processors with $(\log m) - k$ the same bits in their indices, and $k$ bits taking all possible values. Since the positions of the $k$ bits can be arbitrary, there are $\binom{\log m}{k}$ different ways of fixing their positions, and $\binom{\log m}{k} \frac{m}{2^k}$ different, but not separate, $k$-cubes. The number of all such subcubes of different dimensions is $\sum_{k=0}^{\log m} \binom{\log m}{k} 2^{(\log m)-k} = 3^{\log m}$. If we restrict selections to the basic subcubes, then only $\frac{m}{2^k}$ $k$-cubes can be recognized. Thus, an important feature of subcube allocation algorithm is the ability to *recognize* as many subcubes as possible. This is related to the data structure storing information on available processors. The information on free processors can be stored in bit vectors, trees, or lists of available cubes.

Weak recognition ability of certain allocation algorithms should not be mixed with the external processor *fragmentation*. Fragmentation is a term from memory allocation technologies [144, 195, 214, 221]. *Internal fragmentation* arises when the resource is allocated in certain sizes. Here the number of assigned processors is rounded up to the nearest power of 2. If the task requests fewer processors then the difference between the requested size and the nearest power of 2 is the amount of internal fragmentation. In this section, we do not consider internal fragmentation because all tasks request processors in sizes which are powers of 2, and are supported by the allocation methods. In the case of *external fragmentation* the processor resource is divided into many small pieces which together constitute a big number of processors, but none of the pieces alone is big enough to accommodate the request of the arriving task. Consider, e.g., the task assignment in Fig. 5.16a. In this task

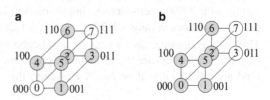

**Fig. 5.16** (a) Example of external fragmentation. (b) Example of weak recognition. Gray nodes are occupied

assignment there are two processors available, but 2-cube cannot be assigned to any task. On contrary in Fig. 5.16b we have a situation in which a cube allocation algorithm exploiting only basic cubes is not able to recognize a free subcube of size 2 on processors $P_3$, $P_7$. Resource fragmentation is a result of allocation, and deallocation of the subcubes. Inability to recognize a free subcube is a weakness of the allocation algorithm.

Another feature of subcube allocation algorithm is *static optimality*. Allocation strategy is said to be statically optimal if it can accommodate any sequence of $n$ subcube requests as long as $\sum_{j=1}^{n} 2^{cube_j} \leq m$. The consequences of deallocation are not considered. It can be proved that statically optimal allocation algorithm is also optimal under LIFO sequence of allocations and deallocations [88].

When the subcubes are released, then almost arbitrary pattern of processor availability may arise. Consequently, the problem of subcube allocation in the dynamic setting is much harder. It must be decided how the released subcubes are coalesced with other free subcubes. With subcube deallocations, the problem of finding subcube of certain size is **NP**-complete, and no online algorithm constructs the optimum allocations [88].

The complexity of cube allocation algorithm depends very much on the implementation and the used data structures. Data structures depend on the way of perceiving the cubes. The simplest data structure is a bit vector representing the free and the occupied processors. Sequential searching for one free processor may take $O(m)$ time in such a bit vector. Other data structures are lists and trees. Implementation issues influencing the allocation algorithm complexity are centralized vs. distributed management of the allocation, using, or not, the fast communication capabilities of the hypercube. By using the capabilities of a hypercube, subcube allocation may be reduced to time $O(\log m)$. Below we present several algorithms for hypercube allocation.

**Buddy Systems (See e.g. [54])** Basic subcubes are the building blocks of buddy systems in which scheduling controllers manage ranges of processor indices. A buddy system is a binary tree with $\log m$ levels (see Fig. 5.17). The root of the tree at level 0 manages all $m$ processors. The $m$ processors are divided into two halves, each associated with one of the root successor nodes. This corresponds to the

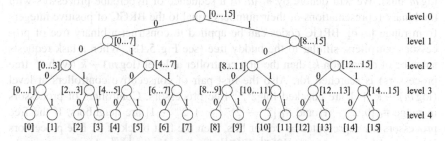

**Fig. 5.17** Buddy system with managed processor index ranges for $m = 16$

division into processors with the first index bit equal 0, and processors with the first index bit equal 1. Note that this matches a division along the first hypercube dimension. The division into the halves is recursively continued until level $\log m$, and each division corresponds to further dividing into processors with bits equal 0 or 1, in the following dimensions. Let $B(i)$ be the binary representation of number $i$. Binary codes used in buddy systems and BRGC defined in the following text are a way of mapping consecutive processor numbers $0, \ldots, 2^m - 1$ to their binary (i.e. hardware) representation. In other words, these are mappings from consecutive processor numbers to the locations in the hypercube. Let $\#_B[a, b]$ denote a sequence of hypercube processors with binary code representation of numbers from range $[a, b]$, i.e. $\#_B[a, b] = (B(a), \ldots, B(b))$. To allocate subcube of dimension $k$, controllers at level $(\log m) - k$ are checked for free processors. This means searching for the first free block of processors in ranges $\#_B[i2^k, \ldots, (i+1)2^k - 1]$, for $i = 0, \ldots, \frac{m}{2^k} - 1$. The processors of the first free controller are granted to the requesting task. If the free processors are recorded in a bit vector, then a sequence of $2^k$ consecutive "available" bits are searched for starting at positions $i2^k$, for $i = 0, \ldots, \frac{m}{2^k} - 1$. The first free block of bits is set to "occupied". When a task is finished, the previously allocated cube is returned to its position in the binary tree, or the availability bits are unset in the bit vector. An advantage of buddy systems is that index ranges correspond to subcubes, and finding some subcube is easy. Buddy system method is statically optimum. A disadvantage of buddy processor systems is weak subcube recognition, and consequently low utilization. Here the allocation is impossible if the free processors forming subcube of certain size are spread between different controllers. In the example in Fig. 5.16b the buddy system does not recognize a free subcube of size 2 on processors $P_3, P_7$.

**Gray Codes Systems [54, 55]** Gray codes can be defined in various ways [54]. One of the common definitions refers to the binary reflected Gray codes (BRGC): Let $G_k$ denote a sequence of BRGC on $k$ bits. It can be constructed recursively in the following way: $G_1 = (0, 1)$. If $G_k = (a_0, a_1, \ldots, a_{2^k-1})$, then $G_{k+1} = (a_0 0, a_0 1, a_1 1, a_1 0, a_2 0, a_2 1, \ldots, a_{2^k-1} 0)$, where $a_i 0, a_i 1$ denotes concatenation of code $a_i$ with bit values 0 and 1, respectively. For example: $G_2 = (00, 01, 11, 10), G_3 = (000, 001, 011, 010, 110, 111, 101, 100)$. Let $G(i)$ be the BRGC representation of number $i$ (in other words it is $i$th BRGC code on $\log m$ bits). We will denote by $\#_G[a, b]$ a sequence of hypercube processors with the binary representations of their numbers equal to the BRGC of positive integers from range $[a, b]$. BRGC codes can be applied to construct a binary tree of processor controllers, similar to the buddy tree (see Fig. 5.18). When a task requests subcube of dimension $k$, then the first controller at level $(\log m) - k$ (with $2^k$ free processors) is searched for. Also the first pair of consecutive controllers at level $(\log m) - k + 1$ are checked for $2^{k-1}$ free processors. Controllers of processors in range $\#_G[0, 2^k - 1]$ and $\#_G[2^m - 2^{k-1} - 1, 2^m - 1]$ are neighbors. If the free processors are represented as vector bits, then the first block of $2^k$ free processors is searched for in ranges $\#_G[i2^{k-1}, i2^{k-1}]$, for $i = 1, \ldots, \frac{\log m}{2^{k-1}}$. As a consequence of using BRGC, the number of recognized subcubes of dimension $k$ is $\frac{m}{2^{k-1}}$, which

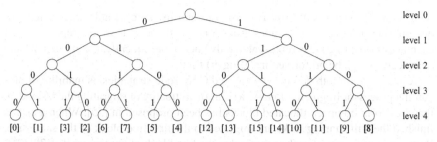

**Fig. 5.18** A binary tree for subcube allocation using BRGC for $m = 16$

is twice as many as in the buddy systems. When a task is finished, appropriate controller(s) switch to state "available", or in the case of bit vector, appropriate bits are unset to "available" value. BRGC strategy is statically optimal [54].

**Improved Binary Tree Systems** Notice that out of $\binom{\log m}{k} \frac{m}{2^k}$ $k$-cubes only $\frac{m}{2^k}$ can be recognized in a buddy system. Analogously, Gray code systems recognize only $\frac{m}{2^{k-1}}$ $k$-cubes. To overcome the weak recognition of free subcubes various extensions were proposed. Let us remind that processors constituting a subcube of dimension $k$ have $k$ bits different and $(\log m) - k$ bits equal. There may be various methods selecting the $(\log m) - k$ constant bits, and this was the way of improving subcube recognition. A change in the selection of these bits has one more interpretation. Observe that each level of the binary tree corresponds to the partition of the hypercube along one of the dimensions. Thus, different selection of constant/variable bits is equivalent to partitioning the hypercube in the binary tree along different dimensions.

In [3] an algorithm was proposed which searched for $2^{k-1}$-cubes adjacent to the cubes in processor ranges $\#_B[i2^{k-1}, \ldots, (i+1)2^{k-1} - 1]$, for $i = 0, \ldots, \frac{m}{2^{k-1}} - 1$ along dimensions $\log m - 1, \ldots, \log m - k + 1$ which allowed for recognizing $((\log m) - k + 1)\frac{m}{2^k}$ $k$-cubes. This has been further improved by shifting the positions of the constant bits $(\log m) - 1, \ldots, (\log m) - k + 1$ to the right, which increased the number of recognized $k$-cubes to $(k(\log m - k) + 1)\frac{m}{2^k}$.

A different way of selecting the $k$ variable bits is by the generalization of Gray codes. Other Gray codes than BRGC may be obtained, e.g., from BRGC by permutation of bits on certain positions [54]. This allows for recognizing different subcubes than in the BRGC. By using *multiple Gray codes* (MRGC) the ability of discovering available cubes is improved. It has been shown in [54] that at most $\binom{\log m}{\lfloor \frac{\log m}{2} \rfloor}$ different Gray codes are necessary to recognize all subcubes in $\log m$-cube. A similar approach was proposed in [62]. To verify all possible subcubes, all possible permutations of the variable and constant bits are checked at each request. The binary address encoding $B$ is the starting point for the permutations.

An algorithm improving the complexity of the Gray code system has been proposed in [209]. Instead of the full binary tree, only a partial tree is used which has branches leading only as deep as to the first free or busy cube. For each dimension $k$ two bidirectional lists of free $k$-cubes are constructed. List real[k] holds the pointers to the $k$-cubes at level $(\log m) - k$, and list $\text{ext}[k]$ holds the pointers to neighboring pairs of $(k-1)$-cubes at level $(\log m) - k + 1$. In this representation each free (or busy) cube is represented only once. Consequently, the allocations and deallocations can be preformed in $O(\log m)$ time.

A downside of both buddy systems, and Gray code strategies, is inability of preventing processor fragmentation. As a solution a strategy of migrating the tasks such that they form compact allocated blocks has been proposed in [55]. When a task is finished the still running tasks are migrated to the first free block of the same size. Precisely, a task using $k$-cube is moved to the free block of processors $\#_G[i\,2^k, i\,2^k]$, with minimum $i$. This can be done in arbitrary order because Gray code strategy is statically optimum. A shortest deadlock free routing for task migration is proposed in [55].

**Free Processor List Systems [88, 143, 202]** A different allocation method follows from other way of representing free cubes. The free cubes can be represented as lists of their addresses. In the $k$-cube address $(\log m) - k$ bits have values 0 or 1, and the $k$ bits in which $k$-cube processors' addresses differ are substituted with symbol "*" meaning "does not matter". See an example of processing a sequence of requests in Fig. 5.19. Here the problem of cube allocation is presented in a different light than in the buddy and BRGC systems. In the earlier two methods cube allocation is equivalent to searching in binary trees. They suffered from weak free cube recognition, severity of which could be alleviated by using different processor number coding schemes [3, 55]. When free cubes are represented by lists of addresses, it has to be decided from which free cube a requested subcube should be excised. When a cube is released, it must be decided with which adjacent cube it should be coalesced.

A good cube selection strategy should avoid processor fragmentation. A set of as big as possible free cubes should be preserved to meet the requests that may arrive in the future. Let $X$ and $Y$ be two sets of disjoint free cubes with the same total number of free processors in an $m$-cube. We will say that $X$ is greater than $Y$, when there exists size $k$ such that the number of $l$-cubes in $X$ and $Y$ is equal for $l = \log m, \ldots, k - 1$, and $X$ has more $k$-cubes than $Y$. A *maximal set of subcubes*

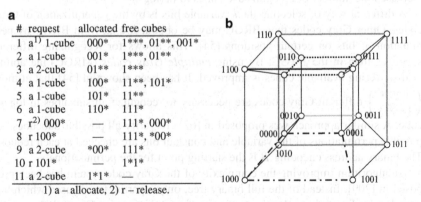

**a**

| # | request | allocated | free cubes |
|---|---------|-----------|------------|
| 1 | a[1] 1-cube | 000* | 1***, 01**, 001* |
| 2 | a 1-cube | 001* | 1***, 01** |
| 3 | a 2-cube | 01** | 1*** |
| 4 | a 1-cube | 100* | 11**, 101* |
| 5 | a 1-cube | 101* | 11** |
| 6 | a 1-cube | 110* | 111* |
| 7 | r[2] 000* | — | 111*, 000* |
| 8 | r 100* | — | 111*, *00* |
| 9 | a 2-cube | *00* | 111* |
| 10 | r 101* | — | 1*1* |
| 11 | a 2-cube | 1*1* | — |

1) a – allocate, 2) r – release.

**Fig. 5.19** Example of free cube list representation for $m = 16$. (**a**) Sequence of requests. (**b**) The resulting processor occupation. Thick edges mark the occupied cubes

(MSS) is a set of disjoint free cubes greater than other sets of disjoint free cubes in $\log m$-cube. MSS need not be unique. A good cube management strategy can be stated as maintaining the greatest MSS after every cube allocation and release. A request for $k$-cube can be processed by BF method assigning the smallest free $l$-cube such that $l \geq k$. A difficulty is maintaining the MSS after a cube release. To facilitate the management of free cubes a concept of *consensus graph* has been proposed in [88]. The nodes of the consensus graph are free cubes, and edges connect the nodes if the two cubes intersect, i.e. share some subset of processors. Construction of the MSS is equivalent to finding maximum independent set in the consensus graph, which is **NP**-hard [88]. In the worst case the construction of the MSS may require exponential time reconstruction of the current set of free cubes after a cube release. Thus, a released $k$-cube is coalesced by a greedy heuristic which works as long as increasing the number of $l$-cubes is possible, where $l \geq k$. Consequently, the set of free cubes is not guaranteed to be an MSS. To compensate for it, additional heuristic searching for a maximum independent set in the consensus graph is used if the allocation by BF fails.

The free processor list systems can be extended to noncubic requests, inclusion, and exclusion of processor sets in the allocation, as well as implemented to run in a distributed fashion [143]. Noncubic requests demand a number of processors which is not a power of 2. In this case a set of adjacent cubes can be assigned to the requesting tasks. The inclusion of certain processor sets is performed by allocating an overlapping cube, and deallocating the unneeded subcubes. The exclusion of (e.g. faulty) processors is done by permanent allocation of some dummy task to these processors. Other heuristics for cube management based on the free processor lists were published in [143,202].

**Lattice Systems [137]** Lattice representation of cubes has been proposed in [137]. Let $P_a, P_b$ be two processors of a hypercube with binary representation of the addresses $a_{m-1} \cdots a_1 a_0$, and $b_{m-1} \cdots b_1 b_0$, respectively. If $a_i \leq b_i$ for $i = 0, \ldots, m - 1$, then we will say that $P_a$ is less than or equal $P_b$, and we will denote it $P_a \trianglelefteq P_b$. Processor set $\mathcal{P}$ and relation $\trianglelefteq$ form a partially ordered set (poset), i.e. a reflexive, antisymmetric, transitive relation on the set of processors. A $glb(X, Y) = W$ in a poset is the greatest lower bound of elements $X, Y$. This means that $W \trianglelefteq X, W \trianglelefteq Y$, and there is no $E$ in the poset such that $W \trianglelefteq E \trianglelefteq X, W \trianglelefteq E \trianglelefteq Y$. A lowest upper bound of two elements $X, Y$ in the poset is $lub(X, Y) = Z$ such that $X \trianglelefteq Z, Y \trianglelefteq Z$, and there is no $E$ in the poset such that $X \trianglelefteq E \trianglelefteq Z, Y \trianglelefteq E \trianglelefteq Z$. A poset in which any pair of elements has a unique $lub$ and a unique $glb$ is called a *lattice*. Processors in a hypercube together with relation $\trianglelefteq$ form a lattice. A subcube can be represented by $lub$ and $glb$ of its processors. The set $[X, Y] = \{P_i : X \trianglelefteq P_i \trianglelefteq Y\}$ is a valid cube, provided that $X \trianglelefteq Y$. For example, in Fig. 5.20a cubes are shown in the lattice form, and their location in the hypercube is shown in Fig. 5.20b. The cube $[X, Y]$ can be equivalently represented by $X$ and bit-wise difference vector (BDV) equal to $X \texttt{xor} Y$. Observe that for cube $[X, Y]$ its representation by $X$ and the corresponding BDV is equivalent to the address of a cube used in the previous free cube list method [88]. For instance, $X = (0001)$, and BDV equal to $(1110)$ together define a cube $[0001, 1111]$ shown in Fig. 5.20, which is equivalent to a cube with the

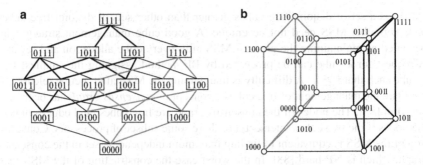

**Fig. 5.20** (**a**) Lattice view of cubes [0001, 1111], and [0000, 1110]. (**b**) Geometric view. Thick lines mark subcubes

address $***1$ used in the MSS method. Processor with address $X$ is the controller of subcube defined by $X$ and the corresponding BDV. The information about the partition into a subcube is held in a distributed manner by the controllers $X$ of the hypercube. When a $k$-cube is requested the smallest free $l$-cube, where $l \geq k$, is searched for, e.g., by broadcasting the requested size in the hypercube. If $l = k$, then the cube is assigned to the requesting task. If $l > k$, then $l$-cube is split into $j$-cubes of sizes $j = l - 1, \ldots, k$, and finally one of the two $k$-cubes is assigned to the requesting task. The process of splitting the $l$-cube initially represented by $X$ and BDV $U$ recursively defines two subcubes: one with controller $X$ and one with controller $W = X \operatorname{or}(U \operatorname{and} U')$. $U'$ is two's complement of $U$, binary operators or, and are bit-wise AND, OR. Notice that $(U \operatorname{and} U')$ has all bits equal to 0 with the exception of the least significant bit of $U$ equal 1. For example, if $U = 01010$, then $U' = 10110, U \operatorname{and} U' = 00010$. In other words, if $a$ is the first bit equal 1 in $U$, then $W$ has bit $a$ equal 1, and $X$ has bit $a$ equal 0. The BDV vectors of both subcubes are $Q = U \operatorname{and} (\overline{U \operatorname{and} U'})$. In other words, the previously defined bit $a$ equal 1 in $U$ is set to 0 in $Q$. The allocation can be completed in $O(\log m)$ time. This algorithm is statically optimal [137].

When the cube defined by $X$, and the corresponding BDV $U$ is released, its controller at address $X$ performs coalescing procedure. The procedure joins only adjacent cubes, and only increasing cube sizes is allowed. This is accompanied by appropriate calculation of the BDV of the coalesced cube. When the controller finds a free subcube (of the same size) with controller $K$ adjacent along dimension $i$, then intermediate BDV of the coalesced cube is set to $NU = (X \operatorname{xor} K) \operatorname{or} U$. This means that since $X$ and $K$ are neighbors along dimension $i$, then bit $i$ is set to 1 in the new BDV. This procedure is repeated iteratively over all possible dimensions for each intermediate subcube. Hence, the complexity of the coalescing procedure is $O(\log^2 m)$. The controller of the coalesced cube has address $(X \operatorname{and} \overline{NU})$ and BDV equal to $NU$.

It should not be forgotten that even the best cube allocation algorithm alone cannot guarantee good performance. The processor resource fragmentation depends on the sequence of cube requests and deallocations. Hence, there is a need for proper task sequencing. It has been demonstrated that utilization of the hypercube processors is very low, and differs only marginally for various allocation systems if the tasks are serviced in FIFO order. Moreover, insufficient free subcube recognition can be overcome by using a good scheduling strategy [153].

## 5.6.2   $C_{\max}$, $L_{\max}$ Criteria

In this, and in the following sections, basic cubes are used rather than the advanced cube allocation methods described in the previous section. In contrast, task sequencing and the duration of the tasks are taken into account.

### 5.6.2.1   Nonpreemptive Schedules, Heuristics with a Guarantee

The results on approximability of scheduling tasks with hypercube shape are collected in Table 5.12. The original names of the heuristics proposed in [247] and [51] are Largest Dimension First (LDF) and Largest Dimension Largest Processing Time (LDLPT), respectively. These names have been substituted by previously used names Nonincreasing Size (NIS), NonIncreasing Size Longest Processing Time (NISLPT), respectively. Other heuristics listed in Table 5.12 are outlined below.

**A–B [158]** We name this algorithm after its two subalgorithms A,B solving two cases of the problem. Tasks are scheduled on normal subcubes only. Let $\mathcal{T}_x$ be a subset of tasks with processing time $p_j \geq x p_{\max}$, where $0 < x < 1$, $p_{\max} = \max_{j \in \mathcal{T}}\{p_j\}$. Let $\mathcal{D}_x = \sum_{j \in \mathcal{T}_x} cube_j$. Algorithm A is applied when $\mathcal{D}_{1-\varepsilon} < \frac{m}{2}$, otherwise algorithm B is applied. Here $0 < \varepsilon < 1$ is some constant.

Algorithm A schedules tasks in $\mathcal{T}_{1-\varepsilon}$ according to the nonincreasing sizes (i.e. using NIS, or LDF rule) on processors in index range $[0, \mathcal{D}_{1-\varepsilon}-1]$. The tasks remaining in $\mathcal{T} - \mathcal{T}_{1-\varepsilon}$ are scheduled according to the nonincreasing sizes using processors in index range $[0, \mathcal{D}_{1-\varepsilon} - 1]$ starting from time $p_{\max}$ and on processors with indices in range $[\mathcal{D}_{1-\varepsilon}, m - 1]$ starting from time 0. The subcube available at the earliest time is used. Algorithm A has the worst-case performance guarantee bounded from above by $(2 - \frac{\varepsilon}{2})$ and $(1 + \frac{\varepsilon}{2(1-\varepsilon)})$ in two different cases.

**Table 5.12**   Approximability of scheduling tasks with hypercube shape

| Problem | Result | Reference |
|---|---|---|
| $P\,|cube_j|\,C_{\max}$ | $R_{NISLPT} = 2 - \frac{2}{m}$ | [51] |
| $P\,|cube_j|\,C_{\max}$ | $R_{NIS} = 2 - \frac{1}{m}$ | [247] |
| $P\,|oll, cube_j|\,C_{\max}$ | $R_{NIS} > \frac{1+\sqrt{6}}{2}$ | [247] |
| $P\,|cube_j, \neg p_j|\,C_{\max}$ | $R_{NIS} = 2 - \frac{1}{m}$ | [103] |
| $Pm\,|cube_j|\,C_{\max}$ | FPTAS | [146] |
| $P\,|cube_j|\,C_{\max}$ | $R_{A-B} = \frac{15}{8}$ | [158] |
| $P\,|olt, cube_j, \neg p_j, p_j(i) = \frac{p(1)}{i}, prec|\,C_{\max}$ | $R_{HC} \sim O(\frac{\log m}{\log\log m})$ | [102] |
| $P\,|cube_j, NdSub|\,C_{\max}$ | $R_{KG} = 3$ | [149] |
| $P\,|cube_j, p_j = 1, \neg prec|\,C_{\max}$ | $R_{NIS} = 2 - \frac{1}{m}$ | [26] |

Algorithm B first builds set $\mathcal{T}'$ of tasks by checking and appending tasks $T_j$ one by one in the order of nonincreasing processing time, as long as the sum of the sizes does not exceed $m$, and $p_j \geq \frac{p_{\max}}{2}$. Tasks in $\mathcal{T}'$ are scheduled in the order of nonincreasing sizes on processors with indices $[0, \sum_{j \in \mathcal{T}'} cube_j - 1]$ starting at time 0. Then, algorithm B considers the tasks in $\mathcal{T} - \mathcal{T}'$ according to their nonincreasing sizes (NIS), and attempts to schedule them on processors with indices in range $[\sum_{j \in \mathcal{T}'} cube_j, m - 1]$ in interval $[0, p_{\max}]$. If it is not possible for certain task $T_j$, then it is moved to set $\mathcal{T}''$. Tasks remaining in $\mathcal{T}''$ are scheduled according to NIS rule on processors in range $[0, m - 1]$ starting from time $p_{\max}$. It has been proved that the performance guarantee of B is bounded by $\frac{7+2\varepsilon}{4}$. For $\varepsilon = \frac{1}{4}$ the bounds of algorithms A and B together give performance guarantee $\frac{15}{8}$.

**Hypercube Heuristic (HC) [102]** This algorithm requires task moldability (in [102] called virtualization), and linear speedup. Thus, a task may be assigned a smaller subcube than required. HC partitions the tasks into classes according to their sizes. It also partitions the hypercube into subcubes dedicated to each of the task classes. A *k-dimensional normal subcube* is a set of processors which have all but the first $k$ coordinates fixed (due to the symmetry of hypercube it can be any fixed set of $k$ coordinates). Let $h$ be the smallest power of 2 such that $h \log h \geq \log m$. Partition tasks into at most $h$ classes $\mathcal{T}_i = \{T_j : \log m - i \log h + 1 \leq cube_j \leq \log m - (i - 1) \log h\}$. Partition the hypercube into at most $h$ normal subcubes $HC_1, \ldots, HC_h$ of dimension $(\log m - \log h)$. Tasks from class $\mathcal{T}_i$ are scheduled on $HC_i$ only, using a subcube of dimension $\log m - i \log h$. Note that in class $\mathcal{T}_i$, task sizes are reduced to $\log m - i \log h$.

**Krishnamurti and Gaur Heuristic (KG) [149]** It is a heuristic for tasks moldable tasks with nondecreasing sublinear speedup, and hypercube shape. The set of admissible task sizes $X_j$ contains only powers of 2. Hence, tasks can be considered moldable tasks with hypercube shape. A lower bound $i_{\min}$ on processor allotment is given. Tasks are assigned minimum number of processors first, and then scheduled according to the LPT rule. If some processors are free and schedule length is determined by a single long task, then its allotment is doubled, and the procedure is repeated. Thus, KG is a modification of Part_Schedule heuristic [16] presented in Sect. 5.4.1.1.

### 5.6.2.2  Preemptive Schedules

Complexity results on preemptive scheduling tasks with hypercube shape are collected in Table 5.13.

$P \,|\, cube_j, pmtn \,|\, C_{\max}$

The algorithms for preemptive scheduling on hypercubes were gradually improved in articles [2, 50, 119, 212, 247]. Early algorithms verified existence of a feasible

**Table 5.13**  Polynomially solvable cases for scheduling tasks with hypercube shape, $C_{max}$, $L_{max}$ criteria

| Problem | Result | Reference |
|---|---|---|
| $P\,|cube_j, pmtn\,|C_{max}$ | $O(n^2 \log^2 m)$ | [212, 247] |
| $Q\,|cube_j, pmtn\,|C_{max}$ | $O(n \log n + nm)$ | [78] |
| $P, win\,|cube_j, pmtn\,|C_{max}$ | $O(n(k + \log m)m \log m)$ | [27] |
| $P\,|cube_j, pmtn, r_j, d_j\,|-$ | $poly(n, m)$ | [196] |

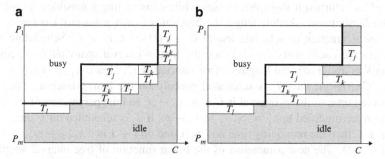

**Fig. 5.21**  (a) Stair-like pattern. (b) Pseudo-stair pattern

schedule for a given schedule length $C$ [2, 50, 119]. We present them first. Tasks are scheduled according to the nonincreasing size, i.e. $cube_1 \geq cube_2 \geq \cdots \geq cube_n$. While scheduling the tasks so-called *stair-like* pattern arises in the profile of processor availability (see Fig. 5.21). Steps in stair-like pattern are called *p*-intervals. *p*-interval $i$ has certain width which follows from the range of processor indices $[a, b]$ it represents, and time moment $\tau(i)$ when all processors of the *p*-interval become idle. In stair-like pattern $\tau(i)$ is nonincreasing in *p*-interval index $i$. The feasibility testing algorithm schedules tasks consecutively. Suppose $T_j$ is about to be scheduled, and $l$ is the last *p*-interval (step). If $C - \tau(l) < p_j$, then the algorithm returns answer "infeasible". Otherwise, task $T_j$ is scheduled starting from the first *p*-interval until filling the time interval $[\tau(i), C]$ completely [50]. If $C - \tau(i) > p_j$, then the remaining part of $T_j$ is assigned on the following *p*-intervals. If the last used *p*-interval is filled only partially by $T_j$, then this part of $T_j$ is shifted to the left such that the remaining processor availability pattern is also a stair-like (Fig. 5.21a). A *p*-interval may be split if the assigned task $T_j$ requires fewer processors than the width of the *p*-interval. This results in $O(n)$ preemptions for a single task, and $O(n^2)$ complexity of the algorithm verifying feasibility of a schedule with length $C$. The number of preemptions has been reduced to $O(n)$ and the complexity of the feasibility verifying to $O(n(\log n + \log m))$ in [119, 212]. Instead of starting the assignment on the first free *p*-interval, the last such that $p_j \geq C - \tau(i)$ is used (Fig. 5.21b). If $p_j = C - \tau(i)$, then $T_j$ fills the *p*-interval completely. Otherwise, the remaining $T_j$ part of length $C - \tau(i)$ is assigned to the next *p*-interval starting as early as possible. The resulting pattern of processor availability is no longer a stair-like pattern. It is called pseudo-stair pattern. Pseudo-stair pattern is equivalent to stair-like pattern in the sense of the length of free intervals and width of the $p$-intervals. Information on free intervals in pseudo-stair pattern may be searched and updated in $O(\log m)$ time using tree-like data structures. Feasibility testing algorithms can be applied in binary search to find optimum schedule length with some given accuracy.

Algorithms determining schedule length directly were proposed in [212, 247]. A vital observation is that in the optimum schedule there exists a task $T_j$ using the entire time on the longest $p$-interval which existed when $T_j$ was scheduled. The above feasibility testing algorithms [119, 212] may be extended such that answer "found" is returned if this event occurs while constructing a feasible schedule. To establish minimum schedule length the free time of each $p$-interval $i$ is represented as a linear function of schedule length $C - \tau(i) = Cx_i + y_i$. Scheduling tasks modifies the coefficients $x_i, y_i$. When the first $p$-interval spans all $m$ processors (no task is assigned), the length of free interval is $C$. Hence $x_1 = 1, y_1 = 0$. If $p_j < Cx_1 + y_1$, then $T_j$ is scheduled entirely on the first $p$-interval. Then, the remaining time of the $p$-interval is $Cx_1 + y_1 - p_j$ and the parameters of the linear function are modified to $x_1' = x_1, y_1' = y_1 - p_j$. If $T_j$ is scheduled on $p$-intervals $i$, and $i + 1$, then the remaining time on $i$ is 0, and on $i + 1$ is $Cx_{i+1} + y_{i+1} - (p_j - (Cx_i + y_i))$. The new parameters of the linear function of free interval length on $i + 1$ are $x_{i+1}' = x_{i+1} + x_i, y_{i+1}' = y_{i+1} + y_i - p_j$. In the following we describe the algorithm from [247]. When $T_j$ is scheduled it is first checked if it should be executed on the first (the shortest) $p$-interval, by checking feasibility for $C = \frac{p_j - y_1}{x_1}$. If the answer is "infeasible", then schedule must be longer. Consequently, in the longer schedule with length $C' > C$ we will have $C'x_1 + y_1 > p_j$ and $T_j$ will be indeed scheduled on the first $p$-interval. If the answer is "found" then the schedule length is optimum, and the algorithm stops. The schedule has been built by the feasibility testing algorithm. If the answer is "feasible", then schedule is too long. After reducing schedule length to $C' < C$ task $T_j$ will not be schedulable on the first $p$-interval, and it must be executed on some $p$-interval $i > 1$. The proper $p$-interval $i$ is binary searched. If $Cx_i + y_i < p_j < Cx_{i+1} + y_{i+1}$, then $T_j$ is scheduled on a pair $(i, i + 1)$ of $p$-intervals. The feasibility testing algorithm is run for $C = \frac{p_j - y_i}{x_i}$. If the answer is "infeasible", then schedule must be longer and $T_j$ is scheduled at most on $p$-interval $i$. If the answer is "found", then the algorithm stops. If the answer is "feasible", then the schedule must be shorter, and $T_j$ is scheduled on $p$-interval greater than $i$. Sorting the tasks according to $cube_j$ is done once in $O(n \log n)$ time. One feasibility test lasts $O(n \log m)$ time. Binary search for the right $p$-interval has at most $O(\log m)$ iterations (for $n > m$). The complexity of the algorithm is $O(n^2 \log^2 m)$.

$P|cube_j, pmtn, r_j, d_j|-$ [196]

The stair-like schedule structure can be used in verifying whether a feasible schedule for tasks with ready times and deadlines exists. Let $e_0 < e_1 < \cdots < e_l$ be the events in the task system, i.e. ready times, and deadlines sorted according to the increasing time value. Tasks are ordered according to the nonincreasing $cube_j$. Basic subcubes are numbered according to the increasing ranges of comprised processor indices. We will denote by $Co(j, f_j)$ the set of basic subcubes which could be used by some tasks from $\{T_1, \ldots, T_{j-1}\}$ and which include basic subcube $f_j$ of dimension $cube_j$. In other words $Co(j, f_j) = \{(j', f_{j'}) : (j' < j) \wedge ((f_{j'} - 1)2^{cube_{j'}} - 1 < f_j 2^{cube_j} - 1 \leq f_{j'} 2^{cube_{j'}} - 1)\}$. Variable $x_{ijk}$ will denote the fraction of task $T_j$ executed on basic subcube $i$ of size $cube_j$ between time moments $e_{k-1}$ and $e_k$. Verifying existence of a feasible schedule can be reduced to a linear program:

$$x_{ijk} = 0 \quad \text{for } j = 1, \ldots, n, \; e_k < r_j, \; i = 1, \ldots, \frac{m}{2^{cube_j}} \qquad (5.24)$$

$$x_{ijk} = 0 \quad \text{for } j = 1, \ldots, n, \; e_{k-1} \geq d_j, \; i = 1, \ldots, \frac{m}{2^{cube_j}} \qquad (5.25)$$

$$\sum_{i=1}^{\frac{m}{2^{cube_j}}} x_{ijk} \leq e_k - e_{k-1} \quad \text{for } j = 1, \ldots, n, \; k = 1, \ldots, l \qquad (5.26)$$

$$\sum_{j=1}^{n} x_{1jk} \leq e_k - e_{k-1} \quad \text{for } k = 1, \ldots, l \qquad (5.27)$$

$$\sum_{k=1}^{l} \sum_{i=1}^{\frac{m}{2^{cube_j}}} x_{ijk} = p_j \quad \text{for } j = 1, \ldots, n \qquad (5.28)$$

$$x_{ijk} + \sum_{j' < j} \sum_{(a,b) \in Co(j,i)} x_{bak} \leq \sum_{j' < j} \sum_{(a,b) \in Co(j,\bar{i})} x_{bak}$$

$$\text{for } j = 1, \ldots, n, \; k = 1, \ldots, l, \; i = 1, \ldots, \frac{m}{2^{cube_j}}, \; \bar{i} < i \qquad (5.29)$$

In the above linear program equations (5.24), (5.25) guarantee that tasks are executed in the interval between respective ready times and deadlines. No task is executed in interval $[e_{k-1}, e_k]$ longer that the interval length by (5.26). Inequalities (5.27) together with (5.29) ensure that in interval $[e_{k-1}, e_k]$ no processor works longer than the interval length. Note that the first $p$-interval in the staircase pattern has the latest completion time. Hence, $\sum_{j=1}^{n} x_{1jk}$ is the biggest load of any cube of size $cube_j$ in interval $[e_{k-1}, e_k]$. Tasks are fully executed by (5.28). To preserve stair-like schedule, processors of basic subcube $i$ of dimension $cube_j$ are allowed to process tasks $T_1, \ldots, T_{j-1}, T_j$, only if the lower indexed subcubes of dimension $d_j$ also process tasks $T_1 \ldots, T_{j-1}$. This is guaranteed by (5.29). In fact, the above algorithm is not polynomial. Though it is polynomial in $n$ and $m$, the dimension of the hypercube is $\log m$, which can be recorded in $O(\log \log m)$ bits.

$Q|cube_j, pmtn|C_{\max}$ [30, 78], $P, win|cube_j, pmtn|C_{\max}$ [27]

Phrase $P, win$ denotes identical processors available in restricted time windows. The problem of preemptive scheduling tasks requiring power of 2 processors, on processors with different speeds, has been considered in a sequence of papers. The technique for scheduling rigid task on uniform processor from [30] has been extended in [78] to tasks requiring $2^{cube_j}$ processors. It has been assumed that processors form $\Delta$-stripes of equal speed, where $\Delta = \max_j\{2^{cube_j}\}$. The methods from [30, 78] can be extended to processors with arbitrary speed, provided that tasks are assigned to basic subcubes only, and the slowest processor in the subcube determines speed of executing the task. Tasks are scheduled according to the nonincreasing dimension $cube_j$ and nonincreasing processing time $p_j$ (NISLPT). Let $PC_i^l = Cb_i^l$ denote processing capacity of $i$th basic subcube of size $l$, where $l$ is a power of 2 for a schedule of length $C$. Initially $C$ is set to a lower bound on schedule length following from processing requirements of tasks and speed of the processors. Processing capacities of the subcubes change as a result of assigning the tasks. When it comes to scheduling tasks in set $T^l$ where $l = 2^k, k = \log m, \ldots, 0$, inequalities (5.8) and (5.9) must be satisfied. In [30,78] a method for scheduling tasks has been applied which maximizes the right side of inequalities (5.8) and (5.9), and keeps them invariant. This means that if (5.8) and (5.9) are satisfied when it comes to scheduling tasks in $T^l$, then (5.8) and (5.8) are satisfied until assigning all tasks in $T^l$. Scheduling of task $T_j$ with size $l = 2^{cube_j}$ is done as follows. Basic subcubes are ordered according to nonincreasing processing capacities. Find a pair of basic subcubes $i, i + 1$ such that $PC_{i+1}^l < p_j \leq PC_i^l$. Calculate time moment $\tau$ such that $T_j$ is executed on $(i + 1)$th basic subcube in interval $[0, \tau]$, and $i$th basic subcube in interval $[\tau, C]$. Combine the two subcubes into a composite subcube $i$ with processing capacity $PC_i^{l'} = PC_i^l + PC_{i+1}^l - p_j$, and remove $(i + 1)$th subcube from the data structure holding information on free subcubes. Notice that in the boundary cases it may happen that $\tau = C$, or that $i$ is the last subcube, i.e. with the smallest processing capacity. In the latter case we assume $PC_{i+1}^l = 0$. If inequalities (5.8) and (5.9), are not satisfied when it comes to scheduling tasks in $T^l$, then schedule must be lengthened by some time. Let $DP_j^l$ denote the amount of processing time by which one of the inequalities (5.8) is violated for some task $T_j$. The schedule must be extended by $C' = \frac{DP_j^l}{\sum_{i \in \mathcal{P}'} b_i}$, where $\mathcal{P}'$ is the set of processors which really contribute their processing power to remove $DP_j^l$. It is hard to predict $\mathcal{P}'$ because its content depends on the way of scheduling tasks $T_1, \ldots, T_{j-1}$. This may further change as a result of lengthening the schedule, because processing capacities grow, and different subcubes may be selected for $T_1, \ldots, T_{j-1}$ then before the lengthening. In [78] an algorithm with complexity $O(n \log n + nm)$ has been proposed which uses special data structures to trace which processors will contribute to the reduction of $DP_j^l$. In [27] conceptually simpler method has been proposed, but for identical processors. The number $m'$ of processors in $\mathcal{P}'$ is in range $[1, m]$. Hence, binary search over $[1, m]$ and verifying existence of schedules with extensions $C' = \frac{DP_j^l}{m'}$ suffices to find the shortest feasible schedule. This resulted in an algorithm with complexity $O(n(k + \log m)m \log m)$, where $k$ is the number of time windows of processor availability. The same reasoning can be applied in the case of uniform processors by applying binary search over denominators of $C'$ in range $[1, \sum_{i=1}^{m} b_i^l]$.

**Table 5.14** Polynomially solvable cases for scheduling tasks with hypercube shape, minsum criteria

| Problem | Result | Reference |
|---|---|---|
| $P\,|cube_j, p_j = 1|\sum w_j c_j$ | $O(n \log n + n \log m)$ | [84] |

### 5.6.3 Minsum Criteria

A polynomially solvable case of scheduling tasks with hypercube shape for minsum criterion is shown in Table 5.14.

$$P\,|cube_j, p_j = 1|\sum w_j c_j \text{ [84]}$$

In the optimum solution for this problem, the first time unit of the schedule is occupied by a processor feasible set of tasks $PFS_1$ with the biggest total weight, and sum of sizes not greater than $m$. The second time unit of the schedule is occupied by the tasks with the biggest total weight in $T - PFS_1$ and sizes not exceeding $m$. This reasoning may be repeated for the following time units of the schedule. Thus, the optimum schedule is a sequence of processor feasible sets of size at most $m$ ordered according to the nonincreasing weights of the tasks. The sequence for size $m$ may be constructed from the sequence of size $\frac{m}{2}$ and $m$-tasks. We start the reasoning for the construction from $m = 1$. The sequence of 1-processor wide PFSes ordered from the heaviest to the lightest is constructed by sorting 1-tasks according to nonincreasing $w_j$. The sequence for 2-processor PFSes can be obtained by merging the sequence of 2-tasks ordered according to the nonincreasing weight and pairs of 1-task wide PFSes. This reasoning may be repeated for increasing task sizes. Finally, the sequence for $m$-processor wide PFSes is obtained by merging the sequence of $m$ tasks ordered according to the nonincreasing weight with the sequence of pairs of $\frac{m}{2}$-processor wide PFSes ordered from the heaviest to the lightest. The complexity of the algorithm is $O(n \log n + n \log m)$.

### 5.6.4 Other Heuristics for Tasks with Hypercube Shape

In this section, we present methods which have no analytical performance guarantees, but turned out to be effective in experimental evaluation. They were designed to achieve more goals than optimizing only the classic makespan or mean completion time criteria. Other performance measures like utilization, number of rejected tasks, resource availability, or slowdown, were also considered.

**Scan [152, 153]** Scan heuristics maintain $(\log m) + 1$ queues, one for each possible cube size. An arriving task $T_j$ joins the queue for size $cube_j$. The scheduler executes all the tasks in one queue before proceeding to the queue with the tasks of the next size. Thus, a Scan heuristic clusters tasks of the same size allowing for easier and more efficient packing of the hypercube. For such homogeneous requests hypercube may be packed without fragmentation. Four types of Scan heuristics were proposed [153]: *ScanUp* proceeds in the direction of increasing cube sizes. After queue $i$ (for the requests of $cube_j = i$), queue $(i + 1)$ mod $(\log m)$ is served. ScanDown proceeds in the direction of decreasing sizes. If certain size $k$ tasks keep arriving while queue $k$ is being served, then the other size requests may starve. To compensate for possible starvation, ScanUpSF (Starvation Free) and ScanDownSF were designed which serve only the tasks waiting in a queue at the time of switching to this queue. The $k$-cube requests arriving during serving queue $k$ must wait for the next scan of the queues by the algorithm. In a series of computational experiments [153] Scan heuristics with simple buddy allocation outperformed FIFO task sequencing even if advanced allocation methods based on free processor lists heuristically building maximum sets of subcubes were used. The effect of precedence constraints and task priorities on mean flow time (among the other criteria) has been studied in [152]. It has been empirically demonstrated that the performance of Scan heuristics is affected less than the performance of FIFO. Out of the four types of Scan heuristics ScanUp on average built the schedules with the smallest mean flow time [153].

It has been observed [187] that Scan heuristics work well when task processing times are roughly equal. In such cases the hypercube contains tasks of almost the same size which reduces fragmentation. If task processing times have wide distribution, then different task sizes may be executed simultaneously. Then, allocation and deallocation of different cube sizes may incur fragmentation anyway. Another disadvantage of Scan may be discrimination against cube size. When certain size is dominating in the input requests, then tasks of other sizes must wait until the tasks with the popular size are finished. Thus, the tasks with rare size may wait for processing longer than the tasks with the dominating size.

**Lazy Scheduling [187]** In static hypercube partitioning the $(\log m)$-cube is partitioned into one $((\log m) - 1)$-cube, one $((\log m) - 2)$-cube, ..., one 1-cube, and two 0-cubes. Tasks requiring certain cube dimensions from range $(\log m) - 1, \ldots, 0$ are assigned to the FIFO queues of the required dimension, and executed on the cube dedicated to the requested dimension. Though static partitioning is simple to implement, and in some circumstances can be effective [187], it may result in poor system utilization and long task waiting times when certain cube requests are very common, and some other are nearly nonexistent.

The lazy scheduling scheme is a modification of static hypercube partitioning designed to overcome the above drawback. For each possible cube size $k$, variable $N_k$ denotes the number of currently allocated $k$-cubes. Initially $N_k = 0$. It is incremented by one when $k$-cube is allocated, and decremented when $k$-cube is released. If the number of tasks waiting in the queue exceeds $N_k$ then it is an indicator that tasks requesting $k$-cubes should be provided more servers. In such a case a new $k$-cube is allocated using buddy system for the tasks from queue $k$. Under certain conditions, tasks of some sizes may starve. To eliminate possibility of starvation another mechanism is used. A task $T_j$ waiting longer than a threshold $d^2(t)\lambda$ is given the highest priority, where $\lambda$ is the task arrival rate and $d(t)$ is the average task queue waiting time. All new assignments of cubes to the tasks are suspended until $T_j$ is scheduled.

In a series of simulations FIFO, Scan, and lazy scheduling have been compared [187]. Scan and lazy scheduling heuristics have much better performance in terms of task waiting time, system utilization, throughput, than FIFO. Yet, lazy scheduling performs better than Scan when task processing times have big variability.

**Buddy/RT and Stacking [9]** These algorithms are dedicated to preemptive on-line scheduling of tasks with deadlines. Buddy/RT extends buddy allocation scheme (Sect. 5.6.1) by maintaining a vector of the earliest availability times (EAT) for each processor. When a new task $T_j$ arrives, then the first subcube with EAT smaller than $d_j - p_j$ is searched for. If found, $T_j$ is scheduled on the selected cube. Otherwise, if the laxity of $T_j$ is greater than the worst-case execution time of the second phase, then the algorithm initiates its second phase. Task laxity is the time remaining to its latest feasible start time. At the arrival $T_j$ laxity is $d_j - r_j - p_j$. If the laxity is too small to initiate the second phase of the algorithm, then $T_j$ is rejected. In the second phase the scheduler tries to reschedule both the currently running tasks and the newly arrived $T_j$. In rescheduling the same algorithm is applied as in the first phase, but tasks are considered in EDD order. If any job cannot meet its deadline, then the current task $T_j$ is rejected. If the rescheduling ends with success, then the new schedule is adopted, and the currently running tasks may be preempted and migrated.

Stacking algorithm tries to minimize fragmentation. When scheduling a request for a $k$-cube it is not using the first available $k$-cube that allows to meet the deadline. Instead, it selects the smallest $h$-cube, where $h \geq k$, and among the equal size $h$-cubes, the one with the smallest EAT. Furthermore, EAT is recorded at cube level in the buddy tree. For each processor the dimension of the last allocated task is recorded which allows for re-using the processors and cubes for the tasks of same dimension.

**Deferred Earliest Deadline First (DEDF) [186]** is an online scheduling discipline for preemptive scheduling tasks with deadlines. Preemption is not a priori planned when scheduling a task as in the algorithms presented in Sect. 5.6.2. It is exploited as the last resort if some task cannot meet its deadline.

Buddy/RT and stacking algorithms schedule tasks immediately as they arrive. DEDF algorithm defers starting of the task until its latest starting time which allows for collecting information. For example, immediate starting task $T_1$ with late deadline may prevent feasible execution of some other task $T_2$ with earlier deadline $d_2 < d_1$, but arriving after $T_1$ ($r_2 > r_1$). In DEDF the new tasks are queued in the arrival queue (AQ). Execution of DEDF is driven by two types of events: exceeding the size of AQ or reaching time greater or equal to $\min_j\{d_j - p_j\} - S_\tau$, where $\min_j\{d_j - p_j\}$ is the first latest starting time of any task, $S_\tau$ is an average task length at time $\tau$. Thus, scheduling operation is triggered $S_\tau$ units of time ahead of the moment when the first task has to be started. This is motivated by a belief that after $S_\tau$ the needed subcube will become available. When the conditions trigger DEDF to run, all tasks from AQ are scheduled according to the increasing values of their deadlines. DEDF uses binary tree as in buddy allocation, but a list of available time windows (ATW) is attached at each tree node representing free time intervals of the subcubes. This has an advantage over EAT because it allows for scheduling tasks in free time intervals before the already made reservations. Also queues with time reservations are maintained for the tasks which execution has already been planned. For a certain task being scheduled the first available subcube is searched for using the ATWs. If the subcube cannot be found, and laxity is sufficient, the algorithm tries to reschedule the currently running tasks, i.e. preempt them, build a new schedule including the new task, and migrate the tasks. It has been shown in a series of computational experiments that DEDF has a smaller ratio of rejected tasks than buddy/RT and stacking.

## 5.7 Tasks with Mesh Shape

This section is dedicated to scheduling parallel tasks with mesh shape. Let us observe that scheduling tasks with mesh shape involves packing one-, two-, or more dimensional objects in the one-, two-, or more dimensional mesh networks of the processors. Therefore, scheduling the tasks with mesh shape is computationally hard not only due to the matching of task processing times and the number of required processors, but also by the hardness of packing task shapes. Consequently, it is hard to expect nontrivial polynomial cases, and the algorithms presented in this section are mostly heuristics. Therefore, we depart here from the presentation of the algorithms along the optimality criteria for which they were constructed. The three types of heuristics are presented in this section: online allocation heuristics, scheduling heuristics for $C_{max}$ criterion with performance guarantee, scheduling heuristics experimentally tested against various criteria.

### 5.7.1 Submesh Allocation

In this section, we present online methods of allocating submeshes requested by the arriving tasks. As in Sect. 5.6.1, the requested submesh must be allocated before considering the next task. In the case of allocation failure the task is rejected, or joins the waiting queue. The allocation methods are constructed with various criteria in mind: maximizing system utilization, minimizing the number of rejected tasks, $\sum c_j$, or mean slowdown $\overline{S}$. It must not be forgotten that the sequence in which tasks are arriving is very important for thus defined performance of allocation algorithms. Here tasks cannot be reordered in a more convenient way. Not surprisingly, FIFO is a bad algorithm for achieving high utilization of the processor resource (cf. Sects. 5.3.3, and 5.6.1). Therefore, allocation methods often work together with some sequencing algorithm, e.g., with backfilling (cf. Sect. 5.3.3). Submesh assignment methods can be divided into two classes. Contiguous assignment methods allocate a singular rectangular area, or at lest a connected area, for the requesting task. Noncontiguous assignment methods may allocate processors in the form of many areas possibly scattered in the system mesh. A disadvantage of contiguous assignments are various kinds of resource fragmentation. Noncontiguous assignments eliminate fragmentation but suffer from contention in message passing which adversely affects communication times.

As already said allocation algorithms often work as a back-end for scheduling algorithms, and cannot modify the sequence of serviced requests, which would result in poor utilization if contiguous allocation were used. Therefore, noncontiguous allocations seem inevitable, to guarantee acceptable utilization of the computers. Another consequence is that it is hard to judge the quality of the allocation algorithm by the quality of the whole schedule, which may be completely determined by the scheduling front-end, and allocation algorithm has no chance of improving bad decisions of the scheduler. As a result in the more recent publications, a different set of optimality criteria is considered, which are more directly related to the geometric quality of the allocations [165, 179]. For a single task it can be measured by the number of processors in a minimum bounding box (in one, two, or three dimensions) enclosing all the processors assigned to the tasks, the sum of sizes of the bounding box along all dimensions, the number of communication links affected by the task (which in 2D is counted as width of the enclosing rectangle times the number of rows occupied by the task plus the height of the enclosing rectangle times the number of occupied columns), the average distance between all pairs of nodes, the longest distance between two allocated processors. For a set of tasks, the average of the above values can be used.

Let us introduce some notions related to the allocation in 2D-meshes. We will be saying that the mesh that is being partitioned is a system or machine mesh. Words block, box, frame, submesh are used interchangeably. The processors in the 2D-mesh are labeled using Cartesian coordinates. Thus, a processor in the lower left corner has coordinates $(0,0)$, and the upper right corner has coordinates $(m_1 - 1, m_2 - 1)$. For the simplicity of presentation we assume that all operations on the processor addresses are bounded to range $[0, m_1 - 1] \times [0, m_2 - 1]$. The processor in the lower left corner of a submesh will be called its *base*. Assume that the arriving task requests a submesh of size $(x, y)$. The set of processors which are allocated to some tasks which arrived before the request for $(x, y)$ is called *busy set*. Busy set may be represented as a bit vector, or a list of allocated areas $(a, b, c, d)$, where $(a, b)$ is the base of the submesh, and $(c, d)$ are coordinates of the upper right corner. In general, it is hard to say which representation, bitmap or a list of areas, is better. Bitmaps have sizes depending on the size of machine mesh which is a disadvantage. Lists of busy regions seem more concise at first glance, but a stream of requests may be constructed which results in allocating the number of regions equal to the number of processors. This may result from many small requests or task departure process. For a request of submesh $(x, y)$, we will say that base $(a, b)$ is free if all processors in the frame $(a, b, a + x - 1, b + y - 1)$ are free. Otherwise, base $(a, b)$ is busy. The set of all processors which cannot be a base for the new request $(x, y)$ because of the overlap with some already assigned processor is called *coverage set*. Coverage set can be computed from the busy set. For example, if processor $(i, j)$ is busy, then all processors in a rectangle $(i - x + 1, j - y + 1, i, j)$ cannot be a free base. For the request $(x, y)$, processors in $(m_1 - x + 1, 0, m_1 - 1, m_2 - 1)$, and $(0, m_2 - y + 1, m_1, m_2)$ cannot be bases, and hence, the search for free bases can be restricted to area $(0, 0, m_1 - x, m_2 - y)$. These two restricted areas are called *reject set*. The requested meshes can be rotated, i.e. a task with dimensions $(x, y)$ may have its side of length $x$ aligned both horizontally and vertically. Though not always explicitly considered, a task rotation can be handled in all the following algorithms by serving request $(x, y)$ first and, if it fails, then the request $(y, x)$. When the search for a free base stops at the first satisfying base, then it is said that the search strategy is *first fit* (FF). If the set of free bases is analyzed to find a base which results in the smallest external fragmentation, then it is said that the search strategy is *best fit*. A difficulty in BF is defining and quantifying the quality of the fit.

### 5.7.1.1  Contiguous Assignments

**2D Buddy System (2DBS) [170,171]**  A two-dimensional buddy system for square meshes of sizes $(2^q, 2^q)$, where $q$ is a positive integer, has been proposed in [171]. It has been assumed that tasks require square meshes. In the opposite case the requested mesh is expanded to a square. Let $(x, x)$ be the mesh requested. The whole mesh of size $2^q$ can be divided into four submeshes of size $2^{q-1}$, which can be further divided into 16 submeshes of size $2^{q-2}$. More generally the mesh network is divided into blocks of processors. A block $B(a, b, k)$ is specified by the location $(a, b)$ of the bottom-left corner processor (its base), and size $2^k$, where $k = 0, \ldots, q$. $B(0, 0, q)$ is a block. If $B(a, b, k)$ is a block, where $k > 0$, then it can be divided into four blocks which are buddies of each other: $B(x, y, k - 1)$, $B(a + 2^{k-1}, b, k - 1)$, $B(a, b + 2^{k-1}, k - 1)$, $B(a + 2^{k-1}, b + 2^{k-1}, k - 1)$. The blocks of free processors are held in $q + 1$ free block lists (FBL), where $FBL_i$ represents free blocks of size $i$. An arriving task is granted a mesh of size $(2^{\lceil \log x \rceil}, 2^{\lceil \log x \rceil})$. If a free block of size $\lceil \log x \rceil$ exists, then it is assigned to the task. Otherwise, the smallest free block capable of covering $(2^{\lceil \log x \rceil}, 2^{\lceil \log x \rceil})$ is split into smaller blocks until size $\lceil \log x \rceil$. When this block is released, it is returned to $FBL_{\lceil \log x \rceil}$. The block is coalesced with its buddies to form a block of size $\lceil \log x \rceil + 1$, if all the three buddies are free. To facilitate the process of searching for the buddies a method of numbering the blocks has been proposed. Note that blocks of size $k$ have base addresses $a, b$ which written in binary $a = (a_{q-1}a_{q-2} \ldots a_0)_2, b = (b_{q-1}b_{q-2} \ldots b_0)_2$ have bits $a_i = b_i = 0$ in positions $k > i \geq 0$. The number of block $B(a, b, k)$ written in binary is $(b_{q-1}a_{q-1}b_{q-2}a_{q-2} \ldots b_k a_k)_2$. If $B(a, b, k)$ is a block with number $N$, then the four buddies arising from splitting $B(a, b, k)$ have numbers $4N, 4N + 1, 4N + 2, 4N + 3$. Examples of block numbering for $k = 1, 2, 3$ are shown in Fig. 5.22. In [170] the implementation of 2DBS has been improved by adding a vector of free blocks which together with the numbering method guaranteed block allocation and release in $O(q) = O(\log m)$ time. Since the requested mesh sizes are rounded up to the nearest power of 2, 2D buddy systems suffer internal fragmentation. Due to the deallocation of the submeshes, external fragmentation (cf. Sect. 5.6.1) may also arise. The fragmentation of the above buddy system was subject of study in [171].

**a**

| 2 | 3 |
|---|---|
| 0 | 1 |

**b**

| 10 | 11 | 14 | 15 |
|----|----|----|----|
| 8  | 9  | 12 | 13 |
| 2  | 3  | 6  | 7  |
| 0  | 1  | 4  | 5  |

**c**

| 42 | 43 | 46 | 47 | 58 | 59 | 62 | 63 |
|----|----|----|----|----|----|----|----|
| 40 | 41 | 44 | 45 | 56 | 57 | 60 | 61 |
| 34 | 35 | 38 | 39 | 50 | 51 | 54 | 55 |
| 32 | 33 | 36 | 37 | 48 | 49 | 52 | 53 |
| 10 | 11 | 14 | 15 | 26 | 27 | 30 | 31 |
| 8  | 9  | 12 | 13 | 24 | 25 | 28 | 29 |
| 2  | 3  | 6  | 7  | 18 | 19 | 22 | 23 |
| 0  | 1  | 4  | 5  | 16 | 17 | 20 | 21 |

**Fig. 5.22** Numbering of buddies in 2DBS for block sizes: (**a**) $\log(\frac{m_1}{2})$, (**b**) $\log(\frac{m_1}{4})$ and (**c**) $\log(\frac{m_1}{8})$

**Frame Sliding [61]** In this method the allocated areas in the mesh are held in a list of records $(a_j, b_j, c_j, d_j)$, where $(a_j, b_j)$ are the coordinates of the lower left corner (base) and $(c_j, d_j)$ of the upper right corner of the mesh already allocated to some task $T_j$. For $n$ tasks already present in the mesh, checking if certain base $(a, b)$ is free can be done in $O(n)$ time by examining if the base $(a, b)$ and the top right corner $(a + x - 1, b + x - 1)$ overlap with the areas of the allocated tasks. Sliding frame algorithm starts with the lowest leftmost free processor, and checks if it is a free base. If it is free, then the processors in the frame are allocated to the requesting task. Otherwise, the algorithm slides the frame in the search for other candidates. The sliding can be viewed as checking bases in two loops: first horizontally (internal loop) and then vertically (external loop). The sliding frame algorithm is not checking all possible bases, but with horizontal stride $x$, and vertical stride $y$. Thus, for $n$ tasks in the system, the complexity of allocating a submesh of size $(x, y)$ is $O(\lfloor \frac{m_1}{x} \rfloor \lfloor \frac{m_2}{y} \rfloor n)$. Sliding frame has an advantage over 2D buddy systems that internal fragmentation is eliminated because sizes of allocated areas are not rounded up. However, due to the use of strides in the search, some existing free bases may be unrecognized.

**Adaptive Scan (AS) [75]** The adaptive scan method is a modification of frame sliding. The search for a free base starts at $(0, 0)$. If this base is busy, then the biggest horizontal coordinate $x'$ of the occupied processor in $(0, 0, x - 1, y - 1)$ is determined, and the frame is slid to base $(x' + 1, 0)$. If also this frame is busy, then the procedure is repeated until reaching $(m_1 - x + 1, 0)$, then the search is continued in the row 1, starting from base $(0, 1)$. The search proceeds in the following rows until finding a free base, or rejecting the request. Thus, the horizontal and vertical strides of frame sliding are eliminated. The complexity of AS is $O(m_1 m_2 n)$.

**2D-Mesh First Fit (2DFF) and 2D-Mesh Best Fit (2DBF) [246]** The 2DFF and 2DBF find all free bases in time $\Theta(m_1 m_2)$. Both 2DFF and 2DBF use two-dimensional *busy array* $B$ of size $(m_1, m_2)$ in which $B[i, j] = 1$ if processor at address $(i, j)$ is busy, and $B[i, j] = 0$, otherwise. When a task of size $(x, y)$ is assigned a frame with base $(a, b)$, then entries $[a, a+x-1] \times [b, b+y-1]$ in $B$ are set to 1. A *coverage array* $C$, of size $(m_1-x+1, m_2-y+1)$, represents the coverage set for the arriving task of size $(x, y)$. Array $C$ can be calculated in $\Theta(m_1 m_2)$ time from array $B$. The 2DFF strategy scans rows of $B$ from right to left, each row only once, to mark the covered areas. Then the columns are scanned from top to bottom, each column only once, to mark covered areas and find free bases. The 2DBF attempts to minimize fragmentation by using the smallest region of available processors. A difficulty here is that these regions may have arbitrary shapes which change as the tasks enter, and depart from the system. Therefore, a heuristic has been proposed which identifies "corners" of the free regions. The heuristic scans the rows of $C$ array for sequences of 0's (0 denotes a free base). For each horizontal sequence, the coordinates of "left" and "right" end are recorded. Then, the columns of $C$ are scanned for sequences of 0s. The bottom and top ends of the vertical sequence are checked if they are also "left" or "right" ends of some horizontal sequence. The coordinates of the positive results are stored as "corners" for the next step of the algorithm. If no "corners" were discovered, then the request for $(x, y)$ is rejected because there is no free base in the mesh. Otherwise, a "corner" with the maximum number of busy neighbors (where also the borders of the mesh are considered busy neighbors) is returned as the BF free base. In a set of computational experiments, it has been discovered 2DBF is not clearly better than 2DFF.

**Allocation in Free Regions [18]** A distinguishing feature of the heuristic proposed here is the use of free regions. It has been applied also in [117, 206, 241]. When a new request for submesh $(x, y)$ arrives its coverage set must be computed. A list of busy regions is used to construct coverage box for each rectangle on the busy list. Then the coverage box is subtracted from the free area, which means that the remaining free space is covered by a set of new rectangles. The covering rectangles are obtained by cutting into pieces the original area along its whole length in parallel to either horizontal or vertical dimension (these kinds of cuts are called guillotine cuts in cutting and packing [177]). This subtraction is performed for each task on the busy list. Finally, the area available for the request $(x, y)$ is represented by a set of rectangles. The procedure can be executed in $O(n^2)$ time, where $n$ is the number of tasks in the mesh. Three heuristics were proposed in [18] to select one of the free rectangles for the request of $(x, y)$: FF – assigns to the region with minimum horizontal coordinate, BF – assigns to the region with the minimum number of remaining free processors, and Worst Fit (WF) – chooses the region with biggest number of remaining free processors. In all three cases the lower left corner of the free rectangle was used as a base for request $(x, y)$. Furthermore, $k$-*lookahead* heuristics were proposed. All the three heuristics FF, BF, WF have their lookahead versions. A lookahead heuristic scans the waiting queue, and selects $k$ tasks requesting the biggest number of processors. When allocating the processors for the current task $T$, the selection is done so that enough space is left to allocate the $k$ waiting tasks. If using the first region selected for $T$ prevents allocation of the $k$ waiting tasks, then the next region is checked for $T$. If none of the free regions in which $T$ can be allocated guarantees a feasible assignment of the $k$ waiting tasks, then allocation returns to the first considered region and assigns it to $T$. Only 1-lookahead heuristics were studied in [18]. The idea covering free space by rectangles has also been presented in [241]. Additionally, stack data structure has been used in [241] to manipulate the free regions during the subtraction process. Let us observe that the method presented here has some deficiencies. There is no unique way of rectangle covering the free area. Furthermore, allocation in two free rectangles touching along one side is not possible, which results in inability to recognize all possible allocations.

**Quick Allocation (QA) [243]** For a request of submesh $(x, y)$ a coverage set must bc calculated. Checking all possible bases for overlapping with the coverage set is not really needed. It is more effective to jump directly to the lower left free base instead. This is facilitated by use of an array $LastCovered[j]$ which stores for each row $j$ the number of the right column in which the coverage set starting at column 0 ends. In other words, $(0, j, LastCovered[j], j)$ is a segment completely included in coverage set of $(x, y)$. $LastCover$ can be calculated by scanning the list of busy areas in $O(nm_2)$ time. $LastCover$ is scanned bottom-up for the first row $j'$ with $LastCover[j'] < m_2 - x$. Here $(j', LastCover[j'] + 1)$ is a free base for the new task. The complexity of QA is $O(nm_2)$.

**Busy List Best Boundary Value (BLBBV) [210]** Previous allocation methods, with the exception of 2DBS, had pseudopolynomial complexity depending on the mesh size. The approach proposed here exploits only adjacent allocations, built using a list of busy regions. Free areas are discovered in $O(n^3)$ (i.e. polynomial) time, where $n$ is the number of tasks present in the mesh, independently of the machine mesh size.

In the current method it is assumed that the requested mesh $(x, y)$ should be positioned in a "corner" of some free area. The new mesh will be directly neighboring with the busy meshes. Consequently, the available areas can be checked by sliding the requested mesh $(x, y)$ along the edges of the allocated meshes (cf. Fig. 5.23). Suppose $(x, y)$ is slid along the edges of $M = (a_1, b_1, c_1, d_1)$ Four areas will be checked: $(a_1 - x, b_1 - y, a_1 - x, d_1 + y - 1)$ (left of $M$), $(c_1 + 1, b_1 - y, c_1 + x, d_1 + y - 1)$ (right of $M$), $(a_1 - x + 1, d_1 + 1, c_1 + x - 1, d_1 + y - 1)$ (above $M$) and $(a_1 - x + 1, b_1 - y, c_1 + x - 1, d_1 - 1)$ (below $M$). While sliding the positions overlapping with at most $n - 1$ other allocated areas are eliminated. Only the positions touching the other allocated areas from left or from right (when sliding $(x, y)$ horizontally), from below or from above (when sliding $(x, y)$ vertically), are calculated and compared for quality of fit. The goodness of the current admissible corner position is evaluated by use of *boundary values*. A boundary value of a processor is the number of its busy neighbors. A boundary value of a free submesh is the sum of boundary values of its processors. When a new corner position is discovered for $(x, y)$, the boundary value is calculated and compared against the previous best position. The position with the biggest boundary value is stored. The algorithm admits rotation of the requested areas. The best positions with the boundary values for $(x, y)$ and $(y, x)$ are compared and the better one is assigned to the requesting task. When the algorithm starts, the mesh is empty, and the first allocated submesh has base $(0, 0)$.

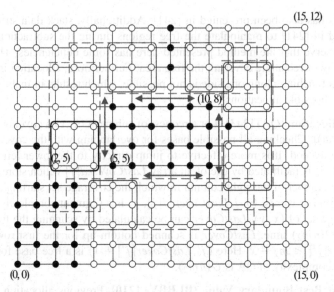

**Fig. 5.23** Computing corner positions for $(3, 3)$ mesh slid around $(5, 5, 10, 8)$ in BLBBV. Black nodes are busy. Sliding areas are marked by dashed lines. Checked admissible "corner" positions are marked with solid lines. Base $(2, 5)$ is selected with the highest boundary value 7

**Processor Allocation by Partitioning (PAP) [185]** The dynamic nature of on-line allocation results in scattering small tasks throughout the mesh. Consequently, external fragmentation occurs preventing allocation of bigger tasks. This problem could be avoided if small tasks were confined to some part of the system mesh. The PAP method assumes square system mesh of size $(2^q, 2^q)$, where $q$ is a positive integer. Mesh $(2^q, 2^q)$ is partitioned into three partitions of size $(2^{q-1}, 2^{q-1})$, and the fourth square is recursively divided into three partitions of size $(2^{q-2}, 2^{q-2})$, three partitions of size $(2^{q-3}, 2^{q-3})$, etc. Finally, there are four partitions of size $(1, 1)$. For each partition size $(2^i, 2^i)$ a queue $Q_i$ of waiting tasks is maintained. For a task requiring submesh $(x, y)$, where $x, y \leq 2^{q-1}$, a free base is searched in the partitions of size $(2^j, 2^j)$, where $j = \lceil \log \max\{x, y\} \rceil$. Within the partition submeshes are allocated using one of the previous methods – FS, 2DFF, etc. If the allocation attempt fails, then the task can be assigned all the smaller partitions of sizes $(2^{j-1}, 2^{j-1}), \ldots, (1, 1)$. If all these partitions are free then together they form a partition of size $(2^j, 2^j)$ which can be assigned to the current task. If this action fails, but three other tasks wait in $Q_j$, then the three waiting tasks and the current task may be allocated together in the bigger partition of size $(2^{j+1}, 2^{j+1})$. The current task joins waiting queue $Q_j$ if all three attempts fail. Alternative methods for partitioning nonsquare meshes were proposed in [185]. The idea of dividing the mesh into separate partitioning for tasks of different sizes is also exploited by several heuristics with performance guarantee in Sect. 5.7.2.

**Restricted Size Reduction (RSR) [47, 48]** This heuristic treats tasks as moldable, and if allocation is unsuccessful the size of the requested mesh is reduced to the next smaller allowable one, and allocation is attempted again. For example, the request for submesh $(x, y)$ can be reduced to $(\frac{x}{2^i}, \frac{y}{2^j})$, where $i = 1, \ldots, \lfloor \log_2 x \rfloor$, $j = 1, \ldots, \lfloor \log_2 y \rfloor$. Usually, $i, j$ are increased one by one to maintain the aspect ratio of the allocated area as similar to the request as possible. The number $k$ of attempted size reductions is limited for each task. RSR needs an allocation method (e.g. Adaptive Scan, QA, 2DFF) to check feasibility of the assignments for the resized requests. A similar policy called **limit-$k$** was proposed in [242]. In [117] a heuristic called **Flexfold** has been proposed which tries assignment of $(x, y)$, the resized requests $(\frac{x}{2}, 2y)$, $(2x, \frac{y}{2})$, and their rotated counterparts.

**Extended Flexible Processor Allocation (EFPA) [206]** This method considers also $L$-shaped areas as possible allocations for the requesting tasks. Let $L(a, b, c, d)$ denote an $L$-shaped area consisting of two rectangles $(a, b)$ and $(c, d)$ touching along the vertical sides, $(a, b)$ to the left of $(c, d)$, with the bottoms aligned. If the request for submesh $(x, y)$ fails, then allocation of $(\frac{x}{2}, 2y)$ and $(2x, \frac{y}{2})$ is tried. If all the three fail, then the algorithm tries the following $L$-shaped areas. Let us assume that $x \geq y \geq 2$. If $x$ is even, then try allocating $L(\frac{x}{2}, y + k, \frac{x}{2}, y - k)$, for $k = 1, \ldots, b-1$. If $x$ is odd, try allocating $L(\lceil \frac{x}{2} \rceil + k, y + \lfloor \frac{x}{2} \rfloor - k, \lfloor \frac{x}{2} \rfloor - k, y - \lceil \frac{x}{2} \rceil - k)$, for $k = 0, \ldots, y - 1 - \lceil \frac{x}{2} \rceil$. The above procedure can be adjusted to construct four rotated versions of the $L$-shaped area. EFPA needs some allocation method to check feasibility of assignments for the above constructed rectangular and $L$-shaped regions. A list of free rectangular and $L$-shaped regions was used for this purpose in [206].

**Right Border Line Segments (RBLS) [57]** This algorithm generalizes the idea of Quick Allocation (QA) heuristic [243]. While QA analyzes, in an FF manner, only one set of free bases located to the right of the continuously occupied area spanning from column 0 to the left, here all such regions are discovered. It is assumed that the incoming request $(x, y)$ is aligned to the right border of some already allocated submesh. Thus, for allocated area $(a, b, c, d)$, possible base locations of the new request are in the rectangle $(c + 1, b - y + 1, c + 1, d)$ which is called *right-border line segment* (RBLS) of $(a, b, c, d)$. The RBLS may overlap with the coverage set. Therefore, from each RBLS the part overlapping with forbidden region around each of the allocated submeshes is subtracted. To speed up the process of subtraction and avoid unnecessary fragmentation of the RBLS the busy regions are analyzed in the order of decreasing vertical coordinate of the upper-right corner. The set of RBLSes remaining from the subtraction procedure is considered for assignment. All RBLSes can be constructed in $(n^2)$ time, where $n$ is the number of tasks in the system mesh. The FF version stops after finding the first nonempty result of subtraction. BF assigns an end node of the shortest RBLS. WF uses an end node of the longest RBLS.

**Leapfrog Method [238]** This method is based on the same ideas as Adaptive Scan (AS) [75] and QA heuristics [243]. A free base for the incoming request of submesh $(x, y)$ is searched for. Similarly to the AS processor addresses are scanned line by line, left to right, and if an occupied area is found, then the search jumps to the

**a**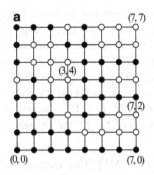

**b**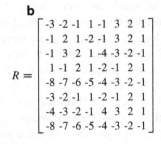

$$R = \begin{bmatrix} -3 & -2 & -1 & 1 & -1 & 3 & 2 & 1 \\ -1 & 2 & 1 & -2 & -1 & 3 & 2 & 1 \\ -1 & 3 & 2 & 1 & -4 & -3 & -2 & -1 \\ 1 & -1 & 2 & 1 & -2 & -1 & 2 & 1 \\ -8 & -7 & -6 & -5 & -4 & -3 & -2 & -1 \\ -3 & -2 & -1 & 1 & -2 & -1 & 2 & 1 \\ -4 & -3 & -2 & -1 & 4 & 3 & 2 & 1 \\ -8 & -7 & -6 & -5 & -4 & -3 & -2 & -1 \end{bmatrix}$$

**Fig. 5.24** Example for leap frog method [238]. (**a**) The occupied mesh. The black nodes are busy. (**b**) The corresponding $R$-array

first free processor in the line. As in QA, the observation is used that a free base is one of the processors directly to the right of coverage set spanning from column 0. However, in leapfrog a different data structure is used to store the information about system mesh occupancy, than in AS, QA. A *run* is a continuous sequence of free or occupied processors. A run-length array (*R-array*) is storing for each processor $(i, j)$ the length of the run to the left of $(i, j)$ including the processor itself (see Fig. 5.24). Occupied runs are represented by negative values, and positive values represent free processors. When checking if $(i, j)$ can be a free base, the algorithm must verify if $R[i, j + k] \geq x$, for $k = 0, \ldots, y - 1$. The above description corresponds with the FF search. A BF version has been also proposed, and the quality of fit is calculated as in 2DBF [246].

### 5.7.1.2  Noncontiguous Assignments

Noncontiguous allocation methods generally do not consider task requests as meshes, and only the number of required processors $xy$ is the description of the request. On the other hand, these algorithms attempt to allocate clusters of closely located processors to take advantage of communication locality.

**Paging [176]** To avoid external fragmentation, which appears as an inevitable consequence of allocating and deallocating a set of different size submeshes, the processors are assigned in units of fixed size square submeshes (pages). Unlike 2DBS or PAP, there is only one submesh size which is a power of 2. Let $(2^k, 2^k)$ be the unit of processor allocation (a page). The pages are held on a Free Page List (FPL), and a task requesting $(x, y)$ mesh is assigned the first $\lceil \frac{xy}{2^k 2^k} \rceil$ free pages. Another constituent of paging method is the mapping from page identifiers to their locations in the system mesh. Several schemes were proposed in [176]: row major, snake-like, and their shuffled versions. The assigned pages need not form a compact area. Thus, paging method departs, from the earlier assumption of scheduling tasks with mesh shape, that the allocated regions are singular rectangles. On the other hand, if $k > 0$ in page dimensions $(2^k, 2^k)$, then paging does not sacrifice completely the contiguity of the assigned areas, and the applications may take advantage of communication locality. Notice, that paging may incur internal fragmentation.

**Multiple Buddy Strategy (MBS) [176]** Similarly to 2D buddy system (2DBS), tasks are assigned squares of sizes which are powers of 2. However, the request is not rounded up to the nearest bigger square, but is split into multiple squares of different sizes. The algorithm starts with partitioning the empty system mesh into blocks of sizes $(2^{\lfloor \log m_1 m_2 \rfloor}, 2^{\lfloor \log m_1 m_2 \rfloor}), \ldots, (2^1, 2^1), (2^0, 2^0)$. Note that block sizes are multiples of each other, and this can be done for arbitrary aspect of the system mesh by a greedy method similar to the one shown in Fig. 5.28b. The information about available areas is stored as Free Block Records (FBR), where $FBR[i].blocknum$ is the number of free $(2^i, 2^i)$-blocks, and $FBR[i].blocklist$ points to a list of these blocks. An arriving request for submesh $(x, y)$ is factored into base 4 number such that $xy = \sum_{i=0}^{\lfloor \log_4(xy) \rfloor} a_i 4^i$, where $a_i$ are the digits of base 4 representation of $xy$. For example, a request for mesh $(7, 5)$, which is a request for $(203)_4$ processors, will be changed to a request for two blocks of size $(4, 4)$, and three blocks of size $(1, 1)$ (i.e. 1-processor). The allocation algorithm attempts to assign to the tasks the first $a_i$ free blocks $(2^i, 2^i)$ from $FBR[i].blocklist$ for $i = \lfloor \log_4(xy) \rfloor, \ldots, 0$. If the attempt fails, then the algorithm tries to make more blocks $(2^i, 2^i)$ by splitting the bigger blocks $(2^j, 2^j)$, for $j > i$. If the number of the produced and the previously existing $(2^i, 2^i)$-blocks is bigger than $a_i$, then the algorithm proceeds to the next size $i$. Otherwise, all $FBR[i].blocknum$ are assigned to the request, and the missing $a_i - FBR[i].blocknum$ blocks are exchanged for a request for additional $4(a_i - FBR[i].blocknum)$ $(2^{i-1}, 2^{i-1})$-blocks. Hence, in such a case the algorithm will try to allocate $4(a_i - FBR[i].blocknum) + a_{i-1}$ blocks of dimension $(2^{i-1}, 2^{i-1})$ in total. The deallocation of the released areas is analogous to 2DBS: free blocks are coalesced if all four buddies are free, $FBRs$ are updated.

**Minimizing Message Passing Contention (MC) [180]** This algorithm uses a concept of shells of growing size, built around free processors. For a request of submesh $(x, y)$, *shell* 0 built around processor $(i, j)$ is a rectangle with coordinates $(i - \lceil \frac{x-1}{2} \rceil, j - \lceil \frac{y-1}{2} \rceil, i + \lfloor \frac{x-1}{2} \rfloor, j + \lfloor \frac{y-1}{2} \rfloor)$. *Shell* $k + 1$ includes all processors around shell $k$. In other words, shell $k + 1$ has coordinates $(i - \lceil \frac{x-1}{2} \rceil - k - 1, j - \lceil \frac{y-1}{2} \rceil - k - 1, i + \lfloor \frac{x-1}{2} \rfloor + k + 1, j + \lfloor \frac{y-1}{2} \rfloor + k + 1)$. Increasing shells are built around $(i, j)$ until some shell $l$ comprises $xy$ free processors. To minimize chance of contention for communication free processors on the shorter sides of the shell are used first, then the processors on the longer sides, and corner processors are used last. For each of the sets of processors constructed in the above way cost $\sum_{h=1}^{l} m'_h h$ is calculated, where $l$ is the last applied shell, $m'_h$ is the number of processors selected in shell $h$. The processor set with the minimum score is selected. For example, in Fig. 5.25 mesh $(2, 3)$ is requested. Shells built around $(3, 4)$, and $(7, 2)$ (here the request is rotated) are shown. The sores of selections built around $(3, 4), (7, 2), (9, 7)$ are 5, 1, 8, respectively. Algorithm MC has the following advantages: requested

**Fig. 5.25** Shells around
$(3, 4)$ for a request of $(2, 3)$
(solid lines) and around $(7, 2)$
for a request of $(3, 2)$ (dashed
lines) in algorithm MC. Black
nodes are busy

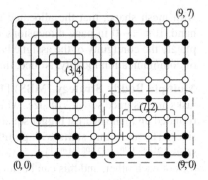

submesh $(x, y)$ is found and assigned if it exists, otherwise a compact set of processors is assigned to the requesting tasks, contention in communication is minimized, external fragmentation is avoided. It has been shown in [17] that a version of MC called MC1x1, which starts building shells around a single processor (as if the request were for submesh $(1, 1)$, not $(x, y)$), is $(4 - \frac{4}{xy})$-approximate algorithm in minimizing total pairwise distance of the selected processors in 2D-meshes. This result can be generalized to meshes with more dimensions.

**Adaptive Non-contiguous Allocation (ANCA) [48]** If allocation of the request $(x, y)$ fails, then it is partitioned into submeshes of smaller size, and then free area is searched for a number of smaller submeshes. The reduced frame sizes are: $(\lceil \frac{x}{2^i} \rceil, \lceil \frac{y}{2^j} \rceil)$, where $i, j$ are iteration numbers. The number of size reductions can be limited, and a version of the algorithm with size reduction limit $k$ is referred to as ANCA-$k$. Due to rounding up the subframe sizes internal fragmentation may arise. To eliminate it, the border submeshes are curtailed to avoid allocating excessive processors. ANCA needs some external allocator algorithm. 2DFF from [246] has been used for this purpose such that feasibility of all the submeshes resulting from $(x, y)$ is checked in one scan of the coverage bitmap.

**Space Filling Curves and One-Dimensional Allocation [165]** The idea of this approach is to transform allocation problem in many dimensions to one-dimensional allocation along a space filling curve such as Hilbert curve (see Fig. 5.26 for an example). As a result of locality in the assignment on the space-filling curve, locality in higher dimensions should also emerge. Notice that the problem considered here is equivalent to constructing a mapping from page numbers to their locations in the machine mesh in the paging algorithm. For the assignment along space filling curve the following rules were used. If task $T_j$ can be allocated contiguously, then apply a standard 1D bin packing algorithm, such as FF, BF, or Sum of Squares allocation, on free intervals treated as bins. The sum of squares allocation chooses the bin which minimizes the sum $\sum_{i=1}^{l} N(i)^2$, where $l$ is the number of different sizes of the remaining free space in the bins (observe that object sizes are discrete, hence $l$ is finite), and $N(i)$ is the number of bins with remaining space $i$. If $T_j$ cannot be allocated contiguously, then the task is assigned a set of curve segments which minimizes the *span* of a task. Span is a measure of allocation dispersion.

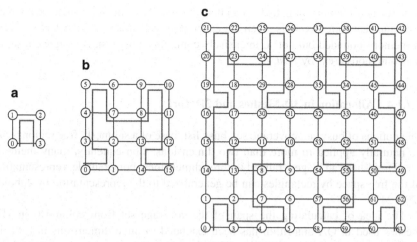

**Fig. 5.26** Example of applying Hilbert space-filling curve to number the processors in a 2D-mesh. The solid line shows the fitting of the Hilbert curve. (**a**) First, (**b**) second, and (**c**) third iteration

For example, for a chain of processors, it can be calculated as $s_j^{\ell} = \max_{i \in M_j} r_i - \min_{i \in M_j} r_i + 1$, where $r_i$ is the rank of the processor, and $M_j$ is the set of processors that are to be assigned to $T_j$. For other topologies, span is calculated on the basis of processor ranking ($r_i$s), which in turn is formulated as integer programming problem of minimizing the distance in the machine network between the processors with close ranks [165].

**Greedy Available Busy List (GABL) [12]**  When the requested submesh $(x, y)$ cannot be allocated, then it is substituted for by a sequence of smaller requests. The smaller submeshes have 1 subtracted from the length of the longer side. For example, if $x \geq y$ then the smaller requested submesh is $(x - 1, y)$. Size reductions may be repeated several times consecutively, to avoid requesting more than $xy$ processors. The submeshes are searched for by RBLS [57] heuristic. The complexity of this allocation algorithm is $O((x + y)n^2)$, where $n$ is the number of tasks in the system mesh.

### 5.7.1.3   Hybrid Strategies

**Hybrid Allocation with modified RSR [49]**  An attempt is made to merge three types of algorithms: Adaptive Scan, RSR, and ANCA. The modification of RSR applied here consists in folding the requested submesh in half only in parallel with the longer dimension, and attempting allocation only along the border of the system mesh to minimize the probability of external fragmentation. Reducing task size in this way increases demand for memory on each CPU. It is postulated that tasks with big memory requirements should not be resized in RSR, while tasks which are intensively communicating should be assigned contiguous processor area. This algorithm recourses to the user-provided directives on the nature of the task. A task declared non-memory-bounded is handled by RSR. A memory-bounded task which communicates intensively is given the exact requested submesh by Adaptive Scan. A memory-bounded but not so intensively communicating task is assigned a set of noncontiguous areas by ANCA.

### 5.7.1.4    Allocation in 3D-Meshes and 3D-Tori

The notions of busy set, coverage set, busy list, base of a submesh, free regions, can be naturally applied in more than two dimensions. Consequently, many methods for 2D-meshes can be generalized to three dimensions. For example, representation of the free space by rectangles can be generalized to the representation by cuboids [201, 241].

The idea of calculating the span of the coverage set from column 0 in 2D-meshes used in QA algorithm has been extended to three dimensions in [58]. In this case, Coverage Status Table (CST) is calculated which is the span of the coverage set from plane $x = 0$ in the direction of growing $x$ (let us denote it $CST[y, z].from$ 0). Since 3D torus is considered in [58], CST is calculated for the span of coverage set from $m_1 - 1$ in the direction of decreasing dimension $x$ (let it be denoted $CST[y, z].from\_m_1$). If there exists a pair $(y, z)$ such that $CST[y, z].from1 + 1 < CST[y, z].from\_m_1$, then the request can be satisfied.

The algorithm of expanding shells MC [180] can be applied in three dimensions to construct noncontiguous allocations, as well.

## 5.7.2    Heuristics with a Guarantee

In Table 5.15 the following notations were used:

- $2D\text{-}mesh_j = (x_j, x_j)$ – Denotes square mesh requirements.
- $2D\text{-}mesh_j = (2^{\lceil \log x_j \rceil}, 2^{\lceil \log x_j \rceil})$ – Represent square requirements with power of 2 sizes.
- $2D\text{-}mesh_j = (2^{\lceil \log x_j \rceil}, 2^{\lceil \log y_j \rceil})$ – Stands for rectangular meshes with side sizes rounded up to the nearest power of 2.
- $E(X)$ – denotes expected schedule length under heuristic $X$, and $E(OPT)$ of the optimum schedule.

The following heuristics have been mentioned in Table 5.15.

### 5.7.2.1    1D-Meshes

**Next Fit Decreasing Height (NFDH) [226]** NFDH is a shelf heuristic assigning tasks in the order of decreasing $p_j$. If the task does not fit in the current shelf, then the current shelf is closed and a new one is opened for the task. Here opening a new shelf means starting a task later.

**Table 5.15**  Approximability results for tasks with mesh shape $C_{\max}$ criterion

| Problem | Result | Reference |
|---|---|---|
| $P\,|\,1D\text{-}mesh_j\,|\,C_{\max}$ | $R_{NFDH} = 2 + \frac{p_{\max}}{C_{\max}^*}$ | [226] |
| $P\,|\,1D\text{-}mesh_j, \neg p_j\,|\,C_{\max}$ | $R_{NIS} \leq 3$ | [103] |
| $P\,|\,1D\text{-}mesh_j, \neg p_j\,|\,C_{\max}$ | $R_{clusters} \leq 2.5$ | [103] |
| $P\,|\,1D\text{-}mesh_j, \neg p_j\,|\,C_{\max}$ | $R \geq 2 - \frac{1}{m}$ | [103] |
| $P\,|\,1D\text{-}mesh_j, \neg p_j, \neg prec\,|\,C_{\max}$ | $ER > \Omega(\frac{\log m}{\log\log m})$ | [208] |
| $P\,|\,1D\text{-}mesh_j, \neg p_j, p_j(i) = \frac{p(1)}{i}, prec\,|\,C_{\max}$ | $R \geq \Omega(\frac{\log m}{\log\log m})$ | [102] |
| $P\,|\,1D\text{-}mesh_j, prec\,|\,C_{\max}$ | $\frac{E(NISBSP)}{E(OPT)} \leq 2$ | [172] |
| $P\,|\,2D\text{-}mesh_j\,|\,C_{\max}$ | $R > 2$ | [169] |
| $P\,|\,2D\text{-}mesh_j\,|\,C_{\max}$ | $R_{LPT-LL} \leq 5 + \frac{4m_1}{8m_2 - m_1}$ | [169] |
| $P\,|\,2D\text{-}mesh_j\,|\,C_{\max}, x_j \leq \frac{m_1}{q}, y_j \leq \frac{m_2}{q}$ | $R_{LPT-LL} \leq 2 + \frac{2}{q-2}$ | [169] |
| $P\,|\,2D\text{-}mesh_j = (x_j, x_j)\,|\,C_{\max}$ | $R_{NIS2DBS} = 4 + \frac{p_{\max}}{C_{\max}^*}$ | [170] |
| $P\,|\,2D\text{-}mesh_j = (2^{\lceil \log x_j \rceil}, 2^{\lceil \log x_j \rceil})\,|\,C_{\max}$ | $R_{NIS2DBS} = 1 + \frac{p_{\max}}{C_{\max}^*}$ | [170] |
| $P\,|\,2D\text{-}mesh_j, \neg p_j\,|\,C_{\max}$ | $R \geq \Omega(\sqrt{\log\log m})$ | [103] |
| $P\,|\,2D\text{-}mesh_j, \neg p_j\,|\,C_{\max}$ | $R_{BP} \leq O(\sqrt{\log\log m})$ | [103] |
| $P\,|\,2D\text{-}mesh_j = (2^{\lceil \log x_j \rceil}, 2^{\lceil \log y_j \rceil}), \neg p_j\,|\,C_{\max}$ | $ER_{sample} = 28$ | [208] |
| $P\,|\,2D\text{-}mesh_j, p_j = 1, \neg prec\,|\,C_{\max}$ | $R_{Level(Pack2D)} \leq \frac{46}{7}$ | [25] |
| $P\,|\,2D\text{-}mesh_j, p_j = 1, \neg prec\,|\,C_{\max}$ | $R > 3.25$ | [25] |
| $P\,|\,2D\text{-}mesh_j, p_j = 1, \neg prec\,|\,C_{\max}$ | $R > 3.859$ | [240] |
| $P\,|\,2D\text{-}mesh_j, p_j = 1, \neg prec\,|\,C_{\max}$ | $R_{N2d} \leq 5.25$ | [240] |
| $P\,|\,2D\text{-}mesh_j, p_j = 1, \neg prec\,|\,C_{\max}$ | $R_{R2d} \leq 4.25$ | [240] |
| $P\,|\,dD\text{-}mesh_j, \neg p_j\,|\,C_{\max}$ | $R_{BP} \leq O(2^d d \log d \sqrt{\log\log m}$ $+ 2^d (d \log d)^d)$ | [103] |
| $P\,|\,dD\text{-}mesh_j, \neg p_j\,|\,C_{\max}$ | $R \geq \Omega(\sqrt{\log\log m})$ | [103] |
| $P\,|\,dD\text{-}mesh_j, \neg p_j\,|\,C_{\max}$ | $ER_{sample} \leq O(4^d)$ | [208] |
| $P\,|\,dD\text{-}mesh_j, \neg p_j, p_j(i) = \frac{p(1)}{i}, \neg prec\,|\,C_{\max}$ | $R_{mesh} \sim O((\frac{\log m}{\log\log m})^d)$ | [102] |

**Clusters [103]**  The set of tasks is partitioned into set $\mathcal{T}'$ comprising tasks requiring at most $\frac{m}{3}$ processors, and $\mathcal{T}'' = \mathcal{T} - \mathcal{T}'$. The mesh is partitioned into segments potentially occupied by up to three tasks called: left, middle, and right. These segments are called clusters. Tasks are dispatched according to the decreasing sizes. Segment sizes decrease as the task sizes are getting smaller. The algorithm starts with one segment. It is intended to maintain efficiency at least $\frac{2}{3}$ in the whole schedule. Efficiency here is the fraction of processors that is executing some tasks. When efficiency falls below $\frac{2}{3}$ in some cluster, then the algorithm tries to provide the missing left, middle, or right task from $\mathcal{T}'$. However, tasks from $\mathcal{T}''$ are preferred over the tasks from $\mathcal{T}'$ as the left task in the leftmost segment. Consequently, tasks from $\mathcal{T}''$ are executed as long as set $\mathcal{T}''$ is nonempty. If all three tasks are present, and efficiency is less than $\frac{2}{3}$, then there must be enough space to accommodate a task from $\mathcal{T}'$. Hence, a new task from $\mathcal{T}'$ is scheduled adjacent to the middle task, and the current cluster is split into two. The remaining tasks from $\mathcal{T}''$ are scheduled at the end of the schedule using the whole mesh as a single segment.

**NonIncreasing size, Binary System Partitioning, Level Scheduling (NISBSP)**
**[172]** Task level is the length of the longest path from the initial vertex in the task
graph to the task. Tasks from level $i$ are executed together before any tasks with level
$i + 1$. Tasks with the same level are executed according to nonincreasing number
of required processors, which are rounded up to the nearest power of 2. The ratio of
expected schedule lengths mentioned in Table 5.15 was obtained under additional
assumption that the task graph is wide, i.e. the length of the longest path is much
smaller than $n$.

### 5.7.2.2  2D-Meshes

**Longest Processing Time, Level by Level (LPT-LL) [169]** Since tasks can be
rotated, it will be assumed that $x_j > y_j$ and $x_j \le m_1, y_j \le m_2$. Tasks are divided into groups such that each group fits in the processor mesh. One group of
the tasks constitutes a level in the schedule. Groups are scheduled one after an-
other without overlapping. Each task $T_j$ requiring $x_j y_j > \frac{m_1 m_2}{4} - \frac{m_1^2}{16}$ processors
is a group itself, and is scheduled alone. The remaining tasks are ordered accord-
ing to the nonincreasing processing times. This sequence of the tasks is divided
into groups $G_1, \dots, G_h$ such that in group $G_i$ the total number of required processors is the biggest possible not exceeding $A' m_1 m_2$, i.e. for group $G_i$ we have
$\sum_{j=n_i}^{n_{i+1}-1} x_j y_j \le A' m_1 m_2$, and $\sum_{j=n_i}^{n_{i+1}} x_j y_j > A' m_1 m_2$, where $n_i = | \cup_{k=1}^{i} G_k|$
is the number of tasks in groups $G_1, \dots, G_i$. Bound $A'$ was set to $\frac{1}{2} - \frac{m_1}{16 m_2}$ in the
general case, and to $(1 - \frac{1}{q})^2$ when task sizes satisfy $x_j \le \frac{m_1}{q}, y_j \le \frac{m_2}{q}$. Tasks in one
group are ordered according to decreasing heights $y_j$, and assigned to the processors
using shelf algorithm NFDH.

**Nonincreasing Size and 2D Buddy System (NIS2DBS) [170]** Tasks are scheduled according to nonincreasing sizes, and a 2D buddy system is used for mesh
allocation. Since square mesh requests are considered here, the order of tasks sizes
is well defined. Note that for a system mesh of size $(2^q, 2^q)$, where $q$ is a positive integer, and tasks requiring squares of sizes which are also powers of 2, NIS
scheduling rule eliminates fragmentation.

**Balanced Parallel (BP) [103]** In the presentation of this algorithm it is assumed
that $m_1 \ge m_2$, and for each task $x_j \ge y_j$. Were it otherwise, then the system mesh,
and task requirements may be rotated to meet this condition. Let $\mathcal{T}^{(l)} = \{T_j :
\frac{m_1}{2^{l+1}} < x_j \le \frac{m_1}{2^l}\}$ be task class $l$. Let $order(\mathcal{T})$ be the number of nonempty task
classes in $\mathcal{T}$. The set of small tasks is $\mathcal{T}' = \{T_j : x_j \le \frac{m_1}{(\log m_1)^2}\}$. The remaining large
tasks are further divided into: $\mathcal{T}'' = \bigcup_{l=0}^{\lceil \log \log \log(m) \rceil} \mathcal{T}^{(l)}$ and $\mathcal{T}''' = \mathcal{T} - \mathcal{T}' - \mathcal{T}''$,
where $m = m_1 m_2$. Actually, three algorithms are applied to tasks of different sizes,
and BP operates on the smallest tasks. Algorithm CLASS schedules a given class
$\mathcal{T}^{(l)}$ on a given mesh of dimension $(a, m_2)$ as follows: The mesh is divided into
submeshes of sizes $(\frac{a}{2^l}, m_2)$. Tasks from $\mathcal{T}^{(l)}$ are scheduled on these submeshes as
on 1D-mesh (disregarding the first dimension) using algorithm NIS over size $y_j$.

**Fig. 5.27** Partitioning mesh
in Balanced Parallel algorithm

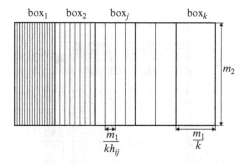

Algorithm SERIAL for a given set of task classes uses CLASS to schedule each
task class separately on the whole $(m_1, m_2)$ system mesh, and the resulting schedules are executed sequentially. Algorithm PARALLEL dynamically repartitions the
mesh into submeshes of sizes $(\lfloor \frac{m_1}{order(T_i)} \rfloor, m_2)$, where $T_i$ is the set of unfinished
tasks. Each task class is scheduled in one of these submeshes using algorithm
CLASS. When the efficiency in the whole $(m_1, m_2)$ mesh falls below $\frac{1}{8}$, then the
running tasks are allowed to finish, but the mesh is repartitioned again, and the remaining tasks are scheduled in the new partitions. Let us remind that efficiency is
understood here, as the fraction of all processors working at some time moment
(as defined in Sect. 5.3.1.3). This loop is finished when all tasks are scheduled.
Algorithm BALANCED PARALLEL is similar to PARALLEL, but uses finer division of the mesh (cf. Fig. 5.27). Instead of waiting until completion of the started
tasks and repartitioning the whole mesh when efficiency is too low, the algorithm
immediately switches to the next one of $k$ submeshes of size $(\lfloor \frac{m_1}{k} \rfloor, m_2)$, where
$k = \lceil \sqrt{\log order(T^a)} \rceil$, and $T^a$ is the initial set of tasks to be scheduled. We will
call these submeshes boxes. The algorithm works as follows: Let $h_{ij} = order(T_{i,j})$,
where $T_{i,j}$ is the set of unscheduled tasks in iteration $i$, and when $j$th box is open for
$j = 1, \ldots, k$. A nonempty class $T^{(l)}$ is scheduled in a submesh of size $(\lfloor \frac{m_1}{kh_{ij}} \rfloor, m_2)$
in box $j$ using algorithm CLASS until the efficiency in box $j$ drops below $\frac{1}{8}$. If
$j < k$, then switch to the next box. Otherwise (the current box is the last one),
wait for completion of all the started tasks, then increase $i$ and restart the algorithm iterating over the boxes. BALANCED PARALLEL stops when all tasks are
scheduled. Algorithm SERIAL applied to large tasks in set $T''$ and PARALLEL
applied to tasks $T'''$ are $O(\log \log \log m)$-competitive. Finally, BALANCED
PARALLEL applied to small tasks in $T'$ is $O(\sqrt{\log \log m})$-competitive. A version
for $d$-dimensional meshes has been also proposed in [103].

**Sample [208]** is a randomized algorithm for online scheduling tasks with unknown
processing times in *square* 2D-meshes, whose sizes are powers of 2. The requested
submeshes are rectangles with side lengths rounded to the nearest power of 2. Tasks
are moldable with linear speedup and a requested mesh $(x_j, y_j)$ can be squashed
to $(x'_j, y'_j)$, where $x'_j \leq x_j, y'_j \leq y_j$. Rotation of the requested submeshes is allowed, and hence it is assumed that $x_j \geq y_j$. Let us partition the tasks into classes

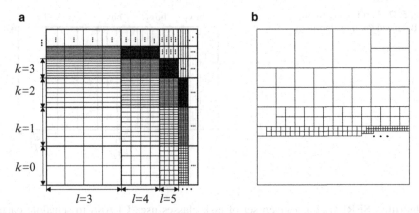

**Fig. 5.28** Mesh partitioning in algorithm sample. (**a**) For sampling in step 4. (**b**) For final processing in step 6

$T^{(l)} = \{T_j : \frac{m_1}{2^{l+1}} < x_j \le \frac{m_1}{2^l}\}$ and subclasses $T^{(l,k)} = \{T_j \in T^{(l)} : \frac{m_1}{2^{l+k+1}} < y_j \le \frac{m_1}{2^{l+k}}\}$. Tasks in $T^{(l,k)}$ request meshes $(\frac{m_1}{2^l}, \frac{m_1}{2^{l+k}})$ because the side sizes of the requested meshes are powers of 2, and the machine mesh is a square. Since $x_j \ge y_j$ any task from class $T^{(l)}$ fits in a submesh $(\frac{m_1}{2^l}, \frac{m_1}{2^l})$. Algorithm Sample first executes the big tasks from classes $T^{(0)}, T^{(1)}, T^{(2)}$ using algorithm CLASS defined in the Balanced Parallel method presented above [103]. The remaining tasks from classes $T^{(l)}$, for $l = 3, \ldots, \log m_1$, are packed, also using algorithm CLASS into $z_l$ squares $H_l$ of sizes $(\frac{m_1}{2^l}, \frac{m_1}{2^l})$, where the number $z_l$ of squares for class $l$ is proportional to the total work $w_l$ of tasks in $T^{(l)}$. The squares can be feasibly allocated in the system mesh using wrap-around layout as shown in Fig. 5.28b because each smaller square size divides the size of the bigger square, and the number of used processors is not greater than $m_1^2$. A key difficulty here is that in this online setting processing times, and hence, the work of the tasks, is unknown until their completion. To overcome it, work in the task classes is sampled. Two further problems arise. How long the sampling should last to have a good work estimate. The estimates of work for different task sizes should be known at once. For the first issue it was decided that sampling lasts until the total processing time of the tasks exceeds twice an estimate of the longest processing time. It is assumed that the longest processing time is at most twice as long as the longest processing time observed in the course of executing the algorithm. If a longer task appears, then the currently running tasks are allowed to finish, and the algorithm is restarted with a doubled estimate of the longest running time. Thus, the schedule is a sequence of parts with consecutively doubled estimates of the longest processing time. In each part the estimation of the longest processing time is $2^h\tau$, where $\tau$ is the initial processing time estimate. To solve the second issue the system mesh is partitioned such that tasks of all different classes may be executed in parallel. First, the system mesh is partitioned into $(\log m_1) - 2$ meshes of sizes $(\frac{m_1}{2^{l-2}}, m_1)$, where each such area is dedicated to class $T^{(l)}$, $l \ge 3$ (see Fig. 5.28a). The above meshes are divided horizontally into submeshes $(\frac{m_1}{2^{l-2}}, \frac{m_1(k+1)}{2^{k+2}})$, for tasks in subclass $T^{(l,k)}$, $k \geq 0$. Observe that these submeshes can be divided into $(k + 1)2^l$ boxes $G_{l,k,j}$ of size $(\frac{m_1}{2^l}, \frac{m_1}{2^{l+k}})$, and $(k + 1)2^l$ tasks from subclass $T^{(l,k)}$ can be executed in parallel. Randomization is used at the beginning of the algorithm to select a sample of tasks from $T^{(l,k)}$ for execution in $G_{l,k,j}$. Algorithm sample for 2D-meshes is summarized in Fig. 5.29 [208]. For simplicity of presentation we assume $\forall T_j$, $p_j > 0$. Instruction **wait** means that the algorithm waits until finishing the currently running tasks.

When system mesh has sizes which are not power of 2, then a modified version of the above algorithm is 44-competitive [208]. A $d$-dimensional version of SAMPLE has been also proposed. If both the system mesh and the requested submeshes are squares with power of 2 sizes, then the $d$-dimensional version of SAMPLE is $O(1)$-competitive, i.e. independent of $d$ and the number of processors in the mesh. When the sizes of system and the requested meshes are arbitrary, then the $d$-dimensional version of SAMPLE is $O(4^d)$-competitive [208].

**Level(Pack_2D) [25]** is an algorithm for online scheduling UET tasks with unknown precedence constraints. It is based on the idea of packing the ready tasks into unit square, which is similar to algorithm level(FF) for rigid tasks using 1D packing (cf. Sect. 5.3.1.3). The arguments and the structure of the algorithm are also similar to LPT-LL [169]. Each used square is equivalent to a unit interval of the schedule. First let us scale the system mesh to a unit square, and the meshes requested by the tasks to rectangles $(x'_j, y'_j) = (\frac{x_j}{m_1}, \frac{y_j}{m_2})$, for $j = 1, \ldots, n$. Tasks requiring area $x'_j y'_j \geq \frac{7}{32}$ are packed into separate squares. The remaining set of tasks ready at time $\tau$ is split into subsets $T^x(\tau) = \{T_j : x'_j \geq y'_j\}$ and $T^y(\tau) = \{T_j : x'_j < y'_j\}$. Tasks in $T^x(\tau)$ are sorted according to decreasing $y'_j$, and further divided into subsets $T^x_1(\tau), T^x_2(\tau), \ldots$ with the total required area $\sum_{j \in T^x_i(\tau)} x'_j y'_j$ between $\frac{7}{32}$ and $\frac{7}{16}$. Each set $T^x_i(\tau)$ is packed into one square using the following shelf algorithm $L^x$. $L^x$ uses shelves that span along horizontal dimension $x$. Tasks with $x'_j \geq \frac{1}{2}$ are put on separate shelves starting at the left border of the square. The remaining tasks are put on the shelves using Next Fit Decreasing Height algorithm. The tasks in $T^y(\tau)$ are treated analogously, but algorithm $L^y$ is applied which builds vertical shelves.

**N2d [240]** This algorithm is applied to online scheduling UET tasks with mesh shape and unknown precedence constraints, as the above Level(Pack_2D). Similarly, each time unit of the schedule is a bin for the ready tasks, but a different packing algorithm is used. Again, let us assume that the system mesh is a square $(1, 1)$, and the requested submeshes are scaled accordingly. Ready tasks are divided into four classes: big tasks $\{T_j : x_j > \frac{1}{2}, y_j > \frac{1}{2}\}$, small tasks $\{T_j : x_j \leq \frac{1}{2}, y_j \leq \frac{1}{2}\}$, long tasks $\{T_j : x_j \leq \frac{1}{2}, y_j > \frac{1}{2}\}$, and wide tasks $\{T_j : x_j > \frac{1}{2}, y_j \leq \frac{1}{2}\}$, and are packed in two steps. In the first step tasks are only assigned to the bins. Big tasks are assigned to separate bins. Long tasks are inserted using (the standard bin packing) FF on widths into partially filled bins if the width does not exceed 1. If a long task does not fit in any existing bin, then a new bin is opened. Wide tasks are assigned to new bins using FF on their heights. Consider all bins with the total area

1: Schedule sequentially classes $T^{(0)}, T^{(1)}, T^{(2)}$ using algorithm CLASS;
   $\tau = \max_{\{T_j \in T^{(l)} | l = 0,1,2\}} \{p_j\}; h = 1; \text{done} = \textbf{false};$

**while** (**not** done) // while not all tasks are scheduled
{
2: **try** // try scheduling with the current estimate $2^h \tau$ of $p_{max}$.
   {
3: **wait**; // allow for finishing the currently running tasks, if any
4: **while** (time elapsed in this step $< 2^{h+1} \tau$) // sampling
   {
   **for all** $l, k, j$ **do in parallel** // mind that $l \geq 3$
   {
   **if** (box $G_{l,k,j}$ is empty, and there is unscheduled task in $T^{(l,k)}$)
      schedule random unscheduled task from $T^{(l,k)}$ on $G_{l,k,j}$
   }
   **wait**;
   **if** (processing time of any task exceeded $2^h \tau$) **throw** new_estimate;
   }
5: **for all** $l, k$
   {
   **if** (there are unfinished tasks in $T^{(l,k)}$)
      {
      set $n_{lk} = $ the number of unfinished tasks in $T^{(l,k)}$;
      set $g_{lk} = $ the smallest $g$ such that the sum of processing times of the first $g$ tasks from
      $T^{(l,k)}$ scheduled in step 4 is at least $2(k+1)2^l 2^h \tau$;
      $w_{lk} = \frac{4n_{lk}(k+1)2^l 2^h \tau}{g_{lk}}$;
      }
   **else** set $w_{lk} = $ sum of processing times of tasks in $T^{(l,k)}$ scheduled in step 4;
   }
   **for all** $l$ $\{w_l = \frac{m_1}{2^l} \sum_{k=0}^{\log m_1} w_{lk} \frac{m_1}{2^{l+k}}\}; w = \sum_{l=3}^{\log m_1} w_l$; //calculate work estimates
   **for all** $l$ $\{proc_l = \frac{47}{48} m_1^2 \frac{w_l}{w}; z_l = \lceil \frac{proc_l}{(\frac{m_1}{2^l})^2} \rceil\}$; // processor assignments for $T^{(l)}$
6: partition the system mesh into $z_l$ squares $H_l$, of sizes $(\frac{m_1}{2^l}, \frac{m_1}{2^l}), l = 3, \ldots, \log m_1$;
7: **for all** $l$ **do in parallel**
   {
   schedule $T^l$ on the collection of $z_l$ squares $H_l$ using algorithm CLASS;
   **if** (tasks in $T^{(l)}$ are finished) **and** (their total work scheduled in this step $< \frac{w_l}{4}$)
   **throw** new_estimate;
   **if** (the length of the schedule built in this step is $\geq \frac{48w}{47m_1^2}$) **throw** new_estimate;
   **if** (processing time of any task exceeded $2^h \tau$) **throw** new_estimate;
   }
   done = **true**;
   } // end of try

   **catch** (new_estimate)  // new estimate of $p_{max}$
   {**wait**; $h = h + 1;$ }     // end the running tasks, double the estimate, continue from step 2:

} // end of while(not done), all tasks scheduled

**Fig. 5.29** Algorithm Sample (on the basis of [208], copyright (1996), with permission from Elsevier)

**Fig. 5.30** Mesh partitioning
in algorithm N2d

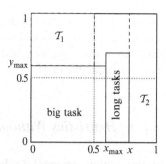

occupied by the assigned tasks strictly smaller than $\frac{1}{2}$. Insert small tasks into these bins using FF on the required area $(x_j y_j)$ such that the total occupied area is at most $\frac{1}{2}$. Open a new bin for the small task if the total area were to exceed $\frac{1}{2}$. In the second step actual layouts of the tasks in the bins are constructed using a Steinberg's 2D packing algorithm $M$ proposed in [219]. Three cases are possible: A bin has no small tasks, then task layout can be easily constructed because big and long tasks assigned to the same bin have width smaller than 1, wide tasks are executed alone and their total height is at most 1. A bin has no big tasks, then it has only long and small tasks or wide and small tasks, and Steinberg's algorithm $M$ can be applied. A bin has a big and small tasks then it is divided into three parts (see Fig. 5.30). The big task is put in the lower-left corner and the long tasks are put to its right. Let $x$ be the total width of the big and long tasks. Small tasks are split into two subsets $\mathcal{T}_1 = \{T_j \in small : x_j > 1 - x\}$ and $\mathcal{T}_2 = \{T_j \in small : x_j \leq 1 - x\}$. Tasks in $\mathcal{T}_1$ are placed using algorithm $M$ in the area of size $(\frac{1}{2}, 1 - y_{max})$ above the big task, and the tasks in $\mathcal{T}_2$ are placed to the right of long tasks in area of size $(1 - x, 1)$ using algorithm $M$, where $(x_{max}, y_{max})$ is the size of the big task. See [240] for the proof of the feasibility and quality of the packing. The performance guarantee of N2d in Table 5.15 is provided without task rotation. If the rotation is allowed, then after rotating the tasks such that $\forall\, T_j, x_j \geq y_j$, the same algorithm named **R2d** has a stronger performance guarantee of 4.25.

### 5.7.2.3 $d$-Dimensional Meshes

Before presenting a heuristic formulated for a general $d$D-mesh, let us remind that algorithms BP, Sample, presented above have their versions for $d$D-meshes.

**Mesh [102]** This algorithm is similar to algorithm HC for scheduling in hypercubes (see Sect. 5.6.2). It is dedicated for scheduling moldable tasks with linear speedup, mesh shape, and precedences on $d$-dimensional mesh, with $p = \sqrt[d]{m}$ processors along each of the dimensions. Let $k$ be the smallest integer such that $k^k > p$. Note that $k$ is $O(\frac{\log p}{\log \log p})$. Tasks are partitioned into $h = k^d$ classes $\mathcal{T}_{(i_1,\ldots,i_d)}$ according to the requested submesh size, where $1 \leq i_l \leq k, l = 1, \ldots, d$. Let $(x_{1j}, \ldots, x_{dj})$ be the size of the submesh requested by $T_j$. $\mathcal{T}_{(i_1,\ldots,i_d)} = \{T_j : \frac{p}{k^{i_l}} < x_{lj} \leq \frac{p}{k^{i_l-1}},$

$l = 1, \ldots, d\}$. The mesh is divided into $h$ submeshes of size $\lfloor \frac{p}{k} \rfloor \times \cdots \times \lfloor \frac{p}{k} \rfloor$. Each task class $\mathcal{T}_{(i_1,\ldots,i_d)}$ has its own queue $\mathcal{Q}_{(i_1,\ldots,i_d)}$ to a dedicated submesh $M_{(i_1,\ldots,i_d)}$. Tasks from $\mathcal{Q}_{(i_1,\ldots,i_d)}$ are scheduled as soon as a submesh of size $\lfloor \frac{p}{k^{i_1}} \rfloor \times \cdots \times \lfloor \frac{p}{k^{i_d}} \rfloor$ becomes available in $M_{(i_1,\ldots,i_d)}$.

### 5.7.3  Heuristics Without a Guarantee

In this section, we present scheduling heuristics which have no guarantees of performance in the worst case, but have been evaluated by simulation. As it has been observed in Sect. 5.7.1, FIFO is not a good choice of task sequencing. An immediate improvement that comes to mind is to combine a sequencing heuristic with some allocation algorithm from Sect. 5.7.1. And indeed, such combinations have been proposed. For example, **NIS/BLFF** [10] schedules tasks according to the nonincreasing sizes, and allocates submeshes using a simplified version of BLBBV algorithm [210]. Here size is the number of requested processors $xy$. The simplification of BLBBV consists in using FF strategy instead of BF on the basis of boundary values. **NDs/2DFF** [242] sequences tasks according to nondecreasing sizes $(xy)$, and allocates meshes with 2DFF [246]. To overcome a preference for small tasks, a limit on the task waiting time is added after exceeding which the task is scheduled first. Other heuristics for scheduling tasks with mesh shape are presented below. Many of the ideas presented in this section can be generalized beyond mesh-connected systems.

**2DFF/RT [244]**  It is a method for online preemptive scheduling of tasks with deadlines and mesh shape. We named this method 2DFF/RT for it combines and extends the features of 2DFF (Sect. 5.7.1) and Buddy/RT (Sect. 5.6.4). An array of processor Earliest Available Times (EAT) is used, where EAT[a,b] is the earliest time at which processor $(a, b)$ becomes free. The indices of currently running tasks are held in set $Q_A$, and the indices of tasks with reservations are held in set $Q_R$. The busy set $B$ is a list of 6-tuples $(a, b, c, d, \tau_1, \tau_2)$, where $(a, b, c, d)$ are corner coordinates of the allocated mesh, $\tau_1$ is the start time, and $\tau_2$ is the finish time of using the submesh. The set of reservations $R$ is held in an analogous way. Let us assume that task $T$ arriving at time $\tau$ requires submesh $(x, y)$, has deadline $d$, and processing time $p$. The algorithm calculates task latest starting time $lst = d - p$ and laxity $d - p - \tau$. In the first phase the algorithm tries to append $T$ to the current schedule. Using EAT table the earliest time $\tau'$ at which some base $(a, b)$ is free for $(x, y)$ is determined. If $\tau' \le lst$, then $T$ is assigned this base for the interval of length $p$. If $\tau' = \tau \le lst$, i.e. the base found is free at the arrival of $T$, then $T$ is added to $Q_A$, and $(a, b, a + x - 1, b + y - 1, \tau, \tau + p)$ is added to the busy set $B$. If $\tau < \tau' \le lst$, then a reservation for $T$ is made: $T$ is added to $Q_R$, and $(a, b, a + x - 1, b + y - 1, \tau', \tau' + p)$ is added to the reservations list $R$. Otherwise, $\tau' > lst$, and $T$ cannot be simply appended to the current schedule. If the laxity is bigger than the worst-case execution time of the second phase then the algorithm initiates its second phase. If the available time is too short $T$ is rejected. In the second phase the algorithm analyzes reservations. Tasks in reservation set $Q_R$ with their laxities greater than the laxity of $T$ are considered together with $T$ for rescheduling. If the attempts succeed, and all tasks meet their deadlines, then all the new reservations are inserted in $R$. Otherwise, the algorithm may attempt its third phase if there is enough laxity. In the third phase a currently running task $T'$ is searched for which can be preempted leaving a free frame for $T$. Thus, $T$ must fit in the area abandoned by $T'$. Furthermore, inserting of the interval $p$ of processing $T$ may affect some tasks executed after $T'$ on the area of processors overlapping with $T'$. All such tasks, and the remaining part of $T'$, must be feasibly rescheduled. If all the tree phases fail, $T$ is rejected. The complexity of this method is $O(m_1 m_2 n^3)$.

**HELM [184]**   The name of this heuristic comes from its High priority queue, Entrance queue, and Lookahead Multiple queues. When a task enters the system it is appended to the entrance queue (EQ). HELM scans EQ from the head to the depth of lookahead window. If the current task in EQ can be allocated, then its execution starts immediately. Feasibility of the allocation is checked by 2DFF algorithm (cf. Sect. 5.7.1). Otherwise, it is moved to one of the lookahead queues (LQs). HELM tries to allocate the next task from EQ, until reaching the end of lookahead window. The depth of the lookahead window is a linear function of the average EQ length. The coefficient of the function must be experimentally tuned. Tasks which join LQs are classified according to the number $xy$ of requested processors. The number of LQs is a tunable parameter. LQs are considered one by one in the order of (e.g.) nonincreasing sizes. If a task from a certain LQ cannot be allocated, then HELM proceeds to the next task in the current queue. However, if the task cannot be allocated for time longer than the upper bound of waiting time (UBWT), then it is moved to HQ. UBWT is a linear function of the average waiting time of the tasks leaving the system. The coefficient of the UBWT function is a tunable parameter of the algorithm. Tasks in HQ have the highest priority, and are scheduled according to FCFS order before tasks from all other queues. Thus, HELM scans queues in the following order: HQ, then LQs according to decreasing sizes, EQ to the depth of lookahead window. The probability of successfully allocating a submesh for big tasks is smaller than for the small tasks. Hence, it is more likely that the waiting time of big tasks will exceed UBWT. By the use of HQ and UBWT, this algorithm has a mechanism to control equality in accessing the processor resource by big and small tasks.

**Multitasking and Multiprogramming ($M^2$) [242]**   The idea of time sharing (cf. Sect. 5.3.3) is applied in mesh-connected computers. The incoming tasks are divided into four classes according to the dimensions $(x, y)$ of the requested submesh: small tasks (here $x \leq \frac{m_1}{2}, y \leq \frac{m_2}{2}$), wide tasks (with $x > \frac{m_1}{2}, y \leq \frac{m_2}{2}$), long task (with $x \leq \frac{m_1}{2}, y > \frac{m_2}{2}$), and large tasks ($x > \frac{m_1}{2}, y > \frac{m_2}{2}$). Classes are executed on the mesh for a time quantum, and switched on the processors one after another in a RR fashion. For each class a FIFO waiting queue is maintained. Allocation of submeshes in each class is performed by 2DFF algorithm.

**2D Packing [125]** Here tasks are moldable. The cost of executing a task consists of two parts: computational part which preserves linear speedup with changing number of processors and communication cost which is proportional to the side sizes of task submesh. This cost should be minimized. The allocation algorithm proposed here boils down to 2D-packing of task rectangles into the system mesh. The tasks are sorted according to some ordering rule. It has been established empirically that the order of decreasing number of requested processors $x_1 y_1 \geq x_2 y_2 \geq \cdots \geq x_n y_n$ is a good ordering rule, and decreasing aspect ratio $\frac{x_1}{y_1} \geq \frac{x_2}{y_2} \geq \cdots \geq \frac{x_n}{y_n}$ is a bad rule. First, a tentative layout of the tasks is constructed by packing the task rectangles $(x_j, y_j)$ into lower left corners of free areas remaining after assigning the preceding tasks. Out of the many possible corner choices, the one which increases the least the width $W$ and desirable height $H = W \frac{m_2}{m_1}$ of the used area is selected. Then, the layout of tasks is scaled to the system mesh in one of two ways. In the first scaling method all the assignments are first scaled by $\frac{m_1}{W}$ horizontally and then by $\frac{m_2}{H}$ vertically. In the second method the layout of the tasks is scaled horizontally and vertically by $\min\{\frac{m_1}{W}, \frac{m_2}{H}\}$ in order to preserve the original aspect ratio of the tasks.

**Reservation and Priority [211]** We propose to name this heuristic after its main features. It combines reservation and priority based on aging with allocation algorithm BLBBV [210]. When a new task arrives in the system, a free submesh is searched for. If the allocation fails the algorithm tries to make a reservation for the task. If the reservation is successful, then the task joins reservation queue. Otherwise, it joins waiting queue. When some task departs from the system, the submesh it was using is not only assigned to the tasks that had reservation there, but also allocating other tasks from the reservation and waiting queues is attempted. There are precautions against starvation in this algorithm. Below we present it in more detail.

The algorithm maintains a list of busy submeshes and a list of reserved submeshes. Allocation works as in BLBBV, but restricted areas include both the currently occupied submeshes and the reserved ones. Here submesh boundary value, which is used by BLBBV, is the number of neighboring allocated or reserved processors including machine mesh boundaries. A submesh with the highest boundary value is assigned to the requesting task.

A processor cannot be reserved twice. Therefore, the already reserved areas must be avoided in BLBBV while searching for a new reservation. The new reservation of submesh $(x, y)$ may be found by sliding $(x, y)$ around the current reservations. A reservation may also overlap currently allocated areas and remain adjacent to the borders of other occupied submeshes. Hence, further possible reservations are obtained by starting sliding the requested rectangle from the base of some allocated area. For a potential reservation $(a, b, c, d)$ a *reservation value* is calculated which is the sum of the boundary value and the number of processors in the submeshes allocated within $(a, b, c, d)$ that happen to share boundary with $(a, b, c, d)$. A potential reservation of submesh $(x, y)$ is rejected if it covers more than $x y \times FREE\_FRAC$ free processors, where $FREE\_FRAC$ is a tunable parameter. The best reservation is chosen using three rules: First, the reservations comprising the fewest free processors are selected. If there is a tie, then the reservations overlapping minimum number of busy submeshes are selected. Finally, the submesh with maximum reservation value is used. For each task $T_j$ joining a waiting queue a counter $no\_supersede[j]$ of the tasks that got allocation or reservation bypassing $T_j$ is created. If $no\_supersede[j] > BPL$ then new allocations and reservations are suspended until $T_j$ gets allocation or reservation. Here bypass limit $BPL$ is a tunable parameter which regulates starvation. The allocation procedure for task $T_i$ can be summarized as follows:

1. Allocate a free mesh using $BLBBV$. If successful goto 3.
2. Attempt making a reservation. If failed goto 4.
3. Increment $no\_supersede[j]$ of all waiting tasks $T_j$. If $no\_supersede[j] > BPL$ for any $T_j$ then suspend any new allocations and reservation. Stop.
4. Append $T_i$ to the waiting queue; $no\_supersede[i] = 0$.

In the deallocation procedure presented below some tasks may get allocation as a consequence of releasing some processors. Therefore, values of counters $no\_supersede[j]$ for the tasks in the waiting queue are updated each time they are bypassed. Furthermore, allocation and reservation suspension is revoked in deallocation procedure as soon as the tasks with $no\_supersede[j] > BPL$ receive allocation or reservation. The procedure of deallocating submesh $(a, b, c, d)$ proceeds as follows:

1. Remove $(a, b, c, d)$ from the busy list.
2. Search the reservation queue and for each reservation overlapping $(a, b, c, d)$ decrease the number of overlapping busy areas. If for some task $T_j$ this number is 0, then assign the reserved region to $T_j$.
3. Attempt allocating tasks remaining in the reservation queue in area $(a, b, c, d)$ and the reservation areas freed by the tasks allocated in this step. Repeat this step as long as any task with reservation gets allocation.
4. Try making allocation for the tasks from the waiting queue in area $(a, b, c, d)$ and the reservation regions released by the tasks allocated in step 3.
5. Scan the waiting queue and try making reservations for the waiting tasks in $(a, b, c, d)$ and the reservation regions released in step 3.

This algorithm can be implemented to perform allocations in $O(n^3)$ time, and deallocations in $O(n^4)$ time, where $n$ is the total number of tasks running in the systems and waiting in the queues.

**Simple Linear Combination (SLC) and Nonlinear Combination with ByPass Value (NLC_BPV) [118]** It has been observed that NIS heuristic constructs schedules with little fragmentation when the variability of task sizes is high. Here NIS heuristic scans the queue of the waiting tasks, and assigns them to the processors disregarding the arrival order. On the other hand, when the dispersion of task sizes is small, or there is a constant stream of big tasks, then some tasks may starve. To eliminate starvation many heuristics introduce some kind of limit on the time the task may wait, or a bypass limit BPL which is the number of times a task may be bypassed. When the limit is exceeded, then these algorithms switch to FIFO until all tasks are below BPL. A disadvantage is that in FIFO mode of operation utilization of the processor resource is small, and hence all other performance metrics are bad. In SLC and NLC_BPV heuristic algorithms a softer method making a transition from NIS to FIFO order has been proposed. Let $NIS(j)$ be task $T_j$ rank in NIS order and $F(j)$ in the arrival (FIFO) order. SLC combines these two orders calculating task priority from formula: $SLC(j) = R(\tau)NIS(j) + (1 - R(\tau))F(j)$, where $R(\tau) = \min\{1, \frac{\sigma(\tau)}{\mu(\tau)}\}$, $\sigma(\tau)$ and $\mu(\tau)$ are standard deviation and mean of task sizes $xy$ at time $\tau$, respectively. The smaller values of $SLC(j)$ represent higher priorities. Thus, in $SLC(j)$ dispersion of task sizes is accounted for, and NIS order is dominating if the dispersion is big. In NLC_BPV task priority is calculated from formula: $NLC\_BPV(j) = R(\tau)(1 - (\frac{bpv(j)}{BPL})^{kBPL})NIS(j) + (1 - R(\tau))(\frac{bpv(j)}{BPL})^{kBPL}F(j)$, where $bpv(j)$ is the number of times task $j$ has been bypassed, and $k$ is a tunable algorithm parameter (in experiments set to $k = 0.2$ [118]). Thus, the closer a task becomes to BPL, the more the arrival (FIFO) order matters.

## 5.8  Multiprocessor Tasks

In this section, we study scheduling multiprocessor tasks, by which we mean parallel tasks requiring a set of processors simultaneously. Alternatively, a family of processor sets on which the task can be executed can be given. This setting is often referred to as scheduling parallel tasks on dedicated processors. Multiprocessor task scheduling has immediate connections with graph theory and graph coloring in particular [157]. There is a rich set of results on this subject, and many of them can be transferred to our scheduling problem. Moreover, scheduling multiprocessor tasks can be considered a special case of scheduling under discrete resource constraints [32, 34]. By adding precedence constraints to the multiprocessor tasks, classic deterministic flow shop, job shop, project scheduling problems can be formulated as special cases of multiprocessor task scheduling problems [22, 39, 40, 131]. Due to space limitations and to preserve integrity of presentation, we do not report all such results.

### 5.8.1  $C_{max}$, $L_{max}$ Criteria

#### 5.8.1.1  Nonpreemptive Schedules, Typical Approaches

The results on complexity of multiprocessor task scheduling for makespan ($C_{max}$), and lateness ($L_{max}$) criteria are collected in Table 5.16. The following notations were used in Table 5.16:

- GDSC – An abbreviation for graph-dependent special cases. Many complexity results follow from hardness or polynomial time solvability of coloring for

**Table 5.16**   Complexity of nonpreemptive multiprocessor task scheduling, $C_{max}$, $L_{max}$

| Problem | Result | Reference |
|---|---|---|
| Single mode tasks | | |
| $P\lfloor fix_j, p_j = 1 \vert C_{max}, \lfloor fix_j \rfloor = 2$ | sNPh | [66, 148] |
| $P\lfloor fix_j, p_j = 1 \vert C_{max}, \lfloor fix_j \rfloor = 2$ | GDSC | [66, 156] |
| $P\lfloor fix_j \vert C_{max}, \lfloor fix_j \rfloor = 2$ | GDSC | [66, 70, 71] |
| $P\lfloor fix_j \vert C_{max}, \lfloor fix_j \rfloor \in \{1, 2\}$ | GDSC | [154] |
| $P3\lfloor fix_j \vert C_{max}$ | sNPh | [28, 121] |
| $P\lfloor fix_j, p_j = 1 \vert C_{max} = 3$ | sNPh | [121] |
| $Pm\lfloor fix_j, p_j = 1 \vert C_{max}$ | $O(n)$ | [121] |
| $P2\lfloor fix_j, chain, p_j = 1 \vert C_{max}$ | sNPh | [121] |
| $P2\lfloor fix_j, r_j \vert C_{max}$ | sNPh | [121] |
| $P4\lfloor fix_j, p_j = 1 \vert C_{max}$ | $O(n)$ | [23] |
| $P5\lfloor fix_j, p_j = 1 \vert C_{max}$ | $O(n^{2.5})$ | [23] |
| $P2\lfloor fix_j \vert L_{max}$ | sNPh | [79] |
| $P3\lfloor fix_j \vert C_{max}, \lfloor fix_j \rfloor = 2$ | $O(n)$ | [156] |
| $P3\lfloor fix_j, chain \vert C_{max}, \lfloor fix_j \rfloor = 2$ | $O(n)$ | [156] |
| $P4\lfloor fix_j, chain, p_j = 1 \vert C_{max}, \lfloor fix_j \rfloor = 2$ | sNPh | [156] |
| $Pm\lfloor fix_j, p_1 = 1, r_j \vert C_{max}$ | $O(k2^k n^{k+1})$ | [41] |
| $P2, win \lfloor fix_j, p_j = 1, r_j \vert C_{max}$ | $O(n + p)$ | [82] |
| $P3, win \lfloor fix_j, p_j = 1 \vert C_{max}$ | $O(n + p)$ | [82] |
| Multimode tasks | | |
| $P2 \vert set_j \vert C_{max}$ | $O(nT^3)$ | [20] |
| $P3 \vert set_j \vert C_{max}, fix_{ij} \neq \{P_1, P_3\}$ | $O(nT^4)$ | [20] |
| $P2 \vert set_j \vert C_{max}$ | $O(nT)$ | [52] |
| $P3 \vert set_j \vert C_{max}, fix_{ij} \neq \{P_1, P_3\}$ | $O(nT^2)$ | [52] |

different graph structures arising in our scheduling problem. Existence of the studies on such relations is marked by the above abbreviation.

- $k$ – The number of different processor sets $fix_j$ which may be requested. Here $k$ is $O(2^m)$, which is fixed for fixed processor number $m$.
- $p$ – The number of processor availability windows.
- $win$ – Processors are available in restricted intervals.
- $T$ – Is an upper bound on schedule length. For example, it can be set to $T = \sum_{j=1}^{n} \min_{fix_i \in set_j} \{p_{ij}\}$.

Below we outline some of the methods used for multiprocessor task scheduling.

## $P\lfloor fix_j \vert C_{max}$

To our best knowledge, the first publication on multiprocessor tasks was [38]. A problem of scheduling in chemical plants, and fabricating shops where in-waiting inventories must be avoided, was analyzed. Though it is not a parallel computing application a similar situation may arise in parallel processing. For example, when a chain of pipelines must be set up in a vector computer, it remains dedicated for a certain application for a relatively long time, similarly to a set of pipes and chemical reactors in a plant. Two tasks $T_i, T_j$ requiring disjoint sets of processors are called compatible, and vice versa if $fix_i \cap fix_j \neq \emptyset$ then $T_i, T_j$ are said to be incompatible. Incompatibility of the tasks can be represented as an *incompatibility graph* (or equivalently by its complement which is a compatibility graph). Note that in the in-/compatibility graphs tasks are represented as nodes. A branch and bound algorithm has been proposed in [38]. A lower bound was calculated as the processing time of incompatible tasks. Notice that this is equivalent to determining a clique in the incompatibility graph, which is a hard combinatorial problem itself. Right from this first publication it can be deduced that multiprocessor task scheduling has close ties with graph theory. It can be easily guessed that nonpreemptive multiprocessor task scheduling is **NP**-hard, because assuming $\forall T_j, p_j = 1$ makes the problem equivalent with **NP**-hard chromatic number problem [110]. Furthermore, each set of properly colored vertices in the incompatibility graph is a set of compatible tasks which can be feasibly executed in parallel. Therefore, heuristics for graph coloring, maximum clique, maximum independent set can be adapted in scheduling multiprocessor tasks [46, 68, 126, 157].

A problem of diagnostic test scheduling has been analyzed in [148]. A set of devices test each other. The tests are nonpreemptive, and involve selected pairs of devices. A graph representation has been used. The devices are represented as nodes, and the tasks (i.e. tests) are edges with weights $p_j$, for task $T_j$. We will call this graph representation a *scheduling graph*. The shortest test schedule is required. This problem is computationally hard because assuming $\forall T_j, p_j = 1$, the diagnostic test scheduling problem becomes equivalent with the chromatic index problem (i.e. classic edge coloring) which is NP-complete [120]. A similar modeling has been used in [66] for file transfer scheduling. An edge represents a file transfer to be performed, and the nodes represent senders and receivers. Since more than one file can be transferred between two processors, there can be parallel edges, and the scheduling graph can be a multigraph. A task requiring only one processor can be represented as a loop in the graph. Observe that scheduling graphs are not easily extensible to tasks requiring more than two processors simultaneously, because it would require a hypergraph representation.

In [23] the incompatibility graph has been extended to a weighted graph in which a node corresponding to $T_j$ has weight $p_j$. This graph was called *constraint graph*. It has been observed in [23] that any feasible schedule imposes orientation on the edges of the constraint graph. And vice versa, any acyclic transitive orientation of the edges in the constraint graph induces a feasible schedule. This has several consequences. First, if the constraint graph is a *comparability graph* then any transitive orientation of the edges defines an optimum schedule, and its length is equal to the weight of the maximum weighted clique. Graph $\mathcal{G} = (V, E)$ is a comparability graph if there exists edge orientation $\mathcal{O}$ such that $\{a, b\}, \{b, c\} \in E$ and $(a, b), (b, c) \in \mathcal{O} \Rightarrow \{a, c\} \in E$ and $(a, c) \in \mathcal{O}$. The second consequence is that if the constraint graph is not a comparability graph, then by adding some edges it can be extended to a comparability graph. Then the problem of constructing the optimum schedule boils down to finding augmentation of the constraint graph into a comparability graph with minimum weight of the maximum weighted clique. The third consequence is that the method of constructing the schedule by finding edge orientation in the constraint or incompatibility graphs is analogous to constructing a schedule in a job shop by finding orientation of the edges in the disjunctive graph [32, 39]. Hence, scheduling multiprocessor tasks is closely related to the classic job-shop problem. The constraint graph representation can be extended to multimode tasks (problem $P|set_j|C_{max}$) [24].

## $Pm|fix_j, p_j = 1|C_{max}$ [121]

This problem can be solved similarly to problem $Pm|size_j, p_j = 1|C_{max}$, by generating all processor feasible sets, and then applying integer linear program analogous to (5.1)–(5.3) to find out how many copies of a given processor feasible set must be used. Here processor feasible sets comprise compatible tasks, or in other words, independent sets in the incompatibility graph. The number of different sets of required processors $fix_j$ is at most $2^m - 1$. Hence, the number of different processor feasible sets is $2^{2^m-1} - 1$, and though this number may be big, it is fixed for $m$ fixed. Consequently, the number of variables in the ILP is also fixed, and it can be solved in $O(n)$ time as formulation (5.1)–(5.3).

## $Pm|fix_j, p_j = 1, r_j|C_{max}$ [41]

This problem can be reduced to calculating the shortest path in some graph $\mathcal{G}$. Let $k \leq 2^m - 1$ be the number of different task types, which is the number of different sets $fix_j$ that may be requested. For a fixed $m$, also $k$ is fixed. We will say that tasks requesting processor set $fix_j$ are of type $j$. Let us denote by $n_j$ the number of tasks of type $j$. For simplicity of presentation we assume that $\min_j\{r_j\} = 0$, and that tasks are ordered according to nondecreasing ready times. Let $T$ be an upper bound on schedule length. Observe that $T$ cannot be bigger than $n$. Otherwise the schedule decomposes into disconnected intervals. Each vertex in $\mathcal{G}$ corresponds with one $(2k + 1)$-tuple $(\tau, i_1, \ldots, i_k, l_1, \ldots, l_k)$, where $\tau = 0, \ldots, T, i_j = 0, \ldots, n_j, l_j \in \{0, 1\}$, and $r_{i_j} \leq \tau$, for $j = 1, \ldots, k$. Tuple $(\tau, i_1, \ldots, i_k, l_1, \ldots, l_k)$ represents a partial schedule of length $\tau$ with $i_j$ tasks of type $j$ started until $\tau$, and $l_j$ tasks of type $j$ finishing at $\tau + 1$. Condition $r_{i_j} \leq \tau$ ensures that ready times are obeyed in the constructed schedule. There are two sets of arcs in $\mathcal{G}$. The first set connects tuples $(\tau, i_1, \ldots, i_k, l_1, \ldots, l_k)$, with $(\tau, i'_1, \ldots, i'_k, l'_1, \ldots, l'_k)$, where $i'_a = i_a + 1, l_a = 0$, $l'_a = 1$ for some $a$ and $i'_j = i_j \; l'_j = l_j$ for all $j \neq a$. Furthermore, if $l_j = 1$ for some $j \neq a$, then task types $j$ and $a$ must be compatible, i.e. $fix_a \cap fix_j = \emptyset$. The weight of such an arc is $\tau + 1$. These arcs represent starting task of type $j$ at time $\tau$. The second set of arcs connects two consecutive starting times $\tau$ and $\tau + 1$ if $\tau + 1 \leq T$. Thus, there is an arc from tuple $(\tau, i_1, \ldots, i_k, l_1, \ldots, l_k)$ to tuple $(\tau + 1, i_1, \ldots, i_k, 0, \ldots, 0)$. Such arcs have weight 0. Here $(0, \ldots, 0)$ is a starting vertex, and $(T, n_1, \ldots, n_k, 0, \ldots, 0)$ is a terminal vertex. A feasible schedule for $Pm|fix_j, p_j = 1, r_j|C_{max}$ corresponds to a path in $\mathcal{G}$. If the length of the path is calculated as a maximum of arc weights $(\tau + 1)$ then the length of the path is also schedule length. Hence, the shortest path in the above sense of distance defines the shortest schedule. There are $O(2^k n^{k+1})$ nodes and at most $O(k2^k n^{k+1})$ arcs in graph $\mathcal{G}$, and the shortest path can be constructed in $O(k2^k n^{k+1})$ time [41].

### 5.8.1.2  Nonpreemptive Schedules, Heuristics with a Guarantee

The approximability results for multiprocessor task scheduling are collected in Table 5.17. The following notations were used in Table 5.17:

- $deg(G)$ – Denotes the degree of diagnostic test graph $G$.
- $\varepsilon > 0$ – An arbitrary constant.
- GDSC – Graph-dependent special cases, where approximability guarantees depend on the existence of special structure of incompatibility graph.

**Table 5.17**  Approximability of nonpreemptive multiprocessor task scheduling, $C_{max}$

| Problem | Result | Reference |
|---|---|---|
| Single mode tasks | | |
| $P|fix_j|C_{max}, |fix_j| = 2$ | $R_{LPT} = 4 - \frac{1}{deg(G)}$ | [148] |
| $P|fix_j|C_{max}, |fix_j| = 2$ | $\frac{4}{3+3\varepsilon} \leq R_{LS} = 2$ | [66] |
| $P3|fix_j|C_{max}$ | $R_{NS} < \frac{4}{3}$ | [28] |
| | $R_{NS} = \frac{4}{5}$ | [72] |
| | $R_{18} \leq \frac{7}{6}$ | [116] |
| $P|fix_j, p_j = 1|C_{max}$ | $R \geq \frac{4}{3}$ | [121] |
| $P|fix_j|C_{max}$ | GDSC | [70, 71] |
| $P4|fix_j|C_{max}$ | $R_{Schedule-P4} \leq 1.5$ | [123] |
| $Pm|fix_j|C_{max}$ | PTAS | [4] |
| $Pm|fix_j, r_j|C_{max}$ | PTAS | [11] |
| $P|fix_j, p_j = 1|C_{max}$ | $\forall \varepsilon > 0, R > m^{\frac{1}{2}-\varepsilon}$ | [106, 107] |
| $P3|fix_j|C_{max}$ | GDSC | [181] |
| $P|oll, fix_j, p_j = 1|C_{max}, |fix_j| \leq \delta$ | $R_{FFS} \leq \delta$ | [126] |
| $P|olt, fix_j, p_j = 1|C_{max}, |fix_j| \leq \delta$ | $R_{FFS} \leq \delta + 1$ | [126] |
| $P|oll, fix_j, p_j = 1|C_{max}$ | $R_{FFS+} \leq 2\sqrt{m}$ | [126] |
| $P|olt, fix_j, p_j = 1|C_{max}$ | $R_{FFS+} \leq 2\sqrt{m} + 1$ | [126] |
| $P|oll, fix_j|C_{max}$ | $R_{FFS} \leq m$ | [126] |
| $P|olt, fix_j|C_{max}$ | $R_{FFS} \leq m + 1$ | [126] |
| $P|fix_j|C_{max}$ | $R_{SRS} \leq 3\sqrt{m}$ | [126] |
| $P|olt, fix_j|C_{max}$ | $R_{SRS+} \leq 6\sqrt{m}$ | [126] |
| Multimode tasks | | |
| $P|set_j|C_{max}$ | $R_{SPTM} = m$ | [20] |
| $Pm|set_j|C_{max}$ | $R_{HSA1} = \frac{m}{2} + \varepsilon$ | [52] |
| $Pm|set_j|C_{max}$ | PTAS | [53, 134] |
| $Jm|set_j, op \leq \mu|C_{max}$ | PTAS | [131] |

- $Jm|set_{ij}, op \leq \mu|C_{max}$ – Denotes a job-shop problem with alternative modes of executing job operations, in each mode a set of processors may be requested simultaneously, and the number $op$ of operations per job is not greater than some constant $\mu$. This problem generalizes $Pm|set_j, chain \leq \mu|C_{max}$, where precedence constraints are chains of at most $\mu$ tasks.

The heuristics mentioned in Table 5.17 are presented below.

**Longest Processing Time (LPT) [148]** The approximability ratio of LPT can be improved for certain graph classes [148].

**LS – Any list scheduling Heuristic** The results in [66] were obtained for a more specific problem in which a processor is capable to serve several simultaneous file transfers.

**Normal Schedule (NS) [28]** This method applies to scheduling on three processors (problem $P3|fix_j|C_{max}$). In the normal schedules tasks requiring the same set of processors are executed consecutively without idle times. There are two methods of constructing normal schedules. In the first method three subschedules are concatenated. In each subschedule 2-tasks (requesting two processors) are executed in parallel with the 1-tasks requiring the third processor. There are three patterns of such a schedule if we exclude symmetric solutions. The second type of normal schedules is obtained by executing 1-tasks in parallel. It is always profitable to start this type of schedule with the 2-tasks of the same kind, followed by 1-tasks. There are six schedules of this type. In all cases tasks are executed as early as possible (i.e. are shifted to the left).

**The Best of 18 Schedules (18) [116]** The solution for $P3|fix_j|C_{max}$ proposed in [116] consists in selecting the shortest of 18 different schedules. Six schedules out of the 18 are normal schedules. The remaining 12 patterns also schedule tasks requiring the same set of processors in a compact block, but one set of 1-tasks is split into a longer and a shorter sub-block.

**Schedule $P4$ [123]** It is a heuristic for $P4|fix_j|C_{max}$. The tasks of the same type are scheduled consecutively. Since tasks requesting four processors may be scheduled consecutively at the beginning of the schedule we do not consider them any more. Let $B_1$ be the sum of processing times of 3-tasks plus $\max(12, 34) + \max(13, 24) + \max(14, 23)$. Here $\max(ij, kl) = \max\{\sum_{T_j \in T^{\{ij\}}} p_j, \sum_{T_j \in T^{\{kl\}}} p_j\}$ is the longer processing time of the 2-tasks in mutually compatible sets. A schedule with 3-tasks and 2-tasks is built first. The 2-tasks are scheduled in parallel with the compatible set of 2-tasks. $B_1$ is the length of this schedule (cf. Fig. 5.31a). Let $B_0$ be a lower bound of schedule length obtained as the maximum of: $B_1$ and the sums of processing times of tasks requesting processor $P_i$, for $i = 1, \ldots, 4$. If the initial schedule has one gap with length greater than or equal to $\frac{B_0}{2}$, then 1-tasks are inserted in the gap between the groups of 2-tasks. If the initial schedule has two gaps with total length greater or equal $\frac{B_0}{2}$, then the partial schedules for 3- or 2-tasks of the same type must be

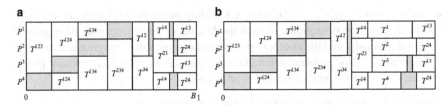

**Fig. 5.31** Approximation algorithm *schedule P4*. (**a**) Initial schedule for 3- and 2-tasks. (**b**) A schedule with 1-tasks inserted

permuted to coalesce the two gaps. Then, again 1-tasks are inserted in the gap. If the initial schedule has no gap of length at least $\frac{B_0}{2}$, then 1-tasks are inserted before the last group of the 2-tasks.

**PTAS for $Pm|fix_j|C_{\max}$ [4]** This polynomial time approximation scheme uses linear programming to build the optimum nonpreemptive schedule for bounded number of long tasks, and possibly preemptive schedule for some limited number of short tasks. The linear program does not distinguish particular short tasks. The short tasks requesting the same set of processors $A$ are treated like one task of type $A$. The short tasks that get preempted are shifted to the end of the schedule and executed in an arbitrary order.

Let $\mathcal{L}$ denote the set of long tasks. For long tasks *relative schedules* are constructed. A relative schedule is a sequence of processor feasible sets (PFSes), i.e. subsets of long tasks that can be executed in parallel. Since the schedule for long task must be nonpreemptive, only sequences in which any long task is present in a single chain of PFSes are admitted as relative schedules. In other words, in a sequence of PFSes there is only one PFS $a_j$ where long task $T_j$ is started, and only one PFS $b_j$ where $T_j$ is finished. In parallel with executing some PFS of long tasks, some set $A$ of processors may be free to execute the short tasks. Such set $A$ of processors may be partitioned to execute various types of short tasks. For a given relative schedule, let us denote by:

$x_i$ – The length of $i$th PFS in the sequence

$M$ – The number of PFSes in the given relative schedule for long tasks, $M \le 2n$

$a_j, b_j$ – The first, and, respectively, the last, PFS including long task $T_j$

$Q_A$ – The set of PFSes of long tasks in which set $A$ of processors is not used by the long tasks

$U_A$ – The set of PFSes of short tasks which can run in parallel on set $A$ of processors

$y_i$ – Duration of PFS $i$ of short tasks

$V_B$ – Set of PFSes of short tasks in $\bigcup_{A \subseteq \{P_1,...,P_m\}} U_A$ which include set $B$ of processors (i.e. task type $B$)

The linear program given below constructs a nonpreemptive schedule for the long tasks and preemptive schedule for the short tasks:

$$\text{minimize} \sum_{i=1}^{M} x_i \qquad \text{subject to} \tag{5.30}$$

$$\sum_{i=a_j}^{b_j} x_i \geq p_j \quad \text{for } T_j \in \mathcal{L} \tag{5.31}$$

$$\sum_{i \in Q_A} x_i \geq \sum_{i \in U_A} y_i \quad \text{for all } A \subseteq \{P_1, \ldots, P_m\} \tag{5.32}$$

$$\sum_{i: \in V_B} y_i \geq \sum_{j \in \{T_j : fix_j = B\}} p_j \tag{5.33}$$

$$x_i, y_i \geq 0 \tag{5.34}$$

The goal of the above formulation is to build the shortest schedule by (5.30) such that all long tasks are fully executed by (5.31), and the intervals not used by the long tasks are able to accommodate the work of short tasks by (5.32) and (5.33). Let us assume that $p_1 \geq p_2 \geq \cdots p_n$. We will denote by $K = (2m\mathcal{B}(m) + 1)^{\frac{1}{\varepsilon}}$, where $\varepsilon$ is the relative distance of the solution build by the PTAS from the optimum, and $\mathcal{B}(m)$ is the $m$th Bell number, i.e. the number of ways in which the set of $m$ objects (here – processors) can partitioned into subsets. $K$ is $O(1)$ for fixed $m$ and $\varepsilon$. The algorithm proceeds in the following steps:

1. Find the smallest $k \leq K$ such that $p_k + \cdots + p_{(2m\mathcal{B}(m)+1)k-1} < \varepsilon \sum_{j=1}^{n} p_j$. Partition tasks into long tasks $\mathcal{L} = \{T_1, T_2, \cdots, T_k\}$, and short tasks $\mathcal{T} - \mathcal{L}$.
2. Enumerate all possible relative schedules for $\mathcal{L}$.
3. Formulate and solve linear program (5.30)–(5.33) for each relative schedule of $\mathcal{L}$. We obtain a feasible schedule for long tasks, and possibly infeasible schedule for some limited number of short tasks which are preempted.
4. Construct a feasible nonpreemptive schedule by shifting the preempted short tasks to the end of the schedule.
5. Choose the shortest schedule among the schedules built on the basis of all the relative schedules of long tasks.

It can be shown that the above procedure runs in $O(n)$ time for each fixed $m$ and $\varepsilon > 0$. The above PTAS can be adapted to solve problem $Pm|size_j|C_{\max}$ [4]. The ideas of partitioning the set of tasks into long and short tasks have been used in [53] to formulate a PTAS for $Pm|set_j|C_{\max}$.

**First Fit Scheduling (FFS) [126]** Here tasks are scheduled in an arbitrary order, and assigned as soon as they are ready, i.e. at time $\tau \geq r_j$ for $T_j$, and the requested set of processors is available.

**First Fit Scheduling+ (FFS+) [126]** Here the set of tasks is divided into $\mathcal{T}^+ = \{T_j : |fix_j| > \sqrt{m}\}$ and $\mathcal{T}^- = \{T_j : |fix_j| \leq \sqrt{m}\}$. As in the FFS algorithm tasks are scheduled greedily as soon as possible, but the tasks of the two sets are executed in different time units. Note that this algorithm is designed for UET tasks.

**Split-Round Scheduling (SRS) [126]** Similarly to the FFS+ heuristic tasks are divided into $T^+ = \{T_j : |fix_j| > \sqrt{m}\}$ and $T^- = \{T_j : |fix_j| \leq \sqrt{m}\}$. Processing times of the tasks in $T^-$ are rounded up to the nearest power of 2, i.e. $p_j$ is replaced with $p'_j = 2^{\lceil \log p_j \rceil}$, for $T_j \in T^-$. Tasks of $T^+$ are scheduled first, using FFS. Then tasks in $T^-$ are ordered according to the nonincreasing $p'_j$, and assigned greedily to the time intervals as in the FFS.

**Split-Round Scheduling+ (SRS+) [126]** This heuristic uses two bins for the tasks: the passive and the active one. At the first ready time all the tasks that just arrived are put in the active bin. Then, the algorithm schedules tasks in the active bin using SRS heuristic, while the arriving tasks are collected in the passive bin. At the time when all tasks from the active bin are scheduled, the roles of the bins are interchanged.

**Shortest Processing Time Mode (SPTM) [20]** This is a heuristic for multimode tasks. It executes the tasks in the shortest processing time mode, i.e. task $T_j$ is executed on the set of processors $fix_i$ for which $p_{ij}$ is minimum.

**Heuristic Schedule Algorithm 1 (HSA1) [52]** This heuristic involves several steps. The assignment of processing modes is a function $\mathcal{B} : T \rightarrow fix_i \in set_j$. This means that the set of processors $fix_i$ must be specified for executing each task $T_j$. Furthermore, assignment $\mathcal{B}$ should minimize maximum load of any processor, i.e. we have to find $\min_{\mathcal{B}}\{\max_{i=1}^m \sum_{\{(k,j):P_i \in fix_k = \mathcal{B}(j)\}} p_{kj}\}$, where $\mathcal{B}(j) \in set_j$ is the set of processors assigned to $T_j$. The assignment problem can be solved by a pseudopolynomial time algorithm in $O(nT^2)$ time, where $T = \sum_{j=1}^n \min_{fix_i \in set_j}\{p_{ij}\}$ is an upper bound on the load of any processor. The pseudopolynomial time algorithm for the assignment problem can be changed to an FPTAS with complexity $O(\frac{n^3}{\varepsilon})$, by scaling the processing times to $\lceil \frac{p_{ij}}{K} \rceil$, where $K = \frac{\varepsilon T}{3n}$. In the first step a solution from the FPTAS is obtained. This determines the assignment of processor sets to the tasks. Given the assignment, it remains to solve the scheduling problem. For $m = 3$, the second step consists in solving problem $P3|fix_j|C_{\max}$. Here tasks are executed in blocks of the same type: 3-tasks are executed first, then 2-tasks, and finally 1-tasks shifted to the left. This approach can be extended to any fixed $m \geq 4$: First schedule tasks requiring more than one processor including $P_1$, then the tasks requiring more than one processor but none of them $P_1$, finally schedule tasks requiring a single processor. A schedule built according to the above procedure has performance guarantee $\frac{m}{2} + \varepsilon$.

### 5.8.1.3  Nonpreemptive Schedules, Heuristics Without a Guarantee

**Divide Uniprocessor Tasks (DUT) [6]** It is a heuristic for $P3|fix_j|C_{\max}$. DUT attempts to schedule some subset of 1-tasks in parallel with the 2-tasks requesting the complementary set of processors. For example, tasks requiring processor $P_1$ are partitioned into sets $T_1^{\{1\}}$ and $T_2^{\{1\}}$. Set $T_1^{\{1\}}$ is constructed such that $\sum_{T_j \in T_1^{\{1\}}} p_j$ is made as close to $\sum_{T_j \in T^{\{2,3\}}} p_j$ as possible. Note that selecting the tasks to $T_1^{\{1\}}$ is itself an **NP**h problem equivalent to the subset sum problem [110].

Thus, $T_1^{\{1\}}$ was constructed by a heuristic which added tasks to $T_1^{\{1\}}$, as long as $\sum_{T_j \in T_1^{\{1\}}} p_j < \sum_{T_j \in T^{\{2,3\}}} p_j$. The remaining two sets $T_1^{\{2\}}, T_1^{\{3\}}$ were constructed analogously. The schedule was a sequence of task sets: $T^{\{1,2,3\}}$, then $T^{\{1,2\}}$ in parallel with $T_1^{\{3\}}$, $T^{\{1,3\}}$ in parallel with $T_1^{\{2\}}$, $T^{\{2,3\}}$ in parallel with $T_1^{\{1\}}$, and finally sets $T_2^{\{1\}}, T_2^{\{2\}}, T_2^{\{3\}}$ in parallel.

### 5.8.1.4 Preemptive Schedules

The results on complexity of preemptive scheduling of multiprocessor tasks for $C_{\max}, L_{\max}$ are collected in Table 5.18, while the results on the approximability of the above problems are summarized in Table 5.19. The following special notations are used in the tables:

- *win* – Processors are available in restricted time windows.
- *p* – Number of processor availability windows.
- $set_j$, $|fix_j| = 2$ – The two symbols appearing together mean that tasks may be executed in alternative modes, but each of the modes uses two processors.
- *T* – An upper bound of schedule length.

**Table 5.18** Complexity of preemptive multiprocessor task scheduling, $C_{\max}, L_{\max}$

| Problem | Result | Reference |
|---|---|---|
| $Pm\|fix_j, pmtn\|C_{\max}$ | $O(poly(n^m))$ | [155] |
| $P2, 3, 4\|fix_j, pmtn\|C_{\max}$ | $O(n)$ | [19] |
| $P\|fix_j, pmtn\|C_{\max}, \|fix_j\| = 2$ | GDSC | [156] |
| $P4\|fix_j, pmtn, p_j = 1, chain\|C_{\max},$ $\|fix_j\| = 2$ | sNPh | [156] |
| $P2, win\|fix_j, pmtn, r_j\|C_{\max}$ | $O(n + p)$ | [21] |
| $P3, win\|fix_j, pmtn\|C_{\max}$ | $O(n + p)$ | [21] |
| $Pm, win\|fix_j, pmtn, r_j\|L_{\max}$ | $O((\log n + \log p)poly(n^m))$ | [21] |
| $P\|fix_j, pmtn\|C_{\max}, \|fix_j\| = 2$ | $poly(n, m)$ | [133] |
| $P\|fix_j, pmtn, r_j\|L_{\max}, \|fix_j\| = 2$ | $poly(n, m)$ | [133] |
| $P\|fix_j, pmtn\|C_{\max}, \|fix_j\| = 3$ | sNPh | [133] |
| $Pm\|fix_j, pmtn\|C_{\max}$ | $O(n)$ | [4] |
| $P2\|set_j, pmtn\|L_{\max}$ | $O(nT^2)$ | [45] |
| $P\|set_j, pmtn\|C_{\max}, \|fix_j\| = 2$ | sNPh | [133] |

**Table 5.19** Approximability of preemptive multiprocessor task scheduling, $C_{\max}$

| Problem | Result | Reference |
|---|---|---|
| $P\|fix_j, pmtn\|C_{\max}$ | $\exists a > 0, R > n^a$ | [133] |
| $P\|fix_j, pmtn\|C_{\max}$ | $\forall a > 0, R > n^{1-a}$ | [133] |
| $Pm\|set_j, pmtn\|C_{\max}$ | FPTAS | [134] |

Complexity of $P|fix_j, pmtn|C_{max}$

The issue of problem $P|fix_j, pmtn|C_{max}$ complexity has been studied in a number of papers. The problem of edge $(a, b)$-multicoloring has been polynomially transformed to $P|fix_j, pmtn|C_{max}$, where $\forall\, T_j, |fix_j| = 2$, in [155, 156]. A graph is edge $(a, b)$-multicolorable if all the edges can be assigned $a$ colors from a set of $b$ colors so that incident edges have disjoint color sets. Edge $(a, b)$-multicoloring is a sNPc problem for $b > 2a$. However, if colors correspond to time units of executing the tasks, then this transformation directly corresponds to schedules in which tasks are preempted only in discrete moments of time. Since tasks in the scheduling problem can be preempted at arbitrary times, possibly rational numbers, while $a, b$ are integers, it raised a question if the transformation applies to the preemptive scheduling problem.

This issue has been further studied in [133]. Problem $P|fix_j, pmtn|C_{max}$ can be formulated as a linear program analogous to (5.5)–(5.7):

$$\text{minimize} \sum_{j=1}^{M} x_j \qquad \text{subject to} \qquad (5.35)$$

$$\sum_{i \in Q_j} x_i \geq p_j \quad \text{for } j = 1, \ldots, n \qquad (5.36)$$

$$x_i \geq 0 \quad \text{for } i = 1, \ldots, M \qquad (5.37)$$

where $M$ is the number of different processor feasible sets (PFSes) of tasks, and $Q_j$ is the set of PFSes including task $T_j$. Note that each PFS is an independent set in the incompatibility graph $\mathcal{G}$. LP (5.35)–(5.37) is a formulation of a problem known in the literature as weighted fractional coloring. It has been proved that weighted fractional coloring is **NPh** for each class of graphs (here incompatibility graphs) for which computing the size of the largest independent set is **NPh**. Hence, problem $P|fix_j, pmtn|C_{max}$ is also **NPh**.

On the other hand if $\forall\, T_j, |fix_j| = 2$, then problem $P|fix_j, pmtn|C_{max}$ can be solved in polynomial time by a reduction to the separation problem of the dual formulation of (5.35)-(5.37). Here the dual LP is:

$$\text{maximize} \sum_{j=1}^{n} p_j y_j \qquad \text{subject to} \qquad (5.38)$$

$$\sum_{j \in PFS_i} y_j \leq 1 \quad \text{for } j = 1, \ldots, M \qquad (5.39)$$

$$y_i \geq 0 \quad \text{for } i = 1, \ldots, n \qquad (5.40)$$

where $PFS_i$ is the $i$th processor feasible set. For a certain LP the separation problem consists in verifying if a given solution is feasible, and if not in determining the violated linear constraint(s). It is known from the theory of linear programming that if the separation problem can be solved in polynomial time for the dual LP (here (5.38)–(5.39)) then also the primal LP (here (5.35)–(5.37)) can be solved in polynomial time. The separation problem for the dual LP can be stated as follows: given vector $(y_1, \ldots, y_n)$ decide if it is a feasible solution, and if not, find the inequality in (5.39) separating $(y_1, \ldots, y_n)$ from the set of feasible solutions. Observe that each inequality (5.39) defines a weighted independent set in $\mathcal{G}$. Thus, the separation problem boils down to finding the biggest weighted independent set in the weighted incompatibility graph, where the node weights are values $y_j$, for $j = 1, \ldots, n$. If the biggest weighted independent set has the sum of weights lower than or equal 1, then the solution is feasible. Otherwise, the vertices in the selected independent set determine the inequality that is not satisfied. Now, the biggest weighted independent set in the incompatibility graph $\mathcal{G}$ can be found in polynomial time if $\forall\, T_j, |fix_j| = 2$. In this case the incompatibility graph has one-to-one scheduling graph equivalent $\mathcal{G}'$. An independent set in the incompatibility graph is a matching in $\mathcal{G}'$. A maximum weighted matching can be found in polynomial time. Thus, problem $P\,|fix_j, pmtn|C_{\max}$ is polynomially solvable if $\forall\, T_j, |fix_j| = 2$. Similar reasoning can be applied to prove polynomial time solvability of problem $P\,|fix_j, pmtn, r_j|L_{\max}$, when $|fix_j| = 2$ [133].

Let us return to formulation (5.35)–(5.37). Observe that tasks of the same type, i.e. requesting the same set of processors (say set $A$), can be converted to a single task with the summary processing times, i.e. $p_A = \sum_{T_j \in \{T_j : fix_j = A\}} p_j$. Thus, the above linear program can be solved only for one task of type $A$. Then the number of processor feasible sets $M$ can be bounded by the $m$th Bell number $\mathcal{B}(m)$ which is the number of ways in which the set of $m$ processors (generally, some objects) can be partitioned into subsets. For fixed $m$, $\mathcal{B}(m)$ is constant, and linear program (5.35)–(5.37) can be solved in constant time. In the actual schedule, tasks of type $A$ can be scheduled one after another in the intervals of time including processor set $A$. In this way tasks can be expanded in the final schedule in $O(n)$ time. Consequently, the problem $Pm\,|fix_j, pmtn|C_{\max}$ can be solved in $O(n)$ time for any fixed $m$ [4].

*$Pm, win\,|fix_j, pmtn, r_j|L_{\max}$ [21]*

Here we present an algorithm for preemptive scheduling of multiprocessor tasks with ready times and duedates, on processors available in restricted time windows, for maximum lateness criterion. This method generalizes the processor feasible set approach proposed in (5.5)–(5.7) and in the above paragraph. Observe that according to the definition of the maximum lateness task $T_j$ cannot be executed after $d_j + L$, where $L$ is some given value of maximum lateness. We will refer to values $d_j + L$ as to deadlines. The contents of processor feasible sets depend on which tasks can be executed in parallel. This in turn depends on the relations between task ready times, task deadlines, and availability of processors. Hence, processor feasible sets change with value of lateness $L$ when for two tasks $T_i, T_j$, $r_j = d_i + L$, or for processor availability window $k$ starting at time $b_k$, $b_k = d_j + L$. There are $O(n^2 + np)$ intervals of maximum lateness values in which the processor feasible sets remain invariant. Let us assume that maximum lateness value $L$ is in one of such intervals $[\underline{L}, \overline{L}]$. In such an interval of maximum lateness also the sequence of events remains the same. Here events are ready times, deadlines, changes in processor availability. Let us denote by

$q \leq 2n + p$ – The number of events.

$e_i$ – For event $i$ representing a ready time or a beginning of processor time window, $e_i$ is equal to the actual time of the event, for event $i$ corresponding to a deadline of some task $T_j$ it is a value of the duedate $d_j$ (without the offset of lateness $L$). For a given interval $[\underline{L}, \overline{L}]$, $e_i$s are constants.

$f_i$ – For event $i$ corresponding to a ready time or a beginning of processor availability window $f_i = 0$, for event $i$ corresponding to a deadline of some task $f_i = 1$.

$M_i$ – The number of processor feasible sets between events $i$ and $i + 1$, for $i = 0, \ldots, q - 1$.

$Q_{ij}$ – The set of processor feasible sets including task $T_j$ between events $i$ and $i + 1$, for $i = 0, \ldots, q - 1$.

$x_{ik}$ – The duration of executing processor feasible set $k$ between events $i$ and $i + 1$.

Our scheduling problem can be formulated as a linear program:

$$\text{minimize } L \quad \text{subject to} \tag{5.41}$$

$$\sum_{k=1}^{M_i} x_{ik} \leq e_{i+1} - e_i + L(f_{i+1} - f_i) \quad \text{for } i = 1, \ldots, q - 1 \tag{5.42}$$

$$\sum_{i=1}^{q-1} \sum_{k \in Q_{ij}} x_{ik} \geq p_j \quad \text{for } j = 1, \ldots, n \tag{5.43}$$

$$\underline{L} \leq L \leq \overline{L} \quad j = 1, \ldots, n \tag{5.44}$$

$$x_{ik} \geq 0 \quad \text{for } i = 1, \ldots, q - 1$$
$$k = 1, \ldots, M_i \tag{5.45}$$

In the above formulation inequalities (5.42) ensure that processor feasible sets fit between corresponding events $i$ and $i + 1$. By (5.43) tasks are fully processed. Inequalities (5.44) guarantee that the sequence of events remains invariant, and processor feasible sets are valid. The optimum schedule is constructed by concatenating partial schedules for the consecutive intervals between events $i$ and $i + 1$, and each partial schedule is a concatenation of intervals of length $x_{ik}$ in which processor feasible set $k$ is executed. Formulation (5.41)–(5.45) may be infeasible, which means that the interval of maximum lateness $[\underline{L}, \overline{L}]$ covered to small values. In such a case an interval with bigger values must be selected. The interval including the optimum value of maximum lateness can be found by binary search over lateness intervals in $O(\log n + \log p)$ calls to formulation (5.41)–(5.45). In the last interval the optimum value of lateness $L$ and the durations $x_{ik}$ of executing processor feasible sets are determined. The number of intervals between the events is at most $2n$. The number of processor feasible sets can be bounded by the number $\binom{n}{m}$ of ways in which at most $m$ tasks out of $n$ can be selected to be run in parallel, which is $O(n^m)$. Hence, the complexity of solving one linear program is $O(poly(n^{m+1}))$, where $poly()$ is a polynomial, and $O(n^{m+1})$ is the number of variables. Thus, whole problem can be solved in $O((\log n + \log p)poly(n^{m+1}))$ time which is polynomial for fixed $m$ [21]. A more precise analysis reveals that the number of processor feasible sets can be bounded by the $m$th Bell number $\mathcal{B}(m)$ [4]. Thus, the number of variables $x_{ij}$ is bounded by $O(n\mathcal{B}(m))$. On the other hand, for fixed $m$ also $\mathcal{B}(m)$ is fixed, the number of variables is $O(n)$, and the whole problem can be solved in $O((\log n + \log p)poly(n))$ time. The above method can be extended to solve similar multimode task scheduling problem $Pm, win|set_j, pmtn, r_j|L_{max}$ [21].

## 5.8.2 Minsum Criteria

The results regarding complexity of scheduling multiprocessor tasks for minimum sum criteria are collected in Table 5.20.

### 5.8.2.1 Nonpreemptive Schedules, Polynomial Cases

$P2|fix_j, p_j = 1| \sum w_j c_j$ [76]

The problem of scheduling UET tasks on two processors for mean weighted completion time can be solved by an adaptation of WSPT order. Tasks requiring $\{P_1\}$

**Table 5.20** Complexity of multiprocessor task scheduling, minsum criteria

| Problem | Result | Reference |
|---|---|---|
| $P2|fix_j, p_j = 1| \sum w_j c_j$ | $O(n \log n)$ | [76] |
| $P2|fix_j| \sum c_j$ | NPh | [121] |
| $P3|fix_j| \sum c_j$ | sNPh | [121] |
| $P|fix_j, p_j = 1| \sum c_j$ | sNPh | [121] |
| $P2|fix_j, chain, p_j = 1| \sum c_j$ | sNPh | [121] |
| $P2|fix_j| \sum w_j c_j$ | sNPh | [121] |
| $P|fix_j, p_j = 1| \sum c_j, |fix_j| = 2$ | sNPh | [156] |
| $P3|fix_j| \sum c_j, |fix_j| = 2$ | $O(n \log n)$ | [156] |
| $P3|fix_j, chain| \sum c_j, |fix_j| = 2$ | $O(n \log n)$ | [156] |
| $P4|fix_j| \sum c_j, |fix_j| = 2$ | NPh | [156] |
| $P4|fix_j, p_j = 1, chain| \sum c_j, |fix_j| = 2$ | sNPh | [156] |
| $P|fix_j| \sum c_j$ | GDSC | [156] |
| $Pm|fix_j, p_1 = 1|\gamma, \gamma \in \{\sum w_j c_j, \sum t_j, \sum w_j u_j\}$ | $O(k 2^k n^{k+1})$ | [41] |
| $Pm|fix_j, p_1 = 1, r_j| \sum c_j$ | $O(k 2^k n^{k+1})$ | [41] |
| $P2|fix_j| \sum c_j$ | sNPh | [44] |
| $P2|fix_j, p_j = 1| \sum c_j, |fix_j| = 2$ | GDSC | [113, 114] |
| $P2|fix_j| \sum c_j, |fix_j| = 2$ | GDSC | [114] |

are matched with tasks requiring $\{P_2\}$ in the order of nonincreasing weight. The matched pairs of 1-tasks and the 2-tasks are executed in the nonincreasing order of weights of the 2-tasks, or the sums of weights for the pairs of 1-tasks.

$Pm|fix_j, p_1 = 1, r_j| \sum c_j$ [41]

This problem can be reduced to constructing the shortest path in a graph, analogously to the algorithm for $Pm|fix_j, p_1 = 1, r_j|C_{max}$ (see Sect. 5.8.1.1). Here a different way of calculating length of the shortest path in graph $\mathcal{G}$ is used. The arcs of the first type connecting tuples $(\tau, i_1, \ldots, i_k, l_1, \ldots, l_k)$ with $(\tau, i'_1, \ldots, i'_k, l'_1, \ldots, l'_k)$ have weight $\tau + 1$. The value of the optimality criterion $\sum c_j$ for a schedule corresponding to a path in $\mathcal{G}$ is equal to the sum of traversed arc weights. Hence, it is necessary to find the shortest path in the sense of the sum of arc lengths. This method can be extended to solve problems $Pm|fix_j, p_1 = 1|\gamma$, where optimality criterion $\gamma$ may be one of: $\sum w_j c_j$, $\sum t_j$, $\sum w_j u_j$.

### 5.8.2.2 Nonpreemptive Schedules, Heuristics with a Guarantee

The results on approximability of nonpreemptive scheduling of multiprocessor tasks for minimum sum criteria are collected in Table 5.21. The following special symbols were used:

- $d_j = d$ – Denotes that all tasks have the same duedate.
- $\sum \hat{u}_j$ – Represents a criterion of maximizing the number of tasks completed before their duedates, studied in [107].

Now we outline the heuristics from Table 5.21.

**H [44]** Problem $P2|fix_j| \sum c_j$ is solved by a two-step procedure. In the first step the problem is relaxed to its preemptive version ($P2|fix_j, pmtn| \sum c_j$). If only 1-tasks were scheduled, then the optimum schedule would be SPT sequences of the tasks in $\mathcal{T}^{\{1\}}$, and in $\mathcal{T}^{\{2\}}$. Similarly, for 2-tasks alone the optimum schedule is built by the

**Table 5.21** Approximability of nonpreemptive multiprocessor task scheduling, minimum sum criteria

| Problem | Result | Reference |
|---|---|---|
| $P2|fix_j| \sum c_j$ | $R_H < 2$ | [44] |
| $P|fix_j, p_j = 1| \sum c_j, |fix_j| = 2$ | $R_{FFC} < 2$ | [113] |
| $Pm|fix_j| \sum c_j$ | PTAS | [1] |
| $Pm|fix_j, r_j| \sum w_j c_j$ | PTAS | [106] |
| $Pm|set_j| \sum w_j c_j$ | PTAS | [105] |
| $P|fix_j, p_j = 1, d_j = d| \sum \hat{u}_j$ | $\sqrt{m} \leq R_{FFI_f} \leq \sqrt{m} + 1$ | [107] |
| $P|fix_j, p_j = 1, d_j = d| \sum \hat{u}_j$ | $\sqrt{m} \leq R_{LFI_f} \leq \sqrt{m} + 1$ | [107] |

SPT rule. In the optimum solution of $P2|fix_j, pmtn| \sum c_j$, 2-tasks are started only at time 0, or when some other task is finished. Therefore, the two sequences of 1-tasks can be converted to a chain of equivalent 2-tasks representing 1-tasks running in parallel. The equivalent 2-tasks span from one completion of a 1-task to the next completion of a 1-task. This reduces problem $P2|fix_j, pmtn| \sum c_j$ to scheduling two chains on a single processor, i.e. to problem $1|chain| \sum c_j$. Consequently, the optimum schedule for $P2|fix_j, pmtn| \sum c_j$ can be built in $O(n \log n)$ time. In the second step heuristic $H$ uses the schedule for $P2|fix_j, pmtn| \sum c_j$, and if a 1-task is preempted by a 2-task, then the starting time of the 1-task is delayed to the moment when the last preempting 2-task finishes.

**First Fit Coloring (FFC) [113]** This heuristic applies to $P|fix_j, p_j = 1| \sum c_j$, where $|fix_j| = 2$. It consists in greedy coloring of the line graph of the scheduling graph. A line graph $L(G)$ of graph $G$ is a graph obtained from $G$ by substituting edges with vertices, two vertices of $L(G)$ are connected if the corresponding edges of $G$ were incident. If $G$ is a scheduling graph, then $L(G)$ is an incompatibility graph. Note that scheduling UET tasks in time units for problem $P|fix_j, p_j = 1| \sum c_j$ with $|fix_j| = 2$ is equivalent to edge coloring of the scheduling graph. The transformation from scheduling graph to its line graph transforms edge coloring to node coloring. The nodes can be colored by a greedy FF algorithm which assigns the smallest possible color to the nodes considered in the arbitrary order. The colors of the nodes in the line graph are the time units of executing the tasks.

**First Fit Increasing for $fix_j$ (FFI$_f$), Last Fit Increasing for $fix_j$ (LFI$_f$) [107]** Tasks are ordered according to the nondecreasing cardinality of $fix_j$, and analyzed in this order. In FFI$_f$ tasks are started as soon as possible, in LFI$_f$ are started as late as possible to be finished in time. If a task cannot meet its duedate, then it is lost (dropped and not processed).

### 5.8.2.3 Preemptive Schedules

In Table 5.22 the complexity and in Table 5.23 the approximability of preemptive scheduling of multiprocessor tasks for minimum sum criteria are outlined.

**Table 5.22** Complexity of preemptive multiprocessor task scheduling, minimum sum criteria

| Problem | Result | Reference |
|---|---|---|
| $P|fix_j, pmtn| \sum c_j, |fix_j| = 2$ | sNPh | [156] |
| $P3|fix_j, pmtn| \sum c_j, |fix_j| = 2$ | $O(n \log n)$ | [156] |
| $P3|fix_j, pmtn, chain| \sum c_j, |fix_j| = 2$ | $O(n \log n)$ | [156] |
| $P4|fix_j, pmtn, chain| \sum c_j, |fix_j| = 2$ | sNPh | [156] |
| $P2|fix_j, pmtn| \sum c_j$ | $O(n \log n)$ | [44] |
| $P2|set_j, pmtn| \sum c_j$ | $O(nT^2)$ | [45] |

**Table 5.23** Approximability
of preemptive multiprocessor
task scheduling, minimum
sum criteria

| Problem | Result | Reference |
|---|---|---|
| $Pm\|fix_j, pmtn, r_j\| \sum w_j c_j$ | PTAS | [1] |

## 5.9  Concluding Remarks on Parallel Task Model

In this chapter, we studied scheduling of parallel tasks. A distinguishing feature of a parallel task is simultaneous use of several processors, while the internals of the task are encapsulated and hidden for the scheduler. Several types of parallel tasks have been distinguished on the basis of the information exposed to the scheduler. The types of information were: the number of required processors (for rigid tasks), processing time functions or speedups (for moldable or malleable tasks), shape of the tasks (on hypercubes and meshes), or the set of required processors (multiprocessor tasks). This distinction of parallel task types, and hence, parallel applications is done on the basis of practical considerations, popularity of research subjects, and the complexity of the typical cases. Yet, in some situations, the above task types may be nonexclusive. Moreover, other classes of scheduling problems may be directly connected with parallel task scheduling. Below we give some examples.

- Dynamic processor partitioning methods AP, AEP, and EQ are presented in different sections here (Sects. 5.4.3, and 5.5.2, respectively) because different assumptions on changing the number of used processors during the execution of the tasks were made. However, in some publications these policies are interchangeably applied to solve one scheduling problem, regardless of the moldable or malleable nature of the application. Hence, in some situations the distinction by runtime changing, or not, the number of used processors may be less important than from the complexity or approximability point of view.
- We assumed that tasks with shape are different than moldable or malleable tasks. However, there are examples in [87, 102, 149, 189] of scheduling problems where tasks with certain shape can be executed on networks of different sizes. There are also examples [67], where tasks executed on 1D-mesh interconnection request a set of processors, rather than some number of processors in a chain shape.
- We analyzed moldable and malleable tasks separately. However they may coexist in one system as analyzed in [124].
- Multiprocessor task model may be applied to generalize classic scheduling models like flow shop, job shop, see e.g. [22, 39, 40, 131]. A parallel flow shop is a system consisting of a number of stages, where each stage is a set of parallel processors. Jobs in parallel flow shop may be composed of a sequence of rigid tasks, as proposed in [193, 215].
- Due to the exceptional flexibility and ability to adapt to various work distributions, malleable tasks are quite similar to the divisible loads studied in Chapter 7. Yet, malleable tasks do not expose the internals of load distribution, which is explicitly analyzed in scheduling divisible loads.

Though the parallel task model departures from the assumptions of the classic deterministic scheduling theory, it inherits methodology, many complexity, and approximability relationships. Consequently, much of the criticism applied to the classic theory can be extended to the parallel task model. Other disadvantages of parallel task model follow from its basic assumption: the lack of knowledge on application internal structure. Therefore, parallel task model is well suited for local and distributed resource managers scheduling parallel applications. It seems less applicable to schedule application level parallelism. Let us note that some of the heuristics for scheduling tasks on hypercubes and meshes address the issues of waiting time, observing deadlines, fairness of scheduling. Hence, as a by-product methods of managing parallel application submissions to any shared high performance facility have been developed.

# References

1. F. Afrati, E. Bampis, A. Fishkin, K. Jansen, and C. Kenyon. Scheduling to minimize the average completion time of dedicated tasks. In S. Kapoor and S. Prasad, editors, *Proceedings of 20th Conference on Foundations of Software Technology and Theoretical Computer Science (FSTTCS'00). LNCS*, volume 1974, pages 454–464, 2000.
2. M. Ahuja and Y. Zhu. An O(nlogn) feasibility algorithm for preemptive scheduling of n independent jobs on a hypercube. *Information Processing Letters*, 35(1):7–11, 1990.
3. A. Al-Dhelaan and B. Bose. A new strategy for processors allocation in an n-cube multiprocessor. In *Proceedings of 8th Annual International Phoenix Conference on Computers and Communications*, pages 114–118, 1989.
4. A.K. Amoura, E. Bampis, C. Kenyon, and Y. Manoussakis. Scheduling independent multiprocessor tasks. *Algorithmica*, 32(2):247–261, 2002.
5. A.K. Amoura. A note on scheduling multiprocessor tasks with precedence constraints on parallel processors. *Information Processing Letters*, 63(3):119–122, 1997.
6. A.K. Amoura, E. Bampis, Y. Manoussakis, and Zs. Tuza. A comparison of heuristics for scheduling multiprocessor tasks on three dedicated processors. *Parallel Computing*, 25(1):49–61, 1999.
7. S.V. Anastasiadis and K.C. Sevcik. Parallel application scheduling on networks of workstations. *Journal of Parallel and Distributed Computing*, 43(2):109–124, 1997.
8. M.J. Atallah, C.L. Black, D.C. Marinescu, H.J. Siegel, and T.L. Casavant. Models and algorithms for coscheduling compute-intensive tasks on a network of workstations. *Journal of Parallel and Distributed Computing*, 16(4):319–327, 1992.
9. D. Babbar and P. Krueger. On-line hard real-time scheduling of parallel tasks on partitionable multiprocessors. In *Proceedings of International Conference on Parallel Processing (ICPP'94)*, pages II–29–II–38. IEEE Computer Society, Los Alamitos, CA, USA, 1994.
10. D. Babbar and P. Krueger. A performance comparison of processor allocation and job scheduling algorithms for mesh-connected multiprocessors. In *Proceedings of 6th IEEE Symposium on Parallel and Distributed Processing (SPDP'94)*, pages 46–53, 1994.
11. E. Bampis and A. Kononov. On the approximability of scheduling multiprocessor tasks with time-dependent processor and time requirements. In *Proceedings of 15th International Parallel and Distributed Processing Symposium (IPDPS'01)*, pages 2144–2151, 2001.
12. S. Bani-Mohammad, M. Ould-Khaoua, I. Ababneh, and L.M. Mackenzie. Non-contiguous processor allocation strategy for 2D mesh connected multicomputers based on sub-meshes available for allocation. In *Proceedings of 12th International Conference on Parallel and Distributed Systems (ICPADS'06)*, pages 41–48, 2006.

13. P. Baptiste. A note on scheduling multiprocessor tasks with identical processing times. *Computers and Operations Research*, 30(13):2071–2078, 2003.
14. P. Baptiste and B. Schieber. A note on scheduling tall/small multiprocessor tasks with unit processing time to minimize maximum tardiness. *Journal of Scheduling*, 6(4):395–404, 2003.
15. A. Bar-Noy, R. Canetti, S. Kutten, Y. Mansour, and B. Schieber. Bandwidth allocation with preemption. *SIAM Journal on Computing*, 28(5):1806–1828, 1999.
16. K. Belkhale and P. Banerjee. An approximate algorithm for the partitionable independent task scheduling problem. In *Proceedings of International Conference on Parallel Processing (ICPP'90)*, volume 1, pages 72–75, 1990.
17. M.A. Bender, D.P. Bunde, E.D. Demaine, S.P. Fekete, V.J. Leung, H. Meijer, and C.A. Phillips. Communication-aware processor allocation for supercomputers. http://arxiv.org/PS_cache/cs/pdf/0407/0407058v2.pdf, 2005 [online accessed 21 October 2007].
18. S. Bhattacharya and W.-T. Tsai. Lookahead processor allocation in mesh-connected massively parallel multicomputer. In *Proceedings of 8th International Parallel Processing Symposium (IPPS'94)*, pages 868–875, 1994.
19. L. Bianco, J. Błażewicz, P. Dell'Olmo, and M. Drozdowski. Scheduling preemptive multiprocessor tasks on dedicated processors. *Performance Evaluation*, 20(4):361–371, 1994.
20. L. Bianco, J. Błażewicz, P. Dell'Olmo, and M. Drozdowski. Scheduling multiprocessor tasks on a dynamic configuration of dedicated processors. *Annals of Operations Research*, 58(7):493–517, 1995.
21. L. Bianco, J. Błażewicz, P. Dell'Olmo, and M. Drozdowski. Preemptive multiprocessor task scheduling with release times and time windows. *Annals of Operations Research*, 70:43–55, 1997.
22. L. Bianco, P. Dell'Olmo, S. Giordani, and M. G. Speranza. Minimizing makespan in a multimode multiprocessor shop scheduling problem. *Naval Research Logistics*, 46(8):893–911, 1999.
23. L. Bianco, P. Dell'Olmo, and M.G. Speranza. Nonpreemptive scheduling of independent tasks with prespecified processor allocations. *Naval Research Logistics*, 41(7):959–971, 1994.
24. L. Bianco, P. Dell'Olmo, and M.G. Speranza. Scheduling independent tasks with multiple modes. *Discrete Applied Mathematics*, 62(1–3):35–50, 1995.
25. S. Bischof. *Efficient Algorithms for On-Line Scheduling and Load Distribution in Parallel Systems*. Ph.D. thesis, Lehrstuhl für Effiziente Algorithmen der Technischen Universität München, 1999. http://tumb1.biblio.tu-muenchen.de/publ/diss/in/1999/bischof.pdf [online accessed 03 October 2007].
26. S. Bischof and E.W. Mayr. On-line scheduling of parallel jobs with runtime restrictions. *Theoretical Computer Science*, 268(1):67–90, 2001.
27. J. Błażewicz, P. Dell'Olmo, M. Drozdowski, and P. Mączka. Scheduling multiprocessor tasks on parallel processors with limited availability. *European Journal of Operational Research*, 149(2):377–389, 2003.
28. J. Błażewicz, P. Dell'Olmo, M. Drozdowski, and M.G. Speranza. Scheduling multiprocessor tasks on three dedicated processors. *Information Processing Letters*, 41:275–280, 1992. Corrigendum: IPL 49, 1994, 269-270.
29. J. Błażewicz, M. Drabowski, and J. Węglarz. Scheduling multiprocessor tasks to minimize schedule length. *IEEE Transactions on Computers*, 35(5):389–393, 1986.
30. J. Błażewicz, M. Drozdowski, G. Schmidt, and D. de Werra. Scheduling independent multiprocessor tasks on a uniform $k$-processor system. *Parallel Computing*, 20(1):15–28, 1994.
31. J. Błażewicz, M. Drozdowski, D. de Werra, and J. Węglarz. Scheduling independent multiprocessor tasks before deadlines. *Discrete Applied Mathematics*, 65(1–3):81–96, 1996.
32. J. Błażewicz, K. Ecker, E.Pesch, G. Schmidt, and J. Węglarz. *Scheduling Computer and Manufacturing Processes*. Springer, Heidelberg, New York, 1996.
33. J. Błażewicz, M. Kovalyov, M. Machowiak, D. Trystram, and J. Węglarz. Preemptable malleable task scheduling problem. *IEEE Transactions on Computers*, 55(4):486–490, 2006.
34. J. Błażewicz, J.K. Lenstra, and A.H.G. Rinnoy Kan. Scheduling subject to resource constraints: Classification and complexity. *Discrete Applied Mathematics*, 5:11–24, 1983.

35. J. Błażewicz and Z. Liu. Scheduling multiprocessor tasks with chain constraints. *European Journal of Operational Research*, 94:231–241, 1996.

36. J. Błażewicz and Z. Liu. Linear and quadratic algorithms for scheduling chains and opposite chains. *European Journal of Operational Research*, 137(2):248–264, 2002.

37. J. Błażewicz, M. Machowiak, J. Węglarz, M. Kovalyov, and D. Trystram. Scheduling malleable tasks on parallel processors to minimize the makespan. *Annals of Operations Research*, 129:65–80, 2004.

38. G. Bozoki and J.-P. Richard. A branch-and-bound algorithm for the continuous-process job-shop scheduling problem. *AIIE Transactions*, 2(3):246–252, 1970.

39. P. Brucker. *Scheduling Algorithms*. Springer, Berlin, 1995.

40. P. Brucker and A. Krämer. Shop scheduling problems with multiprocessor tasks and dedicated processors. *Annals of Operations Research: Mathematics of Industrial Systems I*, 57:13–27, 1995.

41. P. Brucker and A. Krämer. Polynomial algorithms for resource constrained and multiprocessor task scheduling problems. *European Journal of Operational Research*, 90(2):214–226, 1996.

42. P. Brucker and S. Knust. Complexity results for scheduling problems. http://www.mathematik.uni-osnabrueck.de/research/OR/class/, 2006 [online accessed 9 November 2006].

43. P. Brucker, S. Knust, D. Roper, and Y. Zinder. Scheduling UET task systems with concurrency on two parallel identical processors. *Mathematical Methods of Operations Research*, 52(3):369–387, 2000.

44. X. Cai, C.-Y. Lee, and C.-L. Li. Minimizing total completion time in two-processor task systems with prespecified processor allocations. *Naval Research Logistics*, 45(2):231–242, 1998.

45. X. Cai, C.-Y. Lee, and T.-L. Wong. Multiprocessor task scheduling to minimize the maximum tardiness and the total completion time. *IEEE Transactions on Robotics and Automation*, 16(6):824–830, 2000.

46. M. Caramia, P. Dell'Olmo, and A. Iovanella. On-line algorithms for multiprocessor task scheduling with ready times. *Foundations of Computing and Decision Sciences*, 26(3):197–214, 2001.

47. C.-Y. Chang and P. Mohapatra. An adaptive job allocation method for multicomputer systems. In *Proceedings of 16th International Conference on Distributed Computing Systems (ICDCS'96)*, pages 224–231, 1996.

48. C.-Y. Chang and P. Mohapatra. Performance improvement of allocation schemes for mesh-connected computers. *Journal of Parallel and Distributed Computing*, 52(1):40–68, 1998.

49. C.-Y. Chang and P. Mohapatra. Processor allocation using user directives in mesh-connected multicomputer systems. In *Proceedings of 5th International Conference on High Performance Computing (HIPC'98)*, pages 302–309, 1998.

50. G.-I. Chen and T.-H. Lai. Preemptive scheduling of independent jobs on a hypercube. *Information Processing Letters*, 28(4):201–206, 1988.

51. G.-I. Chen and T.-H. Lai. Scheduling independent jobs on partitionable hypercubes. *Journal of Parallel and Distributed Computing*, 12(1):74–78, 1991.

52. J. Chen and C.-Y. Lee. General multiprocessor task scheduling. *Naval Research Logistics*, 46(1):57–74, 1999.

53. J. Chen and A. Miranda. A polynomial time approximation scheme for general multiprocessor job scheduling. *SIAM Journal on Computing*, 31(1):1–17, 2001.

54. M.-S. Chen and K.G. Shin. Processor allocation in an $n$-cube multiprocessor using gray codes. *IEEE Transactions on Computers*, 36(12):1396–1407, 1987.

55. M.-S. Chen and K.G. Shin. Subcube allocation and task migration in hypercube multiprocessors. *IEEE Transactions on Computers*, 39(9):1146–1155, 1990.

56. S.H. Chiang, R.K. Mansharamani, and M.K. Vernon. Use of application characteristics and limited preemption for run-to-completion parallel processor scheduling policies. In *ACM SIGMETRICS Conference on Measurement and Modeling of Computer Systems*, pages 33–44, 1994.

57. G.-M. Chiu and S.-K. Chen. An efficient submesh allocation scheme for two-dimensional meshes with little overhead. *IEEE Transactions on Parallel and Distributed Systems*, 10(5):471–486, 1999.
58. H. Choo, S.-M. Yoo, and H. Y. Youn. Processor scheduling and allocation for 3D torus multicomputer systems. *IEEE Transactions on Parallel and Distributed Systems*, 11(5):475–484, 2000.
59. A.N. Choudhary, B. Narahari, D.M. Nicol, and R. Simha. Optimal processor assignment for a class of pipelined computations. *IEEE Transactions on Parallel and Distributed Systems*, 5(4):439–445, 1994.
60. Ch.Rapine, I. Scherson, and D. Trystram. On-line scheduling of parallelizable jobs. In D. Pritchard and J. Reeve, editors, *Proceedings of Euro-Par 1998. LNCS*, volume 1470, pages 322–327. Springer, Berlin, 1998.
61. P.-J. Chuang and N.-F. Tzeng. An efficient submesh allocation strategy for mesh computer systems. In *Proceedings of 11th International Conference on Distributed Computing Systems*, pages 256–263. IEEE Computer Society, Los Alamitos, CA, USA, 1991.
62. P.-J. Chuang and N.-F. Tzeng. A fast recognition-complete processor allocation strategy for hypercube computers. *IEEE Transactions on Computers*, 41(4):467–479, 1992.
63. W. Cirne and F. Berman. A model for moldable supercomputer jobs. In *Proceedings of 15th International Parallel and Distributed Processing Symposium (IPDPS'01)*, page 10059b. IEEE Computer Society, Los Alamitos, CA, USA, 2001.
64. J. A. Cobb, M. G. Gouda, and A. El Nahas. Time-shift scheduling: Fair scheduling of flows in high speed networks. In *Proceedings of 1996 International Conference on Network Protocols (ICNP '96)*, pages 6–13, 1996.
65. E.G. Coffman Jr., M.R. Garey, and D.S. Johnson. Bin packing with divisible item sizes. *Journal of Complexity*, 14(3):406–428, 1987.
66. E.G. Coffman Jr., M.R. Garey, D.S. Johnson, and A.S. LaPaugh. Scheduling file transfers. *SIAM Journal on Computing*, 14(3):744–780, 1985.
67. G. Confessore, P. Dell'Olmo, and S. Giordani. Complexity and approximation results for scheduling multiprocessor tasks on a ring. *Discrete Applied Mathematics*, 133(1–3):29–44, 2004.
68. G.L. Craig, C.R. Kime, and K.K. Saluja. Test scheduling and control for VLSI built-in self-test. *IEEE Transactions on Computers*, 37(9):1099–1109, 1988.
69. F.A. Barbosa da Silva and I.D. Scherson. Improving throughput and utilization in parallel machines through concurrent gang. In *Proceedings of 14th International Parallel and Distributed Processing Symposium (IPDPS'00)*, pages 121–126. IEEE Computer Society, Los Alamitos, CA, USA, 2000.
70. P. Dell'Olmo, S. Giordani, and M.G. Speranza. An approximation result for duo-processor task scheduling problem. *Information Processing Letters*, 61(4):195–200, 1997.
71. P. Dell'Olmo, M.G. Speranza, and Z. Tuza. Comparability graph augmentation for some multipocessor scheduling problems. *Discrete Applied Mathematics*, 72(1–2), 1997.
72. P. Dell'Olmo, M.G. Speranza, and Z. Tuza. Efficiency and effectiveness of normal schedules on three dedicated processors. *Discrete Mathematics*, 164(1–3), 1997.
73. X. Deng, N. Gu, T. Brecht, and K. Lu. Preemptive scheduling of parallel jobs on multiprocessors. *SIAM Journal on Computing*, 30(1):145–160, 2000.
74. P. Dharwadkar, H.J. Siegel, and E.K.P. Chong. A heuristic for dynamic bandwidth allocation with preemption and degradation for prioritized requests. In *Proceedings of 21st International Conference on Distributed Computing Systems (ICDCS'01)*, pages 547–556, 2001.
75. J. Ding and L.N. Bhuyan. An adaptive submesh allocation strategy for two-dimensional mesh connected systems. In *Proceedings of the International Conference on Parallel Processing (ICPP'93)*, pages 193–200. IEEE Computer Society, Los Alamitos, CA, USA, 1993.
76. G. Dobson and U.S. Karmarkar. Simultaneous resource scheduling to minimize weighted flow times. *Operations Research*, 37(4):592–600, 1989.
77. M. Drabowski. *Szeregowanie zadań w systemach wielomikroprocesorowych*. Ph.D. thesis, Poznań University of Technology, 1985.
78. M. Drozdowski. Scheduling multiprocessor tasks on hypercubes. *Bulletin of the Polish Academy of Sciences, Technical Sciences*, 42(3):437–445, 1994.

79. M. Drozdowski. On complexity of multiprocessor tasks scheduling. *Bulletin of the Polish Academy of Sciences, Technical Sciences*, 43(3):381–392, 1995.

80. M. Drozdowski. Real-time scheduling of linear speedup parallel tasks. *Information Processing Letters*, 57(1):35–40, 1996.

81. M. Drozdowski. Scheduling multiprocessor tasks – an overview. *European Journal of Operational Research*, 94:215–230, 1996.

82. M. Drozdowski. *Selected Problems of Scheduling Tasks in Multiprocessor Computer Systems.* Number 321 in Monographs. Poznań University of Technology Press, Poznań, 1997. http://www.cs.put.poznan.pl/~maciejd/txt/h.ps.

83. M. Drozdowski. New applications of the Munz and Coffman algorithm. *Journal of Scheduling*, 4(4):209–223, 2001.

84. M. Drozdowski and P. Dell'Olmo. Scheduling multiprocessor tasks for mean flow time criterion. *Computers and Operations Research*, 27(6):571–585, 2000.

85. M. Drozdowski and W. Kubiak. Scheduling parallel tasks with sequential heads and tails. *Annals of Operations Research*, 90:221–246, 1999.

86. J. Du and J.Y-T. Leung. Complexity of scheduling parallel task systems. *SIAM Journal on Discrete Mathematics*, 2(4):472–478, 1989.

87. P.F. Dutot, G. Mounié, and D. Trystram. Scheduling parallel tasks: Approximation algorithms. In J.Y. Leung, editor, *Handbook of Scheduling: Algorithms, Models, and Performance Analysis*, pages 26.1–26.24. CRC Press, Boca Raton, 2004.

88. S. Dutt and J. P. Hayes. Subcube allocation in hypercube computers. *IEEE Transactions on Computers*, 40(3):341–352, 1991.

89. J. Edmonds. Scheduling in the dark. *Theoretical Computer Science*, 235(1):109–141, 2000.

90. J. Edmonds, D. Chinn, T. Brecht, and X. Deng. Non-clairvoyant multiprocessor scheduling of jobs with changing execution characteristics. *Journal of Scheduling*, 6(3):231–250, 2003.

91. K. Efe and V. Krishnamoorthy. Optimal scheduling of compute-intensive tasks on a network of workstations. *IEEE Transactions on Parallel and Distributed Systems*, 6(6):668–673, 1995.

92. D.G. Feitelson. Workshops on job scheduling strategies for parallel processing. http://www.cs.huji.ac.il/~feit/parsched/ [online accessed 25 August 2007].

93. D.G. Feitelson. Packing schemes for gang scheduling. In D.G. Feitelson and L. Rudolph, editors, *Proceedings of 2nd Workshop on Job Scheduling Strategies for Parallel Processing. LNCS*, volume 1162, pages 89–110. Springer, Berlin, 1996.

94. D.G. Feitelson. Memory usage in the LANL CM-5 workload. In D.G. Feitelson and L. Rudolph, editors, *Proceedings of 3rd Workshop on Job Scheduling Strategies for Parallel Processing. LNCS*, volume 1291, pages 78–94. Springer, Berlin, 1997.

95. D.G. Feitelson. Parallel workloads archive. http://www.cs.huji.ac.il/labs/parallel/workload/, 2007 [online accessed 20 May 2007].

96. D.G. Feitelson. *Workload Modeling for Computer Systems Performance Evaluation.* 2007. Version 0.10, http://www.cs.huji.ac.il/~feit/wlmod/wlmod.pdf [online accessed 20 May 2007].

97. D.G. Feitelson and L. Rudolph. Distributed hierarchical control for parallel processing. *IEEE Computer*, 23(5):65–77, 1990.

98. D.G. Feitelson and L. Rudolph. Evaluation of design choices for gang scheduling using distributed hierarchical control. *Journal of Parallel and Distributed Computing*, 35(1):18–34, 1996.

99. D.G. Feitelson and L. Rudolph. Metrics and benchmarking for parallel job scheduling. In D.G. Feitelson and L. Rudolph, editors, *Job Scheduling Strategies for Parallel Processing. LNCS*, volume 1459, pages 1–24. Springer, Berlin, 1998.

100. D.G. Feitelson, L. Rudolph, U. Schwiegelshohn, K. Sevcik, and P. Wong. Theory and practice in parallel job scheduling. In D.G. Feitelson and L. Rudolph, editors, *Job Scheduling Strategies for Parallel Processing. LNCS*, volume 1291, pages 1–34. Springer, Berlin, 1997.

101. D.G. Feitelson and A. Mu'alem Weil. Utilization and predictability in scheduling the IBM SP2 with backfilling. In *Proceedings of 12th International Parallel Processing Symposium*, pages 542–546. IEEE Computer Society, Los Alamitos, CA, USA, 1998.

102. A. Feldmann, M.-Y. Kao, J. Sgall, and S.-H. Teng. Optimal online scheduling of parallel jobs with dependencies. *Journal of Combinatorial Optimization*, 1(4):393–411, 1998.
103. A. Feldmann, J. Sgall, and S.-H. Teng. Dynamic scheduling on parallel machines. *Theoretical Computer Science*, 130(1):49–72, 1994.
104. W. Feng and J. Rexford. Performance evaluation of smoothing algorithms for transmitting prerecorded variable-bit-rate video. *IEEE Transactions on Multimedia*, 1(3):302–313, 1999.
105. A. Fishkin, K. Jansen, and L. Porkolab. On minimizing average weighted completion time: A PTAS for scheduling general multiprocessor tasks. In R. Freivalds, editor, *Proceedings of 13th International Symposium on Fundamentals of Computation Theory (FCT'01). LNCS*, volume 2138, pages 495–507, 2001.
106. A. Fishkin, K. Jansen, and L. Porkolab. On minimizing average weighted completion time of multiprocessor tasks with release dates. In F. Orejas, P.G. Spirakis, and J. van Leeuwen, editors, *Proceedings of 28th International Colloquium on Automata, Languages and Programming (ICALP'01). LNCS*, volume 2076, pages 875–886, 2001.
107. A.V. Fishkin and G. Zhang. On maximizing throughput of multiprocessor tasks. In K. Diks and W. Ritter, editors, *Proceedings of 27th International Symposium Mathematical Foundations of Computer Science (MFCS'02). LNCS*, volume 2420, pages 269–279. Springer, Berlin, 2002.
108. C. Flaviu. Understanding fault-tolerant distributed systems. *Communications of the ACM*, 34(2):56–78, 1991.
109. E. Frachtenberg, D.G. Feitelson, F. Petrini, and J. Fernandez. Adaptive parallel job scheduling with flexible coscheduling. *IEEE Transactions on Parallel and Distributed Systems*, 16(11):1066–1077, 2005.
110. M.R. Garey and D.S. Johnson. *Computers and Intractability: A Guide to the Theory of NP-completeness*. Freeman, San Francisco, 1979.
111. E.F. Gehringer, D.P. Siewiorek, and Z. Segall. *Parallel Processing: The $Cm^*$ Experience*. Digital Press, Bedford, 1987.
112. D. Ghosal, G. Serazzi, and S. Tripathi. The processor working set and its use in scheduling multiprocessor systems. *IEEE Transactions on Software Engineering*, 17(5):443–453, 1991.
113. K. Giaro, M. Kubale, M. Małafiejski, and K. Piwakowski. Chromatic scheduling of dedicated 2-processor UET tasks to minimize mean flow time. In *Proceedings of 7th IEEE International Conference on Emerging Technologies and Factory Automation (ETFA'99)*, pages 343–347, 1999.
114. K. Giaro, M. Kubale, M. Małafiejski, and K. Piwakowski. Dedicated scheduling of biprocessor tasks to minimize mean flow time. In R. Wyrzykowski et al., editor, *Proceedings of 4th International Conference on Parallel Processing and Applied Mathematics (PPAM'01). LNCS*, volume 2328, pages 87–96. Springer, 2000.
115. J. Glasgow and H. Shachnai. Channel based scheduling of parallelizable tasks. In *Proceedings of 5th IEEE International Workshop on Modeling, Analysis, and Simulation of Computer and Telecommunications Systems (MASCOTS'97)*, pages 11–16. IEEE Computer Society, Los Alamitos, CA, USA, 1997.
116. M.X. Goemans. An approximation algorithm for scheduling on three dedicated processors. *Discrete Applied Mathematics*, 61(1):49–59, 1995.
117. V. Gupta and A. Jayendran. A flexible processor allocation strategy for mesh connected parallel systems. In *Proceedings of 1996 International Conference on Parallel Processing (ICPP'96)*, pages III.166–III.173, 1996.
118. H.-J. Ho and W.-M. Lin. A performance-optimizing technique for mesh-connected multicomputers based on real-time job size distribution. In *Proceedings of 10th International Conference on Parallel and Distributed Systems (ICPADS'04)*, pages 639–646, 2004.
119. C.P.M. van Hoesel. Preemptive scheduling on a hypercube. Technical Report 8963/A, Erasmus University, Rotterdam, The Netherlands, 1989.
120. I. Holyer. The NP-completeness of edge-coloring. *SIAM Journal on Computing*, 10(4):718–720, 1981.
121. J.A. Hoogeveen, S.L. van de Velde, and B. Veltman. Complexity of scheduling multiprocessor tasks with prespecified processor allocations. *Discrete Applied Mathematics*, 55(3):259–272, 1994.

122. A. Hori, Y. Ishikawa, H. Konaka, M. Maeda, and T. Tomokiyo. A scalable time-sharing scheduling for partitionable distributed memory parallel machines. In *Proceedings of 28th Hawaii International Conference on System Sciences (HICSS'95)*, pages 173–182, 1995.
123. J. Huang, J. Chen, and S. Chen. A simple linear-time approximation algorithm for multiprocessor job scheduling on four processors. In D.T. Lee and S.-H. Teng, editors, Proceedings of *11th International Symposium Algorithms and Computation (ISAAC'00). LNCS*, volume 1969, pages 60–71, 2000.
124. J. Hungershofer. On the combined scheduling of malleable and rigid jobs. In *Proceedings of 16th Symposium on Computer Architecture and High Performance Computing (SBAC-PAD'04)*, pages 206–213. IEEE Computer Society, Los Alamitos, CA, USA, 2004.
125. I. Hwang. An efficient processor allocation algorithm using two-dimensional packing. *Journal of Parallel and Distributed Computing*, 42(1), 1997.
126. A. Iovanella. *On-line algorithms for multiprocessor task scheduling*. Ph.D. thesis, Universitá degli Studi di Roma "La Sapienza", 2002.
127. D. Jackson, Q. Snell, and M. Clement. Core algorithms of the Maui scheduler. In D. Feitelson and L. Rudolph, editors, *Proceedings of 7th Workshop on Job Scheduling Strategies for Parallel Processing. LNCS*, volume 2221, pages 87–102, Springer, Berlin, 2001.
128. K. Jansen. Scheduling malleable parallel tasks: An asymptotic fully polynomial-time approximation scheme. In R. Möhring and R. Raman, editors, *Proceedings of ESA 2002. LNCS*, volume 2461, pages 562–574, Springer, Berlin, 2002.
129. K. Jansen and L. Porkolab. Preemptive parallel task scheduling in $o(n)+\text{poly}(m)$ time. In D.T. Lee and S.H. Teng, editors, *Proceedings of ISAAC 2000. LNCS*, volume 1969, pages 398–409, Springer, Berlin, 2000.
130. K. Jansen and L. Porkolab. Linear-time approximation schemes for scheduling malleable parallel tasks. *Algorithmica*, 32(3):507–520, 2002.
131. K. Jansen and L. Porkolab. Polynomial time approximation schemes for general multiprocessor job shop scheduling. *Journal of Algorithms*, 45(2):167–191, 2002.
132. K. Jansen and L. Porkolab. Computing optimal preemptive schedules for parallel tasks: Linear programming approaches. *Mathematical Programming*, 95(3):617–630, 2003.
133. K. Jansen and L. Porkolab. Preemptive scheduling on dedicated processors: Applications of fractional graph coloring. *Journal of Scheduling*, 7(1):35–48, 2004.
134. K. Jansen and L. Porkolab. General multiprocessor task scheduling: Approximate solutions in linear time. *SIAM Journal on Computing*, 35(3):519–530, 2005.
135. K. Jansen and L. Porkolab. On preemptive resource constrained scheduling: Polynomial-time approximation schemes. *SIAM Journal on Discrete Mathematics*, 20(3):545–563, 2006.
136. K. Jansen and H. Zhang. An approximation algorithm for scheduling malleable tasks under general precedence constraints. *ACM Transactions on Algorithms*, 2(3):416–434, 2006.
137. M. Jeng and H.J. Siegel. A distributed management scheme for partitionable parallel computers. *IEEE Transactions on Parallel and Distributed Systems*, 1(1):120–126, 1990.
138. P. Jędrzejowicz and I. Wierzbowska. Scheduling multiple variant programs under hard real-time constraints. *European Journal of Operational Research*, 127:458–465, 2000.
139. B. Johannes. Scheduling parallel jobs to minimize the makespan. *Journal of Scheduling*, 9(5):433–452, 2006.
140. J. Józefowska and J. Węglarz. Scheduling with resource constraints – continuous resources. In J.Y. Leung, editor, *Handbook of Scheduling: Algorithms, Models, and Performance Analysis*, pages 24.1–24.15. CRC Press, Boca Raton, 2004.
141. B. Kalyanasundaram and K. Pruhs. Dynamic spectrum allocation: The impotency of duration notification. *Journal of Scheduling*, 3(5):289–295, 2000.
142. P.J. Keleher, D. Zotkin, and D. Perkovic. Attacking the bottlenecks of backfilling schedulers. *Cluster Computing*, 3(4):245–254, 2000.
143. J. Kim, C.R. Das, and W. Lin. A top-down processor allocation scheme for hypercube computers. *IEEE Transactions on Parallel and Distributed Systems*, 2(1):20–30, 1991.
144. D.E. Knuth. *The Art of Computer Programming. Volume 1. Fundamental Algorithms.* Addison-Wesley Reading MA, Third Edition, 1997.

145. H. Kopetz and P. Veríssimo. Real time and dependability concepts. In S. Mullender, editor, *Distributed Systems*, pages 411–446. Addison-Wesley and ACM Press, New York, 1994.
146. Y. Kopidakis and V. Zissimopoulos. An approximation scheme for scheduling independent jobs into subcubes of a hypercube of fixed dimension. *Theoretical Computer Science*, 178(1–2):265–273, 1997.
147. E. Koukis and N. Koziris. Memory bandwidth aware scheduling for SMP cluster nodes. In *Proceedings of 13th Euromicro Conference on Parallel, Distributed and Network-Based Processing (Euromicro-PDP'05)*, pages 187–196. IEEE Computer Society, Los Alamitos, CA, USA, 2005.
148. H. Krawczyk and M. Kubale. An approximation algorithm for diagnostic test scheduling in multicomputer systems. *IEEE Transactions on Computers*, 34(9):869–872, 1985.
149. R. Krishnamurti and D.R. Gaur. An approximation algorithm for nonpreemptive scheduling on hypercube parallel task systems. *Information Processing Letters*, 72(5–6):183–188, 1999.
150. R. Krishnamurti and E. Ma. An approximation algorithm for scheduling tasks on varying partition sizes in partitionable, multiprocessor systems. *IEEE Transactions on Computers*, 41(12):1572–1579, 1992.
151. R. Krishnamurti and B. Narahari. An approximation algorithm for preemptive scheduling on parallel-task systems. *SIAM Journal on Discrete Mathematics*, 8(4):661–669, 1995.
152. P. Krueger and D. Babbar. The effects of precedence and priority constraints on the performance of scan scheduling for hypercube multiprocessors. *Journal of Parallel and Distributed Computing*, 39(2):95–104, 1996.
153. P. Krueger, T.-H. Lai, and V.A. Dixit-Radiya. Job scheduling is more important than processor allocation for hypercube computers. *IEEE Transaction on Parallel and Distributed Sysytems*, 5(5):488–497, 1994.
154. M. Kubale. The complexity of scheduling independent two-processor tasks on dedicated processors. *Information Processing Letters*, 24(3):141–147, 1987.
155. M. Kubale. Podzielne uszeregowania zadań dwuprocesorowych na procesorach dedykowanych. *Zeszyty Naukowe Politechniki Śląskiej, Seria:Automatyka z.100, Nr kol. 1082*, pages 145–153, 1990.
156. M. Kubale. Preemptive versus nonpreemtive scheduling of biprocessor tasks on dedicated processors. *European Journal of Operational Research*, 94(2):242–251, 1996.
157. M. Kubale, editor. *Graph Colorings*. American Mathematical Society, Providence, RI, 2004.
158. O.-H. Kwon and K.-Y. Chwa. An algorithm for scheduling jobs in hypercube systems. *IEEE Transactions on Parallel and Distributed Systems*, 9(9):856–860, 1998.
159. O.-H. Kwon and K.-Y. Chwa. Scheduling parallel tasks with individual deadlines. *Theoretical Computer Science*, 215(1-2):209–223, 1999.
160. J. Labetoulle, E.L. Lawler, J.K. Lenstra, and Alexander H.G. Rinnoy Kan. Preemptive scheduling of uniform machines subject to release dates. In W.R. Pulleyblank, editor, *Progress in Combinatorial Optimization*, pages 245–261. Academic, New York, 1984.
161. C.-Y. Lee and X. Cai. Scheduling one and two-processor tasks on two parallel processors. *IEE Transactions*, 31(5):445–455, 1999.
162. W.Y. Lee, S.J. Hong, and J. Kim. On-line scheduling of scalable real-time tasks on multiprocessor systems. *Journal of Parallel and Distributed Computing*, 63(12):1315–1324, 2003.
163. A. Legrand, A. Su, and F. Vivien. Minimizing the stretch when scheduling flows of divisible requests. Technical Report No 2006-19, Laboratoire de l'Informatique du Parallélisme, École Normale Supérieure de Lyon, 2006. Research Report.
164. R. Lepére, D. Trystram, and G. Woeginger. Approximation algorithms for scheduling malleable tasks under precedence constraints. *International Journal of Foundations of Computer Science*, 13(4):613–627, 2002.
165. V.J. Leung, E.M. Arkin, M.A. Bender, D. Bunde, J. Johnston, A. Lal, J.S.B. Mitchell, C. Phillips, and S. Seiden. Processor allocation on Cplant: Achieving general processor locality using one-dimensional allocation strategies. In *Proceedings of the IEEE International Conference on Cluster Computing (CLUSTER'02)*, pages 296–304, 2002.
166. S.T. Leutenegger and M.K. Vernon. The performance of multiprogrammed multiprocessor scheduling policies. In *Proceedings of the 1990 ACM SIGMETRICS Conference on Measurement and Modeling of Computer Systems*, pages 226–236, 1990.

167. K. Li. Analysis of an approximation algorithm for scheduling independent parallel tasks. *Discrete Mathematics and Theoretical Computer Science*, 3(4):155–166, 1999.
168. K. Li. Analysis of the list scheduling algorithm for precedence constrained parallel tasks. *Journal of Combinatorial Optimization*, 3(1):73–88, 1999.
169. K. Li and K.-H. Cheng. Static job scheduling in partitionable mesh connected systems. *Journal of Parallel and Distributed Computing*, 10(2):152–159, 1990.
170. K. Li and K.-H. Cheng. Job scheduling in a partitionable mesh using a two-dimensional buddy system partitioning scheme. *IEEE Transactions on Parallel and Distributed Systems*, 2(4):413–423, 1991.
171. K. Li and K.-H. Cheng. A two-dimensional buddy system for dynamic resource allocation in a partitionable mesh connected system. *Journal of Parallel and Distributed Computing*, 12(1):79–83, 1991.
172. K. Li and Y. Pan. Probabilistic analysis of scheduling precedence constrained parallel tasks on multicomputers with contiguous processor allocation. *IEEE Transactions on Computers*, 49(10):1021–1030, 2000.
173. D.A. Lifka. The ANL/IBM SP scheduling system. In D. Feitelson and L. Rudolph, editors, *Proceedings of 1st Workshop on Job Scheduling Strategies for Parallel Processing. LNCS*, volume 949, pages 295–303, Springer, Berlin, 1995.
174. J.-F. Lin and S.-J. Chen. Scheduling algorithm for nonpreemptive multiprocessor tasks. *Computers and Mathematics with Applications*, 28(4):85–92, 1994.
175. E.L. Lloyd. Concurrent task systems. *Operations Research*, 29(1):189–201, 1981.
176. V. Lo, K.J. Windisch, W. Liu, and B. Nitzberg. Noncontiguous processor allocation algorithms for mesh-connected multicomputers. *IEEE Transactions on Parallel and Distributed Systems*, 8(7):712–726, 1997.
177. A. Lodi, S. Martello, and M. Monaci. Two-dimensional packing problems: A survey. *European Journal of Operational Research*, 141(2):241–252, 2002.
178. U. Lublin and D.G. Feitelson. The workload on parallel supercomputers: Modeling the characteristics of rigid jobs. *Journal of Parallel and Distributed Computing*, 63(11):1105–1122, 2003.
179. J. Mache and V. Lo. The effects of dispersal on message-passing contention in processor allocation strategies. In *Proceedings of 3rd Joint Conference on Information Sciences*, volume 3, pages 223–226, 1997.
180. J. Mache, V. Lo, and K. Windisch. Minimizing message-passing contention in fragmentation free processor allocation. In *Proceedings of 10th International Conference on Parallel and Distributed Computing Systems*, pages 120–124, 1997.
181. R. Mansini, M.G. Speranza, and Z. Tuza. Scheduling groups of tasks with precedence constraints on three dedicated processors. *Discrete Applied Mathematics*, 134(1–3):141–168, 2004.
182. C. McCann, R. Vaswani, and J. Zahorjan. A dynamic processor allocation policy for multiprogrammed shared-memory multiprocessors. *ACM Transactions on Computer Systems*, 11(2):146–178, 1993.
183. M.P. McGarry, M. Maier, and M. Reisslein. Ethernet PONs: A survey of dynamic bandwidth allocation (DBA) algorithms. *IEEE Communications Magazine*, 42(8), 2004.
184. D. Min and M.W. Mutka. Efficient job scheduling in a mesh multicomputer without discrimination against large jobs. In *Proceedings of 7th IEEE Symposium on Parallel and Distributed Processing (SPDP '95)*, pages 52–59, 1995.
185. P. Mohapatra. Processor allocation using partitioning in mesh connected parallel computers. *Journal of Parallel and Distributed Computing*, 39(1):181–190, 1996.
186. P. Mohapatra. Dynamic real-time task scheduling on hypercubes. *Journal of Parallel and Distributed Computing*, 46(1):91–100, 1997.
187. P. Mohapatra, C. Yu, and C. Das. A lazy scheduling scheme for hypercube computers. *Journal of Parallel and Distributed Computing*, 27(1):26–37, 1995.
188. R. Motwani, S. Phillips, and E. Torng. Non-clairvoyant scheduling. *Theoretical Computer Science*, 130(1):17–47, 1994.

189. G. Mounié, C. Rapine, and D. Trystram. A $\frac{3}{2}$ approximation algorithm for scheduling independent monotonic malleable tasks. Technical report, ID-IMAG Laboratory, Grenoble, France, 2002. http://www-id.imag.fr/Laboratoire/Membres/Trystram_ Denis/ publis_malleable/MRT_indepSIAM.pdf [online accessed 10 August 2007].

190. A.W. Mu'alem and D. G. Feitelson. Utilization, predictability, workloads, and user runtime estimates in scheduling the IBM SP2 with backfilling. *IEEE Transactions on Parallel and Distributed Systems*, 12(6):529–543, 2001.

191. V.K. Naik, S.K. Setia, and M.S. Squillante. Processor allocation in multiprogrammed distributed-memory parallel computer systems. *Journal of Parallel and Distributed Computing*, 47(1):28–47, 1997.

192. E. Naroska and U. Schwiegelshohn. On an on-line scheduling problem for parallel jobs. *Information Processing Letters*, 81(6):297–304, 2002.

193. C. Oguz, Y. Zinder, V.H. Do, A. Janiak, and M. Lichtenstein. Hybrid flow-shop scheduling problems with multiprocessor task systems. *European Journal of Operational Research*, 152(1):115–131, 2004.

194. J. Padhye and L. Dowdy. Dynamic versus adaptive processor allocation policies for message passing parallel computers: An empirical comparison. In D.G. Feitelson and L. Rudolph, editors, *Proceedings of 2nd Workshop on Job Scheduling Strategies for Parallel Processing. LNCS*, volume 1162, pages 224–243, 1996.

195. J.L. Peterson and T.A. Norman. Buddy systems. *Communications of the ACM*, 20(6):421– 431, 1977.

196. J. Plehn. Preemptive scheduling of independent jobs with release times and deadlines on a hypercube. *Information Processing Letters*, 34(3):161–166, 1990.

197. G.N.S. Prasanna, A. Agarwal, and B.R. Musicus. Hierarchical compilation of macro dataflow graphs for multiprocessors with local memory. *IEEE Transactions on Parallel and Distributed Systems*, 5(7):720–736, 1994.

198. G.N.S. Prasanna and B.R. Musicus. Generalized multiprocessor scheduling using optimal control. In *Proceedings of 3rd Annual ACM Symposium on Parallel Algorithms and Architectures (SPAA'91)*, pages 216–228, 1991.

199. S.G.N. Prasanna and B.R. Musicus. Generalized multiprocessor scheduling for directed acyclic graphs. In *Proceedings of Supercomputing 1994*, pages 237–246. IEEE Computer Society, Los Alamitos, CA, USA, 1994.

200. S.G.N. Prasanna and B.R. Musicus. Generalized multiprocessor scheduling and applications to matrix computations. *IEEE Transactions on Parallel and Distributed Systems*, 7(6):650 – 664, 1996.

201. W. Qiao and L.M. Ni. Efficient processor allocation for 3D tori. In *Proceedings of 9th International Parallel Processing Symposium (IPPS '95)*, pages 466–471, 1995.

202. S. Rai, J.L. Trahan, and T. Smailus. Processor allocation in hypercube multiprocessors. *IEEE Transactions on Parallel and Distributed Systems*, 6(6):606–616, 1995.

203. E. Rosti, E. Smirni, L.W. Dowdy, G. Serazzi, and B.M. Carlson. Robust partitioning policies of multiprocessor systems. *Performance Evaluation*, 19:141–165, 1994.

204. S. Sahni. Algorithms for scheduling independent tasks. *Journal of the ACM*, 23(1):116–127, 1976.

205. U. Schwiegelshohn, W. Ludwig, J.L. Wolf, J. Turek, and P.S. Yu. Smart SMART bounds for weighted response time scheduling. *SIAM Journal on Computing*, 28:237–253, 1998.

206. K.-H. Seo and S.-C. Kim. Extended flexible processor allocation strategy for mesh-connected systems using shape manipulations. In *Proceedings of International Conference on Parallel and Distributed Systems*, pages 780–787, 1997.

207. S.K. Setia, M.S. Squillante, and S.K. Tripathi. Analysis of processor allocation in multiprogrammed, distributed-memory parallel processing systems. *IEEE Transactions on Parallel and Distributed Systems*, 5(4):401–420, 1994.

208. J. Sgall. Randomized on-line scheduling of parallel jobs. *Journal od Algorithms*, 21(1):149– 175, 1996.

209. D.D. Sharma and D.K. Pradhan. A novel approach for subcube allocation in hypercube multiprocessors. In *Proceedings of 4th IEEE Symposium on Parallel and Distributed Processing*, pages 336–345, 1992.

210. D.D. Sharma and D.K. Pradhan. Submesh allocation in mesh multicomputers using busy-list: A best-fit approach with complete recognition capability. *Journal of Parallel and Distributed Computing*, 36(2):106–118, 1996.

211. D.D. Sharma and D.K. Pradhan. Job scheduling in mesh multicomputers. *IEEE Transactions on Parallel and Distributed Systems*, 9(1):57–70, 1998.

212. X. Shen and E.M. Reingold. Scheduling on a hypercube. *Information Processing Letters*, 40(6):323–328, 1991.

213. D.P. Siewiorek. Fault tolerance in commercial computers. *IEEE Computer*, pages 26–37, 1990.

214. A. Silberschatz, J.L. Peterson, and P.B. Galvin. *Operating Systems Concepts*. Addison-Wesley, Reading MA, USA, 1991.

215. F. Sivrikaya-Serifoglu and G. Ulusoy. Multiprocessor task scheduling in multistage hybrid flow-shops: A genetic algorithm approach. *Journal of the Operational Research Society*, 55(5):504–512, 2004.

216. J. Skovira, W. Chan, H. Zhou, and D. Lifka. The EASY – LoadLeveler API project. In D. Feitelson and L. Rudolph, editors, *Proceedings of 2nd Workshop on Job Scheduling Strategies for Parallel Processing. LNCS*, volume 1162, pages 41–47, Springer, Berlin, 1996.

217. M.S. Squillante. On the benefits and limitations of dynamic partitioning in the parallel computer systems. In D.G. Feitelson and L. Rudolph, editors, *Proceedings of 1st Workshop on Job Scheduling Strategies for Parallel Processing. LNCS*, volume 949, pages 219–238, 1995.

218. S. Srinivasan, V. Subramani, R. Kettimuthu, P. Holenarsipur, and P. Sadayappan. Effective selection of partition sizes for moldable scheduling of parallel jobs. In S. Sahni, V.K. Prasanna, and U. Shukla, editors, *Proceedings of 9th International Conference on High Performance Computing (HiPC'02). LNCS*, volume 2552, pages 174–183, 2002.

219. A. Steinberg. A strip-packing algorithm with absolute performance bound 2. *SIAM Journal on Computing*, 26(2):401–409, 1997.

220. D. Talby and D.G. Feitelson. Supporting priorities and improving utilization of the IBM SP scheduler using slack-based backfilling. In *Proceedings of 13th International Parallel Processing Symposium*, pages 513–517. IEEE, 1999.

221. A.S. Tanenbaum. *Modern Operating Systems*. Prentice-Hall, Upper Saddle River NJ, 2001.

222. A. Tucker and A. Gupta. Process control and scheduling issues for multiprogrammed shared-memory multiprocessors. In *Proceedings of 12th ACM Symposium on Operating System Principles*, pages 159–166, 1989.

223. J. Turek, W. Ludwig, J.L. Wolf, L. Fleischer, P. Tiwari, J. Glasgow, U. Schwiegelshohn, and P. S. Yu. Scheduling parallelizable tasks to minimize average response time. In *Proceedings of 6th Annual ACM Symposium on Parallel Algorithms and Architectures (SPAA'94)*, pages 200–209. ACM, New York, NY, USA, 1994.

224. J. Turek, U. Schwiegelshohn, J.L. Wolf, and P.S. Yu. Scheduling parallel tasks to minimize average response time. In *Proceedings of the 5th Annual ACM-SIAM Symposium on Discrete algorithms (SODA'94)*, pages 112–121. SIAM, Philadelphia PA, USA, 1994.

225. J. Turek, J.L. Wolf, K.R. Pattipati, and P.S. Yu. Scheduling parallelizable tasks: Putting it all on the shelf. *ACM SIGMETRICS Performance Evaluation Review*, 20(1):225–236, 1992.

226. J. Turek, J.L. Wolf, and P. S. Yu. Approximate algorithms for scheduling parallelizable tasks. In *Proceedings of 4th Annual ACM Symposium on Parallel Algorithms and Architectures (SPAA'92)*, pages 323–332. ACM, New York, NY, USA, 1992.

227. B. Veltman, B.J. Lageweg, and J.K. Lenstra. Multiprocessor scheduling with communications delays. *Parallel Computing*, 16:173–182, 1990.

228. V.G. Vizing. About schedules observing dead-lines (in Russian). *Kibernetika*, (1):128–135, 1981.

229. V.G. Vizing. Minimization of the maximum delay in servicing systems with interruption. *U.S.S.R. Computatioanl Mathematics and Mathematical Physics*, 22(3):227–233, 1982.

230. Q. Wang and K.-H. Cheng. List scheduling of parallel tasks. *Information Processing Letters*, 37(5):291–297, 1991.

231. Q. Wang and K.-H. Cheng. A heuristic of scheduling parallel tasks and its analysis. *SIAM Journal on Computing*, 21(2):281–294, 1992.

232. J.B. Weissman, L.R. Abburi, and D. England. Integrated scheduling: The best of both worlds. *Journal of Parallel and Distributed Computing*, 63(6):649–668, 2003.

233. J. Węglarz. Modelling and control of dynamic resource allocation project scheduling systems. In S.G. Tzafestas, editor, *Optimization and Control of Dynamic Operational Research Models*, pages 105–140. North-Holland, Amsterdam, 1982.

234. J. Węglarz. Scheduling under continuous performing speed vs. resource amount activity models. In R. Słowiński and J. Węglarz, editors, *Advances in Project Scheduling*, pages 273–295. Elsevier Science, Amsterdam, 1989.

235. P.R. Wilson, M.S. Johnstone, M. Neely, and David Boles. Dynamic storage allocation: A survey and critical review. In H.G. Baker, editor, *Proceedings of International Workshop on Memory Management (IWMM'95). LNCS*, volume 986, pages 1–116, 1995.

236. Y. Wiseman and D.G. Feitelson. Paired gang scheduling. *IEEE Transactions on Parallel and Distributed Systems*, 14(6), 2003.

237. J.L. Wolf, J. Turek, M.-S. Chen, and P.S. Yu. A hierarchical approach to parallel multiquery scheduling. *IEEE Transactions on Parallel and Distributed Systems*, 6(6):578–590, 1995.

238. F. Wu, C.-C. Hsu, and L.-P. Chou. Processor allocation in the mesh multiprocessors using the leapfrog method. *IEEE Transactions on Parallel and Distributed Systems*, 14(3):276–289, 2003.

239. W. Xing and J. Zhang. Parallel machine scheduling with splitting jobs. *Discrete Applied Mathematics*, 103(1-3):259–269, 2000.

240. D. Ye and G. Zhang. On-line scheduling of parallel jobs with dependencies on 2-dimensional mesh. In T. Ibaraki, N. Katoh, and H. Ono, editors, Proceedings of *14th International Symposium Algorithms and Computation (ISAAC'03). LNCS*, volume 2906, pages 329–338, 2003.

241. B.S. Yoo and C.R. Das. A fast and efficient processor allocation scheme for mesh-connected multicomputers. *IEEE Transactions on Computers*, 51(1):46–60, 2002.

242. B.S. Yoo, C.R. Das, and C. Yu. Processor management techniques for mesh-connected multiprocessors. In *Proceedings of the 24th International Conference on Parallel Processing*, pages 105–112, 1995.

243. S.-M. Yoo and H.Y. Youn. An efficient task allocation scheme for two-dimensional mesh-connected systems. In *Proceedings of the 15th International Conference on Distributed Computing Systems*, pages 501–508, 1995.

244. S.-M. Yoo and H.Y. Youn. An on-line scheduling and allocation scheme for real-time tasks in 2D meshes. In *Proceedings of the 7th IEEE Symposium on Parallel and Distributed Processing (SPDP'95)*, pages 630–637, 1995.

245. B.B. Zhou, R.P. Brent, C.W. Johnson, and D. Walsh. Resource allocation schemes for gang scheduling. In D. G. Feitelson and L. Rudolph, editors, *Proceedings of 5th Workshop on Job Scheduling Strategies for Parallel Processing. LNCS*, volume 1659, pages 129–143. Springer, Berlin, 1999.

246. Y. Zhu. Efficient processor allocation strategies for mesh-connected parallel computers. *Journal of Parallel and Distributed Computing*, 16(4):328–337, 1992.

247. Y. Zhu and M. Ahuja. On job scheduling on a hypercube. *IEEE Transactions on Parallel and Distributed Systems*, 4(1):62–69, 1993.

248. Y. Zinder and V.H. Do. Scheduling unit execution time tasks on two parallel machines with the criteria of makespan and total completion time. In G. Kendall, E.K. Burke, S. Petrovic, and M. Gendreau, editors, *Multidisciplinary Scheduling: Theory and Applications*, pages 83–112. Springer, 2005.

249. Y. Zinder, V.H. Do, and C. Oğuz. Computational complexity of some scheduling problems with multiprocessor tasks. *Discrete Optimization*, 2(4):391–408, 2005.

# Chapter 6
# Scheduling with Communication Delays

In this chapter, we consider scheduling with communication delays. This model assumes that a parallel application is a set of sequential communicating processes (or threads) which can be represented as a directed acyclic graph (DAG). Execution of the tasks in a distributed system causes communication delays if the predecessor and the successor tasks are executed on different processors. Beyond introducing the communication delays, classic scheduling theory assumptions are generally accepted here.

The rest of this chapter is organized in the following way. In Sect. 6.1 motivation for scheduling with communication delays is given with examples of task graphs for parallel algorithms. The scheduling problem is formulated in Sect. 6.2, where variants of the communication delay models are also discussed. A shorthand notation of the scheduling problems is introduced in Sect. 6.3. In Sects. 6.4–6.7 the examined body of knowledge is partitioned according to the limited or unlimited number of processors, and allowed or disallowed task duplication. Scheduling problems are examined along the lines of computational complexity theory. The complexity results and polynomially solvable special cases are presented first. Then, heuristics are discussed. For selected special cases heuristics with performance guarantees exist. Other heuristics have no performance quality guarantees, but provide good solutions on average or solve to optimality certain special cases of the scheduling problem. In Sect. 6.8 we present selected methods of scheduling with communication delays in known interconnection networks. In the following two sections we give examples of scheduling with communication delays under different distributed system models. Thus, in Sect. 6.9 we present scheduling with communication delays in $LogP$ model and in Sect. 6.10 hierarchical delay model. Not all branches of scheduling with communication delays are discussed here. Some approaches not covered in this chapter are mentioned in Sect. 6.11. We conclude this chapter with some general observations in Sect. 6.11.

Other surveys of scheduling with communication delays can be found, e.g., in [29, 35, 76, 110].

M. Drozdowski, *Scheduling for Parallel Processing*, Computer Communications and Networks, DOI 10.1007/978-1-84882-310-5_6,
© Springer-Verlag London Limited 2009

## 6.1   Scheduling with Communication Delays in Practice

Let us start with several simple observations. In the current scheduling model it is assumed that a communication delay must elapse when two tasks: a predecessor and a successor are executed on different processors. Were there no precedence constraints, this model would reduce to classic scheduling because communication delays would disappear. Thus, a task graph or precedence graph is a core input object in scheduling with communication delays. The next feature distinguishing the current scheduling model from the classic one are communication delays. Thus, one may ask what is the practicality and importance of the concepts of task graph and communication delay.

In a program code it is not difficult to observe that a result computed by one operation $T_1$ may be necessary to perform another operation $T_2$. The need for input data introduces partial order between the operations in a program. To represent such an order a concept of *data dependency graph* is used. Two operations $T_1, T_2$ may also be dependent if their outputs have nonempty intersection. For example, if $T_1, T_2$ modify the same variable, then the result of the computation depends on the sequence of executing $T_1, T_2$. This sequence is sometimes determined by the sequence of $T_1, T_2$ in program code. The partial order of operations in the program code is represented by a DAG $\mathcal{G} = (\mathcal{T}, \mathcal{A})$ which is in fact a task graph. The names of *dependence graph* or *flow graph* are often used in the compiler design and automatic program parallelization. For more information on extraction of parallelism and construction of the task graphs see e.g. [35, 44, 103]. In the following discussion we will be assuming that the task graph is given. Below we give examples of algorithms and their possible task graph representation.

A quadratic equation $ax^2 + bx + c = 0$ has two solutions: $x_1 = \frac{-b - \sqrt{b^2 - 4ac}}{2a}$ and $x_2 = \frac{-b + \sqrt{b^2 - 4ac}}{2a}$. Example of a program code for calculating $x_1, x_2$, the corresponding task graph, and schedule are shown in Fig. 6.1.

Another example is calculation of discrete Fourier transform (DFT) by fast Fourier transform (FFT) algorithm. DFT of a sequence $x_0, \ldots, x_{N-1}$ of complex numbers is defined as $Y_k = \sum_{l=0}^{N-1} x_l \omega^{lk}$, for $k = 0, \ldots, N-1$ where $\omega = e^{-\frac{2\pi i}{N}}$. Calculation of DFT from the above definition has complexity $O(N^2)$. Using an observation that $X_k$ is a sum of DFTs for even and for odd values of $x_i$, i.e. $Y_k = \sum_{l=0}^{\frac{N}{2}-1} x_{2l} \omega^{2lk} + \omega^k \sum_{l=0}^{\frac{N}{2}-1} x_{2l+1} \omega^{2lk}$, for $k = 0, \ldots, N-1$, an algorithm with complexity $O(N \log N)$ has been proposed. In Fig. 6.2a example of a code for FFT is given assuming that $N$ is a power of 2, and in Fig. 6.2b its task graph is shown for $N = 4$.

The last example is solving a system of $N$ linear equations with $N$ unknowns by Gauss–Jordan elimination method. The problem consists in solving equation $Ax = b$ for $x$, where $A$ is $N \times N$ matrix, and $b, x$ are vectors of length $N$. The exemplary code is shown in Fig. 6.3a. For simplicity of the code it is assumed that column vector $b$ is concatenated with $A$, and it is in the last $N + 1$th column of $A$. A corresponding task graph for $N = 3$ is shown in Fig. 6.3b.

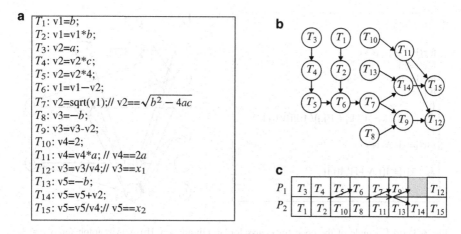

**Fig. 6.1** (a) Code solving a quadratic equation. (b) A corresponding task graph. (c) A schedule assuming that each operation and communication take one unit of time, arcs show interprocessor communications

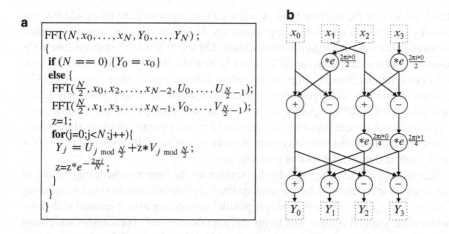

**Fig. 6.2** (a) Example of the code for FFT. (b) A task graph for $N = 4$

From the above examples it can be concluded that in many cases task graphs can be derived before the runtime from the algorithm or from the program code. When the task graph is built at the runtime, then it can be recognized and managed by the runtime environment. Note that task graph may depend on problem size (denoted $N$ in the above two examples).

The second element of scheduling with communication delays are communication delays themselves. To give an impression of the duration of communication delay, let us assume that communication delay is given by formula (3.1), and let us consider just start-up time $S$ examples given in Table 3.1. On the Inmos 30 MHz

**a**
```
GJ(A, b, x); ;
{
for(j=0;j<N;j++)
for(i=0;i<N;i++)
for(k=j;k<N + 1;k++)
if (i!=j)
{
T_jik : A[i,k]=A[i,k]-(A[i,j]/A[j,j])A[j,k]);
};
for(i=0,i<N,i++)
{
T_i : x[i]=A[i,N+1]/A[i,i]
};
```

**b**
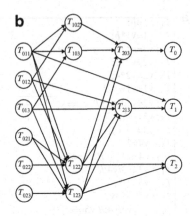

**Fig. 6.3** (a) Example of the code for Gauss-Jordan elimination. (b) A task graph for $N = 3$. Only messages with the results of some computational task $T_{jik}$ are shown. Tasks which are not predecessors of $T_i$ are omitted

T805 Transputer the start-up time of software routing procedure takes 42,000 processor cycles which means that approximately 42,000 instructions can be executed in parallel with the simplest communication. On a 200 MHz PC start-up time took approx. 49,600 instructions, on SGI Origin 3800 with 400 MHz CPU it takes approx. 7,200 instructions. Similar order of the values is reported for other systems in [33]. Communication in wide area networks has even worse start-up times. Only in the best designs of SMP computers, such as vector supercomputers, the time of communication via a local memory is comparable to the instruction cycle time. Thus, communications in distributed systems introduce considerable costs, and ignoring it may result in detrimental loss of performance.

Let us now discuss the most likely position of the current scheduling model in the stack of schedulers in the parallel systems and the relation to other scheduling models. Task graph represents a single parallel application to be executed within the limits of the parallel system. The limits are, e.g., the number of processors which can be imposed either by the hardware or by the scheduler of a parallel system partitioning CPU resources between the submitted jobs. In such environment it is impractical for a global system scheduler to take into account particular tasks existing within all the task graphs of different applications. It is impractical for at least two reasons. First, the parallel application would have to expose to the system scheduler a lot of very specific information. A parallel system scheduler should be omnipotent to deal with such information. This idea is unrealistic. The second reason is that managing and optimizing schedules for many tasks is computationally prohibitive. Thus, only limited amount of information general enough to be provided by all types of parallel applications can be passed to the system scheduler. These can be required number of processors, expected execution time, memory requirements, etc. This description conforms with parallel task model from Chap. 5. On the other hand, it is more viable to allow the programmer or the runtime environment to control execution of the tasks within the parallel application. The programmer or the runtime environment, after analysis of the program code, has the best understanding of the application parallelism and how it can be exploited. The model of scheduling with communication delays most appropriately fits here, i.e. at the application level scheduling. One of the consequences of the above situation is that for a parallel application, and its task graph, it is most rational to minimize schedule length on the given processor number. Therefore, $C_{max}$ is the main optimality criterion in scheduling with communication delays. Example scheduling tools optimizing execution time of the tasks within parallel applications include: Hypertool [124], Task Grapher [81], Parallax [80], Parsa [106], Pyrros [44], and CASCH [6]. A more recent survey of scheduling tools can be found in [25].

## 6.2 Formulation of the Problem

In this section, we formulate the problem of scheduling with communication delays. We use assumptions and terminology of the classic scheduling theory (cf. Sect. 4.1).

### 6.2.1 Notation and Preliminaries

It is assumed that the computing environment is comprised of parallel identical processors. There are only few exceptions where processors are assumed to be uniform. We are given a task graph $\mathcal{G} = (\mathcal{T}, \mathcal{A})$, where $\mathcal{T}$ is the set of tasks and $\mathcal{A}$ is the set of precedence constraints representing communications between the tasks. Here $\mathcal{G}$ is a DAG. Each task is defined by a collection of parameters. In particular, task $T_j \in \mathcal{T}$ has processing time $p_j$. We will denote by $pred(j)$ the set of immediate predecessors of $T_j$ in $\mathcal{G}$. Analogously $succ(j)$ is the set of $T_j$ immediate successors.

Communication cost $c_{ijkl}$ is incurred by precedence $(T_i \rightarrow T_j) \in \mathcal{A}$ when the two tasks $T_i, T_j$ are executed on processors $P_k, P_l$, respectively. There is no communication delay if the predecessor and the successor tasks are executed on the same processor. Thus, task $T_j$ can be started at time $c_i + c_{ijkl}$ or later if $P_k \neq P_l$, where $c_i$ is completion time of $T_i$, or the start time of $T_j$ is at least $c_i$ if $P_k = P_l$. Communication delays $c_{ijkl}$ are given in set $\mathcal{C}$. The amount of available memory at each processor is sufficiently big to hold all the intermediate results and the received messages. On a path $T_i \rightarrow T_j \rightarrow T_k$ the communication from $T_i$ to $T_k$ need not be repeated if tasks $T_j, T_k$ are executed on the same processor. Detailed models determining duration of communication delay are discussed in Sect. 6.2.2.

Let us denote by $cp$ the length of the critical path in $\mathcal{A}$. The length of the critical path includes all the communication delays between tasks executed on different processors. We will denote by $h(j)$ the height, or level of $T_j$ which is the length of the longest path from $T_j$ to its furthest successor in $\mathcal{A}$ including communication delays and processing time $p_j$ of $T_j$ itself. Similarly, let $est(j)$ be the earliest starting time of $T_j$, i.e. the length of the longest path including communication and computation times from any predecessor to $T_j$ excluding processing time of $T_j$. We will denote by $lst(j)$ the latest starting time of $T_j$, i.e. the time at which $T_j$ must be started without increasing the length of the critical path. Tasks $T_j$ satisfying $cp = est(j) + h(j)$, or $est(j) = lst(j)$ are on the critical path, and will be called *critical*.

In the above definitions of $est(j)$, $lst(j)$, $h(j)$ it is tacitly assumed that tasks are already assigned to some processors. A common scheme in scheduling task graphs is to start with tasks assigned to their own processors. Next, the schedule is gradually improved by shifting tasks between processors or by changing their execution interval. A different scheme consists in building a schedule by assigning tasks to processors in the order of some list. If some task $T_j$ is considered for an execution on processor $P_i$, while the assignment of all other tasks remains unchanged, we will denote the earliest starting time by $est(j, i)$. Analogously, $lst(j, i)$ and $h(j, i)$ will denote latest starting time and level of $T_j$ on $P_i$, respectively. We will also denote by $dat(j, i)$ data availability time of $T_j$ on $P_i$. Data availability time is the moment when the latest message from any predecessor of $T_j$ is delivered to processor $P_i$. Note that $est(j, i) \geq dat(j, i)$. However, $est(j, i)$ is not necessarily equal to $\max\{dat(j, i), ft(i)\}$, where $ft(i)$ is the end of the current partial schedule on $P_i$, because $T_j$ may be inserted in some idle interval of the partial schedule on $P_i$. When task $T_j$ is finally scheduled, then $proc(j)$ will denote the index of the processor executing $T_j$.

Let us note that in some publications communication delays are not included in levels, earliest/latest starting times, etc. This may cause confusion. In the case of levels calculated without communication delays, we will be saying that they are *static*. The static values of level, earliest/latest starting time, critical path length will be denoted $h'(j), est'(j), lst'(j), cp'$, respectively. We will explicitly state the difference in the method of calculating levels where necessary.

The fraction of time spent in computation per communication time unit defined as

$$g(T, A) = \min_j \left\{ \frac{\min_{k \in pred(j)}\{p_k\}}{\max_{k \in pred(j)}\{c_{kj}\}}, \frac{\min_{k \in succ(j)}\{p_k\}}{\max_{k \in succ(j)}\{c_{jk}\}} \right\} \tag{6.1}$$

and is often called *granularity* of the input instance. If $g(T, A) \geq 1$ then granularity is called *coarse*. Note that this is a different concept of the grain of parallelism than, e.g., in divisible load models (cf. Chap. 7).

Scheduling with communication delays departs from the classic scheduling theory by allowing for task *duplication*. Duplication means that more than one copy of a task may be executed to avoid or to reduce communication delays. In schedule $S$ a copy of a task is defined by three elements: $(i, k, \tau)$, where $i$ is the index of the task from which the copy is derived, $k$ is the index of the assigned processor, $\tau$ is the execution start time. Each task must have at least one copy. The number of copies must be finite. If $T_i \rightarrow T_j$, then each copy of $T_j$ must receive its input from some copy of $T_i$. The copy of $T_j$ can be started only after the arrival of the earliest message from any copy of $T_i$. Observe that duplication is for free if the number of processors is unlimited. When processor number is limited, duplication increases the amount of performed work, and hence may increase schedule length.

Schedule length is the optimality criterion. Selected results for other criteria will be also mentioned, but the main focus of presentation is on $C_{\max}$ as explained in the previous section. Tasks within the task graph may have their own deadlines or ready times which is a common situation in the distributed real-time systems. However, scheduling for the real-time systems is in general beyond the scope of this book.

Let us distinguish communication delays considered in this chapter from migration delays. Preemption may incur migration costs, and hence a delay in resuming a task on a target processor. We will call it *migration delay*. The problem of scheduling with migration delays was studied in [98]. It has been shown that problem $P\,|pmtn - c = 1|C_{\max}$ is solvable by McNaughton algorithm, where $pmnt - c = k$ denotes migration with delay of length $k$. Problem $P\,|pmtn-c \geq 2|C_{\max}$ is sNPh. In this chapter, we assume that tasks are nonpreemptive, and we do not study migration delays.

## 6.2.2   *Interconnection Topology and Communication Delay Models*

In this section, we discuss several concepts of distributed systems and the resulting communication delay models.

### Standard Delay Model

The early publications [33,90] on scheduling with communication delays explicitly intended to suppress system specific features such as interconnection network. In the simplest formulation of the problem, processors are assumed to be connected by a complete (clique) network. Processors can simultaneously compute, send, and receive messages. On the completion of a task its results are immediately broadcast to all the successors and after the communication delays are considered to be delivered. Reducing perception of the communication network to the communication delay allowed for simplifying analysis of the scheduling problems and for better portability of scheduling algorithms between parallel systems. Other publications incorporated some models of the interconnection but without introducing too many details. We present examples of such extensions in the following text.

Now let us discuss various ways of calculating the duration of the communication delay. The communication delay defined in (3.1) has several components which depend on the sender–receiver pair of processors, and on the amount of transferred data. In our problem it is known what data must be sent from the predecessor task to its successor. Thus, without loss of generality, it may be assumed that communication delay $c_{ijkl}$ depends on sender $T_i$, receiver $T_j$, and the location of processors $P_k$, $P_l$ executing the sender and the receiver, respectively. If the component $Dv$ in Eq. (3.1) related to the distance in the network is small, then communication cost depends on the predecessor $T_i$, and successor $T_j$ pair of tasks, and can be denoted $c_{ij}$.

If also the amount of transferred data $\alpha$ is small, or the bandwidth $\frac{1}{C}$ is big, then communication time mainly consists of start-up time $S$. Consequently, communication delay is constant for all communications in the whole network. In this case notation may be further simplified to $c$.

## $Log P$ Model

A more detailed characterization of communication delay has been proposed in $LogP$ [33] model. $LogP$ is an abstract model of a parallel system with its communication network. It is assumed that communication delay consists of three parameters: $L$ – *latency* is an upper limit on the time of transferring the message data in the communication medium, $o$ – *overhead* is the time of processing the message at the sender and at the receiver sides of the communication, and $g$ – *gap* is the minimum interval in which the sender cannot send and the receiver cannot accept any new message after the initiation of the preceding one. Letter $P$ refers to the number of processors. Here latency $L$ is equivalent to the sum $Dv + C\alpha$ in Eq. (3.1). Overhead $o$ includes the time since issuing the request for sending a message in the application thread at the sender processor to the moment when the first bit of the message appears in the communication medium. It is assumed that equal time elapses at the receiver side, since the last bit of the message disappears from the communication medium to the moment when the message is received at the application thread on the receiver processor. The start-up time $S$ in Eq. (3.1) corresponds to the total overhead $2o$.

$LogP$ model has several scheduling implications. It is assumed that processors cannot perform any other action in the overhead interval $o$. Hence, overhead intervals must be scheduled on processors like tasks of a special type. In this way $LogP$ represents processor involvement in communications. Another consequence is a limit of $\lceil \frac{L}{g} \rceil$ messages which can be in transit from any processor or to any processor in the network at any time. If some processor sends a message to another processor which is in the gap $g$, then the sending processor stalls until the receiver becomes ready to accept a new message. It is assumed that messages are of small fixed size. Long blocks of data require many messages, and hence many overheads, latencies, and gaps, to be delivered. One more important difference between $LogP$ and the basic scheduling with communication delays is that in $LogP$ communications are of point-to-point (or 1-to-1) type. This means that each message has precisely defined receiver, whereas in the standard delay model messages are of broadcast or 1-to-many type. Consequently, if communication delay $c_{ij}$ depends on the predecessor task $T_i$ and the successor task $T_j$, then the processor assignment of $T_j$ is not as crucial in the standard model as in the $LogP$ model. The implications of $LogP$ model for the schedule feasibility are formalized in Sect. 6.9.

Let us note that $LogP$ model is also some approximation of reality. For example, since most of the communication networks work according to the best-effort rule no worst-case limit on communication latency $L$ can be given. It has been also observed that short messages are handled in a different way than long messages [8]. Scheduling for $LogP$ is discussed in Sect. 6.9.

### Hierarchical Systems

It is assumed here that the interconnection of the parallel system has hierarchical structure [11–13]. The parallel computing system consists of connected clusters of processors. Within the local cluster communication is faster. Between the clusters communication is slower. This model can represent a set of CPUs in an SMP system which form a local group of processors with short communication time and a set of SMP computers with longer communication time. Another example is a cluster of workstations connected by a LAN and an intercluster connection via Internet. For a pair of tasks $T_i \rightarrow T_j$ a nonlocal communication takes time $c_{ij}$ and in a local cluster of processors the communication delay is $\kappa_{ij}$. It is generally assumed that $c_{ij} \geq \kappa_{ij}$. Other assumptions of the standard delay model are preserved in the hierarchical communication model. Scheduling with communication delays in hierarchical systems is discussed in Sect. 6.10.

### Processor Networks

There are also publications like [22, 30, 44, 73, 108, 111, 124], and other, which analyze the structure of the underlaying network or the contention in accessing the shared medium by the messages. For example, in [30, 73, 104, 111] it is assumed that communication channel is a resource equivalent to a processor. Thus, two messages cannot use the same communication link simultaneously and must be explicitly sequenced. Thus, in [73, 104] messages are inserted as early as possible into the existing communication schedule so that the previously scheduled messages arrive in time.

We will not consider particular interconnection topologies here. With few exceptions message routing is beyond the scope of this chapter. Examples of algorithms general enough to be executed on any network, but still using a deeper knowledge on the communication system, will be presented in Sect. 6.8. The complexities of the communication network are represented mainly by communication delay times.

Let us note that potential benefits from a more accurate representation of the network in practice must be confronted with the lack of knowledge about the communication subsystem internals and limited control over its activities. Thus, the investment into a better scheduling algorithm makes sense only if adequate information and control of communication is available.

### 6.2.3   Technical Terminology

Before presenting algorithms for scheduling with communication delays let us introduce related terminology.

Some of the heuristics extend the classic list scheduling methods (cf. Sect. 4.3.1.1) in various ways accounting for the communication delays. Examples include ETF [63], MCP [124], and GD/HLFET [7]. These heuristics are often called *single stage* because task to processor assignment and sequencing on the processors are made together.

Some other heuristics have one or more stages of clustering, mapping, and sequencing. *Cluster* is a set of tasks supposed to be executed together on one processor. In the *clustering* (a.k.a. *internalization*) tasks are selected for execution on the same processor to eliminate communication delays and hence to reduce the critical path length. The procedure of removing the communication delay between a predecessor and a successor by including the two tasks in the same cluster is called *arc zeroing*. A cluster is called *linear* if its tasks form a chain in the task graph $\mathcal{G}$ (cf. Figs. 6.12b and 6.18). In a *nonlinear* cluster some tasks may be pairwise independent (see Fig. 6.20d). Note that comprising independent tasks in a nonlinear cluster results in executing them sequentially, and hence limits potential parallelism. A cluster with a single task will be called a *unit* cluster. At the clustering stage a task cluster one-to-one corresponds with a processor. Clustering heuristics generally do not assume any limit on cluster number. Therefore, they will be presented together with heuristics for the unbounded number of processors.

In the *assignment* phase (a.k.a. *mapping*) clusters are assigned to the processors. In the *sequencing* stage execution order of the tasks assigned to the processors is determined. Some heuristics impose the sequence on the tasks in the cluster already at the clustering stage.

## 6.3   Extension of $\alpha|\beta|\gamma$ Notation

In this section, we present extensions of the $\alpha|\beta|\gamma$ notation introduced in [117] to denote problems of scheduling with communication delays.

Sometimes it is assumed that the number of available processors is not bounding in scheduling. It is the case when $m \geq n$. For parallel identical processors this case will be denoted $P\infty$ in the $\alpha$ field of the notation.

The $\beta$ field has been extended by introducing the following set of symbols $\{com, c_{ij}, sct, c_{i*}, c_{*j}, c = 1, \circ\}$ to represent communication delays. The consecutive symbols denote:

    *com* – Communication times can be arbitrary values $c_{ijkl}$.

    $c_{ij}$ – Communication delay is defined for each arc $T_i \rightarrow T_j \in \mathcal{A}$.

    *sct* – Small communication times (SCT) which means that $\max_{(i,j)\in\mathcal{A}}\{c_{ij}\} \leq \min_{T_j\in\mathcal{T}}\{p_j\}$. Thus, *sct* case means that all communication delays are shorter than any processing time. In certain cases this requirement is slightly relaxed.

The *sct* case is also called *coarse grain* case because granularity (cf. Eq. (6.1)) satisfies $g(\mathcal{T}, \mathcal{A}) \geq 1$.

$c_{i*}$ – Communication time depends on the broadcasting task only.

$c_{*j}$ – Communication time depends on the receiving task only.

$c = 1$ – All communication times are equal to one unit of time. The name of this case is often abbreviated to UCT which stands for unit communication times.

○ – Communication delay is negligible.

Let us make an observation on complexity inference for various communication delays. We may expect that a polynomial algorithm for a problem with arbitrary communication delays (denoted *com*) implies a polynomial algorithm for UCT case ($c = 1$). However, a difficulty here is the difference in the length of the input string. Encoding communication delay for each combination of processor and task pairs requires $O(n^2 m^2)$ symbols, while for UCT communication delay is encoded in $O(1)$ symbols. Consequently, it is hard to infer on the complexity without comparing input lengths and their relation with the algorithm complexities. Similarly, it is hard to conclude on polynomial solvability of some UCT problem from the same problem but with communication delays depending on the predecessor–successor pair ($c_{ij}$).

In the online case some of the parameters may be unknown a priori. In such situations we will be preceding the unknown parameter with symbol ¬, as proposed in Sect. 4.4.3. For example, notation $\neg c_{ij}$ is used to represent unknown communication delays.

To denote possibility of task duplication the set of symbols {*dup*, ○} is used. Here *dup* means that task duplication is allowed and ○ that duplication is not allowed.

The extension of $\alpha|\beta|\gamma$ notation, specific to *Log P* and hierarchical models, will be presented in Sects. 6.9 and 6.10, respectively.

## 6.4   Limited Processor Number and No Duplication

In this section, we study scheduling in standard delay model with limited processor number and without duplicating the tasks.

### 6.4.1   Hard Cases

The results on computationally hard cases of scheduling with communication delays on limited number of processors and without task duplication are collected in Table 6.1. The following special notations are used in the this table:

- *bipartite* – A directed bipartite graph
- *binary-tree* – Arbitrary binary tree

**Table 6.1** Hard problems for $m < \infty$, no duplication

| Problem | Result | Reference |
|---|---|---|
| $P\|prec, p_j = 1, c = 1\|C_{max}$ | s**NP**h | [99] |
| $P\|prec, p_j = 1, c = 1\|C_{max} = 4$ | s**NP**h | [60,93] |
| $P\|tree, p_j = 1, c = 1\|C_{max}$ | s**NP**h | [78] |
| $P\|prec, p_j = 1, c \geq 2\|C_{max} = c + 3$ | s**NP**h | [10] |
| $P\|bipartite, p_j = 1, c \geq 2\|C_{max} = c + 3$ | s**NP**h | [10] |
| $P2\|binary\text{-}tree, p_j = 1, c > 1\|C_{max}$ | s**NP**h | [2] |

**Table 6.2** Polynomially solvable problems for $m < \infty$, no duplication

| Problem | Result | Reference |
|---|---|---|
| $P\|bw\text{-}prec, p_j = 1, c = 1\|C_{max}$ | $O(2^w n^{2w})$ | [116] |
| $Pm\|tree, p_j = 1, c = 1\|C_{max}$ | $O(n^{2m-2})$ | [114,115] |
| $P\|prec, p_j = 1, c = 1\|C_{max} = 3$ | $O(n)$ | [60,93] |
| $Pm\|io, p_j = 1, c = 1\|C_{max}$ | $O(mn + n^2)$ | [9,93] |
| $P2\|tree, p_j = 1, c = 1\|C_{max}$ | $O(n)$ | [47,78,93,115] |
| $P2\|sp1, p_j = 1, c = 1\|C_{max}$ | $O(n^2)$ | [40] |
| $Q2\|ck\text{-}tree, p_j = 1, c = 1\|C_{max}$ | $O(n)$ | [21,23] |
| $P\|prec, p_j = 1, c \geq 2\|C_{max} \leq c + 1$ | $O(n^{2c} \log p_{max} \log m)$ | [10] |
| $P\|prec, p_j = 1, c = 2\|C_{max} \leq 4$ | $O(n^2)$ | [10] |
| $P\|io, r_j, p_j = 1, c = 1\|T_{max}$ | $O(n^4 \log n)$ | [118] |
| $P\|io, p_j = 1, c = 1\|T_{max}$ | $O(n^2)$ | [120] |
| $P2\|out - forest, p_j = 1, c = 1\|T_{max}$ | $O(n^2)$ | [122] |
| $P2\|lup.in - forest, p_j = 1, c = 1\|T_{max}$ | $O(n \log n)$ | [122] |
| $P2\|chains, p_j = 1, c = 1\|T_{max}$ | $O(n \log n)$ | [122] |
| $P3\|out\text{-}tree, p_j = 1, c = 1\|C_{max}$ | $O(n)$ | [36] |
| $P2\|ck\text{-}tree, p_j = 1, c > 1\|C_{max}$ | $O(\log n)$ | [2] |

### 6.4.2  Polynomial Cases

The results on polynomially solvable cases of scheduling with communication delays on limited processor number without task duplication are collected in Table 6.2. The following notations are used in the this table:

- bw-prec – The task graph has width bounded by a constant $w$, where width of a task graph is the greatest number of pairwise independent tasks, a pair of tasks $T_i, T_j$ is independent if $(T_i, T_j) \notin \mathcal{A}$ and $(T_j, T_i) \notin \mathcal{A}$.
- io – The task graph is an interval order.
- sp1 – Series-parallel-1 graph (see definition in Sect. 2.1).
- ck-tree – Complete $k$-ary tree.
- $p_{max} = \max_{j=1}^{n}\{p_j\}$.
- $T_{max} = \max_{T_j \in \mathcal{T}}\{0, c_j - d_j\}$ – Maximum tardiness criterion, where $c_j, d_j$ are $T_j$ completion time and duedate, respectively.

- *lup.in-forest* – An in-forest with least urgent parent property which requires that each task has a parent which has a duedate exceeding the duedates of all other parents.

In the following paragraphs we outline selected algorithms from Table 6.2.

$P | bw\text{-}prec, p_j = 1, c = 1 | C_{\max}$ [116]

The algorithm in this case is based on the concept of order ideals. An order ideal $I$ is a set of tasks such that if $T_j \in I$ and $T_i \rightarrow T_j$, then $T_i \in I$. Informally, order ideal comprises some set of tasks with all their predecessors. The number of order ideals is $O(n^w)$, where $w$ is a constant task graph width. A partial schedule can be thought of as some ideal $I_1$ with the last time unit being a column of tasks $T_1$. Adding the next time unit of a schedule is equivalent to constructing a pair $(I_2, T_2)$ of order ideal $I_2$, and column of tasks executed in the last time unit. Note that the following conditions must be satisfied: (a) $I_1 \subseteq I_2, T_2 = I_2 - I_1$. (b) If $T_1 = \emptyset$, then (1) $1 \leq |T_2| \leq m$ and (2) tasks in $T_2$ are pairwise independent. (c) If $T_1 \neq \emptyset$, then either $I_1 = I_2$ (and hence $T_2 = \emptyset$), or the previous conditions (1), (2) are satisfies together with condition (3) for each task in $T_1$ there is at most one direct successor in $T_2$, and vice versa for each task in $T_2$ there is at most one direct predecessor in $T_1$. The above conditions are a set of rules which allow to append new tasks to a partial schedule represented by the pair $(I_1, T_1)$. Constructing a schedule is equivalent to traversing a path between states $(I_1, T_1)$ and $(I_2, T_2)$. Since $T_2 = I_2 - I_1$, the number of such states is at most $O(n^{2w})$. Given some state $(I_1, T_1)$ there are at most $O(2^w)$ transitions to the following states resulting from different ways of selecting $w$ tasks to set $T_2$. Each transition extends the schedule by one unit. The optimum schedule corresponds to the shortest path from $(\emptyset, \emptyset)$ to $(T, T_e)$, where $T_e$ is any subset of exit nodes in the task graph.

$Pm | tree, p_j = 1, c = 1 | C_{\max}$ [114, 115]

The algorithm for the current case builds on the results of [38], where it has been shown that problem $Pm | opposing - forest, p_j = 1 | C_{\max}$ can be solved in $O(n^{2m-2} \log n)$ time. The algorithm in [38] builds a schedule for a limited number of highest trees, and the remaining trees are merged in this schedule in $O(n)$ time. Similar idea can be applied in the current problem of scheduling forests with communication delays. Let us assume that $G$ is an out-forest.

In the first step the original task graph $G = (T, A)$ with communication delays is converted to a *shortest delay free graph* $G_s = (T, A_s)$. Consider some task $T_j$ with its immediate successors in $succ(j)$. In any feasible schedule only one of the immediate successors, say $T_i$, can be scheduled in the first time unit after $T_j$. The remaining tasks in $succ(j) - \{T_i\}$ must be scheduled in the second and latter time units after $T_j$. This situation can be represented as a new graph in which $T_j \rightarrow T_i$, $T_i \rightarrow T_l$ for all $T_l \in succ(j) - \{T_i\}$, and communication delays are removed.

Task $T_i$ is called a favorite child of $T_j$. In the new graph communication delays are substituted by ordinary precedence constraints. Hence it is called a *delay free* graph. It can be shown that for every optimum schedule there is a corresponding delay free graph.

The shortest delay free graph $\mathcal{G}_s$ of a given task graph $\mathcal{G}$ is a delay free graph such that height of every subgraph in $\mathcal{G}_s$ is smaller than or equal to the height of the subgraph containing the same nodes in any other delay free graph for $\mathcal{G}$. The shortest delay free graph $\mathcal{G}_s$ is constructed recursively starting from the roots. Suppose $T_j$ is the currently examined task, and for all tasks $T_l \in succ(j)$ let $\mathcal{G}_l$ be the out-tree rooted in $T_l$. Calculate heights $h'(T_l)$ of $\mathcal{G}_l$ for all $T_l \in succ(j)$. As the immediate successor of $T_j$ select any of the tasks $T_i$ such that $h'(T_i) = \max_{l \in succ(j)}\{h'(T_l)\}$. Add subtrees $\mathcal{G}_l$, for $l \in succ(j) - \{T_i\}$ as successors of $T_i$ (cf. Fig. 6.4). Note that there can be more than one candidate task $T_i$. Hence there may be more than one shortest delay free graph of $\mathcal{G}$.

Let $\mu(\mathcal{G})$ be the height of the $m$th highest tree in the task graph $\mathcal{G}$ plus one (note that here we count only processing times of the nodes on the longest path, communication delays are ignored). The high subgraph $\mathcal{H}_\mathcal{G}$ is the subgraph of $\mathcal{G}$ comprising all the out-trees strictly higher than $\mu(\mathcal{G})$. The trees with height equal or smaller than $\mu(\mathcal{G})$ are in low subgraph $\mathcal{L}_\mathcal{G}$.

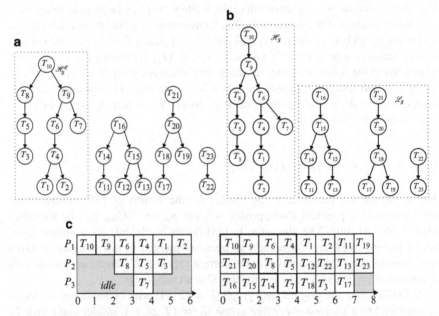

**Fig. 6.4** Example of applying the algorithm for $Pm|tree, p_j = 1, c = 1|C_{\max}$ [114, 115]. (**a**) The initial out-forest $\mathcal{G}$, subgraph $\mathcal{H}_s^e$ is marked with the dotted line. (**b**) The shortest delay free graph of $\mathcal{G}$. Low and high subgraphs are marked by dotted lines. (**c**) The optimum schedule for $\mathcal{H}_s^e$ and the final schedule for the whole task graph. The part remaining from the original schedule for $\mathcal{H}_s^e$ is marked with a bold line

The algorithm constructs the optimum schedule in four steps. First the shortest delay free graph $\mathcal{G}_s$, its high $\mathcal{H}_s$, and low subgraphs $\mathcal{L}_s$ are constructed. The subgraph $\mathcal{H}_s^e$ of the initial task graph $\mathcal{G}$ comprising the tasks from $\mathcal{H}_s$ is also determined. In the second step the optimum schedule is constructed for $\mathcal{H}_s^e$ by full enumeration. In the third step the tasks from $\mathcal{L}_s$ are merged with the optimum schedule of $\mathcal{H}_s^e$ such that assignment of time units is determined for each task. In the final step processors are allocated to the tasks. Now we will present the second and the following steps in more detail.

*Optimum Schedule for $\mathcal{H}_s^e$* Note that it has been shown only that there exists a delay free graph corresponding to an optimum schedule. The high subgraph of $\mathcal{G}_s$ is not necessarily the high subgraph of the delay free subgraph corresponding to the optimum schedule. Hence, to determine the optimum schedule for the tasks in the high subgraph of the original graph, an enumerative approach is used. From the definition of the high trees it follows that there can be at most $m - 1$ of them. A component here is a connected subtree in $\mathcal{G}$. An initial component is an entry task from one of the components. Construction of the optimum schedule for $\mathcal{H}_s^e$ requires computing the optimum schedule for each subgraph of $\mathcal{G}$ with no more than $m - 1$ initial components. There are $O(n^{m-1})$ such subgraphs of $\mathcal{G}$. The construction is done for subgraphs of $\mathcal{G}$ of size increasing from 1 task to all $n$ tasks. Suppose the optimum schedules have been already selected for all the subgraphs of sizes $i - 1, \ldots, 1$. The optimum schedules for all the subgraphs $\mathcal{G}'$ of $\mathcal{G}$ with at most $m - 1$ initial components and of size $i$ are constructed by selecting sets $R$ of tasks to be executed in the first time unit. It is required that $R$ is a subset of entry tasks in $\mathcal{G}'$, $|R| \leq m$, no two sibling tasks are in $R$, and the schedule for $\mathcal{G}' - R$ has minimum length. There are $O(n^{m-1})$ different sets $R$. The schedule for $\mathcal{G}' - R$ is already determined because $|\mathcal{G}' - R| < i$. Hence, the optimum schedule for every subgraph $\mathcal{G}$ with at most $m - 1$ initial components can be computed in time $O(n^{2m-2})$ (see [114, 115] for more details).

*Merging $\mathcal{L}_s$ with the Optimum Schedule for $\mathcal{H}_s^e$* Let $S$ be the optimum schedule for $\mathcal{H}_s^e$, and $S[k]$ be the set of tasks executed in the $k$th time unit of schedule $S$. The low trees from $\mathcal{L}_s$ are merged with schedule $S$ by analyzing consecutive time units of $S$. Let us assume that $k$ is the currently analyzed time unit. If $S[k]$ has free processors then ready tasks of $\mathcal{H}_s^e$ are shifted to the current time unit from time units after $k$ until filling up $S[k]$ completely or until exhausting ready tasks. The resulting set of tasks is $S'[k]$. If there are still available processors, then they are filled with $m - |S'[k]|$ highest ready tasks from $\mathcal{L}_s$. The tasks assigned in time unit $k$ are removed from $\mathcal{H}_s^e$ and from $\mathcal{L}_s$. If after this operation there is a tree $H_i \subseteq \mathcal{H}_s^e$ such that $h'(H_1) = h'(\mathcal{L}_s)$, then $H_1$ is moved to the set of low tasks, and is removed from schedule $S$. If after reaching the last time unit of $S$ there are still some low task unassigned, then they are scheduled in the following time units observing the precedence constraints. The schedule constructed in the above way has schedule length equal to the length of the optimum schedule for $\mathcal{H}_s^e$ (and hence it is optimal), or it has length $\lceil \frac{n}{m} \rceil$ (and it is also optimum). The merging procedure can be run in $O(n)$ time.

*Processor Assignment* The schedule constructed in the previous step determines only the assignment of the tasks to the time units. In the last stage the tasks are assigned to the processors. The tasks from the first time unit are assigned to the arbitrary processors. Let $k$ be the second, or one of the following time units. Tasks which have immediate predecessors from $\mathcal{G}$ in time unit $k - 1$ are assigned to the same processor as the parent task. The remaining tasks are assigned to the remaining processors in an arbitrary way. Processor assignment is determined in $O(n)$ time.

An example of applying the above algorithm is shown in Fig. 6.4.

$P \, | \, prec, p_j = 1, c = 1 | C_{max} = 3$ [60, 93]

Here we consider a decision version of a scheduling problem, by asking if a schedule of length at most three exists. The longest chain in the current case has at most three tasks which have to be executed on the same processor. Only the first task on a 3-task path may have successors which are not on the path. These are executed in the third slot. Only the last task on a 3-task path may have predecessors which are not on the path. These are executed in the first time slot. Tasks which have two or more successors are executed in the first time unit, tasks which have two or more predecessors are executed in the third time unit. What remains to be scheduled are single-level in-trees, single-level out-trees, isolated chains of length 2, and independent tasks (for the sake of simplicity we assume here that all trees have at least two leaves). The root of an out-tree is scheduled in the first time unit, one of the leaves is scheduled in unit 2 on the same processor as the root, the remaining leaves are executed in the unit 3. The root of an in-tree is executed in unit 3, one of its predecessors is in unit 2, the remaining leaves are in time unit 1. Next, the two-task chains and independent tasks are assigned greedily. If the number of processors is sufficient, then a feasible schedule exists.

$Pm \, | \, io, p_j = 1, c = 1 | C_{max}$ [9, 93]

Here the case of scheduling interval orders (cf. Sect. 2.1) of UET tasks with unit communication times is considered. We present the algorithm according to [9]. The algorithm examines ready tasks in the decreasing order of their out-degrees. Let $T_j$ be the currently examined task. The earliest starting time $est(j, i)$ of $T_j$ is calculated for each processor $P_i$. Task $T_j$ is assigned to the processor with the smallest $est(j, i)$. In case of a tie, a processor is selected for which the task executed at time unit $est(j, i) - 1$ has minimum out-degree. The complexity of this algorithm is $O(mn + n^2)$. Thus, it is polynomial algorithm only for fixed number of processors.

$P2|tree, p_j = 1, c = 1|C_{max}$ [47, 78, 93, 115]

Four algorithms for the current problem have been proposed independently in [47, 78, 93, 115]. The methods proposed in [78, 115] can be classified as list scheduling algorithms. The solutions proposed in [47, 93] can be considered clustering algorithms which treat whole subtrees as (non-UET) tasks. The algorithms presented here, after appropriate modifications, can be applied both to in- and to out-forests. Therefore, we can present the algorithms referring to one type of directed trees only.

**The Algorithm of Lenstra, Veldhorst and Veltman [78]** Let us assume that we have an in-forest. The algorithm proceeds in four steps.

First an estimate of the earliest starting time is calculated assuming that processor number is not limited. Thus, $est(j)$ is 0 if $T_j$ is a leaf, if there is exactly one task $T_i \in pred(j)$ such that $\forall T_l \in pred(j) - \{T_i\}, est(l) < est(i)$ then $est(j) = 1 + est(i)$, if there are at least two tasks $T_i, T_k \in pred(j)$ such that $\forall T_l \in pred(j), est(l) \leq est(i) = est(k)$ then $est(j) = 2 + est(i)$.

In the second step priorities $sdist$ of the tasks are calculated from the roots down to the leaves (i.e. opposing the direction of the arcs). The roots $T_j$ have $sdist(j) = 0$. Suppose task $T_j$ has been examined and obtained priority $sdist(j)$. The predecessor $T_i \in pred(j)$ with the maximum $est(i)$ obtains $sdist(i) = 1 + sdist(j)$. If more than one predecessor has maximum $est$, then this procedure is applied to only one of them. The remaining predecessors of $T_j$ receive labels equal to $sdist(j) + 2$.

In the third step a list $L$ of the tasks is constructed. The tasks are examined from the roots down to the leaves of the trees in a breadth-first fashion, and are inserted in front of $L$ (as on a stack). Yet, for the tasks $T_i \in pred(j)$ the predecessor $T_l$ for which $sdist(l) = 1 + sdist(j)$ is inserted before its siblings (thus it is further from the top of $L$).

Finally, in the fourth step tasks from $L$ are scheduled on the processors in the consecutive time units. However, it is disallowed to execute two siblings in the same time unit. In such a case one of the siblings is delayed to the next time unit.

**The Algorithm by Varvarigou, Roychowdhury, Kailath and Lawler [115]** The algorithm converts the initial task graph with communication delays to a shortest delay free graph in which communication delays are substituted by additional arcs. The construction of the shortest delay free graph was described earlier as an element of the method solving problem $Pm|tree, p_j = 1, c = 1|C_{max}$. The shortest delay free forest is scheduled by Hu's algorithm for problem $P|tree, p_j = 1|C_{max}$ (see Sect. 4.3.1.1). It has been shown that in the final schedule any task can be delayed at most $m - 2$ time units with respect to the optimum schedule. Hence, this algorithm builds optimum schedules for $P2|tree, p_j = 1, c_j = 1|C_{max}$. Example of applying this method as a heuristic for $m > 2$ is shown in Fig. 6.10.

**The Algorithm by Picouleau [93]** We present the method for in-trees. Let us denote by $N(j)$ the number of tasks in the subtree $ST(j)$ rooted in task $T_j$ including $T_j$ itself. Without loss of generality let us assume that the root is executed on $P_1$,

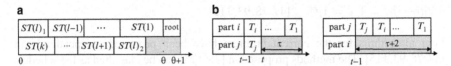

**Fig. 6.5** Structures of partial schedules for $P2|in\text{-}tree, p_j = 1, c = 1|C_{\max}$ in Picouleau algorithm. (**a**) A structure of the schedule for $N(1) \leq \theta$. (**b**) Adding idle time on $P_2$ when $N(1) > \theta$

and it has predecessors $T_1 \ldots, T_k$. We order them according to the nonincreasing subtree cardinalities: $N(1) \geq N(2) \geq \cdots \geq N(k)$. Let $\theta = 1 + \lfloor \frac{\sum_{i=1}^{k} N(i)}{2} \rfloor$.

If $N(1) \leq \theta$ then the subtrees $ST(1), \ldots, ST(k)$ can be scheduled as whole tasks similarly to McNaughton's rule (see Sect. 4.3.1.2). Let $l$ be the first subtree satisfying $\sum_{i=1}^{l} N(i) \geq \theta$. If this condition is satisfied with equality, then the subtrees $ST(1), \ldots, ST(l)$ are executed on $P_1$ in interval $[0, \theta]$, $ST(l + 1), \ldots, ST(k)$ are executed on $P_2$ in interval $[0, \theta - 1]$. If the condition is satisfied with inequality then the subtree of $T_l$ is split into $ST(l)_1$ and $ST(l)_2$. $ST(l)_1$ comprises $N(l) - (\theta - \sum_{i=1}^{l-1} N(i))$ tasks with the biggest distance to $T_l$. $ST(l)_2$ includes the remaining tasks from the subtree. Then, the schedule is constructed in the following way (cf. Fig. 6.5a): Tasks from $ST(l)_1$ followed by $ST(1), \ldots, ST(l - 1)$ are executed on $P_1$. The subtrees $ST(l + 1), \ldots, ST(k)$ followed by $ST(l)_2$ are executed on $P_2$. Processor $P_1$ is used in interval $[0, \theta]$ and $P_2$ in interval $[0, \theta - 1]$. In both cases root is scheduled on $P_1$ at time $\theta$.

Suppose now that $N(1) > \theta$. In this case algorithm has two elements. First an optimum schedule is built for the subtree $ST(1)$. Then, if needed, an idle time is created on one processor to schedule a sequence of the subtrees $ST(2), \ldots, ST(k)$. The optimum schedule for $ST(1)$ is obtained by applying the algorithm recursively on the subtree $ST(1)$, starting with $T_1$ as a root. Without loss of generality let us assume that $T_1$ is executed on $P_1$, and $\tau$ is the number of idle time units on $P_2$. If $\sum_{i=2}^{k} N(i) - \tau + 1 = \mu > 0$ then additional idle time is created by transforming the initial schedule of $ST(1)$. Note that one idle time unit is added on $P_2$ for a communication performed in parallel with $T_1$. Let $t$ be the last busy time unit on $P_2$, let $T_i$ be the task executed in $t$ on $P_1$, and $T_j$ on $P_2$. Two units of idle time are added on $P_2$ by shifting $T_j$ on $P_1$, and swapping between the processors the parts of the schedule in interval $[0, t - 1]$ (cf. Fig. 6.5b). After $\lfloor \frac{\mu}{2} \rfloor$ such transformations sufficient idle time is created on $P_2$ to execute $ST(2), \ldots, ST(k)$.

**The Algorithm by Guinand and Trystram [47]** Assume we have an in-tree. The algorithm starts with calculating cardinalities of subtrees $N(j)$ as in the previous algorithm. The level of $T_j$ is the distance to the root in arcs plus one. Without loss of generality let us assume that the root task is executed on processor $P_1$. Note that in a schedule without unnecessary idle time the number of tasks executed on processors $P_1$ and $P_2$ should differ by two. This results from the fact that no other task can be executed in parallel with the root which is the only exit task, and no task can be executed on $P_2$ in the penultimate time unit because its results cannot be delivered and consumed by the root before the end of the schedule. Thus, the number of tasks

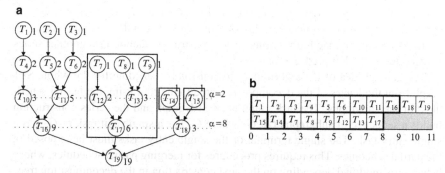

**Fig. 6.6** An example of using algorithm by Guinand and Trystram for $P2|in\text{-}tree, p_j = 1, c = 1|C_{\max}$. (**a**) The task graph. $N(j)$ are shown to the right of the tasks. Subtrees assigned to $P_2$ are shown in boxes. Initial values of $\alpha$ are shown on dotted lines corresponding to levels. (**b**) The schedule. Subtree clusters are shown in boxes

to be executed on $P_2$ should not be greater than $\alpha = \lfloor \frac{n-2}{2} \rfloor$. On the other hand this number may be hard to achieve for certain tree structures. For example, a chain is optimally scheduled on $P_1$ only. Thus the idea of the algorithm is to partition the tree such that one part comprises a number of tasks as close to $\lfloor \frac{n-2}{2} \rfloor$ as possible. Let $\alpha$ denote the number of tasks that still remain to be assigned to $P_2$. The algorithm starts in the root with $\alpha = \lfloor \frac{n-2}{2} \rfloor$ and proceeds through the levels toward the leaves. If there is only one task $T_j$ at the current level $\ell$ then the required ideal partition of the tree is not possible, $\alpha$ is reduced to $\min\{\alpha, \lfloor \frac{N(j)-2}{2} \rfloor\}$, and the algorithm steps to the level $\ell + 1$. If there are more tasks at the current level then they are examined in the order of nonincreasing cardinalities of their subtrees. While there is task $T_i$ with $N(i) \leq \alpha$ its subtree is assigned to $P_2$ and no longer considered by the algorithm, $\alpha$ is reduced by $N(i)$. When the tasks, and hence subtrees, with $N(j) \leq \alpha$ are exhausted at the current level, then the algorithm proceeds to the level $\ell + 1$. The algorithm stops when $\alpha = 0$. Thus an assignment of subtrees to $P_1, P_2$ is determined. The subtrees are executed on the processors in the order of the levels of their roots, the tasks within the subtrees are executed according to the topological order. This algorithm can be extended to problem $P2|tree, p_j \in \{1, \ldots, k\}, c = 1| C_{\max}$ to build a schedule at most $k - 1$ units of time longer than the optimum schedule. An example of applying this method is shown in Fig. 6.6.

## $P2|sp1, p_j = 1, c = 1|C_{\max}$ [40]

The class of series–parallel-1 (SP1) graphs has been defined in Sect. 2.1. Let us remind that an SP1 graph is a special case of the series–parallel graph which allows in series construction joining a predecessor subgraph $G_1$ and a successor subgraph $G_2$ if there is a single exit task in $G_1$ or a single entry task in $G_2$. A special SP1 graph decomposition procedure is proposed in [40] which constructs such decomposition trees that the preceding graph $G_1$ in the series construction is minimal. This means that there is no other series decomposition of $G_1, G_2$ into $G_1', G_2'$ such that $G_1'$ is a subgraph of $G_1$. A consequence of this assumption is that in the decomposition tree of the SP1 graph a node representing series constructor cannot have another series constructor as the left predecessor.

The general idea of the algorithm is to construct a schedule for the whole SP1 graph from the leaves of the decomposition tree to the root using the partial schedules for the subgraphs. The task graph is an SP1 graph and the series construction builds a sequence of subgraphs $G_1, G_2$ where $G_1$ has a single exit task or $G_2$ has a single entry task. The single terminal or the single entry tasks must be exposed in the partial schedules. This requires procedures for merging partial schedules, whose behavior is modified depending on the next construction in the decomposition tree.

We will call a left idle the first time unit of a partial schedule if it has only one busy processor. Analogously, a right idle is the last time unit of a schedule with only one busy processor. The left and the right idles are extremal idles, the other idles are internal idles. Let $SchedPar(S_1, S_2, O)$ denote the procedure scheduling the parallel construction of the SP1 graph, where $S_1, S_2$ are partial schedules for the subgraphs $G_1, G_2$, while $O$ corresponds the next operation in the SP1 graph decomposition tree. The values of $O$ can be one of: $par$ – the next operation is a parallel construction, $ser^-$ (respectively $ser^+$) – the next operation is a series construction and the schedule built by $SchedPar$ is the preceding (the succeeding) graph $G_1$ ($G_2$). Analogously, $SchedSer(S_1, S_2, O)$ schedules a series construction of the SP1 graph. Now let us assume the point of view of the schedule transformation about to be executed. Schedules $S_1, S_2$ must be *nice* for the current transformation. The features of nice schedules with respect to the current type $O$ of schedule transformation are a set of requirements:

1. At least one processor is busy in each time unit.
2. Two consecutive time units cannot have two different processors idle.
3. If $O = par$, then the resulting schedule is optimal with maximum number of extremal idles.
4. If $O = ser^-$ (respectively, $O = ser^+$) then $S_1$ (resp. $S_2$) is the shortest schedule with the right idle (resp. left idle).

The requirements of exposing the right or left idles may result in partial schedules which otherwise are not optimal.

Before discussing procedures $SchedPar, SchedSer$ let us introduce one more procedure used by both of them. Let $S$ be a schedule satisfying nice conditions 1, 2. for an SP1 task graph $G = (\mathcal{T}, \mathcal{A})$. If makespan $C_{max}$ of $S$ is smaller than $|\mathcal{T}|$, then $S$ can be stretched to a feasible schedule of length $C_{max} + l \leq |\mathcal{T}|$, satisfying nice conditions 1, 2. Schedule $S$ can be stretched left or stretched right. Let us consider the stretch-right for $l = 1$. Since $C_{max} < |\mathcal{T}|$ there is at least one time unit when both processors are busy. Let $\tau$ be the last time unit when both processors are busy (cf. Fig. 6.7a). If in time unit $\tau - 1$ a processor is idle then the stretch-right is depicted in Fig. 6.7b. Observe that tasks from time units $\tau, \ldots, C_{max}$ are shifted to the processor which is busy at $\tau - 1$. If both processors are busy in $\tau - 1$ then stretch-right is depicted in Fig. 6.7c and d. Here all moved tasks are shifted to the

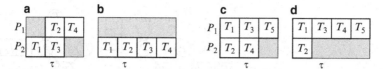

**Fig. 6.7** Two cases of stretching right a schedule in the algorithm for $P2|sp1, p_j = 1, c = 1|C_{max}$. (**a**), (**b**) Initial schedules. (**c**), (**d**) Stretched right schedules

first processor. When $l > 1$ then there must be at least $l$ time units when both processors are working. Let $\tau_1, \ldots, \tau_l$ be the last $l$ time units when both processors are busy. The above constructions for $l = 1$ repeated for each time unit $\tau_i$. Consequently, tasks initially scheduled between $\tau_i$, and $\tau_{i+1}$ are shifted $i$ time units to the right (it can be assumed that $\tau_{l+1} = C_{max}$). In the stretch-left procedure schedule $S$ is analogously extended to the left.

*Scheduling Parallel Construction – SchedPar($S_1, S_2, O$)* Procedure *SchedPar* has too many special cases to present them in extenso. Here we will only outline *SchedPar*. We refer the reader to [40] for the details. Let us denote by $C_{max}^1, C_{max}^2$ the length of schedules $S_1$, $S_2$, by $n_1, n_2$ the number of tasks in $S_1$, $S_2$, respectively, and let $C'_{max} = \lceil \frac{n_1+n_2}{2} \rceil$. Without loss of generality we assume that $n_1 \geq n_2$. Consequently, $C_{max}^2 \leq C'_{max}$. If the next construction $O$ in the task graph is *par* then procedure *SchedPar* builds a schedule of length $C_{max} = \max\{C_{max}^1, C'_{max}\}$. If $O = ser^-$ (resp. $O = ser^+$) then the new partial schedule length is $C_{max} = \max\{C_{max}^1 + \delta, \lceil \frac{n_1+n_2+1}{2} \rceil\}$, where $\delta = 1$ if $S_1$ has no right idle (resp. left idle), $\delta = 0$ otherwise.

Consider the case $O = par$. If $C_{max}^1 < C'_{max}$, then $S_1$ is stretched-left to length $C'_{max}$. The idle time units of $S_1$ are filled with the tasks of $S_2$. If $C'_{max} \geq C_{max}^1$ and $n_1 + n_2$ are even, then start filling from the first time unit in $S_1$. Otherwise ($C'_{max} < C_{max}^1$ or $n_1 + n_2$ is odd), start filling from the second time unit of $S_1$.

Consider the case $O = ser^-$. If $n_1 = n_2 = 1$, then $S_2$ is executed after $S_1$ on processor $P_1$. If $n_1 = n_2 > 1$, then $S_1, S_2$ are stretched to length $C'_{max}$, $S_1$ is executed on $P_1$ in interval $[0, C'_{max}]$ and $S_2$ on $P_2$ in interval $[1, C'_{max} + 1]$. If $n_1 \neq n_2$ then it is checked if $S_1$ has a right idle. If the answer is negative then $S_1$ is stretched right to $C_{max}^1 + 1$. The final schedule must have a left idle. A left idle comes from $S_1$ if $C'_{max} < C_{max}^1$. In the opposite case the left idle must be constructed. If $(n_1 + n_2)$ is even then $S_1$ is stretched left to $C'_{max} + 1$. If $(n_1 + n_2)$ is odd and $C'_{max} > C_{max}^1$ then $S_1$ is stretched left to $C'_{max}$. The current case of $n_1 \neq n_2$ is finished with filling backward the idles of $S_1$ with the tasks of $S_2$ starting from the penultimate time unit of $S_1$. The case of $O = ser^+$ has analogous scheduling method, i.e. all the transformations have opposite directions in time.

*Scheduling Series Construction – SchedSer($S_1, S_2, O$)* By the construction of the SP1 graph decomposition tree used in this algorithm a series construction has no left series predecessor. Hence $O \in \{par, ser^+\}$. Here schedules $S_1, S_2$ are concatenated such that the right idle of $S_1$ and the left idle of $S_2$ are on the same processor. This

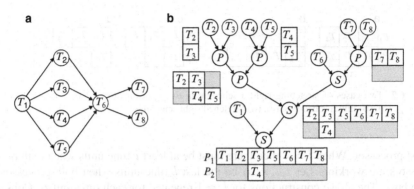

**Fig. 6.8** Example of building a schedule for $P2|sp1, p_j = 1, c = 1|C_{max}$. (a) SP1 task graph.
(b) Task graph decomposition tree with partial schedules built along the tree. $P$ represents parallel
and $S$ series construction

may require renumbering processors in $S_1$ or in $S_2$. If $O = ser^+$ and $S_1$ has no left
idle then the concatenated schedule is stretched left.

 *SchedSer* and *SchedPar* are integrated in recursive procedure *Schedule($R, O$)*.
Parameter $R$ is a node in the SP1 graph decomposition tree, and $O$ is the operation performed by the successor of $R$. If $R$ is a leaf, and hence only one task
must be scheduled, then a trivially optimum schedule for one task is returned.
Let $R$ be an internal node of the decomposition tree with predecessors $R.left$ and
$R.right$. $R$ is representing operation $O \in \{ser, par\}$. If $R$ is representing a parallel construction then *Schedule($R.right, par$)*, *Schedule($R.left, par$)* are called, and
the resulting schedules $S_1, S_2$ are merged in *SchedPar($S_1, S_2, O$)*, where $O$ is the
construction of the successor of $R$. If $R$ is representing a series construction then
*Schedule($R.left, ser^-$)*, *Schedule($R.right, ser^+$)* are called, and the resulting schedules, respectively $S_1, S_2$, are merged in *SchedSer($S_1, S_2, O$)*. *Schedule* is started
in the root of the decomposition tree with empty parameter $O$. The complexity of
the whole algorithm is $O(n^2)$. An example of applying the above algorithm for
$P2|sp1, p_j = 1, c = 1|C_{max}$ is shown in Fig. 6.8.

### $Q2|ck\text{-}tree, p_j = 1, c = 1|C_{max}$ [21, 23]

The problem of scheduling complete $k$-ary tree on two processors differing in speed
is considered. In publication [21] one processor was twice as fast as the second.
In [23] speeds of processors were 1 and $\frac{1}{a}$, where $a \geq 2$ was an integer. Here we
present the more general algorithm from [23].

 Let us denote by $P_f$ the faster and by $P_s$ the slower processor. Thus, tasks are
executed in $a$ time units on $P_s$, and in one time unit on $P_f$. Here we present the case
of an in-tree of height $h$. A size of a subtree is the number of task it comprises. It
can be shown that the root is executed on $P_f$. The remaining tasks, with accuracy of
rounding, are partitioned between $P_f$ and $P_s$ proportionally to their speeds. Thus,

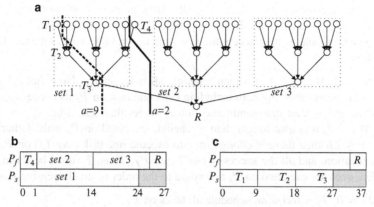

**Fig. 6.9** Example of applying the algorithm for $Q2|ck\text{-}tree, p_j = 1, c = 1|C_{max}$. (**a**) The 3-ary in-tree of height 4, with marked partitioning between $P_s$ and $P_f$ for $a = 2$ and $a = 9$, (**b**) a sketch of the schedule for $a = 2$, and (**c**) a sketch of the schedule for $a = 9$

$LB = \lfloor \frac{(n-1)a}{a+1} \rfloor + 2$ is a lower bound of the schedule length. Term $\lfloor \frac{(n-1)a}{a+1} \rfloor$ is the time of computing on $P_f$, the remaining two units follow from executing the root and either a communication from $P_s$ to $P_f$ or one more task on $P_f$ which results from rounding. The number of tasks executed on the faster processor (not counting the root) is at least $N_f = \lfloor \frac{(n-1)a}{a+1} \rfloor + 1$, the number of tasks run on $P_s$ is $N_s = n - 1 - N_f$. The general framework of constructing the schedule is to partition the task graph between the processors using complete subtrees such that there is one communication from $P_s$ to $P_f$ and several communications from the roots of subtrees executed on $P_f$ to their successors on $P_s$ (see Fig. 6.9). Four cases have been distinguished [23].

*Case $N_s \geq h - 1$* Select for $P_f$ tasks in full binary trees until reaching $N_f$ tasks. Schedule full $k$-ary tress on $P_s$ in the order of decreasing size. Schedule full $k$-ary tress on $P_f$ in the order of increasing sizes. There is only one communication from $P_s$ to $P_f$.

*Case $1 < N_s < h - 1$* Select a path of $N_s$ tasks starting in a leaf and assign it to $P_s$. For simplicity of presentation let us assume that this is the leftmost path in the in-tree. The remaining tasks are executed on $P_f$ in complete $k$-ary subtrees of increasing size. Note that the length of the path from a leaf starting on $P_s$ to the root on $P_f$ is at least $aN_s + 1 + (h - N_s)$. This path is executed feasibly only if $aN_s + 1 + (h - N_s) \leq LB$. In the opposite case the lower bound $LB$ may not be missed. A possible correction consists in moving the last task from $P_s$ and executing it on $P_f$ directly before its successor. This operation increases schedule length to $LB + 1$. Schedule length can be reduced to $LB$ by moving to $P_s$ one of the tasks initially assigned to $P_f$. Let $h_s$ be the height of the last (also the lowest) task executed on $P_s$. Note that due to the symmetry of the tree all tasks of the same level are equivalent. For simplicity of presentation we will consider for the migration from $P_f$ to $P_s$ the tasks on the rightmost path in the task graph. Attempt moving one of the tasks with heights $h_s - 1, \ldots, 2$ from the rightmost path to $P_s$. If this is feasible with respect to communication delays, then accept the first such move. Otherwise, schedule length is $LB + 1$.

*Case $N_s = 1$* If $a + h > LB$ then schedule all tasks on $P_f$. Note that condition $a + h > LB$ means that any path including even one task on $P_s$ its successors, predecessors, and at least one communication is longer than $LB$. Since $N_s = 1$ and $LB = N_f + 1$, it is also longer than a schedule executed on $P_f$ only. Otherwise, if $a + h \leq LB$ then there is enough time to execute one task (say $T_j$) on $P_s$, one communication, and all the successors of $T_j$ on $P_f$. Thus, $T_j$ must be a leaf. The complete trees are executed on $P_s$ according to the order of nondecreasing size.

*Case $N_s = 0$* $P_s$ is too slow, schedule all tasks on $P_f$.

Let us note that the length of the string encoding an instance of this problem is proportional to $\log a + \log k + \log h$. Thus, an algorithm considering tasks one after another has complexity $O(n) = O(k^h)$ which is not polynomial. It can be argued that the above algorithm constructs a pattern of the schedule in which the location of the equivalent tasks (with the same connectivity in the task graph) can be calculated in polynomial time. The same applies to problem $P \mid p_j = 1 \mid C_{\max}$.

$P \mid prec, p_j = 1, c \geq 2 \mid C_{\max} \leq c + 1$ [10]

Since executing any arc on two different processors requires time $c + 2 > c + 1$, dependent tasks must be executed on the same processor (without any communication). Let $\mathcal{T}_i$, for $i = 1 \ldots, k$, be the connected components of the task graph. If $|\mathcal{T}_i| > c + 1$ for any $i$ then a feasible schedule of length at most $c + 1$ cannot exist. In the opposite case an algorithm for problem $P \mid\mid C_{\max}$ with limited number of different task execution times given in [79] should be applied. The complexity of this algorithm is $O(n^{2(l-1)} \log m \log p_{\max})$, where $l \leq c + 1$ is the number of different task processing times and $p_{\max} = \max_{i=1}^{k} |\mathcal{T}_i|$.

$P3 \mid out\text{-}tree, p_j = 1, c = 1 \mid C_{\max}$ [36]

This algorithm builds on the results obtained in [114, 115] for problem $Pm \mid tree, p_j = 1, c = 1 \mid C_{\max}$ (presented at the beginning of this section). The algorithm of [114, 115] would build the optimum schedule in $O(n^4)$ time. It has been shown in [36] that a schedule for the shortest delay free graph can be improved to the optimum schedule in $O(n)$ time.

Let us remind that the shortest delay free graph is obtained by replacing communication delays with additional arcs. The additional arcs inserted in the task graph (here an out-forest) during selecting favorite children are called *false arcs*. The original arcs are called *true*. Let $path(j)$ represent the path from the root of the out-tree to task $T_j$. A path is true if all its arcs are true. Otherwise it is called false. The tasks of the shortest delay free graph can be scheduled, e.g., by Hu's algorithm [62] (Sect. 4.3.1.1). It has been shown in [49, 115] that for $m = 3$ the schedule built in this way is longer than the optimum schedule by no more than 1 unit of time.

Let $S_t$ be the set of tasks executed in time unit $t$. A critical slot in the above schedule is time unit $z$ in which the number of scheduled tasks is smaller than $m$, except the last unit of the schedule. Thus, $S_z \leq 2$. A crucial element of the algorithm is the observation that there is at most *one* false arc on the paths ending in the tasks executed in the critical slot. The algorithm proceeds according to the conditions satisfied by the tasks in the critical slot. The following conditions may arise in the critical slot, optimum schedule conditions are marked with symbol "OPT" [36]:

1. $|S_z| = 1$, OPT;
2. $|S_z| = 2$, let $S_z = \{T_a, T_b\}$
   a. both $T_a$, and $T_b$ have successors
      i. *path*(a) and *path*(b) are true, OPT;
      ii. *path*(a) is false *path*(b) are true;
   b. only $T_a$ has successors
      i. *path*(a) is true, OPT;
      ii. *path*(a) is false
         A. *path*(b) is true;
         B. *path*(b) is false, OPT.

If the algorithm encounters one of the "OPT" cases, then it stops. Otherwise (cases 2.a.ii or 2.b.ii.A) it is verified whether the last time unit of the schedule has more than one task or $T_a$ has only one successor in the shortest delay free graph. Also in theses cases schedule is optimum. If these conditions are not met in cases 2.a.ii or 2.b.ii.A, then a unique false arc $(x, y)$ on the *path*(a) is identified, and the previous favorite child of $T_x$ is substituted with $T_y$. A new delay free out-forest and a corresponding new schedule are built. If the new schedule is shorter, then it is optimum by the results from [49, 115] and the algorithm stops. Otherwise, the algorithm iteratively verifies the above optimality criteria on the tasks in the critical slot, builds an improved schedule, etc. The above iterative algorithm has complexity $O(n^2)$, but it has been shown in [36] that it can be further enhanced to run in $O(n)$ time.

## $P2|ck\text{-}tree, p_j = 1, c > 1|C_{\max}$ [2]

We will present the algorithm for the above complete $k$-ary tree scheduling with an example of a complete binary out-tree ($k = 2$) of height $h$, comprising $n = 2^h - 1$ tasks. It will be assumed that the root of the tree is executed on $P_1$. Let $G_l$ be a tree of height $l$, and $G'_l$ its sibling of the same height, for $l \leq h - 1$. We will denote by $T_{G_l}$, $T'_{G_l}$, the roots of $G_l$ and $G'_l$, respectively. A schedule on two processors with completion times on $P_1$ and $P_2$ differing by at most one unit of time is called balanced. Depending on the communication delay $c$ three cases can be distinguished.

If $c \geq 2^h - 1 - h$, then a sequential schedule on one processor is optimum because any schedule using two processors is longer as it includes a communication delay.

If $2^{h-2} \leq c < 2^h - 1 - h$, then in the optimum schedule at most one communication is performed on any path from the root task to the leaves. Suppose that $h_1$ is the height of the highest subtree $G_{h_1}$ executed on $P_2$. $G_{h_1}$ can be started on $P_2$ no earlier than by $h - h_1 + c$. Were only $G_{h_1}$ executed on $P_2$, then the computations on $P_2$ would be finished by $h - h_1 + c + 2^{h_1} - 1$ and on $P_1$ by $2^h - 2^{h_1}$. To build a balanced schedule computations on $P_2$ should finish no later than 1 unit of time after the completion time on $P_1$. Moreover, the size of $G_{h_1}$ must be as big as possible to distribute the work between the processors as equally as possible. This can be expressed as a requirement:

$$h_1 = \max_{l=1}^{h-1}\{l : 2^{l+1} - l \leq 2^h - h - c + 2\} \tag{6.2}$$

In this case schedule on $P_2$ starts with $h - h_1 + c$ units of idle time, and schedule length is at least $\lceil \frac{2^h - 1 + h - h_1 + c}{2} \rceil$. To make $P_2$ computing continuously beyond the initial idle time subtrees of total size $\lceil \frac{2^h - 1 + h - h_1 + c}{2} \rceil - (h - h_1 + c)$ are scheduled on $P_2$. In other words, number $\lceil \frac{2^h - 1 + h - h_1 + c}{2} \rceil - (h - h_1 + c)$ is decomposed into a sum of sizes of binary trees of heights $h > h_1 > \cdots > h_{k-1} \geq h_k \geq 1$, i.e. $\lceil \frac{2^h - 1 + h - h_1 + c}{2} \rceil - (h - h_1 + c) = 2^{h_1} - 1 + \cdots + 2^{h_{k-1}} - 1 + 2^{h_k} - 1$. The final schedule is constructed in the following way. $P_1$ executes path $T_{G_h}, \ldots, T_{G_{h_1}}, \ldots, T_{G_{h_{k+1}}}$. Trees $G'_{h_1}, \ldots, G'_{h_k}$ are scheduled on $P_2$. If $h_{k-1} = h_k$, then it means that also $G_{h_k}$ is scheduled on $P_2$. The remaining tasks are scheduled without delay on $P_1$ according to the topological order.

If $c \leq 2^{h-2}$, then it is possible to build an optimum schedule with at most two communications on any path from the root to a leaf. Assume that $T_{G_h}$ and $G_{h-1}$ are executed on $P_1$, while $G'_{h-1}$ is executed on $P_2$. The difference between the completion times on the processors is $c > 1$. Then convert such a schedule to a balanced one, $\lfloor \frac{c}{2} \rfloor$ tasks from $G'_{h-1}$ are shifted from $P_2$ to $P_1$. Similarly to the previous case $\lfloor \frac{c}{2} \rfloor$ is decomposed into subtrees of heights $h_1 > \cdots > h_{k-1} \geq h_k \geq 1$. Thus, $P_1$ executes $T_h$ and $G_{h-1}$, $P_2$ executes path $T_{h-1}, \ldots, T_{h_1}, \cdots > T_{h_{k+1}}$ as soon as possible. Then, $P_1$ executes $G'_{h_1}, \ldots, G'_{h_k}$ without undue delay. If $h_{k-1} = h_k$, then it means that also $G_{h_k}$ is on $P_1$. Finally, the remaining tasks of $G_{h-1}$ are scheduled on $P_2$.

Note that $O(\log n)$ symbols are necessary to encode the task data. Thus, this algorithm determines in polynomial time only a structure of the optimum schedule.

### 6.4.3  Heuristics with a Guarantee

The results on approximability of scheduling with communication delays are collected in Table 6.3. The following notations are used in the table:

**Table 6.3** Approximability for $m < \infty$, no duplication

| Problem | Result | Reference |
|---|---|---|
| $P\,\lvert prec, p_j = 1, c = 1\rvert C_{\max}$ | $C_{\max}^{LS} \leq (3 - \frac{2}{m})C_{\max}^* - 1 + \frac{1}{m}$ | [99] |
| $P\,\lvert prec, com\rvert C_{\max}$ | $C_{\max}^{ETF} \leq (2 - \frac{1}{m})C_1 + C_{com}$ | [63] |
| $P\,\lvert prec, p_j = 1, c = 1\rvert C_{\max}$ | $R \geq \frac{5}{4}$ | [60] |
| $P\,\lvert tree, p_j = 1, c = 1\rvert C_{\max}$ | $C_{\max}^{SDF} \leq C_{\max}^* + (m - 2)$ | [115] |
| $P\,\lvert tree, p_j = 1, c = 1\rvert C_{\max}$ | $C_{\max}^{SDF} \leq C_{\max}^* + \lceil \frac{m-2}{2} \rceil$ | [49] |
| $P\,\lvert prec, p_j = 1, c\rvert C_{\max}$ | $R \geq 1 + \frac{1}{c+3}$ | [10] |
| $P2\,\lvert prec, p_j = 1, c = 1\rvert C_{\max}$ | $R_{CG} = \frac{4}{3} + \frac{1(X_0 = \emptyset)}{3C_{\max}^{CG}}$ | [54] |
| $P\,\lvert prec, p_j = 1, c = 1\rvert C_{\max}, m \geq 3$ | $R_{CG} \geq 3 - \frac{6}{m+1}$ | [54] |
| $P\,\lvert out\text{-}tree, c_{ij}\rvert C_{\max}$ | $R_{MCA2} = 1 + \frac{1-1/m}{2-1/(1+\rho)}$ | [87] |
| $P\,\lvert out\text{-}forest, p_j = 1, c = 1\rvert T_{\max}, \forall j, d_j \leq 0$ | $T_{\max} \leq (2 - \frac{2}{m})T_{\max}^* + 1 - \frac{2}{m}$ | [122] |
| $P\,\lvert in\text{-}forest, p_j = 1, c = 1\rvert T_{\max}, \forall j, d_j \leq 0$ | $T_{\max} \leq 2T_{\max}^* + d_{\max}$ | [122] |
| $P2\,\lvert tree, p_j \in \{1, \ldots, k\}, c = 1\rvert C_{\max}$ | $C_{\max}^{CBoS} \leq C_{\max}^* + k - 1$ | [47] |
| $P\,\lvert prec, p_j = 1, c = 1\rvert C_{\max}$ | $R_{FS} = 1 + R_{m=\infty}(1 - \frac{1}{m})$ | [55] |
| $P\,\lvert prec, p_j = 1, c = 1\rvert C_{\max}$ | $R_{FS+MK} = \frac{7}{3} - \frac{4}{3m}$ | [55] |
| $P\,\lvert prec, sct\rvert C_{\max}$ | $R_{FSCT} = 1 + R_{m=\infty}(1 - \frac{1}{m})$ | [55] |
| $P\,\lvert prec, sct\rvert C_{\max}$ | $R_{FSCT+HM1} = \frac{4+3\rho}{2+\rho} - \frac{2+2\rho}{m(2+\rho)}$ | [55] |
| $P2\,\lvert tree, p_j = 1, \underline{c} \leq \neg c_{ij} \leq \bar{c}\rvert C_{\max}$ | $C_{\max}^{PO} \leq C_{\max}^* + \bar{c} - \underline{c}$ | [48] |
| $P\,\lvert prec, p_j = 1, c = 1\rvert \sum c_j$ | $R \geq \frac{6}{5}$ | [58] |

- $C_{\max}^{LS}$ – The worst-case schedule length of any list schedule heuristic
- $C_{\max}^*$ – The optimum schedule length
- $C_1$ – Length of the optimum schedule without communication delays, i.e. for an equivalent instance of problem $P\,\lvert prec\rvert C_{\max}$
- $R \geq k$ – Unless **P=NP**, worst-case performance ratio of any polynomial time algorithm is at least $k$
- $C_{com}$ – The length of the longest path of communications in the schedule built by algorithm ETF
- $C_{\max}^{SDF}$ – The length of an optimum schedule for a shortest delay free forest obtained from the original task graph (which is also a forest)
- $R_{CG}$ – The worst-case performance ratio of the Coffman–Graham (CG) schedule, i.e. a list schedule with task order built by the Coffman-Graham algorithm (see in Sect. 4.3.1.1).
- $1(X_0 = \emptyset)$ – A Function equal to 1 if set $X_0$ is empty in a CG schedule and equal to 0 otherwise; $X_0 = \emptyset$ if in each of the last two time units $C_{\max} - 2, C_{\max} - 1$ of a CG schedule single tasks are executed, and they are mutually independent
- $C_{\max}^{CG}$ – The length of the CG schedule
- $\rho = \frac{\max_{(i,j) \in A}\{c_{ij}\}}{\min_{T_j \in \mathcal{T}}\{p_j\}}$ – A different definition of the reciprocal of granularity
- $T_{\max} = \max_{T_j \in \mathcal{T}}\{0, c_j - d_j\}$ – Maximum tardiness criterion, where $c_j, d_j$ are $T_j$ completion time, and duedate, respectively
- $T_{\max}^*$ – Optimum value of maximum tardiness
- $d_{\max} = \max_{T_j \in \mathcal{T}}\{d_j\}$ – Maximum value of any duedate

- $\underline{c} \le \neg c_{ij} \le \bar{c}$ – Online case: communication times are unknown a priori, hence symbol $\neg c_{ij}$ is used, but they are in bounded range $[\underline{c}, \bar{c}]$
- $R_{m=\infty}$ – The worst-case performance ratio of any approximation algorithm for the same problem on unlimited number of processors
- $C_{\max}^{PO}$ – Length of the processor-ordered schedule, in processor-ordered schedules all messages are sent in the same direction, e.g. from $P_2$ to $P_1$ [48]

Selected heuristics mentioned in Table 6.3 are outlined below.

**Earliest Task First (ETF) [63]** The idea of ETF is to schedule tasks according to the order of their earliest possible starting time. In ETF a task is considered free if all its predecessors are already finished. The earliest starting time is calculated for each free task, taking into account different possible processor assignments and the resulting delays in communication from the predecessors on different processors. The algorithm is event driven. If the starting time $est(i)$ of task $T_i$ selected for execution in the current time moment $\tau_1$ is greater than $\tau_1$ (i.e. $est(i) > \tau_1$) then the decision on starting $T_i$ is postponed until the next time event $\tau_2$ when some processor becomes available. The complexity of the algorithm is $O(mn^2)$. Note that the performance guarantee of ETF mentioned in Table 6.3 is calculated with respect to the solution of the problem instance obtained by removing communication delays.

**Shortest Delay Free graph (SDF) [115]** The performance ratio of this algorithm applies to in- and out-forests. For conciseness of presentation let us refer to out-forests. The first performance guarantee given in [115] has been improved in [49]. The initial task graph with communication delays is converted to a shortest delay free out-forest. The construction of the shortest delay free out-graph is described in Sect. 6.4.2 as an element of the method solving problem $Pm|tree, p_j = 1, c = 1|$ $C_{\max}$. The shortest delay free out-forest is scheduled by Hu's algorithm for problem $P|tree, p_j = 1|C_{\max}$ (see Sect. 4.3.1.1). The complexity of this algorithm is $O(n)$. Examples of schedules on $m = 3$ and $m = 4$ for the task graph from Fig. 6.4a are shown if Fig. 6.10a and b, respectively.

**Munier Clustering Algorithm 2 (MCA2) [87]** This algorithm uses clusters constructed for problem $P\infty|out\text{-}tree, c_{ij}|C_{\max}$ by the algorithm called here MCA1 and introduced in Sect. 6.6.3 [87]. The clusters with a ready task at the head are scheduled as a whole according to the ETF rule.

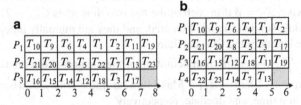

**Fig. 6.10** Example of a schedule by algorithm SDF for the task graph from Fig. 6.4a. (**a**) On $m = 3$ processors. (**b**) On $m = 4$ processors

**Clusters Based on Subtrees (CBoS) [47]**   This algorithm for $P2|tree, p_j \in \{1, \ldots,$ $k\}, c = 1|C_{\max}$ is an adaptation of the algorithm for $P2|tree, p_j = 1, c = 1|C_{\max}$ introduced in Sect. 6.4.2. In the current case the algorithm balances total work assigned to $P_2$. The weights of the subtrees are total processing times. The modifications consist in changing a stopping condition from $\alpha = 0$ to $\alpha = 0$ or $0 < \alpha = i \leq k - 1$ and no task with $p_j \leq i$ is available in the currently available subtrees. Another modification consists in the initialization of $\alpha$ equal to $\lfloor \frac{n-1-p_r}{2} \rfloor$, where $T_r$ is the root of the tree. Let us remind that $\alpha$ is the amount of work remaining to be assigned to $P_2$.

   CBoS can be applied online [48] when the actual communication delays are unknown, but are in bounded range $[\underline{c}, \bar{c}]$. This situation is denoted $\underline{c} \leq \neg c \leq \bar{c}$ in the scheduling problem notation. It has been shown in [48] that all optimum processor-oriented schedules built for problem $P2|tree, p_j = 1, c = 1|C_{\max}$ and then applied to problem $P2|tree, p_j = 1, \underline{c} \leq \neg c_{ij} \leq \bar{c}|C_{\max}$ are longer than the optimum schedule by at most $\bar{c} - \underline{c}$. In the processor-ordered schedules messages are sent *only* from one processor to the other, e.g., from $P_2$ to $P_1$. Algorithm CBoS builds optimum processor-oriented schedules for $P2|tree, p_j = 1, c = 1|C_{\max}$ which can be applied to problem $P2|tree, p_j = 1, \underline{c} \leq \neg c_{ij} \leq \bar{c}|C_{\max}$. In the online case a CBoS schedule preserves from the initial schedule task to processor assignment, sequencing on the processors. Beyond these two restrictions tasks are executed as early as possible.

**FS Algorithm (FS) [55]**   This algorithm uses a schedule with quality guarantee for unbounded processor number to build a schedule with performance guarantee on a system with limited processor number. The key information passed from the schedule on unlimited processor number is about favoring task successors.

   Suppose a schedule on $m = \infty$ is constructed. Let $\tau_i$ denote the time at which $T_i$ is started in this schedule. There can be at most one task $T_j \in succ(i)$ such that $\tau_j < \tau_i + p_i + c_{ij}$. Task $T_j$ is executed on the same processor as $T_i$ in the schedule for $m = \infty$ and is called a *favorite successor* of $T_i$. The binding of a task with its favorite successor is recorded and used in the next algorithm. The schedule for the limited number of processors is built time unit after time unit. Assume the schedule is constructed until time unit $\tau - 1$. In time unit $\tau$ processors are examined consecutively. If there is task $T_i$ executed in time unit $\tau - 1$ on processor $P_l$ with favorite successor $T_j$, then $T_j$ is scheduled at $\tau$ on $P_l$. Otherwise, start at $\tau$ on $P_l$ any schedulable task.

   When the above FS algorithm is combined with the Munier–König approximation algorithm [88] (Sect. 6.6.3) then an approximation algorithm with guarantee $\frac{7}{3} - \frac{4}{3m}$ is obtained (in Table 6.3 shown as algorithm *FS + MK*).

**FS for SCT Algorithm (FSCT) [55]**   This algorithm generalizes the above *FS* algorithm to the case of small communication times (*sct*).

   Suppose a schedule for $m = \infty$ has been constructed, and favorite successors $f(j)$ are determined for each task $T_j$ ($f(j) = \emptyset$ is possible). Let us assume that a partial schedule has been built for interval $[0, \tau)$. We will denote by $\tau_i$ the start time of $T_i$ in the partial schedule, and by $\mathcal{R}$ the set of unscheduled tasks which all predecessors have been scheduled. For any task $T_j \in \mathcal{R}$ the earliest starting time on processors $P_k$ is defined as

$$est(j,k) = \max \left\{ 0, \max_{\{T_i \in pred(j), proc(i) \neq k\}} \tau_i + p_i + c_{ij}, \max_{\{T_i \in pred(j), proc(i) = k\}} \tau_i + p_i \right\}$$

(6.3)

The earliest time at which $T_j$ can be started on any processor is called $T_j$ urgent time $u(j)$. If $pred(j) = \emptyset$ then $u(j) = 0$, otherwise $u(j) = \max_{\{T_i \in pred(j)\}} \{\tau_i + p_i + c_{ij}\}$. Consider a certain processor $P_k$ and the last task $T_i$ scheduled on $P_k$ before $\tau$. Processors are divided into three classes:

1. $P_k$ is busy if $\tau_i + p_i > \tau$.
2. $P_k$ is *awake* if $\tau_i + p_i \leq \tau$ and there is $f(i) \in \mathcal{R}$ such that $est(f(i), k) < u(f(i))$.
3. In all other cases $P_k$ is free.

First, each processor free at $\tau$ is assigned any schedulable task. Next, each awake processor $P_k$ is assigned either a task $T_j$ which is urgent at $\tau$, i.e. satisfying $u(j) < \tau$, or the favorite successor $f(i)$ of the last task $T_i$ on $P_k$, if $est(f(i), k) \leq \tau$. After the assignment of the tasks to processors, set $\mathcal{R}$ is appropriately reduced, and the algorithm proceeds to the next time event at

$$\min \left\{ \min_{i=1}^{m} \{ft(i)\}, \min_{\{T_j \in \mathcal{R}, i=1,\dots,m\}} \{est(j,i) > \tau\}, \min_{\{T_j \in \mathcal{R}\}} \{u(j) > \tau\}, \right\}$$

(6.4)

where $ft(i)$ is the completion time of the computations on $P_i$ at the current stage of schedule construction. Note that awake processors may be left idle if no urgent or favorite task is available.

The above FSCT algorithm combined with the Hanen and Munier approximation algorithm for $P\infty|prec, sct|C_{max}$ [52] gives an approximation algorithm with guarantee $\frac{4+3\rho}{2+\rho} - \frac{2+2\rho}{m(2+\rho)}$ (represented as algorithm $FSCT + HM1$ in Table 6.3). The algorithm in [52] generalizes Munier–König approximation algorithm [88] (Sect. 6.6.3) to the *sct* case.

### 6.4.4  *Heuristics Without a Guarantee*

In this section, we present heuristics which have no worst-case performance guarantee, but have been reported to perform satisfactorily in a series of tests. Exemplary heuristics are described below.

**Sarkar and Hennessy Heuristic (SH) [103]**  The algorithm first clusters the tasks, then assigns the clusters to the processors. In the clustering phase each task starts in a unit cluster (i.e. one task per cluster). For each pair of clusters $(i, j)$ a reduction $\Delta_{CP}(i, j)$ in the critical path length is calculated if clusters $i, j$ were merged.

The algorithm greedily merges the pair of clusters offering the greatest reduction $\Delta_{CP}(i, j)$. This procedure is repeated until no further reduction in the critical path length is possible. The independent tasks within a cluster are ordered by any topological order. This has an important consequence that initially independent tasks are treated as executed sequentially in the calculation of the critical path. In the cluster assignment phase tasks are considered in the topological order again. Assigning task $T_j$ to some processor $P_i$ entails allocating to $P_i$ all the tasks from the cluster comprising $T_j$. For the examined task $T_j$ a processor is selected which results in the shortest partial schedule length.

There is also a slight modification [102] of the above method. Initially all the tasks are in unit clusters. Arcs in $\mathcal{A}$ are analyzed in the order of nonincreasing weights $c_{ij}$. Arc $(i, j)$ is zeroed if it is not increasing the length $cp$ of the critical path. Within a cluster tasks are ordered according to their latest starting times. During the cluster to processor assignment, minimization of the earliest starting time $est(j)$ for the currently examined task $T_j$ is used as a secondary criterion if two different processor assignments result in equal schedule length. The latter version from [102] is sometimes called a Sarkar's heuristic, edge zeroing, or internalization heuristic.

**Modified Critical Path (MCP) [124]**  In MCP latest starting times of the tasks are calculated first, including communication delays as if all tasks were executed on different processors. Then, similarly to Coffman–Graham algorithm, for each task a list of its successors latest starting times ordered decreasingly is constructed. The tasks are ordered according to the decreasing lexicographic order of their lists. Tasks are scheduled according to this sequence. A free processor that allows for starting a task at the earliest time is selected. The same idea was proposed in algorithm GD/HLF [7].

**Dynamic Level Scheduling (DLS) [108]**  For each ready task DLS calculates a dynamic level of executing $T_j$ on $P_i$ as

$$dl(j, i) = h'(j) - \max\{dat(j, i), ft(i)\},$$

where $h'(j)$ is a static level of $T_j$, i.e. the level calculated without communication delays, $dat(j, i)$ is the earliest time at which $T_j$ has received data from all its predecessors to be started on $P_i$, $ft(i)$ is the time by which $P_i$ finishes the last task assigned to it and becomes free. At each stage of building a schedule DLS calculates dynamic levels for all ready tasks on all processors. It is assumed in DLS that a network dependent heuristic exists which determines message routing, and calculates resulting communication delays for the current partial schedules. Task $T_j$ with the highest dynamic level $dl(j, i)$ is scheduled on processor $P_i$ offering this highest level.

Several variants of DLS have been proposed in [108]. DLS has been also extended to scheduling with communication delays on unrelated processors. In this case the algorithm works according to similar concept: An additive priority function of task $T_j$ is calculated which integrates $h'(j)$ and the preference in selecting some processor. The processor preference takes into account processing time of $T_j$ on $P_i$, the cost resulting from executing $T_j$ on $P_i$ and $T_k \in succ(j)$ receiving the greatest amount of data from $T_j$ on a processor different than $P_i$, the cost of not executing $T_j$ on $P_i$ in case processor $P_i$ were assigned to some other task [108]. In [104] it has been proposed to calculate priority according to the formula

$$dl(j,i) = h'(j) - ect(j,i)$$

where $ect(j,i)$ is the earliest completion time of $T_j$ on $P_i$ taking into account idle intervals of sufficient length after $dat(j,i)$. It is also required that the network dependent subsystem takes into account all free intervals in the communication channel schedules connecting the processors running predecessors of $T_j$ and $P_i$.

**Declustering [109]** It has been observed that clustering algorithms are too much oriented toward minimizing communication costs. This may result in construction of clusters which have little communication but long processing times. Thus constructed clusters may cause unavoidable imbalance of the processor load. Declustering was designed with the goal of constructing more balanced schedules on the given processor number. Let us note that task levels are calculated here without communication delays. Therefore, we will refer to them as to static levels. The longest paths are constructed with respect to the static levels too. This algorithm consists of several steps which we describe in the sequel.

*Elementary Cluster Formation*  The first step constructs clusters by determining sets of arcs which represent likely communications separating different clusters. Such arcs will be called *cut arcs*. The tasks which have out-degree greater than one (also called branch nodes, or fork nodes of the graph) are analyzed in the increasing order of their static levels. Consider certain fork node $T_j$. Its immediate successors are ordered according to nonincreasing levels. The two first successors of $T_j$, say $T_a, T_b$, are considered first. An intersection of the sets of all $T_a$'s and $T_b$'s successors is calculated. Two cases are distinguished on the basis of the intersection contents. If the intersection is empty, then the paths stemming from $T_a$, $T_b$ never intersect. The longest paths starting in $T_a$ and in $T_b$ are constructed. Thus, we have a tree (cf. Fig. 6.11a) of $T_j, T_a, T_b$ and the two paths. Then, the algorithm analyzes length of schedules on two processors obtained by removing one arc in the tree. If all such schedules are longer than a schedule on a single processor then the task with higher static level ($T_a$ or $T_b$) is removed from the list of $T_j$ successors. Otherwise, the

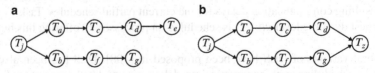

**Fig. 6.11** Declustering algorithm. Two cases of fork task successors in elementary cluster formation. (**a**) Empty intersection. (**b**) Nonempty intersection

arc resulting in the shortest schedule for the tree is recorded as a cut arc. One of tasks $T_a$, $T_b$ which is closer to the selected cut arc is removed from the list of $T_j$ successors. On the other had, if the intersection of the sets of all $T_a$, $T_b$ successors is not empty, then a common successor with the highest level, say $T_z$, is singled out (see Fig. 6.11b). Two paths are constructed: the longest path starting in $T_j$, visiting $T_a$ and ending in $T_z$ and a parallel longest path visiting $T_b$. The algorithm tries all pairs of arcs in an attempt of partitioning the tasks of the two paths into two subsets executed on two processors. If all the pairs result in a schedule longer than on a single processor then the higher static level task ($T_a$ or $T_b$) is removed from the list of $T_j$ successors. Otherwise, the pair of arcs resulting in the shortest two-processor schedule is recorded as cut arcs. The successor of $T_j$ which is closer to one of the selected cut arcs is removed from the list of $T_j$ successors. Next, the algorithm proceeds with the analysis of the next two successors of $T_j$. After considering all the fork tasks, the direction of the arcs is inverted and the same procedure is repeated. The current fork nodes correspond to the tasks with in-degree greater than one in the original task graph (a.k.a. join, or merge nodes). The search for cut arcs is repeated on the inverted graph. Having analyzed the task graph in both directions, all the cut arcs are temporarily removed from the graph. The remaining connected components constitute the elementary clusters.

*Hierarchical Cluster Grouping* In this step a hierarchy of clusters is established in preparation to the next step where clusters are assigned to the processors. The hierarchy is built with a goal of determining groups of clusters with little inter-group communication and with comparable processing times. The elementary clusters from the previous step are considered in the order of increasing total processing times of the comprised tasks. For a cluster $C_1$ with the minimum processing time, a cluster $C_2$ is found which has the biggest total communication time with $C_1$. Ties are broken in favor of shortest candidates. The two clusters are merged into cluster $C_3$. Clusters $C_1$, $C_2$ are removed, and $C_3$ is inserted into the ordered cluster list. Merging is repeated until only one cluster remains. The current step constructs cluster hierarchy only, represented as a sequence of merge operations. It can be viewed as a binary tree with the elementary clusters in the leaves and the internal nodes as merging operations. Cluster merging does not imply scheduling here.

*Cluster Hierarchy Decomposition* The cluster hierarchy from the previous step is decomposed in assigning clusters to processors. Initially all the clusters are executed on a single processor. The list of merge operations is analyzed in the reversed order (from the last merge to the first). The current cluster composed of some clusters $C_a$, $C_b$ is split again. Let $C_a$ be the shorter of the two clusters. Cluster $C_a$ is temporarily moved to a different processor. The set of candidate processors for $C_a$ may include all $m$ processors, or it can be a processor subset selected by an algorithm which recourses to the knowledge on the target computer system and its communication network. The tasks from different elementary clusters assigned to the same processor are executed in the order of nonincreasing static levels. All possible processor assignments for $C_a$ are verified. If moving $C_a$ reduces schedule length then the shortest schedule is accepted. Then the algorithm proceeds to the decomposition of the next cluster in the hierarchy. When all the clusters are considered, two more heuristics are invoked. The first one tries to move to other processors three clusters which most intensively communicate with other processors than with the tasks on the currently assigned processor. The second heuristic attempts shifting clusters from processors which are heavy loaded to the processors which are not. The processor load is calculated as the sum of the total assigned task processing times and sum of all communication times. A processor is heavy loaded if its load exceeds half of the maximum load of any processor. Only these schedule transformations are accepted which reduce schedule length.

*Cluster Breakdown* In this final step an attempt is made of reducing schedule length by breaking the elementary clusters. A *schedule limiting progression* (SLP) is determined which determines schedule length. The SLP is a sequence of tasks and communications which proceed one after another without idle time and in total has the makespan length. In a set of tasks which are in SLP on the same processor, a subset of tasks is identified which is a path in the task graph. The subpaths starting from the last task are considered for a move to a different processor. For example, if a path $T_a \rightarrow \cdots \rightarrow T_x \rightarrow T_y \rightarrow T_z$ exists in SLP on some processor, then paths $(T_z)$, $(T_y \rightarrow T_z)$, $(T_x \rightarrow T_y \rightarrow T_z)$, ... are considered for a shift to a different processor. The target processor can be selected in the same way as in the hierarchy decomposition step.

The total complexity of the declustering algorithm is $O(n^4 + n^3 m)$. In Fig. 6.12 we give an example of applying the declustering method. The input task graph is shown in Fig. 6.12a. The algorithm starts with the analysis of fork task $T_1$. Its successors have nonempty intersection of the sets of successors. Hence pairs of arcs separating two parallel paths $(T_1, T_2, T_6, T_8)$ and $(T_1, T_3, T_7, T_8)$ are searched for.

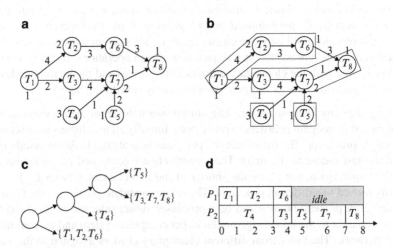

**Fig. 6.12** Example of applying declustering algorithm. (**a**) Input task graph. Task processing times are shown by the task nodes. Communication delays are marked on the arcs. (**b**) Elementary clusters. (**c**) A tree representing hierarchy of clusters. (**d**) A final schedule on $m = 2$ processors

The pair $(T_1, T_3)$, $(T_6, T_8)$ may be selected as the schedule on two processors would have length 8. Then the direction of the arcs is inverted and the algorithm analyzes now the successors for task $T_7$. For a pair of successors $T_3, T_4$ it is profitable to make arc $(T_7, T_4)$ a cut arc because it results in a schedule of length 6 for tasks $T_1, T_3, T_4, T_7$. Then successors $T_3, T_5$ of $T_7$ are analyzed, and adding a cut arc $(T_7, T_5)$ results in a schedule of length 5. The elementary clusters are presented in Fig. 6.12b. The hierarchy of clusters is shown as a tree in Fig. 6.12c. The schedule on $m = 2$ processors is given in Fig. 6.12d. The SLP consists of all the tasks on $P_2$, and another SLP consists of the tasks on $P_1$, communication $T_6 \rightarrow T_8$. Beyond the fact that only $m = 2$ processors are available here, breaking the clusters on $P_2$ does not reduce schedule length.

**Preferred Path Selection (PPS) [85]** In this heuristic tasks are analyzed in the order of increasing static level $h'(j)$. A schedule is built from the terminus of the task graph backward to the entry nodes. First an assignment of the tasks to the processors is constructed. The algorithm proceeds through the processors in a round-robin fashion. For a considered processor $P_i$ an unassigned task with the lowest level is selected satisfying one of the following conditions in the order of preference: (1) has at least one successor on $P_i$, (2) has no successors, and (3) any task at the current level. Let $T_j$ be the selected task. Then, path $(T_a \rightarrow \cdots \rightarrow T_j)$ is also assigned to $P_i$. The selected path can be any path starting in a task without predecessors (here denoted $T_a$), and ending in $T_j$. In constructing the path backward from $T_j$ preference is given to the tasks which already have some successors, other than $T_j$, on $P_i$. Next, the algorithm switches to processor $P_{(i \bmod m)+1}$. The tasks are executed on the assigned processors in a topological order of the task graph obeying communication delays. The complexity of the algorithm is $O(|\mathcal{A}| + n)$.

**Generalized List Scheduling (GLS) [7]** GLS heuristics are modification of the classic list scheduling. Tasks are examined in the order from a given list, and assigned to the processor which guarantees the earliest starting time. Two kinds of GLS heuristics were distinguished depending on the way of calculating the set of tasks ready to run: (a) processor-driven (PD) – the set of tasks ready to run is recalculated on completion of some task and (b) graph-driven (GD) – the set of tasks ready to run is reevaluated when some task is dispatched to a processor and started. The levels of the tasks are calculated by inverting direction of all the arcs in $\mathcal{A}$ and scheduling the tasks in the order in which that become ready. The task completion times in such an inverted schedule are levels for scheduling the original task graph. Let $\vartheta(j)$ denote the level of $T_j$ calculated in the above way. Three GD heuristics with complexity $O(mn^2)$ were proposed within the GLS/GD paradigm.

GD/HLF  – Ready tasks are ordered according to nonincreasing levels $\vartheta(j)$.
GD/HLFET  – Ready tasks are ordered according to nonincreasing values of $\vartheta(j) - est(j, i^*)$, where $P_{i*}$ is a processor on which $T_j$ can be started earliest.
GD/HLFET* – The previous algorithm with an attempt of filling idle time (if any) before the currently dispatched task $T_j$, by inserting in the existing idle intervals an arbitrary ready task with lower priority.

**Chaining [37]** In this algorithm sequences of tasks assigned to a processor are represented as chains of special arcs in the task graph, called $\rho$-arcs. All the tasks are preceded by a dummy task $T_0$, and are succeeded by a dummy task $T_{n+1}$. The algorithm starts with $m$ $\rho$-arcs connecting $T_0$ with $T_{n+1}$ to represent empty task sequences on the processors. For the tasks which have not been examined yet, the earliest starting times and levels are calculated as if the tasks were executed on different processors. Tasks are examined one by one and inserted into the sequences on the processors. For example, if task $T_j$ is inserted between $(T_i, T_k)$ on some processor, then this operation is represented as replacing $\rho$-arc $(T_i, T_k)$ with pairs $(T_i, T_j), (T_j, T_k)$ of $\rho$-arcs, and zeroing communication delays $c_{ij}, c_{jk}$. The selected task, say $T_j$, can be feasibly inserted only into such an arc $(T_i, T_k)$ that neither is $T_i$ a successor of $T_j$, nor is $T_k$ a predecessor of $T_j$. Tasks are examined in the order of nondecreasing relative mobility $rm(j) = \frac{lst(j)-est(j)}{p_j}$. If two tasks have equal relative mobility, then a secondary criterion is maximum value of $\max_{i \in pred(j)}\{c_{ij}\} + p_j + \max_{i \in succ(j)}\{c_{ji}\}$. The concept of relative mobility has been introduced with algorithm MD in [124] (cf. Sect. 6.6.4). For $T_j$ insertion an arc is selected for which $est(j) + p_j + h(j)$ is minimum, and as a secondary criterion maximum value of $cp - (est(i) + p_i + p_k + h(k))$ is used, where $(T_i, T_k)$ is a candidate $\rho$-arc for inserting the examined task. The complexity of the algorithm is $O(n^2 + n|\mathcal{A}|)$.

**Decisive Path Scheduling (DPS) [92]** DPS is a list scheduling heuristic. For simplicity of presentation let us assume that there is only one entry task and only one exit task. This can be achieved by adding dummy entry, and exit nodes with zero processing times, and zero communication costs of the arcs connecting them with the original task graph.

DPS calculates task earliest starting times assuming that they are executed on different processors. The path determining $est(j)$ is called the decisive path of $T_j$. Then, a critical path $CP$ is determined using the earliest starting times. The list of tasks is constructed in the following way. Tasks $T_i \in CP$ are analyzed in the order of increasing $est(i)$. If $T_i$ has predecessors which are not on the list already, then the task graph is recursively searched backward, i.e. from $T_i$ toward the entry nodes, and the predecessors of $T_i$ are inserted in the task list in the topological order. Finally, $T_i$ is inserted after all its predecessors.

Tasks are examined in the order from the above list and are assigned to the processor offering the earliest starting time.

**Radulescu and van Gemund Fast List Scheduling (RGFLS) [96]** This is a generic technique applicable in certain class of list scheduling algorithms proposed to reduce complexity without sacrificing too much performance.

Many list scheduling algorithms can be classified as list scheduling with static priorities (LSSP) or with dynamic priorities (LSDP). In LSSP a priority of a task is calculated first, and then tasks are examined in the order of this priority and assigned to the processor providing the earliest starting time. Examples include HLFET [1] (cf. Sect. 4.3.1.1), MCP [124], GD/HLF [7], and DPS [92] (in this section). In each iteration of LSDP the most suitable pair of a ready task and its processor is determined and scheduled. Examples of LSDP include ETF [63] (Sect. 6.4.3), DLS [108], and GD/HLFET [7] (this section).

If LSSP is realized in a standard way, then its complexity is $O(n \log n + m(n + |\mathcal{A}|))$, where calculating task priorities take $O(n + |\mathcal{A}|)$, sorting tasks and maintaining their order take time $O(n \log n)$, selection of the processor $P_i$ with the minimum $est(j, i)$ for the examined tasks $T_j$ takes total time $O(m(n + |\mathcal{A}|))$. It is proved in [96] that to determine $est(j, i)$ it is sufficient to verify just two processors as $P_i$: processor $P_r$ becoming idle the earliest and the enabling processor $P_e$ executing a predecessor $T_l$ of $T_j$ from which the message would arrive as the last one if $T_j, T_l$ were on different processors. Next, it is argued that for satisfactory performance it is not necessary to maintain a priority queue $Q$ of all ready tasks. It is sufficient to use a priority queue only for a limited number $H$ of tasks. When a task becomes ready and $Q$ has fewer than $H$ members, then the newly ready task is enqueued in $Q$. Otherwise it waits in a FIFO queue. When a task is dequeued from $Q$, then a ready task (if any) is moved from the FIFO queue to $Q$. In a set of computational experiments it has been established that $H = m$ is sufficient. Thus, the complexity of the LSSP heuristic reduces to $O(n \log m + |\mathcal{A}|)$. An MCP heuristic modified in the above way, called Fast Critical Path (FCP), has been proposed and examined in [96].

The above ideas have been extended to LSDP heuristics. It has been determined that for a class of LSDP heuristic the priority of a ready task $T_j$ if executed on $P_i$ is equal to $prio(j, i) = \alpha(j) + \max\{dat(j, i), ft(i)\}$, where $\alpha(j)$ is independent of the scheduling process (e.g. $\alpha(j)$ is calculated using static level or earliest starting time assuming that tasks are assigned to dedicated processors), $dat(j, i)$ is the arrival time of the latest message for task $T_j$ on processor $P_i, ft(i)$ is the time when $P_i$ becomes ready. The pair $(T_j, P_i)$ with the lowest value of $prio(j, i)$ has the highest priority and is selected for scheduling. Let $dat(j)$ denote the arrival time of the last message to $T_j$ if it is executed on a different processor than $P_e$. Note that $dat(j, e) \leq dat(j)$. The above formula for $prio(j, i)$ can be split into

$$prio(j, i) = \begin{cases} \alpha(j) + \max\{dat(j, e), ft(e)\} & \text{for } P_i = P_e \\ \alpha(j) + \max\{dat(j), ft(i)\} & \text{for } P_i \neq P_e \end{cases} \qquad (6.5)$$

For the second case of the above equation an observation that priority is minimized by the processor $P_r$ which first becomes idle is used. Therefore, the second case of Eq. (6.5) can be substituted with and further split into

$$\alpha(j) + \max\{dat(j), ft(r)\} = \begin{cases} \alpha(j) + dat(j) & \text{for } dat(j) \geq ft(r) \\ \alpha(j) + ft(r) & \text{for } dat(j) < ft(r) \end{cases} \qquad (6.6)$$

This gives rise to selecting the pair of a task $T_j$ and processor $P_i$ with the smallest value of $prio(j, i)$ in just three tries which correspond with the first case of Eq. (6.5) and both cases of (6.6). For the enabling processor a priority queue of tasks is maintained. Moreover, processors are ordered according to the priority of the tasks they enable. Thus, if the first case is used in Eq. (6.5) to select the task–processor pair then this can be done in constant time by referring to this set of $m + 1$

queues. The selection in the second case of (6.5) is relaxed because all processors are considered independently whether they are enabling some tasks or not. Two task priority queues are maintained: one ordered according to nondecreasing value of $\alpha(j) + dat(j)$ and one similarly ordered for $\alpha(j) + ft(r)$ as in the two cases of Eq. (6.6). These two queues correspond to the best selection of task–processor pair realizing the second case of Eq. (6.5). Consequently, the best task–processor pair is found in three tries. A ready task is inserted to three priority queues: one corresponding to its enabling processor (the first case of (6.5)) and to two queues corresponding with the processor becoming ready first (the two cases of (6.6)). This reduces complexity of LSDP algorithms from $O(n(n + |\mathcal{A}|)m)$ to $O(n \log m + |\mathcal{A}|)$ if the priority queues have length limited to $m$ as described in the previous paragraph. A DLS heuristic modified in the above way, called Fast DLS (FDLS), has been proposed and examined [96].

## 6.5 Limited Processor Number and Duplication

In this section, we analyze scheduling with communication delays on limited number of processors with duplication of the tasks.

### 6.5.1 Complexity of the Problem

To our best knowledge, quite limited number of publications is dedicated just to scheduling with duplication on a limited number of processors. Some of the **NP**-hardness proofs of scheduling without duplication can be applied also if duplication is allowed. The schedules built in the polynomial transformations have no idle time, or duplication does not reduce the length of the critical paths. In this sense, duplication does not help in such proofs, Thus, **NP**-hardness of $P|prec, p_j = 1, c = 1|C_{\max}$ [60, 93, 99], $P|tree, p_j = 1, c = 1|C_{\max}$ [78] (see Table 6.1) can be transferred to the current case. Also the results from [10] mentioned in Table 6.4 are obtained by equivalence of the two versions of the problem in the **NP**-hardness proof.

### 6.5.2 Heuristics with a Guarantee

Results on approximability of scheduling with duplication on limited processor number are collected in Table 6.5. Heuristic DP is presented below.

| **Table 6.4** Computationally hard cases for $m < \infty$, with duplication | Problem | Result | Reference |
|---|---|---|---|
| | $P|prec, p_j = 1, c, dup|C_{\max}$ | sNPh | [10] |

**Table 6.5**   Approximability results for $m < \infty$, with duplication

| Problem | Result | Reference |
|---|---|---|
| $P\,|\,prec, p_j = 1, c, dup\,|\,C_{\max}$ | $R \geq 1 + \frac{1}{c+3}$ | [10] |
| $P\,|\,prec, p_j = 1, c = 1, dup\,|\,C_{\max}$ | $R_{DP} \leq 2 - \frac{1}{m}$ | [53] |

**D-Path Heuristic (DP) [53]**   This heuristic is based on the concept of a *D-path* in a partial schedule.

We will denote by $\tau_i$ the start time of task $T_i$ in a partial schedule. Suppose the partial schedule includes all predecessors of task $T_j$. A D-path for $T_j$ denoted by $D(j)$ is built as follows. Let $s(j)$ be the latest start time of any predecessor of $T_j$. If exactly one $T_i \in pred(j)$ is started at $s(j)$, then $D(j)$ is the longest path ending in $T_i$ such that for each task $T_k \in D(j)$ and its successor $T_l \in D(j)$, $\tau_l = \tau_k + 1$. Note that only one task $T_l$ can be executed immediately after its predecessor $T_k$, and it requires scheduling $T_l$ on the same processor as $T_k$. Hence, a unique D-path $D(j)$ is defined. If more than one predecessor of $T_j$ is started at $s(j)$, then $D(j) = \emptyset$.

Observe that if some for task $T_k \in D(j)$, processor $proc(k)$ is free in the interval $[\tau_k + 1, s(j) + 2]$, then task $T_j$ can be started on $proc(k)$ at $s(j) + 1$ after duplicating $D(j)$ from $T_k$ to $T_i$ on $proc(k)$. If $T_a$ is the first task in $D(j)$, and some processor $P_b$ is free in interval $[\tau_a, s(j) + 2]$, then again $T_j$ can be scheduled on $P_b$ at $s(j) + 1$ after copying the whole $D(j)$ on $P_b$ in interval $[\tau_a, s(j) + 1]$.

The algorithm builds the schedule, one time unit after another. Let $\tau$ be the length of the already built partial schedule, and let $\mathcal{R}$ be the set of unscheduled tasks whose predecessors have been already scheduled and where at most one predecessor is scheduled at time $\tau - 1$. Tasks from $\mathcal{R}$ are examined in arbitrary order. Let $T_j \in \mathcal{R}$ be the currently examined task. Let us consider the set $\mathcal{P}(j, \tau)$ of processors which may execute $T_j$ starting at $\tau$. If $pred(j) = \emptyset$ or $\tau \geq s(j) + 2$, then $T_j$ may be assigned to any processor, and $\mathcal{P}(j, \tau) = \mathcal{P}$. Otherwise $D(j) \neq \emptyset$ and $\tau = s(j) + 1$, then $T_j$ can be started immediately after the last task of $D(j)$ on the same processor, or on some other processor $P_i$ only if part of $D(j)$ or whole $D(j)$ can be copied to an idle interval on $P_i$ as discussed above. Thus, in the current case $\mathcal{P}(j, \tau)$ comprises all such processor where $T_j$ can be started either after its immediate predecessor or after duplicating some part of $D(j)$. If $\mathcal{P}(j, \tau) \neq \emptyset$ then schedule $T_j$ on any processor from this set instantiating the duplications if necessary.

### 6.5.3   Heuristics Without a Guarantee

**Duplication Scheduling Heuristic (DSH) [70]**   The DSH heuristic tries to reduce schedule length by inserting duplicates of the predecessors of some task if the communication delay time is idle.

The algorithm analyzes the tasks according to the order of decreasing static level $h'(j)$. For each task assignments to all the processors are verified. For a given task $T_j$ and processor $P_i$ the earliest starting time $est(j, i)$ is calculated. If there is an idle interval before $est(j, i)$, then all $T_j$'s predecessors are considered for duplication on $P_i$. Let $T_k$ be the predecessor of $T_j$ whose message arrives at $P_i$ as the last one. If the idle time slot is shorter than $p_k$ then duplication of $T_k$ is not profitable and the algorithm proceeds with the next processor assignment for $T_j$, or the next task $T_j$. Otherwise, $T_k$ is duplicated on $P_i$ and started at the earliest possible time. If possible, $est(j, i)$ is appropriately reduced. Next, the possibility of duplication of $T_k$'s predecessors on $P_i$ is recursively verified. Predecessors whose messages arrive before the beginning of the idle interval on $P_i$ need not be duplicated. After recovering from recursively verifying possibility of duplicating predecessors of $T_j$ on $P_i$, the final value of $est(j, i)$ is recorded. Task $T_j$ is assigned to a processor offering the earliest starting time. The implied duplications are instantiated. Since DSH may produce a lot of redundant task copies, it is possible to eliminate some of them in a postoptimization step. The complexity of the algorithm is $O(n^4)$. In [81] it has been proposed to limit the depth of duplication to the immediate predecessors to reduce the complexity of the algorithm.

**Scalable Task Duplication Based Scheduling Heuristic (STDS) [34]** STDS starts with calculation of static levels $h'(j)$, earliest starting times $est(j)$, latest starting times $lst(j)$ for each task $T_j$ assuming that tasks are assigned to their own processors. A preferred predecessor $fpred(j)$ is selected for each task $T_j$ with $pred(j) \neq \emptyset$. The preferred predecessor satisfies $\forall T_k \in pred(j), est(fpred(j)) + p_{fpred(j)} + c_{fpred(j)j} \geq est(k) + p_k + c_{kj}$. Task $T_{fpred(j)}$ is a candidate to be scheduled on the same processor as $T_j$. The algorithm proceeds in two stages.

In the first stage task clusters are constructed. Tasks not assigned to a cluster are examined according to nondecreasing static levels. The algorithm starts in a given task (initially an exit task) and proceeds backward through the preferred predecessors to an entry node. Visited tasks form a cluster. This rule is realized only if all preferred predecessors are not assigned to some cluster yet. Suppose $T_j$ is the examined task, and $T_{fpred(j)}$ is already assigned to some cluster. If $pred(j) = \{T_{fpred(j)}\}$ or all predecessors of $T_j$ are assigned to some clusters, then $T_{fpred(j)}$ is duplicated in the current cluster, and the algorithm proceeds through the copy of $T_{fpred(j)}$ toward the entry task. Otherwise ($T_j$ has other unassigned predecessors than $T_{fpred(j)}$) it is verified if $T_{fpred(j)}$ resides on a critical path. If $T_{fpred(j)}$ was not a critical task then any unassigned task $T_k \in pred(j)$ is assigned to the current cluster, and the algorithm proceeds through $T_k$ to the entry task. On the other hand if $T_{fpred(j)}$ was a critical task then it is verified if there is another task in $pred(j)$ which could have been selected as the preferred predecessor. If such task $T_l$ exists and it is not assigned to a cluster, then $T_l$ is assigned to the current cluster. If substitute preferred predecessor could not be found, then any unassigned predecessor of $T_j$ is assigned to the current cluster. What is more, pair $(j, cn)$ is recorded, where $cn$ is the current cluster number, to indicate a failure of passing through a preferred predecessor.

In the second stage the number of clusters is adjusted to the available processor number. Let $cn$ denote the number of clusters. If $cn > m$ then the clusters are joined to reduce the number of needed processors. Let $pt(i)$ denote the sum of processing times of the tasks assigned to cluster $i$. Clusters are ordered according to nonincreasing values of $pt(i)$. If $m \leq \frac{cn}{2}$ then the longest cluster is merged with the shortest cluster. The second longest cluster is merged with the second shortest cluster, etc. The merging orders tasks according to nonincreasing static levels and eliminates task duplicates. This procedure reduces the number of clusters by half and is repeated as long as $m \leq \frac{cn}{2}$. If $\frac{cn}{2} < m < cn$ then one more cluster merging iteration is performed, however, only $2(cn - m)$ shortest clusters are merged in the above way. On the other hand, if $cn < m$ after the first phase, then the number of clusters is increased. In this case $m - cn$ pairs $(j, a)$ recording failure of traversing from task $T_j$ through $T_{fpred(j)}$ in cluster $a$ are used. The partial schedule from task $T_j$ to the end of the schedule is copied on a new processor, a copy of $T_{fpred(j)}$ is scheduled before $T_j$ on this new processor, and the preceding sequence of the tasks is constructed as in the first phase of the algorithm by traversing the task graph toward an entry task. The complexity of STDS is $O(n^2)$. A modification of STDS to schedule task graphs in SMP systems with a single bus has been proposed in [67].

**Economical Critical Path Fast Duplication (ECPFD) [5]**  ECPFD is a version of the earlier CPFD heuristic [3] adjusted to the limited processor number. Here we make reference to the notation introduced in the description of CPFD heuristic in Sect. 6.7.4.

One adaptation of CPFD consists in using a new processor in procedure attempt duplication $AD(j)$ only if an unused processor is still available. Another modification was applied in out-branch nodes (OBNs) scheduling. When examining an OBN task $T_i$ its critical child is determined which is task $T_j \in succ(i)$ such that $c_{ij}$ is maximum in $succ(j)$. Procedure attempt duplication $AD(i)$ is applied to the pair $T_i, T_j$ and the set of already used processors. A processor $k$ for which $est(j, k) + est(i, k)$ is minimum is a candidate for scheduling $T_i$. If no such processor is found, then scheduling $T_i$ on an unused processor $P_l$ is attempted (here duplication rule $DR(i, l)$ is applied). If an unused processor does not exist then $T_i$ is scheduled on a processor executing one of $T_i$'s predecessors such that the increase of the schedule length is minimum.

A heuristic called Selective Duplication (SD) using similar ideas has been proposed in [16]. A recursive nature of CPFD/ECPFD is substituted by examining tasks in the order built around critical path while preserving precedence constraints. Only immediate predecessors of the examined task $T_j$ are considered for duplication on the currently verified processor $P_i$. Duplication which is not strictly reducing $est(j, i)$ is rejected. This reduces algorithm complexity to $O(\max_j\{indeg(j)\}mn^2 + |\mathcal{A}|)$. What is more, SD is capable of taking into account the processor interconnection. In such a case the set of candidate processors for scheduling task $T_j$ is restricted to the processors executing tasks in $pred(j)$ and their nearest neighbor processors.

**Scalable Scheduling with DFRN (SDFRN) [91]**  It is a modification of DFRN heuristic originally designed for unlimited processor number (see in Sect. 6.7.4). Here the modification consists in using a new processor only if it is still available.

## 6.6  Unlimited Processor Number and No Duplication

In this section, it is assumed that the number of processors is not restricting for the schedule construction. The algorithms select the most appropriate processor number.

### 6.6.1  Hard Cases

Computationally hard cases of scheduling with communication delays for unlimited processor number and without task duplication are presented in Table 6.6. Special symbols were used to denote:

- $2l.out\text{-}tree, 2l.in\text{-}tree$ – Task graph is an out-tree or an in-tree, respectively, with two levels (i.e. the longest chain has two arcs and three tasks).
- $m : C_{max} = C_{max}^*$ – The problem consists in finding minimum number of processors such that schedule length is optimum.
- $\mathbf{FP^{NP[\log n]}c}$ – The class of complete problems in $\mathbf{FP^{NP[\log n]}}$, where $\mathbf{FP^{NP[\log n]}}$ is the class of problems which can be decided in polynomial time by making $O(\log n)$ calls to an oracle solving any problem from class $\mathbf{NP}$.

### 6.6.2  Polynomial Cases

The results on polynomially solvable cases of scheduling with communication delays when processor number is not bounding, without duplication, are collected in Table 6.7. The following notations are used in Table 6.7:

- $poly(x)$ – Polynomial function of $x$
- $1l.tree$ – A single level in- or out-tree, a.k.a. *join* and *fork* graphs, respectively
- $sp11$ – Series–parallel-11 graph (cf. Sect. 2.1)

**Table 6.6**  Hard problems of scheduling with communication delays, $m = \infty$, no duplication

| Problem | Result | Reference |
| --- | --- | --- |
| $P\infty\lvert prec, c_{ij}\rvert C_{max}$ | **NPh** | [27] |
| $P\infty\lvert in\text{-}tree, p_j = 1, c > 1\rvert C_{max}$ | **sNPh** | [64] |
| $P\infty\lvert 2l.in\text{-}tree, c_{ij}\rvert C_{max}$ | **NPh** | [28] |
| $P\infty\lvert 2l.out\text{-}tree, c_{ij}\rvert C_{max}$ | **NPh** | [28] |
| $P\infty\lvert prec, p_j = 1, c = 1\rvert C_{max} = 6$ | **sNPc** | [60] |
| $P\infty\lvert prec, sct\rvert C_{max}$ | **sNPh** | [94] |
| $P\infty\lvert sp, p_j = 1, c_{ij} \in \{0, 1\}\rvert C_{max} = 6$ | **sNPc** | [86] |
| $P\infty\lvert prec, p_j = 1, c = 1\rvert m : C_{max} = C_{max}^*$ | $\mathbf{FP^{NP[\log n]}c}$ | [59] |
| $P\infty\lvert prec, p_j = 1, c \geq 3\rvert C_{max} = c + 4$ | **sNPc** | [45] |

**Table 6.7** Polynomial cases of scheduling with communication delays, $m = \infty$, no duplication

| Problem | Result | Reference |
|---|---|---|
| $P\infty\|in\text{-}tree, sct\|C_{\max}$ | $O(n)$ | [26] |
| $P\infty\|out\text{-}tree, sct\|C_{\max}$ | $O(n)$ | [26] |
| $P\infty\|1l.tree, c_{ij}\|C_{\max}$ | $O(n \log n)$ | [27] |
| $P\infty\|prec, p_j = 1, c = 1\|C_{\max} = 5$ | $O(poly(n))$ | [60] |
| $P\infty\|sp11, sct\|C_{\max}$ | $O(n^2)$ | [29,93] |
| $P\infty\|bipartite, sct\|C_{\max}$ | $O(n^2 \log n)$ | [29,93] |
| $P\infty\|ck\text{-}tree, p_j = 1, c > 1\|C_{\max}$ | $O(n)$ | [41,42] |
| $P\infty\|prec, p_j = 1, c \geq 2\|C_{\max} \leq c + 2$ | $O(n^2)$ | [10] |
| $P\infty\|sp, c = 1\|C_{\max}$ | $O(n + \|\mathcal{A}\|)$ | [86] |
| $P\infty\|sp, c = 1\|\sum w_j c_j$ | $O(n^3)$ | [86] |

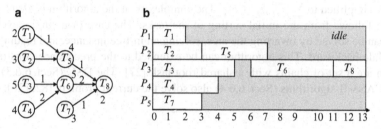

**Fig. 6.13** (a) Exemplary instance of $P\infty\|in\text{-}tree, sct\|C_{\max}$. Processing times and communication delays are shown by the task nodes and arcs, respectively. (b) A schedule

- *bipartite* – Directed bipartite graph
- *ck-tree* – Complete $k$-ary tree

Below we outline selected problems listed in Table 6.7.

### $P\infty\|in\text{-}tree, sct\|C_{\max}$ [26]

Suppose task $T_j$ is a root of an in-tree and has immediate predecessors $T_a, \ldots, T_b$. The algorithm for the above problem is based on the observation that predecessors $T_a, \ldots, T_b$ of $T_j$ are executed on different processors, and one of them is executed on the same processors as $T_j$. Any schedule not satisfying the above condition can be transformed to satisfy it without increasing schedule length. If two predecessors $T_a, T_b$ of $T_j$ are executed on the same processor, then the first of them, say $T_a$, can be moved to a different processor without increasing schedule length because $c_{aj} \leq p_b$ (as we have *sct*). This allows for decomposing the construction of the optimum schedule for an in-tree to a recursive algorithm scheduling the in-trees rooted in $T_a, \ldots, T_b$ on disjoint processor sets, and then scheduling the root $T_j$ on a processor guaranteeing the shortest feasible schedule. Example of a schedule built according to this method is shown in Fig. 6.13. The same algorithm can be applied to solve also problem $P\infty|out\text{-}tree, sct|C_{max}$ by first inverting direction of the arcs, solving the resulting instance of in-tree scheduling problem, and reading the obtained schedule backward. The current problem is also solved by algorithms DSC (Sect. 6.6.3), MCP (Sect. 6.4.4), and ETF (Sect. 6.4.3) [126].

### $P\infty|1l.tree, c_{ij}|C_{max}$ [27]

In the current problem the precedence constraints form single-level trees. Let us assume that we have an out-tree rooted in $T_1$, and that tasks are numbered such that $c_{12} + p_2 \geq c_{13} + p_3 \geq \cdots \geq c_{1n} + p_n$. The algorithm executes first $k$ tasks on the same processor as $T_1$, and tasks $T_{k+1}, \ldots, T_n$ are executed on separate processors. Here $k$ is the maximum index satisfying $p_1 + \sum_{j=2}^{k} p_j \leq p_1 + p_k + c_{1k}$. which can be simplified to $\sum_{j=2}^{k-1} p_j \leq c_{1k}$. The complexity of the algorithm is $O(n \log n)$ which follows from the initial sorting of the tasks. The case of a single-level in-tree can be solved by inverting the arcs, solving an in-tree instance, and reading the schedule backward. This algorithm can be extended to the precedence constraints which are a set of chains with a shared root task [27]. The DSC (Sect. 6.6.3) and MD CASS-II algorithms (Sect. 6.6.4) also solve the current problem [82, 126].

### $P\infty|prec, p_j = 1, c = 1|C_{max} = 5$ [60]

A decision version of the scheduling problem is considered here. We ask if a feasible schedule of length at most 5 exists. This problem has been reduced to a special case of the problem of verifying whether a polyhedron defined by a linear system of inequalities is nonempty.

### $P\infty|sp11, sct|C_{max}$ [29, 93]

Series–parallel-11 (SP11) graphs were defined in Sect. 2.1. Let us remind that SP11 graphs are constructed in a sequence of operations which by convention we called series and parallel constructions. The construction of an SP11 graph may be represented as a tree. The algorithm for the current problem builds the optimal schedule by applying special procedures for the parallel and the series parts of the task graph. Let $par(G_1, \ldots, G_k)$ be the subgraph of the task graph obtained from the subgraphs $G_1, \ldots, G_k$ by applying parallel construction (see Fig. 2.2). Let us denote by $C_{max}^q$ the length of the optimum schedule for subgraph $G_q$. We will denote by $T_{s_i}, T_{f_i}$ the entry task and exit task, respectively, of the subgraph $G_i$. Let $T_0$ be the fork task and $T_{k+1}$ the join task of $par(G_1, \ldots, G_k)$. It can be shown that in the optimum schedule independent tasks should be executed on different processors. Hence $G_1, \ldots, G_q$ are executed on different processor sets. If $T_0$ is executed on the same processor as $T_{s_i}$, and $T_{k+1}$ is executed on the same processor as $T_{f_j}$, then the length of the schedule is

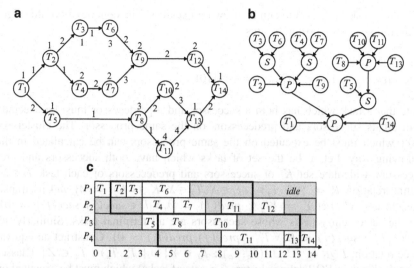

**Fig. 6.14** Example of solving problem $P\infty|sp11, sct|C_{max}$. (**a**) Initial task graph. Processing times and communication delays are marked by the nodes and arcs, respectively. (**b**) Series–parallel task graph decomposition tree. (**c**) A schedule

$$C_{max}^{ij} = p_0 + \max_{q\in\{1,\dots,k\}}\{c_{0s_q}(1 - \delta_{s_i,s_q}) + C_{max}^q + c_{f_q,k+1}(1 - \delta_{f_q,f_j})\} + p_{k+1}$$

where $\delta_{a,b} = 1$ if $a = b$ and $\delta_{a,b} = 0$ otherwise. Thus, the optimum schedule for $par(G_1, \dots, G_k)$ can be computed by analyzing all pairs $(i, j)$ and choosing the one for which the value of $C_{max}^{ij}$ is minimum. In the case of series construction $ser(G_0, G_1)$ the optimum schedules for $G_0, G_1$ are concatenated such that the tasks $T_{f_0}$ and $T_{s_1}$ are on the same processor. Example of applying this algorithm is shown in Fig. 6.14.

## $P\infty|bipartite, sct|C_{max}$ [29, 93]

In the directed bipartite graph all paths have just two tasks. Since it is profitable to execute independent tasks on different processors, and each communication is shorter than any processing time, each processor executes either one or two tasks. Pairs of tasks executed on the same processor correspond to a matching $M$ in $\mathcal{A}$ because no task is duplicated. For a given matching $M$ schedule length is $C_{max}(M) = \max\{\max_{(i,j)\in M}\{p_i + p_j\}, \max_{(i,j)\notin M}\{p_i + c_{ij} + p_j\}\}$. It is profitable to execute on the same processor arcs $(i, j)$ with the greatest value of $p_i + c_{ij} + p_j$. An algorithm for the current problem sorts the arcs in the order of decreasing value of $p_i + c_{ij} + p_j$, and selects the greatest number of them such that they form a matching. Pairs of tasks adjacent to a selected arc are executed on the same processor. The remaining tasks are executed on their own processors. The complexity of this algorithm follows from sorting the arcs.

$P\infty|prec, p_j = 1, c \geq 2|C_{\max} \leq c + 2$ [10]

Note that a task which has both a successor and a predecessor must be executed with all its successors and predecessors on the same processor. The clusters of tasks which must be executed on the same processors can be calculated in the following way. Let $X$ be the set of tasks which have both successors and predecessors. Calculate set $K_i$ of successors and predecessors of each task $T_i \in X$. Define relation $R = \{(T_i, T_j) : T_i \in X, T_j \in X, K_i \cap K_j \neq \emptyset\}$ and its transitive closure $R^*$. Let $Y = \{T_j : pred(j) = \emptyset, \forall T_i \in succ(j), succ(T_i) = \emptyset\}$, i.e. the set of entry tasks whose successors are all terminal tasks. Similarly, let $Z = \{T_j : succ(j) = \emptyset, \forall T_i \in pred(j), pred(T_i) = \emptyset\}$. Construct an equivalence relation: $EQR = R^* \cup \{(T_a, T_a) : T_a \in Y\} \cup \{(T_a, T_a) : T_a \in Z\}$. Classes of equivalence in $EQR$ define clusters (i.e. sets of tasks) which must be executed on the same processor. There is a feasible schedule if and only if:

1. No cluster has more than $c + 2$ tasks.
2. In each cluster there is at most one entry task preceding some tasks not included in the current cluster.
3. In each cluster there is at most one exit task succeeding some tasks not included in the current cluster.

The clusters must be executed on separate processors. The remaining tasks are executed as early as possible on their own processors.

$P\infty|ck\text{-}tree, p_j = 1, c > 1|C_{\max}$ [41,42]

The algorithm is presented for binary in-trees, but it can be modified to any complete $k$-ary in- or out-tree [41,42]. For simplicity of presentation let us assume that the binary in-tree is oriented. Thus, the left and the right immediate successors of a nonleaf are distinguished. The nodes at a certain level are ordered from left to right. The algorithm has an invariant that any partial schedule is optimum for the scheduled subtree. The algorithm builds the schedule in two stages.

In the first stage a schedule is built bottom-up on processor $P_1$ for the leftmost subtree of the task graph. More precisely, the algorithm starts with scheduling the two leftmost leaves at times 0, 1, and their successor is scheduled at time 2. The leftmost unscheduled leaf is appended at the end of the schedule. While some internal task of the in-tree has its predecessors scheduled it is appended at the end of the schedule on $P_1$. These steps are repeated until building a schedule on $P_1$ strictly longer than the communication delay $c$. Then, the algorithm switches to the second stage.

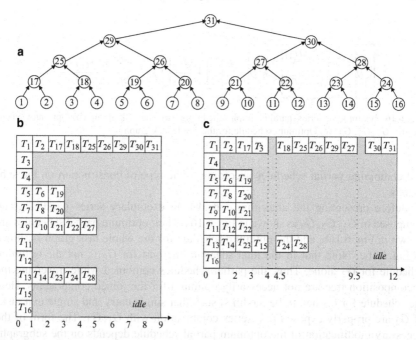

**Fig. 6.15** Examples of schedules for problem $P\infty|ck\text{-}tree, p_j = 1, c > 1|C_{max}$. For brevity, only task indices are shown. (**a**) The task graph. (**b**) Schedule for $c = 2$. (**c**) Schedule for $c = 3.5$

Suppose $\tau$ is the length of the current partial schedule on $P_1$, and $C_{max}^*(i)$ is the length of the optimum schedule for a subtree of height $i$. In the second stage the algorithm determines height $h$ of the highest in-tree satisfying $\tau > C_{max}^*(h) + c - 1$. Height $h$ can be determined using the currently constructed partial schedule because of the invariant optimality of the partial schedules. The leftmost unscheduled task $T_j$ on level $h + 1$ is scheduled at time $\max\{\tau, C_{max}^*(h) + c\}$ on $P_1$. If the left predecessor subtree of height $h$ is still unscheduled, then it is scheduled on unused processors by copying the existing schedule for the leftmost subtree of the same height. The same operation is applied to the right subtree of $T_j$. This procedure is repeated until reaching the root of the in-tree (the exit task).

Examples of applying the above algorithm to a binary in-tree of height 4, for $c = 2$ and $c = 3.5$, are shown in Fig. 6.15b and c, respectively.

## $P\infty|sp, c = 1|C_{max}$ [86]

Before presenting the algorithm for the current case of (general) series–parallel graphs let us remind that these graphs may be represented by binary decomposition trees with tasks in the leaves, and nodes representing series and parallel constructions (see Sect. 2.1 for notation). The construction of the schedule for the whole task graph consists in traversing the decomposition tree from the leaves to the root,

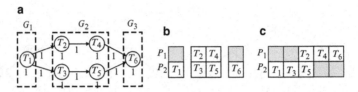

**Fig. 6.16** Example of series–parallel graph scheduling. (**a**) The task graph. (**b**) Optimum schedules for $G_1, G_2, G_3$. (**c**) Optimum schedule for the whole task graph

and combining partial schedules according to the type of construction on the subgraphs.

Before presenting the algorithm consider an exemplary series–parallel graph composed of $G_1, G_2, G_3$ as shown in Fig. 6.16a. Their optimum partial schedules are shown in Fig. 6.16b, and the optimum schedule for the whole task graph is shown in Fig. 6.16c. Note that in the final schedule the part for $G_2$ is not the optimum schedule for $G_2$ alone. Thus, the partial schedules combined while traversing the decomposition tree are not necessarily optimum for the joined components. Here the schedule for $G_2$ had to be modified such that single entry and single exit tasks of $G_2$ are properly exposed to a series combination with $G_1, G_3$. The form of the necessary modification of the optimum partial schedule depends on the subgraphs and the type of construction. It has been shown in [86] that two partial schedules suffice for each subgraph.

Let us denote by $S$ a partial schedule for subgraph $G$. We will denote by $C_{max}(S)$ the length of $S$. Let $left(S)$ be the number of tasks executed at time 0 in $S$ and $right(S)$ be the number of tasks completed at $C_{max}(S)$ in $S$. Schedule $S$ will be called *strongly optimal* for $C_{max}$ criterion if it satisfies two conditions:

1. $C_{max}(S)$ is optimum for $G$.
2. $right(S)$ is minimum among all schedules satisfying 1.

For each subgraph $G$ two schedules may be used in the joining construction: the strongly optimal schedule $S(G)$ and schedule $\bar{S}(G)$ which is strongly optimal among all schedules $S$ of $G$ with $left(S) = 1$. Let $S^{+1}$ be a schedule obtained from $S$ by delaying the start time of every task by a time unit. For two partial schedules $S_1, S_2$, let $S_1 || S_2$ denote parallel juxtaposition of the two schedules on independent processors such that start times of the tasks remain unchanged. Similarly, for two partial schedules $S_1, S_2$ let $S_1 \lhd S_2$ be a schedule obtained by concatenation of $S_1, S_2$ such that tasks from $S_2$ are delayed by $C_{max}(S_1)$.

Procedure *SchedPar*$(G_1, G_2)$ corresponding to the parallel construction $G = par(G_1, G_2)$ is defined as follows: $S(G) = S(G_1) || S(G_2)$, for $\bar{S}(G)$ choose the shorter of $\bar{S}(G_1) || S(G_2)^{+1}$, and $\bar{S}(G_2) || S(G_1)^{+1}$.

Procedure *SchedSer*$(G_1, G_2)$ for the series construction $G = ser(G_1, G_2)$ is defined as follows. If $right(S(G_1)) \geq 2$ then $S(G) = S(G_1) \lhd S(G_2)^{+1}$, i.e. the two schedules for $G_1, G_2$ are executed one after another with a separating unit idle time. When $right(S(G_1)) = 1$, then $S(G) = S(G_1) \lhd \bar{S}(G_2)$. To construct $\bar{S}(G)$ the same procedure is applied with $\bar{S}(G_1)$ in the position of $S(G_1)$.

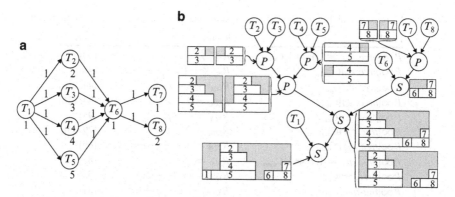

**Fig. 6.17** Example of series–parallel graph scheduling. (**a**) The task graph. (**b**) The decomposition tree with partial schedules. Only task indices are shown in the partial schedules. Schedule $S(G)$ is shown to the left (or above), $\bar{S}(G)$ is shown on the right (or below). Only one schedule is shown if $S(G) = \bar{S}(G)$

The algorithm starts in the leaves of the decomposition tree with trivial schedules for single tasks which are both $S(G)$ and $\bar{S}(G)$. Then, it proceeds toward the root of the decomposition tree applying procedures $SchedSer, SchedPar$ as necessary. An example of applying the above algorithm is presented in Fig. 6.17. The above algorithm may be implemented to run in $O(n + |\mathcal{A}|)$ time. It has been also extended to the mean weighted completion time criterion, i.e., to problem $P\infty|sp, c = 1|\sum w_j c_j$ [86].

### 6.6.3   Heuristics with a Guarantee

The results on approximability of scheduling with communication delays are collected in Table 6.8. The following notations are used in this table:

- $R_{lin}$ – Worst-case performance ratio of any heuristic building linear clusters.
- $g(\mathcal{T}, \mathcal{A})$ – Granularity of the instance as defined in (6.1).
- $\rho = \frac{\max_{(i,j)\in\mathcal{A}}\{c_{ij}\}}{\min_{T_j\in\mathcal{T}}\{p_j\}}$, for the *sct* case $\rho < 1$; note that $\frac{1}{\rho}$ is defined differently than the granularity in (6.1), and hence $\rho \geq \frac{1}{g(\mathcal{T}, \mathcal{A})}$.
- $h$ – Height of the in- or out-tree.

Algorithm PLW is considered in Sect. 6.7.3, other heuristics alluded to in Table 6.8 are presented below.

**Linear Clustering (LC) [43,69]**   The LC algorithm greedily clusters the tasks constituting the longest path in the task graph. More formally, LC can be defined as follows. Initially all arcs in the task graph are marked unexamined. The longest path is determined assuming that tasks are assigned to different processors. The tasks on

**Table 6.8** Approximability of scheduling with communication delays, $m = \infty$, no duplication

| Problem | Result | Reference |
|---|---|---|
| $P\infty\|prec, p_j = 1, c = 1\|C_{\max}$ | $R \geq \frac{7}{6}$ | [60] |
| $P\infty\|prec, c_{ij}\|C_{\max}$ | $R_{lin} \leq 1 + \frac{1}{g(\mathcal{T}, \mathcal{A})}$ | [43] |
| $P\infty\|prec, c_{ij}\|C_{\max}$ | $R_{DSC} \leq 1 + \frac{1}{g(\mathcal{T}, \mathcal{A})}$ | [44, 126] |
| $P\infty\|prec, sct\|C_{\max}$ | $R_{DSC} \leq 2$ | [44, 126] |
| $P\infty\|prec, sct\|C_{\max}$ | $R_{SCT} = 1 + \rho$ | [94] |
| $P\infty\|tree, c_{ij}\|C_{\max}$ | $R_{SDR} = h - 1$ | [29, 93] |
| $P\infty\|tree, c_{ij}\|C_{\max}$ | $R_{PLW} \leq 1 + \frac{1}{1 + g(\mathcal{T}, \mathcal{A})}$ | [89] |
| $P\infty\|prec, p_j = 1, c = 1\|C_{\max}$ | $R_{MK} = \frac{4}{3}$ | [88] |
| $P\infty\|prec, sct\|C_{\max}$ | $R_{HM1} = 1 + \frac{1}{1 + 2/\rho}$ | [52] |
| $P\infty\|out\text{-}tree, c_{ij}\|C_{\max}$ | $R_{MCA1} = 1 + \frac{1}{1 + 1/\rho}$ | [87] |
| $P\infty\|prec, p_j = 1, c = 1\|\sum c_j$ | $R \geq \frac{8}{7}$ | [58] |
| $P\infty\|prec, p_j = 1, c \geq 3\|C_{\max}$ | $R \geq \frac{c+5}{c+4}$ | [45] |
| $P\infty\|prec, p_j = 1, c \geq 2\|C_{\max}$ | $R \leq \frac{2(c+1)}{3}$ | [45] |

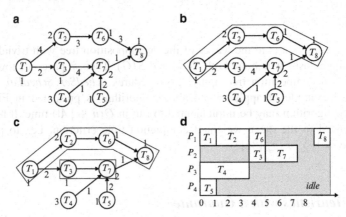

**Fig. 6.18** Example of linear clustering. (**a**) Initial task graph. (**b**), (**c**) Linear clustering. (**d**) A schedule

the longest path are clustered together in a single linear cluster. The arcs incident with the new cluster are marked examined. The procedure is repeated until examining all arcs. Clusters are executed on separate processors, tasks in the clusters are started as early as possible. The complexity of LC is $O(n(n + |\mathcal{A}|))$. An example of applying LC is shown in Fig. 6.18. For clarity of the picture unit clusters are not shown.

**Dominant Sequence Clustering (DSC) [44, 125, 126]** DSC pseudocode is presented in Fig. 6.19. This algorithm builds nonlinear clusters. The path lengths, task levels in the tasks graph are calculated including the communication delays existing in the current state of clustering. An arc is added between the last task in the cluster and the just included task if they were independent of the original DAG. To distinguish the critical path existing in the original task graph from the critical path

---

1: $EG = \emptyset, UEG = T, FL = \{T_j : prec(j) = \emptyset\};$// initially all tasks are in unit clusters
2: compute $h(j)$ for each task, and $\forall T_j \in FL$ set $est(j) = 0$;
3: **while** $(UEG \neq \emptyset)$ {
4:      $j_x = head(FL);$ // $T_{j_x}$ has the highest priority $PRIO$
5:      $j_y = head(PFL);$ // $T_{j_x}$ has the highest priority $pPRIO$
6:   **if** $(PRIO(j_x) \geq pPRIO(j_y))$
7:         { call minimization procedure to reduce $est(j_x)$ }
8:   **else**
9:         { call minimization procedure to reduce $est(j_x)$ with constraint $DSRW$ };
10:  if no zeroing is accepted, $T_{j_x}$ remains alone in a cluster;
11:  update priorities of $T_i \in succ(j), EG = EG \cup \{T_j\}, UEG = UEG - \{T_j\}$;
12: } // end of while

---

**Fig. 6.19** Pseudocode of DSC (on the basis of [126], ©[1994] IEEE)

in the final schedule including task sequencing a name of *dominant sequence* (DS) is used.

The algorithm analyzes the task graph in a single sweep without backtracking. This is accomplished by maintaining set *EG* of tasks which are already examined, and set *UEG* of tasks which are not yet examined. Initially all tasks are in the unit clusters. A task is free if all its predecessors are in set *EG*. Free tasks from *UEG* are analyzed in the topological order of $\mathcal{A}$ giving priority to task $T_j$ with the greatest value of $PRIO(j) = est(j) + h(j)$. Note that $\max_j\{PRIO(j)\}$ is also the makespan for the whole task graph, and tasks $T_i$ with $PRIO(i) = \max_j\{PRIO(j)\}$ are on dominant sequence (DS). Task $T_j$ is included in the cluster of its predecessor if it does not increase schedule length. If there is more than one possible way of zeroing an arc to $T_j$, then $T_j$ is included in cluster $k$ which reduces $est(j, k)$ in the maximum degree. Note that if arc $T_x \rightarrow T_j$ is zeroed then $est(i)$ changes only for tasks $T_i \in succ(j)$.

Suppose $T_a \rightarrow T_b$ is an arc on the DS, $T_c$ is earlier topologically than $T_b$, but $T_c$ is not on DS. Since tasks are examined in the topological order and arc zeroing is accepted if it is not increasing schedule length then $T_c$ may be included in $T_a$'s cluster and prevent $T_b$ from joining this cluster. Thus, DS may not be reduced in the expected way. To avoid such a situation priority is defined for tasks which are not free: $pPRIO(b) = h(j) + \max_{a \in PRED(b) \cap EG}\{est(a) + p_a + c_{ab}\}$. If there is task $T_b$ with $pPRIO(b) > PRIO(c)$, then the free tasks $T_c$ cannot join the cluster of the $T_b$ predecessor until $T_b$ is examined and moved to $EG$.

To improve the performance of DSC while dealing with single-level in-trees (a.k.a. join graphs) more than one arc may be zeroed in a single step. This special case is equivalent to problem $P\infty|1l.tree, c_{ij}|C_{max}$ presented above. Assume $T_j$ is the currently examined task. DSC orders the tasks $T_i \in pred(j)$ according to nonincreasing values of $est(i) + p_i + c_{ij}$. Without loss of generality let us assume that tasks in $pred(j)$, according to the above order, are $T_1, T_2, \ldots, T_h$. Only those predecessors which are in the cluster of $T_1$, or have $T_j$ as the unique successor, are allowed for further analysis. DSC finds by binary search the maximum

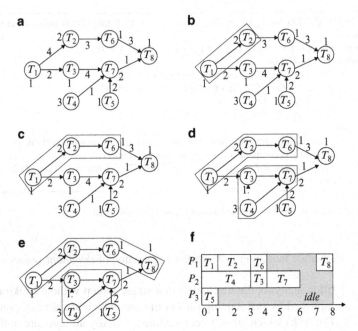

**Fig. 6.20** Example of clustering by DSC algorithm. (**a**) Initial task graph. (**b**)–(**e**) Steps of clustering. Unit clusters are not shown for clarity of presentation. (**f**) A schedule

$k \in \{1, \dots, h\}$ satisfying $\sum_{j=1}^{k-1} p_j \leq c_{kj}$. Tasks $T_1, \dots, T_k, T_j$ are included in $T_1$ cluster, and arcs are added between the initially independent tasks such that their order coincides with the order of earliest starting times.

It is suggested in [126] that DSC should be executed for the original task graph, and for the task graph with all arcs inverted with the resulting schedule read backward. The better schedule is presented as the final solution. The complexity of DSC is $O((n + |\mathcal{A}|) \log n)$.

An example of applying DSC is shown in Fig. 6.20. Tasks are examined in the order $(T_1, T_2, T_3, T_6, T_4, T_5, T_7, T_8)$. Clustering of $T_3$ with $T_1$ is rejected because it increases schedule length. While examining task $T_7$ (Fig. 6.20d) arcs $T_3 \rightarrow T_7, T_4 \rightarrow T_7$ are zeroed in a single step, and pseudo-arc $T_4 \rightarrow T_3$ is added.

Though DSC is a clustering method which does not take the processor limit into account, presenting it as a method for scheduling on unlimited processor number may be confusing, because it has been applied in PYRROS system [44] for scheduling in real distributed systems. In the real computing systems, obviously, the number of processors is limited. This required a method of imposing processor limitations, and sequencing tasks if two clusters were assigned to the same processor. While assigning the clusters to $m < \infty$ processors in PYRROS the clusters from DSC were treated as sequential tasks with processing times equal to the sum of the processing times of the included tasks. Then, the assignment was done in a greedy way resembling LPT heuristic. When several clusters are assigned to the same processor, then some mutually independent tasks must be sequenced. It has been proposed in [44, 125] to execute first ready tasks with the greatest level $h(j)$ including the communication delays.

**Small Communication Time Heuristic (SCT) [94]** Given the instance $I$ of problem $P\infty|prec, sct|C_{\max}$, the algorithm constructs an instance $I'$ of problem $P\infty|prec|C_{\max}$ where $p'_j = (1 + \rho)p_j$, for $j = 1, \ldots, n$, where $\rho = \frac{\max_{(i,j)\in A}\{c_{ij}\}}{\min_{T_j\in T}\{p_j\}}$ $< 1$. Observe that in instance $I'$ we have no communication delays. An optimum schedule for $I'$ is constructed greedily. Let $\tau'_j$ be the starting time of task $T'_j$ in $I'$. A schedule for $I$ is constructed by starting tasks $T_j$ at time $\tau'_j$ on their own processors. By the selection of processing times $p'_j$ in $I'$ it is guaranteed for any arc $T_i \to T_j$ that $\tau_j \geq \tau_i + p_j + c_{ij}$, where $\tau_j$ denotes starting time of $T_j$ in a schedule for $I$. Hence, the schedule for instance $I$ is feasible. Let $C'_{\max}$ denote schedule length for instance $I'$, $C^*_{\max}$ optimum schedule length for instance $I$, $C^1_{\max}$ schedule length for instance $I$ scheduled without communication delays (i.e. tasks have length $p_j$). We have $C'_{\max} = (1 + \rho)C^1_{\max}$, $C^*_{\max} \geq C^1_{\max}$. Since $C'_{\max}$ is also length $C_{SCT}$ of the schedule built $SCT$ heuristic we obtain $\frac{C_{sct}}{C^*_{\max}} = \frac{C'_{\max}}{C^*_{\max}} \leq \frac{(1+\rho)C^1_{\max}}{C^1_{\max}} = 1 + \rho$.

**SDR Heuristic (SDR) [29, 93]** This heuristic is defined for scheduling in- or out-trees, i.e. problem $P\infty|tree, c_{ij}|C_{\max}$. Let us assume that we have an out-tree. Suppose $T_j$ is a root of a single-level subtree with leaves in $succ(j)$. The algorithm schedules this out-tree optimally in makespan $C_{\max}(j)$ using the algorithm for $P\infty|1l.tree, c_{ij}|C_{\max}$. The partial schedules for the subtrees are treated as single tasks of length $C_{\max}(j)$, on which the same algorithm is applied recursively. SDR applies this procedure bottom-up until reaching the root of the whole task graph.

**Munier and König Heuristic (MK) [88]** This heuristic builds a schedule for UET-UCT case on the basis of linear programming solution.

Let us first formulate the current problem as an integer linear program. In the following formulation $\tau_j$ is a variable representing start time of task $T_j$. For each pair $(i, j) \in A$ we introduce binary variable $x_{ij}$ equal to 1 if and only if $T_j$ is a preferred successor of $T_i$ executed immediately after $T_i$ on processor $proc(i)$. Problem $P\infty|prec, p_j = 1, c = 1|C_{\max}$ can be formulated as an integer linear program:

$$\text{minimize } C_{\max} \text{ subject to} \tag{6.7}$$

$$\tau_i + 2 - x_{ij} \leq \tau_j \quad \forall (i, j) \in A \tag{6.8}$$

$$\sum_{j \in succ(i)} x_{ij} \leq 1 \quad \forall T_i \in \{T_l : succ(l) \neq \emptyset\} \tag{6.9}$$

$$\sum_{i \in pred(j)} x_{ij} \leq 1 \quad \forall T_j \in \{T_l : pred(l) \neq \emptyset\} \tag{6.10}$$

$$\tau_j + 1 \leq C_{\max} \quad \forall T_j \in T \tag{6.11}$$

$$\tau_j \geq 0 \quad \forall T_j \in T \tag{6.12}$$

$$x_{ij} \in \{0, 1\} \quad \forall (i, j) \in A \tag{6.13}$$

In the above formulation equation (6.8) guarantees that the time between finishing predecessor $T_i$ and starting its successor $T_j$ is zero only if $T_j$ is the preferred successor. Inequalities (6.9) and (6.10) guarantee that there is at most one preferred successor. The above ILP in general cannot be solved in polynomial time unless $\mathbf{P} = \mathbf{NP}$. By replacing constraints (6.13) with $0 \leq x_{ij} \leq 1$ we obtain an LP which can be solved in polynomial time. Let $x'_{ij}, \tau'_j$ denote the values of $x_{ij}, \tau_j$, respectively, in the optimum solution of the relaxed LP formulation.

A schedule is constructed in the following way. Tasks without predecessors are started at time 0 on separate processors. Let $\mathcal{T}'$ be the set of tasks which are not scheduled yet, and $t_i$ be the start time assigned to $T_i$ which is already scheduled. Task $T_j \in \mathcal{T}'$ can be started at time $\theta > 0$ if one of the two conditions is satisfied:

1. If $\forall\, T_i \in pred(j), t_i \leq \theta - 2$, then $T_j$ can be scheduled on any free processor.
2. If there exists exactly one task $T_k \in pred(j)$ such that $t_k = \theta - 1$ and $\forall\, T_i \in pred(j) - \{T_k\}, t_i \leq \theta - 2$, then $T_j$ is started on the same processor as $T_k$. However, if there is more than one successor task $T_j$, satisfying the current conditions with exactly the same predecessor task $T_k$, then all such tasks $T_j$ cannot be started at $\theta$ on the same processor. In such a case the task with maximum $x'_{kj}$ is scheduled at $\theta$ on the same processor as $T_k$.

It can be shown that $\forall\, T_j \in \mathcal{T}, t_j \leq \frac{4}{3}\tau'_j$. Hence, the approximability ratio $\frac{4}{3}$. This method has been extended to the small communication time case (*sct*) in [52] (in Table 6.8 denoted as heuristic $HM1$).

**Munier Clustering Algorithm 1 (MCA1) [87]** This algorithm builds clusters for out-trees using a method similar to Papadimitriou–Yannakakis algorithm [90] (see Sect. 6.7.3), but instead of predecessors, the successors are analyzed.

We will introduce now a method of calculating a lower bound $\theta(j)$ on the length of the schedule for the out-tree rooted in task $T_j$. For tasks $T_i$ with $succ(i) = \emptyset$ let $\theta(i) = p_i$. Suppose that $succ(j) \neq \emptyset$ and all the successors of $T_j$ have their lower bounds already calculated. Let us assume that the value of the lower bound is $\tau$. Any successor $T_k$ of $T_j$ satisfying $p_j + c_{jk} > \tau - \theta_k$ cannot meet its lower bound $\theta_k$ unless it is executed on the same processor as $T_j$. Let $N(\tau, j)$ denote the subset of $T_j$ successors which for the given $\tau$ must be executed on the same processor as $T_j$, and for each such successor $T_k$ there is a path from $T_j$ to $T_k$ including only tasks from $N(\tau, j)$. Note that if we invert direction of the time axis, then the feasibility of the schedule for the tasks in $N(\tau, j) \cup \{T_j\}$ is equivalent to problem $1\,|\,in\text{-}tree, r_j\,|\,C_{\max}$, where $\theta(k) - p_k$ are ready times of the tasks in $N(\tau, j)$, and the ready time of $T_j$ is 0. Let the tasks in $N(\tau, j)$ be ordered according to decreasing values of $\theta(k) - p_k$. The minimum schedule length is equal to $C_{\max}(\tau, j) = p_j + \max_{k=1}^{|N(\tau,j)|}(\theta(k) + \sum_{l=1}^{k-1} p_l)$. Hence, $\theta(j) = \arg\min_\tau\{\tau : C_{\max}(\tau, j) \leq \tau\}$, where $\arg\min_x\{f(x) : y\}$ is the smallest $x$ which minimizes $f(x)$ under conditions $y$.

The tasks which are in the set $N(\theta_j, j)$ constitute a cluster together with $T_j$, for all $T_j \in \mathcal{T}$. Clusters are scheduled as early as possible on their own processors. Tasks $T_k$ in a cluster are executed in the order of decreasing $\theta(k) - p_k$.

**Giroudeau, König, Moulaï and Palaysi Expansion Heuristic [45]** This heuristic solves problem $P\infty|prec, p_j = 1, c \geq 2|C_{max}$ with performance ratio at most $\frac{2(c+1)}{3}$. Here Munier and König heuristic [88] presented above is used for the same task graph and communication delays $c = 1$. Then, starting times of the tasks are multiplied by $\frac{c+1}{2}$ to obtain feasible starting times of the task in problem $P\infty|prec, p_j = 1, c \geq 2|C_{max}$. Processor assignments remain unchanged.

### 6.6.4 Heuristics Without a Guarantee

In this section, we present selected clustering heuristics for scheduling on unlimited processor number without task duplication.

**Mobility-Directed Scheduling (MD) [124]** The algorithm starts with the calculation of the earliest starting times $est(j)$, latest starting times $lst(j)$, and relative mobility $rm(j) = \frac{lst(j) - est(j)}{p_j}$, for all the tasks as if they were executed in unit clusters.

Tasks are assigned to clusters in the order of increasing relative mobility. Let $T_j$ be the currently examined task. Let $k$ be a cluster comprising tasks $T_a, \ldots, T_b$, where $est(a) \leq est(a+1) \leq \cdots \leq est(b)$. Task $T_j$ can be assigned to cluster $k$ if its interval $[est(j, k), lst(j, k) + p_j]$ does not intersect with similar intervals of the tasks already assigned to the cluster. If interval $[est(j, k), lst(j, k) + p_j]$ intersects with some of the intervals of tasks $T_a, \ldots, T_b$, then it is verified if $T_a, \ldots, T_b$, and $T_j$ can be executed together. If there exists a task $T_i, a \leq i \leq b + 1$, for which inequality

$$\max\{est(j, k), est(i - 1) + p_{i-1}\} + p_j \leq \min\{lst(j, k) + p_j, lst(i)\} \quad (6.14)$$

is satisfied, then $T_j$ is inserted before the first task $T_i$ for which the inequality holds, and the $est(j)$ is set to $\max\{est(j, k), est(i - 1) + p_{i-1}\}$. In inequality (6.14) it is assumed that $est(a - 1) + p_{a-1} = 0$ and $lst(b + 1) = \infty$. $T_j$ cannot be inserted in an interval after its successor or before its predecessor. If the gap before $T_i$ results in such a violation of the precedence constraints then the next interval satisfying (6.14) is searched for. If $T_j$ cannot be assigned to the first cluster, then it is checked if the assignment to the second cluster is possible, and so on until finding a feasible cluster. In the boundary case a unit cluster is created for $T_j$. After assigning $T_j$ to a particular cluster the weights of the arcs between tasks $T_a, \ldots, T_b$ and $T_j$ are zeroed. Arcs $(T_{i-1}, T_j), (T_j, T_{i+1})$ with weight 0 are added. The values of earliest starting times and latest starting times are recalculated for the tasks which still need to be assigned. The complexity of this algorithm is $O(n^3)$.

**Dynamic Critical Path (DCP) [72]** This algorithm builds linear clusters using similar ideas to the above MD heuristic.

The earliest and the latest starting times are calculated after each clustering operation taking into account current set of communications and the resulting delays.

Tasks are analyzed in the order of increasing $lst(j) - est(j)$, ties are broken in favor of the tasks with smaller $est(j)$. Initially each task is in an unexamined unit cluster. After examining a task its unit cluster is merged with some other cluster or it is moved to a set of already examined unit clusters. Tasks which are not on the critical path may be inserted into any examined cluster. Tasks which are on the critical path are inserted only into the clusters which comprise their predecessors or their successors. To feasibly insert a task into some cluster condition (6.14) must be satisfied. Moreover, tasks which are not critical are not allowed to change the earliest starting times of the tasks which are already examined. If no cluster exists into which a task can be inserted, then it remains in a unit cluster. If there is more than one possible cluster assignment, then its critical successor is taken into account. A critical successor has minimum difference between the latest and the earliest starting times. For example, let $T_j$ be the currently analyzed task, and let $T_k$ have minimum value of $lst(k) - est(k)$ among successors of $T_j$. For $T_j$ cluster $i$ is chosen for which the sum of $est(j, i) + est(k, i)$ is minimum. In an alternative version [4] a critical successor is task $T_k$ which has the longest communication time $c_{jk}$. The complexity of this algorithm is $O(n^2(n + |\mathcal{A}|))$.

**Clustering And Scheduling System-II (CASS2) [82]**  The algorithm computes clusters by examining the task graph bottom-up, i.e. from the exit nodes toward the entry nodes.

The algorithm starts with the calculation of $est(j)$ assuming that each task is in a unit cluster. To control clustering, CASS2 calculates functions $f$ and $l$ for the tasks. Let $f(j) = p_j$ for the exit tasks $T_j$. Each exit task is comprised in a unit cluster. The *examined* tasks have their $f(j)$ and cluster assignment determined. The tasks with all their successors examined will be called *current*. For each current task $T_i$ value of $f$ is tentatively set to $f(i) = p_i + \max_{j \in succ(i)}\{f(j) + c_{ij}\}$. The successor $T_k$ which determines the value of $f(i)$ is called a *dominant successor* of $T_i$. A single task may be a dominant successor of many tasks. Let $head(k)$ be the first task in the cluster comprising task $T_k$. Value $l(i) = est(i) + f(i)$ is calculated for each current task. Current tasks $T_i$ are ordered according to nonincreasing values of $l(i)$. For this purpose a priority queue is used in CASS2 [82]. Let $T_i$ be the current task with the highest value of $l(i)$. $T_i$ is examined for the assignment at the head of its dominant successor cluster. Thus, for $T_i$ the value of function $f$ would be set to $f'(i) = p_i + f(head(k))$. If $f'(i) > f(i)$ then $T_i$ is placed in a unit cluster, and $f(i)$ remains unchanged. Otherwise ($f'(i) \leq f(i)$), $T_i$ is put at the head of its dominant successor cluster, and $f(i)$ is set to $f'(i)$. This procedure stops after determining $f$ and clusters for all the tasks. The complexity of CASS2 is $O(|\mathcal{A}| + n \log n)$.

An example of applying CASS2 is shown in Fig. 6.21. For the instance in Fig. 6.21a two solutions may be built by CASS2. After clustering $T_6$, with $T_8$, task $T_2$ has $f(2) = 7, est(2) = 5, l(2) = 12$, and task $T_7$ has $f(7) = 4, est() = 8$, $l(7) = 12$. If $T_7$ is chosen as this step as the most critical task, then the solution in Fig. 6.21c and d is built. If $T_2$ is chosen, then the solution in Fig. 6.21e and f is built.

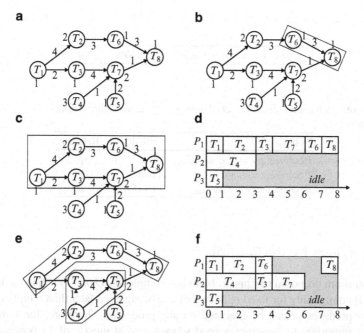

**Fig. 6.21** Example of clustering by CASS2 algorithm. (**a**) Initial task graph. (**b**) The pivotal step. (**c**) Clustering for solution 1, $T_4$, $T_5$ are in unit clusters. (**d**) Schedule for solution 1. (**e**) Clustering for solution 2, $T_5$ is in a unit cluster. (**f**) Schedule for solution 2

## 6.7 Unlimited Processor Number and Duplication

In this section, we examine scheduling with communication delays with nonrestrictive processor number and allowed task duplication.

### 6.7.1 Hard Cases

The results on the hardness of scheduling with communication delays on systems with not limiting processor number and allowed task duplication are shown in Table 6.9.

### 6.7.2 Polynomial Cases

The results on polynomially solvable cases of scheduling with communication delays are collected in Table 6.10. Problems mentioned in the above table are outlined below.

**Table 6.9**  Hardness of scheduling with communication delays, $m = \infty$ with duplication

| Problem | Result | Reference |
|---|---|---|
| $P\infty\|prec, p_j = 1, c > 1, dup\|C_{\max}$ | sNPh | [90] |

**Table 6.10**  Polynomial cases of scheduling with communications delays, $m = \infty$ with duplication

| Problem | Result | Reference |
|---|---|---|
| $P\infty\|prec, p_j = 1, c, dup\|C_{\max}$ | $O(n^{c+1})$ | [65] |
| $P\infty\|prec, sct, dup\|C_{\max}$ | $O(n^2)$ | [31] |
| $P\infty\|out\text{-}tree, c_{ij}, dup\|C_{\max}$ | $O(n^2)$ | [5,28] |

## $P\infty\|prec, p_j = 1, c, dup\|C_{\max}$ [65]

The algorithm proposed for this problem has complexity $O(n^{c+1})$ which means that it is polynomial only for fixed $c$. Note that a task executed later than $c$ units of time after its predecessor can be executed on any processor. Therefore, for some task $T_j$, it is important to construct a good sequence of at most $c$ of $T_j$ predecessors. Let us assume that task indices correspond with the topological order in $\mathcal{A}$, and the shortest schedules $\mathcal{S}_{j-1}$ for tasks $T_1, \ldots, T_{j-1}$ are already generated. The idea of the dynamic programming algorithm proposed in [65] is to analyze all possible extensions of $\mathcal{S}_{j-1}$ by sequences of at most $c$ tasks preceding $T_j$ which are feasible in $\mathcal{A}$, and selecting the ones with the earliest starting time of $T_j$.

## $P\infty\|prec, sct, dup\|C_{\max}$ [31]

The notation of the problem is slightly more demanding than necessary because in the current problem it is precisely required that communication times satisfy $\forall\, T_j, \min_{\{i \in pred(j)\}}\{p_i\} \geq \max_{\{i \in pred(j)\}}\{c_{ij}\}$. This is actually a weaker requirement than for small communication times (*sct*) case.

The algorithm proceeds in two steps. In the first one the earliest starting times are calculated for the tasks. The tasks without predecessors have their earliest starting times equal to 0. Let $T_j$ be a task which all predecessors have the earliest starting times calculated. Let $k = \arg\max_i\{est(i) + p_i + c_{ij} : i \in pred(j)\}$, where $\arg\max_x\{f(x) : y\}$ is the smallest $x$ which maximizes $f(x)$ under conditions $y$. The earliest starting time of $T_j$ is

$$est(j) = \max\{est(k) + p_k, \max_i\{est(i) + p_i + c_{ij} : T_i \in pred(j) - \{T_k\}\}\} \quad (6.15)$$

From the method of calculating $est(j)$ it can be concluded that at most one predecessor of task $T_j$ can satisfy condition $est(k) + p_k + c_{kj} > est(j)$. If the condition

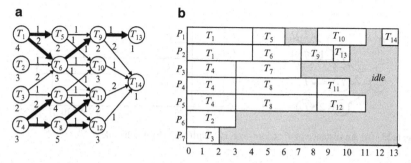

**Fig. 6.22** (**a**) Exemplary instance of $P\infty|prec, sct, dup|C_{max}$. Processing times and communication delays are shown by the task nodes and arcs, respectively. Bold arcs are critical. (**b**) A schedule

is satisfied, then arc $(T_k, T_j)$ is called critical, and tasks $T_k, T_j$ must be executed on the same processor. Moreover, since there is only one predecessor which may be on a critical arc, the set of all critical arcs forms an out-forest. A path in such an out-forest is identified by its leaf.

In the second step of the algorithm each critical path is executed on a separate processor, the remaining tasks are started at their earliest starting times on free processors. The number of used processors is at most $n$, and the complexity of the algorithm is $O(n^2)$. Example of applying the above algorithm is shown in Fig. 6.22.

The conditions of the optimality of the schedules built by the above algorithm have been extended in [17]. Let tasks $T_j, T_k$ be defined as in Eq. (6.15), and let $T_l$ be the task for which $\max_i\{est(i) + p_i + c_{ij} : T_i \in pred(j) - \{T_k\}\}$ is maximum in Eq. (6.15). The above algorithm builds optimum schedules also if $p_k \geq c_{lj} + \max\{0, est(l) - est(k)\}$ is satisfied when $est(j)$ is calculated. Another condition of optimality is based on the idea of calculating the earliest starting time in Papadimitriou–Yannakakis heuristic [90] (see Sect. 6.7.3 for definitions and notation). If $C_{max}(est(j) - 1, j) \geq est(j)$, where $est(j)$ is calculated in Eq. (6.15), then again the schedule is optimum.

The current scheduling problem $P\infty|prec, sct, dup|C_{max}$ is also solved by the PLW algorithm [89] (cf. Sect. 6.7.3). In publication [30] it has been also shown that in a system with a complete interconnection network (clique) the above algorithm guarantees contention-free message scheduling if $\forall T_j, \min_{\{i \in succ(j)\}}\{p_i\} \geq \max_{\{k \in succ(j) - \{i\}\}}\{c_{jk}\}$, which is satisfied in the $sct$ case as defined in Sect. 6.3.

## $P\infty|out\text{-}tree, c_{ij}, dup|C_{max}$ [28]

Without loss of generality let us assume that $T_1 \rightarrow T_2 \rightarrow \cdots \rightarrow T_j$ is a path in the out-tree. The earliest starting time of $T_j$ is $est(j) = \sum_{k=1}^{j-1} p_k$. A schedule which achieves this lower bound for each task $T_j$ is constructed by duplicating tasks on all paths from the root to any leaf. Note that communication delays are meaningless in this special case. The complexity of the algorithm is $O(n^2)$ because

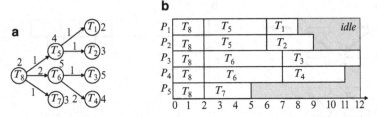

**Fig. 6.23** (a) An instance of $P\infty|out\text{-}tree, c_{ij}, dup|C_{max}$. (b) A schedule

**Table 6.11** Approximability of scheduling with communication delays, $m = \infty$ with duplication

| Problem | Result | Reference |
|---|---|---|
| $P\infty|prec, c_{j*}, dup|C_{max}$ | $R_{PY} \leq 2$ | [90] |
| $P\infty|prec, c_{ij}, dup|C_{max}$ | $R_{PLW} \leq 1 + \frac{1}{1+g(\mathcal{T},\mathcal{A})}$ | [89] |

at most $n$ paths of $O(n)$ tasks must be built. Example of applying this algorithm is shown in Fig. 6.23. This problem is also solved by algorithm CPFD [5] presented in Sect. 6.7.4.

### 6.7.3  Heuristics with a Guarantee

The results on approximability of scheduling with communication delays are collected in Table 6.11. Below we present the algorithms mentioned in the above table.

**Papadimitriou and Yannakakis Heuristic (PY) [90]** This algorithm starts with the calculation of the estimate of the task earliest starting times which is done in the following way.

For all tasks without predecessors set earliest starting times equal to 0. Now consider task $T_j$ which all predecessors have their earliest starting times already established. For each ancestor $T_{i_a}$ (not necessarily immediate) compute $f(i_a) = est(i_a) + p_{i_a} + c_{i_a j}$, and sort them according to the nonincreasing order of $f$: $f(i_1) \geq f(i_2) \geq \cdots$. Suppose task $T_j$ is about to be started by time $\tau$. Then the ancestors with $f(i) > \tau$ must be scheduled on the same processor as $T_j$. Let $N(\tau, j)$ be the subgraph of the task graph including all the tasks $T_i$ such that $f(i) > \tau$, and there is a path from $T_i$ to $T_j$ containing only tasks in $N(\tau, j)$. Let us assume that $|N(\tau, j)| = k$. All the tasks in $N(\tau, j)$ must be scheduled on the same processor as $T_j$ before $\tau$. Verifying feasibility of such a schedule is equivalent to scheduling problem $1|prec, r_j|C_{max}$, where $est(i)$ corresponds to the ready time for $T_i \in N(\tau, j)$. Here a feasible schedule exists if $C_{max}(\tau, j) = \max_{i=1}^{k}\{est(i) + \sum_{l=1}^{k} p_l\} \leq \tau$. Thus, $est(j) = \arg\min_{\tau}\{\tau : C_{max}(\tau, j) \leq \tau\}$, where $\arg\min_x\{f(x) : y\}$ is the smallest $x$ which minimizes $f(x)$ under conditions $y$. Tasks in $N(\tau, j)$ are executed on the same processor as $T_j$. The remaining predecessors of $T_j$ are executed on other processors.

It can be shown that $T_j$ can be feasibly started by $2est(j)$. Thus, the required worst-case performance ratio is achieved by starting $T_j$ by $2est(j)$, for $j = 1, \ldots, n$.

**Palis, Liou, and Wei Heuristic (PLW) [89]** This algorithm builds clusters for each task $T_j$ using a lower bound on the task earliest start time $lb\_est(j)$ as a guide.

The values $lb\_est(j)$ are calculated by selecting tasks $T_j$ in the topological order. For the entry tasks $lb\_est(j) = 0$. Now consider some task $T_j$ which is not an entry node and its cluster comprising $\{T_{i_1}, \ldots, T_{i_k}\}$ a subset of $T_j$ ancestors. Tasks $T_{i_1}, \ldots, T_{i_k}$ have their $lb\_est$ values already calculated. Similarly to the above PY method assume that task $lb\_est(i_i), \ldots, lb\_est(i_k)$ are equivalent to ready times. Determining the earliest start time of $T_j$, which must be executed after tasks $T_{i_1}, \ldots, T_{i_k}$, is equivalent to solving problem $1|in\text{-}tree, r_j|C_{\max}$. This can be done in $O(n)$ time. Let us denote by $lb1\_est(j)$ the value of $T_j$ calculated in the above way. If some task $T_i$ in the cluster has a predecessor $T_l$ outside the cluster, then it can be started no earlier than by $lb\_est(l) + p_l + c_{li}$. Let $lb2\_est(j)$ be the maximum of the values calculated in this way for all tasks in the cluster including $T_j$. If $lb2\_est(j) > lb1\_est(j)$ then there is a chance that including more tasks to the cluster of $T_j$ will reduce the start time of $T_j$. Thus, the cluster of $T_j$ is extended by considering the predecessors of the tasks already included in the cluster. The predecessors are selected in an arbitrary order. If after including in the cluster some task $T_h$ from outside the cluster condition $lb2\_est(j) > lb1\_est(j)$ is still satisfied, then the extension process is continued, otherwise it stops. The lower bound $lb\_est(j)$ is the smallest of the values $lb2\_est(j)$, $lb1\_est(j)$ obtained in the course of cluster building.

Note that as a result of the above procedure each task has its own cluster. This may result in excessive task duplication. To limit the excessive duplication, only clusters which comprise unique copies of some tasks are executed. To determine the necessary clusters the task graph is searched from the exit tasks toward the entry tasks. The clusters of the exit tasks are included in the schedule, and all their tasks are marked as scheduled. Now the algorithm proceeds to the predecessors from the outside of the just analyzed cluster. If the predecessor is not marked as scheduled, then its whole cluster is included in the schedule and its tasks are marked as scheduled. This process is continued until marking all tasks as scheduled. Eventually, each cluster included in the final solution is executed as early as possible on its own processor. The complexity of the algorithm is $O(n(n\log n + |\mathcal{A}|))$.

It can be shown that for granularity satisfying condition $g(\mathcal{T}, \mathcal{A}) \geq \frac{1-\varepsilon}{\varepsilon}$ the actual start time of task $T_j$ is not later than $(1 + \varepsilon)lb\_est(j)$. The constraint on granularity can be reformulated to $\varepsilon \geq \frac{1}{1+g(\mathcal{T},\mathcal{A})}$. Hence, the worst-case performance ratio is $1 + \frac{1}{1+g(\mathcal{T},\mathcal{A})}$ if $\varepsilon$ satisfies the former inequality as an equation. This algorithm can be applied in scheduling trees without duplication [89].

### 6.7.4 Heuristics Without a Guarantee

Here we present selected heuristics for scheduling on unlimited processor number with task duplication.

**Linear Clustering with Task Duplication (LCTD) [107]** This algorithm combines linear clustering (LC) introduced in Sect. 6.6.3 with duplication.

LCTD constructs a set of linear clusters as in LC heuristic and assigns each cluster to an individual processor. In the next step tasks in each cluster are examined in the topological order. Let $T_j$ be the currently analyzed task. The predecessors of $T_j$ which are out of the current cluster are examined for duplication on the current cluster. The predecessor of $T_j$ which duplication results in the largest reduction of the starting time of $T_j$ is indeed duplicated in the current cluster. This step is repeated as long as there are parents of $T_j$ which duplication on the current cluster reduces start time of $T_j$. Then the algorithm proceeds to the next task, and after examining all tasks in the cluster, to the next cluster.

Though LCTD is declared in [107] as a heuristic for unbounded number of processor it has one more step which optimizes processor usage. The algorithm attempts merging pairs of cluster. The merging must observe task topological order and earliest starting times. If schedule length is not increased by merging two clusters then the new combined cluster is accepted in the schedule. It is suggested to try merging clusters which are assigned to the neighboring processors in the interconnection network. If the interconnection is a clique then merging all pairs of processors is attempted. The sequence of merging operations is not determined in [107]. The complexity of LCTD can be bounded by $O(n^3 \log n)$.

**Critical Path Fast Duplication (CPFD) [3,5]** This heuristic improves DSH (see in Sect. 6.5.3) by using duplication focused around the critical path and the paths leading to the critical path. The elements of CPFD will be presented now in the bottom-up fashion.

A very important parent of task $T_j$, when executed on processor $P_i$, is a task in $pred(j)$ whose message arrives to $T_j$ as the last one. The very important parent will be denoted $VIP(j, i)$, and the time when the message arrived will be denoted $dat(j, i)$. Note that $est(j, i)$ may be determined not by the communication delay from $VIP(j, i)$ but by the time when tasks on $P_i$ scheduled before $T_j$ are finished.

Duplication rule $DR(j, i)$ is a procedure verifying if the very important predecessors of task $T_j$ can be duplicated on processor $P_i$ without deteriorating schedule quality. Let $\tau_k$, for $k = 1, \ldots, n_i$ denote the start times of tasks already assigned to processor $P_i$. To insert task $T_j$ on $P_i$ a free interval of length at least $p_j$ must exist on $P_i$. This is verified by formula

$$\tau_{k+1} - \max\{\tau_k + p_k, dat(j, i)\} \geq p_j \tag{6.16}$$

where $k = 0, \ldots, n_i$, $\tau_0 + p_0 = 0, \tau_{n_i+1} = \infty$. If (6.16) is satisfied for some $k$, then $T_j$ can be inserted after the $k$th task on $P_i$. Observe that this is slightly reformulated condition used in the algorithm MD (cf. Sect. 6.6.4, and inequality

(6.14)). The earliest start time of $T_j$ on $P_i$ is $est(j,i) = \max\{dat(j,i), \tau_{k'} + p_{k'}\}$, where $k'$ is the minimum $k$ satisfying (6.16). Inequality (6.16) is always satisfied for $k = n_i$ but it is not always equivalent to a feasible schedule. If task $T_j$ is a predecessor of some task $T_l$ considered for execution on $P_i$, $T_j$ is considered for duplication on $P_i$, then such duplication is possible only if $T_j$ can be finished before $T_l$, i.e. $est(j,i) + p_j < est(l,i)$. If this condition is not satisfied then we assume $est(j,i) = \infty$. The $DR(j,i)$ proceeds as follows. The value of $est(j,i)$ and $VIP(j,i)$ is determined. If $est(j,i) = \infty$, or $VIP(j,i)$ does not exist or is executed on $P_i$ then $est(j,i)$ cannot be reduced by duplication of $VIP(j,i)$ on $P_i$. Otherwise, attempt inserting $VIP(j,i)$ on $P_i$. If $est(j,i)$ does not increase then $VIP(j,i)$ is recorded on the duplication node list $DNL(j,i)$, $VIP(j,i)$ substitutes the role of $T_j$, and the procedure is recursively repeated for the very important parent of $VIP(j,i)$.

Procedure attempt duplication $AD(j)$ checks the possibility of scheduling task $T_j$ with duplication of its predecessors. The processors running the immediate predecessors of $T_j$ and one unused processor are tested for scheduling $T_j$. Duplication rule $DR(j,i)$ is applied to all such processors $P_i$ and task $T_j$. The results of speculative duplication for processor $P_{i'}$ providing the smallest $est(j,i')$ are instantiated. This means that all the task duplicates specified on $DNL(j,i')$ are scheduled on $P_{i'}$ as planned in procedure $DR(j,i')$. Note that in a special case a task without a predecessor is scheduled on its own processor at time 0.

Procedure trace ancestor $TR(j)$ recursively traverses the task graph from the current task $T_j$ via its unscheduled parents toward the entry tasks. The recursion stops in the task without unscheduled immediate predecessors. On recovering from the recursion procedure $AD(j)$ is called. Thus, due to the recursion all the predecessors of $T_j$ are already scheduled, and $T_j$ is also scheduled before returning from $TR(j)$.

An out-branch node (OBN) is a task which is neither on the critical path, nor is it on any path of the task graph ending in a critical task. OBN binding is a procedure assigning numbers to the OBN tasks according to the topological order.

Algorithm CPFD is integrating all the above elements. A critical path in the task graph is calculated assuming that tasks are executed on different processors (consequently, all communication delays are included). Ties are broken in favor of paths with greater sum of processing times. Procedure $TR(j)$ is applied to the tasks of the critical path in the order of their precedence. Thus, after examining all the tasks of the critical path, their predecessors are also scheduled. The remaining tasks are OBNs. The OBN binding is performed, and procedure $TR(j)$ is applied to the OBN tasks according to their numbers obtained in OBN binding. The complexity of the CPFD is $O(\max_j\{indeg(j)\}|\mathcal{A}|n^2)$, where $indeg(j)$ is the biggest in-degree in the task graph. A version of the current algorithm called ECPFD has been proposed for limited number of processors in [5]. An example of using CPFD is shown in Fig. 6.24.

**Duplication First Reduction Next (DFRN) [91]** DFRN first orders tasks according to the increasing distance in arcs (hops) from the entry tasks in the task graph. Tasks with equal distance are ordered according to the nonincreasing processing times. Let $VIP(j)$ for task $T_j$ be its immediate predecessor $T_i$ from which the

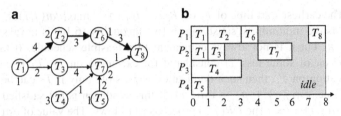

**Fig. 6.24** Example of scheduling with duplication by CPFD algorithm. (**a**) Input task graph. Thick arrows indicate the critical path. (**b**) A schedule

message arrives as the last one assuming that $T_j, T_i$ are executed on different processors. A task is called a *join* node if it has more than one predecessor.

Let us assume that $T_j$ is the currently analyzed task. Its $VIP(j)$, and processor $proc(VIP(j))$ executing $VIP(j)$ are identified. Suppose $T_j$ is not a join node, then two cases may happen:

(a) If $VIP(j)$ is the last task scheduled on $proc(VIP(j))$, then $T_j$ is scheduled on $proc(VIP(j))$ immediately after $VIP(j)$.

(b) If $VIP(j)$ is not the last task scheduled on $proc(VIP(j))$, then the part of the schedule from time 0 to the completion of $VIP(j)$ is copied from $proc(VIP(j))$ to an unused processor, and $T_j$ is scheduled immediately after its predecessor.

Suppose $T_j$ is a join node. Again two cases were distinguished:

(a) If $VIP(j)$ is the last task on $proc(VIP(j))$, then procedure $dfrn(proc(VIP(j)), j)$ is called (explained in the following text).

(b) If $VIP(j)$ is not the last task on its processor, then the part of the schedule on $proc(VIP(j))$ is copied from time 0 to the end of $VIP(j)$ to an unused processor $P_b$. Then procedure $dfrn(b, j)$ is called.

Procedure $dfrn(x, y)$ first greedily duplicates predecessors of $T_y$ on processor $P_x$ and then removes unnecessary duplicates. More precisely, it has two subroutines $try\_duplication(x, y)$ and $try\_deletion(x, y)$. In $try\_duplication(x, y)$ all the predecessors $T_a$ of $T_y$ are analyzed in the order of decreasing $mat(a, y)$. Here $mat(a, y)$ is the arrival time of the message from $T_a$ to $T_y$. If $proc(a) = proc(y)$ then $mat(a, y)$ is the completion time $c_a$ of $T_a$, otherwise it is $c_a + c_{ay}$. If $T_a$ is not executed on $P_x$ then $try\_duplication(x, a)$ is called recursively. Otherwise (all predecessors of $T_y$ are already on $P_x$), $T_y$ is scheduled as the last task on $P_x$. Procedure $try\_deletion(x, y)$ removes from $P_x$ any task $T_i$ satisfying one of the two conditions:

(1) Completion time of task $T_i$ on $P_x$ is greater than message arrival time $mat(i, l)$ from some other copy of $T_i$ not executed on $P_x$, $T_l$ is a successor of $T_i$ present on $P_x$.

(2) Let $T_l$ be the tasks for which $mat(T_l, T_y)$ is the second biggest message arrival time of $T_y$. Remove task $T_i$ if the completion time of $T_i$ on $P_x$ is greater than $mat(T_l, T_y)$. Note that in this case $VIP(y), T_y$ are already on the same processor $P_x$, and executing some task beyond the second latest arrival time of a message to $T_y$ is counterproductive.

The complexity of DFRN is $O(n^3)$. There is a modification of DFRN called Scalable scheduling DFRN (SDFRN) which works for a limited number of processors. The modification consists in copying parts of the schedule used in the above cases (b) only if an unused processor is still available. Otherwise the examined task is treated as in cases (a).

## 6.8  Scheduling in Processor Networks

Heuristics presented in this section take into account some information on the underlaying communication network. This can be done in various ways. For example, message routing is usually handled by a separate heuristic which provides just communication delay values. Heuristic DLS [108] introduced in Sect. 6.4.4 can be adjusted to the underlying communication network when provided with network-dependent communication delays. Similar idea is used in [111] where list scheduling is combined with communication delays resulting from message routing. Another approach is to limit the set of candidate processors for scheduling a task to the processors executing the immediate predecessors of the task and their neighboring processors. This idea is used in heuristic SD [16]. Other heuristics go beyond this simple network perception and rely even more on the information on the underlaying communication subsystem. Below we present examples of the heuristics for scheduling task graphs in arbitrary interconnection networks.

**Mapping Heuristic (MH) [39]**  MH combines greedy scheduling based on the earliest starting times and adaptive routing in a heterogeneous system with arbitrary interconnection network.

It is assumed that processors are uniform (cf. Sect. 4.1). For $(T_i \rightarrow T_j) \in \mathcal{A}$ let $\alpha(i, j)$ denote the amount of data sent from task $T_i$ to task $T_j$. For a pair of processors $P_k$, $P_l$ we will denote by $hop(k, l)$ the number of hops on the path from $P_k$ to $P_l$. Let $C$ be the inverse of bandwidth and $S$ the communication start-up time in the communication between two neighboring processors (cf. Eq. (3.1)). The communication delay $c_{ijkl}$ incurred by precedence $(T_i \rightarrow T_j) \in \mathcal{A}$ when tasks $T_i$, $T_j$ are executed on processors $P_k$, $P_l$, respectively, is equal to

$$c_{ijkl} = (\alpha(i, j)C + S)hop(k, l) + D(k, l) \tag{6.17}$$

The last term $D(k, l)$ approximates extension of the communication delay resulting from contention en route.

The scheduling part assigns the tasks with all predecessors scheduled to the processor which guarantees the earliest starting time considering communication delays from the predecessors. If there is more than one ready task then the ready tasks are ordered according to decreasing level primarily and to decreasing number of successors secondarily. Two versions of level ordering were proposed: one using static levels and one assuming that all tasks are on different yet neighboring processors.

The adaptive routing part of *MH* communicates with the scheduling part via component $D(k, l)$ of the communication delay (6.17). The information about the routing status is held in a routing table. An entry $(k, l)$ for a route from $P_k$ to $P_l$ has three fields:

$hop(k, l)$ – The number of hops on the path from $P_k$, to $P_l$, initially it is the length of the shortest path in hops from $P_k$ to $P_l$

$L(k, l)$ – The first processor on the path from $P_k$ to $P_l$

$D(k, l)$ – Communication delay due to contention initially equals 0

When a message from $T_i$ on $P_k$ is sent to $T_j$ on $P_l$, then $D(k, l)$ is increased by $(\alpha(i, j) + S)hop(k, l)$. Similarly, for all processors $P_a$ on the route from $P_k$ to $P_l$ the delay due to contention $D(a, l)$ is increased by $(\alpha(i, j) + S)hop(a, l)$. While the message is in transit, the communication delays are different than expected for empty network. Therefore, all neighbors of the just established path recalculate the shortest paths to other processors assuming that $D(a, b)$ is the length of the route from $P_a$ to $P_b$. Consequently, new routes may be established which results in modifications of $hop(a, b)$, $L(a, b)$, $D(a, b)$ in the routing table. When the communication delay of the message expires, then all $D(a, l)$ are decreased by $(\alpha(i, j) + S)hop(a, l)$. This is applied to $D(k, l)$, too. What is more, the neighbors of the released communication path again recalculate the cheapest routes to other processors.

Observe that the method of calculating $c_{ijkl}$ in Eq. (6.17) gives only some approximation of the communication delay because it is not aware of the time remaining to the end of the contending communication. For example, suppose that $T_i$, $T_j$ established a path without contention from $P_k$ to $P_l$ at time $\tau_1$. Then $D(k, l)$ is set to $c_{ijkl}$ for the whole interval $[\tau_1, \tau_1 + c_{ijkl})$. If the same path is to be used at time $\tau_2 \in [\tau_1, \tau_1 + c_{ijkl})$, then component $D(k, l)$ in Eq. (6.17) is invariant no matter how close $\tau_2$ is to $\tau_1 + c_{ijkl}$. This simplification was a design choice made in [39] to reduce the complexity of the algorithm.

**Bubble Scheduling and Allocation (BSA) [73]** In the first step a sequence of the tasks is constructed. A critical path is calculated assuming that all tasks are executed on different processors. The first position in the sequence is assigned to the first task on the critical path. The tasks of the critical path are examined in the topological order. If the current critical task $T_j$ has all parents already in the sequence, then it is appended at the end of the sequence. Otherwise (some parents are not in the sequence yet), the algorithm recursively traverses the task graph backward until all ancestors of $T_j$ are numbered and in the sequence. Thus, if $T_i \in pred(j)$ is not in the sequence, then the backward search is started in $T_i$ and then $T_i$ is appended to the sequence. Finally, when all the predecessors of $T_j$ are in the sequence also $T_j$ is appended. The remaining tasks, which are neither critical nor on any path leading to a critical task, are appended in a topological order at the end of the sequence. Note that the same method of sequencing tasks was used in heuristics DPS [92] (in Sect. 6.4.4), CPFD [5] (Sect. 6.7.4).

In the second step the above sequence of all tasks is assigned to a processor called a *pivot* processor. The processor with the greatest number of communication ports is selected as the pivot processor.

In the next step tasks are moved from the pivot processor to the further processors in an attempt of reducing schedule length. Processors are examined in the breadth-first order conforming with growing distance in communication links (hops) from the pivot processor. If the starting time $\tau_j$ of some task $T_j$ on the currently analyzed processor $P_i$ is greater than the $est(j, i)$, then $T_j$ is considered for execution on a different processor. If there is an unexamined processor $P_h$ adjacent to $P_i$ for which $est(j, h) < \tau_j$ then $T_j$ is moved to $P_h$. If $est(j, h) \geq \tau_j$ but a parent of $T_j$ whose message arrives to $T_j$ as the last one is executed on $P_h$ then $T_j$ is moved to $P_h$.

In determining $est(j, h)$ two elements are taken into account. The messages of length $c_{ij}$ from some $T_i \in pred(j)$ executed on some processor $P_l$ are scheduled on communication links as on resources analogous to processors. The method of determining the earliest starting time for communication $T_i \rightarrow T_j$ on communication link $P_l - P_h$ and for execution of $T_j$ on $P_h$ is analogous to inserting a task in a cluster of tasks in method MD (cf. Sect. 6.6.4 and inequality (6.14)). More precisely, a time slot is searched for in which communication $T_i \rightarrow T_j$ can be inserted into the sequence of communications on the link $P_l - P_h$ without violating the feasibility of the schedule for the already assigned communications and without increasing the earliest starting times of other tasks. The latest arrival time of the messages for $T_j$ on $P_h$ is the beginning of the interval in which executing $T_j$ on $P_h$ is possible. Then, the same method is used to find the earliest time slot for $T_j$ between the tasks already assigned to $P_h$ without violating their schedule. The beginning of this time slot is $est(j, h)$. The complexity of BSA is $O(m^2 n|\mathcal{A}|)$.

## 6.9 Scheduling in *Log P* Model

In this section, we examine scheduling under *LogP* model. This model of a distributed system has been introduced in Sect. 6.2.2. Here we first formalize requirements for the schedule feasibility, and slightly extend the $\alpha|\beta|\gamma$ notation to express scheduling model concisely. Then, complexity results and approximation algorithms are presented.

### 6.9.1 Notation

#### 6.9.1.1 Feasible Schedule

As already mentioned in Sect. 6.2.2 communication overheads must be explicitly scheduled on the sender and the receiver processors. Therefore, the definition of a feasible schedule must be extended to include these operations. We will call *overhead tasks* the operations corresponding to the overheads at the sending and at the receiving side.

In some papers (e.g. [24,66]) it is allowed that messages had different overheads and/or latencies depending on the sender and the receiver. In other publications (e.g. [8]) it is advised to combine many short communications into a single long one to take advantage of shorter communication overheads. We will stick to the original assumption of [33] that all messages have length limited by some small constant. Greater amounts of data are transferred in multiple messages. The results obtained under different assumptions on the communication delay structure will be explicitly mentioned. In this section, $c_{ij}$ will denote here the number of messages sent from task $T_i$ to task $T_j$ whenever arc $T_i \rightarrow T_j$ exists in $\mathcal{A}$. If all tasks send the same number of messages, then this number will be denoted as $c$. Each message requires scheduling one overhead task at the sender and one at the receiver side. Let $proc(j)$ be the processor executing task $T_j$. Let *SEND* be the set of send operations defined as follows:

$$SEND = \{snd(i, j, k, q) : (T_i, T_j) \in \mathcal{A}, k = proc(i), 1 \leq q \leq c_{ij}\} \qquad (6.18)$$

where $snd(i, j, k, q)$ represents the $q$th overhead task corresponding to a message sent from task $T_i$ executed on processor $k$ to task $T_j$. Analogously, let *RECEIVE* be the set of all receive operations which are executed during the computation:

$$RECEIVE = \{rec(i, j, k, q) : (T_i, T_j) \in \mathcal{A}, k = proc(j), 1 \leq q \leq c_{ij}\} \qquad (6.19)$$

where $rec(i, j, k, q)$ is a receive operation defined analogously to $snd(i, j, k, q)$.

For simplicity of presentation let us assume that tasks are nonpreemptive. Let $\tau_j$ denote the time of starting task $T_j \in \mathcal{T}$, $\tau_{snd(i,j,k,l)}$ the start time of overhead task $snd(i, j, k, l) \in SEND$, $\tau_{rec(i,j,k,l)}$ the start time of overhead task $rec(i, j, k, l) \in RECEIVE$. A feasible schedule must satisfy all the standard requirements such as: no processor executes two or more tasks at the same time, each task is executed by only one processor (we have nonpreemptive schedule), all tasks must be fully executed. Assume that there is an arc $T_i \rightarrow T_j \in \mathcal{A}$, task $T_i$ is executed on processor $P_k$, and task $T_j$ is executed on $P_l \neq P_k$. Let us remind that length of the gap interval starts with the initiation of the overhead task. Beyond the standard conditions, it is required that

1. $\tau_{snd(i,j,k,q)} \geq \tau_i + p_i$, for $q = 1, \ldots, c_{ij}$
2. $\tau_{rec(i,j,l,q)} = \tau_{snd(i,j,k,q)} + o + L$, for $q = 1, \ldots, c_{ij}$
3. $\tau_{snd(i,j,k,q)} + \max\{o, g\} \leq \tau_{snd(i,j,k,q+1)}$, for $q = 1, \ldots, c_{ij} - 1$
4. $\tau_{rec(i,j,l,q)} + \max\{o, g\} \leq \tau_{rec(i,j,k,q+1)}$, for $q = 1, \ldots, c_{ij} - 1$
5. $\tau_j \geq \tau_{rec(i,j,l,c_{ij})} + o$

The first requirement decrees that send overhead be executed after the task that sends the message. The second condition states that the receive operation is started *exactly* $o + L$ units of time after its send operation. In some publications (e.g. [24])

this condition is relaxed and it is allowed that $\tau_{rec(i,j,l,q)} \geq \tau_{snd(i,j,k,q)} + o + L$. Note that this relaxation implicitly allows buffering arbitrary number of messages at the receiver side. The third and fourth requirements state that there is a sequence of send and receive operations which do not overlap. The fifth condition demands to start $T_j$ after all receive tasks involved in the communication from $T_i$ to $T_j$. We will say that above requirements define a *complete communication* from $T_i$ to $T_j$.

Let us now comment on the implications of the above definition of a feasible schedule. Note that tasks from $\mathcal{T}$ can be executed in the span of the gap $g$ between overhead tasks.

The existence of a sequence of $2c_{ij}$ overhead tasks for each arc $(T_i, T_j) \in \mathcal{A}$, where $c_{ij}$ is a number encoded in $O(\log c_{ij})$ bits, poses a question whether scheduling under *LogP* is in class **NP** at all. It will be assumed that $\forall (T_i, T_j) \in \mathcal{A}, c_{ij} \leq q(n, \log p_{max})$, where $q$ is a polynomial. This means that values $c_{ij}$ are bounded by a polynomial in the length of the input string, and the existence of the overhead tasks does not preclude constructing schedules in polynomial time.

Consider a broadcast communication in which some task $T_a$ distributes the same information to its successors $T_b, T_c$ which are assigned to the same processor $proc(b) = proc(c)$. Since send and receive operations defined in (6.18) and (6.19) require transferring a message from a task to a task it may seem that the same message is sent twice to $proc(b) = proc(c)$. In such a case we assume that the message is sent from $proc(a)$ to $proc(b)$ only once, delivering data to two or more tasks if they are on the same processor. Consequently, the same pair of overhead tasks is used by the tasks receiving a broadcast from a different processor.

Let us observe that broadcast messages may be relayed between the processors. In other words, a broadcast message may be received not from the initiator but from some intermediate processor. This feature is called *forwarding* [127]. In the case of forwarding a receiving task $T_d$ may be started after a sequence of complete communications linking the broadcast initiator $T_a$ with $T_d$ via immediate successors of $T_a$. Unless stated otherwise, we assume that forwarding is not used.

If duplication is allowed then a copy of each task must receive the necessary data in complete communications from some copies of the predecessors.

### 6.9.1.2   More $\alpha|\beta|\gamma$ Notation

In this section, we extend the $\alpha|\beta|\gamma$ notation to quickly express scheduling problems in *LogP* model. Since the parameters $L, o, g$ represent the communication subsystem, and, more generally, to computing environment, we extend the first ($\alpha$) field.

The general form of the notation extension is $P(w, x, y)z$, where $w, x, y, z$ take the following values:

- $w \in \{L, number\}$ – Position $w$ represents latency, letter $L$ means that latency is given in the instance of the problem, *number* means that latency is fixed to value *number*.

- $x \in \{o, number\}$ – Position $x$ represents overhead, letter $o$ means that overhead is given in the instance of the problem, *number* means that overhead is fixed to value *number*.
- $y \in \{g, number\}$ – Position $y$ represents gap, letter $g$ means that gap is given in the instance of the problem, some *number* on position $y$ means that gap is equal to *number*.
- $z \in \{o, \infty, number, \}$ – Position $z$ represents processor number in a standard way for $\alpha|\beta|\gamma$ notation: $z = o$, where $o$ is a symbol representing empty place, means that processor number $m$ is given in the instance of the problem, $z = number$ means that $m$ is fixed to *number* for all instances of the problem, $z = \infty$ denotes unbounded processor number.

We allow for inserting simple conditions which must be satisfied by latency, overhead, gap, processor number in the $w, x, y, z$ positions. For example, prefix $P(L, o, g \geq o)| \ldots$ represents scheduling problems under the $LogP$ model where all communication delay parameters and processor numbers are given in the instances, but the duration of the gap must be at least as long as the overhead task. Prefix $P(2, 1, 1)\infty| \ldots$ represents the problems of scheduling with latency equal to 2 units of time, overhead and gap of one unit of time, and unlimited processor number.

Let us observe that broadcasting is possible if the same information is sent to all the recipients. Hence it is allowed in problems which have the same number of messages in all communications, or if the number of sent messages depends on the sender only. These cases are denoted $c$, or $c_{j*}$, in the $\beta$ field of the notation. It will be implicitly assumed that the scheduling problems with single level out-trees, a.k.a. fork graphs, and number of messages denoted $c$, or $c_{j*}$, involve broadcasting.

### 6.9.2  Hard Cases

The hard cases of scheduling under $LogP$ are listed in Table 6.12. The following special notations have been used:

- $1l.tree$ – A single level out- or in-tree
- $1l.in\text{-}tree$ – A single level in-tree, a.k.a. a *join* graph
- $1l.out\text{-}tree$ – A single level out-tree, a.k.a. a *fork* graph

**Table 6.12**  Hard problems of scheduling under $LogP$ model

| Problem | Result | Reference |
|---|---|---|
| $P(0, 0, g)\infty|1l.tree, c = 1|C_{max}$ | sNPh | [119, 121] |
| $P(0, 0, g)2|1l.in\text{-}tree, c = 1|C_{max}$ | sNPh | [127] |
| $P(0, o > 0, g)2|1l.out\text{-}tree, c = 1|C_{max}$ | NPh | [127] |

### 6.9.3 Polynomial Cases

The polynomially solvable problems of scheduling under $LogP$ are listed in Table 6.13. Symbol $(*)$ is used to note that forwarding is allowed. Let us observe that for the last two problems in the above table the string encoding task data have length $O(\log n)$ because it suffices to record task number $n$. Thus, the two last problems are polynomial in $n$, which is of necessary complexity to actually execute the tasks, but not in the length of the string encoding the instance. The algorithms for problems mentioned in Table 6.13 are outlined below.

$P(L, o, g) \infty | 1l.in\text{-}tree, p_j = p, c_{ij} | C_{\max}$ [120]

Let us assume that the root task is $T_n$ and it is executed on $P_1$, while the remaining tasks are ordered according to nondecreasing number of their messages: $c_{1n} \leq c_{2n} \leq \cdots \leq c_{n-1,n}$.

In the optimum schedule entry tasks with the shortest communications are executed on their own processors. Some entry tasks are executed on $P_1$ starting at time 0 without idle times. Then a sequence of receive operations is executed on $P_1$. The receive operations may be interleaved with other entry tasks. Finally, $T_n$ is executed as the last task. Let $n'$ be the number of entry tasks executed on their own processor, and let $k$ be the number of entry tasks executed between the receive operations. Schedule length is determined by $n'$ and $k$. Let us express schedule length as a function of $n'$ and $k$.

Tasks executed on processors different than $P_1$ require $C(n') = \sum_{j=1}^{n'} c_{jn}$ receive operations on $P_1$. Let $\alpha = \frac{\max\{o,g\}-o}{p}$. Between two consecutive receive operations $\lfloor \alpha \rfloor$ entry tasks can be executed without delaying the receive operations. Also no more than $\lceil \alpha \rceil$ entry tasks are executed between two consecutive receive operations, because any extra entry tasks can be scheduled at the beginning of the schedule without increasing makespan. If $k > (C(n') - 1)\lfloor \alpha \rfloor$, then the receive operations are delayed with respect to their earliest start time by $\delta(k) = \max\{0, k - (C(n') - 1)\lfloor \alpha \rfloor\}(\lceil \alpha \rceil p - (\max\{o, g\} - o))$. Thus, schedule length as a function of $n', k$ is equal to

$$C_{\max}(n', k) = \max\{(n-k-n')p, p+o+L\} + (C(n')-1)\max\{o, g\} + o + \delta(k) + p$$

Since both $n'$ and $k'$ are smaller than $n$, the optimum schedule length can be found by full enumeration of $n', k$ in time $O(n^2)$.

**Table 6.13** Polynomially solvable cases of scheduling under $LogP$ model

| Problem | Result | Reference |
| --- | --- | --- |
| $P(L, o, g) \infty | 1l.in\text{-}tree, p_j = p, c_{ij} | C_{\max}$ | $O(n^2)$ | [120] |
| $P(L, o, g) | 1l.out\text{-}tree, p_j = p, c | C_{\max}$ | $O(n^3)$ | [120, 121] |
| $P(L, o, g) | 1l.out\text{-}tree, p_j = 1, c = 1 | C_{\max} (*)$ | $O(n^2)$ | [127] |

$P(L, o, g)|1l.out\text{-}tree, p_j = p, c|C_{\max}$ [120, 121]

Since the number of processors used in the optimum schedule is not greater than $\min\{n, m\}$ it is enough to build the optimum schedules for each processor number $m' = 1, \ldots, \min\{n, m\}$, and choose the shortest one.

Let $m'$ denote the examined processor number. Without loss of generality the entry (root) task $T_1$ is scheduled on processor $P_1$ at time 0. For simplicity of presentation we assume that $p_1 = p$, but the algorithm remains correct for arbitrary processing time of $T_1$. A schedule on $m'$ processors must execute at least one exit task on each of $m'$ processors. Let these tasks be denoted $T_2, \ldots, T_{m'}$. There is no advantage in delaying the communication operations. Therefore, send operations $send(1, i, i, l)$ to $P_i$ precede operations $send(1, i + 1, i + 1, k)$ to $P_{i+1}$, for all $k, l$, and $i = 2, \ldots, m - 1$. Analogously, operation $send(1, i, i, l)$ precedes $send(1, i, i, l + 1)$ for $l = 1, \ldots, c - 1$.

Let $\alpha = \frac{\max\{o, g\} - o}{p}$. As many as $\lfloor \alpha \rfloor$ exit tasks can be executed between two consecutive send operations without delaying the start of the exit tasks on processors $P_2, \ldots, P_{m'}$. It is not profitable to execute more than $\lceil \alpha \rceil$ exit tasks between two consecutive send operations, because the excess of such tasks can be moved to the end of the schedule on $P_1$ without increasing schedule length. Assume that $n_1 > (c(m' - 1) - 1)\lfloor \alpha \rfloor$ exit tasks are scheduled between the send operations on $P_1$. Hence, the start of availability of processors $P_2, \ldots, P_{m'}$ will be delayed in relation to executing only groups of $\lfloor \alpha \rfloor$ exit tasks on $P_1$. The time remaining for executing exit tasks on $P_2, \ldots, P_{m'}$ is the biggest when $k = n_1 - (c(m' - 1) - 1)\lfloor \alpha \rfloor$ blocks of $\lceil \alpha \rceil$ exit tasks are scheduled between the last $k$ communication intervals on $P_1$. The start of processor $P_i$, for $i = 2, \ldots, m'$, availability interval is delayed by

$$\delta(i) = \max\{0, n_1 - (c(m' - 1) - 1)\lfloor \alpha \rfloor - (m' - i)c\}(\lceil \alpha \rceil p - (\max\{o, g\} - o))$$

Consequently, $P_i$ can start executing exit tasks at

$$\tau_i = p + (c(i - 1) - 1)\max\{g, o\} + \delta(i) + 2o + L$$

Processor $P_1$ is free to start executing exit tasks from time

$$\tau_1 = p + (c(m' - 1) - 1)\max\{g, o\} + o + \delta(m')$$

For the given $m', n_1$ optimum schedule length $C_{\max}(m', n_1)$ is the smallest integer which satisfies

$$C_{\max}(m', n_1) \geq \tau_{m'} \quad \text{and} \quad \sum_{i=1}^{m'} \left\lfloor \frac{C_{\max}(m', n_1) - \tau_i}{p} \right\rfloor \geq n - n_1 - 1$$

The optimum $C_{max}(m', n_1)$ can be calculated in $O(n)$ time for each pair $m', n_1$. Hence, the best schedule selected over all admissible values of $m', n_1$ is constructed in $O(n^3)$ [121].

$P(L, o, g)|1l.out\text{-}tree, p_j = 1, c = 1|C_{max}$ with Forwarding [127]

We consider here a special case of problem $P(L, o, g)|1l.out\text{-}tree, p_j = p, c|C_{max}$ analyzed in the preceding paragraph. However, it is allowed to forward the messages in broadcasting from the root task. The algorithm relies on the optimum broadcasting method for *LogP* machine proposed in [68]. If an optimum broadcast schedule is known for some given number $m'$ of processors, then the optimum schedule for the tasks in $\mathcal{T}$ can be constructed by executing them greedily as early as possible. For a given $m'$ a schedule can be built in $O(m' + n)$ time. Thus, the optimum schedule can be constructed in $O(n^2)$ time by analyzing all processor numbers $m' \leq \min\{m, n\}$.

### 6.9.4   Heuristics with a Guarantee

The results on approximability of scheduling under *LogP* are collected in Table 6.14. The following symbols were used:

- $R_{lin}$ – The worst-case performance ratio of any algorithm building linear clusters; methods for constructing linear clusters were presented in Sect. 6.6.3 and in publications [43, 69].

- $\rho_1 = \min_{T_j \in \mathcal{T}} \left\{ \frac{\min_{T_i \in pred(j)}\{p_i\}}{\max_{T_i \in pred(j)} com(i,j)} \right\}$, where

$$com(i, j) = \sum_{T_k \in succ(i)} (2(c_{ik} - 1) \max\{o, g\} + 2o + L)$$
$$+ \sum_{T_k \in pred(j)} (2(c_{kj} - 1) \max\{o, g\} + 2o + L),$$

**Table 6.14**   Approximation algorithms for scheduling under *LogP* model

| Problem | Result | Reference |
|---|---|---|
| $P(L, o, g)\infty|prec, c_{ij}|C_{max}$ | $R_{lin} \leq 1 + \frac{1}{\rho_1}$ | [83] |
| $P(L, o, g \leq o)\infty|1l.in\text{-}tree, c_{ij}|C_{max}$ | $R_{URGS} \leq 3$ | [119] |
| $P(L, o, g \leq o)|1l.in\text{-}tree, c_{ij}|C_{max}$ | $R_{RRGS} \leq 3 + \varepsilon$ | [119] |
| $P(L, o, g)|1l.out\text{-}tree, c|C_{max}$ | $R_{FGS} \leq 2$ | [119, 121] |
| $P(L, o, g)|d.in\text{-}tree, c|C_{max}$ | $C_{max}^{DFS} \leq (3 - \frac{6}{m+2})C_{max}^* +$ | |
| | $(d(d - 1)(m - 1) - 1) \times$ | |
| | $(L + o + \max\{c_{ij}\} \max\{o, g\})$ | [119] |
| $P(L, o, g)|prec, c_{ij}|C_{max}$ | $R_{any'} \leq (1 + \frac{1}{\rho_1})R_{any}$ | [66] |
| $P(L, o, g)|1l.in\text{-}tree, c = 1|C_{max}$ | $R_{ZLT1} \leq 3 + \varepsilon$ | [127] |
| $P(L, o, g)|1l.out\text{-}tree, c = 1|C_{max}(*)$ | $R_{ZLT2} \leq 2 + \varepsilon$ | [127] |

here $\rho_1$ is yet another definition of granularity.

- $\varepsilon$ – An arbitrary constant greater than 0.
- $d.in\text{-}tree$ – $d$-ary in-tree.
- $C_{max}^{DFS}$ – Length of a schedule constructed by algorithm Decomposition Forest Scheduling (DFS) [119].
- $(*)$ – Denotes that forwarding is allowed.
- $R_{any}$ – Performance ratio of any approximation algorithm for problem $P|prec|C_{max}$, or problem $P|prec, c_{ij}|C_{max}$.
- $R_{any'}$ – Performance ratio of schedules built by inserting necessary overhead tasks and communication latencies into a schedule for $P|prec|C_{max}$, or $P|prec, c_{ij}|C_{max}$ built by a heuristic with performance ratio $R_{any}$ [66].

Selected approximation algorithms mentioned in Table 6.13 are outlined below.

**Unrestricted Receive Graph Scheduling (URGS) [120]** In [120] a join graph is called receive graph. Hence, the name of the algorithm. Without loss of generality let us assume that the exit task (the root) is $T_n$, and it is executed on processor $P_1$. The structure of the optimum schedule for the current problem of scheduling a join graph on an unrestricted processor number, for $g \leq o$, satisfies the following conditions:

1. All entry tasks executed on $P_1$ are scheduled before any receive operation.
2. Each entry task not executed by $P_1$ is executed on its own processor.
3. If tasks $T_i, T_j$ are not executed by $P_1$, and $p_i < p_j$ then the receive operations of $T_i$ precede on $P_1$ all receive operations of $T_j$.
4. Tasks $T_j$ with processing times $p_j \leq c_{jn}o$ are scheduled on $P_1$.
5. If $\forall j, p_j \geq c_{jn}o \Rightarrow \sum_{i=1}^{n-1} p_i \leq (c_{jn} + 1)o + L + p_j$ then the sequential schedule on $P_1$ only is optimum.

Thus, if the schedule on a single processor is not guaranteed to be optimum by the last condition, then a schedule on $1 + |\mathcal{T}_1|$ processors is built, where $\mathcal{T}_1 = \{T_j : p_j > c_{jn}o\}$. Tasks from $\mathcal{T}_1$ are executed on their own processors starting at time 0. Tasks from $\mathcal{T} - \mathcal{T}_1$ satisfy the fourth condition and hence are executed on $P_1$. They are followed by receive operations from the tasks in $\mathcal{T}_1$ ordered according to the increasing execution time of the sender tasks. $T_n$ is executed as the last task on $P_1$. The complexity of URGS heuristic is $O(n \log n)$.

**Restricted Receive Graph Scheduling (RRGS) [120]** Without loss of generality let us assume that the exit task (the root) is $T_n$. Let $\mathcal{T}_1 = \{T_j \in \mathcal{T} - \{T_n\} : p_j > c_{jn}o\}$ be the set of computationally intensive tasks. The tasks from $\mathcal{T}_1$ are scheduled on $m$ processors using a PTAS for $P||C_{max}$ [56] presented in Sect. 4.3.1.1. The remaining entry tasks are scheduled on processor $P_1$. After them the receive operations of the tasks executed on processors $P_2, \ldots, P_m$ are executed. The last task in the schedule is $T_n$ on $P_1$. The worst-case performance ratio of RRGS is $R + 2$, where $R = 1 + \varepsilon$ is the performance ratio of the PTAS for $P||C_{max}$ (see Sect. 4.3.1.1). Since the complexity of the PTAS is quite high it is possible to reduce the total complexity of RRGS at the cost of worse quality guarantees by exploiting other heuristics for $\mathcal{T}_1$.

**Fork Graph Scheduling (FGS) [121]** The algorithm presented here has performance guarantee for fork graphs, with the communication delay (i.e. the number of sent messages) equal to $c$.

The number of used processors in the optimum schedule is not greater than $\min\{n, m\}$. Hence, the algorithm constructs schedules for all processor numbers $1 \le m' \le \min\{n, m\}$. Without loss of generality let the root of the fork graph be scheduled on processor $P_1$ at time 0. For each given processor number $m'$ a schedule is built in the following way. First $c$ messages are sent to each of $m' - 1$ processors. Thus, $c(m' - 1)$ send operations are scheduled on $P_1$. On each of processors $P_2, \ldots, P_{m'}$, $c$ receive operations are performed as soon as the latency elapses, after which one of the exit task is scheduled. If there are still $n - (m - 1) > 0$ unscheduled tasks, then they are considered in an arbitrary order and scheduled as early as possible on the processors which become free. The shortest schedule from the schedules built for processor numbers $m' = 1, \ldots, \min\{n, m\}$ is returned as the final solution. The complexity of this algorithm is $O(n^2 \log n)$.

**Algorithm 1 by Zimmermann, Löwe, and Trystram (ZLT1) [127]** ZLT1 is an algorithm for join graphs and tasks sending only one message. The structure of a schedule is similar to the schedules constructed by RRGS algorithm presented above.

Without loss of generality let us assume that root is executed on $P_1$, and that tasks are ordered according to the nonincreasing processing times: $p_1 \ge p_2 \ge \cdots \ge p_n$. The longest $n_1$ tasks are scheduled on $P_2, \ldots, P_m$ using the PTAS for $P||C_{max}$ [56] (cf. Sect. 4.3.1.1). The remaining tasks are executed on $P_1$. Let $C'$ be the length of the schedule built so far. Next, all the communication operations are executed starting from time $C'$ without unnecessary delay. Finally, the root is executed on $P_1$. ZLT1 chooses the best solution among the schedules constructed for all possible numbers $0 \le n_1 \le n$ of tasks executed on $P_2, \ldots, P_m$. The performance ratio of the algorithm is $2 + R$, where $R = 1 + \varepsilon$ is the worst-case performance ratio of the PTAS for $P||C_{max}$ [56]. Complexity of ZLT1 is $O(n \left(\frac{n}{\varepsilon}\right)^{\lceil 1/\varepsilon^2 \rceil} (\log n + \log p_{max}))$. Other heuristics can be also applied for the $n_1$ longest tasks with appropriately modified complexity and approximation ratio [127].

**Algorithm 2 by Zimmermann, Löwe, and Trystram (ZLT2) [127]** ZLT2 is an algorithm for scheduling fork graphs, tasks sending only one message, when message forwarding is allowed.

The structure of the schedule is the following. Let $m' \le \min\{m, n\}$ be the number of exploited processors. Schedule the root task at time 0 on $P_1$. Construct an optimum broadcast schedule for $m'$ processors using the algorithm from [68]. Schedule the tasks from $\mathcal{T}$ on $m'$ processors using some heuristic for $P||C_{max}$. ZLT2 chooses the best solution from the schedules built for $m' = 1, \ldots, \min\{m, n\}$. If the heuristic used for scheduling tasks in $\mathcal{T}$ is the PTAS for $P||C_{max}$ [56] (see Sect. 4.3.1.1) then the worst-case performance ratio is $2 + \varepsilon$, and the complexity can be bounded by $O(n (n/\varepsilon)^{\lceil \frac{1}{\varepsilon^2} \rceil} (\log n + \log p_{max}))$. Other heuristics for the tasks in $\mathcal{T}$ were also analyzed in [127].

### 6.9.5   Heuristics Without a Guarantee

In this section, we present selected heuristics without performance guarantees for scheduling under *LogP* model.

**Two-Pass Earliest Task First (2ETF) and Earliest Task First with Reservation (ETFR) [66]**  Both 2ETF and ETFR are adaptations of ETF [63] (see Sect. 6.4.3) to *LogP* machines.

It was assumed in [66] that the durations of the overhead tasks and the latencies depend on the sender and the receiver. The gap time was assumed to be equal to the overhead time. Hence, a message from task $T_i$ to its successor $T_j \in succ(i)$ is delivered in time $o(i, j) + L(i, j) + o(i, j)$ if $proc(i) \neq proc(j)$.

Moreover, it was assumed that after task $T_j$ generating some results all its send overhead tasks are immediately executed. This poses a difficulty in constructing ETF schedule because overhead tasks are executed only if a message is delivered to a different processor than the one executing $T_j$. Thus, to calculate task earliest starting times it is necessary to know a priori which successors of $T_j$ are executed on $proc(j)$, and which successors are executed on other processors. To overcome this difficulty two approaches were proposed.

In 2ETFS the schedule is built first by ETF algorithm for the standard delay model assuming communication delays $\forall (i, j) \in \mathcal{A}, c_{ij} = 2o(i, j) + L(i, j)$, and then necessary overhead tasks are inserted into this schedule.

In ETFR it is assumed that all successor tasks are executed on different processors than their predecessors. Therefore, for each task $T_i \in \mathcal{T}$ an interval of length $\sum_{T_j \in succ(i)} o(i, j)$ is reserved after each task $T_i$ for inserting send tasks if necessary. If $T_j \in succ(i)$ is supposed to be executed on a different processor than $T_i$, then the earliest start time is calculated assuming that the send overhead task is scheduled at the end of the send overhead tasks in the reserved interval. Since the resulting schedule may have unnecessarily reserved idle intervals, a version ETFRGC (ETFR with garbage collector) was proposed which shifts tasks as early as feasible in after they are assigned to processors and sequenced.

**Boeres, Nascimento, and Rebello Heuristic (BNR2) [24]**  This is a clustering heuristic for problem $P(L, o, g)\infty|prec, c_{ij}, dup|C_{\max}$.

It was assumed in [24] that overhead tasks have different durations $o_s, o_r$ for sending and receiving, respectively, latency depends on the sender and the receiver and hence it is denoted $L(i, j)$ for $(i, j) \in \mathcal{A}$, there are no broadcasts in the task graph. It was also assumed that each receive task has duration $\max\{g, o_r\}$. Observe that in *LogP* model clustering has more complex nature than in the standard delay model. In the standard delay model inclusion of some task in a cluster increases the total processing time in the cluster. In *LogP* inclusion of a predecessor of some task in the cluster eliminates one receive overhead task. Consequently, the length of the cluster may be reduced.

BNR2 construction bears some similarity to PLW algorithm (cf. Sect. 6.7.3). A dedicated cluster is constructed for each task $T_j$. Thus, $T_j$ is called an owner of its cluster. The following set of rules is applied in BNR2:

1. Only the owner of the cluster may send a message to another cluster.
2. Each cluster has only one successor, thus for each arc $(i, j) \in \mathcal{A}$ there is a unique copy of $T_i$ cluster.
3. Receive overhead tasks are executed just before the task from $\mathcal{T}$ receiving the message.
4. The receive overhead tasks are executed in the order of their arrival as they were queued in the communication subsystem.

Note that design choices (1) and (2) may result in extensive task duplication.

In the first stage of BNR2 clusters are constructed. Tasks are analyzed in the topological order. Let $\tau_i$ be the starting time of task $T_i$ in its final cluster. If $pred(i) = \emptyset$ then $\tau_i = 0$. Let $T_j$ be the currently examined task. Since clusters are constructed in the topological order the start times of all $T_j$ predecessors are already established. Let $cpred(j)$ be the set of immediate predecessors of the tasks included in $T_j$ cluster which themselves are not in this cluster. Let $pt(j)$ denote the total processing time of the tasks included in the $T_j$ cluster (including receive overhead tasks). BNR2 analyzes all tasks $T_i \in cpred(j)$ and attempts inserting them before their immediate successors in $T_j$ cluster. Hence, $T_j$ cannot be scheduled earlier than $maxc(i) = \tau_i + p_i + o_s + L(i, k) + o_r + pt(k, j)$, where $T_i \in cpred(j)$, $T_k \in succ(i)$ is included in $T_j$ cluster, $pt(k, j)$ is the processing time of all the tasks in $T_j$ cluster in the sequence starting from $T_k$ till the last task before $T_j$ (including overhead tasks). The algorithm chooses task $T_a$ which has maximum value of $maxc(a)$ in $cpred(j)$. If $maxc(a) \leq pt(j)$ then cluster construction stops. Otherwise $maxc(a) > pt(j)$, and the total processing time of the cluster is recalculated with task $T_a$ included in the cluster. If after inserting $T_a$ condition $maxc(a) < pt(j)$ is satisfied, then $T_a$ is removed from the cluster and its construction is finished. In the opposite case including $T_a$ reduces $est(j)$ and $T_a$ is included in the cluster just before its immediate successor. Since the cluster formation rules are not equivalent to building a cluster with minimum makespan, it is suggested in [24] to record the shortest cluster which was built in the above stage.

In the second stage of BNR2 the unnecessary clusters are eliminated as in the PLW method. Other rules for limiting the number of used processors were also mentioned in [24]. The complexity of BNR2 is $O(n^5)$. BNR2 can be also applied in the standard delay model [24].

## 6.9.6 Remarks on Scheduling in *Log P* Model

Here we make some comments and draw some conclusions on scheduling under the *LogP* model. Observe that even simple scheduling problems are **NP**-hard under *LogP*, polynomial optimization algorithms and approximation algorithms with performance guarantee are known only for a limited set of quite restricted problems.

Let us observe that there is no firmly established consensus on the definition of *LogP* as a scheduling model. There are propositions [8] of combining many short messages into a long one. Some papers, like [24,66], assume overheads and latencies depending on the sender and receiver, but other publications, e.g. [119,120], assume that messages have small constant length, and the number of messages depends on the sender and the receiver. Another degree of freedom is introduced by explicitly scheduling communications as in forwarding [127]. This lack of unanimity results in incomparability of the obtained results. On the other hand, variants of *LogP* allow for more detailed perception of a parallel system. However, this precision of system representation comes at considerable price of additional complexity and results incomparability.

## 6.10   Scheduling with Hierarchical Communication

In this section, we present the problems of scheduling task graphs in hierarchical distributed systems with nonuniform communication delays. As discussed in Sect. 6.2.2 in such systems communication delays have two grades: shorter for local communications and longer distant communications.

In the following parts of this section we first introduce some useful notation. Then we present results on the complexity and approximability of scheduling in the current model.

### 6.10.1   Problem Formulation and Notation

We will denote by $\kappa_{ij}$ local communication delay for $(T_i, T_j) \in \mathcal{A}$. The intercluster communication delay will be denoted by $c_{ij}$ for the same arc. In general it is assumed that $c_{ij} \geq \kappa_{ij}$. Other assumptions of the standard delay model (Sect. 6.2.2) are accepted here. Thus, the results of task $T_i$ are available for $T_j$ on each local processor after delay $\kappa_{ij}$ and on each nonlocal processor after $c_{ij}$. Processors are not involved in message passing.

The number of processor clusters (nonlocal machines) is denoted by $m_c$, and the number of processors in each processor cluster is equal to $m_l$. Hence, we assume symmetric structure of the hierarchical system. Let us remind that we distinguish processor clusters from task clusters.

We will slightly extend the $\alpha|\beta|\gamma$ notation to express scheduling problems with hierarchical communication. The extension allows for expressing numbers of the local and nonlocal machines and the durations of the local and nonlocal communication delays.

The processing environment field may take form $P(a, b)$, where symbols $a, b$ represent processor numbers in a standard way for $\alpha|\beta|\gamma$ notation. The first symbol $a$ applies to the number of clusters, and the second symbol $b$ corresponds to the number of processors in each cluster. For example, $P(\infty, 4)$ will denote unlimited number of quad-processor clusters. $P(, 2)$ will represent limited number of duo-processor clusters, where the number of processor clusters $m_c$ is given in the instance of the problem.

In the task field a pair of symbols $(x, y)$ will be used to represent the intercluster communication delay $x$ and the local communication delay $y$. The form of symbols $x, y$ will be the same as for the standard communication delay model. For example:

- $(c_{ij}, \kappa_{ij})$ – Denote that intercluster and local communication delays depend of the sender and the receiver tasks, their values are given in the instance of the problem.
- $(c, \kappa)$ – Denote that the all intercluster communications take the same time $c$, while local communications take time $\kappa$, values of $c, \kappa$ are given in the instance of the problem.
- $(c, \kappa) = (a_1, a_2)$ – The intercluster and the local communication delays take $a_1, a_2$ units of time, respectively.
- $(c_{ij}, \kappa) = (sct, 0)$ – The intercluster communication delays are small, which means that $\max_{(i,j)\in\mathcal{A}}\{c_{ij}\} \leq \min_{T_j \in T}\{p_j\}$, communication delays in the cluster take no time.

## 6.10.2  Complexity of the Problem

In this section, we present results of the complexity analysis for scheduling with hierarchical communication model. Hard problems of scheduling with hierarchical communication delays are listed in Table 6.15.

Let us observe that scheduling with communication delays on hierarchical distributed system is a special case of standard delay model. By assuming that $c_{ij} = \kappa_{ij}$ we obtain the standard delay model problems. Hence, all the results considering hardness of scheduling with standard communication delay model are valid also in the current model of hierarchical system.

Polynomially solvable cases of scheduling with hierarchical communications are collected in Table 6.16. Problems mentioned in the above table are presented below.

**Table 6.15**  Hard problems of scheduling in hierarchical systems

| Problem | Result | Reference |
|---|---|---|
| $P(\infty, 2)|prec, (c, \kappa) = (1, 0), p_j = 1|C_{max} = 4$ | sNPh | [12] |

**Table 6.16**  Polynomially solvable cases of scheduling in hierarchical systems

| Problem | Result | Reference |
|---|---|---|
| $P(\infty, 2)\|prec, (c, \kappa) = (1, 0), p_j = 1, dup\|C_{\max}$ | $O(n^2)$ | [11] |
| $P(\infty, 2)\|prec, (c, \kappa) = (1, 0), p_j = 1\|C_{\max} = 3$ | $O(n^3)$ | [12] |

### $P(\infty, 2)\|prec, (c, \kappa) = (1, 0), p_j = 1, dup\|C_{\max}$ [11]

The algorithm for the current problem is an adaptation of the algorithm for problem $P\infty\|prec, sct, dup\|C_{\max}$ [31], considered in Sect. 6.7.2. Similarly to [31] task starting times will be calculated, and then a critical subgraph of the task graph will be used to identify tasks which must be executed on the same processor cluster.

In the first stage a lower bound on the task earliest start times is calculated. Simultaneously critical arcs are added to the critical graph. Let us denote by $pred(a, b)$ the distance $a$ predecessors of $T_b$, i.e. $pred(1, b) = pred(b)$, and for $a > 1$ $pred(a, b) = \{T_j \in pred(k) : T_k \in pred(a - 1, b)\}$. For the tasks $T_i$ without predecessor $est(i) = 0$. Suppose $T_j$ is the currently examined task which all predecessors have their earliest starting times already calculated. Let $e_j = \max_{T_i \in pred(j)}\{est(i)\}$ and $S_j = \{T_i \in pred(j) : est(i) = e_j\}$. Three cases may arise in determining $est(j)$:

1. $|S_j| = 1$, and let $S_j = \{T_k\}$, then $est(j) = e_j + 1$, and arc $(k, j)$ is added to the critical graph.
2. $|S_j| = 2$, and let $S_j = \{T_k, T_l\}$, observe that $T_k, T_l$ can be executed immediately before $T_j$ and on the same processor cluster only if there are together only two predecessors of $T_k, T_l$. This applies also to the predecessors of the predecessors, and so on until the entry tasks. Thus if $\forall h, |pred(h, k) \cup (pred(h, l)| \leq 2$ then $est(j) = e_j + 1$, and critical arcs $(k, j), (l, j)$ are added to the critical graph. Otherwise, $est(j) = e_j + 2$ and no arc is added to the critical graph.
3. $|S_j| \geq 3$, then $est(j) = e_j + 2$ and no arc is added to the critical graph.

Note that in the critical graph constructed in the above way each task has at most two predecessors. Furthermore, by traversing the critical graph from the exit nodes to the entry nodes clusters of tasks are constructed which must be executed on the same processor cluster. Observe that in no moment is it necessary to use more than $m_l = 2$ processors in the same processor cluster because of the second case of the $est(j)$ calculation method. The complexity of this algorithm is $O(n^2)$.

### $P(\infty, 2)\|prec, (c, \kappa) = (1, 0), p_j = 1\|C_{\max} = 3$ [12]

An instance of this problem can be scheduled in $C_{\max} = 3$ when there are no paths longer than three tasks in the task graph. Let us partition the set of tasks into four subsets:

1. $A = \{T_j \in T : pred(j) = succ(j) = \emptyset\}$

2. $B = \{T_j \in \mathcal{T} : pred(j) \neq \emptyset, succ(j) = \emptyset\}$
3. $C = \{T_j \in \mathcal{T} : pred(j) = \emptyset, succ(j) \neq \emptyset\}$
4. $D = \mathcal{T} - (A \cup B \cup C)$

Note that tasks in $D$ with all their predecessors and successors must be executed on the same processor cluster, because adding any communication delay $c = 1$ renders the instance unschedulable in $C_{\max} = 3$. For each task $T_j$ in $D$ define $K_j = pred(j) \cup \{T_j\} \cup succ(j)$. Define a relation $R \subseteq \mathcal{T} \times \mathcal{T}$ such that $(T_k, T_l) \in R$ if and only if $T_k \in K_i, T_l \in K_j$ and $K_i \cap K_j \neq \emptyset$. Let $R^*$ be the transitive closure of $R$. An equivalence relation is defined by $R^*$. A group of tasks in the same equivalence class must be processed on the same processor cluster. Let $\mathcal{T}_i$ denote a group of tasks in the same equivalence class. A feasible schedule of length 3 exists only if $|\mathcal{T}_i \cap B| \leq 2$, $|\mathcal{T}_i \cap C| \leq 2$, $|\mathcal{T}_i \cap D| \leq 2$, for each equivalence class $\mathcal{T}_i$. The tasks (from sets $A, B, C$) which are not included in any equivalence class of $R^*$ can be scheduled at time 0 on any unused processor cluster for the tasks in sets $A, C$, or at time 2 for the tasks in set $B$.

### 6.10.3  Heuristics with a Guarantee

In this section, we study approximability of scheduling with hierarchical communication. The results on approximability of this problem are collected in Table 6.17. In Table 6.17 $\rho$ is granularity defined as $\rho = \frac{\max_{(i,j) \in A} \{c_{ij}\}}{\min_{T_j \in \mathcal{T}} \{p_j\}}$. Below we expand selected results from the table.

**Bampis, Giroudeau, and König heuristic (BGK) [13]**  This heuristic extends the technique of Munier and König [88] (Sect. 6.6.3) based on rounding fractional solutions of a fractional relaxation of an integer linear programming formulation of the problem.

Let us first formulate the current problem as an integer linear program. In the following formulation $\tau_j$ is a variable representing start time of task $T_j$. For each pair $(i, j) \in A$ we introduce binary variable $x_{ij}$ equal to 1 if and only if $T_j$ is executed on a different processor cluster than $T_i$, and equal to 0 if $T_j$ is executed immediately after $T_i$ on the same processor cluster as $T_i$. Our problem can be formulated as an integer linear program:

**Table 6.17**  Approximability results for scheduling in hierarchical systems

| Problem | Result | Reference |
| --- | --- | --- |
| $P(\infty, 2)\|prec, (c, \kappa) = (1, 0), p_j = 1\|C_{\max}$ | $R \geq \frac{5}{4}$ | [12] |
| $P(\infty, 2)\|prec, (c, \kappa) = (1, 0), p_j \geq 1\|C_{\max}$ | $R_{BGK} = \frac{8}{5}$ | [13] |
| $P(\infty, m_l)\|prec, (c, \kappa) = (1, 0), p_j \geq 1\|C_{\max}$ | $R_{BGK} = 1 + \frac{2m_l - 1}{2m_l + 1}$ | [13] |
| $P(\infty, 2)\|prec, (c_{ij}, \kappa) = (sct, 0)\|C_{\max}$ | $R_{BGK} = 1 + \frac{11\rho}{12 + \rho}$ | [14] |

$$\text{minimize } C_{max} \text{ subject to} \tag{6.20}$$

$$\tau_i + p_i + x_{ij} \le \tau_j \quad \forall (i,j) \in \mathcal{A} \tag{6.21}$$

$$\sum_{j \in succ(i)} x_{ij} \ge |succ(i)| - 2 \quad \forall T_i \in \{T_i : succ(i) \ne \emptyset\} \tag{6.22}$$

$$\sum_{i \in pred(j)} x_{ij} \ge |pred(j)| - 2 \quad \forall T_j \in \{T_j : pred(j) \ne \emptyset\} \tag{6.23}$$

$$\tau_j + p_j \le C_{max} \quad \forall T_j \in \mathcal{T} \tag{6.24}$$

$$x_{ba} + x_{bc} + x_{dc} + x_{de} \ge 1 \quad \forall (T_a, T_b, T_c, T_d, T_e):$$
$$\{(b,a),(b,c),(d,c),(d,e)\} \subseteq \mathcal{A} \tag{6.25}$$

$$x_{ab} + x_{cb} + x_{cd} + x_{ed} \ge 1 \quad \forall (T_a, T_b, T_c, T_d, T_e):$$
$$\{(a,b),(c,b),(c,d),(e,d)\} \subseteq \mathcal{A} \tag{6.26}$$

$$\tau_j \ge 0 \quad \forall T_j \in \mathcal{T} \tag{6.27}$$

$$x_{ij} \in \{0,1\} \quad \forall (i,j) \in \mathcal{A} \tag{6.28}$$

In the above formulation inequalities (6.21) guarantee sufficient distance between starting times of the predecessor and the successor task to make the necessary communication. By inequalities (6.22) and (6.23) not more than $m_l = 2$ tasks are executed immediately after their predecessors or before their successors. By (6.24) no task is processed after the end of the schedule. Inequalities (6.25) and (6.26) correspond with $W$ and $M$ structures in the task graph (see Fig. 6.25). It is easy to observe that at least one of the five tasks in such structures must be executed in a different processor cluster than the remaining four tasks. Integer linear programs (6.20)–(6.28) can be formulated in polynomial time in $n$, but in general cannot be solved in polynomial time unless $\mathbf{P} = \mathbf{NP}$. However, the fractional relaxation (6.20)–(6.27), with additional constraint $0 \le x_{ij} \le 1$, $\forall (i,j) \in \mathcal{A}$, can be solved in polynomial time. Let $x'_{ij}, \tau'_{ij}$ be the solutions of the fractional linear program, corresponding to variables $x_{ij}, \tau_{ij}$ of ILP, respectively.

The second stage of the algorithm consists in rounding $x'_{ij}$ to binary variables such that a feasible schedule is defined. In the first step $x_{ij}$ is set to 1 if $x'_{ij} \ge 0.25$ and to $x_{ij} = 0$ otherwise. Arc $(i,j)$ is called a 0-arc if $x_{ij} = 0$ and a 1-arc in the opposite case. The first step rounding does not define a feasible schedule in general. For the second step a critical path $CP$ is calculated including both task processing times and values $x_{ij}$ as weights of the arcs. Let $A_j = \{(i,j) : T_i \in pred(j), (i,j) \in CP\}$. If task $T_i$ is an entry node then values of $x_{ij}$, for $T_j \in succ(i)$ remain unchanged. Suppose that all predecessors of $T_j$ have been examined. If $A_j$ comprises a 0-arc then set $x_{jk} = 1$ for all arcs $(j,k)$, where $T_k \in succ(j)$. If $A_j$ comprises no 0-arc

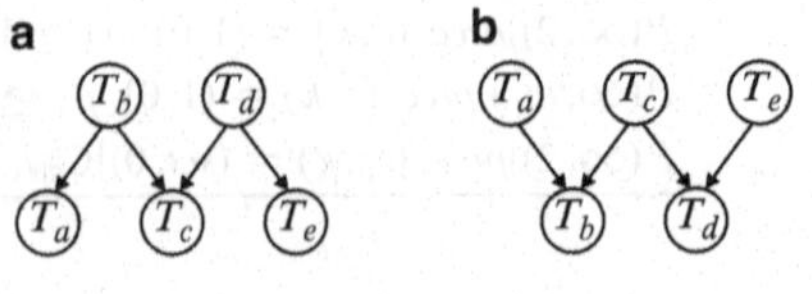

**Fig. 6.25** (a) $M$ and (b) $W$ structures in the task graph

then $x_{jk}$ remain unchanged for all arcs $(j, k)$, where $T_k \in succ(j)$, while for the incoming 0-arcs $(i, j)$, where $T_i \in pred(j)$, set $x_{ij} = 1$. It can be shown that task $T_j$ starting times $\tau_j$ resulting in the precedence constraints, and the above defined values of variables $x_{ij}$, are not greater than $\frac{8}{4}\tau'_j$.

The above heuristic can be generalized to deal with processor clusters comprising arbitrary fixed number of processors [13] and to the case of small intercluster communication delays (*sct*) [14].

## 6.11  Further Reading and Conclusions

In this section, we give some final remarks on scheduling with communication delays. Not all branches of this model have been discussed in this chapter. Therefore, we will provide some examples of other research directions in scheduling with communication delays. We finish this section with some comments on this scheduling model and its utility.

### 6.11.1  Other Branches of Scheduling with Communication Delays

Since all problems considered in this chapter are computationally hard in general, a number of heuristics have been presented. We have not compared these heuristics to select the best performers because it is beyond the scope of this book. Comparisons of this kind can be found, e.g., in [4, 5, 75]. A difficulty here is the lack of portability of the results between systems and instances, as well as the fact that no heuristic fits all needs. Therefore, the results of such studies must be taken with caution as soft indicators of quality rather than recommendation of the ultimate scheduling algorithm. For similar reasons, and as explained in Sect. 2.3.4, we do not present metaheuristics solving problems of scheduling with communication delays. Examples of metaheuristics for scheduling with communication delays can be found in [32, 74, 76, 105, 110, 112, 123, 128].

Possible extensions of the scheduling problems considered in this chapter follow from the classic scheduling theory methodologies. For example, problems with task ready times and deadlines are introduced in [95, 118, 120, 122]. Heterogeneous computing systems can be naturally expected within the lines of classic scheduling theory. Examples of the studies on scheduling with communication delays in heterogeneous systems can be found in [18–20, 50, 71, 95, 105].

Another group of extensions in scheduling with communication delays deals with alternative criteria and multicriterial optimization. For example, in [51] the criteria of the schedule length and the number of task duplicates are considered, in [77] schedule length and the number of sent messages, and in [105] schedule length and schedule robustness, where robustness is measured as expected dispersion of the makespan. In [84, 100] scheduling for maintaining maximum number of tasks ready for execution is considered.

In this chapter, we analyzed scheduling with standard communication delay model and under two extensions introduced in Sects. 6.9 and 6.10. However, also other models of communication delay, distributed system, and the application were proposed. A review of models for scheduling with communication delays which appeared until mid-1990s was given in [15]. In [57, 61] a model similar to *LogP* has been proposed but with slightly different representation of communication delay and processor involvement in message transfer. Scheduling with communication delays under bulk-synchronous parallel (BSP) model [113] has been studied in [46]. Limitations on communication medium capabilities have been introduced, e.g., in [20, 67]. Finally, let us note that there are also combinations of more remote models. In [97, 101] parallel task model (Chap. 5) is blended with scheduling with communication delays.

### 6.11.2  Observations on Scheduling with Communication Delays

It can be observed that scheduling with communication delays is a playground of combinatorial optimization. Though some polynomially solvable cases and heuristics with performance guarantees were identified, they have rather limited applicability. A general message for a practitioner is that scheduling with communication delays is computationally hard, and realistic problem instances can be solved only by heuristics. Consequently, a question arises what heuristics should be used. As we noted in the previous section there is no single panacea for all the scheduling needs, and selecting appropriate heuristic requires understanding the distributed system, application, and scheduling method peculiarities.

In this chapter, we examined standard model of scheduling with communication delays and its two extensions. Other variants and more diverse models were also proposed, and we mentioned them in the previous section. It can be observed that the simplest model attracted the greatest attention of the researchers, while the number of publications on more detailed models is smaller. Moreover, the more detailed a model is the more difficult is applying it. For example, in *LogP* parameters $L, o, g$ of the communication system are measured at considerable cost, but are not portable between different computer systems. On the other hand, this effort is not offset by better scheduling algorithms because scheduling under *LogP* is not computationally easier than in the basic model. Thus, it can be concluded that solving some scheduling problem is a matter of good models which are a compromise of precision and tractability. A more detailed model is not necessarily better.

A critique of scheduling with application DAG model has been submitted in [25]. Programs usually have loops and branches that must be unrolled which result in oversized task graphs. Moreover, application DAGs very often depend on problem size. Hence, each new problem size results in a different DAG. These features limit scalability of the task graph model. Current scheduling model seems not suitable for wide area or grid systems which have high degree of autonomy, heterogeneity, and long unpredictable communication delays. Consequently, scheduling tools based on the model considered in this chapter does not seem to have wide use in practice [25].

Still, let us observe that scheduling should not be considered without the context of time. The model of scheduling with communication delays originated in late 1980s when massively parallel (MPP) architectures with limited (from the current point of view) communication capabilities dominated. In such technology context this model was reasonable and justified.

# References

1. T.L. Adam, K.M. Chandy, and J.R. Dickson. A comparison of list schedules for parallel processing systems. *Communications of the ACM*, 17(12):685–690, 1974.
2. F. Afrati, E. Bampis, L. Finta, and I. Milis. Scheduling trees with large communication delays on two identical processors. *Journal of Scheduling*, 8(2):179–190, 2005.
3. I. Ahmad and Y.-K. Kwok. A new approach to scheduling parallel programs using task duplication. In *Proceedings of the International Conference on Parallel Processing (ICPP'94)*, volume 2, pages 47–51, 1994.
4. I. Ahmad and Y.-K. Kwok. Analysis, evaluation, and comparison of algorithms for scheduling task graphs on parallel processors. In *Proceedings of the 1996 International Symposium on Parallel Architectures, Algorithms and Networks (ISPAN'96)*, pages 207–213, 1996.
5. I. Ahmad and Y.-K. Kwok. On exploiting task duplication in parallel program scheduling. *IEEE Transactions on Parallel and Distributed Systems*, 9(9):872–892, 1998.
6. I. Ahmad, Y.-K. Kwok, M.-Y. Wu, and W. Shu. CASCH: A tool for computer-aided scheduling. *IEEE Concurrency*, 8(4):21–33, 2000.
7. M. Al-Mouhamed and A. Al-Maasarani. Performance evaluation of scheduling precedence-constrained computations on message-passing systems. *IEEE Transactions on Parallel and Distributed Systems*, 5(12):1317–1322, 1994.
8. A. Alexandrov, M.F. Ionescu, K.E. Schauser, and C. Scheiman. LogGP: Incorporating long messages into the LogP model for parallel computation. *Journal of Parallel and Distributed Computing*, 44(1):71–79, 1997.
9. H.H. Ali and H. El-Rewini. An optimal algorithm for scheduling interval ordered tasks with communication on N processors. *Journal of Computer and System Sciences*, 51(2):301–306, 1995.
10. E. Bampis, A. Giannakos, and J.-C. König. On the complexity of scheduling with large communication delays. *European Journal of Operational Research*, 94(2):252–260, 1996.
11. E. Bampis, A. Giroudeau, and J.-C. König. Using duplication for the multiprocessor scheduling problem with hierarchical communications. *Parallel Processing Letters*, 10(1):133–140, 2000.
12. E. Bampis, A. Giroudeau, and J.-C. König. On the hardness of approximating the UET-UCT scheduling problem with hierarchical communications. *RAIRO Operations Research*, 36(1):21–36, 2002.
13. E. Bampis, A. Giroudeau, and J.-C. König. An approximation algorithm for the precedence constrained scheduling problem with hierarchical communications. *Theoretical Computer Science*, 290(3):1883–1895, 2003.
14. E. Bampis, A. Giroudeau, and A. Kononov. Scheduling tasks with small communication delays for clusters of processors. *Annals of Operations Research*, 129(1–4):47–63, 2004.

15. E. Bampis, F. Guinand, and D. Trystram. Some models for scheduling parallel programs with communication delays. *Discrete Applied Mathematics*, 72(1–2):5–24, 1997.

16. S. Bansal, P. Kumar, and K. Singh. An improved duplication strategy for scheduling precedence constrained graphs in multiprocessor systems. *IEEE Transactions on Parallel and Distributed Systems*, 14(6):533–544, 2003.

17. S.K. Baruah. The multiprocessor scheduling of precedence-constrained task systems in the presence of interprocessor communication delays. *Operations Research*, 46(1):65–72, 1998.

18. S. Baskiyar and C. Dickinson. Scheduling directed a-cyclic task graphs on a bounded set of heterogeneous processors using task duplication. *Journal of Parallel and Distributed Computing*, 65(8):911–921, 2005.

19. O. Beaumont, V. Boudet, and Y. Robert. The iso-level scheduling heuristic for heterogeneous processors. In *Proceedings of the 10th Euromicro Workshop on Parallel, Distributed and Network-based Processing (EUROMICRO-PDP'02)*, pages 335–350, 2002.

20. O. Beaumont, V. Boudet, and Y. Robert. A realistic model and an efficient heuristic for scheduling with heterogeneous processors. In *Proceedings of the International Parallel and Distributed Processing Symposium (IPDPS'02) Workshops*, page 0088, 2002.

21. J. Błażewicz, P. Bouvry, F. Guinand, and D. Trystram. Scheduling complete in-trees on two uniform processors with communication delays. *Information Processing Letters*, 58(5):255–263, 1996.

22. J. Błażewicz, M. Drozdowski, and K. Ecker. Management of resources in parallel systems. In J. Błażewicz, K. Ecker, B. Plateau, and D. Trystram, editors, *Handbook on Parallel and Distributed Processing*, pages 263–341. Springer, Berlin, 2000.

23. J. Błażewicz, F. Guinand, B. Penzand and D. Trystram. Scheduling complete trees on two uniform processors with integer speed ratios and communication delays. *Parallel Processing Letters*, 10(4):267–277, 2000.

24. C. Boeres, A. Nascimento, and V.E.F. Rebello. Cluster-based task scheduling for the LogP model. *International Journal of Foundations of Computer Science*, 10(4):405–424, 1999.

25. J. Cao, A.T.S. Chan, Y. Sun, S.K. Das, and M. Guo. A taxonomy of application scheduling tools for high performance cluster computing. *Cluster Computing*, 9(3):355–371, 2006.

26. P. Chrétienne. A polynomial algorithm to optimally schedule tasks on a virtual distributed system under tree-like precedence constraints. *European Journal of Operational Research*, 43(2):225–230, 1989.

27. P. Chrétienne. Task scheduling with interprocessor communication delays. *European Journal of Operational Research*, 57(3):348–354, 1992.

28. P. Chrétienne. Tree scheduling with communication delays. *Discrete Applied Mathematics*, 49(1-3):129–141, 1994.

29. P. Chrétienne and C. Picouleau. Scheduling with communication delays: A survey. In P. Chrétienne, E.G. Coffman Jr., J.K. Lenstra, and Z. Liu, editors, *Scheduling Theory and Its Applications*, pages 65–90. Wiley, Chichester, 1995.

30. J.-Y. Colin and P. Colin. Scheduling task and communication on a virtual distributed system. *European Journal of Operational Research*, 94(2):271–276, 1994.

31. J.Y. Colin and P. Chrétienne. C.P.M. scheduling with small communication delays and task duplication. *Operations Research*, 39(4):680–684, 1991.

32. R.C. Corrêa, A. Ferreira, and P. Rebreyend. Scheduling multiprocessor tasks with genetic algorithms. *IEEE Transactions on Parallel and Distributed Systems*, 10(8):825–837, 1999.

33. D.E. Culler, R.M. Karp, D. Patterson, A. Sahay, E.E. Santos, K.E. Schauser, R. Subramonian, and T. Eicken. LogP: A practical model of parallel computation. *Communications of the ACM*, 39(11):78–85, 1996.

34. S. Darbha and D.P. Agrawal. A task duplication based scalable scheduling algorithm for distributed memory systems. *Journal of Parallel and Distributed Computing*, 46(1):15–27, 1997.

35. A. Darte, Y. Robert, and F. Vivien. *Scheduling and Automated Parallelization*. Birkhäuser, Boston, 2000.

36. M. Dell'Amico and L. Finta. A linear time algorithm for scheduling outforests with communication delays on three processors. *Journal of Algorithms*, 44(2):287–307, 2002.

37. G.L. Djordjević and M.B. Tošić. A heuristic for scheduling task graphs with communication delays onto multiprocessors. *Parallel Computing*, 22(9):1197–1214, 1996.
38. D. Dolev and M.K. Warmuth. Profile scheduling of opposing forests and level orders. *SIAM Journal on Algebraic and Discrete Methods*, 6(4):665–687, 1985.
39. H. El-Rewini and T.G. Lewis. Scheduling parallel program tasks onto arbitrary target machines. *Journal of Parallel and Distributed Computing*, 9(2):138–153, 1990.
40. L. Finta, Z. Liu, I. Millis, and E. Bampis. Scheduling UET-UCT series–parallel graphs on two processors. *Theoretical Computer Science*, 162(2):323–340, 1996.
41. L. Gao, A.L. Rosenberg, and R.K. Sitaraman. Optimal architecture-independent scheduling of fine-grain tree-sweep computations. In *Proceedings of the 7th IEEE Symposium on Parallel and Distributed Processing (SPDP'95)*, pages 620–629, 1995.
42. L. Gao, A.L. Rosenberg, and R.K. Sitaraman. Optimal architecture-independent scheduling of fine-grain tree-sweep computations. Technical Report UM-CS-1997-037, Dept. of Computer Science, University of Massachusetts, Amherst, 1997.
43. A. Gerasoulis and T. Yang. On the granularity and clustering of directed acyclic task graphs. *IEEE Transactions on Parallel and Distributed Systems*, 4(6):686–701, 1993.
44. A. Gerasoulis and T. Yang. Efficient algorithms with a software tool for scheduling parallel computation. In P. Chrétienne, E.G. Coffman Jr., J.K. Lenstra, and Z. Liu, editors, *Scheduling Theory and Its Applications*, pages 111–143. Wiley, Chichester, 1995.
45. R. Giroudeau, J.C. König, F.K. Moulaï, and J. Palaysi. Complexity and approximation for the precedence constrained scheduling problem with large communication delays. In P.D. Medeiros and J.C. Cunha, editors, *Proceedings of Euro-Par 2005. LNCS*, volume 3648, pages 252–261. Springer, Berlin, 2006.
46. A. Goldman, G. Mounie, and D. Trystram. Near optimal algorithms for scheduling independent chains in BSP. In *Proceedings of the 5th International Conference on High Performance Computing (HIPC'98)*, pages 310–317, 1998.
47. F. Guinand and D. Trystram. Scheduling UET trees with communication delays on two processors. *RAIRO Operations Research*, 34(2):131–144, 2000.
48. F. Guinand, A. Moukrim, and E. Sanlaville. Sensitivity analysis of tree scheduling on two machines with communication delays. *Parallel Computing*, 30(1):103–120, 2004.
49. F. Guinand, C. Rapine, and D. Trystram. Worst case analysis of Lawler's algorithm for scheduling trees with communication delays. *IEEE Transactions on Parallel and Distributed Systems*, 8(10):1085–1086, 1997.
50. T. Hagras and J. Janecek. A high performance, low complexity algorithm for compile-time task scheduling in heterogeneous systems. *Parallel Computing*, 31(7):653–670, 2005.
51. C. Hanen and A. Munier Kordon. Minimizing the volume in scheduling an out-tree with communication delays and duplication. *Parallel Computing*, 28(11):1573–1585, 2002.
52. C. Hanen and A. Munier. An approximation algorithm for scheduling dependent tasks on *m* processors with small communication delays. In *Proceedings of INRIA/IEEE Symposium on Emerging Technologies and Factory Automation (ETFA '95)*, volume 1, pages 167–189, 1995.
53. C. Hanen and A. Munier. Using duplication for scheduling unitary tasks on m processors with unit communication delays. *Theoretical Computer Science*, 178(1–2):119–127, 1997.
54. C. Hanen and A. Munier. Performance of Coffman–Graham schedules in the presence of unit communication delays. *Discrete Applied Mathematics*, 81(1–3):93–108, 1998.
55. C. Hanen and A. Munier. An approximation algorithm for scheduling dependent tasks on *m* processors with small communication delays. *Discrete Applied Mathematics*, 108(3):239–257, 2001.
56. D.S. Hochbaum and D.B. Shmoys. Using dual approximation algorithms for scheduling problems: Theoretical and practical results. *Journal of the ACM*, 34(1):144–162, 1987.
57. L. Hollermann, T.-S. Hsu, D.R. Lopez, and K. Vertanen. Scheduling problems in a practical allocation model. *Journal of Combinatorial Optimization*, 1(2):129–149, 1997.
58. H. Hoogeveen, P. Schuurman, and G.J. Woeginger. Non-approximability results for scheduling problems with minsum criteria. *INFORMS Journal on Computing*, 13(2):157–168, 2001.

59. H. Hoogeveen and G.J. Woeginger. A very difficult scheduling problem with communication delays. *Operations Research Letters*, 29(3):241–245, 2001.
60. J.A. Hoogeveen, S.L. van de Velde, and B. Veltman. Three, four, five, six or the complexity of scheduling with communication delays. *Operations Research Letters*, 16(3):129–137, 1994.
61. T.-S. Hsu, J.C. Lee, D.R. Lopez, and W.A. Royce. Task allocation on a network of processors. *IEEE Transactions on Computers*, 49(12):1339–1353, 2000.
62. T.C. Hu. Parallel sequencing and assembly line problems. *Operations Research*, 9(6):841–848, 1961.
63. J.-J. Hwang, Y.-C. Chow, F.D. Anger, and C.-Y. Lee. Scheduling precedence graphs in systems with interprocessor communication times. *SIAM Journal on Computing*, 18(2):244–257, 1989.
64. A. Jakoby and R. Reischuk. The complexity of scheduling problems with communication delays for trees. In O. Nurmi and E. Ukkonen, editors, *Proceedings of the 3rd Scandinavian Workshop on Algorithm Theory (SWAT'92)*. *LNCS*, volume 621, pages 165–177. Springer, Berlin, 1992.
65. H. Jung, L. Kirousis, and P. Spirakis. Lower bounds and efficient algorithms for multiprocessor scheduling of dags with communication delays. In *Proceedings of the 1st Annual ACM Symposium on Parallel Algorithms and Architectures (SPAA'89)*, pages 254–264. ACM, New York, NY, USA, 1989.
66. T. Kalinowski, I. Kort, and D. Trystram. List scheduling of general task graphs under LogP. *Parallel Computing*, 26(9):1109–1128, 2000.
67. O.H. Kang and D.P. Agrawal. Scalable scheduling for symmetric multiprocessors (SMP). *Journal of Parallel and Distributed Computing*, 63(3):273–285, 2003.
68. R.M. Karp, A. Sahay, E.E. Santos, and K.E. Schauser. Optimal broadcast and summation in the LogP model. In *Proceedings of the 5th Annual ACM Symposium on Parallel Algorithms and Architectures (SPAA'93)*, pages 142–153, 1993.
69. S.J. Kim and J.C. Browne. A general approach to mapping of parallel computation upon multiprocessor architectures. In *Proceedings of the International Conference on Parallel Processing*, volume 3, pages 1–8, 1988.
70. B. Kruatrachue and T. Lewis. Grain size determination for parallel processing. *IEEE Software*, 5(1):23–32, 1988.
71. Y.-K. Kwok. Parallel program execution on a heterogeneous PC cluster using task duplication. In *Proceedings of the 9th Heterogeneous Computing Workshop (HCW'00)*, pages 364–374, 2000.
72. Y.-K. Kwok and I. Ahmad. A static scheduling algorithm using dynamic critical path for assigning parallel algorithms onto multiprocessors. In *Proceedings of the International Conference on Parallel Processing (ICPP'94)*, volume 2, pages 155–159, 1994.
73. Y.-K. Kwok and I. Ahmad. Bubble scheduling: A quasi dynamic algorithm for static allocation of tasks to parallel architectures. In *Proceedings of the 7th Symposium on Parallel and Distributed Processing (SPDP'95)*, pages 36–43, 1995.
74. Y.K. Kwok and I. Ahmad. Efficient scheduling of arbitrary task graphs to multiprocessors using a parallel genetic algorithm. *Journal of Parallel and Distributed Computing*, 47(1):58–77, 1997.
75. Y.K. Kwok and I. Ahmad. Benchmarking and comparison of the task graph scheduling algorithms. *Journal of Parallel and Distributed Computing*, 59(3):381–422, 1999.
76. Y.K. Kwok and I. Ahmad. Static scheduling algorithms for allocating directed task graphs to multiprocessors. *ACM Computing Surveys*, 31(4):406–471, 1999.
77. C. Lahlou. Approximation algorithms for scheduling with a limited number of communications. *Parallel Computing*, 26(9):1129–1162, 2000.
78. J.K. Lenstra, M. Veldhorst, and B. Veltman. The complexity of scheduling trees with communication delays. *Journal of Algorithms*, 20(1):157–173, 1996.
79. J.Y. Leung. On scheduling independent tasks with restricted execution times. *Operations Research*, 30(1):163–171, 1982.
80. T. Lewis and H. El-Rewini. Parallax: A tool for parallel program scheduling. *IEEE Parallel & Distributed Technology: Systems & Applications*, 1(2):62–72, 1993.

81. T.G. Lewis, H. El-Rewini, J. Chu, P. Fortner, and W. Su. Task grapher: A tool for scheduling parallel program tasks. In *Proceedings of the 5th Distributed Memory Computing Conference*, volume 2, pages 1171–1178, 1990.

82. J.-C. Liou and M.A. Palis. A new heuristic for scheduling parallel programs on multiprocessor. In *Proceedings of the 7th International Conference on Parallel Architectures and Compilation Techniques (PACT'98)*, pages 358–365, 1998.

83. W. Löwe and W. Zimmermann. Upper time bounds for executing PRAM-programs on the LogP-machine. In *Proceedings of the 9th International Conference on Supercomputing (ICS'95)*, pages 41–50, 1995.

84. G. Malewicz, A. L. Rosenberg, and M. Yurkewych. Toward a theory for scheduling dags in internet-based computing. *IEEE Transactions on Computers*, 55(6):757–768, 2006.

85. B.A. Malloy, E.L. Lloyd, and M.L. Soffa. Scheduling DAGs for asynchronous multiprocessor execution. *IEEE Transactions on Parallel and Distributed Systems*, 5(5):498–508, 1994.

86. R.H. Möhring and M.W. Schäffter. Scheduling series–parallel orders subject to 0/1-communication delays. *Parallel Computing*, 25(1):23–40, 1999.

87. A. Munier. Approximation algorithms for scheduling trees with general communication delays. *Parallel Computing*, 25(1):41–48, 1999.

88. A. Munier and J.-C. König. A heuristic for a scheduling problem with communication delays. *Operations Research*, 45(1):145–147, 1997.

89. M.A. Palis, J.-C. Liou, and D.S.L. Wei. Task clustering and scheduling for distributed memory parallel architectures. *IEEE Transactions on Parallel and Distributed Systems*, 7(1):46–55, 1996.

90. C.H. Papadimitriou and M. Yannakakis. Towards an architecture-independent analysis of parallel algorithms. *SIAM Journal on Computing*, 19(2):322–328, 1990.

91. G.-L. Park, B. Shirazi, and J. Marquis. Mapping of parallel tasks to multiprocessors with duplication. In *Proceedings of the 31st Hawaii International Conference on System Sciences (HICSS'98)*, volume 7, pages 96–105, 1998.

92. G.-L. Park, B. Shirazi, J. Marquis, and H. Choo. Decisive path scheduling: A new list scheduling method. In *Proceedings of the 1997 International Conference on Parallel Processing (ICPP'97)*, pages 472–480, 1997.

93. C. Picouleau. *Etude de Problemes d'Optimisation dans les systemes distribues*. Ph.D. thesis, Universite Paris VI, 1992.

94. C. Picouleau. New complexity results on scheduling with small communication delays. *Discrete Applied Mathematics*, 60(1–3):331–342, 1995.

95. X. Qin and H. Jiang. Dynamic, reliability-driven scheduling of parallel real-time jobs in heterogeneous systems. In *Proceedings of the 2001 International Conference on Parallel Processing (ICPP'01)*, pages 0113–0122, 2001.

96. A. Radulescu and A.J.C. van Gemund. Low-cost task scheduling for distributed-memory machines. *IEEE Transactions on Parallel and Distributed Systems*, 13(6):648–658, 2002.

97. T. Rauber and G. Runger. Compiler support for task scheduling in hierarchical execution models. *Journal of Systems Architecture*, 45(6–7):483–503, 1998.

98. V.J. Rayward-Smith. The complexity of preemptive scheduling given interprocessor communication delays. *Information Processing Letters*, 25:123–125, 1987.

99. V.J. Rayward-Smith. UET scheduling with interprocessor communication delays. *Discrete Applied Mathematics*, 18(1):55–71, 1987.

100. A. Rosenberg. On scheduling mesh-structured computations for internet-based computing. *IEEE Transactions on Computers*, 53(9):1176–1186, 2004.

101. A. Rădulescu, C. Nicolescu, A.J.C. van Gemund, and P.P. Jonker. CPR: Mixed task and data parallel scheduling for distributed systems. In *Proceedings of the 15th International Parallel and Distributed Processing Symposium (IPDPS'01)*, page 1039b, 2001.

102. V. Sarkar. *Partitioning and Scheduling Parallel Programs for Multiprocessors*. MIT Press, Cambridge, MA, USA, 1989.

103. V. Sarkar and J. Hennessy. Compile-time partitioning and scheduling of parallel programs. In *Proceedings of the 1986 SIGPLAN symposium on Compiler construction*, pages 17–26, ACM, New York, NY, USA, 1986.

104. S. Selvakumar and C. Siva Ram Murthy. Scheduling precedence constrained task graphs with non-negligible intertask communication onto multiprocessors. *IEEE Transactions on Parallel and Distributed Systems*, 5(3):328–336, 1994.
105. Z. Shi. *Scheduling tasks with precedence constraints on heterogeneous distributed computing systems*. Ph.D. thesis, University of Tennessee, Knoxville, 2006. http://www.cs.utk.edu/~shi/thesis.pdf [online accessed 2 September 2008].
106. B. Shirazi, H.B. Chen, K. Kavi, J. Marquis, and A.R. Hurson. PARSA: A parallel program software development tool. In *Proceedings of the 3rd Symposium on Assessment of Quality Software Development Tools*, pages 96–111, 1994.
107. B. Shirazi, H.B. Chen, and J. Marquis. Comparative study of task duplication static scheduling versus clustering and nonclustering heuristics. *Concurrency: Practice and Experience*, 7(5):371–389, 1995.
108. G. Sih and E. Lee. A compile-time scheduling heuristic for interconnection constrained heterogeneous processor architectures. *IEEE Transactions on Parallel and Distributed Systems*, 4(2):175–187, 1993.
109. G. Sih and E. Lee. Declustering: A new multiprocessor scheduling technique. *IEEE Transactions on Parallel and Distributed Systems*, 4(6):625–63, 1993.
110. O. Sinnen. *Task Scheduling for Parallel Systems*. Wiley, Hoboken, New Jersey, 2007.
111. O. Sinnen and L.A. Sousa. Communication contention in task scheduling. *IEEE Transactions on Parallel and Distributed Systems*, 16(6):503–515, 2005.
112. A. Świecicka, F. Seredynski, and A.Y. Zomaya. Multiprocessor scheduling and rescheduling with use of cellular automata and artificial immune system support. *IEEE Transactions on Parallel and Distributed Systems*, 17(3):253–262, 2006.
113. L. Valiant. A bridging model for parallel computation. *Communications of the ACM*, 33(8):103–111, 1990.
114. T.A. Varvarigou, V.P. Roychowdhury, and T. Kailath. Scheduling in and out forests in the presence of communication delays. In *Proceedings of the 7th International Parallel Processing Symposium (IPPS'93)*, pages 222–229, 1993.
115. T.A. Varvarigou, V.P. Roychowdhury, T. Kailath, and E. Lawler. Scheduling in and out forests in the presence of communication delays. *IEEE Transactions on Parallel and Distributed Systems*, 7(10):1065–1074, 1996.
116. B. Veltman. *Multiprocessor scheduling with communication delays*. Ph.D. thesis, Technical University Eindhoven, 1993.
117. B. Veltman, B.J. Lageweg, and J.K. Lenstra. Multiprocessor scheduling with communications delays. *Parallel Computing*, 16:173–182, 1990.
118. J. Verriet. Scheduling interval orders with release dates and deadlines. Technical Report UU-CS-1996-12, Department of Information and Computing Sciences, Utrecht University, 1996. http://www.cs.uu.nl/research/techreps/repo/CS-1996/1996-12.pdf [online accessed 29 June 2008].
119. J. Verriet. *Scheduling with communication for multiprocessor computation*. Ph.D. thesis, Universiteit Utrecht, The Netherlands, 1998.
120. J. Verriet. Scheduling interval-ordered tasks with non-uniform deadlines subject to non-zero communication delays. *Parallel Computing*, 25(1):3–21, 1999.
121. J. Verriet. Scheduling outtrees of height one in the LogP model. *Parallel Computing*, 26(9):1065–1082, 2000.
122. J. Verriet. Scheduling tree-like task systems with non-uniform deadlines subject to unit-length communication delays. *Discrete Applied Mathematics*, 101(1–3):269–289, 2000.
123. L. Wang, H.J. Siegel, V.P. Roychowdhury, and A.A. Maciejewski. Task matching and scheduling in heterogeneous computing environments using a genetic-algorithm-based approach. *Journal of Parallel and Distributed Computing*, 47(1):8–22, 1997.
124. M.-Y. Wu and D.D. Gajski. Hypertool: A programming aid for message-passing systems. *IEEE Transactions on Parallel and Distributed Systems*, 1(3):330–343, 1990.
125. T. Yang and A. Gerasoulis. List scheduling with and without communication delays. *Parallel Computing*, 19(12):1321–1344, 1993.

126. T. Yang and A. Gerasoulis. DSC: Scheduling parallel tasks on an unbounded number of processors. *IEEE Transactions on Parallel and Distributed Systems*, 5(9):951–967, 1994.
127. W. Zimmermann, W. Löwe, and D. Trystram. On scheduling send-graphs and receive-graphs under the LogP-model. *Information Processing Letters*, 82(2):83–92, 2002.
128. A. Zomaya and G. Chan. Efficient clustering for parallel task execution in distributed systems. *International Journal of Foundations of Computer Science*, 16(2):281–299, 2005.

# Chapter 7
# Divisible Loads

In this chapter, we study scheduling of divisible loads (DL). This model of parallel processing assumes that the computation can be *divided* into parts of arbitrary sizes, and these parts can be *independently* processed in parallel. The two assumptions on arbitrary divisibility and independence of execution are in fact very strong. The grains of parallelism determine possible partitions of the parallel computations. Consequently, in divisible computations the grains of parallelism are negligibly small. The nature of the algorithm executed in a distributed manner determines how often the distributed threads must communicate, and hence synchronize. Here the need for communication between remote processors can be ignored. The above assumptions match easily data parallel computations which are processing great amounts of similar data units. In the following sections examples of data parallel applications conforming with divisible load model will be presented. The data are commonly called *load*. The area of parallel processing dedicated to the analysis of divisible applications is called *divisible load theory* (DLT).

In a simple form divisible applications can be performed in the following way: Initially, some amount of load resides on a processor called an *originator*. The originator divides the load and sends it to its neighbors for remote processing. The originator's neighbors intercept some part of the load for local processing, and relay the rest of the load to the still inactive processors for remote execution. This load scattering procedure is continued until activating all the processors taking part in the computation. After completion of the computations, the results may be returned to the originator. The goal is to scatter the load so that communications and computations finished in the shortest time. Thus, in the DLT communication delays are explicitly taken into account. This generic organization of a distributed divisible computation will be detailed in the following sections.

DLT originated in the late 1980s with publications [2, 36]. In the first paper an effective distribution of parallel computation on a network of workstations was sought for. A general mathematical programming formulation was the tool for solving the problem. It could be reduced to a linear program in a special case. In the second paper a chain of intelligent sensors was considered, and the practical question was how

M. Drozdowski, *Scheduling for Parallel Processing*, Computer Communications and Networks, DOI 10.1007/978-1-84882-310-5_7,
© Springer-Verlag London Limited 2009

to distribute processing of the arriving measurements. The authors faced a dilemma: Parallel computations may be finished earlier, but distributing data costs time. How much load should be distributed, and how much processed locally? The mathematical model was reduced to a set of linear equations. This mathematical simplicity may have contributed to the initial interest in the DLT model. Later DLT developed in many new directions. At the time of writing these words, DLT comprises over 160 scientific publications and two patents [96]. Unfortunately, not all of them can be mentioned here. Surveys of divisible load theory can be found in [21, 22, 39, 94, 95].

In this chapter, we depart from the framework of the classic scheduling theory, because in majority of DLT publications only single load is considered. Consequently, beyond schedule length ($C_{max}$), the classic optimality criteria have little applicability. Moreover, the research did not follow the framework of the classic scheduling theory. Instead, DLT has been expanded and generalized in many other ways. In the following sections, we present the orthogonal directions in which the DLT developed. We start with the basic model of processing divisible load in a star network where terminology and notations are introduced. The following sections consider using DLT in diversified settings. Examples of applying DLT in practice are given in the penultimate section, when the DLT concepts and terminology are already known.

## 7.1   Star – Basic Formulation

In this section, we present a simple model of processing divisible load in a star network, a.k.a. a single level tree (cf. Fig. 7.1a). Star network can be a reference model for the DLT. A simple initial formulation will be generalized in the following paragraphs.

### 7.1.1   Base Model

Let us assume that initially amount $V$ of load is held by the originator $P_0$ (here also called root, master). The originator divides the load into parts $\alpha_1, \ldots, \alpha_m$ to

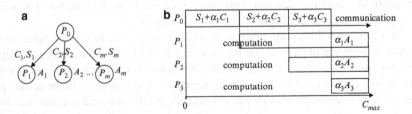

**Fig. 7.1** (a) Star interconnection. (b) A schedule without returning the results

be processed on worker processors $P_1, \ldots, P_m$. The processors are numbered according to the order of receiving the load. Implicitly we assumed that the originator performs a role of a scheduler, and does no computing. The worker processors receive their whole share of the load from the originator first, and then start computing. There are no communications between processors $P_1, \ldots, P_m$. The star network can model a variety of parallel systems using master–slave, or master–worker, paradigm: a set of CPUs sharing a bus in an SMP system [10], a network of workstations connected by a single segment of Ethernet [2,48], a set of computing clusters connected via Internet to a master controller [13]. In the case of bus interconnection a simplifying assumption is often made that communication links are identical. A piece of load $\alpha_i$ is transferred to $P_i$ in time $S_i + \alpha_i C_i$. Thus, the communication delay is an affine function with two components: a constant start-up time $S_i$ (expressed, e.g., in seconds) and a part linearly increasing with the amount of the transferred load. Here $C_i$ is reciprocal of bandwidth and is expressed, e.g., in seconds per byte. Load $\alpha_i$ is processed by $P_i$ in time $\alpha_i A_i$. Parameters $A_i, C_i, S_i$ depend on the application and computing system. Let us assume, for the time being, that the time of returning the results to the originator is negligibly small, or that the results of the computation need not be returned. In this case an *optimality principle* proved in [10, 13, 21, 29, 36, 99] states that all processors taking part in the computation should stop computing in the same moment of time. Now, the problem is to find load partition $\alpha_1, \ldots, \alpha_m$ such that the time of communication and computation is the shortest possible. Notice that in this case the time of computing on a processor activated earlier is equal to the time of sending the load to the next processor and computing the load (cf. Fig. 7.1b). After adding a requirement that all the load must be processed, the problem of determining load sizes $\alpha_1, \ldots, \alpha_m$ reduces to solving a linear system:

$$\alpha_i A_i = S_{i+1} + \alpha_{i+1}(A_{i+1} + C_{i+1}) \quad \text{for } i = 1, \ldots, m-1 \qquad (7.1)$$

$$\sum_{i=1}^{m} \alpha_i = V \qquad (7.2)$$

The above system of linear equations can be solved in $O(m)$ time due to its special structure. For example, $\alpha_i$ (for $i = m, \ldots, 1$) can be expressed as a linear function $k_i \alpha_m + l_i$ of $\alpha_m$, where $k_m = 1, l_m = 0, k_i = k_{i+1} \frac{A_{i+1} + C_{i+1}}{A_i}, l_i = \frac{S_{i+1}}{A_i} + l_{i+1} \frac{A_{i+1} + C_{i+1}}{A_i}$. Then we have

$$\alpha_m = \frac{V - \sum_{i=1}^{m} l_i}{\sum_{i=1}^{m} k_i} \qquad (7.3)$$

If $\forall i, S_i = 0$, then load distribution is simpler to calculate, so that even *closed-form solutions* exist [9]. Note that $k_i = \prod_{j=i}^{m-1} \frac{A_{j+1} + C_{j+1}}{A_j}$, for $i < m$, and $l_i = 0$ in this case. The load sizes for $i = m, \ldots, 1$ can be calculated from equations

$$\alpha_i = V \frac{\prod_{j=i}^{m-1} \frac{A_{j+1}+C_{j+1}}{A_j}}{\sum_{h=1}^{m} \prod_{j=h}^{m-1} \frac{A_{j+1}+C_{j+1}}{A_j}} \tag{7.4}$$

For identical processors $\forall i$, $A_i = A, C_i = C$, Eq. (7.4) reduces to $\alpha_i = V \frac{\phi^{m-i}(\phi-1)}{\phi^m-1}$, where $\phi = \frac{A+C}{A}$. Closed-form solutions quite often can be derived when start-up times are negligible, or when the system is homogeneous.

In the preceding discussion we assumed that the originator does no computing. The computing capability of the originator may be represented as an additional processor. If the originator is able to communicate and compute simultaneously, then $P_0$ receives the load as the first one, over a "link" with communication parameters $S_0 = C_0 = 0$. If the originator is not able to compute and communicate simultaneously, then the load is sent to $P_1, \ldots, P_m$ first, and then load $\alpha_0$ is "sent" in no time to $P_0$.

## 7.1.2   Start-Up Times, Message Sequencing, Complexity

In the solution of equation system (7.1)–(7.2), $\alpha_m$ may be negative (cf. also (7.3)). This means that system (7.1)–(7.2) is infeasible, and load $V$ is too small to activate all processors $P_1, \ldots, P_m$. Consequently, some processors should be eliminated from the computing set, or alternatively, the load size $V$ must be sufficiently big to exploit all the processors. Similar situation appears in other topologies and other divisible load scheduling cases if start-up times are nonzero. This rises two questions: (1) which processors from set $\mathcal{P}$ should be used and (2) what is the optimum sequence of sending the load to the processors. To answer these questions let us first consider the case of negligible start-up times ($\forall i, S_i = 0$). Notice that if $\forall i, S_i = 0$, then $\forall i, l_i = 0$ in Eq. (7.3), and $\alpha_m$ is non-negative. Thus, equation system (7.1)–(7.2) is always feasible, and arbitrarily big number of processors may take part in the computation. Such a situation is unrealistic because the inevitable costs of parallelism prevent activation of arbitrarily big numbers of computers in finite time. For the same case of negligible start-up times ($\forall i, S_i = 0$), it has been shown in several independent publications [17, 19, 29, 72] that the order of activating the processors resulting in the shortest schedule is the order of nondecreasing communication rates ($C_1 \leq C_2 \leq \cdots \leq C_m$). This result may be considered surprising because the speed of processors (reciprocals of $A_i$s) is meaningless in this case. Nevertheless, it may be concluded that the sequence of sending the load to the processors does matter.

Let us now consider nonzero start-up times ($\forall i, S_i \geq 0$). The problem of selecting the optimum set of processors taking part in the computation, the sequence of communications, and the sizes of the load parts can be expressed as the following mixed quadratic mathematical programming formulation:

$$\text{minimize } C_{\max} \text{ subject to} \qquad (7.5)$$

$$\sum_{k=1}^{i}\sum_{j=1}^{m} x_{kj}(S_j + \alpha_j C_j) + \sum_{j=1}^{m} x_{ij}\alpha_j A_j \le C_{\max} \text{ for } i = 1,\dots,m \qquad (7.6)$$

$$\sum_{i=1}^{m} x_{ij} \le 1 \text{ for } j = 1,\dots,m \qquad (7.7)$$

$$\sum_{j=1}^{m} x_{ij} \le 1 \text{ for } i = 1,\dots,m \qquad (7.8)$$

$$\sum_{i=1}^{m}\sum_{j=1}^{m} x_{ij}\alpha_i = V \qquad (7.9)$$

$$\alpha_i, C_{\max} \ge 0 \qquad (7.10)$$

$$x_{ij} \in \{0,1\} \qquad (7.11)$$

In the above formulation $\alpha_i, C_{\max}, x_{ij}$ are variables. Here $x_{ij} = 1$ if and only if processor $P_j$ participates in the computation, and is activated as the $i$th in the communication sequence, otherwise $x_{ij} = 0$. Value $\sum_{k=1}^{i}\sum_{j=1}^{m} x_{kj}(S_j + \alpha_j C_j)$ is the duration of the first $i$ communications. Hence, inequalities (7.6) guarantee that all computations finish by the end of the schedule. Inequalities (7.7) and (7.8), respectively, ensure that each processor is activated at most once, and only one processor takes the $i$th position in the communication sequence. All the load is processed by Eq. (7.9).

The complexity of selecting the optimum set of processors remained open for quite long time, finally it has been shown in [110] that selecting the optimum set of processors is **NPh** even if $\forall i, C_i = 0$. For this particular case a pseudopolynomial algorithm has been given [110]. For identical communication links ($\forall i, C_i = C, S_i = S > 0$) the processors should be activated in the order of decreasing computing speed ($A_1 \le A_2 \le \cdots \le \cdots A_m$) [29]. In [53] various processor sequencing methods have been compared experimentally.

Similarly to the communication start-up times, computation start-up times $z_i$ for processor $P_i$ may be included in the mathematical model, see e.g. [6,17,25,41,111]. These can be accounted for by adding appropriate computation start-up times on both sides of Eq. (7.1). For the simplicity of presentation, with few exceptions, we do not consider computation start-up times in the following sections.

## 7.1.3   Communication Options

So far we assumed that the time of returning the results may be ignored. Returning the results may be included in the DLT model (see Fig. 7.2) if the sequence of

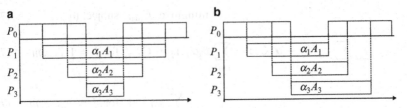

**Fig. 7.2** (a) Returning the results in the LIFO order. (b) Returning the results in the FIFO order

returning the results and their amounts are known. For example, suppose that the computation produces $\beta_1 + \beta_2\alpha$ units of results (e.g. bytes) per $\alpha$ units of input load, and the processors return the results in the inverted order of the activation (last in first out, see Fig. 7.2a). Here $\beta_1, \beta_2$ are application-specific constants. Then Eq. (7.1) should be substituted with

$$\alpha_i A_i = 2S_{i+1} + \alpha_{i+1}(A_{i+1} + C_{i+1}) + C_{i+1}(\beta_1 + \beta_2\alpha_{i+1}) \qquad (7.12)$$

for $i = 1, \ldots, m - 1$. If the results are returned in the order of activating the processors (first in first out, Fig. 7.2b), Eq. (7.1) should be substituted with

$$\alpha_i A_i + S_i + C_i(\beta_1 + \beta_2\alpha_{i+1}) = S_{i+1} + \alpha_{i+1}(A_{i+1} + C_{i+1}) \qquad (7.13)$$

for $i = 1, \ldots, m - 1$.

If the processors have sufficiently effective communication subsystem, then the computations may start while receiving the load [71]. This means that as soon as the first grain of parallelism which can be feasibly processed according to the logic of the application is received, the computations may be started. This mode of operation is called *nonblocking communication* or *simultaneous start* of computation and communication. Let $\phi_i$ denote the time of transferring a grain of parallelism to processor $P_i$. In the current case computing on processor $P_{i+1}$ may be started after sending the whole load to $P_i$, and the starting grain of load to $P_{i+1}$. Hence, to find the distribution of the load, one should substitute (7.1) with the following equations:

$$\alpha_i A_i = S_i + \alpha_i C_i + \phi_{i+1} + \alpha_{i+1} A_{i+1} \quad \text{for } i = 1, \ldots, m - 1 \qquad (7.14)$$

One more variation in the star network is allowing for simultaneous communication over all links from the originator to processors $P_1, \ldots, P_m$ (see e.g. [29,94]). In this case communications to the processors start simultaneously, and computations finish computationally. This leads to the substitution of Eq. (7.1) by

$$S_1 + \alpha_1(A_1 + C_1) = S_i + \alpha_i(A_i + C_i) \quad \text{for } i = 2, \ldots, m \qquad (7.15)$$

Hence, $\alpha_i = \alpha_1 \frac{A_1 + C_1}{A_i + C_i} + \frac{S_1 - S_i}{A_i + C_i}$, and $\alpha_1$ can be found by substitution of $\alpha_i$s in Eq. (7.2).

### 7.1.4  Equivalent Speed

For the end of this section let us note that having calculated the load partition $\alpha_1, \ldots, \alpha_m$ we can reduce the whole star to an equivalent processor with processing rate $A_{eq} = \frac{\alpha_1(C_1+A_1)+S_1}{V}$. The equivalent processing rate has qualitatively different nature depending on the start-up times. If $\forall i, S_i = 0$ then $A_{eq}$ is a constant which can be calculated using (7.4). On the other hand, if $\exists S_i \neq 0$, then the feasibility of equation systems (7.1) and (7.2) depends on load size $V$. Consequently, $A_{eq}$ is also a function of $V$.

## 7.2  Interconnection Topologies

In this section, we examine how DLT can be applied to partition the load in various interconnection topologies. For simplicity of formulation we assume that the time of returning the results to the originator can be neglected. This does not limit generality of the considerations because results returning can be added to the model as presented in Sect. 7.1. It seems that applying DLT in some interconnection network boils down to designing an appropriate load scattering algorithm.

### 7.2.1  Chains

The chain or linear network of processors has been first studied in [36]. Here only neighboring pairs $(P_i, P_{i+1})$ of processors, for $i = 1, \ldots, m-1$, are able to communicate. The network is depicted in Fig. 7.3a. Assume that $P_1$ is the originator, and

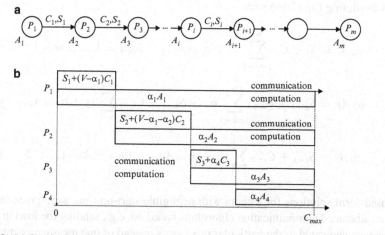

**Fig. 7.3** (a) Chain of processors. (b) A schedule for processors with communication front-end

that all processors are capable of communicating and computing simultaneously. The latter means that the processors are equipped with a communication front-end hardware (such as NIC and DMA) performing communications when the CPU is computing. A message sent from processor $P_i$ to processor $P_{i+1}$ includes load for processors $P_{i+1}, \ldots, P_m$. On the receipt of the load, $P_{i+1}$ immediately starts processing its load share $\alpha_{i+1}$, while the rest of the load is simultaneously sent to $P_{i+2}$. If the result returning time is negligible, then the time of computing on $P_i$ is equal to the time of sending the load to $P_{i+1}$ and computing on it (see Fig. 7.3b). Thus, the distribution of the load may be calculated from the linear system:

$$\alpha_i A_i = S_i + C_i \sum_{j=i+1}^{m} \alpha_j + \alpha_{i+1} A_{i+1} \quad \text{for } i = 1, \ldots, m-1 \quad (7.16)$$

$$\sum_{i=1}^{m} \alpha_i = V \quad (7.17)$$

Suppose that processors are not able to communicate and compute simultaneously. Then, each processor $P_i$ sends the load to its neighbor first, and only then can it start computing its share $\alpha_i$. In this case Eq. (7.16) should be replaced with

$$\alpha_i A_i = S_{i+1} + C_{i+1} \sum_{j=i+2}^{m} \alpha_j + \alpha_{i+1} A_{i+1} \quad \text{for } i = 1, \ldots, m-2 \quad (7.18)$$

$$\alpha_{m-1} A_{m-1} = \alpha_m A_m \quad (7.19)$$

If load originates from the interior of the network, then the load may be distributed in two directions. Suppose $P_k$, where $1 < k < m$, is the originator and the message to $P_{k+1}$ is sent before the message to $P_{k-1}$. The computations should stop simultaneously in both branches of the chain. Therefore, load partition may be calculated by substituting Eq. (7.16) with

$$\alpha_i A_i = S_i + C_i \sum_{j=i+1}^{m} \alpha_j + \alpha_{i+1} A_{i+1} \quad \text{for } i = k, \ldots, m-1 \quad (7.20)$$

$$\alpha_k A_k = S_{k+1} + C_{k+1} \sum_{j=k+1}^{m} \alpha_j + S_{k-1} + C_{k-1} \sum_{j=1}^{k-1} \alpha_j + \alpha_{k-1} A_{k-1} \quad (7.21)$$

$$\alpha_i A_i = S_{i-1} + C_{i-1} \sum_{j=1}^{i-1} \alpha_j + \alpha_{i-1} A_{i-1} \quad \text{for } i = k-1, \ldots, 2 \quad (7.22)$$

Closed-form solutions for a chain with negligible start-up time were given in [84]. More advanced communication algorithms based on, e.g., sending the load in many messages dedicated to the particular processors instead of one message aggregating the load, sending the load to processors in the order from the end of the chain toward the originator, multi-installment load distribution (cf. Sect. 7.3), and circuit switching commutation have been studied in [23, 39, 57, 76].

## 7.2.2 Trees

Tree topology was considered first in [35]. The distribution of the load can be found by combining the ideas applied in star and chain topologies. A subtree with leaves and a common predecessor is a single level tree or a star. On each path from the originator $P_0$, which is the root of the tree, to any internal node $P_i$ a message is carrying load for $P_i$ and all its successors. Let us consider the case when the results are not returned to the originator, processors can communicate and compute simultaneously, but only one message may be sent at a given time. Let us denote by $AS(i)$ the set of $P_i$ and all its successors (not necessarily immediate). $Pre(i)$ is the processor which shares a parent with $P_i$ but receives its load just before $P_i$. If $P_i$ receives the load first among the siblings, then $Pre(i)$ is the parent of $P_i$. The above sets represent the tree structure and communication schedule. Without loss of generality, let $P_1$ be the first processor which receives the load from the originator. The communication parameters of a link arriving at $P_i$ are $C_i, S_i$, for $i = 1, \ldots, m$. Since the results are not returned computations on all processors must stop simultaneously. The load distribution can be calculated from the linear system

$$\alpha_{Pre(i)} A_{Pre(i)} = S_i + C_i \sum_{j \in AS(i)} \alpha_j + \alpha_i A_i \quad \text{for } i = 2, \ldots, m \qquad (7.23)$$

$$\sum_{i=1}^{m} \alpha_i = V \qquad (7.24)$$

In the above description we assumed that all processors take part in the computation, and that the sequence of communications is known. If $\exists i, S_i > 0$, then load $V$ may be too small to activate all the processors. The problem of selecting the optimum set of processors participating in the computation is **NPh** [110] already for a star topology, hence it is computationally hard also for trees.

When the start-up times are negligible ($\forall i, S_i = 0$), then partitioning of the load in a tree can be conveniently found by applying the concept of equivalent processor to each subtree, and folding the tree bottom-up from the leaves to the root. More precisely, each subtree with just some leaves and a common root $P_i$ can be reduced to an equivalent processor with equivalent processing rate $A_{i,eq}$. Note that $P_i$ is computing, and its processing capability must be included in $A_{i,eq}$. From the discussion in Sect. 7.1 we know that in the current case (cf. (7.4)), $A_{i,eq}$ is a constant independent of the assigned load. This procedure may be applied recursively to fold up the whole tree to the root $P_0$ and its direct neighbors representing their subtrees. Then, the load distribution is calculated as for a star. The load part assigned to a particular equivalent processor is again partitioned between its successors using the star topology. This procedure applied recursively unfolds the tree and determines the load distribution for a whole tree. This method has been applied e.g. in [9, 11, 12, 14, 31, 112].

Divisible load processing with or without communication front end, with or without returning of the results, has been analyzed in [35]. Low-order complexity heuristics to find the set of active processors and communication sequence were proposed in [6]. Specific trees were foundation of load scattering in other interconnection topologies. We will present them in the following text.

### 7.2.3 Meshes

In this section, we assume that the meshes are homogeneous. The computing rate is $A$, and communication link parameters are $C$, $S$, for communication rate and start-up time, respectively. Processors can communicate and compute simultaneously. Originator $P_0$ takes part in the computation. The time of returning the results is negligible.

Divisible load processing algorithms for meshes were built on the basis of various load scattering algorithms. The first publication on divisible load scheduling in meshes [28] assumed that the originator is located in the center of a 2D-mesh, communication start-up costs is negligible ($S = 0$), the load is distributed in a store-and-forward manner from a processor to a processor. The sets of processors activated in the same iteration of load distribution formed *layers* of rectangular shape around the originator (Fig. 7.4a). The whole layers may be treated as processors connected in a chain. By the use of the equivalent speed of the whole layer of processors, performance limits of a 2D-mesh network with store-and-forward load scattering have been analyzed (compare the analysis for a chain in Sect. 7.12.2).

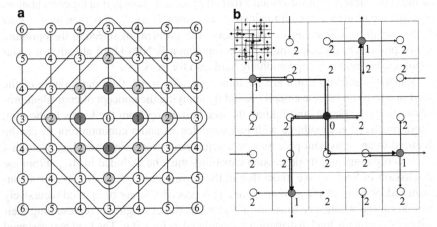

**Fig. 7.4** Load scattering in a 2D-mesh (**a**) using store-and-forward routing and (**b**) using circuit switching and $p = 4$ ports

A different set of scattering algorithms were proposed for circuit-switched and wormhole routing. In circuit switching and wormhole routing the communication delay does not depend on the distance between the sender and the receiver (cf. Sect. 3.1.3). As a result it is possible to send the load very far from the originator, and then to redistribute it in remote parts of the network. A 2D-mesh broadcasting algorithm taking advantage of such a structure of communication delay was proposed in [91]. It was adopted as a scattering algorithm for divisible loads, and generalized in a series of publications [3, 39, 40, 52, 58]. The method of load scattering for 2D-toroidal mesh, based on [91] and used in [3], is presented in Fig. 7.4b. Each scattering iteration has two steps: chess queen moves and then cross moves using the torus wrap-around connections. Note that the pattern of load distribution recursively repeats itself in submeshes of five times smaller side size. Furthermore, all communication ports of the already activated processors are used in each step of load distribution. Let $p$ denote the number of processor ports used in each step of load distribution. Examples of load scattering patterns for different numbers of ports $p$, 2D-, and 3D-meshes are shown in Fig. 7.5. Also here the communication path patterns are repeated in submeshes with $p + 1$ times shorter side size, and all $p$ ports of the active processors are busy in each communication step. More examples for 3D-meshes and various number of ports $p$ used simultaneously can be found in [39].

Let us now make some observations on the general structure of the scattering patterns presented in Figs. 7.4b and 7.5. The processors act synchronously, and all processors activated in iteration $i$ receive load simultaneously. In the first scattering step the originator distributes load to $p$ processors. In the next step each activated processor sends load to $p$ new processors. Thus, $p(p + 1)^{i-1}$ processors receive load in step $i$ of scattering. At the end of step $i$ the number of active, and hence

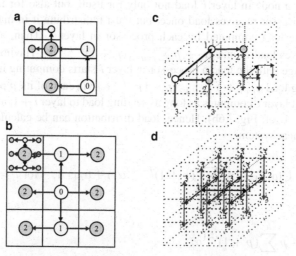

**Fig. 7.5** Load scattering in meshes using circuit switching, and different numbers of ports $p$: (**a**) 2D-mesh, $p = 1$ (**b**) 2D-mesh, $p = 2$ (**c**) 3D-mesh, $p = 1$ and (**d**) 3D-mesh $p = 2$

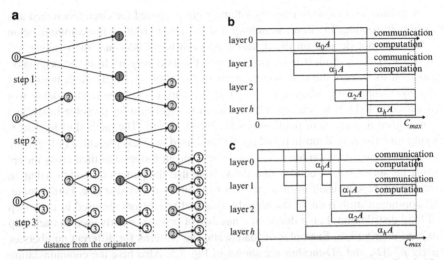

**Fig. 7.6** (a) 3-Nomial tree spread along the distance in the network. (b) A schedule for simple load scattering in $(p + 1)$-nomial tree. (c) A schedule for LLF scattering strategy

already computing, processors is $(p + 1)^i$. The scattering can be viewed as a tree which can be called a $(p + 1)$-nomial tree. Let us call a *layer* the set of processors activated in the same step, and hence on the same level of the $(p + 1)$-nomial tree. Let $h = \log_{p+1} m$ be the last level in the tree (the tree has $h + 1$ levels including the root at level 0). Each node at levels $0, \ldots, i < h$ has exactly $p$ successors at level $i + 1$. This is illustrated in Fig. 7.6a. A processor activated in iteration $i < h$ has successors in layers $i + 1, \ldots, h$. Each of the successors in layers $i + 1, \ldots, h$ must receive from a node in layer $i$ load not only for itself, but also for its successors. Hence, a processor receives load once, but must redistribute it in many steps. Let $\alpha_i$ denote the load computed by each processor in layer $i$. Then, a processor in layer $i$ receives load of size $\alpha_i + p \sum_{j=i+1}^{h} (p + 1)^{j-i-1} \alpha_j$. Having received the whole message with the load a processor in layer $i$ starts computing its part $\alpha_i$, and redistributing load $\alpha_{i+1} + \sum_{j=i+2}^{h} (p + 1)^{j-i-2} \alpha_j$ via each of its $p$ ports. It can be observed that layer $i$ computes as long as sending load to layer $i + 1$, and computing on layer $i + 1$ (cf. Fig. 7.6b). Hence, load distribution can be calculated from the following linear system:

$$\alpha_i A = S + C\left(\alpha_{i+1} + p \sum_{j=i+2}^{h} (p + 1)^{j-i-2} \alpha_j\right) + \alpha_{i+1} A, \quad \text{for } i = 0, \ldots, h - 1$$

$$(7.25)$$

$$V = \alpha_0 + p \sum_{i=1}^{h} (p + 1)^{i-1} \alpha_i \qquad (7.26)$$

Closed-form solutions for the above equations were derived in [40].

A different load distribution strategy on $(p + 1)$-nomial trees has been proposed in [58] and later in [52]. Instead of starting computations as soon as any load arrives to a processor, the whole communication network is exploited to activate selected layer of processors. It has been shown [58] that *Largest Layer First* (LLF) method activating the layers in the order of decreasing number of processors (see Fig. 7.6c) has the shortest schedule length among all possible activation orders. Let us analyze communication time in activating layer $i$. Layer $i$ receives load in $i$ steps. Processors in layer $i$ receive load $p(p + 1)^{i-1}\alpha_i$ in total. In the first step originator sends load $p(p + 1)^{i-2}\alpha_i$ over each of its $p$ ports to layer 1 which will be redistributed from layer 1, via layers $2, \ldots, i - 1$ to layer $i$. The remaining load $p(p + 1)^{i-2}\alpha_i$ is sent from the originator to layer $i$ via layers $2, \ldots, i - 1$, bypassing layers $1, \ldots, i - 2$, respectively. More generally, in step $j < i$ all active processors send to layer $j$ load of size $p(p + 1)^{i-j-1}\alpha_i$. Hence, the total time of communication to layer $i$ is $Si + C\alpha_i(1 + p\sum_{j=1}^{i-1}(p + 1)^{i-j-1}) = Si + C(p + 1)^{i-1}\alpha_i$. The load partitioning between the processors can be found by solving the following set of equations:

$$\alpha_0 A = Sh + C(p + 1)^{h-1}\alpha_h + \alpha_h A \tag{7.27}$$

$$\alpha_i A = S(i - 1) + C(p + 1)^{i-2}\alpha_{i-1} + \alpha_{i-1}A, \quad \text{for } i = h, \ldots, 2 \tag{7.28}$$

$$V = \alpha_0 + p\sum_{i=1}^{h}(p + 1)^{i-1}\alpha_i \tag{7.29}$$

It was shown in [52] that if messages have restricted sizes imposed, e.g., by limited sizes of communication buffers, then LLF is not always the best load scattering strategy. In this case *Nearest Layer First* (NLF) activation order which is opposite of LLF may be advantageous.

### 7.2.4 Hypercubes

In this section, we assume that the system is homogeneous, processors can communicate and commute simultaneously, originator takes part in the computation, the time of returning the results is negligible. Similarly to the networks presented above, a load scattering algorithm is necessary as an intermediary between the interconnection topology and divisible load processing model. The load in a hypercube may be distributed by activating processors along consecutive hypercube dimensions. For example, $P_0$ sends load to processor $P_1$ along dimension 0, then $P_0$, $P_1$ send load to $P_2$, $P_3$, respectively, along dimension 1, etc. This scattering method uses binomial tree embedded in the $\log m$-dimensional mesh of side size 2. Note that this is a special case of $(p + 1)$-nomial tree, for $p = 1$, presented in Sect. 7.2.3. A disadvantage of this approach is that only one path is used to activate a processor.

Hypercube scattering algorithms taking advantage of dense network structure have been proposed in [27, 39]. We will present here only two simple algorithms. Before proceeding with further presentation let us remind some features of hypercube network (cf. Sect. 3.1.3). Let $d = \log m$. Each processor of the hypercube may be labeled with $d$-bit binary number such that neighboring nodes differ in exactly one bit. Thus, there are $\log m$ ports in each node. Suppose originator $P_0$ has label 0. Then, its direct neighbors have exactly one bit equal 1 in their labels. The processors in a distance of two hops from the originator have two bits equal to 1 in their labels. Analogously, processors with $i$ 1s in their labels are $i$ hops away from the originator. Let us call a *layer* the set of processors in equal distance from the originator. The number of processors in layer $i$ is $\binom{d}{i}$. Since the neighboring processors differ only in one bit, each node in layer $i$ can be reached via $i$ ports. A processor in layer $i$ may send load to layer $i + 1$ through $d - i$ ports.

In the first scattering algorithm load is passed from layer to layer in a store-and-forward manner as if in a chain. The originator sends the load for layers $2, \ldots, d$ over its $d$ ports in the first communication step. Then processors in layer 1 (counting from 0) intercept their load part $\alpha_1$, and relay the remaining load to layer 2. In the same way processors in layer $i > 1$ capture $\alpha_i$ units of the load from the received messages, and send the remaining load to layer $i + 1 \leq d$. When held in layer $i$ the load for layers $i + 1, \ldots, d$ is equally distributed between all $\binom{d}{i}$ processors of layer $i$. This load is relayed in equal sizes to $d - i$ ports. Since the time of returning the results is negligible, all processors should stop computing simultaneously. Consequently, the time of computing in layer $i$ is equal to the time of sending to layer $i + 1$, and computing on it. Load partitioning can be calculated from the following linear system:

$$\alpha_i A = S + C \frac{\sum_{j=i+1}^{d} \binom{d}{j} \alpha_j}{(d-i)\binom{d}{i}} + \alpha_{i+1} A \qquad \text{for } i = 0, \ldots, d-1 \quad (7.30)$$

$$V = \sum_{i=0}^{d} \binom{d}{i} \alpha_i \qquad (7.31)$$

A different scattering algorithm takes advantage of circuit-switching routing and partitions the load in the intermediate layers without storing it. A processor in layer $i$, having received its part of the load from $i$ predecessors, immediately starts computing. The remaining load is relayed to $d - i$ output ports in equal shares without storing in layer $i$. Hence, the messages to layers $i + 1, \ldots, d$ reach their destinations nearly immediately after departing the originator, and the bandwidth of the $d$ output ports of the originator is determining the communication delay. Hence, the distribution of the load can be found from the following equations:

$$\alpha_i A = S + \alpha_{i+1} \left( \frac{C}{d} \binom{d}{i+1} + A \right) \qquad \text{for } i = 0, \ldots, d-1 \quad (7.32)$$

$$V = \sum_{i=0}^{d} \binom{d}{i} \alpha_i \qquad (7.33)$$

Other methods of divisible load scheduling in hypercube networks were considered in [39].

## 7.2.5   Arbitrary Graphs

Scheduling divisible loads in an arbitrary graph $G = (\mathcal{P}, E)$, where $\mathcal{P}$ is the set of processors and $E$ the set of communication links between them, depends on the scattering algorithm. Very often trees are embedded in the graphs, and the communications take place via the edges of the tree. If the load is distributed in some given tree then equations (7.23) and (7.24) can be applied to find optimum load distribution [29]. Yet, a key difficulty here is to find a tree in which the scattering is performed most effectively. Let us notice similarities with the Steiner tree problem which is **NP**-hard [56]. Hence, finding a good scattering tree is computationally hard in general.

A heuristic called resource-aware optimal load distribution optimum sequence (RAOLD-OS) following the above lines has been proposed in [112]. It first builds a minimum spanning tree (MST) rooted in the originator assuming that the weight of edge $(i, j)$ is $C_{ij}$, i.e. transfer rate of the communication link between $P_i$ and $P_j$. Here the communication start-up times are all zero ($\forall\, (i, j) \in E, S_{ij} = 0$)). Hence, it is possible to fold up the MST using the equivalent processor concept as described in Sect. 7.2.2. In the RAOLD-OS the sequence of activating the processors in each single level subtree is the sequence of nondecreasing communication rate (i.e. the sequence of decreasing bandwidth). A different version of this algorithm called RAOLD has also been proposed in [112] to deal with the trees in which the processor activation sequence in the single level subtrees is predetermined and cannot be changed. In [55] three more methods building spanning trees were analyzed. The first method builds a tree which is a union of the shortest paths from each node to the originator. Here the weight of an edge $(i, j)$ is $C_{ij}$. The second method uses the same rule, but counts the number of hops, that is the edge weights are 1. The third method uses Prim's algorithm which starts with MST including only the originator, and then appends to the MST a vertex which is connected to the originator by an edge of the lowest cost. This procedure is repeated for the following vertices: vertex $j$ is appended to the MST if it has the cheapest connection to any node $i$ already in the MST. In the third method the cost of edge $(i, j)$ is $\xi_{ij} = \lambda_i h_i + (1 - \lambda_i)(\xi_i + C_{ij})$, where $\lambda_i = 1 - \frac{h_i}{e_1}$, $h_i$ is the length of the shortest path from the originator to vertex $i$ in hops, $e_1$ is the length of the longest shortest path from originator to any node in the network, $i$ is already in MST, and $j$ is a candidate for the inclusion.

## 7.3   Multi-installment Processing

In *multi-installment* divisible load processing (also called *multi-round* processing) the load is sent to a processor in more than one *chunk*. The following example demonstrates that distributing the load in many chunks may be advantageous. Load $V = 10$ is to be sent from originator $P_0$ to a single processor $P_1$. The parameters of $P_1$ are: $A_1 = C_1 = 1, S_1 = 0$. Were the load sent in one piece, the schedule length

| $P_0$ | $S_1+C_1\alpha_{11}$ | $\cdots$ | $S_i+C_i\alpha_{ij}$ | $\cdots$ | $S_m+C\alpha_{mj}$ | $S_1+C\alpha_{1,j+1}$ | $\cdots$ | $S_i+C_i\alpha_{i,j+1}$ | |
|---|---|---|---|---|---|---|---|---|---|
| $P_1$ | | $A_1\alpha_{11}$ | | $\cdots$ | | $A_1\alpha_{1j}$ | $A_1\alpha_{1j+1}$ | | $\cdots$ |
| $\vdots$ | | | | | | | | | |
| $P_i$ | | | $\cdots$ | | | $A_i\alpha_{ij}$ | | $A_i\alpha_{i,j+1}$ | $\cdots$ |
| $P_m$ | | | | $A_m\alpha_{m,j-1}$ | $A_m\alpha_{mj}$ | | | | $\cdots$ |

**Fig. 7.7** Part of a schedule for multi-installment processing in a star

would be $S + CV + AV = 20$. However, if we divide the load into $k$ pieces the whole processing time would be $\frac{CV}{k} + AV$. Thus, processor $P_1$ starts the computation earlier, and the whole schedule is shorter. More generally, multi-installment processing allows for earlier activation of the processors, and eliminates processor idle time during communications. Distributing the load in many installments was analyzed first in [20].

In the following discussion we will mean by an installment one iteration of load distribution. Hence, an installment has $m$ load chunks. Let us denote by $k$ the number of installments and by $\alpha_{ij}$ the size of the load chunk sent to $P_i$ in the $j$th installment. We assume that the pattern of communications is the following: Processors are activated in a round-robin fashion ($P_1, P_2, \ldots, P_m, P_1, P_2, \ldots, P_m, \ldots$, repetitively), and all processors receive $k$ chunks (cf. Fig. 7.7). If the results are not returned to the originator all processors must stop computations simultaneously. In the last installment the load sizes must satisfy the standard relationship in a star demanding that computing on $P_i$ lasts as long as communication to $P_{i+1}$, and computing on $P_{i+1}$. In the preceding installments processor $P_i$ should compute as long as it takes to send load to processors $P_{i+1}, \ldots, P_m, P_1, \ldots P_i$. Thus, load chunk sizes can be calculated from the following linear system:

$$\alpha_{ik}A_i = S_{i+1} + (A_{i+1} + C_{i+1})\alpha_{i+1,k} \quad \text{for } i = 1, \ldots, m-1 \quad (7.34)$$

$$\alpha_{ij}A_i = \sum_{l=i+1}^{m} (S_l + C_l\alpha_{lj}) + \sum_{l=1}^{i}(S_l + C_l\alpha_{l,j+1})$$
$$\text{for } i = 1, \ldots, m, j = 1, \ldots, k-1 \quad (7.35)$$

$$V = \sum_{j=1}^{k}\sum_{i=1}^{m}\alpha_{ij} \quad (7.36)$$

Closed-form solutions for multi-installment processing and performance limits for $m \to \infty$ and $k \to \infty$ were studied in [20]. In [107] is has been shown that for a network with negligible start-up times, in the limit $k \to \infty$, multi-installment processing may reduce schedule length to $\frac{e-1}{e} \approx 0.632$ of the initial length. In the above equations (7.34)–(7.36) it is tacitly assumed that there is no idle time in the sequence of communications nor in computing the load on the processors. Only recently, has it been analytically proved in [110] that this intuition is indeed correct.

The problem of optimally selecting the set of processors participating in the computation is **NP**-hard [110]. Hence, a number of heuristics have been proposed in the literature. In the heuristic *uniform multi-round* (UMR) [111], as it is defined for heterogeneous systems, it is assumed that the time of processing load chunks in a given installment (round) is equal on all processors. Thus, $\alpha_{ij} A_i = \tau_j$, for $i = 1, \ldots, m$, where $\tau_j$ is the time of computing in the $j$th installment. Simultaneously with computing the $j$th installment the originator has to send off the load for the next installment. Hence, $\sum_{i=1}^{m} (\alpha_{i,j+1} C_i + S_i) = \tau_j$, for $j = 1, \ldots, k-1$. Moreover, it is assumed that the load $\sum_{i=1}^{m} \alpha_{ij} = V_j$ processed in installment $j$ is a quasi geometric sequence: $V_j = \theta^{j-1}(V_1 - \eta) + \eta$, where $\theta, \eta$ are constants depending on the parameters $(A_i, C_i, S_i)$ of the distributed system. The problem of finding the load chunk sizes is formulated as a nonlinear optimization problem with the objective of minimizing schedule length and the constraint that all the load must be processed. As the results $V_1$ and the near-optimum number of installments $k$ are determined. In the heterogeneous systems, if all $m$ processors cannot be exploited without introducing idle times, then the processors were included in the computing set in the order of decreasing communication speed. For the homogeneous systems it is assumed that all processors receive chunks of equal size in the same installment. A hybrid algorithm combining genetic search and linear programming to select the set of computing processors, the sequence of communications, and the chunk sizes has been proposed and evaluated in [43].

## 7.4 Memory Constraints

In this section, we consider memory limitations in processing divisible loads. Limited memory sizes were dealt with in various ways in DLT. Key distinctions are whether the load is sent in single or multiple installments, and if the memory system is hierarchical or flat. We present these cases in the following.

### 7.4.1 Single Installment Processing

In the single installment processing a processor receives only a single load chunk. The memory subsystem must be able to accommodate the arriving amount of load. This may impose limitations on the size of the load chunk, or reduce computing speed if the load chunk is very big.

#### 7.4.1.1 Flat Memory Model

In the case of flat memory model, access time is constant for all memory cells. This may be an approximation of a more complex hierarchical memory structure by restriction to just one memory level (see Sect. 3.1.2), or it may be a result of the system architecture as in some embedded and mobile devices. Consequently, computing speed is independent of the size of used memory block. Yet, memory is a limited resource, and only some amount of it can be accessed in constant speed. Let $B_i$ denote the size of the memory available at processor $P_i$. The above assumptions on the constant memory bandwidth, and hence computing speed, are satisfied if $\alpha_i \leq B_i$, for all processors $P_i$. For simplicity of presentation, let us assume that the load can be feasibly accommodated on the available processors, and there is more than one feasible solution, i.e. $\sum_{i=1}^{m} B_i > V$. We also assume that the time of returning results is negligible.

In the first publication [79] considering limited memory sizes an Incremental Balancing Strategy (IBS) heuristic has been proposed for star interconnection with negligible communication start-up time ($\forall i, S_i = 0$). In the IBS processor loads are iteratively increased up to the limits $B_i$. Let $\alpha_i$ be the load already assigned to $P_i$, $B_i' = B_i - \alpha_i$ the space remaining on $P_i$, $V' = V - \sum_{i=1}^{m} \alpha_i$ the amount of load remaining to be assigned, $\mathcal{P}_f$ the set of processors whose load is still below $B_i$. IBS finds the assignments $\alpha_i'$ of the remaining load $V'$ in $\mathcal{P}_f$ using basic formulation (7.1)–(7.2) as if there were no memory limits. If $\forall i, \alpha_i' \leq B_i'$, then the currently calculated $\alpha_i'$ are added to the previous assignments, and algorithm stops. Otherwise, the load assignments are scaled down to $\alpha_i' Y$, where $Y = \min\{\frac{B_i'}{\alpha_i'} : P_i \in \mathcal{P}_f\}$. Note that at least one processor has its buffer filled completely, and is removed from $\mathcal{P}_f$. This procedure is repeated until assigning all the load. IBS does not build optimum solutions in general which was shown in [50].

A different approach based on the following linear program has been proposed in [50]:

$$\text{minimize } C_{\max} \text{ subject to} \tag{7.37}$$

$$\alpha_i A_i + \sum_{j=1}^{i} (S_j + \alpha_j C_j) \leq C_{\max} \quad \text{for } i = 1, \dots, m \tag{7.38}$$

$$\alpha_i \leq B_i \quad \text{for } i = 1, \dots, m \tag{7.39}$$

$$\sum_{i=1}^{m} \alpha_i = V \tag{7.40}$$

$$\alpha_i, C_{\max} \geq 0 \tag{7.41}$$

In the above formulation inequalities (7.38) guarantee that no processor computes after the end of schedule. Note that the sum on the left side of inequality (7.38) is the duration of all communications preceding the start of computation on $P_i$. By (7.39) memory limitations are obeyed, and by (7.40) no load is left unprocessed. Using the above formulation the influence of the memory limitations on the schedule length was studied in [50]. It turned out that the memory limits have the biggest influence on $C_{\max}$ when load size $V$ is small, and computing is fast ($A_i$ are small). On the other hand, with growing load size and for computationally intensive problems ($A_i$ are big), memory limits have smaller influence on the performance, provided that the given load $V$ fits in memory at all.

Note that both in the IBS and in the linear program we tacitly assumed that all
processors take part in the computation, and that the sequence of activating the computations on the processors is given. When start-up times $S_i$ are nonzero and size
$V$ of the load is too small some processors may be dropped from the computation
which has been observed already in Sect. 7.1. The problem of selecting optimum
set of processors, the optimum communication sequence and load part sizes may be
expressed by the formulations (7.5)–(7.11) with additional requirements

$$\alpha_i \le B_i \text{ for } i = 1,\dots,m. \tag{7.42}$$

Scheduling divisible loads with nonzero communication start-up times and limited
memory buffers has been shown to be **NP**-hard in [53] and sNPh in [15]. Various
methods solving the above problem have been proposed and compared experimentally in [53]. Note that formulations (7.5)–(7.11) with the constraint (7.42) reduce
to linear programs (7.37)–(7.41) if $x_{ij}$ are set, i.e. if the communication sequence
is known. Using this observation a branch and bound algorithm selecting the set of
computing processors and their activation sequence has been proposed in [53]. Also
a set of heuristics selecting the set of active processors and the sequence of activation
supplemented with linear programs (7.37)–(7.41) have been proposed. It appeared
that heuristics based on communication transfer rates ($C_i$s) were superior in most of
the cases. However, for certain instances (e.g. if all $C_i$ were very small) also other
parameters ($A_i$, $B_i$) could influence the optimum order of activating the processors.
An extended version of IBS heuristic called IBSC has been proposed. The original version of IBS could not be applied when $\forall i, S_i > 0$ because some processors
may have to be dropped from the computing set. In IBSC processors were ordered
according to nondecreasing $C_i$s, and only the processors from the head of this list
receiving positive load in linear systems (7.1)–(7.2) took part in the computation.
IBSC appeared to be competitive with the heuristics using linear programming.

Scheduling divisible loads in trees with memory limitations has been considered
in [31]. The proposed algorithm called push–pull optimal load distribution (PPOLD)
is a heuristic which blends the IBS heuristic with recursive folding and unfolding of
the tree using the method of equivalent processor (Sect. 7.2.2). Here it is assumed
that $\forall i, S_i = 0$. Each subtree rooted in $P_i$ with direct successors in set $\mathcal{P}(i)$ is
folded to an equivalent processor with memory size equal to $\min_{P_j \in \{P_i, \mathcal{P}(i)\}} \{\frac{B_j}{a_j}\}$,
where $a_j$ is fraction of the load assigned to $P_j$ from the whole load $V_i$ assigned to
the subtree rooted in $P_i$. Note that since $\forall i, S_i = 0$, the value of $a_i$ is a constant
independent of the load $V_i$, and can be calculated assuming $V_i = 1$.

### 7.4.1.2 Hierarchical Memory Model

In the preceding section it was assumed that processing speed is constant on condition that the load assignments $\alpha_i$ are not greater than some strict limit $B_i$. However,
contemporary computer systems have hierarchical memory systems. If the out-of-
core storage, such as magnetic disks, is used then the load sizes may be huge at

**Fig. 7.8** Approximation
of computing time with a
piecewise linear function

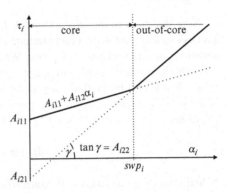

relatively low costs. Yet, out-of-core computations suffer much slower computing speed. Thus, a different approach to processing with memory constraints is possible. Instead of strictly limiting load assignments $\alpha_i$, it is possible to allow unlimited loads processed at smaller computing speed. This is illustrated in Fig. 7.8. As long as $\alpha_i$ is smaller than the admissible core memory usage the load is processed at the maximum speed. A soon as $\alpha_i$ exceeds certain limit external storage starts to be used and processing time increases much faster due to smaller computing speed. The dependence of the computing time on the size of assigned load can be approximated by a piecewise linear function $\tau_i = \max_j\{A_{ij1} + A_{ij2}\alpha_i\}$, where $\tau_i$ is the time of computing on $P_i$, $\alpha_i$ is the size of load assigned to $P_i$, $A_{ij1}$, $A_{ij2}$ are coefficients of a linear function approximating computing time on memory level $j$. We will assume that computing speed decreases with increasing level number $j$. Note that $\tau_i$ is a convex function of $\alpha_i$. Furthermore, $A_{i11}$ is equivalent to the computation start-up time. In [51] just two memory levels were considered: core memory (i.e. semiconductor RAM) and out-of-core memory (e.g. virtual memory swap area on a hard disk). The size of load at which the computer system starts using disk swap and the two approximations of processing time are equal has been called swap point $swp_i$, i.e. $A_{i11} + swp_i A_{i21} = A_{i21} + swp_i A_{i22}$. Let us assume that all processors take part in the computation, their activation sequence coincides with the processor numbers, and just two memory levels are used. The optimum load distribution can be found from the following linear program [51]:

$$\text{minimize } C_{\max} \text{ subject to} \tag{7.43}$$

$$\sum_{j=1}^{i}(S_j + \alpha_j A_j) + \tau_i \le C_{\max} \text{ for } i = 1,\ldots,m \tag{7.44}$$

$$A_{i11} + A_{i21}\alpha_i \le \tau_i \text{ for } i = 1,\ldots,m \tag{7.45}$$

$$A_{i12} + A_{i22}\alpha_i \le \tau_i \text{ for } i = 1,\ldots,m \tag{7.46}$$

$$\sum_{i=1}^{m}\alpha_i = V \tag{7.47}$$

$$\alpha_i, C_{\max} \ge 0 \tag{7.48}$$

Inequalities (7.45) and (7.46) together represent the piecewise linear function of the processing time $\tau_i$. When one of the constraints (7.45) and (7.46) is satisfied with equality, then the computing time is exactly equal to the piecewise linear approximation of the computing time. If none of inequalities (7.45) and (7.46) is satisfied with equality for certain processor $P_i$, then it means that processor $P_i$ is idle in some interval. The above nonlinear model of hierarchical memory has been compared in [51] against multi-installment processing with only one memory level. It appears that multi-installment processing is faster as long as communication speed is greater than the combined speed of all the processors, and it is possible to start computations during one communication cycle to the processors (more precisely if $\forall i, A_{i11} < \sum_{i=1}^{m} S_i$).

Let us note that the above method was the first attempt of representing nonlinear dependence of processing time on the load size. Any convex nonlinear function of processing time may be approximated in the above way by a piecewise linear function, and the load distribution may be found by linear programming.

### 7.4.2 Multi-installment Processing

As suggested in the section on hierarchical memory model it is possible to avoid slowing down the computations by dividing the load into many small chunks which fit in the core memory. The gain is twofold: slow out-of-core storage is not used and since messages are shorter, also the initial idle waiting for any load is shorter. A key requirement which must be satisfied is that the load residing at any processor does not exceed memory limit $B_i$. This further poses a question how the memory usage is counted.

In the simplest model, only the currently processed chunk is included in the memory space of the divisible load processing application. This implies that $\alpha_{ij} \leq B_i$, where $\alpha_{ij}$ is the size of the $j$th load chunk sent to processor $P_i$ (cf. Fig. 7.9a). The problem of finding load assignments may be reversed by asking what memory size is required for divisible load processing. By solving linear systems (7.34)–(7.36) for certain number of installments $k$ maximum load chunk sizes may be calculated. Since the load chunk sizes decrease with $k$, it is also possible to find minimum $k$

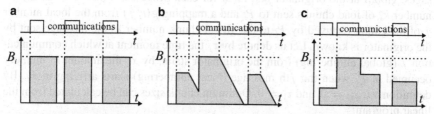

**Fig. 7.9** Memory occupancy models for multi-installment processing. (**a**) One chunk at a time. (**b**) Chunks overlap, memory continuously released. (**c**) Chunks overlap, block memory releases

for which $\forall i, j, \alpha_{ij} \le B_i$. This approach has been pursued in [49]. Yet, it is only an approximation of the reality because the memory usage by messages arriving in the background of computing is not taken into account. Consequently, overlap of load chunks must be ignored, or $B_i$ must be at least equal to the doubled biggest $\alpha_{ij}$ to leave room for at least one message to arrive, or the chunk overlap should be explicitly forbidden (e.g. by assuming that processors cannot simultaneously communicate and compute). The idea of limiting $\alpha_{ij}$ to at most a half of $B_i$ has been used in a heuristic Multi-Installment Balancing Strategy (MIBS) proposed in [18]. It first calculates load assignments $\alpha_{i1}$ as if there were no memory constraints. If $\alpha_{i1} > B_i$ for some processor $P_i$, then the assignment is reduced to $\alpha_{i1} = \frac{B_i}{2}$. The remaining load is distributed iteratively assuming that processors have release times resulting from processing the previously assigned load. The methods of calculating load assignments when processors have release times, or more generally, varying speed of communication and computation are presented in Sect. 7.7. In the second and the following iterations the calculated load chunks are distributed only to the processors which have become ready sufficiently early to accept a new load chunk. The remaining load is moved to the next installment. If no processor finished its previous assignment then time is progressed to the first completion time of computation on any processor, and the procedure is repeated.

A more detailed memory usage model allowing for the chunk overlap and choosing chunk sizes according the load already present at a processor has been proposed in [42]. It has been assumed that a memory block is obtained from the operating system pool at the beginning of a communication. As the computations progress, memory is gradually released to the operating system in grains of parallelism. Here a grain of parallelism is an application-specific smallest unit of data which can be processed alone, and cannot be divided any further. Considering small size of the grain of parallelism, and big size of the load chunk it can be assumed, with acceptable accuracy, that memory occupation decreases linearly as the load is being processed (see Fig. 7.9b). This allows for formulating the problem of optimum chunk sizes selection as a linear program. For the simplicity of presentation let us assume that results are not returned to the originator, simultaneous computation and communication are possible, all processors (except the originator) take part in the computation, and the communication sequence is given in a vector of chunk destinations $\overline{d} = (d_1, \ldots, d_k)$, where $d_i$ is the index of the processor receiving the $i$th chunk, $k$ is the number of chunks. We will use two ways of numbering the messages: *global* at the originator and *local* for each processor. Since $\overline{d}$ is given, the number $k_i$ of load chunks sent to $P_i$ and a mapping $g(i, j)$ from the local number $j$ of the chunk received by $P_i$ to the global chunk number as the message sent by the originator is known. Let us denote by $\tau_j$ the time moment at which communication $j$ (global numbering) from the originator starts, by $x_{ij}$ the amount of memory occupied at $P_i$ when the $j$th message (local numbering) starts arriving in $P_i$. By definition $\forall i, x_{i1} = 0$, and $\tau_1 = 0$. Optimum chunk sizes can be calculated from the linear program:

minimize $C_{max}$ subject to (7.49)

$$x_{i,j-1} + \alpha_{g(i,j-1)} - \frac{1}{A_i}(\tau_{g(i,j)} - \tau_{g(i,j-1)}) \leq x_{ij}$$

$$\text{for } i = 1, \ldots, m, \ j = 2, \ldots, k_i \qquad (7.50)$$

$$\alpha_{g(i,j-1)} - \frac{1}{A_i}(\tau_{g(i,j)} - (\tau_{g(i,j-1)} + S_i + C_i\alpha_{g(i,j-1)})) \leq x_{ij}$$

$$\text{for } i = 1, \ldots, m, \ j = 2, \ldots, k_i \qquad (7.51)$$

$$\tau_i + S_{d_i} + \alpha_i C_{d_i} \leq \tau_{i+1} \quad \text{for } i = 1, \ldots, k-1 \qquad (7.52)$$

$$\tau_{k_i} + S_i + C_i\alpha_{g(i,k_i)} + A_i(\alpha_{g(i,k_i)} + x_{ik_i}) \leq C_{max} \quad \text{for } i = 1, \ldots, m \quad (7.53)$$

$$x_{ij} + \alpha_{g(i,j)} \leq B_i \qquad \text{for } i = 1, \ldots, m, \ j = 1, \ldots, k_i \qquad (7.54)$$

$$\sum_{i=1}^{k} \alpha_i = V \qquad (7.55)$$

$$\alpha_i, C_{max}, \tau_j, x_{ij} \geq 0 \qquad (7.56)$$

In the above linear program inequalities (7.50) and (7.51) specify the amount of load $x_{ij}$ at processor $P_i$ at the moment when $j$th load starts arriving in $P_i$. Observe that load in chunk $j-1$ received at $P_i$ can be computed only after fully receiving it which reduces computing interval by $S_i + C_i\alpha_{g(i,j-1)}$. The two sets of inequalities represent two possible cases: processing of the previously remaining load $x_{i,j-1}$ finished after the end of receiving the $(j-1)$th load chunk (inequalities (7.50)), or before the end or receiving it (inequalities (7.51)). Inequalities (7.52) ensure that communications do not overlap. Inequalities (7.53) guarantee that all computations finish before the end of the schedule. Note that memory occupation is biggest when a new load chunk starts arriving. Thus, by (7.54) memory occupation does not exceed limit $B_i$. All load is processed by (7.55). Linear programs (7.49)–(7.56) have been used as an element of branch and bound and genetic search algorithms in [42]. The two algorithms were used to search for a good communication sequence $\overline{d}$, and (7.49)–(7.56) were applied to calculate chunk sizes. It has been observed that with growing heterogeneity of the system, good solutions are increasingly hard to be found.

High fluency in releasing the memory assumed in the preceding paragraph many seem unnatural in many cases. More often memory is requested and released as blocks of certain sizes (cf. Fig. 7.9c), and it is not possible to return to the operating system parts of such a memory block. Scheduling divisible loads according to this model has been formulated in [44] as a mixed quadratic mathematical programming problem for a given communication sequence $\overline{d}$. Even if $\overline{d}$ is known, it is still unknown which load chunks received by a processor coincide in the memory. We will use binary variables $y_{ijl}$ to specify chunk overlapping. Here $y_{ijl} = 1$ will denote that on processor $P_i$, chunk $j$ is still unfinished when chunk $l > j$ (local numbers) starts arriving. Value $y_{ijl} = 0$ will mean that computing chunk $j$ is finished when chunk $l$ starts arriving at $P_i$. Variable $f_{ij}$ will denote time moment when processing of chunk $j$ (local number) on $P_i$ finishes. Let $M$ denote a constant greater than schedule length, e.g. $M > V(\max_i C_i + \max_i A_i) + k \max S_i$. In the following formulation we use the notation introduced in the preceding paragraph. Optimum load chunk sizes can be calculated from the following mathematical programming formulation:

$$\text{minimize } C_{\max} \qquad\qquad \text{subject to} \qquad\qquad\qquad (7.57)$$

$$\tau_i + S_{d_i} + \alpha_i C_{d_i} \leq \tau_{i+1} \qquad \text{for } i = 1,\ldots,k-1 \qquad\qquad (7.58)$$

$$\tau_{g(i,j)} + S_i + \alpha_{g(i,j)}(C_i + A_i) \leq f_{ij} \quad \text{for } i = 1,\ldots,m,\ j = 1,\ldots,k_i \qquad (7.59)$$

$$f_{i,j-1} + \alpha_{g(i,j)} A_i \leq f_{ij} \qquad \text{for } i = 1,\ldots,m,\ j = 2,\ldots,k_i \qquad (7.60)$$

$$f_{ij} \geq \tau_{g(i,l)} - (1 - y_{ijl})M \qquad \text{for } i = 1,\ldots,m,$$
$$j = 1,\ldots,k_i - 1,\ l = j+1,\ldots,k_i \quad (7.61)$$

$$f_{ij} \leq \tau_{g(i,l)} + y_{ijl}M \qquad \text{for } i = 1,\ldots,m,$$
$$j = 1,\ldots,k_i - 1,\ l = j+1,\ldots,k_i \quad (7.62)$$

$$y_{ijl} \leq y_{ihl} \qquad \text{for } i = 1,\ldots,m,\ j = 1,\ldots,k_i - 1,$$
$$l = j+2,\ldots,k_i, h = j+1,\ldots,l-1 \quad (7.63)$$

$$y_{ijl} \geq y_{ijh} \qquad \text{for } i = 1,\ldots,m,\ j = 1,\ldots,k_i - 1,$$
$$l = j+1,\ldots,k_i, h = l+1,\ldots,k_i \qquad (7.64)$$

$$\alpha_{g(i,j)} + \sum_{l=j+1}^{k_i} y_{ijl}\alpha_{g(i,l)} \leq B_i \qquad \text{for } i = 1,\ldots,m,\ j = 1,\ldots,k_i \qquad (7.65)$$

$$\sum_{i=1}^{k} \alpha_i = V \qquad\qquad\qquad\qquad\qquad (7.66)$$

$$f_{ik_i} \leq C_{\max} \qquad\qquad \text{for } i = 1,\ldots,m \qquad\qquad (7.67)$$

$$y_{ijl} \in \{0,1\};\ \alpha_i, C_{\max}, \tau_j, f_{ij} \geq 0 \qquad\qquad\qquad (7.68)$$

In the above formulation inequalities (7.58) guarantee that the sequence of communications is obeyed, and they do not overlap. Computations on a chunk of load may finish after fully receiving it by inequalities (7.59) and after finishing the preceding load chunk (7.60). Constraints (7.61) and (7.62) guarantee together that on processor $P_i$ chunks $j, l$ overlap, or not, as set by variable $y_{ijl}$. Note that for a given value of $y_{ijl}$, only one of the inequalities (7.61) and (7.62) may be active. Inequalities (7.63) and (7.64) guarantee consistency of $y_{ijl}$ values. Chunk $j$ overlapping with chunk $l > j + 1$ overlaps also with all intermediate chunks by (7.63). Chunk $j$ completed before chunk $l > j$ cannot become undone again by (7.64). Memory limits are obeyed and all load is processed due to (7.65) and (7.66), respectively. Computations finish before the schedule end thanks to (7.67). In [44] the above mathematical programming formulation was embedded in a branch and bound algorithm searching in the set of possible communication sequences $\overline{d}$, and overlaps $y_{ijl}$.

## 7.5  Processing Cost Optimization

### 7.5.1  Negligible Start-Up Times

The trade-off between the cost of processor usage and schedule length has been considered first in [101]. The cost may be of monetary nature, or it may represent energy consumption. The cost was assumed to be proportional to the time of using a processor. For example, if $P_i$ is used for $\alpha_i A_i$ time units, then it costs $f_i' \alpha_i A_i$, where $f_i'$ is the cost per time unit. To simplify the notation we will use the cost per load unit $f_i = f_i' A_i$. The problem of cost optimization was presented in two settings:

1. For a given schedule length $\overline{C_{\max}}$, find the least costly schedule.
2. For a given cost limit $H$, find the shortest schedule.

Let us assume that the load is processed in a star system, with communication front-ends, in a single installment mode, the start-up time is negligibly small, communication links are identical ($\forall i, S_i = 0, C_i = C$), and that computations on all processors finish simultaneously. Solving both above problems requires determining:

- The set of used processors
- The sequence of activating the processors
- Load part sizes $\alpha_i$

To determine the cheapest processor activation sequence let us consider the conditions under which interchanging two processors $(P_i, P_{i+1})$ activated consecutively reduces computing cost. In both arrangements the same load $V'$ must be processed in the same time $\tau$. Let $\alpha_i, \alpha_{i+1}, H$ denote load sizes and cost, respectively, for the sequence $(P_i, P_{i+1})$ and $\alpha_i', \alpha_{i+1}', H'$ for sequence $(P_{i+1}, P_i)$. Load chunk sizes must satisfy conditions (cf. Fig. 7.10):

$$H = \alpha_i f_i + \alpha_{i+1} f_{i+1} \tag{7.69}$$

$$H' = \alpha_i' f_i + \alpha_{i+1}' f_{i+1} \tag{7.70}$$

$$\tau = \alpha_i (C + A_i) = \alpha_{i+1}' (C + A_{i+1}) \tag{7.71}$$

$$V' = \alpha_i + \alpha_{i+1} = \alpha_i' + \alpha_{i+1}' \tag{7.72}$$

$$\alpha_i A_i = \alpha_{i+1} (C + A_{i+1}) \tag{7.73}$$

$$\alpha_{i+1}' A_{i+1} = \alpha_i' (C + A_i) \tag{7.74}$$

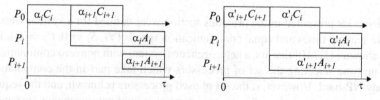

**Fig. 7.10**  Interchange of processors to reduce computing cost

It can be derived from the above conditions that $H \leq H'$ if and only if $f_i \leq f_{i+1}$. Thus, if $\forall i, C_i = C, S_i = 0$ then processors should be activated in the order of increasing cost per load unit [101].

Let us assume now that processors are ordered according to the nondecreasing cost of use, i.e. $f_1 \leq f_2 \leq \cdots \leq f_m$. Problem 1 can be solved by adding processors, one at a time, until collecting sufficient load [101]. Processor $P_1$ computes load $\alpha_1 = \frac{C_{max}}{A_1 + C}$, and its communications finish by $\tau_1 = \alpha_1 C$. Suppose processors $P_1, \ldots, P_i$, for $i \geq 1$, received load $\sum_{j=1}^{i} \alpha_i$, in time $\tau_i$. If the collected load $\sum_{j=1}^{i} \alpha_i < V$ and $\tau_i > \overline{C_{max}}$, then the instance is infeasible. If $\sum_{j=1}^{i} \alpha_i < V$ and $\tau_i < \overline{C_{max}}$, then processor $P_{i+1}$ is appended to the communication sequence and it receives load $\alpha_{i+1} = \frac{\overline{C_{max}} - \tau_i}{A_{i+1} + C}$. If $\sum_{j=1}^{i} \alpha_i > V$, then sufficient load has been collected on the cheapest processors, and load $\alpha_i$ of the costliest processor is reduced to $\alpha_i = V - \sum_{j=1}^{i-1} \alpha_i$. The remaining processors $P_{i+1}, \ldots, P_m$ (if any) receive no load.

For solving problem 2 let us observe that schedule length is nonincreasing and the computing cost is nondecreasing in the number of used processors. Problem 2 can be solved by first determining the maximum number of processors $m' \leq m$ for which the cost of processor usage is at most $H$. The value of $m'$ may be found by binary search over the number of processors and load distributions for $m'$ from Eqs. (7.1)–(7.2). If the cost for using $m'$ processors does not exceed $H$, then the cost may be further increased to $H$ by using one more processor and reducing schedule length. The algorithm for problem 1 described in the preceding paragraph together with binary search over schedule lengths may provide minimum schedule length for which the cost limit is not exceeded.

Simultaneous minimization of the communication and computation costs was considered in [34]. The costs were assumed to be linear in the amount of transferred and computed load. The transfer and computation times were linear in load sizes, without start-up times. Conditions were sought for under which swapping a pair of processors in the communication sequence reduces the cost of processing. A set of four conditions were proposed. Unfortunately, these conditions are not covering all possible situations. The four conditions gave rise to the construction of a greedy algorithm improving the communication sequence by pairwise interchange of the processors neighboring in the communication sequence.

## 7.5.2  Nonzero Start-Up Times

The methods presented in the previous section were defined for a system with negligible start-up times and equal communication speeds ($\forall i, S_i = 0, C_i = C$). It has been shown [41, 110] that for a heterogeneous system with nonzero communication start-up time selecting the set of processors which take part in the computation is already **NP**-hard. However, if the set of used processors is known, and the sequence of communications is given then a more general case of heterogeneous systems can be solved by use of linear programming [41]. Let us denote by $\bar{d}$ the vector of message destinations. For simplicity of notation we assume that all $m$ processors take part in the communication, and the load is received once (single installment). Let us combine the cost of communication to and computation on processor $P_i$ in an affine function $l_i + \alpha_i f_i$ of the assigned load. This cost function can be changed to a function of the time of resource usage because the time of communication and computation are also affine functions of $\alpha_i$. The linear program for calculating the shortest schedule on condition that the cost does not exceed limit $H$ can be formulated as follows:

$$\text{minimize } C_{\max} \qquad\qquad \text{subject to} \qquad (7.75)$$

$$\sum_{j=1}^{i} (S_{d_j} + \alpha_j C_{d_j}) + \alpha_i A_{d_j} \leq C_{\max} \qquad i = 1, \ldots, m \qquad (7.76)$$

$$\sum_{j=1}^{m} (l_j + \alpha_j f_j) \leq H \qquad (7.77)$$

$$\sum_{j=1}^{m} \alpha_j = V \qquad (7.78)$$

$$\alpha_i \geq 0 \qquad (7.79)$$

In the above linear program the LHS of (7.77) is the total cost of system usage. Note that the above formulation may be infeasible if the cost limit $H$ is set too low [41].

## 7.6 Multiple Tasks

In this section, we present application of DLT in scheduling multiple divisible loads. Two types of models are presented: for loads originating in the same processor and for loads originating in multiple sources.

### 7.6.1 Single Source Loads

Scheduling multiple divisible loads was first studied in publication [98]. It was assumed that set $\mathcal{T}$ of $n$ divisible loads of sizes $V_1, \ldots, V_n$ was processed on a star network. Let us name the $n$ loads as tasks. The sequence of processing the tasks was predetermined by the order of their arrival. It was assumed that the processors are heterogeneous, but identical for the tasks, i.e. communication and computation speeds do not depend on the task. Two strategies for processing the tasks were analyzed. In the *single-task* strategy, loads were processed one at a time. In the *multitask*

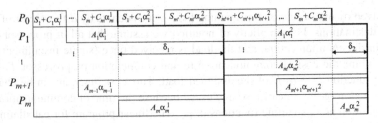

**Fig. 7.11**  Processing multiple loads in multitask strategy

strategy, load distribution of one task overlapped with the computing of the preceding task (cf. Fig. 7.11). A method of calculating the distribution of the load has been proposed. In both strategies the first task $T_1$ is scheduled according to the standard methods (see Sect. 7.1), as if it were the only task. Below we present the way of calculating the load distribution for $T_2, \ldots, T_n$ in multitask strategy.

Let us assume that the tasks are numbered according to the sequence of processing them. It is assumed that the loads originate in the center of the star, the originator does no computing, all processors take part in the computation, the order of activating the processors coincides with their numbers, the results are not returned to the originator, computations for a certain task simultaneously finish on all processors. Let us denote by $\alpha_i^j$ the size of $T_j$ load part sent to processor $P_i$, and by $\delta_j$ the length of the interval from the end of communication for $T_j$, till the completion of computations for $T_j$ (see Fig. 7.11). The distribution of the load for $T_1$ is found from (7.1)–(7.2). Hence, $\delta_1 = A_m \alpha_m^1$. Suppose that while processing $T_{j-1}$ the load of $T_j$ has been sent to $m'$ processors. Thus, processors $P_1, \ldots, P_{m'}$ can start computations on $T_j$ immediately after the completion of computations on $T_{j-1}$. Processors $P_{m'+1}, \ldots, P_m$ must wait for the arrival of the new load. Since all processors stop computations simultaneously the distribution of the load can be found from the following set of linear equations:

$$\alpha_1^j A_1 = \alpha_i^j A_i \quad \text{for } i = 1, \ldots, m' \tag{7.80}$$

$$\alpha_1^j A_1 = \sum_{i=1}^{m'+1} (S_i + \alpha_i^j C_i) + A_{m'+1} \alpha_{m'+1}^j - \delta_{j-1} \tag{7.81}$$

$$\alpha_i^j A_i = S_{i+1} + \alpha_{i+1} (A_{i+1} + C_{i+1}) \quad \text{for } i = m' + 1, \ldots, m - 1 \tag{7.82}$$

$$\sum_{i=1}^{m} \alpha_i^j = V_j \tag{7.83}$$

The distribution of the load can be found in $O(m)$ for a given $m'$ [98]. The value of $m'$ can be found iteratively as the maximum $m'$ for which the solutions of (7.80)–(7.83) are non-negative, and the length of communications for the first $m'$ processors is not greater than $\delta_{j-1}$. The complexity of this method is $O(m^2 n)$.

The multitask strategy has been combined with multi-installment processing in [103]. Suppose the interval $\delta_{j-1}$ is sufficiently long to send $T_j$ load to all $m$

processors in just one installment (i.e. $m' = m$). Then the linear system (7.80)–(7.83) reduces to just (7.80) and (7.83), from which we obtain

$$\alpha_i^j = \frac{V_j}{\sum_{l=1}^{m} \frac{A_i}{A_l}} \tag{7.84}$$

If $\delta_{j-1} \geq \sum_{i=1}^{m}(S_i + \alpha_i^j C_i)$ then indeed this scenario is feasible. Otherwise, the load may be divided into many installments so that load part sizes are smaller, all processors receive their loads earlier, and consequently idle time in computations may be avoided. Now let us denote by $\alpha_{il}^j$ the size of task $T_j$ part sent to processor $P_i$ in installment $l$. Let $k_j$ be the number of installments for $T_j$. A condition to avoid idle time in computation is that sending the first installment to the processors should last no longer than $\delta_{j-1}$:

$$\sum_{i=1}^{m}(\alpha_{i1}^j C_i + S_i) = \delta_{j-1} \Rightarrow \alpha_{i1}^j = \frac{\delta_{j-1} - \sum_{l=1}^{m} S_l}{A_i \sum_{l=1}^{m} \frac{C_l}{A_l}} \tag{7.85}$$

where the RHS of the implication was obtained using (7.80). Analogously, the load transmitted in installment $q \geq 2$ must be delivered in time of computation on the preceding installment. Hence we have

$$\sum_{l=1}^{m}(\alpha_{iq}^j C_l + S_l) = A_1 \alpha_{1,q-1}^j \Rightarrow \alpha_{iq}^j = \frac{A_1 \alpha_{1,q-1}^j - \sum_{l=1}^{m} S_l}{A_i \sum_{l=1}^{m} \frac{C_l}{A_l}} \tag{7.86}$$

The load delivered in $k_j$ installments to each processor $P_i$ must be equal to the amount of load $\alpha_i^j$ determined by (7.84) because all processors start and stop computing simultaneously. Therefore, the number of installments $k_j$ may be calculated from such a condition formulated for any processor, e.g. for $P_1$:

$$\sum_{q=1}^{k_j} \alpha_{1q}^j = \alpha_1^j. \tag{7.87}$$

Here $k_j$ can be solved numerically, or an analytical formula for $\alpha_{iq}^j, k_j$ may be derived. The above reasoning simplifies when $\forall i, S_i = 0$, which was the case considered in [103]. It should come as no surprise that positive (and hence feasible) solutions for $\alpha_{iq}^j$ not always exist. To deal with such cases four heuristics were proposed in [103]. Let us observe that the above methods (single- and multi-installment) can be used to partition divisible loads if the processors are ready not at time 0, but at some release time $\delta_{j-1}$.

The complexity of scheduling multiple divisible loads on a star system has been analyzed in [45, 46]. Note that different tasks may perceive speeds of processors differently. Therefore, analogously to the classic deterministic scheduling theory three types of processors were distinguished. *Unrelated processors* have their communication link and processor parameters perceived differently by different tasks.

Hence these parameters are denoted $C_{ij}$, $S_{ij}$, $A_{ij}$ for processor $P_i$ and task (load) $T_j$. *Uniform processors* are the type of heterogeneous processors considered so far in this section. Uniform processors and their communication links are different, but all tasks perceive these differences identically. Hence notation $C_i$, $S_i$, $A_i$ is appropriate. Finally, *identical processors* have all respective parameters equal $\forall i$, $A_i = A$, $C_i = C$, $S_i = S$. It has been established [46] that if returning of the results must be explicitly scheduled, and the processors are unrelated then scheduling multiple loads on just one ($m = 1$) unrelated processor is **NPh**. Note that the communication medium acts like one more unrelated processor here. If returning of the results needs no explicit scheduling, then the problem of scheduling multiple loads on $m = 1$ processor is equivalent to classic scheduling problem $F2||C_{max}$ which can be solved by Johnson algorithm [68]. For $m = 2$ processors this problem is already s**NPh**. In the case of uniform processors with the additional requirement that computations of each task must finish simultaneously on all the used processors, scheduling two loads ($n = 2$) is **NPh**. Finally, it has been shown in [45] that scheduling on identical processors is **NPh** if tasks (loads) are different. To construct a schedule for multiple divisible loads on a star network the following decisions must be made: (1) the sequence of executing the tasks, (2) the set of used processors for each task, (3) the sequence of activating the processors for a given task, and (4) selecting the load chunk sizes. Using multi-installment processing introduces more degrees of freedom in the scheduling decision process: (5) the number of installments for each task, (6) matching of the processors with the installments for each task, and (7) the sequence of installments from different tasks in the communication medium and on the processors. The above decisions have combinatorial nature. However, if the above decisions are taken load chunk sizes may be calculated using linear programming. For simplicity of the presentation let us assume that processors are unrelated the loads are processed in single installment mode, the sequence of distributing the loads from the originator is $T_1, \ldots, T_n$, and the sequence of computing the loads on the processors is the same. We will denote by $\mathcal{P}_j \subseteq \mathcal{P}$ the set of processors exploited by task $T_j$, and by $f(j, i)$ the index of the processor receiving the $i$th chunk of task $T_j$. The optimum load chunk sizes may be calculated from the following linear program:

$$\text{minimize } C_{max} \qquad\qquad \text{subject to} \qquad\qquad (7.88)$$

$$\sum_{l=1}^{j-1}\sum_{i=1}^{|\mathcal{P}_l|}(S_{f(l,i)l} + \alpha^l_{f(l,i)}C_{f(l,i)l}) + \sum_{i=1}^{h}(S_{f(j,i)j} + \alpha^j_{f(j,i)}C_{f(j,i)j})$$

$$+ \sum_{l=j}^{n}\alpha^l_{f(j,h)}A_{f(j,h)l} \le C_{max} \quad \text{for } j = 1, \ldots, n, \ h = 1, \ldots, |\mathcal{P}_j| \quad (7.89)$$

$$\sum_{i=1}^{|\mathcal{P}_j|}\alpha^j_{f(j,i)} = V_j \qquad\qquad \text{for } j = 1, \ldots, n \qquad\qquad (7.90)$$

$$\alpha^j_i \ge 0 \qquad\qquad\qquad\qquad (7.91)$$

In the above inequalities (7.89) the first two sums on the LHS express the communication time until sending the $h$th load chunk of task $T_j$, the last sum on the LHS is the computation time on the processor receiving load chunk $f(j, h)$ including task $T_j$ and the following tasks. It has been observed in [46] that in the optimum solution of (7.88)–(7.91) the completion times of tasks preceding the last one may be different on different processors. This is against the common assumption in DLT that all processors stop computing a single load simultaneously. Furthermore, if the communication speed is much bigger than the combined computation speed (i.e. $C \ll \frac{A}{m}$ for identical processors) then in the optimum solutions the processors may be nearly equally loaded, but a particular task may be processed sequentially on one processor only. Though such a solution may be optimum for a set of tasks, it neglects any gains from parallelism for the particular parallel applications. Linear programs (7.88)–(7.91) may be modified to introduce additional requirement that the computations on all the exploited processors finish simultaneously [46]. It has also been shown that on identical processors with negligible start-up ($\forall i, S_i = 0$) a greedy equipartitioning algorithm constructs a schedule not worse than twice the length of the optimum schedule.

Scheduling multiple divisible loads on a chain of heterogeneous processors was analyzed in [88]. Single- and multi-installment load partitioning strategies similar to the above ones were proposed. The loads were rearranged according to Smallest Load First (SLF) or Largest Load First (LLF) orders (these can be considered local flavors of SPT, LPT orders). Note that if tasks (loads) have ready times, deadlines, then standard heuristics like EDD for deadline scheduling can be applied. Moreover, to meet the deadline a minimum number of necessary processors may be calculated and applied to process a divisible load, as proposed in [82]. This results in processors with different release times resulting from processing the preceding loads. For the end of this section let us observe that in the above considerations, different loads are isolated from each other on the processors. In other words they do not merge or coalesce.

### 7.6.2 Multiple Source Load

Let us observe that the case when the loads originating from many sources are different and isolated from each other is similar to multicommodity network flow problem which is **NPh** [56]. The similarity to multicommodity network flow was also mentioned in [97].

The problem of scheduling multiple divisible loads originating from multiple sources in an arbitrary graph has been studied in [114]. When several chunks arrive at a certain node, then they constitute volume of load which is processed with the same speed. Thus, the loads originating from the different nodes do not compete for the computing resources, but they merge as if belonging to the same application. It is assumed that the load is distributed from a node via virtual paths representing computing and communication capabilities of the neighboring nodes. For example, the length of the path representing local computing capability of a processor $P_i$ is $\tau_i^{\max} + A_i\alpha_i$, where $\tau_i^{\max}$ is the time moment when the last piece of load arrives at $P_i$. This time moment depends on the amount of load $\alpha_{ji}$ transferred to $P_i$ from its direct neighbor $P_j$. Here $\tau_i^{\max}$ can be calculated as $\tau_i^{\max} = \max_{P_j \in N(i)}\{\tau_j^{\max} + \sum_{k \in O(j,i)} C_{jk}\alpha_{jk}\}$, where $N(i)$ is the set of $P_i$ neighbors, and $O(j,i)$ is the set of processors receiving load from $P_j$ not after $P_i$. An algorithm has been proposed which iteratively recalculates partition of the load until the lengths of all virtual paths are equal. The equal length of the virtual paths translates to equal completion time of the computations on all processors. When some path is longer than the shortest one then it means that too much load is processed by a certain processor. Then the length of the shorter path is increased by transferring some load from the longer path. It may be also said that the algorithm proposed in [114] is a completion time balancing algorithm built on the basis of DLT.

In [108] processing loads originating from multiple sources in a network which is a complete bipartite graph is considered (Fig. 7.12a). One of the node sets in the bipartite graph are originators. The other set contains computing processors. Let $m_1$ be the number of the originators and $m_2$ the number of computing processors. The $i$th originator has $V_i$ load to process. Let us denote by $C_{ij}$ the communication transfer rate from the $i$th originator to the computing processor $P_j$, and by $\alpha_{ij}$ the amount of load transferred from originator $i$ to processor $P_j$. For simplicity of presentation we assume that there are no communication nor computation start-up times, and that $C_{ij} < A_j$. In [108] it is assumed that computations may start in parallel with receiving the load as proposed in [71] (cf. Sect. 7.1.3). Consequently, the computations start and finish simultaneously on all processors (Fig. 7.12b). The distribution of the load must satisfy conditions:

$$\sum_{i=1}^{m_1} \alpha_{i1} A_1 = \sum_{i=1}^{m_1} \alpha_{ij} A_j \quad \text{for } j = 1, \dots, m_2 \tag{7.92}$$

$$\sum_{j=1}^{m_2} \alpha_{ij} = V_i \quad \text{for } i = 1, \dots, m_1 \tag{7.93}$$

$$\alpha_{ij} \geq 0 \tag{7.94}$$

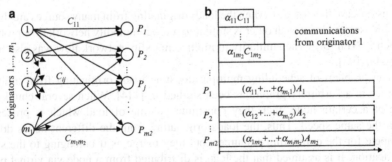

**Fig. 7.12** Multiple loads originating in a complete bipartite network. (**a**) The network and (**b**) exemplary schedule

Since the above constraints are not sufficient to calculate $\alpha_{ij}$, because there are $m_1 m_2$ variables and $m_1 + m_2$ constraints, it was additionally required in [108] that $\alpha_{ij} = \alpha_j V_i$. Under this assumption it can be calculated that $\alpha_j = \dfrac{1}{A_j \sum_{j=1}^{m_2} \frac{1}{A_j}}$.

This model of scheduling loads originating from multiple sources was extended to the case when each processor $P_j$ has memory buffer limit $B_j$, and the total load processed by $P_j$ cannot exceed it. A heuristic extending IBS [79] (see Sect. 7.4.1) algorithm was used to calculate the load distribution. Let us remind that IBS calculates load distribution iteratively. In each iteration the unassigned load is partitioned as if there were no memory constraints. Then, the loads are proportionately scaled down (if needed) to saturate the smallest memory buffer. The remaining load and memory buffers are distributed in the following iterations. Note that both problems, with and without memory constraints, can be solved by linear programming without imposing constraint $\alpha_{ij} = \alpha_j V_i$. Such a linear programming formulation has been proposed in [89], for complete bipartite network with two originators, and computations starting after receiving the whole message with the load. The sequence of receiving the load chunks, however, was given.

The above model of scheduling divisible loads originating from multiple sources in a complete bipartite network was a foundation of heuristic Resource-Aware Dynamic Incremental Scheduling (RADIS) [106]. RADIS performs a similar function as the algorithms presented in Sects. 5.6.4 and 5.7.3. The tasks arriving at the originators have different ready times $r_j$, deadlines $d_j$, and load sizes $V_j$. Each originator has one task, or load, to process. RADIS consists of several components. Admission control heuristic accepts the newly arrived task $T_j$ if it can be processed before its deadline $d_j$ considering the load $V_j$, the loads of the tasks already allowed into the system, and the average computing speed. Local schedulers at the processors predict memory availability using the past data, inform a central controller about the predicted memory availability, receive load distribution information from the central controller, request the load from the selected originators, and finally compute the load. The central controller works iteratively. In each iteration it calculates partitioning of the loads from the chosen sources on the basis of computing speeds and available memory sizes. The sources are chosen from the ones admitted to processing using one of three rules: EDD – the loads with the smallest deadline are distributed, progressive scheme – the loads at risk of missing their deadlines are distributed, noninterleaved scheme – all the admitted loads are distributed. The performance of RADIS heuristic was evaluated by simulation [106].

## 7.7 Time-Varying Environment

DLT has been applied to analyze time-varying computing systems. By time-varying systems we mean that communication and computation speeds may change in time. This may result from the existence of other flows competing for the communication medium, the existence of other tasks competing for the computing power, or predetermined maintenance periods. Changes of the communication and computation media were represented in various ways in different publications.

Time-varying environments were first studied in [100] for a star network with negligible start-up times. Processors with release times were studied in [18, 24, 39, 104]. When all processors become available at a certain time $\tau$, then finding distribution of the load is similar to the case of scheduling task after task, where the first task leaves processors occupied until moment $\tau$. This situation was considered in Sect. 7.6.1. For example, in [24] a multi-installment strategy for processors with equal release times is used. In the first installment some part of load is sent to the processors before the release time, and it is partitioned such that processors start computing at their release times, and stop computing simultaneously. The remaining load (if any) is distributed in the next and the following installments. If processors become available in different time moments, then a method based on binary search over the number of used processors and linear programming is proposed in [39]. It has been shown in [41] that scheduling divisible loads on processors with release times, or with upper limits of availability intervals, is computationally hard. However, if the set of processors that must be used and the sequence of their activation are given then optimum load distribution can be found by use of linear programming. Below we outline the method proposed in [100] for a bus.

Since the problem of selecting the set of processors is **NP**-hard [41, 110] we will assume that all processors participate in the computation, and the order of activating them coincides with their numbers. The processing rate of processor $P_i$ changes in time moments $0 < \gamma_{i1} < \cdots < \gamma_{ia_i}$ (see Fig. 7.13). Let $A_i^j$ be the processing rate of $P_i$ in the interval $[\gamma_{i,j-1}, \gamma_{ij}]$. More generally processing rate of $P_i$ is a function $A_i(t)$ in time $t$. In interval $[x, y]$, where $x \in [\gamma_{i,j-1}, \gamma_{i,j}]$ and $y \in [\gamma_{i,l-1}, \gamma_{i,l}]$, for some $0 < j \leq l \leq a_i$, $P_i$ is able to process load

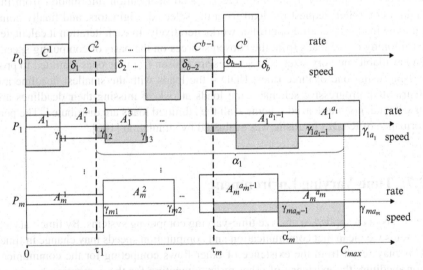

**Fig. 7.13** Time-varying environment. Boxes above the horizontal axes are processing rates, boxes below the axes represent speeds. The shaded area is equal to the transferred or computed load

$$\alpha_i(x, y) = \int_x^y \frac{dt}{A_i(t)} = \begin{cases} \frac{\gamma_j - x}{A_i^j} + \sum_{k=j+1}^{l-1} \frac{\gamma_k - \gamma_{k-1}}{A_i^k} + \frac{y - \gamma_{l-1}}{A_i^l} & \text{for } j < l \\ \frac{y - x}{A_i^j} & \text{for } j = l \end{cases} \quad (7.95)$$

Observe that for fixed $x$, $\alpha_i(x, y)$ is a piecewise linear nondecreasing function of $y$, and for fixed $y$, $\alpha_i(x, y)$ is a piecewise linear nonincreasing function of $x$.

It is assumed that the communication network is a bus. Consequently the communication medium is shared and all processors perceive the same changes of communication speed. Let $0 < \delta_1 < \cdots < \delta_b$ denote the time moments when the speed of communication changes (Fig. 7.13). The communication rate in interval $[\delta_{j-1}, \delta_j]$ is $C^j$, for $j = 1, \ldots, b$. Also here it may be said that communication rate is a function $C(t)$ of time $t$. For simplicity of presentation we assume that communication start-up times are negligible $\forall i$, $S_i = 0$. Analogously to Eq. (7.95) the amount of load $V'(x, y)$ that may be transferred from the originator to the processors in time $[x, y]$, where $x \in [\delta_{j-1}, \delta_j]$ and $y \in [\delta_{l-1}, \delta_l]$, for some $0 < j \le l \le b$, is equal to

$$V'(x, y) = \int_x^y \frac{dt}{C(t)} = \begin{cases} \frac{\delta_j - x}{C^j} + \sum_{k=j+1}^{l-1} \frac{\delta_k - \delta_{k-1}}{C^k} + \frac{y - \delta_{l-1}}{C^l} & \text{for } j < l \\ \frac{y - x}{C^j} & \text{for } j = l \end{cases} \quad (7.96)$$

Observe that $V'(x, y)$ is the same type of piecewise linear function as $\alpha_i(x, y)$s.

It is assumed that there are idle times neither in the communications, nor in the computations, and that all processors stop computing simultaneously. We will denote by $\tau_i$ the time moment when communication to $P_i$ finishes, for $i = 1, \ldots, m$. The distribution of the load may be found using the following procedure:

---

1: Find $\tau_m$ from equation $V = V'(0, \tau_m)$; // cf. equation (7.96)
2: Express $C_{max}$ as a function of $\alpha_m$ using equation $\alpha_m = \alpha_m(\tau_m, C_{max})$; // cf. (7.95)
3: **for** $i = m - 1$ **downto** 1 **do**
   {
4:   Express $\tau_i$ as a function of $\alpha_m$ using equation $V - \sum_{j=m}^{i+1} \alpha_j = V'(0, \tau_i)$;
5:   Express $\alpha_i$ as a function of $\alpha_m$ using equation $\alpha_i = \alpha_i(\tau_i, C_{max})$;
   };
6: Using normalization equation $V = \sum_{i=1}^m \alpha_i$ find $\alpha_m$, and from $\alpha_m$ find $\alpha_i$ for $i = 1, \ldots, m - 1, C_{max}$.

---

Observe that the above procedure is quite complex because it requires operations on $C_{max}, \alpha_1, \ldots, \alpha_{m-1}$ which are piecewise linear functions of $\alpha_m$. The above approach requires a priori knowledge about the changes of communication and computation speeds in the future. A probabilistic analysis has been conducted in [100] which accounts for changing communication and computation rates by the use of average communication rate and average computation rate.

## 7.8 Expected Search Time

In the preceding sections we assumed that by the nature of the application it is required that all the load must be processed from the beginning to the very end. However, in the case of searching in a flat file database the operation may be terminated as soon as the first matching record is found [73]. Similarly, for other search and decision problems the computation may be finished when sufficient information is gathered. This poses a question of the expected schedule length.

The problem of evaluating the expected schedule length has been studied in [73]. Below we outline this approach. For simplicity of presentation let us assume that the load is processed in a star network, and is partitioned according to the linear systems (7.1) and (7.2). Let $x(i) = \sum_{j=1}^{i} \alpha_j$ be the load assigned to processors $P_1, \ldots, P_i$, and $\tau_i = \sum_{j=1}^{i} (S_j + \alpha_i C_i)$ the time of starting computations on $P_i$. Let $\mathbf{X}$ be a random variable representing the position of the searched object in the volume of load $V$. After normalizing the positions to the size of load it can be assumed that $\mathbf{X} \sim U(0, 1)$, i.e. the normalized position has uniform distribution in range $[0, 1]$. The random variable of the searched object position may be mapped to a random variable $\mathbf{Y}_i$ of the amount of time till the object is found on processor $P_i$, for $i = 1, \ldots, m$. The random variable of search time on processor $P_i$ is given by function

$$\mathbf{Y}_i = (\mathbf{X} - x)A_i + \tau_i \quad \text{for } \mathbf{X} \in [x(i-1), x(i)] \tag{7.97}$$

The mapping $\mathbf{X} \to \mathbf{Y}$ from the random variable of the object position to the random variable of the object search time is

$$\mathbf{Y} = \sum_{j=1}^{m} \mathbf{Y}_i \tag{7.98}$$

The expected search time is $E(\mathbf{Y}) = \int_0^{C_{\max}} y p(y) \, dy$, where $y$ is finish time, $p(y)$ is probability density function (pdf) of $y$. From (7.98) and by Bayes' Theorem $p(y) = \sum_{i=1}^{m} p(y|P_i) p(P_i)$, where $p(y|P_i)$ is the pdf for finishing the search at time $y$ on $P_i$, and $p(P_i) = \frac{\alpha_i}{V}$ is the probability that the searched object is on $P_i$. Note that $p(y|P_i)$ is a pdf of $\mathbf{Y}_i$. By Eq. (7.97) $p(y|P_i) = \frac{1}{C_{\max}-\tau_i}$ for $y \in [\tau_i, C_{\max}]$, and 0 otherwise. Inserting all the above functions into the formula for the expected search time we obtain

$$E(\mathbf{Y}) = \int_0^{C_{\max}} y \left[ \sum_{i=1}^{m} p(y|P_i) \frac{\alpha_i}{V} \right] dy = \sum_{j=1}^{m} \frac{\alpha_i}{V} \left[ \int_0^{C_{\max}} y p(y|P_i) dy \right]$$

$$= \sum_{j=1}^{m} \frac{\alpha_i}{V} \left[ \frac{\int_{\tau_i}^{C_{\max}} y \, dy}{C_{\max} - \tau_i} \right] = \sum_{j=1}^{m} \frac{\alpha_i (C_{\max}^2 - \tau_i^2)}{2V(C_{\max} - \tau_i)} = \sum_{j=1}^{m} \frac{\alpha_i (C_{\max} + \tau_i)}{2V} \tag{7.99}$$

Intuitively, the expected search time in Eq. (7.99) is weighted average completion time of all processors. In [73] also the expected time for searching multiple records has been analyzed.

## 7.9  Steady-State Divisible Load Scheduling

In multi-installment processing of very big loads the number of installments may be very big. After initialization of the computations in a finite time, the process of communicating and computing the load may stabilize in this sense that a periodic pattern of communications and computations arises. This behavior has been called a *steady state* in [14]. Since the number of installments tends to infinity, schedule length criterion may be substituted with the criterion of maximizing the throughput $\rho$ which is the amount of load processed in time unit (e.g. in bytes per second). Now the problem is how to divide the stream of arriving load between the communication paths and the processors. Scheduling divisible loads in the steady state may be considered a special case of multi-installment processing. However, since the steady state opens a host of new options in divisible load scheduling, we present it as an independent approach in the DLT.

### 7.9.1  Single Originator

Steady-state divisible load scheduling for a star has been studied for trees in [14]. We start the presentation with a star network assuming that the time of returning the results is negligible, the originator does no computing, it is connected with its parent via a link with communication rate $C_0$, simultaneous communication and computation is possible, and the start-up times are negligible. Let $\rho_i$ denote the throughput of load directed to processor $P_i$, $m'$ the number of used processors. The problem of maximizing throughput $\rho$ in steady state may be formulated as a linear program:

$$\text{maximize } \rho \quad \text{subject to} \tag{7.100}$$

$$\rho = \sum_{i=1}^{m'} \rho_i \tag{7.101}$$

$$\rho \le \frac{1}{C_0} \tag{7.102}$$

$$\rho_i \le \frac{1}{A_i} \quad \text{for } i = 1, \ldots, m' \tag{7.103}$$

$$\sum_{i=1}^{m'} \rho_i C_i \le 1 \tag{7.104}$$

$$\rho_i, \rho \ge 0 \tag{7.105}$$

In the above formulation (7.101) is a load conservation condition, inequalities (7.102) and (7.103) are bandwidth constraints. Inequality (7.104) is a transformed condition $\sum_{i=1}^{m'} \alpha_i C_i \leq \tau$ demanding that the load can be sequentially sent to the processors in the period $\tau$ in which communication and computation pattern repeat, $\alpha_i$ is the load sent to $P_i$ in time $\tau$, $\rho_i = \frac{\alpha_i}{\tau}$. In (7.104) this condition has been normalized to a unit of time. Linear program (7.100)–(7.105) has the following constructive solution [14]: Order the processors according to the nondecreasing $C_i$. Choose $l$ as the largest index such that $\sum_{i=1}^{l} \frac{C_i}{A_i} \leq 1$. If $l < m$ then set $\varepsilon = 1 - \sum_{i=1}^{l} \frac{C_i}{A_i}$, otherwise set $\varepsilon = 0$ and $C_{l+1} = 1$ (for simplicity of presentation). Then, the optimum throughput assignments are: $\rho = \min\{\frac{1}{C_0}, \sum_{i=1}^{l} \frac{1}{A_i} + \frac{\varepsilon}{C_{l+1}}\}$, $\rho_i = \frac{1}{A_i}$ for $i = 1, \ldots, l$, $\rho_{l+1} = \frac{\varepsilon}{C_{l+1}}$. If $l+1 < m$, then $\rho_i = 0$ for $l+2 \leq i \leq m$. To construct a feasible periodic load distribution pattern from $\rho, \rho_i$ it is proposed to calculate period length $\tau$ as the least common multiple of $\{A_1, \ldots, A_l, C_0, C_{l+1}\}$. The load received by the star is $\alpha_0 = \rho\tau$, and the size of load part sent to processor $P_i$ is $\alpha_i = \rho_i \tau$. To stabilize this pattern it is proposed to send loads $\alpha_i$ to the idle processors in the first period. In the second, and the following periods distribution of new loads in sizes $\alpha_i$ is overlapped with processing of the load received in the preceding iteration. Observe that period $\tau$ calculated in this way may be quite big (even exponential in the input size), which may impose high requirements on memory subsystems to hold $\alpha_i$s between the consecutive periods of the schedule. Values $\alpha_i$ calculated in this way are integer, and such a solution can be applied to schedule discretely divisible loads (cf. Sect. 7.11). A more general formulation of the steady-state scheduling of divisible loads with communication and computation start-up times, with or without communication–computation overlap, has been analyzed in [17]. It has been shown that the steady-state model delivers asymptotically optimum solutions, where asymptotically refers here to $V \to \infty$. A number of heuristics based on linear programming have been proposed and evaluated by simulation.

The star can be considered as equivalent to a single processor with speed $\rho = \frac{1}{A_{eq}}$, where $A_{eq}$ is an equivalent processing rate. Hence, the above analysis can be applied recursively to a tree of processors. A subtree consisting of a set of leaves and a common predecessor (which is a star) may be replaced with an equivalent processor, and the whole tree may be analyzed by folding it bottom-up. A set of *bandwidth-centric* distributed heuristics which build for a tree a schedule close to the optimum in steady state were proposed in [74]. We present them in Sect. 7.10.3. A procedure building optimum steady-state schedule for a tree using the above model of a star and a depth-first traversal of the tree was proposed in [4]. A different approach has been proposed in [17], where the whole tree is represented in a single linear program. Variants of the steady-state scheduling in trees, including or excluding communication overlap with computation, various numbers of communication ports, communication and computation start-up times, have been analyzed in [17].

Scheduling steady-state computations on arbitrary graphs was studied in [5]. Finding optimum load flows was reduced to linear programming, and multiple paths connecting the originator with the processors were possible. If only spanning trees can be used to deliver the load to the processor, then it can be shown that constructing a spanning tree giving maximum throughput is **NPh**, and a solution using spanning trees (instead of multiple parallel communication paths) can be arbitrarily bad [5]. The same problem was reduced to finding maximum network flow for which a distributed algorithm was proposed in [66].

### 7.9.2   Multiple Originators

Scheduling multiple divisible loads originating from different sources in the arbitrary interconnection network under the steady state has been analyzed in [85]. It has been assumed that the communication network consists of routers only. The processors are connected to the network via routers. The routes between the processors are fixed and consist of a chain of communication links. In a communication link $l_i$ at most $mc_i$ connections may be opened each with bandwidth at most $bw_i$ (cf. communication delay considerations in Sect. 3.1.3). There are $n$ applications (tasks) $T_1, \ldots, T_n$. For simplicity of presentation let us assume that there are $n \leq m$ processors in set $\mathcal{P}_A$, where $P_i \in \mathcal{P}_A$ is the originator for $T_i$. Let $\rho_i$ be the throughput (e.g. in bytes per second) at which the load of $T_i$ originating at processor $P_i \in \mathcal{P}_A$ is processed, and let $\rho_{ij}$ be the throughput of the load sent off from $P_i \in \mathcal{P}_A$ to some other $P_j \in \mathcal{P}$. Let $R_{ij}$ be the sequence of communication links composing the route from $P_i$ to $P_j$. Since the routes in the network are fixed it is possible to determine the minimum bandwidth of any link on the route from $P_i$ to $P_j$. Consequently, it is also possible to determine the time $C_{ij}$ of transferring one load unit (e.g. byte) of task $T_i$ from originator $P_i$ to some other processor $P_j$ over one opened connection. More than one connection may be opened between a pair of processors. Let $\beta_{ij}$ be the number of connections opened between processor $P_i$ where load of $T_i$ originates, and some other processor $P_j$. Processors which are not originators do not relay the load, and hence $\rho_{ij}, R_{ij}, \beta_{ij}$ are not defined for $i > n$. Let $A_{ij}$ denote the time of processing one load unit (e.g. byte) from $T_i$ on processor $P_j$. The applications have priorities $w_i$. The objective function is to maximize the weighted processing throughput observed by any application. The steady-state scheduling under the above assumptions may be formulated as the following mixed linear programming problem

$$\text{maximize} \quad \min_{j=1}^{n} \{\rho_j w_j\} \quad \text{subject to} \tag{7.106}$$

$$\rho_i = \sum_{j=1}^{m} \rho_{ij} \quad \text{for } i = 1, \ldots, n \tag{7.107}$$

$$\sum_{i=1}^{n} \rho_{ij} A_{ij} \leq 1 \quad \text{for } j = 1, \ldots, m \tag{7.108}$$

$$\sum_{i=1, i \neq j}^{n} \rho_{ij} C_{ij} + \sum_{i=1, i \neq j}^{n} \rho_{ji} C_{ji} \leq 1 \quad \text{for } j = 1, \ldots, n \tag{7.109}$$

$$\sum_{\{(i,j):l_a \in R_{i,j}\}} \beta_{ij} \le mc_a \quad \text{for } i = 1, \ldots, n, j = 1, \ldots, m \qquad (7.110)$$

$$\rho_{ij} C_{ij} \le \beta_{ij} \quad \text{for } i = 1, \ldots, n, j = 1, \ldots, m \qquad (7.111)$$

$$\rho_{ij} \ge 0 \quad \text{for } i = 1, \ldots, n, j = 1, \ldots, m \qquad (7.112)$$

$$\beta_{ij} \in Z^+ \quad \text{for } i = 1, \ldots, n, j = 1, \ldots, m \qquad (7.113)$$

In the above formulation (7.107) is the load conservation requirement. By inequalities (7.108) processors are able to compute the inflow of load. Constraints (7.109) demand that the flow of load departing from some originator $P_i$ and the load of other tasks than the local one can be feasibly transferred between $P_i$ and the network. The number of connections opened between the processors may not exceed the capacity of any link by inequality (7.110). Analogously, the bandwidth required to transfer load from $P_i$ to $P_j$ is not exceeded by (7.111). The above formulation is a mixed linear program because $\rho_{ij}$ are rational, and $\beta_{ij}$ are integer variables. This means in practice that (7.106)–(7.113) is hard to solve. Therefore, heuristic algorithms solving (7.106)–(7.113) have been proposed and evaluated in [85].

An idea of a different heuristic partitioning the load originating from multiple sources in an arbitrary graph was proposed in [97]. Distribution of the load is to be found for each originator separately using linear communication delay and processing times (no start-up times). The flow of the load is analogous to the flow of current in linear electric circuits. In linear electric circuits currents from different sources may be superimposed. Analogously, flows of the loads from different sources may be superimposed on each other, and the flows in opposite directions can cancel each other out. Consequently, the network may be partitioned into domains around the originator where its load is processed.

## 7.10   Online Scheduling

In the preceding sections it was assumed that the parameters of the distributed system are known and certain. In the real systems the parameters may be unknown, known with some degree of uncertainty, or be drifting with time. To account for this uncertainty various types of heuristic algorithms were proposed.

### 7.10.1   Measuring Heuristics

The idea of the algorithms presented here is to measure system parameters first, and then to apply the standard DLT methodology using the most up-to-date measurement results.

**Probing and Delayed Distribution (PDD) [61]** First short chunks of size $\lceil \frac{V\eta}{m} \rceil$ are sent to the processors, where $0 < \eta < 1$ is a tunable parameter of the algorithm.

Having received the load processors send communication task completion (CTC) message to the originator. Analogously processing task completion (PTC) message is sent to the originator on completion of the computations. Knowing the length of communication, computation, and the amount of load, the originator calculates $A_i, C_i$. The rest of the load is partitioned according to the standard DLT methodology, e.g. using (7.1) and (7.2). The initial probing may last unnecessarily long. If one of the processors is very slow, then the start of the processing the remaining load is delayed until the response from such a processor. Furthermore, this strategy is not able to adapt to a significant change in the system parameters after the probing stage.

**Probing and Continuous Distribution (PCD) [61]** The load $V$ is partitioned into $\frac{1}{\eta}$ equal installments (or batches). Each processor receives a chunk of size $\frac{V\eta}{m}$ from each started installment. The originator keeps distributing the load in installments until receiving the last PTC message from the first installment. Then, the originator stops distributing the installments, and calculates $A_i, C_i$. Note that in the probing stage some load may have accumulated on the processors. Thus, some load is already present on the processors and it must be computed first. Therefore, the load partitioning should be calculated assuming that processors have release times equal to the time needed to compute the accumulated load (cf. Sect. 7.7). This strategy avoids idling the processors in the probing stage, but does not account for system changes after the last distribution step.

**Probing and Selective Distribution (PSD) [61]** As in the previous strategy the probing installments with chunks of size $\frac{V\eta}{m}$ are being sent until receiving the first PTC message from some processor $P_a$. Then parameters $A_a, C_a$ are calculated, and load $V\eta$ is sent to $P_a$. After receiving the second PTC message from some processor $P_b$, parameters $A_b, C_b$ are known, and load of size $2V\eta$ is partitioned between $P_a$ and $P_b$ according to the DLT methods. Analogously, after receiving $i$ PTC messages from some set $\mathcal{P}'$ of processors load $iV\eta$ is distributed to the processors in $\mathcal{P}'$. This procedure is continued until partitioning all the remaining load. With each PTC message the information on processor speed should be updated, to be used in the next load partitioning calculation. If some processors return no PTC messages until processing the whole load, then their load may be redistributed again to the final set of working processors.

### 7.10.2  Loop Scheduling

Let us observe that the same problem as in online divisible load scheduling must be confronted in scheduling *independent* loops which is often called *loop scheduling*. The loop scheduling problem consists in distributing some number $V$ of loops between $m$ processors such that the total processing time is the shortest possible. The execution time of a loop is unpredictable. Two difficulties must be overcome: saturation of the loop distributor (equivalent of saturating the communication medium) and imbalance in the computation completion time of the processors. We present this special case of loop scheduling here because loop scheduling algorithms are immediately applicable in the divisible load case. The names of loop distributor and the originator are used interchangeably. The costly synchronization in the access to the loop distributor is equivalent to communication time with dominating start-up times. Hence, most loop scheduling algorithms try to minimize the number of accesses to the loop distributor, or in other words, the number of messages. Since grains of parallelism exist in the applications, the chunk sizes must be integer multiples of the grain size. If not stated explicitly, it is assumed that fractional chunk sizes are rounded up, and the last chunk receives the remaining load which may be smaller than the fractional assignment. Brief surveys of independent loop scheduling algorithms can be found in [32, 37, 83].

**Static Chunk** Each processor receives a chunk of size $\frac{V}{m}$. This method is also called *static scheduling* or *equipartitioning* in DLT. An advantage of static chunk scheduling is that there are only $m$ accesses to the originator. A disadvantage is that it does not account for heterogeneity or any change in the system. Hence arbitrarily bad solutions may arise. An algorithm similar to static chunk is present in OpenMP [90] programming environment (see Sect. 3.2). Pragma schedule(static, *chunk_size*) assigns equal number of *chunk_size* iterations to each thread.

**Self-Scheduling [75]** Each processor is assigned a unit load at a time. The unit load may be one grain of parallelism, or one loop. After computing it, the processor requests a new load unit. In a variant of self-scheduling load is sent in chunks of fixed size $\alpha > 1$. This method was also presented under names *dynamic chunk scheduling*, *chunk self-scheduling*, *fixed size chunking* [32], *DA2* [39]. If chunk sizes are equal to 1, then this method gives the best possible balance of processor completion times. It is also able to adapt to the changing environment because faster processors request and receive load more often. Yet, if load chunk $\alpha$ is too small then the communication with the originator may become a bottleneck. Optimum chunk sizes were analyzed using statistical models in [75]. There is an equivalent of self-scheduling in OpenMP [90] (Sect. 3.2). Pragma schedule(dynamic, *chunk_size*) assigns *chunk_size* iterations to a thread requesting new work.

**Guided Self-Scheduling [33]** Let $V'$ be the amount of the remaining load. A processor requesting work is assigned a chunk of size $\max\{1, \lceil \frac{V'}{m} \rceil\}$. An equivalent of guided self-scheduling is present in OpenMP [90] (Sect. 3.2). Pragma schedule(guided, *chunk_size*) determines that a thread requesting work receives $\max\{\lceil V'/m' \rceil, chunk\_size\}$ iterations, where $m'$ is the number of threads.

**Trapezoid Self-Scheduling [102]** Here the chunk sizes linearly decrease with the consecutive requests for work from initial size $\alpha_I$ to the final size $\alpha_F$. The chunk size decreasing step is $\frac{\alpha_I - \alpha_F}{\lceil \frac{2V}{\alpha_F + \alpha_I} \rceil - 1}$. Here $\alpha_I, \alpha_F$ are tunable parameters. Sizes $\alpha_I = \frac{V}{2m}$ and $\alpha_F = 1$ were proposed in [102].

**Factoring Self-Scheduling [67]** Here load is distributed in batches. In iteration $j \geq 0$ a batch of $\frac{1}{l_j}$ of the remaining load is distributed in equal chunks to the processors. Thus, load $\alpha_j = \max\{1, \lceil \frac{V'}{ml_j} \rceil\}$ is sent to all the processors. It has been proposed to choose $l_j$ on the basis of the existing statistics on the execution time of the loops. Let $\mu, \sigma$ denote the mean and standard deviation of loop execution time. Then $l_j$ can be calculated from the formulae: $l_0 = 1 + b_0^2 + b_0 \sqrt{b_0^2 + 2}$, $l_j = 2 + b_j^2 + b_j \sqrt{b_j^2 + 4}$, for $j > 1$, where $b_j = \frac{m\sigma}{2\sqrt{V'}\mu}$. If no statistics of the loop execution time are known then $l_j = 2$ has been recommended in [67]. Factoring tries to limit the imbalance in the processor computation time that could have arisen if the load chunk sizes changed too rapidly.

**Adaptive Factoring Self-Scheduling [32]** Here the statistics on the loop execution times are collected during the execution of the algorithm. It starts with arbitrary load chunk size $\alpha$. Let $\mu_i, \sigma_i$ denote the most recent estimate of the mean execution time and standard deviation of loop execution time for processor $P_i$. Let $D = \sum_{i=1}^{m} \frac{\sigma_i^2}{\mu_i}$, $E = \sum_{i=1}^{m} \frac{1}{\mu_i}$. The next chunk size sent to $P_i$ is

$$\alpha_i = \left( D + 2\frac{V'}{E} - \sqrt{D^2 + 4D\frac{V'}{E}} \right) / (2\mu_i).$$

**Safe Self-Scheduling [83]** It is assumed that statistics on execution time of the loops are available. As in the factoring load is distributed in batches. In the first stage processors receive chunks of size $\max\{\alpha_F, \lceil \beta \frac{V}{m} \rceil\}$, where $\alpha_F$ is the minimum chunk size. The $i$th processor requesting load receives a chunk of size $\max\{\alpha_F, \lceil (1 - \beta)^{\lceil i/m \rceil} \frac{V}{m} \rceil\}$. It is proposed to calculate $\beta$ from the formula $\beta = \frac{1}{2}(1 + p(\tau_{max}) + p(\tau_{min})\frac{\tau_{min}}{\tau_{max}})$, where $p(x)$ is the probability of executing a loop in time $x$, while $\tau_{max}, \tau_{min}$ are the longest and the shortest loop execution time. Let us note that here batch sizes change in stages like in the factoring, and the sizes decrease exponentially similarly to guided self-scheduling.

**Affinity Scheduling [86]** In the first stage of the algorithm processors are assigned load $\lceil \frac{V}{m} \rceil$. The load is fetched for computing from the local buffer in chunks of size $\max\{1, \lceil \frac{V'_i}{l} \rceil\}$, where $V'_i$ is the load remaining at processor $P_i$, and $l$ is a tunable parameter. In the final stage, when processor $P_i$ runs out of work it finds the processor $P_j$ with the biggest remaining amount of load, and removes load $\max\{1, \lceil \frac{V'_j}{m} \rceil\}$ from $P_j$ buffer. This algorithm has load balancing features which bypass the originator in the transfers of the load, and it requires a method for distributed election of the most loaded processor.

Interesting enough is to note which of the above algorithms found their way to the practice of parallel processing in the form of OpenMP implementation.

## 7.10.3  Other Heuristics

**Distribution Algorithm 1 (DA1) [39]** Processors $P_1, \ldots, P_m$ receive load chunks, compute them, and then turn to the originator to return the results (if any) and to request a new load chunk. Algorithm DA1 measures duration between the accesses of each processor to the originator. Let $\delta_i$ be the length of the interval between the previous and the current request of $P_i$, and let $\alpha_i$ be the size of the load chunk sent to $P_i$ in the previous iteration. DA1 intends to maintain a constant gap $\tau$ between the processor accesses to the originator. If a processor returns in time $\delta_i < \tau$ then its load assignment is increased proportionately and vice versa, it is proportionately decreased if $\delta_i > \tau$. This algorithm has two tunable parameters: $\alpha$ – the size of the first load chunk sent to all processors and $\tau$. If $m\alpha > V$ then the whole load would be distributed in just one iteration. Hence, $\alpha$ should be much smaller than $\frac{V}{m}$. If the parameters of the processors differ very much, then one processor may still process the first load chunk of size $\alpha$ when the other processors compute all the load. Thus, an arbitrarily big difference in the completion times may arise. If $\tau$ is too small then the algorithm intends to set very short interval between the processor accesses, and the originator becomes a bottleneck. The advantage of DA1 is that it requires no initial knowledge on the computing environment, it can continuously adapt itself to changing system parameters. Yet DA1 is sensitive to the choice of parameters $\alpha, \tau$. DA1 may be summarized as follows:

---

1: Send to all $m$ processors load $\alpha_i = \alpha$;
2: **while** there is load to process
 { **if** $P_i$ is asking for load { send load max$\{1, \lfloor \alpha_i \frac{\tau}{\delta_i} \rfloor\}$ to $P_i$ }};

---

**Distribution Algorithm 3 (DA3) [39]** This algorithm tries to correct deficiencies of DA1 by adjusting the length of the access interval $\tau$. If the communication medium from the originator to the processors is working without idle time, then it is a bottleneck. This is verified by checking if in the interval between two accesses of one selected processor (say $P_1$) the originator became free. If the originator is continuously sending load in the second or latter iteration then $\tau$ is increased $m$ times. On the other hand, if the currently serviced processor is about to receive its second or latter chunk greater than max$\{1, \lceil \frac{V'}{m} \rceil\}$, where $V'$ is the load remaining to be distributed, then the access interval is reduced to $\frac{\tau}{m}$. It has been demonstrated in simulations [39] that though DA3 is less susceptible to bad choice of parameters $\alpha, \tau$, there are combinations of system parameters for which DA3 performs as bad as DA1. DA3 is summarized in the following pseudocode:

---

1: Send to all $m$ processors load $\alpha_i = \alpha$; *toobusy*=**true**;
2: **while** there is load to process
 {
3: **if** no processor requests load { *toobusy*=**false**};
4: **if** $P_1$ is asking for load **and** *toobusy* {$\tau = m\tau$};
5: **if** $P_1$ is asking for load {*toobusy*=**true**}; // reset flag
6: **if** $P_i$ is asking for load **and** ($\lceil \alpha_i \frac{\tau}{\delta_i} \rceil > $ max$\{1, \lceil \frac{V'}{m} \rceil\}$) { $\tau = \frac{\tau}{m}$ };
7: **if** $P_i$ is asking for load { send load max$\{1, \lceil \alpha_i \frac{\tau}{\delta_i} \rceil\}$ to $P_i$ };
 };

---

**Robust Uniform Multi-Round (RUMR) [109]**   This is a combination of algorithm UMR [111] already presented in Sect. 7.3 and factoring for loop scheduling from Sect. 7.10.2. It is assumed that the system is homogeneous, processor and communication parameters $A, C, S$ are known but only with limited certainty. The result of this uncertainty is schedule length divergence from the expectation. Let $\varepsilon > 0$ be the normalized relative difference between the expected and the real execution time. The value of $\varepsilon$ may be initially known, e.g. from the past observations of the system. The algorithm can be also formulated without the earlier knowledge on $\varepsilon$. In the first phase algorithm UMR is used, in the second phase factoring is applied to distribute the remaining load. In switching from UMR to factoring three rules are used in the following order: (1) If $\varepsilon = 0$, then only UMR is used. (2) If $\varepsilon > 1$ then only factoring is used. (3) If $\frac{\varepsilon VA}{m} \geq (S + mz)$ where $z$ is computation start-up time, then the final $\varepsilon V$ load is scheduled in the second phase (factoring), else factoring is not used. If $\varepsilon$ is unknown, then it was established by simulation that $0.8V$ should be scheduled by UMR, and $0.2V$ by factoring. It was also proposed to bound the chunk size from below in the factoring. The chunks should not be smaller than $\frac{S+mz}{A\varepsilon}$ if $\varepsilon$ is known, and not smaller than $\frac{S+mz}{A}$ otherwise.

**Autonomous Protocol for Bandwidth-Centric Scheduling (APBCS) [74]**   The heuristic presented here are inspired by the main feature of optimum solutions for steady-state load partitioning in stars (see Sect. 7.9.1). The load is distributed from the originator to the processors according to the order of decreasing communication speed which is called a *bandwidth-centric principle*. The considered network topology is a tree, and the APBSC is a distributed scheduling algorithm executed on each processor (i.e. tree node). Two types of APBCS heuristics were considered in [74]: with nonpreemptive and with preemptive communication. We present here the second type which turned out to be more effective. Communication buffers at the processors are key element of APBCS heuristics. A processor requests a new load unit (a load of size equal to the grain of parallelism) when one of its buffers becomes empty. A buffer may become empty as a consequence of starting the computation on the load unit, sending it to a child node. A set of rules have been proposed to adjust the number of buffers to the conditions during the computation. However, experimental results indicate that three buffers suffice. In managing communications with its children $P_i$ gives preference to the successor $P_j$ with the greater communication speed (i.e. smaller $C_{ij}$). A communication with a processor with a slower link is interrupted and suspended by a request for a load from a faster communicating successor. After the end of the communication with the faster communicating processor, the suspended communication is resumed and continued from where it left off. Consequently, one communication buffer is necessary for each successor node (beyond the three mentioned earlier). It has been verified in simulations that APBCS heuristic with preemptive communication builds load distributions very close to the steady-state optimum.

## 7.11  Toward Discrete Load Granularity

In this chapter, we generally assumed that the load is arbitrarily divisible. However, from the perspective of the application the load is not truly arbitrarily divisible. Usually there exist some smallest amount of data in data-parallel application which cannot be further divided without violating the logic of the application. These are often called *grains of parallelism*. Let us assume that the size (e.g. in bytes) of a parallelism grain is a unit. Thus, in practical applications the load part sizes should be integer multiples of such a unit. The solutions of the standard DLT formulations like linear systems (7.1) and (7.2), or linear programs (7.37)–(7.41) are not expected to provide integer load part sizes $\alpha_i$. Hence, some additional precautions must be taken to obtain integer part sizes. An immediate solution could be to add a requirement (e.g. to (7.1) and (7.2) or to (7.37)–(7.41)) that $\alpha_i$ must be integer. This would make the problem considerably harder to solve because integer linear programming is in general **NP**-hard (see Sect. 2.3.3). A more tractable approach is to use some heuristic rounding method, and try to bound the increase in the schedule length. Below we outline the methods of dealing with granular loads.

### 7.11.1  Rounding Techniques

The first attempt analyzing the increase in the schedule length has been made in [3]. Divisible load processing in a 2D-toroidal mesh with scattering over 5-nomial tree (compare Sect. 7.2.3) has been considered in [3]. While scattering in 5-nomial trees messages with load are sent from one tree node to another node where they are further partitioned and redistributed, until reaching the level of leaves. It was observed that if the message sizes are rounded up to the nearest integer, and load sizes are rounded up to $\lceil \alpha_i \rceil$, then the extension of the schedule length is not greater than $Ch + A$, where $h$ is the greatest number of consecutive messages carrying the load to some processor. In other words $h$ is the length of the longest path in the 5-nomial tree.

A more careful analysis has been preformed in [105] for a homogeneous star with single- and multi-installment processing. To support the analysis a concept of *direct flow graph* (DFG) has been introduced (Fig. 7.14). The nodes of DFG

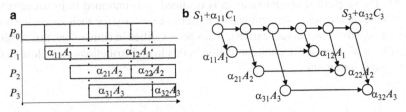

**Fig. 7.14** Exemplary Directed Flow Graph (DFG). (**a**) Gantt chart and (**b**) the corresponding DFG

represent communications and computations. Arcs connect the nodes representing communications and computations in their precedence order. For example, the communication nodes form a chain according to the sequence of their distribution from the originator. Similarly, in multi-installment processing a chain of nodes represents the sequence of chunk computations on a processor. DFG is a graph with weights on nodes. The weight is the duration of communication or computation corresponding to the node. The weights (durations) are calculated from the fractional solutions such as (7.1) and (7.2). The deviation from the timings calculated in (7.1) and (7.2) arising due to rounding the load parts can accumulate. A path in the DFG provides information which load part sizes contribute to the eventual change of completion time on a processor. Thus, the longest path in DFG with the worst possible load size deviation can be used to calculate the worst-case schedule length extension. The algorithms proposed in [105] round the fractional $\alpha_i$s up or down to $\alpha_i'$ depending on the amount of a residue accumulated in the rounding process. For a single-installment distribution the initial residue is $res_1 = 0$ and $\alpha_1' = \lceil \alpha_1 \rceil$. If $res_{i-1} + \lceil \alpha_i \rceil - \alpha_i < 1$ then $\alpha_i' = \lceil \alpha_i \rceil$, otherwise $\alpha_i' = \lfloor \alpha_i \rfloor$, for $i = 2, \ldots, m$. Here $res_i = res_{i-1} + \alpha_i' - \alpha_i$, for $i = 2, \ldots, m$. It has been shown that the maximum schedule length increase is $C + A$ in homogeneous system. For multi-installment processing similar approach is used. Yet, the threshold of the residue switching from rounding up to rounding down is set to 0.5 (instead of 1). The two algorithms PIA (Processor based Integer Approximation) and IIA (Installment based Integer Approximation) differ in the sequence of rounding the load chunks. In PIA the rounding is carried processor-wise between the consecutive chunks received by the same processor. After reaching the last chunk on processor $P_i$ the residue is carried to the first chunk received by $P_{i+1}$. In IIA the sequence of chunk rounding follows their sequence of departing from the originator, the residue is carried between the chunks in the same order. It has been shown that the schedule extension is not bigger than $\frac{m}{2}C + A$, or $\frac{k}{2}C + A$, depending on the applied algorithm, where $k$ is the number of installments [105].

An algorithm for trees rounding the fractional solutions was proposed in [7]. The load part sizes are analyzed in the breadth-first search order. We denote by $\alpha^i$ the amount of load assigned to a subtree rooted in $P_i$ according to a fractional solution, by $IS(P_i)$ the set of $P_i$ immediate successors. In the rounding process we will treat in the same way all processors in set $X_i = \{P_i, IS(P_i)\}$, processor $P_i$ with load $\alpha_i$ as well as its immediate successors in $IS(P_i)$ with load $\alpha^i$ representing a whole subtree. For each node $P_j \in X_i$ load $\alpha_j$ is rounded down. Let $res_i = \alpha^i - \sum_{P_j \in X_i} \lfloor \alpha^j \rfloor$. A relative change $rc_j$ of the load is calculated for each processor in $X_i$. There are two ways of calculating the relative change. In algorithm Quantify 1 it is $rc_j = \frac{\lfloor \alpha_j \rfloor - \alpha_j}{\alpha_j}$, in Quantify 2 it is $rc_j = \frac{\lfloor \alpha_j \rfloor + 1 - \alpha_j}{\alpha_j}$. The processors in $X_i$ are sorted according to the nondecreasing values of $rc_j$, and the load of the fist $res_i$ processors is rounded up to $\lceil \alpha_j \rceil$. This procedure is applied recursively to the following tree nodes until reaching the level of the leaves. The shorter of the two solutions generated by algorithms Quantify 1 and Quantify 2 is chosen as the final solution. The above method can be generalized to multi-installment load scattering for trees and buses. It has been shown that for single-installment distribution on a bus Quantify increases schedule length by at most $\lfloor \frac{m+1}{2} \rfloor \max_i C_i + \max_i A_i$. In the case of multi-installment processing schedule length is increased by at most $\lceil \frac{k}{2} \rceil \max_i A_i + \lfloor \frac{k}{2} \rfloor \max\{C, 2A_i\}$, here $k$ is the number of installments, and the communication links are assumed to be homogeneous, i.e. $\forall i, C_i = C$. Algorithm Quantify has also been evaluated in a series of computational experiments [7].

Application of genetic algorithm to build a solution with integer part sizes is mentioned in [38].

### 7.11.2  Discretely Divisible Loads

Here we discuss a scheduling model accepting all the DLT assumptions but with a vital difference that the load is a set of identical indivisible tasks. This means that the load is granular or discrete. We will say that this is *discretely divisible load* (DDL). The difference between DL and DDL is essential because even simple polynomially solvable cases in DL model tend to be computationally hard for DDL model. What is more, for DL it seems hard to present a generally applicable rule which would allow for deciding whether certain load distribution algorithm builds the optimum solution. Hence, a variety of scattering algorithms adjusted to the topologies, message routing, and switching techniques. On the other hand, as in DDL, if the number $V$ of load units (i.e. tasks) is finite then it is possible, at least in principle, to enumerate all possible schedules for the finite number of load units and decide which solution is optimum. The concept of DDL is also present in the bag-of-task model of a parallel application [1]. The bag-of-task applications consist of a big number of similar, but importantly, discrete work units. Thus, the idea of the bag-of-tasks is equivalent to discretely divisible loads. Below outline several results for DDL scheduling.

Scheduling DDL in a star with heterogeneous processors and identical communication links was analyzed in [16]. Instead of the standard makespan minimization for a given amount of load $V$, a dual formulation requiring maximization of the processed load under limited schedule length $C_{\max}$ is examined. Various models of necessary communications were assumed. If just one communication of duration $S$ is necessary to start the computations, then maximizing the processed load boils down to the maximum weighted matching in a bipartite graph: The first set of nodes represents processors in $\mathcal{P}$, and the second set of nodes represents positions in the activation sequence. An edge $(i, j)$ joining processor $P_i$ with the $j$th position has weight $\frac{C_{\max} - jS}{A_i}$ equal to the amount of load processed on $P_i$ if it is activated as the $j$th processor. The maximum weight matching can be constructed in $O(m^{2.5})$. If one communication of duration $S$ is needed to start the computations, and to return the results, then scheduling DDL in a heterogeneous star is sNPh [16]. Let us observe that were the load arbitrarily divisible then this problem is solvable by using $\min\{m, \lfloor \frac{C_{\max}}{2S} \rfloor\}$ processors and activating them in the order of decreasing computing speed while the results should be collected in the LIFO order (cf. Fig. 7.2). If a communication of duration $S$ is needed before each grain of the load, then a heuristic solution similar to the steady-state schedule for a star is proposed (see Sect. 7.9.1). A communication pattern of length $\tau$ is built, and it is repeated as many times as possible in $C_{max}$. This algorithm is asymptotically optimum in maximizing the processed load with $C_{max}$ tending to infinity. Assume that the processors are ordered according to the decreasing computing speed, i.e. $A_1 \leq A_2 \leq \cdots \leq A_m$. Let $l$ be the maximum integer satisfying $\sum_{i=1}^{l} \frac{S}{S+A_i} \leq 1$. If $l = m$ then the length $\tau$ of the period is the least common multiple of $A_1 + S, \ldots, A_m + S$, and processors receive loads $\alpha_i = \frac{\tau}{S+A_i}$, for $i = 1, \ldots, m$. If $l < m$, then the length $\tau$ of the period is the least common multiple of $S, A_1 + S, \ldots, A_l + S$. Processors receive $\alpha_i = \frac{\tau}{A_i+S}$ load units for $i = 1, \ldots, l$, $\alpha_{l+1} = \frac{\tau}{S} - \sum_{i=1}^{l} \alpha_i$, $\alpha_i = 0$ for $i > l$. The originator sends the above numbers of load units to the processors consecutively, i.e. $\alpha_1$ load units to $P_1$, then $\alpha_2$ to $P_2$, etc. After sending the loads $\alpha_1, \ldots, \alpha_l$ the communication pattern is repeated. Processors compute their load assignments as soon as they are received. This approach can be generalized to the case when one communication per load unit is also necessary to return the results.

When memory sizes are limited DDL scheduling in a heterogeneous star is sNPh [15]. If the network is a heterogeneous tree then scheduling DDL is sNPh even if the time of returning the results may be neglected [54]. The DL versions of both problems are polynomially solvable.

## 7.12 DLT and Performance Evaluation

DLT has been applied to model performance of distributed systems. Below we present applications of DLT in performance evaluation.

### 7.12.1 DLT and the Classic Performance Measures

Let us observe that schedule length can be calculated from the distribution of the load. For example, in the case of a star network, solution to Eqs. (7.1)–(7.2) gives schedule length $C_{max} = S + \alpha_1(A_1 + C_1)$. Knowing schedule length we can calculate speedup $\varsigma(m)$, efficiency, and other performance measures (cf. Sect. 2.4). In Fig. 7.15, we give examples of applying DLT to analyze performance of parallel processing. In Fig. 7.15a dependence of the processing time $C_{max}$ on $V$ and the number of processors for a homogeneous mesh with 5-nomial tree scattering (cf. Sect. 7.2.3) are shown [3]. The system parameters are $A = 1E - 6$, $C = 1E - 8$, $S = 1E - 3$. This can be translated as follows: One byte of the load is processes in 1μs, the bandwidth is 100MB/s, the start-up time is 1ms. Thus, computations are quite demanding and slow, communication network is fast but the start-up time is an important component of the communication delay. The processing time increases with $V$, and decreases with $m$ as can be expected. Yet, the gains from adding processors are diminishing which can be seen in the decreasing gap between the lines for

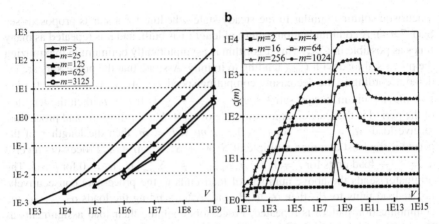

**Fig. 7.15** Performance of divisible applications. (**a**) $C_{\max}$ vs. $V$ in a mesh and (**b**) speedup vs. $V$ in a star with hierarchical memory

different processor numbers. For small load sizes the difference in processing time for various processor numbers is unnoticeable. Moreover, to activate certain number of processors load size $V$ must be sufficiently big. In Fig. 7.15b dependence of speedup on $V$ for various processor numbers in a homogeneous star system with hierarchical memory is shown (cf. Sect. 7.4.1). The system parameters were $\forall i$, $A_{i12} = 1E - 3$, $\frac{A_{i22}}{A_{i12}} = 10$, $swp_i = 1E8$, $C_i = 1E - 6$, $S_i = 1E - 3$. Thus, the speeds of processing in the core memory and out-of-core differ by an order of magnitude. As it can be seen $V$ must be sufficiently big to start computations on certain processor number $m$. What is more, a "bump" of superlinear speedup can be observed for load sizes in range $[swp_i, m \times swp_i]$. To explain this phenomenon note that speedup $\varsigma(m)$ in Eq. (2.12) has processing time on a single processor in the numerator. For $V \in [swp_i, m \times swp_i]$, a single processor has no option but start using out-of-core memory. The $m$ parallel processors are able to accommodate the load in their core memories at the cost of communication, and computing is faster. It can be said that this comparison is unfair, and the superlinear "bump" would not have existed if the single processor used as a reference in Eq. (2.12) had sufficient memory sizes. On the other hand it may be argued that single processor systems with such a big core memory do not exist, and the phenomenon of faster processing due to the existence of memory hierarchy is real. This was one of the foundations of the Gustafson's speedup "law" [65]. Hence, performance study on the basis of speedup must be given considerable care.

The existence of closed-form solutions, or calculation of equivalent speed for the whole network (see Sect. 7.12.2), allowed for calculation of ultimate speedup achievable in certain networks by some load scattering algorithms. For example, in 3D-meshes with scattering over embedded $p$-nomial trees (cf. Sect. 7.2.3) a speedup limit is $\lim_{m \to \infty} \varsigma(m) = 1 + \frac{pA}{C}$, for $AV \gg S$ [40]. The results of this kind very often demonstrate that achievable speedup depends on the bandwidth $\frac{p}{C}$ between the originator and the rest of the network.

One more approach to the analysis of parallel computer system performance is to consider the whole computing system as equivalent to a queuing system. The maximum allowable arrival rate for an M|M|1 system, where the whole star network was considered equivalent to a processor, was analyzed in [8].

### 7.12.2 Equivalent Processors and Ultimate Performance

Ultimate performance limits of a distributed system can be calculated using a concept of equivalent processor. The whole computing network may be substituted by a single processor with the same speed. This idea has been introduced first for chains and binary trees in [11, 93]. We have already presented it for finite networks in Sects. 7.1, and 7.2.2. Below we show how it can be applied in very big networks.

Let us start with an example of a chain of processors. We will assume that the computing system is homogeneous, with processing rate $A$ and communication rate $C$, while the start-up times are negligible. Suppose that the number of processors tends to infinity. Then in a sub-chain $(P_i, P_{i+1}, \ldots, P_m)$, processors $P_{i+1}, P_{i+2}, \ldots, P_m$ may be replaced with an equivalent processor $P_{eq}$ with processing rate $A_{eq}$. Let us calculate the distribution of the load $V'$ between $P_i$ which gets $\alpha_i$, and $P_{i+1}, \ldots, P_m$. From Eqs. (7.16) we have

$$\alpha_i A = (V' - \alpha_i)(A_{eq} + C) \tag{7.114}$$

$$\alpha_i = \frac{V'(A_{eq} + C)}{A_{eq} + A + C} \tag{7.115}$$

Schedule length for the subchain is $\alpha_i A = \frac{V' A (A_{eq} + C)}{A_{eq} + A + C}$, and equivalent processing rate for the whole subchain starting at $P_i$ is $\frac{\alpha_i A}{V'} = \frac{A(A_{eq} + C)}{A_{eq} + A + C}$. Note that $\alpha_i$ is a constant fraction of the load $V'$ assigned to subchain $P_i, \ldots, P_m$. Thus, load distribution scales proportionately with $V'$. In other words, it may be said that ratios of load sizes are independent of load units used.

For the whole chain $P_1, \ldots, P_m$, the equivalent processing rate must be equal to the processing rate of the pair $(P_1, (P_2, \ldots, P_m))$. Thus, the equivalent processing rate must satisfy

$$A_{eq} = \frac{A(A_{eq} + C)}{A_{eq} + A + C} \tag{7.116}$$

which has a solution

$$A_{eq} = \frac{-C + \sqrt{C^2 + 4AC}}{2} \tag{7.117}$$

Equivalent processor speed $\frac{1}{A_{eq}}$ is an ultimate limit of system performance at $m$ tending to infinity. Observe that $A_{eq}$ is independent of $V$.

A similar analysis of equivalent processor speed has been applied for stars and busses [25, 62, 77], trees [9, 11, 12, 14, 31, 77], meshes [28, 76, 77], hypercubes [27, 77] to calculate limits on speedup achievable in some network for some scattering algorithm and other features of processor networks.

Unfortunately, the above reasoning cannot be applied when start-up times are nonzero. Let $S > 0$ be the start-up time of all communication links. Then Eq. (7.114) becomes $\alpha_i A = S + (V' - \alpha_i)(A_{eq} + C)$, its solution is $\alpha_i = \frac{S + V'(A_{eq} + C)}{A_{eq} + A + C}$. Here $\frac{\alpha_i}{V'}$ depends on $V'$, loads $\alpha_i$ are not a constant fraction of the load $V'$ assigned to $P_i, \ldots, P_m$. It may be said that $S > 0$ introduces a yardstick which prevents proportional load distribution scaling. Consequently, there is no single value of equivalent speed for each pair $(P_i, (P_{i+1}, \ldots, P_m))$, but a sequence of equivalent speeds for each such pair. A solution of the equation equivalent to (7.116) for the subchain starting at $P_i$ is $A_{eq} = \frac{1}{2}\left(-C + \sqrt{C^2 + 4(AC + \frac{SA}{V'})}\right)$, which again depends on the assigned load.

### 7.12.3  Isoefficiency

One of the recent concepts in revealing performance relations in parallel processing is the isoefficiency function. It has been observed that efficiency (see Sect. 2.4) of parallel computation decreases with growing number of used processors $m$, and increases with problem size $V$. Originally isoefficiency was defined in [63, 64] as the function $ief(E, m)$ of the problem size $V$ required to maintain efficiency $E$ while using $m$ processors. DLT allows to calculate the efficiency $E$ of distributed computation for given $V$ and $m$. Hence it is possible to depict isoefficiency $ief(E, m)$ as a set of points with efficiency $E$ on the plane $V \times m$. An example of isoefficiency function in $V, m$ for a homogeneous system with $A = 1, C = 0.02, S = 0.1$ is shown in Fig. 7.16a. Discontinuities of the isoefficiency lines for certain values of

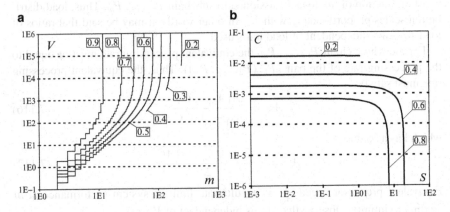

**Fig. 7.16** Isoefficiency functions. (**a**) vs. $V$ and $m$ and (**b**) vs. $S, C$

$E$ result from the fact that certain values of efficiency cannot be obtained for some combinations of $A, C, m, S, V$. It can be concluded from Fig. 7.16a that for small $V$ the number of processors $m$ and the size of the problem $V$ are mutually related. With growing $m$ also $V$ should grow to maintain constant efficiency. However, for big values of $V$ efficiency depends on $m$ only. The concept of isoefficiency has been generalized in [47]. Beyond just $V$ and $m$, also other combinations of the system parameters may be considered. For example, in Fig. 7.16b dependence of efficiency on $C, S$ is depicted (for $m = 8, V = 1E - 5, A = 1E - 2$). As it can be seen the area where the computations can be performed efficiently ends very abruptly with growing $C$ or $S$. Moreover, there is no area where $C$ and $S$ would compensate for each other which means that reduction in $S$ does not substitute for the increases in $C$ and vice versa. A tool for generating other isoefficiency charts is available on web page [70].

## 7.13 Divisible Loads in Practice

In this section, we present practical applications of DLT which serve as a motivation for considering this model. Divisible load model may represent many real applications involving data parallelism on big input volumes such as massive experimental data processing, image processing, linear algebra, combinatorial optimization, parameter-sweep computations. Applications involving processing a big number of independent loops also conform with the assumptions of DLT. Applicability of DLT in flat-file database processing has already been described in Sect. 7.8. An implementation of middleware which supports processing divisible loads in GRID environment has been presented in [92]. Below we report in a more detailed way on other works where DLT models have been explicitly applied. We will also discuss accuracy of the DLT predictions.

### 7.13.1 Divisible Applications

#### 7.13.1.1 Processing Measurement Data

Already the first paper [36] from which the DLT started analyzes processing measurements in a chain of processors. In [113] heterogeneous star with simultaneous distribution of the load to the computing processors and simultaneous result collection is considered to schedule event reconstruction from the measurement data collected at Solenoidal Tracker At RHIC (RHIC is a Relativistic Heavy Ion Collider at Brookhaven National Laboratory).

### 7.13.1.2   Linear Algebra

Distributed matrix–vector multiplication was analyzed in [59,60]. The problem consisted in calculating product $x = Yz$, where $x$ is a column vector of size $a$, $Y$ is a matrix of size $a \times b$, and $z$ is column vector with $b$ entries. For the purpose of the distributed computation, vector $x$ and matrix $Y$ are row-partitioned. This means that a unit of load, or a grain of parallelism, is the computation of one entry in $x$, e.g., the $i$th element $x_i = \sum_{j=1}^{b} Y_{ij} z_j$. A processor computes a range of $x$. Thus, the load size here is $V = a$, while load part size $\alpha_i$ is the number of rows assigned to processor $P_i$, for $i = 1, \ldots, m$. Observe that load is not arbitrarily divisible here. Still, considering the size of the output, the results of rounding $\alpha_i$s are negligible. Distributed computation of the matrix–vector product in the above way requires delivering $z$ to all processors, some range of $Y$ rows to certain processors, and collecting the resulting parts of $x$. Four different communication strategies for a star network were analyzed in [59,60]. Similar row-partitioning is used to calculate sizes of the load parts in multiplying square matrices in [38].

### 7.13.1.3   Image and Vision Processing

Application of DLT in computer image and vision processing has been reported in [26,80]. Very often image processing algorithms consist in computing transforms for each pixel, or for local groups of pixels. These can be various types of filtering (smoothing, edge detection, color enhancements), calculating histograms, FFTs, feature extractions, compression, etc. The image may be partitioned, and its parts can be processed independently in parallel. In most of the algorithms the image is partitioned row-wise, column-wise, or block-wise, possibly with a cyclic interleave. Essentially, however, the load was equipartitioned without considering communication delays or possible heterogeneity of the computing system. The DLT does not change the method of partitioning the image here, but allows for adjusting the load (image) part sizes according to the speeds of communication and computation which results in shorter schedules. One more aspect of distributed image processing is communication between the processors. Consider, e.g., a processor assigned to apply some algorithm to range $[a, b]$ of image rows. The processor may additionally require rows $a - 1$ and $b + 1$. The required rows are usually provided by exchanging messages between the processors. This introduces additional precedence constraints in processing grains of parallelism. Such precedence constraints are not easily managed in DLT. To eliminate them the image parts overlapping by some margin with the part of the neighboring processor are sent at the load distribution stage. It means in our example that the processor receives rows in range $[a - 1, b + 1]$ as the input, but only rows in range $[a, b]$ are computed as the output. Thus, load distribution can be found from (7.1) and (7.2), but some constant delay must be added in the communication time to account for transferring the overlapping load margins.

Application of DLT in video encoding has been considered in [38,78,81,92]. One of possible ways of employing DLT in encoding digital video is to partition a digital video file into chunks comprising compact ranges of video frames, these ranges are compressed in parallel, and the resulting compressed video files are concatenated into a single file. A theoretical analysis of this approach is presented in [38, 81]. Practical experiments on MPEG encoding are reported in [38, 92]. A different approach is assumed in [78]. One of the operations in video compression is motion compensation. In reducing the size of encoded video an observation is used that in the short sequences of frames parts of the images are repeated, possibly with some shift resulting from the motion in the picture. A reference frame is used to reconstruct several following frames. This is done by recognizing motion of blocks of pixels in the sequence of frames. To discover motion vectors of the areas of pixels, a video frame is partitioned into blocks of certain size (e.g. 16×16 pixels). A block of pixels existing in the current (latter) frame is searched in the reference (earlier) frame. This is accomplished by searching in the area of the current block and some margin of pixels in horizontal and vertical direction. A shift of the block which results in the smallest value of a difference criterion is the searched motion vector. Then the motion vectors may be used to reconstruct the current frame from the reference frame. The operation of motion vectors calculation may be parallelized by partitioning the current and the reference frames. In the algorithms proposed in [78] the current frame is partitioned into stripes of blocks spanning horizontally across the whole frame. Thus, in a frame of $x \times y$ blocks of size, e.g., 16×16 pixels, a unit of load is a stripe of $y$ blocks each in size of 16×16 pixels. Using DLT, the number of stripes $\alpha_i$ of the reference and the current frame assigned to a processor $P_i$ are calculated.

### 7.13.1.4 Sequence Alignment

The alignment problem consists in searching for similarities in two DNA or protein sequences by aligning them in the best possible way. More precisely, two sequences $E = (e_1, \ldots, e_g)$ and $F = (f_1, \ldots, f_h)$ of symbols are given. The symbols may be nucleic acids, amino acids, or any symbols from a finite alphabet. Informally, the strings are stretched along each other such that the number of equal positions is maximum. This may involve inserting some gaps in the strings. To solve the alignment problem a Smith-Waterman algorithm is used in [87]. Smith-Waterman algorithm is a dynamic programming algorithm which calculates scores $H(i, j)$ for the best alignment of subsequences $(e_1, \ldots, e_i)$ and $(f_1, \ldots, f_j)$, for $i = 1, \ldots, g, j = 1, \ldots, h$. The algorithm can be formulated such that $H(i, j)$ depends on cells $(i - 1, j), (i, j - 1), (i - 1, j - 1)$ only [87]. The problem now is partitioning the range of calculated scores between processors in a star network. It is assumed that sequences $E, F$ are already present at the processors. Matrix $H$ of scores is partitioned row-wise between $m$ processors, and column-wise between $Q$ iterations (see Fig. 7.17a). Computations start on $P_1$ with calculation of $H_{11}$. Then $P_1$ sends the last row of $H_{11}$ to $P_2$, and starts computing $H_{12}$. More generally, at the end of iteration $k$ processor $P_i$ sends to $P_{i+1}$ the last row of submatrix $H_{ik}$. An example Gantt chart for communications and computations is shown in Fig. 7.17b.

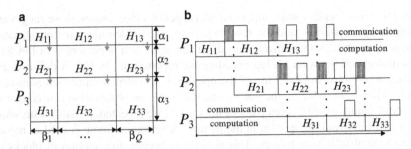

**Fig. 7.17** Divisible load processing in sequence alignment. (**a**) Partitioning of $H$ range and (**b**) Gantt chart, dashed boxes are interprocessor communications

To avoid idle times in the communications and computations it is required that computations on iteration $k$ on $P_i$ and sending the last row of $H_{ik}$ to $P_{i+1}$ last as long as computing iteration $k - 1$ on $P_{i+1}$ and receiving the last row of $H_{i,k-1}$ from $P_i$. Thus, $\alpha_i \beta_k A_i + C\beta_k = C\beta_{k-1} + \alpha_{i+1}\beta_{k-1}A_{i+1}$, for $i = 1, \ldots, m-1, k = 2, \ldots, Q$. Furthermore, the communications between the processors and returning of the resulting submatrices $H_{ik}$ to the originator must fit in the interval of computations. Hence, it is required that $C \sum_{i=1}^{m-1} \alpha_i \beta^{k-1} + C \sum_{i=1}^{m-1} \beta_{k-i} \leq \alpha_1 \beta_k A_1$. In the above formulations it was assumed that all communication links have zero start-up time and equal bandwidth. Since, the above problem is quite constrained, heuristics were proposed in [87] to solve it.

## 7.13.2   Empirical Confirmations of DLT

Here we report on experiments verifying correctness of DLT. In most of the cases the parallel application execution time predicted by DLT was compared against the actual execution time. Yet, to formulate a prediction of the execution time parameters of the system and application like $A_i, C_i, S_i$ are needed. Therefore, measurements of communication times, computation times, and the amounts of returned results as function of assigned load were done first. This allowed for calculating the partition of the load and the predicted schedule length. The calculated load partitioning was applied in practice, and the actual schedule length was measured.

In [2] distributed multiplication of $100 \times 100$ matrices on $m = 8$ processors was partitioned according to the DLT indications. Each processor received selected rows of one matrix and all of the second matrix, computed part of a result matrix, and returned the computed rows to the originator. The communication times for sending the data and reporting the results were assumed to be affine functions of the number of matrix rows (i.e. load size). The relative difference between processing time predicted by the DLT model and the real processing time ranged from 0.5% on a single processor to 6% on eight processors.

Distributed search for a pattern in a text file was a divisible application considered in [30]. The goal of the study was to verify the difference between the schedule length calculated according to Eqs. (7.2) and (7.12) and the real execution time.

The experiments were conveyed on a 12 CPU, T805 Transputer system. Transputers were CPUs, conceived in 1980s, including some memory and basic hardware for communication. By CPU to CPU connections bigger networks like meshes and hypercubes could be built. In the experiments reported in [30] communications were performed in a tree embedded in the underlying mesh topology. To calculate load part sizes $\alpha_i$, parameters $A_i, C_i, S_i$ are needed for each processor $P_i$. The processing rates $A_i$ were measured as average time of searching per one byte of the input data. Parameters $C_i, S_i$ were calculated using linear regression from a set of pairs (communication time, message size) for various message sizes. The measured parameters $A_i, C_i, S_i$ were plugged in (7.2) and (7.12) to calculate $\alpha_i$s and schedule length $C_{max}$. The input file was partitioned according to the calculated part sizes $\alpha_i$ and sent to CPUs for distributed processing. The real execution time was compared against the expected schedule length $C_{max}$. A relative difference between the two vs. problem size $V$ (for one of the studied settings) is shown in Fig. 7.18a. In the cases

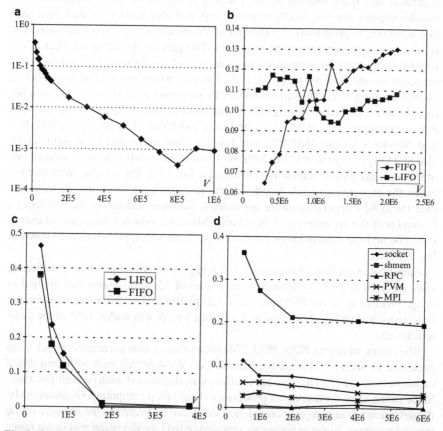

**Fig. 7.18** Relative difference between theoretical and real schedule length. (**a**) Transputer system, search for a pattern, (**b**) IBM SP2, PVM, compression, (**c**) WinNT, MPI, Join and (**d**) Origin 3000, search for a pattern. $V$ is in bytes

not covered by Fig. 7.18a, the difference was in range $\pm1.5\%$ [30]. The very good coincidence of the expectation and the real execution times can be attributed to the simple nature of the application and fact that the Transputer system was running *only* the user applications (i.e. without any operating system).

The same methodology as in [30] has been applied in [48, 107] to verify viability of the DLT on a much wider set of parallel platforms and applications. The applications included distributed search for a pattern, compression, join of two relations in a database, graph coloring by a genetic algorithm. The compression application consisted in sending parts $\alpha_i$ of input file to processors, remotely compressing the parts, and concatenating the results at the originator. The amount of returned results was proportional to size of the input part. In the join application two relations $X$ (e.g. a list of supplier identifiers with their addresses) and $Y$ (e.g. a list of products names with suppliers ids) are subject of an operation similar to a conditional Cartesian product. For each record $x_i \in X$ and $y_j \in Y$, pair $(x_i, y_j)$ is created if one field in records $x_i, y_j$ is equal (e.g. a list of products with the supplier addresses is created only if the supplier ids in $x_i$ and in $y_j$ are equal). In this application the smaller relation was sent to all computers first, and only parts $\alpha_i$ of the bigger relation were sent to processors $P_i$. The size of the results was proportional to $\alpha_i$. The results were concatenated on the originator. The genetic algorithm (cf. Sect. 2.3.4) consists in applying the genetic operators on a set of $V$ solutions. A population of $V$ solutions was divided into parts of size $\alpha_i$, and the parts were modified in parallel on distributed computers. The same number of genes was returned to the originator before the next iteration of the algorithm. The parallel processing platforms included Sun workstations with PVM, PCs with Linux and PVM, IBM SP2 with PVM, PCs with Windows NT and MPI, PCs with Java on Windows or on Linux, and in [107] also SGI Origin 3000 with PVM, MPI, sockets, shmem. Only selected combinations of the applications and platforms were tested in [48, 107]. The relative difference between the expected schedule length and the real execution times ranged from less than 1% to 30% depending on the application, platform, and size of the problem $V$. Examples of the dependence of the relative difference between the expected execution time and the measurement for various systems and applications are shown in Fig. 7.18b–d.

Empirical evaluation of the model and comparison with equal load partitioning were reported in [80]. A heterogeneous cluster of 15 workstations was applied in image processing on the PVM (see Sect. 3.2) platform. The difference between the expected schedule length and the real schedule length was within 10% of the theoretical value.

The online strategies PDD, PCD, PSD measuring system parameters which were presented in Sect. 7.10.1 were implemented on WindowsXP, with MPI, and tested experimentally [61]. The test application was distributed matrix multiplication. Since in the ideal conditions all processors should stop computing simultaneously, the deviation of the computer completion times can be treated as the measure of the method accuracy. In the experiments reported in [61] the deviation was in the range 4.60%–7.84% of the mean completion time.

# 7.14 Concluding Remarks on DLT

In this section, we will make some final comments on divisible load scheduling model. The DLT proved itself to be a generic and versatile method of representing various factors influencing scheduling decisions in parallel processing. Interconnection topology, communication algorithms, memory limitations, monetary cost of computation, variability of the environment can all be represented within the DL model. The model parameters $m, V, A, C, S$ are easy to obtain. Moreover, the basic formulation is conceptually simple and computationally tractable. Despite this simplicity, experiments confirm that DLT is capable of representing real computations accurately. Hence, it may be concluded that DLT is a good compromise between technical detail and accuracy. Obviously, DLT is not a panacea because it is dedicated to a specific kind of parallel applications.

With the inclusion of discrete objects like start-up times, discretely divisible load, combinatorial aspects emerged, e.g., in sequencing of the communications. Then, many DL scheduling problems turned out to be computationally hard, and the initial impression of computational tractability became less justified. Let us observe that without communication start-up times, solutions expressing load partitioning are often determined by quotients of $C_i$s and $A_i$s. It may be said that it makes no difference whether the application involves computing of Mega- or Terabytes of input data. The relationships between load part sizes remain the same. Inclusion of start-up times in the communication delays changes the nature of DL scheduling problem not only from the complexity point of view, but also introduces a yardstick which cannot be relativized. Consequently, equivalent processor speeds are no longer constant, but depend on load sizes (cf. Sect. 7.12.2). DLT assumes that load is arbitrarily divisible, but in reality it is not. The practical experiments demonstrate that despite this inconsistency, the schedules and the predictions are often acceptable. Moreover, discrete nature of the load is accounted for in several ways: the online heuristics consider grains of parallelism explicitly, fractional solutions may be rounded to integer solutions with limited loss of schedule quality, or the discrete grains of load may be scheduled explicitly.

By the nature of the parallel application and the proposed approaches DLT has connections with other scheduling models, and the line separating them is vague. For example, scheduling discretely divisible loads considered as a set of separate tasks can be considered equivalent to classic problem $Q||C_{max}$ (but communications are ignored) or to scheduling with communication delays $Q|c_{1j}|C_{max}$ (a dummy "originator" task precedes other tasks). Finally, let us point to one more similarity. In the steady-state scheduling the fractional throughputs which are "timeless" numbers must be converted to schedules where discrete objects such as packets are manipulated in time. The difference between the actual throughput and the planned one should be as small as possible. A similar problem is posed in just in time sequencing, e.g., car production. What is even more interesting, obtaining a good schedule for just in time sequencing is equivalent to the apportionment problem which is fair assignment of the seats in a parliament [69].

# References

1. M. Adler, Y. Gong, and A.L. Rosenberg. Sharing bags of tasks optimally in heterogeneous clusters. In *Proceedings of the 15th Annual ACM Symposium on Parallel Algorithms and Architectures (SPAA'03)*, pages 1–10, 2003.
2. R. Agrawal and H.V. Jagadish. Partitioning techniques for large-grained parallelism. *IEEE Transactions on Computers*, 37(12):1627–1634, 1988.
3. J. Błażewicz, M. Drozdowski, F. Guinand, and D. Trystram. Scheduling a divisible task in a two-dimensional toroidal mesh. *Discrete Applied Mathematics*, 94(1–3):35–50, 1999.
4. C. Banino. A distributed procedure for bandwidth-centric scheduling of independent-task applications. In *Proceedings of the 19th IEEE International Parallel and Distributed Processing Symposium (IPDPS'05)*. IEEE Computer Society, Los Alamitos CA, USA, 2005.
5. C. Banino, O. Beaumont, L. Carter, J. Ferrante, A. Legrand, and Y. Robert. Scheduling strategies for master–slave tasking on heterogeneous processor platforms. *IEEE Transactions on Parallel and Distributed Systems*, 14(4):319–330, 2004.
6. G. Barlas. Collection-aware optimum sequencing of operations and closed-form solutions for the distribution of a divisible load on arbitrary processor trees. *IEEE Transactions on Parallel and Distributed Systems*, 9(5):429–441, 1998.
7. G. Barlas and B. Veeravalli. Quantized load distribution for tree and bus connected processors. *Parallel Computing*, 30(7):841–865, 2004.
8. S. Bataineh and M. Al-Ibrahim. Load management in loosely coupled multiprocessor systems. *Dynamics and Control*, 8(1):107–116, 1998.
9. S. Bataineh, T.-Y. Hsiung, and T.G. Robertazzi. Closed form solutions for bus and tree networks of processors load sharing a divisible job. *IEEE Transactions on Computers*, 43(10):1184–1196, 1994.
10. S. Bataineh and T.G. Robertazzi. Bus-oriented load sharing for a network of sensor driven processors. *IEEE Transactions on Systems, Man, and Cybernetics*, 21(5):1202–1205, 1991.
11. S. Bataineh and T.G. Robertazzi. Ultimate performance limits for networks of load sharing processors. In *Proceedings of the 26th 1992 Conference on Information Sciences and Systems*, Princeton NJ, pages 794–799, 1992.
12. S. Bataineh and T.G. Robertazzi. Performance limits for processor networks with divisible jobs. *IEEE Transactions on Aerospace and Electronic Systems*, 33(4):1189–1198, 1997.
13. O. Beaumont, H. Casanova, A. Legrand, Y. Robert, and Y. Yang. Scheduling divisible loads on star and tree networks: Results and open problems. *IEEE Transactions on Parallel and Distributed Systems*, 16(3):207–218, 2005.
14. O. Beaumont, L. Carter, J. Ferrante, A. Legrand, and Y. Robert. Bandwidth-centric allocation of independent tasks on heterogeneous platforms. In *Proceedings of the International Symposium on Parallel and Distributed Processing (IPDPS'02)*, pages 67–72, 2002.
15. O. Beaumont, A. Legrand, L. Marchal, and Y. Robert. Independent and divisible tasks scheduling on heterogeneous star-shaped platforms with limited memory. Technical Report 2004-22, Laboratoire de l'Informatique du Parallélisme, École Normale Supérieure dy Lyon, 2004.
16. O. Beaumont, A. Legrand, and Y. Robert. The master–slave paradigm with heterogeneous processors. *IEEE Transactions on Parallel and Distributed Systems*, 14(9):897–908, 2003.
17. O. Beaumont, A. Legrand, and Y. Robert. Scheduling divisible workloads on heterogeneous platforms. *Parallel Computing*, 29(9):1121–1152, 2003.
18. V. Bharadwaj and G. Barlas. Scheduling divisible loads with processor release times and finite size buffer capacity constraints in bus networks. *Cluster Computing*, 6(1):63–74, 2003.
19. V. Bharadwaj, D. Ghose, and V. Mani. Optimal sequencing and arrangement in distributed single-level tree networks with communication delays. *IEEE Transactions on Parallel and Distributed Systems*, 5(9):968–976, 1994.
20. V. Bharadwaj, D. Ghose, and V. Mani. Multi-installment load distribution in tree networks with delays. *IEEE Transactions on Aerospace and Electronic Systems*, 31(2):555–567, 1995.

21. V. Bharadwaj, D. Ghose, V. Mani, and T.G. Robertazzi. *Scheduling Divisible Loads in Parallel and Distributed Systems*. IEEE Computer Society, Los Alamitos, CA, 1996.

22. V. Bharadwaj, D. Ghose, and T.G. Robertazzi. Divisible load theory: A new paradigm for load scheduling in distributed systems. *Cluster Computing*, 6(1):7–17, 2003.

23. V. Bharadwaj, D. Ghose, and V. Mani. An efficient load distribution strategy for a distributed linear network of processors with communication delays. *Computers and Mathematics with Applications*, 29(9):95–112, 1995.

24. V. Bharadwaj, H.F. Li, and T. Radhakrishnan. Scheduling divisible loads in bus networks with arbitrary processor release times. *Computers and Mathematics with Applications*, 32(7):55–77, 1996.

25. V. Bharadwaj, X. Li, and C.C. Ko. Design and analysis of load distribution strategies with startup costs in scheduling divisible loads on distributed networks. *Mathematical and Computer Modeling*, 32(7-8):901–932, 2000.

26. V. Bharadwaj, X. Li, and C.C. Ko. Efficient partitioning and scheduling of computer vision and image processing data on bus networks using divisible load analysis. *Image and Vision Computing*, 18(11):919–938, 2000.

27. J. Błażewicz and M. Drozdowski. Scheduling divisible jobs on hypercubes. *Parallel Computing*, 21:1945–1956, 1995.

28. J. Błażewicz and M. Drozdowski. Performance limits of two-dimensional network of load-sharing processors. *Foundations of Computing and Decision Sciences*, 21(1):3–15, 1996.

29. J. Błażewicz and M. Drozdowski. Distributed processing of divisible jobs with communication startup costs. *Discrete Applied Mathematics*, 76(1–3):21–41, 1997.

30. J. Błażewicz, M. Drozdowski, and M. Markiewicz. Divisible task scheduling – concept and verification. *Parallel Computing*, 25(1):87–98, 1999.

31. B. Veeravalli and J. Yao. Divisible load scheduling strategies on distributed multi-level tree networks with communication delays and buffer constraints. *Computer Communications*, 27(1):93–110, 2004.

32. R.L. Cariño and I. Banicescu. Dynamic scheduling parallel loops with variable iterate execution times. In *Proceedings of the International Parallel and Distributed Processing Symposium (IPDPS'02) Workshops*, pages 239–246, 2002.

33. C.D. Polychronopoulos and D.J. Kuck. Guided self-scheduling: A practical scheduling scheme for parallel supercomputers. *IEEE Transactions on Computers*, 36(12):1425–1439, 1987.

34. S. Charcranoon, T.G. Robertazzi, and S. Luryi. Parallel processor configuration design with processing/transmission costs. *IEEE Transactions on Computers*, 49(9):987–991, 2000.

35. Y.-C. Cheng and T.G. Robertazzi. Distributed computation for a tree network with communication delays. *IEEE Transactions on Aerospace and Electronic Systems*, 26(3):511–516, 1990.

36. Y.-C. Cheng and T.G. Robertazzi. Distributed computation with communication delay. *IEEE Transactions on Aerospace and Electronic Systems*, 24(6):700–712, 1988.

37. A.T. Chronopoulos, R. Andonie, M. Benche, and D. Grosu. A class of loop self-scheduling for heterogeneous clusters. In *Proceedings of the 3rd IEEE International Conference on Cluster Computing (CLUSTER'01)*, page 282, 2001.

38. N. Comino and V.L. Narasimhan. A novel data distribution technique for host–client type parallel applications. *IEEE Transactions on Parallel and Distributed Systems*, 13(2):97–110, 2002.

39. M. Drozdowski. *Selected Problems of Scheduling Tasks in Multiprocessor Computer Systems*. Number 321 in Monographs. Poznań University of Technology Press, Poznań, 1997. http://www.cs.put.poznan.pl/~maciejd/txt/h.ps.

40. M. Drozdowski and W. Głazek. Scheduling divisible loads in a three-dimensional mesh of processors. *Parallel Computing*, 25(4):381–404, 1999.

41. M. Drozdowski and M. Lawenda. The combinatorics of divisible load scheduling. *Foundations of Computing and Decision Sciences*, 30(4):297–308, 2005.

42. M. Drozdowski and M. Lawenda. Multi-installment divisible load processing in heterogeneous systems with limited memory. In R. Wyrzykowski, J. Dongarra, N. Meyer, and J. Wasniewski, editors, *Proceedings of the 6th International Conference on Parallel Processing and Applied Mathematics (PPAM'05). LNCS*, volume 3911, pages 847–854. Springer, Berlin, 2006.

43. M. Drozdowski and M. Lawenda. Multi-installment divisible load processing in heterogeneous distributed systems. *Concurrency and Computation: Practice and Experience*, 19(17):2237–2253, 2007.

44. M. Drozdowski and M. Lawenda. A new model of multi-installment divisible loads processing in systems with limited memory. In R. Wyrzykowski et al., editor, *Proceedings of the 7th International Conference on Parallel Processing and Applied Mathematics (PPAM'07). LNCS*, volume 4967, pages 1009–1018. Springer, Berlin, 2008.

45. M. Drozdowski and M. Lawenda. Scheduling multiple divisible loads in homogeneous star systems. *Journal of Scheduling*, 11(5):347–356, 2008.

46. M. Drozdowski, M. Lawenda, and F. Guinand. Scheduling multiple divisible loads. *The International Journal of High Performance Computing Applications*, 20(1):19–30, 2006.

47. M. Drozdowski and Ł. Wielebski. Efficiency of divisible load processing. In R. Wyrzykowski, J. Dongarra, M. Paprzycki, and J. Wasniewski, editors, *Proceedings of the 5th International Conference on Parallel Processing and Applied Mathematics (PPAM'03). LNCS*, volume 3019, pages 175–180. Springer, 2000.

48. M. Drozdowski and P. Wolniewicz. Experiments with scheduling divisible tasks in clusters of workstations. In A. Bode, T. Ludwig, W. Karl, and R. Wismuller, editors, *Proceedings of 6th Euro-Par Conference. LNCS*, volume 1900, pages 311–319. Springer, 2000.

49. M. Drozdowski and P. Wolniewicz. Processing time and memory requirements for multi-installment divisible job processing. In R. Wyrzykowski, J. Dongarra, M. Paprzycki, and J. Waśniewski, editors, *Proceedings of the 4th International Conference on Parallel Processing and Applied Mathematics (PPAM'01). LNCS*, volume 2328, pages 125–133. Springer, Berlin, 2002.

50. M. Drozdowski and P. Wolniewicz. Divisible load scheduling in systems with limited memory. *Cluster Computing*, 6(1):19–29, 2003.

51. M. Drozdowski and P. Wolniewicz. Out-of-core divisible load processing. *IEEE Transactions on Parallel and Distributed Systems*, 14(10):1048–1056, 2003.

52. M. Drozdowski and P. Wolniewicz. Performance limits of divisible load processing in systems with limited communication buffers. *Journal of Parallel and Distributed Computing*, 64(8):960–973, 2004.

53. M. Drozdowski and P. Wolniewicz. Optimum divisible load scheduling on heterogeneous stars with limited memory. *European Journal of Operational Research*, 172(2):545–559, 2006.

54. P.F. Dutot. Complexity of master–slave tasking on heterogeneous trees. *European Journal of Operational Research*, 164(3):690–695, 2005.

55. D. England, B. Veeravalli, and J.B. Weissman. A robust spanning tree topology for data collection and dissemination in distributed environments. *IEEE Transactions on Parallel and Distributed Systems*, 18(5):608–620, 2007.

56. M.R. Garey and D.S. Johnson. *Computers and Intractability: A Guide to the Theory of NP-completeness*. Freeman, San Francisco, 1979.

57. W. Głazek. Scheduling divisible loads on a chain of processors. In *Proceedings of the International Conference on Principles of Distributed Systems (OPODIS '97)*, pages 123–136, Paris, 1997. Editions Hermes.

58. W. Głazek. A multistage load distribution strategy for three-dimensional meshes. *Cluster Computing*, 6(1):31–39, 2003.

59. D. Ghose and H.J. Kim. Load partitioning and trade-off study for large matrix–vector computations in multicast bus networks with communication delays. *Journal of Parallel and Distributed Computing*, 55(1):32–59, 1998.

60. D. Ghose and H.J. Kim. Computing BLAS level-2 operators on workstation clusters using the divisible load paradigm. *Mathematical and Computer Modeling*, 41(1):49–70, 2005.

61. D. Ghose, H.J. Kim, and T.H. Kim. Adaptive divisible load scheduling strategies for workstation clusters with unknown network resources. *IEEE Transactions on Parallel and Distributed Systems*, 16(10):897–907, 2005.

62. D. Ghose and V. Mani. Distributed computation with communication delays: Asymptotic performance analysis. *Journal of Parallel and Distributed Computing*, 23(3):293–305, 1994.

63. A.Y. Grama and V. Kumar. Scalability analysis of partitioning strategies for finite element graphs: A summary of results. In *Proceedings of Supercomputing '92*, pages 83–92. IEEE Computer Society, Los Alamitos CA, USA, 1992.

64. A. Gupta and V. Kumar. Performance properties of large scale parallel systems. *Journal of Parallel and Distributed Computing*, 19(3):234–244, 1993.

65. J.L. Gustafson. Reevaluating Amdahl's law. *Communications of the ACM*, 31(5):532–533, 1988.

66. B. Hong and V.K. Prasanna. Distributed adaptive task allocation in heterogeneous computing environments to maximize throughput. In *Proceedings of the 18th International Parallel and Distributed Processing Symposium (IPDPS'04)*, 2004.

67. S. Flynn Hummel, E. Schonberg, and L.E. Flynn. Factoring: A method for scheduling parallel loops. *Communications of the ACM*, 35(8):90–101, 1992.

68. S.M. Johnson. Optimal two- and three-stage production schedules with setup times included. *Naval Research Logistics*, 1(1):61–68, 1954.

69. J. Józefowska, Ł. Józefowski, and W. Kubiak. Characterization of just in time sequencing via apportionment. In H. Yan, G. Yin, and Q. Zhang, editors, *Stochastic Processes, Optimization, and Control Theory Applications in Financial Engineering, Queuing Networks, and Manufacturing Systems, International Series in Operations Research & Management Science*, volume 94, pages 175–200. Springer, 2006.

70. M. Kaftański and M. Drozdowski. Isoefficiency modeling. http://www.cs.put. poznan.pl/mdrozdowski/divisible/, 2007 [online accessed 15 December 2007].

71. H.J. Kim. A novel optimal load distribution algorithm for divisible loads. *Cluster Computing*, 6(1):41–46, 2003.

72. H.J. Kim, G. Jee, and J.G. Lee. Optimal load distribution for tree network processors. *IEEE Transactions on Aerospace and Electronic Systems*, 32(2):607–612, 1996.

73. K. Ko and T.G. Robertazzi. Signature search time evaluation in flat file databases. *IEEE Transactions on Aerospace and Electronic Systems*, 44(2):493–502, 2008.

74. B. Kreaseck, L. Carter, H. Casanova, and J. Ferrante. Autonomous protocols for bandwidth-centric scheduling of independent-task applications. In *Proceedings of the 17th International Parallel and Distributed Processing Symposium (IPDPS'03)*. IEEE Computer Society, Los Alamitos CA, USA, 2003.

75. C. Kruskal and A. Weiss. Allocating independent subtasks on parallel processors. *IEEE Transactions on Software Enggineering*, SE-11(10):1001–1016, 1985.

76. K. Li. Improved methods for divisible load distribution on k-dimensional meshes using pipelined communications. *IEEE Transactions on Parallel and Distributed Systems*, 14(12):1250–1261, 2003.

77. K. Li. Parallel processing of divisible loads on partitionable static interconnection networks. *Cluster Computing*, 6(1):47–55, 2003.

78. P. Li, B. Veeravalli, and A.A. Kassim. Design and implementation of parallel video encoding strategies using divisible load analysis. *IEEE Transactions on Circuits and Systems for Video Technology*, 15(9):1098–1112, 2005.

79. X. Li, V. Bharadwaj, and C.C. Ko. Processing divisible loads on single-level tree networks with buffer constraints. *IEEE Transactions on Aerospace and Electronic Systems*, 36(4):1298–1308, 2000.

80. X. Li, V. Bharadwaj, and C.C. Ko. Distributed image processing on a network of workstations. *International Journal of Computers and Applications*, 25(2):1–10, 2003.

81. T. Lim and T.G. Robertazzi. Efficient parallel video processing through concurrent communication on a multi-port star network. In *Proceedings of the 40th Conference on Information Sciences and Systems*, 2006.

82. X. Lin, Y. Lu, J. Deogun, and S. Goddard.  Real-time divisible load scheduling for cluster computing. In *Proceedings of the 13th IEEE Real Time and Embedded Technology and Applications Symposium (RTAS'07)*, pages 303–314, 2007.

83. J. Liu, V.A. Saletore, and T.G. Lewis.  Safe self-scheduling: A parallel loop scheduling scheme for shared-memory multiprocessors. *International Journal of Parallel Programming*, 22(6):589–616, 1994.

84. V. Mani and D. Ghose.  Distributed computation in linear networks: Closed-form solutions. *IEEE Transactions on Aerospace and Electronic Systems*, 30(2):471–483, 1994.

85. L. Marchal, Y. Yang, H. Casanova, and Y. Robert.  A realistic network/application model for scheduling divisible loads on large-scale platforms. In *Proceedings of the 19th IEEE International Symposium on Parallel and Distributed Processing (IPDPS'05)*, page 48b, 2005.

86. E.P. Markatos and T.J. LeBlanc.  Using processor affinity in loop scheduling on shared-memory multiprocessors. *IEEE Transactions on Parallel and Distributed Systems*, 5(4):379–400, 1994.

87. W.H. Min and B. Veeravalli.  Aligning biological sequences on distributed bus networks: A divisible load scheduling approach. *IEEE Transactions on Information Technology in Biomedicine*, 9(4):489–501, 2005.

88. W.H. Min, B. Veeravalli, and G. Barlas.  Design and performance evaluation of load distribution strategies for multiple divisible loads on heterogeneous linear daisy chain networks. *Journal of Parallel and Distributed Computing*, 65(12):1558–1577, 2005.

89. M.A. Moges, D. You, and T.G. Robertazzi.  Grid scheduling divisible loads from multiple sources via linear programming. In *Proceedings of the 16th IASTED International Conference on Parallel and Distributed Computing and Systems*, pages 423–428, 2004.

90. OpenMP application program interface. http://www.openmp.org/drupal/mp-documents/spec25.pdf, 2005.

91. J.G. Peters and M. Syska.  Circuit-switched broadcasting in torus networks. *IEEE Transactions on Parallel and Distributed Systems*, 7(3):246–255, 1996.

92. K. van der Raadt, Y. Yang, and H. Casanova.  Practical divisible load scheduling on grid platforms with APST-DV. In *Proceedings of the 19th IEEE International Parallel and Distributed Processing Symposium (IPDPS'05)*, page 29.b, 2005.

93. T.G. Robertazzi.  Processor equivalence for daisy chain load sharing processors. *IEEE Transactions on Aerospace and Electronic Systems*, 29(4):1216–1221, 1993.

94. T.G. Robertazzi.  Ten reasons to use divisible load theory. *IEEE Computer*, 36(5):63–68, 2003.

95. T.G. Robertazzi. *Networks and Grids: Technology and Theory*. Springer, New York, 2007.

96. T.G. Robertazzi.  Divisible load scheduling. http://www.ee.sunysb.edu/~tom/dlt.html, 2008 [online accessed 29 September 2008].

97. T.G. Robertazzi and D. Yu.  Multi-source grid scheduling for divisible loads. In *Proceedings of the 40th Annual Conference on Information Sciences and Systems*, Princeton University, Princeton NJ, USA, pages 188–191, 2006.

98. J. Sohn and T.G. Robertazzi.  A multi-job load sharing strategy for divisible jobs on bus networks.  CAES Technical Report 697, Department of Electrical Engineering, SUNY at Stony Brook, Stony Brook, New York 11794, 1994.

99. J. Sohn and T.G. Robertazzi.  Optimal divisible job load sharing for bus networks. *IEEE Transactions on Aerospace and Electronic Systems*, 32(1):34–40, 1996.

100. J. Sohn and T.G. Robertazzi.  Optimal time-varying load sharing for divisible loads. *IEEE Transactions on Aerospace and Electronic Systems*, 34(3):907–927, 1998.

101. J. Sohn, T.G. Robertazzi, and S. Luryi.  Optimizing computing costs using divisible load analysis. *IEEE Transactions on Parallel and Distributed Systems*, 9(3):225–234, 1998.

102. T.H. Tzen and L.M. Ni.  Trapezoid self-scheduling: A practical scheduling scheme for parallel compilers. *IEEE Transactions on Parallel and Distributed Systems*, 4(1):87–98, 1993.

103. B. Veeravalli and G. Barlas.  Efficient scheduling strategies for processing multiple divisible loads on bus networks. *Journal of Parallel and Distributed Computing*, 62(1):132–151, 2002.

104. B. Veeravalli and W.H. Min. Scheduling divisible loads on heterogeneous linear daisy chain networks with arbitrary processor release times. *IEEE Transactions on Parallel and Distributed Systems*, 15(3):273–288, 2004.
105. B. Veeravalli and N. Viswanadham. Suboptimal solutions using integer approximation techniques for scheduling divisible loads on distributed bus networks. *IEEE Transactions on Systems, Man, and Cybernetics – Part A: Systems and Humans*, 30(6):680–691, 2000.
106. S. Viswanathan, B. Veeravalli, and T.G. Robertazzi. Resource-aware distributed scheduling strategies for large-scale computational cluster/grid systems. *IEEE Transactions on Parallel and Distributed Systems*, 18(10):1450–1461, 2007.
107. P. Wolniewicz. *Divisible Job Scheduling in Systems with Limited Memory*. Ph.D. thesis, Poznań University of Technology, 2003. http://www.man.poznan.pl/~pawelw/phd.pdf [online accessed 14 January 2008].
108. H.M. Wong, D. Yu, B. Veeravalli, and T.G. Robertazzi. Data intensive grid scheduling: Multiple sources with capacity constraints. In *Proceedings of the IASTED International Conference on Parallel and Distributed Computing and Systems (PDCS'03)*, 2003.
109. Y. Yang and H. Casanova. RUMR: Robust scheduling for divisible workloads. In *Proceedings of the 12th IEEE International Symposium on High Performance Distributed Computing (HPDC'03)*, pages 114–123, 2003.
110. Y. Yang, H. Casanova, M. Drozdowski, M. Lawenda, and A. Legrand. On the complexity of multi-round divisible load scheduling. Research Report 6096, INRIA Rhône-Alpes, 38334 Montbonnot Saint Ismier, France, 2007.
111. Y. Yang, K. van der Raadt, and H. Casanova. Multiround algorithms for scheduling divisible loads. *IEEE Transactions on Parallel and Distributed Systems*, 16(11):1092–1102, 2005.
112. J. Yao and B. Veeravalli. Design and performance analysis of divisible load scheduling strategies on arbitrary graphs. *Cluster Computing*, 7(2):191–207, 2004.
113. D. Yu and T.G. Robertazzi. Divisible load scheduling for grid computing. In *Proceedings of the IASTED International Conference on Parallel and Distributed Computing and Systems (PDCS'03)*, 2003.
114. Z. Zeng and B. Veeravalli. Distributed scheduling strategy for divisible loads on arbitrarily configured distributed networks using load balancing via virtual routing. *Journal of Parallel and Distributed Computing*, 66(11):1404–1418, 2006.

# Chapter 8
# Back to Scheduling Models

In the preceding chapters we presented some technical background of scheduling in parallel systems. This included both the "technology" of mathematical analysis tools and the technology of parallel processing. Four different views of scheduling for parallel processing were analyzed in the form of four different scheduling models. In this chapter, we will make some remarks on the models and algorithms for scheduling parallel computations. We will use previous chapters as the basis for our considerations. The goal of this chapter is not to criticize the results presented earlier in the book, but to draw conclusions and generalize the knowledge beyond the limits of particular scheduling models. Probably these conclusions cannot be called enlightening, but we believe that it is worthwhile to present them so that the previous discussions are put into a wider context. We also hope that these observations may be helpful in future considerations on scheduling models, problems, and algorithms.

Let us return to Fig. 1.2. It illustrates the relation between real scheduling problems, their models, theoretical scheduling problems, algorithms, and schedules. Figure 1.2 also corresponds with the process of transforming knowledge on real scheduling problem into a schedule. All the steps in the development of a schedule have their peculiarities. In the rest of this chapter we will discuss some pitfalls in the above process of developing schedules for parallel applications.

## 8.1 On Scheduling Models

As we already observed, a scheduling model imposes some perception of a parallel application, computing system, and the way they should be managed to obtain desired performance. In the following subsections we give examples of misunderstandings, unexpected situations, and difficulties which may arise in formulating a new scheduling model.

M. Drozdowski, *Scheduling for Parallel Processing*, Computer Communications and Networks, DOI 10.1007/978-1-84882-310-5_8,
© Springer-Verlag London Limited 2009

## 8.1.1  What Is a Parallel Application?

In many discussions regarding parallel processing and scheduling for parallel processing in particular, presumed views on the nature of parallel applications result in
misunderstandings. Let us consider two examples.

Distributed branch and bound (B&B) algorithms solve various combinatorial optimization problems (cf. Sect. 2.3.1). An important feature of B&B algorithms is
that they have unpredictable data-dependent search trees. Processing one node in
the B&B search tree usually requires a short time, but the number of nodes may
be overwhelming. As a result, the demand for computations in a distributed B&B
algorithm is hard to predict. A scheduling algorithm must manage this irregularity
and efficiently shift the computations between the available processors. The size and
timing of communications is unpredictable. Bursty data transfers are likely.

The second example are parameter-sweep computations consisting in executing
the same algorithm for a range of input datasets. The amount of transferred data is
to a large extent predictable. Though execution time of the algorithm may be different for different datasets, for a big number of datasets the differences cancel out.
A scheduling algorithm must efficiently partition the dataset between the available
computers, taking into account their computing and communication performance.
Map-reduce [3] and scientific work flow applications have similarly predictable execution times resulting from processing a big volume of data. On the other hand,
the sheer volume of data may impose a different restriction. Namely, the scheduling
algorithm must decide where to store the intermediate results.

The above two types of parallel applications require different scheduling models
and algorithms. Differences in understanding a parallel application may be observed
in the scheduling models presented earlier in the book:

- In the classic deterministic scheduling and in scheduling with communication
  delays (see Chaps. 4 and 6) a job (which is a theoretical equivalent of a parallel
  application) is a directed acyclic graph. Thus, the application has some internal
  structure.
- In the parallel task model (Chap. 5) the application is a rectangle which must
  placed in the time × processors space.
- In the divisible load model (Chap. 7) a parallel application consists in streaming
  data through communication system and processors, like a liquid flushed through
  pipes and vessels.

These concepts of parallel applications are obviously different and can be feasibly
used only in certain situations. Thus, the differences in the nature of parallel applications will result in different scheduling algorithms.

It can be concluded that before choosing a scheduling model or constructing
a new one, sufficient knowledge should be collected on the nature of the parallel application. Presumed beliefs on the nature of the parallel application tend to
be misleading. Therefore, it is necessary to verify, e.g., if the application internal

structure is important in scheduling, if the work of the application is divisible, it is also advisable to know resource usage: demand for computation, communication, storage, their time usage pattern, and stability of this pattern.

## 8.1.2  Parallel Systems in Scheduling Models

At the first glance it may seem that each of the scheduling models presented in Chaps. 4–7 is a collection of theoretical scheduling problems unified by the same perception of the parallel application. However, each of these scheduling models encompasses, explicitly or implicitly, some vision of both the application and the computing system. For example:

- In the classic deterministic scheduling a parallel computing system is similar to an SMP system.
- In scheduling with communication delays, a default parallel system is a set of identical processors with constraining communication network similar to an MPP system.
- Formulation of $LogP$ [2] model of a parallel system resulted in creating a new branch of scheduling with communication delays (see Sect. 6.9).
- In the parallel task model the computing system is a set of centralized shared resources with queues where jobs are submitted. This corresponds with batch queuing systems of an MPP or cluster supercomputer.
- The divisible load model assumes that a parallel system is a set of processors with stable speed connected by communication links of stable speed which resembles a cluster or a grid system.

Obviously, the above description ignores a lot of details in the models. However, it proves that all the scheduling models discussed in the book make some assumptions on the nature of the parallel system.

## 8.1.3  On Bridging the Models

Here we will show that different scheduling models easily blend or overlap.

There is a natural tendency to make the existing scheduling models more and more general. If a scheduling model successfully addresses one problem new details are being included in the model to solve yet another problem with the same conceptual tools. For example, consider three types of parallel tasks: rigid tasks, tasks with shape, and multiprocessor tasks (cf. Chap. 5). Rigid tasks are just boxes in the time×processors space. Rigid task model can be generalized to the tasks with shape by adding more dimensions to better fit the underlying communication network of the computer system or the communication channels in the application. Multiprocessor tasks by requesting a *set* of processors, which is the most general case in this context, may form arbitrary pattern in the processor space. With each such generalization the internal structure of the application is becoming more visible in the resource usage. Note that in the generalization process we have slipped from tasks without internal structure (rigid tasks), via the tasks with some "corners" (tasks with shape), to the tasks with almost arbitrary structure (multiprocessor tasks). Thus, the perception of the parallel application has changed completely in the generalization process.

Let us examine malleable (cf. Sect. 5.5) and divisible tasks (Chap. 7). Malleable tasks a are special type of parallel tasks which can change the number of used processors while being executed. This may be achieved by spawning many threads which are shifted between the CPUs by the operating system. One kind of parallel application conforming with the malleable task model is processing a big volume of data in data-parallel style. Data-parallel applications are also typical of the divisible load model. Yet, a different view of the computing system is assumed in each case. Hence, the model of malleable parallel tasks has some similarities with divisible load model because both models may represent the same parallel application.

In [14, 17] a scheduling model has been proposed which combines parallel tasks and scheduling with communication delays. This was dictated by the need of scheduling an application which has a complex structure of parallel tasks which communicate their results to other parallel tasks. Thus, two apparently different scheduling models have been connected.

From the above discussion we conclude that different scheduling models may have overlapping areas of application, or can be fused as a result of generalizations, perceiving the same thing in various ways, or due to the complex nature of the real problems. Consequently, it leads to difficulties in constructing pure classifications, and to confusion in understanding and comparing research results or algorithms.

## 8.1.4   The Case of Granularity

Granularity is one of the frequently used parallel processing concepts. Almost all scheduling models have some concept of the smallest unit of computation. However, there is no unanimity in defining it. Let us give examples.

- In [6, 9] granularity is defined as the frequency of synchronization between the tasks. A *grain of parallelism* is a nonpreemptive task. The measure of granularity is the number of instructions executed between synchronizations (i.e. communications). In this case, granularity can be expressed in CPU clock ticks, CPU instructions, program code statements, etc. We say that granularity is fine, medium, or coarse, depending on the number of instructions in a task.
- In the model of scheduling with communication delays granularity is defined as the ratio of communication delay and task processing time (see Eq. (6.1)). Hence, it is a dimensionless fraction. Here granularity can be either fine or coarse depending on what is bigger: communication delay or task processing time.

- The divisible load model follows, in a sense, the first granularity concept. The synchronizations are performed before and after processing a unit of data. A grain of parallelism is an indivisible unit of data. Thus, granularity can be expressed in bytes.

Hence, the granularity concept is shared by many scheduling models. Though it can be claimed that the above concepts express the same idea in different ways, they are qualitatively different. This results in incomparability of scheduling models.

Let us present one more difficulty related to granularity. In the divisible load model it is assumed that work is infinitely (arbitrarily or continuously) divisible. This assumption allows us to reduce the scheduling problem to solving a simple set of linear equations. However, real computations are not arbitrarily divisible. Introducing discrete indivisible units of load complicates the model in many ways. Firstly, in the discrete version scheduling divisible loads is intractable (i.e. **NP**-hard). Moreover, discrete units of load result in indivisible components of computing time thus introducing an irreducible yardstick of time (communication start-up time has a similar effect). Without such a discrete time unit, divisible load schedules are determined by ratios of computing and communication speeds and volume of load is irrelevant. Even if we allow for arbitrary divisibility of the work at the model level, and then we try to convert the solutions to indivisible units, we may obtain a nontrivial problem related to fair apportionment of the seats in a parliament [10].

We might expect that with decreasing granularity discrete and continuous models of load would fuse. Unfortunately, nothing like this happens because discrete and arbitrarily divisible loads result in qualitatively different models, algorithms, and solutions. The issue when to switch from one interpretation of the load to another boils down to the question, whether something is so small that it can be considered continuous. Although this question may seem funny, academic, or philosophical, it has practical consequences.

We conclude with an observation that granularity serves as an example of objects or ideas that seem superficially simple and similar in all scheduling models, but prove to be very complex and diversified at closer inspection.

## 8.1.5   Criteria and Constraints

An important element of a scheduling model is a concept of the desired performance attributes. This is expressed in terms of objective functions and additional constraints imposed on the solutions.

It appears that certain objective functions have unexpected side-effects. Let us consider the following examples.

- Equipartitioning presented in Sect. 5.5.2 is very effective in scheduling malleable parallel tasks for the mean flow time criterion. However, under heavy load conditions the number of tasks sharing the processors may be so big that parallel execution is effectively eliminated.

- An analogous observation has been made in [4] for the optimum schedules of chains of parallel tasks. There are optimum schedules where at most $m - 1$ tasks can take advantage of parallel execution. Similar observations were made in [5] for the optimum schedules of multiple divisible tasks.
- In managing queuing systems for parallel tasks (see e.g. Sect. 5.6.4 or Sect. 5.7.3) the mean flow time criterion is commonly used. The value of this criterion can be improved by giving preference to tasks with short computation time and small processor demands. Thus, big computing tasks are unfairly penalized by this criterion.

Thus, single criteria of $C_{max}$ or the mean flow time are insufficient to express what is desired in a good schedule. As it has been observed in [8] it is unrealistic to expect that a single number (i.e. a single criterion) would express the whole complexity of parallel application performance. Hence, additional optimality criteria and constraints must be used to make scheduling models more realistic. It renders the scheduling problem inherently multicriterial. This road has been already chosen in many studies of scheduling problems. We outlined some ideas in Sect. 4.4.2.

Let us summarize these considerations on formulation of scheduling models. Scheduling models are built around some concept of the parallel application, or the computing system, but in most cases of both of them. Partitions between scheduling models tend to be fuzzy, fusions of models are possible, and the same real world scheduling problem may be represented by different nonexclusive models. The way of perceiving performance in a scheduling model is evolving, and classic single optimality criteria may be insufficient. A good scheduling model must be a compromise between precision and tractability (we discuss tractability in the next section).

## 8.2  On Scheduling Algorithms

Let us assume that the process of conceptualizing a real scheduling problem is over. We know the nature of the application, of the computing system, the desired performance criteria and solution constraints. We even have an algorithm. But the algorithms require input data and resources to run. Therefore, we will now turn our attention to some implementability issues.

### 8.2.1  Computational Costs

Usually, a scheduling algorithm is part of the services provided by the computing environment. The execution time of a scheduling algorithm as a service cannot be too long.

Some scheduling algorithms incur costs which cannot be accepted in practice. Exponential algorithms are practically unusable except for small instances. There are examples of scheduling algorithms with complexity polynomial in $O(n^m)$ (e.g.

in Sect. 5.3.1.1) or $O(n^c)$ (in Sect. 6.7.2). More generally, there are polynomial algorithms with complexity $O(poly(N(I)^{k_1}))$, where *poly* is a polynomial, $N(I)$ is the length of the string encoding instance $I$, and $k_1$ is a huge constant possibly depending on some part of the instance. Such algorithms remain polynomial only if $k_1$ remains constant, which may require fixing some part of the input instance. Otherwise such algorithms are exponential. Even if $k_1$ can be reasonably expected to be constant but it is big, the complexity of the above algorithm is very high. On one hand such algorithms provide very important qualitative information on the nature of the problem: it is solvable in polynomial time. On the other hand, such polynomial algorithms are hardly usable.

Another difficulty which may arise in practical implementations is dealing with big amounts of information. For example, a task graph of a big parallel application may consist of thousands of nodes and at least the same number of arcs. Even a polynomial algorithm handling big amounts of data may have unacceptable complexity. Hence, there is a need for algorithms which build good quality solutions by exploiting only partial information on the scheduling problem. Heuristics DSC, RGFLS presented in Sect. 6.4.4 are examples of such algorithms.

It can be concluded that scheduling algorithms must have low running time. This may be achieved by using heuristics and/or by using only partial information from the instance. Some algorithms are simple because their scheduling model perceives the real scheduling problem in a simpler way.

## 8.2.2 Where Is My Scheduling Information?

One of the obstacles in applying scheduling algorithms is inaccessibility of input data or lack of control mechanisms for executing schedules. The scheduling information may be hard to find, or may be inaccurate. Consider examples.

- In all the presented models it is assumed that processing time $p_j$ of task $T_j$ is given. Yet, execution of an application in a computer system is determined by so many interactions that dispersion of execution time is inevitable. Whether this can be ignored is a matter of long discussion on the foundations of the deterministic scheduling theory. On the other hand, providing reasonably accurate estimates of the running times is necessary for guaranteeing quality of service in shared computing systems (e.g. in distributed batch systems).
- The structure of the task graph is fundamental scheduling information. This structure is well defined for some parallel applications (e.g. FFT, linear algebra), but is highly unpredictable for some other applications (e.g. distributed branch and bound).
- It is assumed that the parameters of the computing system are known. However, the exact status of the computing system is influenced by factors which are beyond our control or even observability. Hence, computing and communication system parameters are known with limited precision.

- The instrumentation monitoring a computing system changes the observed system. Costs of increasing observation resolution may easily exceed the gains from obtaining more accurate information.
- Scheduling information obtained in one computing system is not easily portable to some other computing system.

It seems that only practice may verify whether precision of the input data is satisfactory. Hence, it is a reasonable direction to restrict scheduling efforts to models and algorithms which require only information which is easily obtained.

Even being aware of the inevitable costs of obtaining information and its lack of precision is not the end of the story. The scheduling information is available from specific sources and the results of scheduling algorithms are best applied in specific environment. Let us give examples.

- The task graph is best known by the programmer or the compiler.
- The number of processors required by the application is best known by the programmer, compiler, or the application runtime environment.
- The status of the computing system (availability, computing and communication speeds) is known by the instrumentation of computing system.
- Parallel applications differ, and some type of information may be nonexistent in some types of parallel applications.
- Also parallel systems differ, and some types of information may be unavailable in certain types of parallel systems.

Shifting information between different incompatible levels of abstraction in the application and the operating system may be very costly. Therefore, it is advisable to make scheduling decisions and to implement them at certain level of abstraction where scheduling information is best available and scheduling decisions are easiest to implement. For example, scheduling task graphs seems most suitable at the application level because task graphs need not be communicated to the operating systems. Scheduling parallel tasks requires just the number of processors and processing times. This is enough to communicate job requirements to the operating system. Application level scheduling requires information on the status of the computing environment which is maintained by the computer system instrumentation.

The same application may be handled by several different scheduling algorithms using different scheduling models. In other words, different scheduling models and algorithms reside on different levels of abstraction of the computing environment. Scheduling parallel application may be thought of as a stack of scheduling models and algorithms. There are low-level scheduling policies of the operating system presented in Sect. 3.3.1 at the bottom of the stack. In the next layer runtime environment is implementing application level scheduling, i.e. the scheduling model used in the programming language, library, or by the programmer. On top of the scheduling stack there are algorithms used by distributed batch systems managing whole applications. Such a scheduling stack is an interesting analog of the stack of communication protocols.

We finish this discussion on implementability of scheduling algorithms with the following conclusions. Scheduling algorithms need to be not only polynomial, but also sufficiently fast in processing the amounts of input data typical for their area of application. Scheduling algorithms should be implemented on the appropriate level of abstraction so that necessary information is easily exchanged between the scheduler and its environment.

## 8.3   It Is a Matter of Time

New technologies are developed at a stunning pace. We have already seen the centralized single-CPU single-user computers, multiuser computers, multiprocessors, MPP systems, grids, and mobile computing. The changes in hardware resulted in changes in scheduling paradigms: from single queue batch processing, via time sharing, space sharing, to jobs on virtualized computers floating from one real computer to another. Thus, scheduling models and their perception of the computing environment is a result of the current state of technology. Let us give more detailed examples.

- Time sharing algorithms of round-robin and multilevel feedback type invented in 1960s [1, 13] provide short response time for interactive programs, but penalize computationally intensive applications with long execution times. With the advent of MPP systems this kind of scheduling was no longer sufficient for parallel applications. Hence, scheduling efforts shifted from the time quantum optimization to other mechanisms such as processor space sharing or communication optimization.
- Initial efforts in scheduling for MPP systems were oriented toward matching the communication pattern of the application with the communication network. With the progress in the performance of the communication subsystem and increasing isolation of a programmer from the underlying network this issue is becoming less important. It seems likely that the practical need for scheduling parallel tasks with shape may diminish.
- The number of computers which can be harnessed in a parallel virtual machine is constantly increasing. Consequently, scheduling efforts may shift away from processor utilization optimization. It has been pointed out in [7] that in the context of real time systems optimizing processor utilization is not a crucial issue. This observation is meaningful also in the context of high performance computing. Though there are applications able to consume any computing power, the growing availability of computing resources is changing the scheduling context. For example, if computing power is relatively easily available, but communication delays are long and unpredictable, then new optimality criteria may arise to represent these two facts. The number of tasks available for execution may be maximized, as proposed in [12, 15, 16], to prevent stalls in the computations

due to waiting for completion of some preceding tasks or communications. Furthermore, scheduling efforts may shift toward minimizing software development costs, increasing reliability of the schedules, etc.

Unfortunately, mathematical models for managing parallel applications and for the analysis of parallel performance lag behind the progress in computing hardware. While in the field of computer hardware 2–3 years make a generation, scheduling models are developed in decades.

We conclude this section with an observation that since the progress in technology is not likely to suspend, the scheduling context will keep changing. New scheduling models may be expected to emerge, and others may become obsolete. This situation has been summarized in [11] for the computer benchmarks:

> "Good benchmarks drive industry and technology forward. At some point, all reasonable advances have been made. Benchmarks can become counter productive by encouraging artificial optimizations. So, even good benchmarks become obsolete over time."

This can be also said about scheduling models.

## 8.4   Toward Scheduling Problem Taxonomy Anyway?

At the beginning of this book we dismissed the idea of a taxonomy of scheduling problems in parallel processing. However, within reasonable limits taxonomies may be useful. For example, $\alpha|\beta|\gamma$ notation (introduced in Sect. 4.2) initially was also a scheduling problem taxonomy. The latter extensions introduced in the $\alpha|\beta|\gamma$ notation made it more a language of the scheduling society than a taxonomy. Below we summarize some remarks and recommendations regarding the scheduling taxonomies.

- Scheduling models differ fundamentally, so it seems hard to expect a good taxonomy which spans several different models.
- The same real scheduling problem may be solved on the grounds of different scheduling models and may have several incomparable solutions.
- Scheduling models need not exclude one another if they operate on different levels of abstraction, similarly to different ecological niches.
- A scheduling taxonomy should take into account the area of application of the scheduling algorithm and availability of input data.
- A scheduling taxonomy should recognize parallel applications with different structure, e.g., with discrete internal structure, or with divisible work, or black box applications with attributes.
- A scheduling taxonomy should take into account possible existence of communication delays.
- A scheduling problem taxonomy should not mix a scheduling problem with the tools for solving the problem.

We hope the above remarks may be useful in future attempts to organize the knowledge on scheduling for parallel processing.

# References

1. E.G. Coffman and L. Kleinrock. Feedback queueing models for time-shared systems. *Journal of the ACM*, 15(4):549–576, 1968.
2. D.E. Culler, R.M. Karp, D. Patterson, A. Sahay, E.E. Santos, K.E. Schauser, R. Subramonian, and T. Eicken. LogP: A practical model of parallel computation. *Communications of the ACM*, 39(11):78–85, 1996.
3. J. Dean and S. Ghemawat. MapReduce: Simplified data processing on large clusters. In *Proceedings of the 6th Symposium on Operating System Design and Implementation (OSDI'04)*, pages 137–150, 2004.
4. M. Drozdowski and W. Kubiak. Scheduling parallel tasks with sequential heads and tails. *Annals of Operations Research*, 90:221–246, 1999.
5. M. Drozdowski, M. Lawenda, and F. Guinand. Scheduling multiple divisible loads. *The International Journal of High Performance Computing Applications*, 20(1):19–30, 2006.
6. E.F. Gehringer, D.P. Siewiorek, and Z. Segall. *Parallel Processing: The $Cm^*$ Experience*. Digital Press, Bedford, 1987.
7. W.A. Halang. Contemporary research on real-time scheduling considered obsolete. *Annual Reviews in Control*, 28(1):107–113, 2004.
8. R.W. Hockney. *The Science of Computer Benchmarking*. SIAM, Philadelphia, 1996.
9. K. Hwang. *Advanced Computer Architecture: Parallelism, Scalability, Programmability*. McGraw-Hill, New York, 1993.
10. J. Józefowska, Ł. Józefowski, and W. Kubiak. Characterization of just in time sequencing via apportionment. In H. Yan, G. Yin, and Q. Zhang, editors, *Stochastic Processes, Optimization, and Control Theory Applications in Financial Engineering, Queuing Networks, and Manufacturing Systems, International Series in Operations Research & Management Science*, volume 94, pages 175–200. Springer, New York, 2006.
11. C. Levine. TPC-C: The OLTP benchmark. In *SIGMOD'97, Industrial Session*, 1997. http://www.tpc.org/information/sessions/sigmod/indexc.htm [online accessed 22 September 2008].
12. G. Malewicz, A.L. Rosenberg, and M. Yurkewych. Toward a theory for scheduling dags in internet-based computing. *IEEE Transactions on Computers*, 55(6):757–768, 2006.
13. J.A. Michel and E.G. Coffman Jr. Synthesis of a feedback queueing discipline for computer operation. *Journal of the ACM*, 21(2):329–339, 1974.
14. T. Rauber and G. Runger. Compiler support for task scheduling in hierarchical execution models. *Journal of Systems Architecture*, 45(6–7):483–503, 1998.
15. A. Rosenberg. On scheduling mesh-structured computations for internet-based computing. *IEEE Transactions on Computers*, 53(9):1176–1186, 2004.
16. A. Rosenberg and M. Yurkewych. Guidelines for scheduling some common computation-dags for internet-based computing. *IEEE Transactions on Computers*, 54(4):428–438, 2005.
17. A. Rădulescu, C. Nicolescu, A.J.C. van Gemund, and P.P. Jonker. CPR: Mixed task and data parallel scheduling for distributed systems. In *Proceedings of the 15th International Parallel and Distributed Processing Symposium (IPDPS'01)*, page 1039b, 2001.

# Appendix A
# Summary of the Notation

| | |
|---|---|
| $\alpha_i$ – | Size of load assigned to processor $P_i$ (e.g. in bytes, Chap. 7) |
| $\alpha_{ij}$ – | Size of load assigned to processor $P_i$ in the $j$th installment (e.g. in bytes, Chap. 7) |
| $\delta_j$ – | Upper bound on the number of processors which may be used by parallel task $T_j$ (Chap. 5) |
| $\kappa_{ij}$ – | Local communication delay between task $T_i$ and task $T_j$ in the hierarchical model of a distributed system (Chap. 6) |
| $\varsigma_j(i)$ – | Speedup of task $T_j$ on $i$ processors, also speed of processing $T_j$ on $i$ processors |
| $\Sigma = \sum_{j=1}^n p_j$ | |
| $\mathcal{A}$ – | Set of arcs in a task graph |
| $A_i$ – | Processing rate of processor $P_i$ (e.g. seconds per byte, Chap. 7) |
| $B_i$ – | Size of memory on processor $P_i$ (Chap. 7) |
| $C_i$ – | Communication rate of processor $P_i$ (e.g. seconds per byte, Chap. 7) |
| $c_j$ – | Completion time of task $T_j$ |
| $c_{ij}$ – | Communication delay between tasks $T_i, T_j$ (Chap. 6) |
| $c_{ijkl}$ – | Communication delay between tasks $T_i$ executed on $P_k$, and task $T_j$ on processor $P_l$ (Chap. 6) |
| $C_{max}$ – | Schedule length |
| $cp$ – | Length of the critical path including communication delays assuming default, or current, processor assignment (Chap. 6) |
| $cp'$ – | Length of the static critical path (without communication delays, Chap. 6) |
| $dat(j, i)$ – | Data availability time, i.e. the earliest start time of task $T_j$ on processor $P_i$ considering only communication delays from its predecessors (Chap. 6) |
| $d_j$ – | Duedate or deadline of task $T_j$ |
| $est(j)$ – | Earliest start time of $T_j$ including communication delays assuming default, or current, processor assignment (Chap. 6) |
| $est(j, i)$ – | Earliest start time of task $T_j$ on processor $P_i$ including communication delays (Chap. 6) |

379

| | |
|---|---|
| $f_j = c_j - r_j -$ | Flow time of task $T_j$ |
| $ft(i) -$ | The end of the partial schedule on $P_i$ (Chap. 6) |
| $g(\mathcal{T}, \mathcal{A}) -$ | Granularity of computations (see Eq. (6.1) in Chap. 6) |
| $h(j) -$ | Level of task $T_j$ including communication delays assuming default, or current, processor assignment (Chap. 6) |
| $h(j, i) -$ | Level of task $T_j$ on processor $P_i$ including communication delays (Chap. 6) |
| $h'(j) -$ | Static level of task $T_j$ (i.e. without communication delays) (Chap. 6) |
| $\bar{i} = (i_1, \ldots, i_n) -$ | Vector of numbers of processors assigned to moldable tasks $T_1, \ldots, T_n$ (Chap. 5) |
| $indeg(j) -$ | In-degree of node $j$ in a graph |
| $lst(j) -$ | Latest start time of task $T_j$ including communication delays assuming default, or current, processor assignment (Chap. 6) |
| $lst(j, i) -$ | Latest start time of $T_j$ on processor $P_i$ including communication delays (Chap. 6) |
| $m -$ | Number of processors |
| $n -$ | Number of tasks |
| $outdeg(j) -$ | Out-degree of node $j$ in a graph |
| $\mathcal{P} -$ | Set of processors |
| $P_i -$ | The $i$th processor |
| $p_j(i) -$ | Processing time function of parallel task $T_j$ on $i$ processors |
| $p_j -$ | Processing time of task $T_j$ (when the number of used processors is fixed) |
| $p_{max} = \max_j\{p_j\} -$ | The longest processing time |
| $p_{min} = \min_j\{p_j\} -$ | The shortest processing time |
| $proc(j) -$ | Number of the processor executing task $T_j$ (Chap. 6) |
| $r_j -$ | Ready time of task $T_j$ |
| $\bar{R}_j = [R_{1j}, \ldots, R_{sj}] -$ | Resource requirements of task $T_j$ |
| $S_i -$ | Communication start-up time on the link to processor $P_i$ (Chap. 7) |
| $s_j -$ | Slowdown of task $T_j$ |
| $\mathcal{T} -$ | Set of tasks |
| $T_j -$ | The $j$th task |
| $V -$ | Size of load (Chap. 7) |
| $W_j(i) -$ | Work of parallel task $T_j$ executed on $i$ processors (Chap. 5) |
| $w_j -$ | Weight of task $T_j$ |
| $X_j -$ | Set of admissible sizes of moldable task $T_j$ (Chap. 5) |

# Index